Creating a New World Economy

FORCES OF CHANGE AND PLANS FOR ACTION

Creating a New World Economy

FORCES OF CHANGE & PLANS FOR ACTION

Edited by
GERALD EPSTEIN
JULIE GRAHAM
JESSICA NEMBHARD
for the
Center for
Popular Economics

FOREWORD BY SAMUEL BOWLES

Temple University Press Philadelphia

Temple University Press, Philadelphia 19122
Copyright © 1993 by Temple University. All rights reserved
Published 1993
Printed in the United States of America

The paper used in this publication meets the minimum
requirements of American National Standard for Information
Sciences—Permanence of Paper for Printed Library Materials,
ANSI Z39.48-1984

The Center for Popular Economics is located
in Amherst, Massachusetts (Box 785).

Library of Congress Cataloging-in-Publication Data
Creating a new world economy : forces of change and plans for
    action / edited by Gerald Epstein, Julie Graham, Jessica Nembhard
    for the Center for Popular Economics.
        p.   cm.
    Includes bibliographical references and index.
    ISBN 1-56639-053-2 (cloth : alk. paper)—ISBN
1-56639-054-0 (pbk. : alk. paper)
        1. Developing countries—Foreign economic relations. 2.
Developing countries—Economic conditions. 3. International
business enterprises. 4. International trade. I. Epstein, Gerald
A. II. Graham, Julie, 1945–   . III. Nembhard, Jessica
Gordon. IV. Center for Popular Economics (U.S.).
HF1413.C73 1993   92-30977
337'.0917'4—dc20   CIP

For Tom Riddell

Contents

Figures and Tables

FIGURES

xi

TABLES

SAMUEL BOWLES

Foreword

In November 1990 the apparel business's trade journal *Bobbin* ran an ad featuring a photo of a woman sewing a man's shirt, with the caption in bold type: "Rosa Martinez Produces Apparel for United States Markets on Her Sewing Machine in El Salvador. *You* Can Hire Her for 57 Cents an Hour." And then, in smaller type: "Rosa is more than just colorful. She and her coworkers are known for their industriousness, reliability, and quick learning. They make El Salvador one of the best buys." The ad urged United States textile companies to "find out more about sourcing in El Salvador." It was an invitation for U.S. firms to relocate their production or, as industry double-talk would prefer, to "outsource."

Martinez's pitiful wage and diligent work ethic did not come about because the people of El Salvador are happy to work long hours for little pay. Readers of the *Bobbin* probably did not need to be reminded that over the previous ten years the government of El Salvador had carried out a brutal repression of trade unionists, priests, and any others who would speak out against the exploitation of workers like Martinez. According to Salvadoran Catholic church sources, more than five thousand trade unionists had been killed and many more silenced or run out of the country. During this period the U.S. government had spent $4 billion supporting the government of El Salvador, offering as a justification the threat of communism in the region.[1] In August 1991, the *Bobbin* ran the identical advertisement, with just one difference: one could now hire Martinez for $.33 an hour. It was an offer that many U.S. garment businesses would find hard to refuse.

In the United States, garment workers averaged $5.77 an hour in 1989 for sewing men's shirts (U.S. Department of Commerce 1991: table 669). U.S. garment workers are among the most productive in the world, producing on the average more than four shirts an hour. But productivity is not that much different in El Salvador or in Sri Lanka or in Bangladesh, or wherever shirts are made. A sewing machine is a sewing machine, and skilled stitchers are about as good whether their names are Martinez or Rahman or Rankin. In Bangladesh, for example, workers average about two and a half shirts an hour; they are paid about what Rosa Martinez gets.[2]

In 1980 there were a million and a quarter garment workers in the United States. Nine years later there were barely a million: 190,000 jobs had been lost. This was despite the fact that the average wage in the U.S. garment industry, like Rosa Martinez's wage, was not keeping up with inflation. The buying power of the average garment worker's wage in the United States fell 10 percent in just nine years (U.S. Department of Commerce 1991: table 669).

Particularly galling to U.S. textile workers is the fact that they have been forced to pay for their own undoing. Although the fortunate few who work full-time take home less than $10,000 a year (well below the poverty line for a family of four), as a group they gave up more than $20 million of their tax dollars to support the repressive government of El Salvador. Their tax dollars paid for the death squads that eliminated leaders of the Salvadoran trade-union movement, crushing Rosa Martinez's hopes for a decent wage. Some of their tax dollars may well have paid for the ad in the *Bobbin* seeking to lure their employers to the business-friendly environment to the south.

Textile workers are not alone in this complaint; autoworkers, steelworkers, and even office workers have found themselves in the same bind, as U.S. business has taken the global road to profit making. New York Life Insurance Company, for example, processes claims in Castleisland, Ireland, with the keyboards of Irish clerical workers connected by computer link to New York Life's service center in Clinton, New Jersey. "More and more, companies are looking at foreign countries as extensions of the United States," observed Paul Coombes of McKinsey and Company, the consulting firm. "Technology has enabled corporate managements to make sourcing and location decisions internationally in ways they could not before" (Lohr 1988).

The jet-set mentality has captivated U.S. business for a simple reason: there is more money to be made somewhere else. "The United States does not have an automatic call on our resources," remarked Cyrill Siewert, chief financial officer at the Colgate Palmolive Company. "There is no mindset that puts this country first" (Uchitelle 1989b).

And why should there be? Flag waving and hand wringing to the contrary, a business is a business, not a support group for the nation where its headquarters are located. Do U.S. corporations need to worry about lagging productivity in the United States? Here is how the president of the National Cash Register Company put it: "I was asked the other day about United States competitiveness and I replied that I don't think about it at all. We at NCR think of ourselves as a globally competitive company that happens to be headquartered in the United States." NCR made 60 percent of its $6 billion in revenue in 1988 from sales of products made outside the United States—computers made in Germany, automatic teller machines made in Scotland, and computerized cash registers made in Japan (Uchitelle 1989a).

When asked about the choice of Kuala Lumpur, Malaysia, as the location for its plant producing telephone pagers, as well as for the engineering and design center for the beepers, Motorola's chairman remarked: "We'd try to make a balanced decision that took everyone into consideration, Malaysians and Americans. We need our Far Eastern customers. . . . We must treat our employees all over the world equally" (Uchitelle 1989b).

Good point. Rosa Martinez needs her job too—as much, maybe more, than those who lost their jobs in North Carolina. So do NCR's workers in Germany and Japan, and Motorola's assemblers and engineers in Malaysia and New York, Life's keyboard operators in Ireland. Those who would drum up nationalist fervor to stem business flight on the grounds that "American jobs" should have priority will have to answer to Rosa Martinez.

Global hypermobility has given business a trump card in its bargaining with workers and with communities. The logic of its hard bargain is that to keep jobs in the United States we must mimic the working conditions that lure these footloose firms away. Can living standards and economic security be maintained in the United States now that all economies are irreversibly part of the global economy? The answer, surprisingly, is yes. But it will take an about-face in economic thinking and policy.

The first step is to recognize that the key to sustainable living standards in the United States is the productivity of the U.S. work force; and this requires ongoing investment in skills, research, education, new machinery and equipment, and modern systems of communication and transportation. Little of this can be accomplished by complacent reliance on trickle-down stimulus to the private sector; much of it will require government-funded investment in human resources and public infrastructure.[3]

Getting the U.S. economy out of the productivity doldrums also requires a rejection of the dog-eat-dog economy sometimes euphemistically called free enterprise, with its widening gap of wealth and poverty. A country that put three times more additional prisoners behind bars than it put additional teachers into the classroom over the last decade should ask questions about its favored economic dogmas before it starts blaming some other country's good fortune for its own distress.

In this respect, we might ponder the lessons of the very global business hypermobility that concerns us. When U.S. firms leave the United States, they go primarily to Europe and Canada, regions of the world where wages are on the average higher, not lower, than in the United States and where governments spend more, not less, than here (U.S. Department of Commerce 1991; U.S. Department of Labor 1991). According to U.S. Commerce Department data, only a quarter of all U.S. direct foreign investment is in the poor countries of Africa, Asia, and Latin America (Eisner and Pieper 1991). It goes to Europe because the workers there do calculus and the trains do one hundred miles an hour on modernized road beds—in short, because of the skills of the work force and the quality of the public infrastructure, not to mention the rapidly growing markets made possible by high and rising wages. Low wages are a draw to other parts of the world, to be sure, but the key is productivity, and this requires high wages and an adequately funded public sector.

The second step is to recognize that from the standpoint of the living standards of the vast majority of the people of the United States, the U.S. government has been on the wrong side of many, even most, of its interventions abroad since the end of the Second World War. With the cold war at its height, many were led to think that they had a personal stake in U.S. government support for reactionary regimes that create "good business climates" to attract international investment by eliminating labor unions, denying democratic rights, and tolerating—even bidding for—environmentally destructive, so-called development projects. But the "evil empire" no longer motivates us, and the country it once referred to no longer exists. It is easier to see that most people's interests would be favored by policies throughout the world to raise wages, support democratic governments, even if they are "unfriendly" to U.S. businesses, and protect the global environment. In the long run, a decent wage for Rosa Martinez is the best guarantee for decent wages of workers in the United States.

Perhaps this is why so many in the United States are coming to doubt that the free enterprise policies and the support of repressive regimes favored by U.S. multinational corporations are in the interests of anyone but a tiny minority of people anywhere in the world. Perhaps this is why, for example, the Amalgamated Clothing and Textile Workers Union in the United States has taken up the cause of people like Rosa Martinez, defending the rights of trade unionists in Central America and successfully pressuring the U.S. Congress to cut off financial support to the government of El Salvador. Other unions, churches, environmental groups, and ordinary citizens have done the same.

The book you hold in your hands was written by a group of outstanding economists. On the basis of their years of research and their experience teaching activists from community movements, labor unions, environmental, feminist, and other groups, they have assembled here a look into the emerging global economy designed for those who think that the purpose of knowledge is to change the world for the better. I hope that many who share this view throughout the world will read this book and will find in it facts and ideas that empower them to take the steps necessary eventually to restructure the world economy. For only in this way will it come to pass that Rosa Martinez need not fear either for her livelihood or for her life, and that others in countries more fortunate will welcome her productivity rather than fear losing their jobs as a result of the import of the shirts she sews.

NOTES

1. U.S. Government Accounting Office 1991a, 1991b. Two excellent sources on U.S. military and economic aid (most of it indirectly related to military objectives) can be found in Arms Control and Foreign Policy Caucus 1985 and 1988.

2. Samuel Bowles and Richard Edwards (1992: chap. 13) present an analysis of global inequalities in living standards and the uneven development of the world economy. See also Walter Russel Mead 1990.

3. A program for restoring sustainable growth in living standards is presented in Bowles, Gordon, and Weisskopf 1991.

BIBLIOGRAPHY

Arms Control and Foreign Policy Caucus. 1985. *U.S. Aid to El Salvador: An Evaluation of the Past, A Proposal for the Future.* Washington, D.C.: U.S. Congress.
———. 1988. *Bankrolling Failure.* Washington, D.C.: U.S. Congress.
Bowles, Samuel, and Richard Edwards. 1992. *Understanding Capitalism: Competition, Command, and Change in the U.S. Economy.* New York: Harper Collins.
Bowles, Samuel, David Gordon, and Thomas Weisskopf. 1991. *After the Waste Land: A Democratic Economics for the Year 2000.* Armonk, N.Y.: M. E. Sharpe.
Eisner, Robert, and Paul Pieper. 1990. The World's Greatest Debtor Nation. *North American Review of Economics and Finance* 1(1): 9–32.
Lohr, Steve. 1988. The Growth of the Global Office. *New York Times*, 18 October, D1.
Mead, Walter Russel. 1990. *The Low Wage Challenge to Global Growth.* Washington, D.C.: Economic Policy Institute.
Uchitelle, Louis. 1989a. Trade Barriers and Dollar Swings Raise Appeal of Factories Abroad. *New York Times*, 26 March, 1.
———. 1989b. U.S. Business Loosens Link to Mother Country. *New York Times*, 21 May, 1.
U.S. Department of Commerce. 1991. *Statistical Abstract of the United States.* Washington, D.C.: U.S. Government Printing Office.
U.S. Department of Labor. 1991. *International Comparisons of Hourly Compensation Costs for Production Workers in Manufacturing, 1990.* Washington, D.C.: U.S. Government Printing Office.
U.S. Government Accounting Office. 1991a. El Salvador Aid Compensates for Eco-

nomic Losses but Achieves Little Growth. Report to the chairman of the Subcommittee on Western Hemisphere Affairs. Committee on Foreign Affairs, House of Representatives. Washington, D.C., 19 February.

———. 1991b. El Salvador Military Assistance Has Helped Counter but Not Overcome the Insurgency. Washington, D.C., April.

Acknowledgments

This book is a project of the Center for Popular Economics (CPE) in Amherst, Massachusetts. A nonprofit educational organization, the center, for more than fifteen years, has taught and learned from thousands of political activists involved in the struggle for peace and social justice. Our greatest debt in writing this book has been to these thousands of activists who have taught us so much about the way our economy and society really work and who, through their actions, have given us hope that we can make our world a better place.

Unfortunately, organizations are not sustained and books do not get written by ideas alone. Many individuals and organizations have given generous financial support for this book.

First, we thank the United Church Board for World Ministries (United Church of Christ), which gave us seed money to begin the International Project at the CPE out of which we developed the idea for this book. During the time we were writing our book, three foundations gave CPE substantial grants that helped to fund our International Project: the Northshore Unitarian/Universalist Veatch Program, the Limantour Fund, and the Samuel Rubin Foundation. We thank them all.

Many other foundations and individuals have given generously to our organization during the time we have been working on our International Project. We are grateful to them all. Without them, the Center for Popular Economics and its work would not exist.

A number of individuals have helped us complete this book, not with money but with the sweat of their brows. James Boyce generously gave us editorial assistance on part of the manuscript. Gail Joy, Ann Lucas, and Carol Vogel typed several of the chapters. We thank them for efforts above and beyond the call of duty.

Without Kevin Crocker, the book would still be an assorted jumble of misspelled words and undecipherable tables. We cannot thank Kevin enough for his tireless and efficient efforts in producing the final manuscript.

While this book was being written, the CPE staff happily and productively kept our organization working. We thank all the administrative staff of the CPE for their great efforts on our behalf. We especially thank Natasha Harmon, the executive director of the Center for Popular Economics, whose work and inspiration have kept our organization educating for social justice for more than five years.

Last, and far from least, we thank Tom Riddell, who recently finished his term as staff director of the Center for Popular Economics. Tom has been director of the center virtually from its inception more than fifteen years ago. He has been the rock—the center of the Center—who has kept it going through thick and thin, and thinner. Being staff director has in many ways been a thankless task. But we would like to thank him anyway. We dedicate this book to Tom: Thanks for everything.

Acronyms and Abbreviations

AID	Agency for International Development
BCCI	Bank of Credit and Commerce International
BLS	Bureau of Labor Statistics
CBERA	Caribbean Basin Economic Recovery Act
CBI	Caribbean Basin Initiative
CMEA	Council for Mutual Economic Assistance
COMECON	Council for Mutual Economic Assistance
CPE	Center for Popular Economics
DAC	Development Assistance Committee
DC	developed country
DEA	Drug Enforcement Administration
DFI	direct foreign investment (same as FDI)
ECLA	U.N. Economic Commission for Latin America
EIU	Economist Intelligence Unit
ENDA	Environmental Development Action for United Nations
EOI	export-oriented industrialization
ERP	*Economic Report of the President*
ESF	Economic Support Fund
FDI	foreign direct investment
Fed	Federal Reserve Bank
FMLN	Frente Farabundo Martí para la Liberación Nacional
FRELIMO	Frente de Libertação de Moçambique
FTA	Free Trade Agreement
G7	Group of Seven
GATT	General Agreement on Tariffs and Trade
GSP	Generalized System of Preferences; or gross social product
IADB	Inter-American Development Bank
IBRD	International Bank for Reconstruction and Development
IFC	International Finance Corporation
ILO	International Labor Office (or Organization)
IMF	International Monetary Fund
ISI	import-substituting industrialization
JIT	just-in-time

LDC	less-developed country
MDB	multilateral development bank
MITI	Ministry of International Trade and Industry [Japan]
MNC	multinational corporation
MOF	Ministry of Finance
NACLA	North American Congress for Latin America
NAFTA	North American Free Trade Agreement
NBER	National Bureau of Economic Research
NIC	newly industrialized(-ing) country
NIEO	New International Economic Order
NNP	net national product
ODA	official development assistance
OECD	Organization for Economic Cooperation and Development
OPIC	Overseas Private Investment Corporation
PRC	Peoples Republic of China
QC	quality control
RENAMO	Mozambican National Resistance
SAL	structural adjustment loan
SAP	structural adjustment program
SDR	special drawing right
SSA	social structure of accumulation
TAA	trade adjustment assistance
TNC	transnational corporation
UNCTAD	United Nations Conference on Trade and Development
UNCTC	United Nations Centre on Transnational Corporations
UNEP	United Nations Environment Program
VER	Voluntary Export Restraint
WCED	World Commission on Environment and Development
WIDER	World Institute for Development Economics Research

Creating a New World Economy

FORCES OF CHANGE AND PLANS FOR ACTION

GERALD EPSTEIN
JULIE GRAHAM
JESSICA NEMBHARD

Introduction

Five International and Domestic Problems

With the end of the cold war and the elimination of economic and political barriers in Western Europe, it sometimes seems that we are on the verge of a new world, a global community where dreams of harmony are suddenly made real. But just as our dreams have become globalized, we are reminded that many of our problems and fears are global as well. The fall of the Berlin Wall and transformations in the Soviet Union and Eastern Europe are generating poverty, violence, and chaos along with the possibility of greater political freedom. The destruction and the deadly aftermath of the Persian Gulf War remind us that despite the apparent end of the cold war, *global militarization* is an ongoing process with no end in sight. With trepidation we read the latest reports of ozone depletion over Antarctica and of deforestation in Brazil while keeping a watchful eye on our thermometers at home as we brace ourselves for the expected warming of the planet. The *environmental crisis* is a global problem that has finally seized the world's attention and seems to demand a global solution.

Averting environmental disaster by slowing world economic growth, as some have suggested, is complicated by a third profound global problem: enormous *global inequality*. The annual income of the United States and Canada, for example, is greater than the annual income of all the developing countries put together (United Nations 1991). And while wealthy nations have almost tripled their per capita income since 1950, per capita income for the poorest countries has stagnated (Worldwatch Institute 1990:136–37). Almost one quarter of the world's population, or 1.2 billion people, lived in absolute poverty in 1989—reflecting a substantial deterioration during the 1980s (World Bank 1990:1; Worldwatch Institute 1990:139). Slowing growth in the countries of the Third World, which comprise 77 percent of the world's population, can only lead to the maintenance of widespread misery. Hence, addressing the world environmental crisis must go hand in hand with solving the problem of global inequality.

1

For those of us living in the United States, a fourth and very serious problem threatens to divert our attention from the environmental crisis and global inequality or, worse, to actively inhibit solutions to these problems. The U.S. *economic decline* is negatively affecting the lives of millions of U.S. citizens in more direct and immediate ways than these other seemingly distant and less palpable problems. The average real wage for U.S. workers has not risen since 1973. In 1988, 13 percent of the population lived below the poverty line (Kidron and Segal 1991:128). Hardest hit have been children; 12 million live in poverty. The United States, one of the richest nations on earth, has a higher infant mortality rate than Spain, Austria, and Hong Kong (Children's Defense Fund 1990). As Americans see the quality of their lives stagnate or, more likely, decline, it becomes difficult to convince them that other—global—problems must take priority. This fear has led some, in fact, to suggest turning away from the global economy and reducing the United States' interaction with the rest of the world at a time when major problems call out for global solutions. In this context, it is difficult to persuade Americans to contribute to the solution of global problems. And because of the great military and economic power of the United States, a problem for the United States can become a problem for the world.

Indeed, increasingly, Americans are blaming globalization for their own economic problems. International competition, particularly from Japan, is blamed for the loss of jobs and erosion of living standards at home. Headlines about foreign takeovers of the U.S. movie industry or of Rockefeller Center raise the specter of foreign *corporate control* over our economy.

Yet it seems to us that the focus on foreign corporations is misplaced. Increasing foreign corporate investment in the United States is just a symptom of the expanding role of global corporations—both U.S. and foreign—around the world. U.S. citizens are simply joining the ranks, long filled with citizens from the Third World and smaller industrial nations like Canada, of those concerned with their lack of control over large and footloose multinational firms.

These five international and domestic problems—global militarization, the environmental crisis, global inequality, U.S. economic decline, and corporate control over the economy—illustrate the profound ways in which global and domestic problems interact and the ways in which the solutions to global problems depend on solutions to domestic ones and vice versa. In short, to solve the problems we face, we must think locally and globally at the same time if we are to act at all. This means that progressive analysis and discussion of the global economy is now more important than ever. The need for progressive analysis is heightened by the fact that mainstream academics, policymakers, and business leaders are developing a consensus about the nature of global problems and the appropriate global and local solutions. Moreover, they are not simply developing this consensus in theory. Through the governments of the major industrial powers, and through international agencies such as the World Bank and the International Monetary Fund, they are implementing it. From our perspective, this consensus, which stresses *competitiveness*, *deregulation*, and *corporate control*, is unlikely to solve the global problems we describe. Indeed, it will only make things worse.

The Conservative Consensus on Global Problems

The conservative consensus, emanating from world power centers such as the World Bank, the International Monetary Fund, and conservative think tanks, offers a simple explanation for the major problems faced by the world's citizens, including those in the United States. According to this consensus, around the globe there has been too much government control of the economy and too little control by the market. The solution is equally simple: reduce government interference in the market and allow "free enterprise," competing on a global scale, to solve the problems we face.

This analysis and the proposed solutions that derive from it are most familiar, of course, in the context of Eastern Europe. There, and in many parts of the former Soviet Union, state-owned industries are being "privatized": sold off to the highest bidders, preferably foreign corporations from Europe, Japan, or the United States. Government controls over prices, exchange rates, and interest rates are being lifted. Government protection of workers, income subsidies for the poor, and subsidies on food and other basic necessities are being reduced or even eliminated. These policies, it is hoped, will generate an investment boom in which foreign corporations will buy and build factories, hire workers, and sell products on the domestic and international markets, thereby unleashing a hurricane of entrepreneurial energy and a tidal wave of economic growth.

Although Eastern Europe is the best known example of this strategy, it is far from the only one. Indeed, it is not an exaggeration to say that in one form or another this analysis and strategy is being applied today in the vast majority of the world's countries. The strategy is based on the premise that corporate control, instead of being a problem facing the world's economies, is the solution to our economic ills. Reducing or eliminating government involvement in the economy, from Bucharest to Boston—by selling government-owned enterprises to private corporations (privatization), reducing regulation of the financial sector (deregulation), and opening economies to multinational corporate investment and products from abroad (free trade)—is the only way to restore economic growth.

Enhancing the role of the market and increasing corporate control will also solve the problem of global inequality. According to the emerging consensus, the only hope poorer countries of the world have for sustained economic growth is to attract investment from foreign corporations to modernize their economies. And the only way to do that is to reduce government involvement in the economy and open themselves to free trade in investment and goods. The market is not the cause but the cure for global inequality.

The solution for U.S. economic decline, likewise, is less government involvement. Less involvement will lead to productivity growth, reduced waste, and greater international competitiveness. Increasing our competitiveness will expand exports, create jobs, and raise the standard of living at home. Anything that reduces our competitiveness—from increased government intervention to increased taxes to increased environmental regulation—will only exacerbate U.S. decline.

Yet it is clear that this new conservative consensus, which stresses deregulation, corporate control, and competitiveness, has several gaping holes. For no one believes that the unregulated market and corporations that are primarily focused on competition can possibly solve the environmental crisis. Similarly, as private corporations rush to sell more arms abroad, even in the wake of the Gulf War, corporate control and deregulation can hardly be seen as solutions to the problem of global militarization. Solving these problems requires more regulation, less corporate control, and cooperation rather than competitiveness. This contradiction should give us pause. Might the conservative consensus offer false hope for the other problems as well?

Critique of the Conservative Consensus

The conservative consensus says that letting the market work both domestically and internationally will solve the problems we face. This view is based on three major assumptions about markets: that they are efficient, neutral, and characterized by an absence of power. The first assumption implies that markets will allocate resources to maximize social welfare at both the national and international levels. The second implies that markets do not favor one group or class over another. And the third implies that markets will foster freedom, eliminating exploitation and abuses of power. All three of these assumptions turn out to be false.

The problems with the first assumption—markets are efficient—are nowhere clearer than in an analysis of environmental destruction. The unabashed pursuit of profit, far from protecting the environment, often causes its degradation. Firms pollute the water, foul the air, and destroy the soil because it is profitable, even though it is not socially efficient. Profitability and social efficiency coincide only under very special circumstances. Government regulation of the market is often necessary to make profitability and efficiency coincide.

The environment is not the only area where the market fails to guarantee social efficiency. Financial deregulation has fostered billions of dollars of speculative investment by banks, savings and loans, and other financial

institutions. These institutions invested heavily in Third World countries, risky real estate deals, and corporate mergers and acquisitions. In the end, many of their loans went sour, creating massive hardship for the citizens of debtor countries, for workers in merged companies, and ultimately for U.S. taxpayers, who have had to bail out the insolvent financial institutions. Meanwhile, credit has been extremely costly or unavailable for companies or communities that have wanted to invest productively in new factories, infrastructure and mass transit, or education.

The United States is not the only place where financial deregulation and market domination of the financial system has had devastating results. In Chile, Argentina, and other countries of the South, the details are different but the basic story is the same. Unregulated financial markets can hardly be said to foster efficiency.

The assumption that power is absent from markets is a central tenet of the new consensus—illustrated by the title of Milton Friedman's popular book, *Free to Choose*. If workers, for example, can choose to leave their jobs and get other jobs, the argument goes, then capitalists have no power over workers—the "labor market" is a realm of freedom, not coercion. Exploitation and domination cannot occur; for if they did, workers would leave and find a job where there was none. Markets liberate, governments coerce; or so the new consensus says.

In a world characterized by inequality of wealth and income and by high unemployment, however, markets are hardly a realm of liberation. If there is high unemployment, workers who are subject to dangerous or exploitative jobs can quit, but they may not be able to find other jobs. Families may be forced to live near toxic waste dumps because they cannot afford to live anywhere else. In this context, markets coerce; and the government, or community organizations, can liberate.

Differential power in market relations also undermines the neutrality of markets; markets tend to reproduce inequality, rather than reduce it, contrary to what the conservative consensus would say. The biased, rather than neutral, role of markets is clearly illustrated by an important component of the new consensus: the "free mobility" of capital within and between nations, the ability of corporations to invest their funds virtually anywhere around the globe. To the extent that governments try to create more and more freedom for corporations to move capital, it will be increasingly easy for corporations to pick up and move. Labor, however, has no such ability. The result is that workers continue to depend on their own communities to provide them with good jobs, education, housing, and safe environments—things that corporations and the government typically provide in a capitalist economy—but U.S. corporations have less and less interest in providing these things. Instead, corporations use the threat of moving abroad or to some other region of the nation to get lower wages, lower taxes, eased environmental standards, and less control by unions. In the end, the free market in capital leads to a great imbalance in power between corporations on the one hand and communities and workers on the other.

In sum, while markets and competition can have important benefits, completely unregulated markets are not power-free, neutral, or efficient, contrary to the assertions of the conservative consensus.

Progressive Alternatives to the Conservative Consensus

Progressive alternatives to the conservative consensus vacillate between two extreme positions. Some progressives deny that the economy has become globalized at all and suggest that old national solutions to economic problems are still viable. We call these the *National Keynesians*. They argue that nations are largely insulated from the vagaries of the international economy. National governments can and should pursue national policies of full employment and high economic growth without worrying about the way the international economy constrains their policy choices. In short, policy options facing large countries like the United States have not changed much since the 1960s.

Other progressives accept the reality of globalization but view nations and communities as totally helpless in its wake. The international mobility of capital allows multinational corporations and banks to pick up and leave in response to any attempt by governments to control them. Corporations, not nation-states, are sovereign. For these *Global Pessimists*, progressive policy to raise the standard of living of workers and protect the environment is virtually impossible.

A third group, the *New Competitors*, by contrast, agree that too much has changed in the international economy for us simply to go back to the 1960s. But, from their perspective, we do not have to be pessimistic about the ability of nations to foster economic development as long as they accept the rules of the game outlined in the conservative consensus—competition in the international marketplace is the path to economic prosperity. Industrial policy and more public expenditure on education and research and development will make "our" corporations more competitive. Being more competitive will solve the economic problems we face.

We find all of these alternatives unsatisfying. The world has changed too much to go back to the policies of the 1960s. But the world has not changed so much that nations and communities are totally helpless in the face of multinational corporations. Despite the increased internationalization of the economy, nations, citizens, and workers still have a great deal of power to affect economic and political outcomes.

Yet if we just accept the New Competitors' premise that markets and international competition are the path to prosperity, we will squander this potential to control our destinies. With so many problems of global dimensions—environmental destruction, to name just one—it would be globally destructive to foster economic nationalism.

The authors of the chapters in this book do not propose a single alternative analysis and policy program to those of the conservatives, National Keynesians, Global Pessimists, or New Competitors. Indeed, given the diversity of conditions and problems faced by people and countries around the globe, and considering the complexity of these conditions and problems, it is unlikely that any single, simple list of principles could be anything more than suggestive. The authors do, however, share some critical perspectives and a number of insights that call into question the assumptions underlying these other perspectives and that can help point the way to alternative plans of action for solving national and global problems.

Some of the principles shared by many of the authors include the following:

First, inequalities of power are central to international economic relations. Powerful nations are able to use military and economic carrots and sticks to win attractive economic concessions that further widen the gap between themselves and the poorer nations. Markets do not eliminate these inequalities. On the contrary, they harness, transform, and often exacerbate them. As we mentioned above, for example, multinational corporations use the international capital market to exploit and ultimately increase the inequalities in power that exist between workers and owners. In such a setting, the unregulated markets advocated by some of the New Competitors will not necessarily reduce power inequalities but will often make them worse.

Second, even though the economy is becoming increasingly internationalized, national governments and local communities are not so powerless as the Global Pessimists imply. On the contrary, the international economy still develops on a national basis. This is most visible where military power is central to economic relations, as we have recently witnessed in the Persian Gulf War. The military power of the United States has become central to the market for oil—one of the world's most important internationally traded commodities, dominated by some of the world's largest multinational corporations.

But the importance of national power in international economic relations is manifest in subtler ways as well. Nations and communities have a great deal of power to confront corporations. This power derives from the resources they have that corporations need for survival—labor, natural resources, and consumers. Nations and communities can use this power to control the operations of corporations for the benefit of the community as a whole. They can say, if you want access to these resources, you must operate more in the interests of our communities.

Third, while national power is still central to the world economy, the increasing integration of the international economy has made it more difficult for a single country, operating alone, to exert control over its economy and solve national problems. It is much easier for a group of countries to exert leverage over multinational corporations than it is for one country by itself. It is much easier for a group of countries to control environmental pollution that knows no borders than for any country alone.

This brings us to the fourth major point: international cooperation is essential to achieving solutions to national and international problems. The need for international cooperation is clear in the case of environmental protection, where coolants used in one country destroy the ozone layer protecting another. But international cooperation is equally important in other realms as well. Reducing the trend toward global militarization requires cooperation among arms-selling nations to restrict arms sales; otherwise, arms suppliers in one nation will simply fill the gaps left by restrictions in another one. International cooperation to reduce negative aspects of international capital mobility is another example. Without it, all nations will suffer, as communities and nations compete for investment by lowering wages and environmental standards, with little or no increase in the total amount of investment undertaken.

Fifth, and finally, cooperation that benefits the majority of citizens requires democratic control over institutions at both the local and international levels. Otherwise, cooperation will be cooperation among the few and the powerful. The International Monetary Fund and the World Bank, for example, are already institutions of international cooperation, but they are primarily clubs controlled by the banks and corporations of the wealthy nations. Hence, the type of cooperation they undertake is likely to benefit those that control them, rather than the bulk of the world's population.

To summarize: power is central to international economic relations; the international economy is built on the power of nation-states, but with increasing globalization, nations individually have less power than they need to solve the problems they face; so more international cooperation, not just competition in international markets, is needed to solve global problems; and cooperation requires democracy.

Domestic and Global Problems: Strategies and Suggestions

The authors of this volume do not offer any blanket solutions to world problems. They believe that the list of approaches or solutions is open-ended and that successful approaches are not restricted to a particular social scale. Thus, international agencies can devise approaches to inequality, but so can local people in their communities worldwide. And international coordination can take place among grass-roots organizers as well as among nations. In their individual chapters the authors offer proposals or provide examples of strategies for dealing with one or more global and U.S. problems. In the rest of this introduction, we briefly outline some of the suggestions and approaches put forward in the chapters to come.

Global Inequality

Many authors offer proposals that are aimed at reducing inequality in the world's distribution of wealth. In an interesting examination of hours worked, Juliet B. Schor (Chapter 9) argues that a shorter work week in the United States and other wealthy countries would not only increase leisure in those countries but could also decrease consumption and growth. Other countries might then have greater access to the resources wealthy countries currently consume.

Offering a novel suggestion for redistributing population as a means of redistributing wealth, Bob Sutcliffe (Chapter 4) proposes that freedom of movement, a basic right in democratic countries, be extended to all people around the world. Although illegal immigration now functions as a way of gradually promoting equalization of wealth, we should work toward the opening of borders worldwide. At the very least, the presence of new immigrants may make wealthier people more conscious of the great poverty many immigrants are fleeing.

Other approaches to poverty and inequality fall into the category of economic development strategies. José Távara (Chapter 21) argues that local survival strategies in debt-ridden and impoverished Latin American countries point the way toward a new model of economic development. Távara suggests that rather than rely on foreign aid and expertise to promote projects that may ultimately increase local dependency, national governments and international agencies should find ways to foster and promote the local initiatives that are already taking place. Brenda Wyss and Radhika Balakrishnan (Chapter 23) supplement Távara's inventory of local development initiatives, citing innovative efforts of Third World women to remake their economic situations through a variety of organizational and entrepreneurial means. These existing initiatives are the potential foundations of an equitably and democratically transformed world economy.

Robin Broad and John Cavanagh (Chapter 20) echo this conception on a slightly different note. They criticize the "sin of universality" in development strategies and suggest thinking about development in terms of the existing strengths and orientations of Third World economies. Instead of imposing a model of development derived from the industrial experiences of the developed world, or a vision of the recent success of South Korea, Singapore, and Hong Kong, aid agencies and others could help the many existing nongovernmental organizations to promote agriculture and related industries in which most Third World producers are concentrated. This conception is supported and extended by Jessica Nembhard's analysis in Chapter 16. Her study suggests that foreign aid can be constructive and helpful, rather than destructive (exacerbating and causing dependencies and inequalities, and wasting precious resources), when it is controlled more by the recipients themselves and by democratic, local institutions. Aid giving may be justified when it is directed toward alleviating long-term poverty and inequalities and toward productive projects that are in the national and regional interest of the recipients and are self-sustaining, empowering, and locally sensitive.

For Carmen Diana Deere and Stan Malinowitz (Chapter 22), the emphasis is not so much on economic development strategies as on the forms of social and economic organization that could allow equitable economic development to take place. For Third World nations attempting to eliminate poverty and inequality at home, this means that a democratic socialism is on the agenda, to ensure that the wealth of a society is generated and distributed equitably under democratic conditions.

From a slightly different perspective, Wyss and Balakrishnan (Chapter 23) argue that inequalities within countries are often drawn along gender and ethnic lines. Grass-roots organizing among Third World women both in the United States and in their countries of origin is an essential ingredient of a real redistribution of power and wealth.

Environmental Crisis

Although many of the papers in this collection have environmental implications, some are directly focused on the global environmental crisis as a worldwide problem of resource depletion or, more specifically, as a problem that threatens the livelihoods of Third World peoples. Juliet B. Schor's chapter (Chapter 9) on working hours versus leisure time points to the possible global environmental benefits of greater leisure (and associated lower incomes and consumption) for people in the wealthier countries of the world.

Héctor Sáez (Chapter 18) and Anthony Guglielmi (Chapter 17) articulate certain principles for democratic responses to environmental crisis in the Third World. These principles, which have emerged from the ongoing debate in Third World countries over the causes of and remedies for environmental degradation, include self-sufficiency, regional economic planning and delinking, sustainable development, and popular participation in economic and environmental planning. Sáez and Guglielmi present the environment as an integral part of the economic picture, associating positive environmental effects with democratic and participatory approaches to economic development. When the environment is seen as an integral aspect of the economy, the opposition between economic and environmental goals disappears.

Global Militarization

Tom Riddell (Chapter 5) and Maribel Aponte-García (Chapter 19) take on the problem of global militarization and the major role of the United States in this ongoing process. Riddell suggests that the United States should pull back from its self-assigned role as global cop, eliminating armed forces in foreign countries and reallocating the enormous resources devoted to global policing functions to domestic economic and social development goals. Although this reallocation will require conversion of personnel and production facilities to nonmilitary uses in the United States, Aponte-García points out that it will also require economic conversion in the Third World. Many Third World countries have been drawn into the U.S. military industrial complex, producing goods and services for the U.S. military. The U.S. peace movement, which is currently very interested in economic conversion in the United States, should also consider the effects of demilitarization upon workers and communities in the Third World. Conversion plans that will help people deal with the dislocating effects of reduced military production are necessary for all parts of a militarized globe.

U.S. Economic Decline

Although this book presents neither a comprehensive analysis of U.S. economic decline nor a blueprint for reversing it, several chapters do contain important suggestions for increasing the benefits of international integration for the citizens of the United States. These chapters avoid the perspectives of both the Global Pessimists and the New Competitors. They suggest policies that people in the United States can pursue to improve their standard of living without eliminating U.S. interactions with the rest of the world and without pursuing destructive forms of international competition. At the same time, they reject the neoclassical view that letting the free market reign and adopting pure "free trade" and free international capital mobility is the solution to the economic problems of the United States.

Gerald Epstein (Chapter 10) identifies an important source of U.S. economic decline: the increasing degree to which international capital mobility has created incentives for multinational corporations—including U.S. corporations—to see their health and welfare as independent of the prosperity of the communities in which they operate. The result of this increasing lack of coincidence between the interests of corporations and communities is capital flight, lost jobs, lost tax revenues, impoverished government budgets, and growing indebtedness. The solution, according to Epstein, is to establish tax and regulatory policies that will allow multinational corporations, both U.S. and foreign, to operate only if they take into account the effects of their policies on communities and workers.

James Crotty (Chapter 8) also analyzes the problems that unregulated international capital mobility creates for the U.S. economy. The ability of wealthy individuals and institutions to send money abroad can act as a veto power over domestic economic policies, such as low interest rates, that are perceived as being against the interests of the rich. (See also Ilene Grabel's contribution on this same issue, in Chapter 3). Crotty points out that some countries, such as Japan and South Korea, have successfully used government "capital controls" to stem the tide of international capital flows.

Mehrene Larudee (Chapter 2) shows that, for the United States over its recent history, free trade can be seen as a major contributor to economic decline. In her discussion of the North American Free Trade Agreement (NAFTA), Larudee develops an alternative strategy for implementing trade policy. She urges labor and environmental activists from the United States, Mexico, and Canada to join forces in shaping international trade negotiations and in pushing governments to pursue policies that "level up" wages, environmental standards, and social spending rather than level them down to the lowest common denominator among the three countries.

While identifying unregulated international capital mobility as a potentially destructive economic force, Julie Graham (Chapter 11) reminds us that international capital mobility and capital flight are not characteristic of all firms or industries. Forms of internationalization differ from industry to industry, and there are many other causes of economic decline besides the internationalization of production. It is therefore not necessarily a good idea to limit international capital mobility, which is often a vehicle for workers in other countries to become employed and which may participate in reducing global inequality. Instead, it is important to protect workers and communities from the devastating effects of industrial change, whether it is caused by capital flight or by a range of other causes of industrial transformation.

Chapter 12, by Emily Kawano, looks at the Japanese approach to production, which is commonly viewed as a prominent source of Japanese competitiveness and U.S. economic decline. She argues that the Japanese production system is not necessarily a panacea for the United States, or at least not for the problems of U.S. workers. If U.S. firms are moving toward adopting this system, as they seem to be doing, U.S. workers will need to struggle for greater worker control, the right to unionize and to assert union power, and the inclusion of all workers in the benefits of this new approach to production.

On the international scale, the United States must also come to terms with Japan's new position in the world economy if destructive economic, political, and even military competition is to be avoided. Lyuba Zarsky

(Chapter 13) argues that reversing the economic decline of the United States is itself necessary if the nation is to stop blaming Japan for its problems and learn to deal with Japan in a constructive way. Zarsky points out, however, that the United States will not be able to reverse its economic decline until it abandons its ideological obsession with "free market" capitalism and embraces—as Japan has done—aspects of industrial policy and other limited forms of economic planning. Julie Graham likewise suggests more community control over investment decisions as a way of dealing with U.S. economic decline.

Finally, Juliet B. Schor (Chapter 14) argues that U.S. economic decline, when seen relative to the economic performance of other countries, may be more a function of the development and growth of other industrialized countries than a function of problems in the United States. Workers and communities in the United States need assistance in adjusting to ongoing changes in the international division of labor, but we should not try to restore our economic hegemony at the expense of people in other parts of the world.

Corporate Control

The emerging conservative consensus in favor of letting the market rule allows little space for either progressive coordination from above or for community power from below. Rather, free markets grant maximum freedom to large corporations to invest where they want, and how they want, subject only to the competition of other rich and powerful corporations. The benefits of this competition may on occasion trickle down, but often at the expense of environmental degradation, inequality, and insecurity.

Diane Flaherty (Chapter 7) describes the costs of implementing the "free market" vision in the emerging "capitalist" nations of Eastern Europe (and, by extension, the nations of the former Soviet Union). She argues that administering the so-called shock therapy of the free market and corporate control overnight will only create chaos in these nations. According to Flaherty, however, markets are not necessarily destructive, as long as they operate within a context of worker control of firms, rather than in the context of concentrated ownership by a wealthy few.

Third World nations that have chosen a socialist path are confronted with the fallout from the breakup of the Soviet Union and the associated institutional structures that bound Eastern Europe together. As Deere and Malinowitz argue in Chapter 22, these countries are experimenting with a variety of approaches that mix markets, planning, and democratic control to develop their economies, albeit under extremely difficult circumstances—including opposition by capitalist nations and the demise of their trading ties with the Eastern bloc nations.

A similar search for new approaches to markets is being pursued in

Latin America, according to Távara (Chapter 21). Here, too, different communities are experimenting with various mixtures of markets, private property, and community control to forge a more dynamic yet more equitable model of development than is offered by Western calls for corporate control and laissez-faire.

Such alternative models are also being pursued by women in Third World nations, according to Wyss and Balakrishnan (Chapter 23). They cite numerous examples of women organizing for changes: female multinational factory workers in the Philippines have organized unions; informal-sector women workers in Jamaica have formed two national associations; Indian women have organized to play a more powerful role in determining policies with respect to reproductive rights.

International Cooperation and Coordination

As the world's problems and hopes become more interdependent, so too must our solutions and actions. Neither unilateral national actions nor the actions of business operating through markets will be adequate to address many of the problems we face. In the following chapters, numerous areas are identified that require coordinated action among nations and citizens across national boundaries.

Environmental destruction is, perhaps, the most obvious example of a problem requiring international coordination. Sáez (Chapter 18) argues that concerted action among both the industrialized and the developing nations will be necessary before the dumping of environmental problems onto the poorer nations of the world can be halted.

Zarsky (Chapter 13) points out that restoring healthy economic growth in the United States will not be sufficient to avoid destructive economic and political competition with Japan. A new framework of cooperation between the two nations must be created, one that recognizes their greater degree of equality, as well as their common interests. Indeed, creating institutions of cooperation and coordination to overcome the destructive competition of the marketplace is important on a world scale, and not simply in Japanese–U.S. relations.

Managing the world's trading and financial system to maintain equitable, stable, and environmentally sustainable growth also requires the creation of institutions that will allow for international cooperation. Crotty (Chapter 8) describes how increasingly integrated financial markets make domestic macroeconomic policy less effective in achieving its traditional goal of maintaining full employment. One solution to this problem is for each country to institute capital controls that limit the ability of banks, corporations, and wealthy individuals to send money abroad.

Ilene Grabel (Chapter 3) addresses a similar problem, namely, the difficulties faced by nations that try to achieve national goals of high employment and an equitable distribution of income in a world dominated by the uncoordinated actions of a few powerful countries and in the context of international financial markets governed by rapid speculative movements. The result has been high world interest rates and an erratic distribution of credit to those countries and sectors of the world that are most productive and most needy. Grabel makes the case for more international coordination of global financial policies.

Manuel Pastor's discussion in Chapter 15 of the International Monetary Fund (IMF) and the Third World debt crisis makes this point abundantly clear. The IMF is an example of an international institution that coordinates policies; but, as Pastor shows, it coordinates them in the interests of the wealthy and the powerful in both the capitalist industrialized nations and, to a lesser extent, in the Third World. In the case of Third World debt, the goal of the IMF has been to help the Western banks get repaid and to force political and economic changes on Third World countries to make them safe for multinational banks and corporations and the "free market" system. Here, the problem has not been lack of coordination but coordination in the interests of the powerful few against the vast majority of the citizens of these nations. Pastor and Kiaran Honderich (Chapter 6) call for debt forgiveness by lending countries such as the United States as a way of allowing debt-ridden countries to use their scarce financial resources for their own development.

To address the need for more equitable credit and financial institutions, Grabel proposes a global bank that will create and distribute world credit equitably and efficiently. She insists that this global bank must be democratically controlled by representatives of all the world's people, and not dominated by the major industrialized countries, as is currently the case with the International Monetary Fund and the World Bank. Both Grabel and Pastor argue that democratic global institutions will not suffice to make the international financial system serve people rather than corporate interests. Local, grass-roots initiatives, such as those to fight IMF austerity and to promote an equitable and efficient North American Free Trade Agreement, will remain important in helping to ensure that international coordination is accountable.

As Deere and Malinowitz remind us in Chapter 22, "international coordination" of policies and grass-roots activities also involves, as a central component, international solidarity among progressive forces around the globe. Such international solidarity at the grass roots must include a continued commitment to prevent military and political intervention by powerful capitalist countries, particularly the United States, that attempt to prevent socialist, democratic, and anticorporate forces from coming to power in Third World countries.

What's to Come

The rest of the chapters in this book offer more focused analyses of particular problems and issues presented by the international economy. In Part I, "The Global Economy: International Flows and National Dilemmas," after Gerald Epstein (Chapter 1) provides some of the historical background and conceptual tools necessary to understand international economic issues, the other chapters address problems and opportunities created by international integration. Part II, "Changes in the Industrialized World: Nations and Multinationals," explores the difficulties facing U.S. workers and communities as they confront the power of global corporations and competition from other industrialized nations. Part III, "The Third World in the Global Economy: Failed Models and New Approaches," covers a range of issues from militarization to debt to environmental degradation. Each chapter in the book attempts to analyze a particular international issue or problem and to provide some insight into ways in which these have been or might be addressed.

ACKNOWLEDGMENT

We would like to thank Sam Bowles for his helpful comments on an earlier draft of this introduction.

BIBLIOGRAPHY

Children's Defense Fund. 1990. *Child Poverty in America*. Washington D.C.: Children's Defense Fund.
Kidron, Michael, and Ronald Segal. 1991. *The New State of the World Atlas*. 4th ed. New York: Simon & Schuster.
United Nations. 1991. *World Economic Survey*. New York: United Nations.
World Bank. 1990. *World Development Report 1990: Poverty*. New York: Oxford University Press (for the World Bank).
Worldwatch Institute. 1990. *State of the World 1990*. New York: W.W. Norton.

THE GLOBAL ECONOMY: INTERNATIONAL FLOWS AND NATIONAL DILEMMAS

1

GERALD EPSTEIN

Power, Profits, and Cooperation in the Global Economy

Sometimes it seems that we are on the verge of a new era. Around the globe, millions of people are moved by the power of two ascendant ideas: capitalism and globalization. Politicians and businesspersons from the United States have declared victory in the cold war: capitalism won, they shout. The collapse of communism and the rush to create private property and "free" markets in previously Communist countries are compelling testimony to this claim of capitalist victory.

If capitalism seems on the rise, it is of a particular brand. The same politicians, economists, and business consultants who tout the victory of free markets tell us that we are witnessing the creation of a truly global capitalism—where the goal of businesses and nations around the world is to become "competitive" in the global marketplace; the key is to attract investment from around the globe; the challenge is to export products; and the winners will be the countries that can fight it out, lean and mean, in the global economy.

If there is a debate about these ideas, it is a debate about what type of capitalism will best serve the needs of global competitiveness: a free market, "laissez-faire" brand, where the government interferes as little as possible, or one based on "industrial policy," where government is involved in picking winners and losers. But both sides of this debate accept the idea that global capitalism is the wave of the future, if not the present.

Yet, despite the increasing dominance of these two ideas, the reality is far more complicated. Eastern Europe and the former Soviet Union face enormous difficulties in their transition from communism to capitalism; the continuing power of Islam in many areas of the world belies the global character of capitalist ideology; in the United States, one of the main bastions of capitalism, the rise of protectionist sentiment threatens to block the ideology of globalization and free trade. And with the global economy enmeshed in a period of recession and, perhaps, longer-term stagnation, questions abound about the viability of this "new" idea and reality.

19

This complex picture is as it should be, for the idea of global capitalism is not a new one; nor is the unevenness of its sway or of its performance
unique to this period. Since its inception, capitalism on a global scale has
been a system characterized by fits and starts, by uneven development in
both ideas and reality, and by growth, stagnation, and contradiction.

It is true, however, that with the collapse of communism in Eastern
Europe and the Soviet Union, these ideas are now less challenged than they
have been for a century. And the reality of a global capitalism—a system of
capitalist nations highly integrated into a global economy—is probably
more plausible now than it has been at any time since the First World War.

It is imperative, then, to understand how this potentially emerging
global capitalism works. What is its structure? What are its problems or
contradictions? Who gains and who loses from this system? What can nations, workers, and communities do to make sure that the global economy
serves their needs, rather than the needs of the few?

In order to begin answering these important questions, it is necessary
to analyze the role of profits, power, and cooperation in the global economy. In an international capitalist economy, profit seeking is the engine
that makes the economy grow and drives firms to expand their international
operations. At the same time, international profit making is impossible
without the exercise of power. Power, however, is distributed highly
unequally in the world economy: just consider the difference between
the United States and Bangladesh. Because power plays a central role in
international transactions, the distribution of the benefits of international
transactions will be strongly influenced by who has that power and who
does not.

In the end, however, economies cannot run on power alone. International cooperation is therefore also important to the structure of the international economy. But the terms of that cooperation itself will be strongly
influenced by the distribution of power in the economy.

Sometimes the structure of power and cooperation stabilizes profits at
a high level in the international economy, and a period of strong economic
growth occurs, as it did in many parts of the world in the so-called Golden
Age of the 1950s and 1960s; sometimes the structure of power and cooperation breaks down, profits stagnate, and a period of economic crisis and
political conflict emerges, as in the 1930s and 1940s. In short, this system
based on profit seeking, power, and cooperation is potentially very powerful, but it is also fragile and erratic. The same system delivers the vast economic growth of the 1950s to 1970s and World War II of the 1940s.

Wars and crisis are not the only costs of this global capitalist system.
Even during periods of growth and stability, as long as the underlying
structure of the economy is primarily dependent on profits and power, the

world economy will neglect the interests of vast numbers of the world's population and future generations. A new structure—one that is based on a more equal distribution of power, that can lead to democratic cooperation by the world's citizens, and that can, at least partially, replace private profits as the driving force of economic activity—will be necessary to reduce the glaring inequalities and periodic crises that global capitalism inevitably offers us.

Capitalism on a Global Scale

Capitalism is not a new economic system, and from its beginning, capitalism has had a tendency to expand beyond its regional and national boundaries, bursting onto the global scene. Ever since Adam Smith, economists have known that the search for profits would lead individuals and businesses anywhere they could in search of even more profits. This has led not only to Adam Smith's truck, barter, and trade but also to billions of dollars of lending and borrowing (credit flows) across national borders by huge international banks, to huge conglomerates like General Motors setting up shops in country after country (foreign direct investment), and to people moving from one country to another in search of work or investment opportunities. And through these international flows of people, goods, and money, the fates of different national economies—and peoples—become linked to one another, and national economies become part of a global economy. These links have been happy ones for some and extremely unhappy ones for others. And whether happy or unhappy, they have evolved in uneven ways, producing ups and downs for virtually all nations that have been a part of the global chain.

Figure 1.1 shows the ups and downs of the global economy from 1900 to 1987. As the chart indicates, the world has been characterized by periods of rapid expansion and periods of relatively stagnant growth. The periods of expansion have generally been accompanied by increases in living standards for countries involved in the global system, but periods of decline have been associated with great hardship and, on occasion, calamitous war or economic destruction.

But even within periods of up or down, not all countries or groups interconnected in the global economy fare the same. Figure 1.2 shows that over a long sweep of capitalist history, from 1860 to 1959, some regions have fared far better than others. Income per capita grew fivefold in North America over that period, whereas income per capita grew hardly at all in most of Asia. Some groups enter into international interaction by choice; others, like Africans in the Atlantic slave trade, are dragged kicking and screaming into the world economy, and with the most dire consequences.

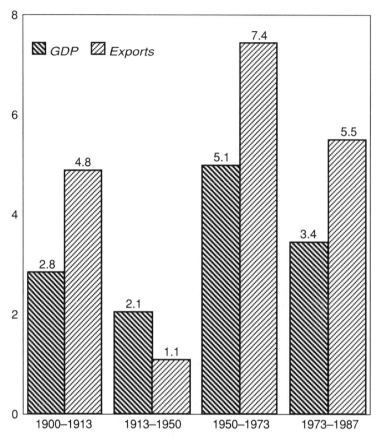

Figure 1.1 Annual average percentage growth rate in GDP and exports, 1900–1987. These data are for a sample of 32 countries from North America, Asia, and Latin America. *Source:* Maddison 1989:32.

Some groups find their incomes rising and their ways of life becoming more secure, while others find devastation of their standard of living or the way of life they and their ancestors might have known for hundreds of years.

This process of uneven development is one of the dominant features of the international economy. Figure 1.3 shows some indicators of uneven development on an international scale. Income per capita in the United States in 1987 was almost thirty times what it was in Nigeria. In 1987, the infant mortality rate was only 7 per 1,000 live births in Sweden; in Nigeria the rate was 174 per 1,000.

In recent years, these extremes in the distribution of income and welfare around the world are getting much worse. As Figure 1.4 shows, among the world's nations, the ratio of income of the richest 20 percent to that

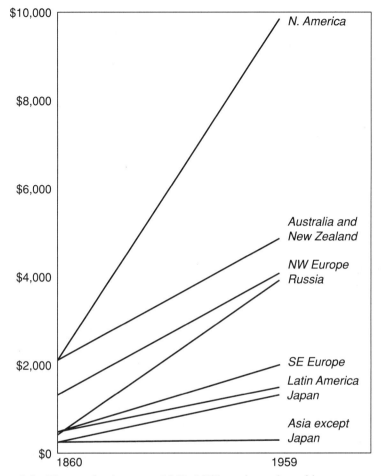

Figure 1.2 Uneven development, 1860–1959, as shown in real income per capita in 1990 dollars. *Source:* Bowles and Edwards 1992.

of the poorest 20 percent was 30:1 in 1960. By 1990, this difference had doubled, to 60:1. In the decade of the 1980s alone, the disparity between the richest and poorest countries leaped by one-third, from 45:1, to 60:1. As Figure 1.4 makes abundantly clear, growth and change do not come to all at the same time, or in the same way.

Not only does the rate of economic growth appear to have its ups and downs, so does the intensity of international economic interactions. Figure 1.5 shows the growth of world trade over the period 1850 to 1989. It shows that the rate of growth of world trade has its ups and downs, plummeting to a virtual standstill during the Great Depression of the 1930s,

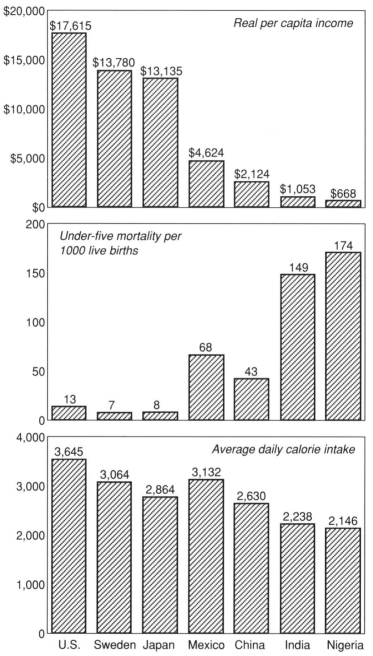

Figure 1.3 Uneven development among nations, 1987. *Source:* Bowles and Edwards 1992.

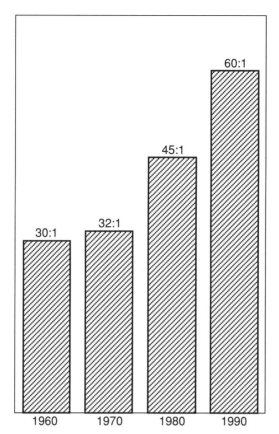

Figure 1.4　Income per capita ratio between the richest 20 percent and poorest 20 percent of the world's countries. *Source:* United Nations 1992.

rising dramatically between the end of the Second World War and 1970, falling again in the last several decades. As one can see from the graph, there are periods of quite remarkable expansion and periods of equally remarkable contraction of international economic links.

Sometimes these ebbs and flows in international links reflect choices made by governments to reduce or increase their countries' connections to the global economy. An example is the decision by many Latin American countries to reduce their links to the global economy after the devastating effects of the decline in world trade caused by the Great Depression of the 1930s. Figure 1.6 shows the decline in imports faced by Latin American and the richer Western countries between 1929 and 1932. By 1932, because of the huge loss in income associated with its dependence on exports during the Great Depression, Latin America faced a decline in the imports

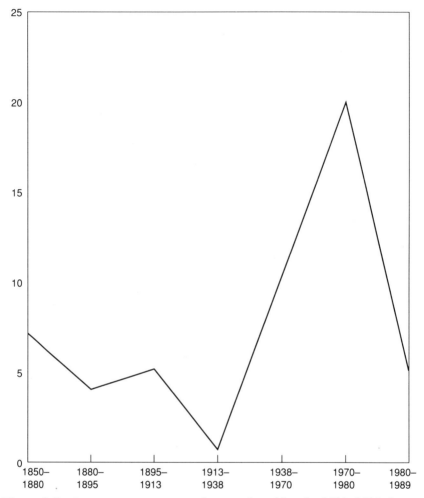

Figure 1.5 Average percentage growth rates of world trade, 1850–1989. *Sources:* Gordon, Edwards, and Reich 1982:table 2.3; UNCTAD 1991:table 1.5.

it could purchase to only 40 percent of what it could buy in 1929. As a result, many Latin American countries decided to delink—reduce their dependence on exports and imports—and looked inward to develop their economies somewhat independently of links to the global economy. Figure 1.7 shows that Latin American countries were able to recover more rapidly from the Great Depression than were many of the richer industrialized countries. It would be fair to speculate that this was due, at least in part, to the decision of the Latin American countries to delink.

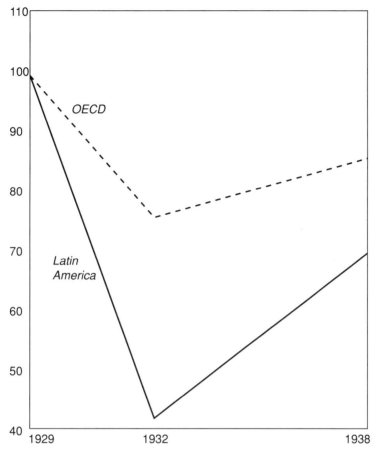

Figure 1.6 Index of real imports to Latin America and OECD countries, 1929–1938 (1929 = 100). *Source:* Maddison 1989:57.

Thus, there has been an enormous variety of historical experiences with international capitalism: sometimes it grows rapidly; sometimes it declines into recession or depression. Sometimes nations and groups benefit from being involved in it; sometimes they lose miserably. Sometimes governments decide to integrate their countries as much as possible into the international economy; sometimes they choose to delink from it, close themselves to international trade and financial interactions.

This variety of experiences makes clear that despite what the ideologies say, throwing one's self or one's nation into the global economy headfirst is not always the best strategy: it can go down as well as up. And even if *it* goes up, that does not necessarily mean that all participants will go up with it.

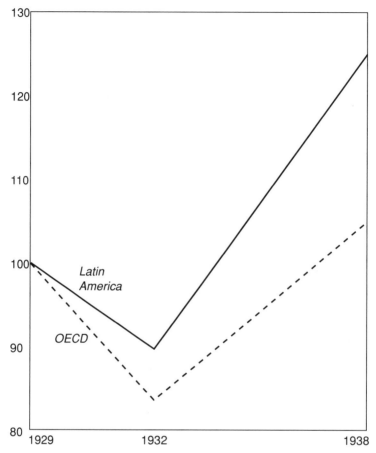

Figure 1.7 Index of real GDP growth rate in Latin America and OECD countries, 1929–1938 (1929 = 100). *Source:* Maddison 1989:57.

How can we make progress in understanding these three trends of the global economy: the ups and downs, the uneven development among and within countries, and the expansion and contraction of international interactions among nations?

The key is to understand the importance of three ideas for international capitalism: profits, power, and cooperation. Profits are the driving force for a capitalist economic system, power underlies the production and distribution of profit, and cooperation is necessary to prevent the competitive struggle for profits from breaking down into chaos on an international scale.

Profits

The search for profits by business people (capitalists) is the driving force of the capitalist economy, and understanding this process is the secret to understanding the dynamics of the economic system, both at the national level and at the level of the international system.

At one level, the search for profits is all very simple and follows common sense. Capitalists start with some money, either their own or some borrowed money (say from a bank). They use this money to buy raw materials, invest in equipment, and hire workers. They organize production to get these workers to produce a product. And then they find or create a market for the product and sell it. If the amount of money they make by selling the product is greater than what it cost them to produce it, they have made a surplus, or a profit. If not, they have made a loss. If they see that they have made a great profit, they start the circuit again; indeed, they may invest in more plants and equipment, hire more workers, and produce more next time in the hope of making even more profits. If they have made a loss or not as much profit as they expected, they may cut back on production and lay off workers; at that point they may look for some other line of business, or they may go out of business altogether. This is the industrial circuit of profits.

The key idea is that if profits are expected to be high, capitalists invest and the economy expands; if profits are expected to be low, capitalists may cut back on investment and production, and the economy will tend to decline (Gordon 1978; Gordon, Edwards, and Reich 1982; Bowles, Gordon, and Weisskopf 1991; Marglin and Schor 1990).

Note that in addition to this industrial circuit of profits, there is also a financial circuit; the capitalists may have initially borrowed money from banks to buy equipment, factories, or raw materials. Banks earn their profits from the interest that the firms pay them. If firms are doing well, then the banks will tend to have little trouble getting their interest payments and their borrowed money returned. If firms are losing money, however, they may stop paying interest and default on their loans. Banks, too, do well when business profits are high.

The Circuit of Capital Internationally

This same logic applies at both the national and international levels. Indeed, it helps explain why capitalism quickly becomes an international system, a system of national economies linked together by markets. The way that capitalists make more profit is by buying raw materials and equipment more cheaply; by hiring workers who, for a given level of productivity, require lower wages or, for a given level of wages, have higher productivity;

and by finding markets for their products where they can sell more, or more easily, or at a higher price. And the way banks make more money is by finding new customers to borrow and pay interest.

It is easy to see why some firms would want to buy raw materials, like oil, at the cheapest price possible: they might choose to import oil from the Middle East so that they can make a higher profit on the products they sell. It is easy to see why some firms might decide to become multinational, having operations in more than one country: they can produce abroad and find cheaper or more productive labor. It is easy to see why some firms may look for foreign markets: they can sell more of their products or sell the ones they have at higher prices.

Some firms might find it easier to market their products abroad by actually becoming multinational and setting up shop there—that is, by undertaking foreign direct investment (FDI). Thus, the search for profit leads firms to internationalize—to import from abroad, to move abroad, and to try to sell more abroad. Similarly, banks, looking for new customers to borrow money and pay interest, may well look for new customers in foreign lands.

Table 1.1 illustrates these circuits of industrial and financial capital. When these circuits are applied to the international economy, several complications arise; these require explanation before we can return to the discussion of profits, power, and cooperation. These complications affect profits and profit making and are peculiar to international economic relations: (1) international money and the balance of payments, (2) the terms of trade, and (3) exchange rates.

TABLE 1.1
International Circuits of Financial and Industrial Capital: M→C→C'→M'

M	M→C	C→C'	C'→M'
finance (borrowing; foreign direct investment [MNCs]; international money)	buy inputs (buy imports or domestic goods and foreign or domestic labor power)	production (at home or MNC abroad)	sell output (sell domestically, export, or MNC sell in foreign markets)

M = money; M' = money greater than M; M' − M = profit
C = commodities, including but not limited to raw materials and labor power
C' = commodities with a value greater than C, including but not limited to final products

International Money and the Balance of Payments

When this circuit is applied to a country operating in the international economy, the money (M) the country uses to buy commodities from abroad, that is, to import goods, has to have a particular characteristic: it has to be international money. That means that it has to be money that is accepted by the foreign business people from whom goods are being bought. Mexicans cannot, as a rule, pay for imports of machinery from the United States with the Mexican currency, pesos. They need to pay in a currency that U.S. exporters want, dollars.

It turns out that one of the most important aspects of inequality in the world economy stems from the fact that some nations—like the United States, Great Britain, Germany, and Japan—can create money that is accepted for payment internationally, whereas others—for example, Mozambique, Nicaragua, Bolivia, and Morocco—cannot.

Compare the constraints facing Mexico and the United States, for example. If Mexico wants to import more goods than it is exporting, it is running a trade, or balance-of-payments, deficit. How can it find the money to pay for these imports or finance its balance-of-payments deficit when its export earnings are not sufficient to pay for them? Mexico must borrow dollars from foreign banks, or it must sell off some of its domestic resources—such as its corporations or oil fields—in order to get the dollars to pay for these imports. If foreigners are not willing to lend dollars, except at exorbitant interest rates, or to buy domestic resources, except at bargain basement prices, then Mexico must cut back on its imports; that is, it must adjust its balance-of-payments deficit. Cutting back on necessary imports can only be accomplished by cutting back spending, investment, or consumption, by tightening the belts of people or institutions in the economy. Where spending is severely reduced, these policies are called austerity measures.

The United States is not in such a difficult position. Since it can pay for its imports in dollars, it need not persuade others to lend it money or buy its resources.[1] So belt tightening and austerity are not so necessary.

Moreover, the fact that only some countries produce international money (like the dollar) and all countries need it gives banks from the international money countries an important edge: countries that need international money will usually want to borrow money from these banks and are willing to pay high fees and interest rates in the process. If these countries are able to repay their loans, the banks can make a high profit, through the international financial circuit of capital.

Terms of Trade

When this circuit of capital is applied to an economy with important trade and financial interactions with the rest of the world, the terms of trade become a very important determinant of profits and, therefore, investment. The terms of trade measure how many export goods a country must sell in order to buy one import good. The fewer export goods it must sell to buy one import good, the cheaper are the imports, and therefore, the more goods a country can buy with its exports.

In other words, the terms of trade are the price of a country's imports relative to its exports. For example, if a typical import good costs $20 and the typical export good costs $100, then the terms of trade are $20/$100 = 1/5. This says that it costs one-fifth of the export good's value (or twenty cents to the dollar) to buy one import good. Assume that the price of the import good goes up to $50. The terms of trade facing this country have changed to $50/$100 = 1/2. Now the home country must sell half a good for each import good; each import good now costs fifty cents to the dollar; its price has more than doubled. In this case we say that the terms of trade facing this country have *deteriorated*; imports are more expensive compared with exports. The total amount of goods and services this country can buy has now gone down.

In terms of algebra, let P* equal the price of the import good. Let P equal the price of the export good. Then the terms of trade are given by the proportion P*/P.

Who will bear the burden of this decline in total amount of goods and services available? Workers may bear part of it; that is, since imports are more expensive relative to what the workers produce, the purchasing power of their wages could fall. Capitalists, owners of firms, may find that their profits fall as a result of the increased costs of imports (e.g., oil, plant, and equipment) compared with the revenue they make from the goods they sell.

Who bears how much of the burden will depend on a number of factors. Most important is the distribution of power in the political economic system. If workers are able to maintain their wages, the brunt will be borne by the owners; if owners have all the power, the workers will bear the entire burden. Usually the outcome is somewhere in between.

Exchange Rates

There is one complication to this picture that must be taken into account. One of the key factors that distinguish international economic relations from domestic ones is that in international economic relations, different countries use different currencies. Germans use deutsche marks, Mexicans use pesos, Japanese use yen, the British use pounds. However, in order to figure out how much one good costs in relation to another, you cannot measure one in marks and the other in yen. That would be like comparing grapefruit and watermelon. When comparing prices, they have to be put into a common unit. For example, prices of German goods have to be translated from deutsche marks to dollars. Similarly, if a German tourist visits the United States and goes to McDonald's, he or she must pay in dollars, not deutsche marks. The tourist must *exchange* deutsche marks for dollars.

The rate at which one country's money can be exchanged for another country's money is called the exchange rate. Using the exchange rate, we can now translate foreign prices into domestic prices. So, for example, assume U.S. cars cost $10,000 and British cars (in Great Britain) cost £5000. What are the terms of trade? It is impossible to say without translating dollars into pounds or vice versa.

Each pound is worth about $2. We will call that E, the exchange rate between dollars and pounds. So, British cars cost £5,000 at $2/pound = $10,000, or $E \times P^*$. So the terms of trade are $(E \times P^*)/P = $10,000/$10,000 = 1$.

What if the exchange rate changes? Say it moves to $4 a pound. Then the terms of trade would become $(E \times P^*)/P = ($4/pound \times £5,000)/$10,000 = $20,000/$10,000 = 2$. Now the terms of trade have deteriorated; the home country must send twice as many cars to Great Britain as it had previously for every car it gets back.

Is that good or bad for the home country? The implication of the previous analysis is that an increase in the cost of a British pound from $2 to $4 would be bad for the home country, in this example, the United States. Since imports cost more, the home country has access to fewer goods; so wages or profits, or both, will have to decline.

But here we have to recognize that under some conditions, an increase in the cost of foreign products can have some positive effects that can offset the negative effects of a deterioration in the terms of trade. How? By making home-produced goods more competitive and increasing the demand for them. That can increase production at home and increase the number of jobs available to home country workers.

To summarize: when the home currency appreciates in value, the cost of import goods falls and that of export goods increases; when the home currency depreciates in value, the opposite occurs.

Appreciations of the currency, then, cause a deterioration in competitiveness and improvement in the terms of trade; a depreciation of the currency causes an improvement in competitiveness but a deterioration in the terms of trade. Which is better for wages and profits depends on whether the demand for the products is highly responsive to changes in prices.

As an example, take an appreciation of the exchange rate. If the demand for domestic exports falls a great deal when a country's export prices go up, then even though that country can import more per unit of exported goods, the total amount it can sell abroad goes down; so the country cannot really benefit from an improvement in the terms of trade.

What Determines Exchange Rates?

As the previous section suggests, the exchange rate is important because it can affect competitiveness and terms of trade, both of which can have an important effect on the economy. But what determines exchange rates? One would think that since exchange rates are so important for the trade of goods and services, trade in goods and services would determine exchange rates. But, in fact, that is not so. For what determines exchange rates is the demand for and supply of financial assets—like bonds, stocks, and bank accounts—measured in different currencies. One estimate puts the *daily* value of foreign-exchange market transactions at $250 billion in 1987, whereas the daily volume of world trade was only $10 billion. (Schor 1992:2; UNCTAD 1991:4). So, for example, if interest rates are high in the United States, Germans will want to invest their money in the United States—perhaps put their money in U.S. bank accounts or buy U.S. government bonds. To do that, they must first sell their deutsche marks and buy dollars, since they need dollars to open a U.S. bank account. When they sell their deutsche marks, it drives down the value of the deutsche mark; and when they buy dollars, that drives up the value of the dollar. So, that makes goods produced in the United States more expensive, worsening U.S. competitiveness but improving the U.S. terms of trade.

German investors may want to sell deutsche marks and buy dollars not just because U.S. interest rates are higher in the United States than in Germany. They might also want to buy dollars because they expect the value of the dollar to go up over the next year. For example, if the current value of the dollar is DM2 and it doubles to DM4 next year, an investor could sell DM2 and buy $1 now; a year later the same investor could sell the $1 and get DM4. The original investment has doubled, not because interest rates were high in the United States but because the investor decided to gamble that the dollar would go up in value over the next year. In that sense, buying foreign currency can be like any other speculative investment in the stock market or land or condos: you buy them now hoping you can sell them later at a higher price.

In short, we have discovered a paradox: exchange rates can have an enormous impact on a country by affecting the cost of imported goods and by affecting the competitiveness of a country's products; yet the exchange rate is not determined by the demand for and supply of these products, but rather by the demand for and supply of paper assets—by financial markets.

The fact that exchange rates have a huge impact on trade and profits in goods and services, yet are determined by financial markets, has important consequences for the way the international economy works. The reason is that the foreign-exchange market, like the stock market, is essentially one big gambling casino. It is driven by whim, fear, and greed, not careful consideration of long-run efficiency or profitability. When whim and fancy rule production and investment decisions, an economy is not likely to be very productive and healthy, however much money is made in financial dealings. The millions made by junk bond specialists Kravis and Kohlberg, while many companies they bought were destroyed, shows that speculative financial profits do not necessarily a productive economy make.

Since financial markets are driven by whim and fancy, rumor and speculation, they operate like casinos. Exchange rates, like prices on the stock exchange, can go up and down like a roller coaster, on a track with no apparent plan or reason. Such ups and downs in exchange rates can hurt the economy by making goods overly expensive or overly cheap. This erratic movement in exchange rates may also, therefore, cause similar erratic movements in profits and power.

This movement occurs under a system of flexible exchange rates. Sometimes governments, in an effort to avoid such erratic and destructive movements, fix the exchange rate at a given value. The international economy has gone through periods of fixed exchange rates (as under the Bretton Woods system, 1944–71) and flexible exchange rates (as under today's system). Usually, systems of fixed and flexible exchange rates operate side by side, with some countries having one and some the other. For example, in the current period, the Japanese, German, and U.S. exchange rates are flexible relative to one another, but most African countries fix their exchange rates vis-à-vis at least one major industrialized country's currency.

The world economy has gone through long periods when most of the industrial countries had fixed exchanged rates, followed by periods when most had flexible rates. These periods of flexible rates have in turn been followed by a move back to fixed rates. Why has there been this cycle up and down, back and forth? To some extent it might simply be a case of the grass looking greener on the other side of the fence.

But a better explanation is that these different exchange-rate "systems" are connected with entirely different regimes of international regulation of the world economy, regimes that in turn rise and eventually fall with the power of nations in the world. The fixed exchange-rate system of 1880–1914 (the international gold standard) was connected with the dominant economic and political power of Great Britain. The floating exchange-rate period of the 1920s and the 1930s was associated with a competitive struggle among the world's major capitalist powers—Great Britain, Germany, France, and the United States. During the period of the Bretton Woods system of fixed exchange rates, 1944–71, the United States had supreme economic and military power among the capitalist economies. And the floating period of 1973 to the present is again one of economic competition and lack of a dominant economic power (see Table 1.2).

These ebbs and flows of hegemonic power among different countries are mirrored, to some extent, by the countries' relative positions in interna-

TABLE 1.2
Exchange-Rate Regimes and International Political Power

	Exchange-Rate Regime	Hegemony/ Competition
1880–1914	fixed (gold standard)	Great Britain
1920–1944	intermittent (flexible and fixed)	competition/war
1944–1971	fixed (Bretton Woods)	United States
1973–	flexible	competition

tional trade. Figure 1.8 shows the share of world manufacturing exports held by each of three major powers—the United States, the United Kingdom, and Japan—since 1899. The United Kingdom, dominant in the nineteenth century, has now greatly declined, first overcome by the United States, which in turn has now been matched by Japan.

Power

Now we can return to the main trail of our story: the role of power, profits, and cooperation in the international economy. So far we have described the role of profits. We have seen important examples that demonstrate that this process of profit making is strongly affected by who has power in the international economy and, indeed, whether the international economy is characterized by a strong center of power at all.

We have seen that banks in countries that have the power to issue international currency have an advantage in getting profitable banking business and that countries lacking the power to issue international money have many fewer options for dealing with balance-of-payments problems. Similarly, we have seen that countries that have the power to improve their terms of trade can also improve the profitability or living standards of their corporations and citizens. Finally, we have seen that the dynamics of exchange rates are strongly affected by the existence or absence of a single overwhelmingly powerful country, or hegemon.

All of these examples indicate that power plays a central role in the international economy, and it also affects how the economy functions, who is advantaged and who is disadvantaged. Indeed, the nature and existence of this power affects whether the international economy will function at all.

So, to complete our story of the international circuits of capital, we must take into account this factor that makes these circuits work: power. In

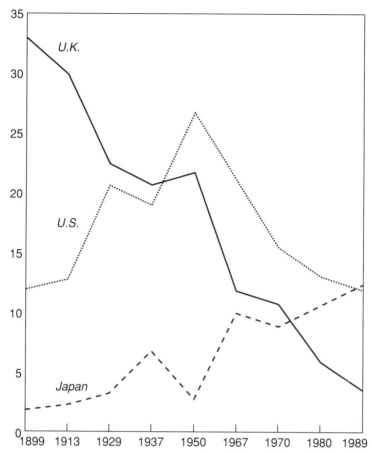

Figure 1.8 Percentage share of world manufacturing exports for Japan, the United Kingdom, and the United States, 1899–1989. *Sources:* Beaud 1983:151; UNCTAD 1991:table A13; International Bank for Reconstruction and Development 1991:tables 14 and 16.

the domestic and the international economies, power plays a central role in both the production and distribution of profits.

And here is where political economy and mainstream economics part ways. Mainstream economics contends that this circuit of capital, if it is controlled by markets and competition, is one where freedom and individual choice reign supreme, whereas political economists argue that although markets are important, they operate only in the context of power relations among people and groups.

The classic example of this analysis of the importance of power is the "labor market." According to mainstream economics, workers sell their labor power to the highest bidder; if they do not like their jobs, either because the jobs pay too little or are unsafe or because the hours are too long, they simply find others. If they feel they are exploited, they simply quit; they find other jobs where they will not be exploited.

Political economists, however, from the time of Karl Marx, have pointed out that workers do not necessarily have such freedom to choose; if jobs are in scarce supply, a worker may be forced to take a job or starve. Workers' lack of ownership of wealth and property, combined with high levels of unemployment, gives them little power to choose a job and working conditions, whereas it gives the employer much more power in that situation. Indeed, it is hard to understand why, if power were unimportant or equally distributed, we would have a society divided into a class of capitalists who make a profit and a class of workers who only work for wages.

If power is central to profit making at the national level, it is even more important in international economics. For in the domestic sphere, economic relations—buying and selling, lending and borrowing—operate within a legal system enforced by police and courts of law. If a contract is violated, the injured parties can bring a lawsuit against the alleged perpetrator and get redress. However, in the international economy, there is no overriding set of laws, no international police to enforce them, no courts to adjudicate them. In such a situation, it is remarkable that any international commerce occurs at all.

Since there is no international court of law, military power is crucial in structuring international economic relations. The use of military force changes from period to period—from colonization by European powers in the eighteenth and nineteenth centuries to occasional intervention and constant threat of intervention in the late twentieth century (e.g., the Gulf War). Military power is not always used simply for immediate economic gain; it often provides a less direct framework for economic and political interactions on the global scale.

But military power is a blunt and destructive instrument. Simply the threat of war can achieve economic and political gains. But even there, threatening war to achieve every gain will quickly undermine the credibility of such threats, as happened to the credibility of the boy who cried wolf a few times too many.

The use of economic carrots and sticks—payoffs and penalties—is another means by which power enhances the circuit of profit. The promise of economic aid to the former Soviet Union in exchange for opening up their oil and gas fields to exploitation by Western multinational corporations is one example of the use of economic power to enhance profitability on the international scale.

However, international economic relations cannot operate on power and competition alone. Other means of organizing and structuring international relations are necessary to a stable and profitable world economy. These other mechanisms involve cooperation. Nevertheless, it is important to remember that underlying cooperation are these very same inequalities of political, economic, and military power.

Cooperation

International cooperation takes many forms. The creation of the United Nations, the International Monetary Fund, and the World Bank at the end of the Second World War and recent environmental summits are examples of "multilateral" cooperation, when more than two countries agree to work together to achieve some international goal: stable exchange rates, redistribution of world resources, or the protection of the environment. The potential for cooperation stems from the likelihood that the independent actions of different nations will achieve a situation inferior to what could be achieved if the nations worked together; this is called a coordination failure.

The classic case is the so-called prisoner's dilemma.[2] Take the example of trade negotiations. The United States and European countries are bargaining over whether to have trade barriers that protect their least efficient, most politically powerful domestic industries. If only the United States has protection, its corporations' profits will be highest (see Table 1.3). If the European countries protect their industries while the United States does not, that is the best situation for Europe's industries and the worst for the United States. If each country makes its decision in isolation, each will pick its best policy from its own point of view. The end result, however, would be reciprocal protection, the worst of all possible worlds from the point of view of industry. Therefore, it is in the interest of both countries' capitalists to negotiate and try to coordinate their policies so they can reach the no-protection–no-protection solution: the second-best solution for them all.

Here, the worst solution, which would be arrived at independently, indicates a coordination failure. The potential exists for negotiation and co-

TABLE 1.3
Prisoner's Dilemma: Protecting Industries

		EUROPEAN ACTION	
		Protect	*Do nothing*
U.S. ACTION	*Protect*	Worst for both	Best for U.S. Worst for Europe
	Do nothing	Worst for U.S. Best for Europe	Second best for both

operation to improve profits for the firms involved in the bargaining. If there were such cooperation and compromise, the two countries might end up taking no action whatsoever, which would be better for both.

It was with this in mind that institutions such as the IMF and the World Bank were created after the Second World War. Cooperative institutions were established for the benefit of firms operating in the major countries, to improve their profitability over and above what they would have achieved from unconstrained competition.

Those groups without sufficient power are not even allowed at the bargaining table. The poorest countries have relatively little power in the International Monetary Fund or the World Bank; workers from the United States, likewise, have very little say in the agreements that are reached there. And while free trade might be better for the corporations in our example, it is not necessarily in the best interests of workers who work for them. So the nature and results of cooperation will depend largely on the distribution of power in the world economy that determines who will be represented at the bargaining table and what the agenda will be. Hence, although cooperation is an important component of the international structure of profit making, the distribution of international power will leave an indelible mark on the nature of that cooperation and who benefits from it.

Social Structure of Accumulation (SSA)

As we have seen, making profits and investing are riddled with problems and conflicts. There are conflicts between capitalists and workers, between capitalists of different nations, and between workers of different nations. And the possible problems that can arise in the international economy are even greater. For example, the prices of raw materials (C) might suddenly increase, markets (M') might suddenly collapse, and borrowers might not be able to repay debts (M' →M). All these problems interrupt the flow of the circuits of capital and endanger profits and investment in an economy totally dependent on the profit motive for its health. If the economy is going to prosper, these problems have to be reduced.

A social structure of accumulation (SSA) is a set of institutions and rules of the game, domestic and international, that structure these conflicts and problems (Bowles, Gordon, and Weisskopf 1991). The set of institutions uses a combination of power and cooperation. Examples of SSA institutions are the International Monetary Fund, the World Bank, and the hegemonic role of the United States. When they reduce conflicts and stabilize the international economy, it is easier for capitalists to make profits, investment tends to be higher, and the world economy, or at least some parts of it, tends to grow more rapidly. When these institutions cease to work, conflicts become more important, the economy becomes destabilized, and it becomes harder to make profits. As a result, there is less investment and growth.

It is important to note that each SSA is structured around a set of institutions and rules of the game that imply certain power relations among countries and groups; consequently, these rules of the game work to the advantage of some groups and countries and to the disadvantage of others. Historically, these social structures of accumulation have been structured around one or a few very powerful countries that have established the rules of the game and the set of institutions—often based on their military power and economic might. For example, in the nineteenth century, Great Britain was the dominant economic and military power. As a result, this period came to be known as Pax Britannica. Similarly, the United States was the dominant power in the middle twentieth century and presided over a time known as Pax Americana (see Table 1.4).

For several reasons these institutions and structures eventually break down. One such reason is competition from other capitalists asserting their power. For example, in the late nineteenth and early twentieth centuries, capitalists from Germany, the United States, and Japan began winning the competitive struggle with banks and industry from Great Britain. Great Britain ceased to be the dominant power, and international arrangements that were built around Great Britain's dominance, such as the international gold standard, began to collapse. Similarly, competition from industries in Germany and Japan have greatly reduced the competitive dominance of U.S. firms in the latter part of the twentieth century. This in turn has upset arrangements established at the end of the Second World War, such as the Bretton Woods system of fixed exchange rates.

A second group that can create opposition to the structures and rules of the game is composed of workers and others resistant to the domination and exploitation that may be associated with the rules of the game. Examples of this opposition include anticolonial wars of liberation against Great

TABLE 1.4
Social Structures of Accumulation

	Period	*Regime*	*Center country*
1880–1914	Pax Britannica	hegemonic	Great Britain
1919–1944	economic and political crisis	no hegemony	
1944–1971	Pax Americana	hegemonic	United States
1973–	?	?	?

Britain in India and a number of African countries, and also the Vietnam War against the United States in the 1960's.

When the old rules and institutions cease to function properly, the world economy often enters a period of instability—as it did in the 1920s and 1930s—until a new set of institutions is put in place. The ebb and flow of these SSAs helps to explain the ups and downs of the world economy that we saw in Figure 1.1 above. At present, Pax Americana has broken down. Yet a new social structure of accumulation has yet to emerge. What form will it take? There are a variety of views of the current and emerging international structure, none of which is completely correct. Below I identify five such views.

In the abstract, the SSA approach, by itself, cannot indicate who gains and who loses from the structure of the global economy. Only by filling in the structure and looking in detail at how it operates can one discover the sources and likely outcomes of uneven development in the international system. That is why understanding alternative possible structures of the global SSA is critical to understanding the operations of the system.

Alternative Structures of the World Economy

The first of the five structures is what I call the *free trade view* of the emerging world economy. This free trade view is the dominant one among economists and policymakers at institutions that "manage" the world economy, such as the IMF and the World Bank. This view makes a number of key assumptions: first, all actors are essentially equal (except, perhaps, for differences in size, income, and wealth, which are of no consequence except for initial difference in the standard of living). Free trade and finance lead to improvements in the standard of living of all involved and bring about convergence of living standards in the world economy, or, in other words, *even development*.

The second view implies a rather strong critique of the first, the free trade view. According to this dependency view, the "developed" (Northern) countries are more powerful than the "undeveloped" (Southern) countries. Military power is essential here in enforcing and maintaining unequal relations among these countries. But economic processes also structure the inequality. Trade and commercial relations between the North and South hurt the South and help the North. For example, the terms of trade systematically turn against the Southern countries, raising the cost of products that the Southern countries buy from the North, while lowering the prices of products the Southern countries sell to the North, thereby raising the standard of living in the Northern countries. Workers as well as capitalists in the North gain from "imperialism," that is, the exploitation of the Southern countries by the Northern ones. In this view the Northern countries are more or less united against the Southern ones. This view could be summarized as one of *uneven and exploitative development.*

The third view is the *Marxist imperialist view.* According to this view, international finance and trade between the North and the South undercuts noncapitalist relations in the Southern countries and spreads capitalism throughout the world. As such, capitalists in all countries benefit at the expense of all workers and other noncapitalist groups. This structure is subject to instability and crisis of the capitalist system (problems in the circuit of capital on a world scale) and intercapitalist rivalries among the major capitalist countries. This view can be summarized as *uneven and combined development.* In this view, capitalists exploit workers both in the North and the South. But Northern capitalists exploit both Northern and Southern workers. The South develops, but in a capitalist (and perhaps distorted) fashion.

A fourth view is the *stateless corporation* view of the world economy. The first three views see nation-states as important actors: the first in making trade and taxation policy, the second two in also possessing and utilizing military power. In the stateless corporation view, by contrast, states are overwhelmed by the operations of multinational corporations who roam the planet free of any state control. Here, only the owners of multinational corporations dominate and gain from the structure of the world economy. Moreover, they are helped by organizations like the IMF and the World Bank; rivalry among countries is of secondary importance, since the world's multinational corporations have an interest in maintaining openness and stability. Citizens and workers compete with each other for jobs from multinational corporations. Here virtually all workers and citizens in the world suffer from the concentration of power in the hands of global corporations.

The final view I consider is that of the *corporate-led state.* According to this view, which I call *multinational corporate capitalism,* nation-states are still extremely important in the international economy because they are the locus of significant power: military and economic. However, increasingly, state power is being used as a weapon in the global competitive battle among large multinational corporations from the three emerging major (blocs of) countries: the United States, Europe, and Japan. The large corporations from each of these blocs are vying for profits and using their states to promote their interests. Often these interests involve organizing relations with other parts of the world to give their corporations a competitive advantage in those areas; for example, the United States is trying to negotiate a U.S–Mexican Free Trade Agreement to give U.S. multinational corporations a competitive advantage vis-à-vis European and Japanese corporations in the Mexican and Latin American markets.

In the world of multinational corporate capitalism, the state-led corporate structure exerts pressure on government to direct policy toward maintenance of corporate profitability vis-à-vis its rivals on the global scene. This system often works against the interests of the citizens of the nations themselves. Corporate threats to leave the economy ratchet down wages, taxes, and environmental protections in country after country.

The key difference between the corporate-led state and the stateless corporation views is that the corporate-led view recognizes that nation-states still have significant power in the international economy. However, as this discussion of global problems and cooperation implies, many global problems cannot be solved without international cooperation. In the corporate-led world of multinational corporate capitalism, this cooperation takes place between representatives of the large corporations.

The alternative to the state-led corporate world is a citizen-led global economy. For a truly citizen-led world economy to emerge, citizens will have to take back the international institutions of cooperation and negotiation. This implies that citizens continue to have a political and institutional mechanism within the nation-state to gain control over their economic destiny.

I end with the questions with which I started. What is the structure of this new global capitalism? What are its problems or contradictions? Who gains and who loses from this system? What can nations, workers, and communities do to make sure that the global economy serves their needs, rather than the needs of the few?

As I have suggested, although we cannot be sure what the emerging structure will be, multinational corporate capitalism is as good a bet as any. Here, corporations from the three major blocs, Europe, Japan, and the United States, will attempt to use their state governments and international agencies to promote their profits and interests. Is this likely to lead to sustainable economic growth and improvement in welfare for the bulk of the world's population? It seems unlikely. If past history is much of a guide, the answer must be in the negative. Profit seeking and competition at best can lead only to temporary gains for some, even if the three emerging powerful blocs can develop new cooperative structures for stabilizing the international economy. But even in that case, state-led multinational capitalism is unlikely to lead to benefits for the bulk of the world's population. The ratcheting down of wages, taxes, and environmental standards as corporations threaten to move abroad, and the attempt to use government power only to further corporate ends, will only lead to increasing concentration of wealth and power among a relative few of the world's population.

The alternative model is a citizen-led global economy. Here, nation-states, independently and in cooperation with one another, are organized to serve the interests not of major multinational corporations but of the citizenry. The goal for citizens of the United States, Europe, and Japan must be to take back control of their states in order to make the corporations act in their interest, rather than the other way around. And citizens in other countries throughout the world must do the same. International institutions, where governments represent the interests of their citizens, must then negotiate cooperative institutions to ensure that if profit making remains a force in the world, it will be used for the ends of equitable and sustainable growth for all.

ACKNOWLEDGMENT

I would like to thank Trish Kelly for helpful research assistance.

NOTES

1. This is not strictly true, since foreigners will take the dollars in payment and then invest them in the United States, buying government or private bonds, land, or corporations. But since dollars are accepted as international money, foreigners are much more willing to make these investments without demanding exorbitant rates of return.

2. This discussion follows closely that in Bowles and Edwards 1992.

BIBLIOGRAPHY

Beaud, Michel. 1983. *A History of Capitalism, 1500–1980*. New York: Monthly Review Press.

Bowles, Samuel, and Richard Edwards. 1992. *Understanding Capitalism*. 2nd ed. New York: Harper & Row.

Bowles, Samuel, David Gordon, and Thomas Weisskopf. 1991. *After the Waste Land: A Democratic Economics for the Year 2000*. Armonk, N.Y.: M. E. Sharpe.

Gordon, David M. 1978. Up and Down the Long Roller Coaster. In *U.S. Capitalism in Crisis*, ed. Lourdes Beneria, 22–35. New York: Union for Radical Political Economics.

Gordon, David M., Richard Edwards, and Michael Reich. 1982. *Segmented Work, Divided Workers: The Historical Transformation of Labor in the United States*. London: Cambridge University Press.

International Bank for Reconstruction and Development. 1991. *World Development Report: The Challenge of Development*. New York: Oxford University Press.

Maddison, Angus. 1989. *The World Economy in the Twentieth Century*. Paris: OECD.

Marglin, Stephen A., and Juliet B. Schor, eds. 1990. *The Golden Age of Capitalism: Reinterpreting the Postwar Experience*. Oxford: Clarendon Press.

Schor, Juliet B. 1992. Introduction. In *Financial Openness and National Autonomy*, ed. Tariq Banuri and Juliet B. Schor, 1–14. Oxford: Clarendon Press.

United Nations. 1992. *Human Development Report.* New York: Oxford University Press.

United Nations Conference on Trade and Development (UNCTAD). 1991. *Handbook of International Trade and Development Statistics.* New York: United Nations.

2 MEHRENE LARUDEE

Trade Policy: Who Wins, Who Loses?

If we ask, what is the best trade policy for the United States to adopt? we must then ask, "for whom?" A trade policy, such as free trade or protectionism, does not benefit all groups equally. Labor may be hurt by free trade, while stockholders in multinational corporations may benefit. Consumers, domestic business, and politicians may be affected differently by trade policy, as may business and labor in other countries. In this essay we ask who wins and who loses from a variety of trade policies, and we seek the policy that is best for the large majority of the population.

The Problem for Labor, the Problem for Multinational Business

What is the problem that trade policy is supposed to solve? The usual answer is, declining U.S. competitiveness, or (almost the same thing) the U.S. trade deficit. But the trade deficit does not fall equally on labor and capital. The problem that labor faces is not the same problem that capital faces, so the solutions they propose also differ.

To say the United States has a trade deficit means that U.S. businesses, government, and consumers are buying (importing) more goods from abroad than they are selling (exporting) to businesses, governments, and consumers abroad. This translates into hiring abroad and layoffs at home. A recent study estimated that the 1987 U.S. trade deficit of $171 billion meant 5.1 million jobs lost here. The figure looms large when compared to the official number of 7.4 million unemployed in 1987. The same study showed that it is disproportionately the higher-paid jobs that are disappearing (Duchin and Lange 1988:1–2). And it is not just a loss of individual jobs; whole communities are devastated when plants shut down, and the families of the unemployed often go through hell, suffering higher rates of divorce, alcoholism, and suicide.

Lost jobs also mean lost income, even to those not laid off, as the

47

higher rate of unemployment, along with threats that employers will run away, undercut labor's bargaining strength and drive down wages even in the plants that end up staying where they are. Real weekly earnings for U.S. production workers ("real" means adjusted for inflation to reflect actual purchasing power) fell 14 percent between 1978 and 1990 (*ERP* 1990: 336), a decline for which international competitive pressures bear part of the blame.

When U.S. labor advocates that we "buy American" or that the government impose protectionist tariffs or quotas, it does so in order to save jobs and income. And any other trade policy, however good for business, can only hope to win the support of labor if it answers the need to protect jobs and income.

Multinational Corporations and the Trade Deficit

Trade is often talked about as if nations—not Exxon or IBM, Honda or Mercedes-Benz, your family or mine—were the buyers and sellers of goods that cross borders. And the trade deficit is talked about as if it were a problem for the *nation*—for rich as well as poor, owners as well as workers. The trade deficit is a problem for U.S. labor because it hurts jobs and income. But does the trade deficit hurt U.S. corporations? To be sure, domestic businesses such as small textile or apparel makers can be hurt if consumers buy imported textiles or clothes. But multinational corporations (MNCs), such as Levi-Strauss, are not necessarily hurt by the trade deficit; in fact, the very process by which they become multinational, producing abroad, can make the trade deficit worse while it increases their own profitability.

When plants run away, this can bloat the U.S. trade deficit in two ways. First, if the exports from the plant abroad substitute for exports from the United States, this raises the trade deficit by reducing U.S. exports while imports remain unchanged. This is what happens when Ford trucks, say, that used to be shipped out from U.S. ports are now produced and sold abroad. Second, if the foreign subsidiaries of U.S. firms export back to the United States, this also raises the trade deficit, by increasing U.S. imports while exports remain unchanged. This can happen when Levi's jeans that used to be produced and sold in the United States are produced abroad and then sold back to the United States.[1]

In fact, the declining competitiveness of goods *produced in the United States* has not meant declining competitiveness of goods *produced by U.S.-based multinational corporations* (produced either in their U.S. plants or their subsidiaries abroad). On a world scale, U.S.-based multinationals have held their own. From 1966 to 1984 the share of world manufactured exports produced by U.S.-based MNCs *rose*, from 17.7 percent to 18.1 percent. It was just that the production of these goods fled from the United States abroad, so that the share of total world manufactured exports produced *in the United States* fell in this same period from 17.5 percent to 14 percent (Lipsey and Kravis 1987:151).

If the trade deficit is not the problem for U.S.-based multinational corporations, what problem is it that they hope to solve when they propose free trade? The perennial problem is profitability: they want greater market share and lower costs. Toward countries like Mexico that MNCs expect to dominate, they propose a policy of free trade; toward Japan, which is a much more formidable competitor, they propose restrictions on trade.

Free Investment

The picture is even more complex than this, however, since measures that are really policies of free investment are often smuggled in under the slogan of "free trade." Corporations seek not just to ship goods made in the United States wherever buyers can be found, but to build plants and hire workers wherever it suits them to do so. Free investment coupled with free trade quite often means the freedom for corporations to hire low-wage labor elsewhere and sell the product back to U.S. consumers; this in turn means runaway shops and lost U.S. jobs. Ultimately, U.S.-based MNCs advocate those policies that allow them to exercise the most power and earn the most profits, whether or not these benefit the people of the United States.

Free trade—and the policies piggybacked onto it that are more than just free trade—is not the road to paradise that its proponents make it out to be. If we say free trade has its problems, however, that is not to advocate circling our protectionist wagons and ignoring the rest of the world. Protectionism as usually practiced can be as inequitable and problematic as MNC-backed free trade. Instead, the best strategy for labor and for the majority of people would actively seek to raise income, strengthen workers' rights, and protect environmental standards in other countries while maintaining those in the United States.

Free Trade: The History, the Theory

Pure free trade means no barriers of any kind to imports and no subsidies on exports: nothing but raw, unbridled competition. When trade is not "free," barriers may take the form of tariffs or quotas, or other nontariff barriers. A tariff is a tax on imported goods. A quota is a limit on the total quantity of a good that is allowed to be imported into a country in a given year. Nontariff barriers, apart from quotas, include such diverse regulations as limits on pesticide residues in imported fruit, requirements specifying that certain information be printed on the labels of food or clothing, and the like.

Economists have been singing odes to free trade for many decades.

But though economists sing to free trade, no one has ever been fool enough to implement it in every sector of the economy. Traditionally, each country reserves special privileges to its own merchant marine to carry cargo in its own waters. In aviation, likewise, not even airline companies advocate throwing open the skies to any airline that wishes to fly; rather, all agree that regulatory control, at least of who flies which routes, is needed to forestall total chaos. Even the United States, in its recent sweeping proposals to the General Agreement on Tariffs and Trade (GATT) to open up trade further, was quite careful not to touch these traditional preserves (Farnsworth 1990).

The History of U.S. Trade Policy

Then who advocates free trade, when, and why? In general, the strong advocate free trade when they know it will help them dominate the weak. When England held sway in the nineteenth century, it upheld free trade, whereas its struggling former colony, the United States, hung on to protectionist policies, sheltering its fledgling producers from the tempest of world trade. After World War II, the tables were turned, and the United States pushed to break down tariff barriers so that it could export more of its goods to Europe and the rest of the world.

GATT, founded in 1948, was the vehicle for this policy. GATT is a written agreement to which a growing number of countries (over one hundred at last count) are now party, laying down principles that all members agree to follow in trade with each other. In general, GATT calls for freer trade, though a number of exceptions, such as special restrictions on trade in textiles, have been allowed. Periodic rounds of negotiations, usually five years in length, are held among member countries to try to further dismantle trade barriers; the most recent was the Uruguay round, which began in 1986.

GATT has worked to a great degree: tariff and nontariff barriers have been greatly reduced since World War II. And during the couple of decades after World War II, U.S. exports penetrated the whole world. In this period, trade liberalization and expansion was on balance a benefit to workers and consumers in the United States; since few plants ran away, few jobs were lost, and a variety of cheap foreign goods became available. Much of the profits earned from U.S. exports were reinvested in the United States, raising employment, incomes, and growth here. This made it easier for capital and labor more or less to agree on trade policy, as long as free trade mainly meant more exports. But as free trade turned into free investment abroad, and increasing numbers of jobs were exported, especially to overseas auto plants, the AFL-CIO switched from its long-standing support for free trade. By 1970, it was testifying in favor of protectionist policies (Baldwin 1986). From this point on, the economic interests of labor and multinational capital with respect to trade policy increasingly diverged.

How the Theory of Free Trade Works

Mainstream economic theory has long held that free trade is a boon to everyone, just as it holds that free markets are the most efficient way to organize the economy. The idea is that through specialization, each country produces what it is relatively better at producing, using the fewest resources and making goods available more cheaply to all people in all countries. There is truth in this view: to the extent trade does encourage specialization that economizes on resources, it is possible for consumers to benefit.

Imagine two countries, Riceland and Beanland, separated by a large body of water. Before boats are invented, each produces its own rice and beans. Riceland is blessed with a wet climate ideal for growing rice, but its bean fields require constant, backbreaking work to drain the soil and keep the beanstalks from rotting. Beanland's climate is ideal for growing beans, but growing rice is a headache, since its people have to sweat and strain, day in and day out, hauling water to the rice fields.

Then a drastic change occurs: boats are invented, trade opens up, and Riceland's producers are delighted to specialize in growing rice, selling half of it to Beanland, while Beanland's producers specialize in growing beans and sell half the beans to Riceland. The combined populations save the time it used to take both to drain Riceland's bean fields and to haul water to Beanland's rice fields; they can use their extra time and energy to sing, dance, and compose odes to free trade. Or, if they work the same number of hours as before, but now spend that time growing what they are best at growing (rice in Riceland, beans in Beanland), they are able to grow both more rice and more beans than before free trade. In between these two extremes (putting the gain entirely into leisure or putting the gain entirely into additional production), any wages that agricultural producers lose from reduced working hours should be more than counterbalanced by a fall in rice and bean prices, so that purchasing power actually rises.

Moreover, the theory of free trade says that even if Riceland's resources—in this case its climate—were better for growing *both* rice and beans, and even if Beanland specialized in growing beans anyway (because it could grow beans more easily than rice), both countries would still be better off with trade than without it. To get to this surprising conclusion, the theory has to assume that all labor and resources are always fully employed and that capital cannot shift from one country to another. The punch line, then, is that free trade is *always* a good idea. The full argument, a little too intricate to reproduce here, is the first lesson on comparative advantage in any undergraduate textbook on international trade.

In whose interest, then, is free trade? The answer that theorists of free trade give is that it is in everyone's interest, since in the economy as a whole, consumers gain (in the form of cheaper goods) at least as much as workers lose (in the form of wages). The key to the argument lies in efficiency increases, called gains from trade—that is, increases that specialization makes possible by using the same resources (labor, energy, materials, tools, land) to produce more output than before.

What's Wrong with the Theory of Free Trade

Much is wrong with the theory of free trade, however. It assumes, for one thing, that plants do not relocate from one country to the other, and neither do workers. It assumes, too, that there is no unemployment. Thus, the theory does not even consider the possible danger that production will all move to the country that is more technologically advanced or more blessed with natural resources, while that country's trading partner will end up with massive unemployment. When trade opens up and less-efficient plants in one country are shut down, unable to compete with more-efficient plants in the country's trading partner, the theory of free trade pretends that laid-off workers will find jobs in other industries, even if at lower wages.

Proponents of free trade also talk as if low wages—for example, those in Mexico—were a "comparative advantage" just like a favorable climate for growing melons or a well-developed industrial base. But when the "comparative advantage" consists solely of low wages, what appear to be gains from trade are just a shift in income from wages to profits. This point is explained more fully later in this chapter in discussing the North American Free Trade Agreement.

Moreover, the theory says that protectionism is an expensive way to save jobs and income. It argues that consumers benefit so much from free trade that even if some jobs are lost, it would be cheaper to compensate those laid off by taxing consumers and using the money to hire laid-off workers than it would be to protect those jobs with a tariff. Sure, there are winners and losers, so the story goes, but (the story continues) if we adopt free trade, it is possible for the winners to pay back the losses suffered by the losers, and everyone ends up better off than under any other policy. Up to this point the theory is not far wrong, but the catch is that the theory says free trade is better even when the winners do not *actually* compensate the losers—so long as the winners gain enough so that in principle they *could* compensate them. If laid-off workers were actually compensated and retrained, as they are to a much greater degree in Europe, one of labor's problems with free trade might disappear.

Free Trade and Developing Countries

The theory of free trade is used not only to win support for U.S. policy but to persuade developing countries to drop their trade barriers and take their chances in the world market, producing whatever is dictated by their existing "comparative advantage." Here, too, the theory deceives. It imagines a world of small-scale producers in competition, with each country taking advantage of its own native resources. In fact, however, resources are made as much as they are given by nature. Early nineteenth-century economist David Ricardo, in his classic work on the benefits of free trade, pointed to Portugal's advantage in producing wine and England's advantage in producing cloth. However, although Portugal may have become a wine producer because it had a fine climate for growing grapes, England certainly did not become a manufacturer of cotton textiles because it had a good climate for growing cotton. Its advantage was created through its industrial revolution.

If the United States had followed the prescriptions of present-day free trade theorists, it would have specialized in furs, starting in early colonial days. Instead, the United States deliberately established tariffs to protect its infant manufacturing industries and thereby developed the capacity to make tools and machinery that it was previously unable to produce at competitive prices. It did not just use its advantage in the resources it already had, it took conscious steps to *develop* its resources. Other developing countries have every reason to do the same.

Moreover, in industries where there are economies of scale, whichever country industrializes early has a great advantage in the world market. In automobile manufacture, for most operations the production cost per unit produced does not approach a minimum until a single plant is producing at least one hundred thousand units and by some estimates, for some operations, several hundred thousand or more (Shapiro 1992:57). So whichever country gets there first with integrated production of more than a hundred thousand cars will be able to undersell smaller auto producers. That is why struggling local industries in poor countries often need temporary protection from international competition—in the form either of protective tariffs or of government subsidies to export industries—if they are ever to develop. In pursuing such policies, they are doing no more than following in the footsteps of the developed countries.

The reality of trade is far from the ideal picture painted by theory of small producers bound to each country and subject to the workings of the market. In reality, trade is a complex game in which large multinational corporations adopt (and pressure governments to adopt) whatever strategy will strengthen their hand against corporate competitors, against their own employees, and against threats of government regulation. Toward Mexico that policy may be "free trade" (and free investment), while toward Japan it may not be free trade. It may be protectionism at one point in history and free trade at another.

Free Trade: What's in It for the MNCs?

One gain to multinational corporations from free trade has little to do with the theory. A significant fraction of U.S. trade is intrafirm trade, that is, trade among different subsidiaries of the same multinational corporation. For example, in 1982, affiliates of U.S.-based companies accounted for more than a fifth of all U.S. imports, and in the auto industry U.S. firms' imports from their own subsidiaries accounted for 46 percent of imports (Karier 1990:10). MNCs with global factories gain from free trade both because it reduces the cost of sending raw materials, components, and capital goods from suppliers in one country to assembly plants in another and because it reduces the cost of the product when it is exported from its final assembly plant. The more tariff barriers exist, the more costs there are to globalization of production; free trade, by eliminating these tariffs, helps MNCs more than national corporations and therefore helps MNCs against at least their smaller competitors.

But perhaps the biggest gains to MNCs from free trade are gains in bargaining power, or strategic advantage. At this writing a North American Free Trade Agreement (NAFTA) is in the process of being negotiated among Mexico, the United States, and Canada. Canada and the United States have already concluded a separate free trade agreement, in effect since 1989, gradually reducing tariffs and nontariff barriers between them. U.S. MNCs wanted trade and investment among all three countries to be free. But they also wanted the agreement to include rules of origin that would reserve the lion's share of NAFTA's benefits to North American MNCs. These rules would allow foreign investors to use Mexico as a low-wage export platform to the United States only if a large percentage, such as 65 percent, of the value of the goods produced originated in the free trade area (the United States, Canada, or Mexico). The effect, it was hoped, would be to secure the benefits of North American free trade and investment to U.S.-based MNCs while placing them out of reach of their strongest competitors. U.S.-based MNCs could cut production costs by producing in Mexico and still have full access to the U.S. market. But their foreign competitors would find it more difficult to locate in Mexico because unless they moved virtually their entire integrated production process there, they would not be permitted to sell to the lucrative U.S. market. In advocating rules of origin, MNCs reveal that they have no commitment to free trade in principle—only where it works to their advantage.

NAFTA would also provide MNCs with a powerful bargaining chip against their own employees. U.S. hourly compensation in manufacturing is about eight times that in Mexico. Until recently, the Mexican government placed severe restrictions on U.S. foreign investment in Mexico, such as limiting foreigners to only minority stock ownership, except in the *ma-*

quiladora region just south of the Mexican border. Now 100 percent foreign ownership is permitted in a wide range of industries, and NAFTA would assure investors that these conditions would persist, since a treaty has the force of law and could not easily be changed even by a much more populist Mexican government (Campbell 1991:23). After NAFTA, U.S.-based MNCs could use Mexico's more favorable investment climate to threaten their U.S. employees much more convincingly with picking up and moving to Mexico if unions did not yield to lower wages and worse working conditions.

These MNCs would gain power over labor and reduce their labor costs whether or not they actually moved. Not only could corporations pit U.S. workers against Mexican workers, they could throw workers in U.S. plants into competition with one another to see who could offer the company a better deal. General Motors, for instance, pitted workers in its Arlington, Texas, assembly plant against those in its Willow Run plant in Ypsilanti, Michigan, in deciding which would shut down. The Arlington workers offered greater concessions, so GM decided to shut the Willow Run plant (Patterson 1992:1).

Harmonization of Environmental and Consumer Regulations

Multinationals also gain power over consumer and environmental regulations through negotiations for free trade. The U.S. proposal to GATT for harmonization of environmental and consumer protection standards among member countries is one example. The idea of harmonization is that it is unfair for one country to impose more stringent requirements on imported goods than other countries impose. If Mexico tolerates higher levels of pesticides on melons than does the United States, then U.S. melons can be sold to Mexico, whereas Mexican melons cannot be sold to the United States, giving an "unfair" advantage to U.S. melon producers, or so the story goes. The U.S. proposal was defined by two principles:

1. Standards for food and other products could be set only on the basis of "scientific evidence," not social or economic considerations, or consumer opinion.
2. The U.N. agency, Codex Alimentarius, would be the main judge of what is scientific evidence. Any national standards that were stricter than this code would have to be brought down to its level, or else other nations would be authorized to retaliate by applying tariffs to goods imported from the country with stricter standards (Ritchie 1990:20–22).

Under harmonization, the proposed European Community (EC) ban on bovine growth hormone, used in growing beef cattle, would be threatened. Likewise, 16 percent of Codex pesticide tolerance standards are weaker than U.S. standards, so that the stricter U.S. standards would be in jeopardy from harmonization. Food industries have avidly lobbied for these changes, and at a Codex meeting, the U.S. delegation included corporate executives from Nestle, Coca Cola, Pepsi, Hershey, CPC International, Ralston Purina, and Kraft, as well as several food industry associations (Ritchie 1990:22). Not only do they want harmony, they want to call the tune.

The North American Free Trade Agreement (NAFTA)

NAFTA illustrates both the possibilities and the dangers of "free trade." The major corporations leading the lobbying effort for NAFTA include Ford and Chrysler (the two leading private-sector exporters from Mexico to the United States), IBM and Texas Instruments, and other corporations with large, long-established Mexican subsidiaries (Orme 1991: 11–12). Although automakers have kept a low profile to avoid angering the autoworkers' union, they have big plans for shifting production to Mexico, and much more so if NAFTA is approved. Even without NAFTA, Big Three automaker executives expect Mexican industry to produce two million vehicles by the year 2000, double its present production. And the president of Ford's Mexican subsidiary has said that with NAFTA, by that year Mexico could be making three million vehicles or more.

Mexico is a classic example of how free investment combined with free trade can mean runaway jobs. In the mid-1980s, Mexico abandoned its long-standing policy of limiting foreign investment and maintaining high tariffs. It sharply reduced its tariffs and allowed 100 percent foreign ownership in many industries. As a result, even without NAFTA, automakers continued to shift operations there, such as the 549 jobs in engine production that GM planned in 1992 to move from Moraine, Ohio, to Toluca (Detroit South 1992:98).

Will this bring about gains from trade, so that everyone in both the United States and Mexico is better off? To the extent that Mexico's "comparative advantage" lies in low wages, it will not. With average hourly compensation (wages plus benefits) for production workers in manufacturing at $14.83 in the United States and at $1.85 in Mexico, imagine a plant moving south of the border and paying the same number of workers for the same number of hours to produce the same number of cars as before and selling them at the same price. This is fairly realistic, since productivity has been found to be about three-quarters as high in the newer Mexican plants as in comparable plants to the north (Shaiken 1988:8). As auto production shifts south, there is no efficiency gain, then, but the wage difference goes directly into profits. Corporate stockholders gain at the expense of workers, as money once paid out as wages to U.S. workers goes to profits on operations at Mexican plants.

Proponents of NAFTA wax euphoric about the expanding Mexican market for U.S. goods that would result from more Mexican jobs, and are blind to the much larger shrinkage in the domestic market for U.S. goods that would result from lost wages in the United States. Only sleight of hand can subtract $14.83 in wages here, add $1.85 there, and get an expansion in the market for U.S. goods.

To claim that such a change would benefit U.S. workers is like saying U.S. workers would benefit if wages were slashed to $1.85 an hour in some state, say Michigan. The claim would be that the greater investment that would flow into Michigan (taking advantage of its newly lowered wages) would raise employment and income there, so that Michigan residents would buy more goods from other states. This, the fanciful story goes, would create more jobs in other states to produce these goods, and everyone would be better off.

But if lowering wages in Michigan would make everyone wealthier, then why not lower wages in California too and make everyone more prosperous yet? Or better still, why not lower wages in all fifty states and make us all blissfully rich? Such is the logic of NAFTA proponents.

Win Some, Lose Some

It is possible that trade and output will rise in Mexico as a result of NAFTA, but it would be a mistake to interpret that as success from the standpoint of the world economy. The Mexican government views NAFTA as a means of attracting investment, including investment from outside North America. If they succeed, some of what will appear to be the success of NAFTA will come from robbing Peter to pay Paul—as the United States buys sugar more from Mexico and less from the Caribbean islands, and as electronics assembly plants are set up in Mexico instead of in East Asia. To a degree, Mexico's gain will be the Caribbean's loss, or East Asia's loss; and the real winners will be those corporations that, wooed by many suitors, can choose the one willing to pay the highest bride-price.

And even if trade and output rise, it is not at all certain that either employment or wages will rise, even in Mexico. A recent study estimates that when U.S. and Canadian corn flood Mexican markets and displace Mexican corn producers, the resulting migration to cities will create so much unemployment that the jobs resulting from new investment will be insufficient to employ those who lost jobs. And the decline in rural incomes in Mexico, coupled with an unemployment rate that stays the same or rises, will undermine workers' bargaining power and result in lower Mexican wages (Koechlin and Larudee 1992).

Protectionism? Buy American? Or Support Workers' Rights Abroad?

If free trade has its problems, should we advocate protectionism, such as tariffs or quotas on imports? Protectionism can save jobs in the industries protected—it is true. In the United States, for example, quotas on imports of textiles have kept the U.S. textile industry in business. But protectionism has its drawbacks.

First, if other countries retaliate by raising their own trade barriers (tariffs or quotas, for instance), the effect of protection may be nullified or worse, and everyone may end up no better off than before. Moreover, protectionism often comes packaged with a narrow-minded, self-righteous, racist nationalism that has taken the form most recently of anti-Asian sentiment and Japan bashing. Such sentiments are ugly in themselves and often lead to violence, even war.

In addition, protectionism against countries whose standard of living is far lower than that of the United States, such as South Korea, fosters the ugly suspicion that we feel we are justified in keeping the rest of the world poor so that we can live much more comfortably than they do. One pillar of South Korea's development strategy has been exporting to the huge and lucrative U.S. market. South Korea has been a successful exporter, fulfilling the ideal held up by the International Monetary Fund, and cited as a model for developing countries. Yet the United States has criticized it sharply and pressured it to avoid a trade surplus with the United States. This pressure has helped slow Korean growth.

An argument that mainstream economists make against protectionism has some truth to it: that wherever protective tariffs or quotas save jobs, the cost to consumers is great, in the form of higher prices (both for imports and for the domestic goods sold in the same market with imports). They say those jobs could be saved more cheaply by taking funds out of tax revenues for a trade adjustment assistance (TAA) program to retrain workers for jobs in more buoyant industries. Federal Trade Commission studies say that each $29,000 job saved in the steel industry by import restraints cost consumers $114,000; each $27,000 job saved in the auto industry by Japan's Voluntary Export Restraint (VER) cost $241,000 in higher car prices; and each $19,000 job saved in the sugar industry cost consumers $53,000 (DeLay 1987:62).

Both consumers and workers would be better off, then, if Japanese cars entered the U.S. market freely, and if the money consumers had been paying out in higher prices were used to compensate each laid-off auto worker up to $241,000 per year for income support and retraining. The catch is that no administration in the United States has yet offered to pay anything like this amount for TAA.

On the contrary, TAA in the United States has always been under-funded and inadequate. At most a few thousand dollars per worker has ever been allocated. It is corporations, not workers, that have the most influence on Congress; when management has made common cause with workers, as in the textile industry, the alliance has often swung enough weight to pass the trade policy they desired. But once plants have shut down, workers left high and dry have relatively little clout and get only the leavings after the main budget banquet. And a 1986 study showed that of workers laid off by plant closings, over a quarter of those who did eventually find full-time jobs suffered at least a 20 percent pay cut (Kamel 1990:21).

If the United States had top-notch unemployment and retraining benefits like those in some European countries, so that being laid off did not mean a personal disaster for workers, one potent objection to free trade would be removed.

Buy American?

Is "buy American" a good alternative? When labor unions talk about buying American, they are mainly talking about cars, the big-ticket item in every family's budget. But what is "American"? Is the Dodge Stealth, built by Mitsubishi, an American car? Even GM, Ford, and Chrysler cars built in the United States are full of components from all over the world. The Toyota Corolla and the Chevrolet Geo Prizm are built on the same assembly line in Fremont, California, in the GM–Toyota plant there, and are practically indistinguishable. Which is the American car?

In 1988 the hottest-selling imported car in Japan was the Honda Accord, a "U.S. export" produced by Honda in Ohio. The runner-up was the Ford Probe, manufactured in Michigan by Mazda, in which Ford has 25 percent ownership. The situation is so confusing that the Environmental Protection Agency no longer announces mileage ratings for "domestic" and "foreign-made" cars as separate categories, since it is impossible to decide which is which. Trade negotiators for the United States and Japan have found it difficult to agree on a definition of what a "domestic" American car is for tariff purposes. "Nobody knows what anyone is talking about," said Commerce Secretary Robert Mosbacher (Patterson 1991:A1; White and Mitchell 1991; Kline 1989:25–32).

The auto companies use the confusion to their advantage, defining the same car as an import for one regulatory purpose and a domestic car for another. Ford, by defining its big gas-guzzling Crown Victoria as an import on the grounds that some of its parts are made in Mexico, averages it in with the fuel-efficient imported Festiva and avoids paying a federal penalty for failing to meet fuel efficiency standards on its domestic fleet. Corporations use their putative nationality as a protective cloak, donning it when it serves them to do so, hanging it in the closet when it does not (Stateless Corporation 1990).

Protecting Workers' Rights

Are there forms of protectionism, or other policies, that are better?

In the 1980s the labor movement took a strong stand in support of workers' rights abroad and won enactment of trade restrictions, in theory anyway, against governments that violated those rights. But because labor is weak, enforcement of these laws has been lax and selective.

A minor breakthrough came with a provision in the 1983 Caribbean Basin Initiative (CBI) stating that in deciding which countries would receive the CBI-mandated trade privileges, the president had to consider the degree to which workers in these countries had reasonable working conditions and the right to organize and bargain collectively.

The 1984 renewal of the Generalized System of Preferences (GSP) prescribed five slightly more detailed requirements that countries had to meet in order to qualify for trade privileges. These were:

1. the right to free association;
2. the right to organize and bargain collectively;
3. prohibition of compulsory labor;
4. prohibition of child labor; and
5. acceptable working conditions with regard to minimum wages, working hours, and occupational health and safety, though these need not be the same standards as in the United States.

In 1985, in renewing legislation creating the Overseas Private Investment Corporation, Congress said OPIC could provide risk insurance only for corporate subsidiaries located in countries that meet these conditions.

Enforcement of these laws has been feeble, and has been biased against left-leaning countries. Still, these laws offer a foothold that labor could use as an organizing tool.

A Social Charter

In Europe, farsighted labor and community leaders anticipated the danger that hard-won high wages, strong labor laws, and consumer and environmental protections would be leveled down to the lowest common denominator when poorer countries such as Spain and Portugal joined the EC. They drew up a social charter setting a floor under wages and environmental and labor regulations, to maintain the standard of living in the new, larger European Community. Following that example, a coalition of groups in the United States is developing the idea of a social charter to be applied to any free trade area to which the United States becomes a party.

Trade has always been a tough issue. We want U.S. workers to keep their jobs and income levels without fostering the racism that often accompanies protectionism. We want the people of the rest of the world to get the good life, without losing it ourselves.

Free trade has the same potential benefits that the free market has: more efficient production, since goods are produced using the fewest material resources, and hence lower prices to consumers. But free trade has its dangers:

If "comparative advantage" lies in low wages, there will be no gains from trade, but only a shift from wages to profits.

When coupled with free investment, free trade often means both lost jobs and lost income as shops run away.

Since full employment does not exist, workers laid off from firms that lose out in world competition can be badly hurt; unless fully adequate adjustment programs exist (and they do not now in the United States), free trade can be damaging.

Free trade, and policies that are not free trade but hide under the slogan of free trade, can work to strengthen the power of multinational corporations against their own employees and against consumer and environmental regulation.

The threat of runaway shops will disappear only when wages and working conditions become fairly equal around the world. We help ourselves most by working actively to raise standards around the world—workers' rights, democratic rights, human rights, and environmental and consumer protection standards. Trade does have the potential to benefit us all, but only if the majority of people assert themselves to prevent free trade from becoming a banner beneath which the multinational corporations strengthen their power against labor and against consumer and environmental protections.

Developing a social charter like that in Europe might be a promising strategy for progressives, with NAFTA on the table and a free trade agreement with all Latin American countries waiting in the wings. But whatever the specific trade policy we choose, it must be based on a vision of a future world in which everyone has a decent living standard and in which worldwide justice and equality form the foundation of permanent peace. We cannot reach this world by adopting policies that keep the rest of the world poor. Instead, we can maintain our own standard of living only by actively supporting improvements in others', through enforcing and strengthening laws supporting workers' rights and environmental and consumer protections everywhere. International cooperation among people, uniting across borders to control the arbitrary power of corporations, can bring the benefits of trade without its problems.

NOTE

1. However, the extent to which plants abroad still receive machinery and materials from suppliers in the United States partially offsets the increase in the trade deficit due to the two reasons cited in the text.

It is true, also, that there is at least one way in which the trade deficit hurts MNCs. If a persistent trade deficit undermines confidence in the U.S. economy and drives down the value of the dollar, the dollars that MNCs use to buy up foreign firms, equipment, raw materials, or labor will buy less. MNCs would prefer to avoid this loss of purchasing power if possible. On the other hand, they can put some of their holdings into German marks or Japanese yen and reduce the damage. And on balance, MNCs have not appeared very vulnerable to a decline in the dollar's value. From 1985 to 1991 the U.S. government allowed the dollar to fall in value by about a third, and many MNCs gained substantially. The prices of their goods produced in the United States fell abroad so that their exports from the United States increased (Ansberry 1991; Nasar 1991:1).

BIBLIOGRAPHY

Ansberry, Clare. 1991. U.S. Exports Turn into Ports in a Storm. *Wall Street Journal*, 17 January, A6.
Baldwin, Robert E. 1986. The Changing Nature of U.S. Trade Policy since World War II. In *International Trade and Finance*, 3d ed., ed. Robert E. Baldwin and J. David Richardson, 143–60. Boston: Little, Brown.
Campbell, Bruce. 1991. Beggar Thy Neighbor. *Report on the Americas* 24 (May): 22–29.
DeLay, Tom. 1987. Trade Policy: A Republican's View. In *Trade Policy and U.S. Competitiveness*, ed. Claude Barfield and John Makin, 62. Washington, D.C.: American Enterprise Institute.
Detroit South, Mexico's Auto Boom: Who Wins, Who Loses. 1992. *Business Week*, 16 March, 98–103.
Duchin, Faye, and Glenn-Marie Lange. 1988. Trading Away Jobs: The Effects of the U.S. Merchandise Trade Deficit on Employment. Working paper no. 102. Economic Policy Institute, Washington, D.C.
ERP (Economic Report of the President). 1990. Washington, D.C.: U.S. Government Printing Office.
Farnsworth, Clyde H. 1990. U.S. Changes Its Tune on Liberalizing Trade. *New York Times*, 29 October, D1, D4.
Kamel, Rachael. 1990. *The Global Factory*. Philadelphia: American Friends Service Committee/Omega Press.
Karier, Thomas. 1990. *Trade Deficits and Labor Unions: Myths and Realities*. Washington, D.C.: Economic Policy Institute.
Kline, John M. 1989. Trade Competitiveness and Corporate Nationality. *Columbia Journal of World Business* 24(3): 25–32.
Koechlin, Timothy, and Mehrene Larudee. 1992. Effect of the North American Free Trade Agreement on Investment, Employment, and Wages in Mexico and the U.S. Photocopy (T. Koechlin, Economics Department, Skidmore

College; or M. Larudee, Economics Department, University of Massachusetts–Amherst).

Lipsey, Robert E., and Irving B. Kravis. 1987. The Competitiveness and Comparative Advantage of U.S. Multinationals, 1957–84. *Banca Nazionale del Lavoro Quarterly Review*, no. 161.

Nasar, Sylvia. 1991. Boom in Manufactured Exports Provides Hope for U.S. Economy. *New York Times*, 21 April, 1, 22.

Orme, William A., Jr. 1991. The Sunbelt Moves South. *Report on the Americas* 24 (May): 10–19.

Patterson, Gregory. 1991. Foreign or Domestic? Car Firms Play Games with the Categories. *Wall Street Journal*, 11 November, A1, A6.

———. 1992. How GM's Car Plant in Arlington, Texas, Hustled to Avoid Ax. *Wall Street Journal*, 6 March, A1, A4.

Ritchie, Mark. 1990. Trading Away Our Environment: GATT and Global "Harmonization." *Journal of Pesticide Reform* 10 (Fall): 20–22.

Shaiken, Harley. 1988. Wages, Productivity, and Trade: The Auto Industry in Mexico, Canada, and the United States. Paper presented at Allied Social Science Association annual meeting, New York, December.

Shapiro, Helen. 1992. Automobiles: Trade and Investment Flows in Brazil and Mexico. January. Harvard Business School. Photocopy.

The Stateless Corporation. 1990. *Business Week*, 14 May, 98–105.

White, Joseph B., and Jacqueline Mitchell. 1991. Detroit Rolls Out Old Ploy: Quotas. *Wall Street Journal*, 14 January, B1.

3 ILENE GRABEL

Crossing Borders: A Case for Cooperation in International Financial Markets

By the end of the 1980s, many people, from academics to government officials to progressive activists, had begun to recognize the need for bold action to rein in international financial markets. The flight of capital from the United States to low-wage centers (and paradoxically, from these same centers to the relative security of U.S. bank accounts), unpredictable gyrations in currency exchange rates, and the meddling of the International Monetary Fund in the affairs of developing nations—all signaled an international financial system out of the control of domestic policymakers worldwide.

But the same evidence that gave rise to these concerns also proved daunting for most observers. What developments gave birth to this apparent chaos, and how could it ever be tamed? Whose interests were being served by the modern international financial system, and how could its operation be reoriented to serve those who do not trade dollars for deutsche marks or hold portfolios of exotic financial instruments? And what policies, if any, could be implemented domestically and internationally to take control of a system that increasingly defied comprehension?

This chapter explores this terrain. At the broadest level, much of the current disorder of the international financial system stems from the practices and opportunities licensed by worldwide financial deregulation. In contrast to the sanguine sales pitch hawked by "free-marketeers," the rewards of breakneck competition for the spoils of speculative trading are not equally available to all individuals and nations; nor do they trickle down to the economically disadvantaged. In short, in a world economy fraught with inequalities of political and economic power both within and among nations, global financial deregulation is not the messenger of robust and equitable economic growth.

The disorder of the international financial system has contributed significantly to several global economic problems. These include (1) the chaotic and destabilizing fluctuations in currency exchange rates (see Figure 3.1) and international capital flows; (2) the absence of national control over

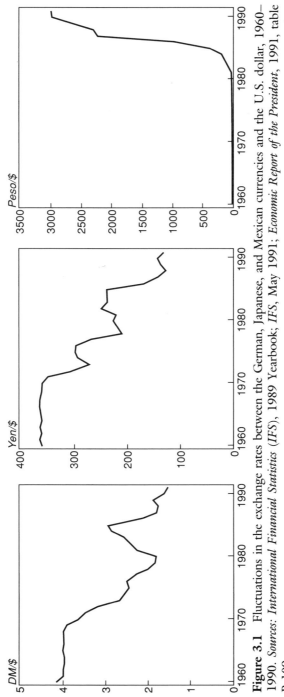

Figure 3.1 Fluctuations in the exchange rates between the German, Japanese, and Mexican currencies and the U.S. dollar, 1960–1990. *Sources: International Financial Statistics (IFS), 1989 Yearbook; IFS, May 1991; Economic Report of the President, 1991, table B-109.*

fiscal and monetary policy; (3) the stagnation of economic growth in developed and less-developed countries (DCs and LDCs, respectively) in the 1980s (see Figure 3.2); and (4) increasing income inequality, within and among nations.

Piercing the surface of financial markets, I explore how the particular features of the present-day international financial scene contribute directly to the disorder. Three salient and interrelated features of the international financial landscape contribute to and exacerbate the problems cited here.[1] The first of these is the *restrictive and uncoordinated monetary policies of the world's industrial powers*. An important consequence of this is the slower growth rates in LDCs throughout the 1980s (see Figure 3.2). The second feature concerns the degree to which the *international financial system is based on one currency*. One dramatic consequence of the "single-currency reserve" system is the pressure to maintain interest rates above a level that would support economic growth. High interest rates have profound deleterious macroeconomic consequences and particularly detrimental effects on those without resources. The third is the *high degree of capital mobility*. The ability and willingness of capital holders to veto a progressive social agenda by exporting their wealth has imposed strict limitations on domestic-policy options.

These three characteristics of the financial scene are interrelated. The confidence of the international financial community in the strength and stability of a nation's currency rests on the maintenance of (among other things) high domestic interest rates. It is in this manner that domestic interest rates are held hostage to the expectations of the financial community. These high interest rates cripple economic growth and have disastrous consequences for economically vulnerable groups and nations. Moreover, the threat of massive capital flight prevents any one nation from pursuing expansionary monetary policies. A radical democratic program to redress these problems must take account of these complex linkages.

Obviously, progressive reform of the international financial system is predicated on political will and a broad-based visionary program to transform the world economy (see Pollin 1989). This chapter is limited strictly to financial matters, one critical element of any such realignment. It is intended both as a primer on the financial sector's contribution to the global economic disorder and as an outline of a progressive reform program. The goals of this reform include the furtherance of equitable economic growth and the introduction of stability into international financial markets.

Interest in Dollars and Dollars in Interest

Reading modern business press accounts of monetary arbitraging and cabalistic meetings of nervous central bankers, it is sometimes hard to remem-

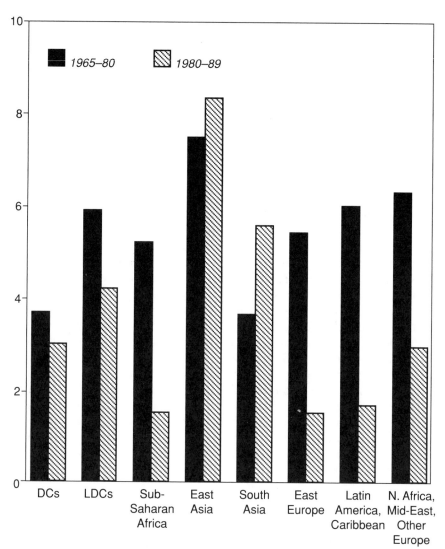

Figure 3.2 Real GDP growth rates in percentages. *Source: World Development Report*, 1990.

ber that not so long ago the value of each nation's currency was fixed relative to others by international accord. American currency was at the center of the post–World War II reconstruction of the world economy. Placing the dollar and, by extension, the United States at the center of the world economic order during those heady days seemed certain to orchestrate world prosperity. But today U.S. attempts to direct the international financial order are often overwhelmed by circumstances far beyond Washington's control. What went wrong?

From Bretton Woods to Lost in the Woods

In July of 1944, delegates from forty-four nations, led by the United States and Britain, gathered at a resort in Bretton Woods, New Hampshire.[2] Their mandate was to establish a plan for global economic management. The financial turbulence of the 1920s had engendered in these delegates a consensus that, in the words of Charles Kindleberger, "for the world economy to be stabilized, there has to be a stabilizer, one stabilizer" (quoted in Moffit 1983:19). Only the United States, emerging from World War II economically, militarily, and politically hegemonic, could act simultaneously as global banker, marshal, and governor.

The Bretton Woods accord enshrined the U.S. dollar as the world's reserve currency (i.e., as the currency accumulated by other nations to settle their accounts with one another). The dollar's status was ensured by the U.S. Treasury's pledge to redeem dollars for a specified amount of gold. All countries were required to set their currency's exchange rate in relation to the price of an ounce of gold. Under this system of fixed exchange rates, countries could change the value of their currencies by more than 1 percent only upon securing the permission of the Bretton Woods–chartered International Monetary Fund (IMF) (Moffit 1983:21).

Until the mid-1960s the Bretton Woods economic order appeared to provide a sturdy foundation for global economic development. Global economic reconstruction was sustained by a hearty diet of U.S. dollars, goods, and services. But the success of the Bretton Woods regime ultimately eroded the conditions for its own survival. In order to keep the dollar spigot open to facilitate world economic growth, the United States had to run chronic balance-of-payments deficits (i.e., import more goods than it sold). These chronic deficits undermined the world's confidence in the ability of the United States to redeem dollars for gold at a fixed rate (Epstein 1985:628).[3] Thus, under the conditions set out in the Bretton Woods accord, the United States was at once central and yet vulnerable to the workings of the postwar economic order.

By the 1960s other problems had set in. Skyrocketing inflation in the United States had eroded the competitiveness of its manufactures on the world market. The success of European reindustrialization shrank the market for U.S. goods. The resulting decline in Western European purchases of U.S. goods slowed the flow of dollars back to the United States. Consequently, the United States was pressed to underwrite the global economic order through sales of its dwindling gold stock. At the same time, a reconstructed Western Europe mounted economic and political challenges (e.g., Charles de Gaulle purposely exposed the vulnerability of the system and thereby embarrassed the United States by presenting large stocks of U.S. dollars for redemption when he knew that U.S. gold reserves were dangerously low). Moreover, the substantial costs of the Vietnam War swelled the U.S. balance-of-payments deficit, further undermining the confidence of other nations in the United States' ability to redeem dollars for gold.

By the late 1960s the gold rush was on. The Bretton Woods accord was finally pronounced dead in August 1971, when President Nixon declared that the United States would no longer redeem dollars for gold.

After the Gold Rush

There was no postmortem regrouping in Bretton Woods, New Hampshire, no attempt (apart from a few feeble gestures in 1971–73) to salvage the gold standard as the basis for maintaining fixed exchange rates. Since 1973, exchange rates have been free to float with the whims, fears, and expectations of the banking establishment. In the wake of Bretton Woods, the international financial system remains dollar-centered. But no longer as good as gold, the dollar's centrality rests on the state of the world financial community's confidence in its high and stable value, that is, its exchange rate.

The exchange rate is the price of one nation's currency in terms of some other currency. For example, the U.S. dollar–Mexican peso exchange rate refers to the number of dollars that must be sold in order to purchase one peso. A dollar–peso exchange rate of 3:1 means that three U.S. dollars buys one peso. Under a floating-exchange-rate regime, exchange rates are driven by supply and demand conditions in currency markets. A currency is said to appreciate (i.e., "strengthen") in value whenever an increase in demand for that currency raises its "price," and to depreciate (i.e, "weaken") whenever a decline in the demand for that currency reduces its price in terms of other currencies. Neither sunspots nor laws of logic drive the desirability of one nation's currency on world financial markets. Frenzied waves of buying and selling are galvanized by rumor, speculation, or political conditions—strikes, elections, reports on the inflation rate, or fluctuations in interest rates can trigger run-ups or sell-offs (Aliber 1987:57). Of these, the interest rate is critical to determining a currency's desirability on world financial markets.

Taking the case of the United States as an example, the decision of the Federal Reserve Bank (i.e., the United States' central bank, hereafter the Fed) to pursue a restrictive or high-interest-rate monetary policy makes U.S. financial assets (e.g., government bonds) more attractive to foreign wealth holders (as long as confidence in the stability of the dollar is maintained). In order to purchase U.S. assets, buyers must obtain U.S. dollars. The increased demand for U.S. dollars causes an appreciation of the dollar.

The 1970s

Double-digit inflation in the United States during the 1970s and the concomitant loss of confidence in the stability of the U.S. economy triggered frenzied dollar sell-offs by currency traders and foreign governments. By 1979, dollar sales soared as the U.S. economy nosedived. Facing a dollar panic (i.e., large-scale sales of dollar-denominated assets) and political failure, an embattled President Jimmy Carter sought to restore the world financial community's confidence in U.S. banks and dollars. That boost in confidence came with the appointment of Paul Volcker, a hard-nosed banker's banker, as chairperson of the Fed.

Volcker immediately took action to restore the dollar's desirability on the international financial market by driving up U.S. interest rates (see Figure 3.3). By 1980, U.S. nominal interest rates had reached an extraordinary high of 20 percent.[4] Attracted by these new high rates of return, foreign investors demanded dollars in order to purchase dollar-denominated assets. And so the tight money resolution of the 1970s dollar panic "strengthened" the U.S. dollar while expanding the wealth portfolios of banks and investors. The wealth of this minority was greatly enhanced by the spiraling returns on bank loans and bonds.

Who, exactly, is weakened by the dollar's strengthening, and how are their lives affected by the prerogatives of the dollar?

Monetary Policy: Marching to the Tune of Asset Markets

Highly restrictive (or "tight") monetary policy has far-reaching (but often obscure) primary and secondary effects. Domestically, the increased cost and scarcity of credit associated with high interest rates hurts those individuals and industries (e.g., automobile and housing) heavily dependent on debt to finance their activities. It is in this manner that low- and middle-income consumers, small businesses, and farmers are driven out of the credit market by tight monetary policy. The costs to the economy are measured in lost output, rising unemployment due to business cutbacks, and declining purchasing power, which can combine to produce a self-sustaining cycle of economic contraction. The victims of this turn of events include fired workers, consumers, farmers, small businesses, and the poor—in short, those most vulnerable to the effects of economic decline. If these, then, are the victims, who are the victors? These include wealthy individuals and financial institutions (e.g., banks and brokerage firms). The return (i.e., interest income) available to these bondholders and loan providers is enhanced when they lend money at higher interest rates. Globally, debtors are squeezed by rising interest rates as "credit rationing" diminishes their access to new borrowing at the same time that debt-service obligations (i.e., inter-

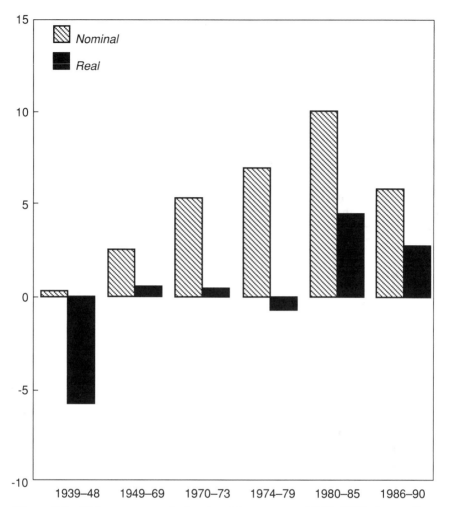

Figure 3.3 U.S. average nominal and real interest rates, 1939–1990. *Sources: Economic Report of the People*, Center for Popular Economics, 1986; *Economic Report of the President*, 1991.

est and charges due on a debt, including payment of the original amount borrowed) expand.

The link between interest rates and debt-service obligations has become more direct in recent years. In the aftermath of the inflation of the 1970s, the vast majority of domestic and international loan agreements have been contracted at variable interest rates. From the banks' perspective, the beauty of variable-interest-rate loans is that they mitigate the uncertainty inherent in long-term contracts. With variable-rate loans, debt-service obligations increase as the prime rate (or the rate of interest banks charge their best corporate customers) increases. LDC debtors are particularly vulnerable to upward trends in world interest rates; it has been estimated that some 40 percent of total LDC debt, and up to 75 percent for the largest borrowers, was contracted at variable interest rates (Makhijani and Browne 1985–86:64). Under these circumstances, rising interest rates have had devastating effects on LDC economies.

The Fed's tight monetary policy also triggered an international ratcheting of interest rates. The globalization of "free" (i.e., deregulated) financial markets constrains the ability of domestic policymakers to pursue *independent* monetary policies. Fearful of currency panics (similar to the United States in 1978–79), industrialized nations were forced to follow the U.S. lead in raising interest rates. In the words of former West German chancellor Helmut Schmidt, "In country after country, the Fed's policies have led to the highest rates of interest since the birth of Jesus Christ" (Moffit 1983:202).

The restrictive monetary policy of the United States was defended by its architects as a straightforward application of a necessary technocratic fix. But in the words of financial journalist William Greider, "Monetary policy is not just a deliberation over supply-and-demand conditions in credit markets; it is a political debate over the nation's economic priorities" (1988: 591). The global wave of monetary austerity of the 1980s, then, is a component of a strategy to prop up the dollar while inflating bank profits and the wealth of asset holders. This same policy, however, has the inevitable effect of penalizing the economically vulnerable (e.g., the poor, small businesses, and LDC debtors).

Repairing the economic and social dislocation arising out of monetary austerity requires loosening the grip of monetary policy. The interdependence of nations demands a global economic vision that transcends the boundaries of the nation-state (Wachtel 1986:9; 1987). This vision should be based not simply on shoring up the values of financial assets but on some shared standard of justice within and among nations (Greider 1988:608). Depending on the particular policies pursued by the world's industrialized nations, a lowering of U.S. interest rates could stimulate output and employment while mitigating the debt burdens facing U.S. and LDC debtors. Such a move by the United States could also create the conditions for less restrictive monetary policies in other nations.[5]

It should be clear that monetary expansion in one country is no substitute for a globally orchestrated easing of credit. In fact, the historical record unambiguously demonstrates that such national experiments are quickly undermined by footloose capital. A decision by one nation to pursue an expansionary monetary policy—in the absence of stringent controls on capital movements—will result in the flight of capital to nations providing a climate more hospitable to holders of financial assets. (The issue of controls on international capital movements will be addressed in the section "Jetsetting Capital.") Thus, international coordination[6] of monetary policy would eliminate one key catalyst for the dramatic movements of short-term capital, known as capital flight.

Or Dancing to the Beat of Social Objectives

Of course there is nothing inherently progressive about policy coordination per se. Recasting monetary policy to provide the wherewithal for the achievement of shared social objectives is predicated on both a dramatic shift in the political climate and, as many progressive analysts have noted, the establishment of a *fully representative transnational financial institution*. In the absence of democratization of international financial institutions, monetary policy will continue to operate in accordance with the imperatives of a powerful minority—capital.

The mandate for a democratic "Global Bank" has been outlined by Wachtel (1986, 1987) and Greider (1988). The Global Bank would be charged with policy coordination and monitoring. It would therefore replace the presently existing IMF, a decidedly undemocratic institution in terms of both its governance (by elites in DCs) and its interventions (in the affairs of LDCs).[7] The Global Bank would exert influence over the macroeconomic policies pursued by *both* DCs and LDCs. Policy adjustment—which in the current context refers to adherence to harsh IMF conditionality by LDCs—would be forced on those countries with excessively tight financial policy as well as on the profligate. In short, adjustment would be enforced symmetrically (Buira 1984:47; Greider 1988:607). The bank would be empowered to mete out penalties for excessively tight monetary policy and succor (in the form of increased credit) to those suffering as a consequence of monetary contraction on the part of their trading partners (Greider 1988:607–8).[8] The Global Bank would also be empowered to stabilize and coordinate national macroeconomic policies and to avert liquidity crises by acting as a lender-of-last-resort to governments in need of funds.

The Dollar Habit

The Bretton Woods accord enshrined the U.S. dollar as king. Although no longer atop its throne of gold, the dollar today remains at the center of the international financial system. In the jargon of international finance, the dollar is the world's principal reserve currency. A reserve currency is an international money accumulated by other nations in order to settle their accounts with one another (Block 1977:256). The increasing use of the Japanese yen and the German deutsche mark (DM) in settling international transactions may suggest a long-term movement toward a tripolar (namely, a U.S., Japanese, and German) or a multicurrency reserve system (i.e., one in which the currencies of several nations serve as reserve currencies). But even though the yen and especially the deutsche mark are increasingly being used in international transactions, evidence suggests that the U.S. dollar remains the predominant currency (see Tavlas 1990; Tavlas and Ozeki 1991). What, then, are the costs of one nation's currency serving in this capacity, and what are the alternatives to a national reserve currency?

A reserve currency must be of high and stable value in order to maintain the confidence of foreign investors and its attractiveness as an asset. On the surface, these attributes appear innocuous. In point of fact, the maintenance of a "strong" and stable currency subjugates domestic to international economic performance and inextricably links performance of both to the condition of the reserve currency.

When, for example, the dollar appreciates with respect to the peso, the number of dollars it takes to purchase one peso falls. Using the example provided previously, an appreciation of the dollar would be reflected in a shift from 3:1 to 2:1 in the dollar–peso exchange rate. Since the peso has, in a sense, become "cheaper" for U.S. dollar holders, Mexican goods in effect have become less expensive for U.S. citizens, while U.S. goods have become more expensive for Mexicans (because more pesos must be given up in order to purchase one U.S. dollar). In general, then, when the U.S. dollar appreciates relative to other currencies, U.S. exports decrease due to a decline in the competitiveness of American-produced goods on the world economy, while U.S. imports of foreign-produced goods increase.

Having to maintain a currency of high and stable value thus forces a reserve-currency country into a paradoxical position. A "strong" currency encourages imports and reduces the competitiveness of a country's goods on the world economy and thereby has adverse effects on the trade balance and domestic employment. The high interest rates required to support the domestic currency further dampen domestic economic activity by reducing domestic investment, construction, borrowing, and spending.

Since globalization wears down the boundaries among national economies, high interest rates and the resulting economic stagnation in the reserve currency country have significant feedback effects on world economic performance. The experience of the 1980s may be recast as the fallout of the United States' reserve-currency status. Burdened by competition from less expensive imports, domestic manufacturing contracted, with severe effects on idled production workers. Industries that rely heavily on debt (such as farming) or whose consumers borrow to finance purchases (such as housing or automobiles) were likewise stung by tight monetary policy. Much the same could be said of the LDCs, which found in the crippled U.S. economy little demand for their exports while they faced rising debt burdens. The financial community, on the other hand, reaped untold rewards.

Reserve-currency status necessarily implies a trade-off between the interests of the financial community and the interests of those lacking resources. The former collect high rates of return while the latter suffer the consequences of economic stagnation. In view of these inherent trade-offs, there is general consensus among progressive economists that the international financial system could be made more accountable to the nonwealthy majority by liberating the dollar from its reserve-currency role.

We should be advised, however, that a planned transition to a multicurrency reserve system is not a satisfactory resolution to the present state of affairs. In fact, it has been argued that a multicurrency reserve system is potentially fraught with even greater difficulties (see Epstein 1985:646–47). As with the single-currency reserve system, national economic performance would continue to be held hostage to the prerogative of maintaining the high value of the reserve currencies. This prerogative frustrates the ability of nations to lower interest rates. Additionally, the monetary status quo would remain in force. The international financial system would continue to remain in the hands of the financial community of the most powerful DCs. And finally, a multicurrency reserve system is likely to be characterized by a greater degree of exchange-rate instability (with the concomitant "real" effects discussed above) than that which already prevails. One can easily imagine flights from one reserve currency to another as competing nations wreak economic "warfare" on one another by means of minuscule changes in their interest rates.

Kicking the Dollar Habit
In recognition of the constraints inherent in a single-currency (or multicurrency) reserve system, and in the interests of expanding world liquidity and stability, many progressive economists have proposed that the international financial system move toward the adoption of a truly international reserve currency. The IMF's special drawing right (SDR), though not widely used at present, has emerged as a prime candidate for a "stateless" reserve currency (see, e.g., Bergsten 1984; Epstein 1985; Kenen 1983). The SDR is a reserve asset created by the IMF in 1967 whose value is calculated as a weighted average of sixteen countries' exchange rates. It is accepted in settlement of official debts between member nations of the IMF (see Bergstrand 1984). The outlines of an SDR-based international financial system have been developed by progressive and mainstream economists (see, e.g., Epstein 1985; Group of Thirty 1980; Kenen 1983).

World Money
In order to promote the use of the SDR as the world's principal reserve asset, the Global Bank (described in the section "Dancing to the Beat") could require mandatory deposits of foreign-exchange reserve holdings (particularly dollar-denominated holdings) into a specially created sub-

stitution account. The creation and maintenance of the substitution account would facilitate an orderly transition to an SDR-based international money system, since it would discourage the full-scale unloading of dollar holdings by central banks and official holders (Epstein 1985:647; Group of Thirty 1980). Freshly minted SDR-denominated claims or certificates would be issued in return for foreign-exchange reserve deposits (Kenen 1983). Widespread use of and confidence in SDRs as the principal reserve currency could be stimulated by paying interest on SDR claims in the substitution account (Group of Thirty 1980), and by encouraging nations to accept SDRs when drawing on the general resources of the Global Bank (see Kenen 1983:357).

Transition to an SDR reserve asset system, in conjunction with the other financial reforms discussed here, could address a great many institutional inequities and would be part of a broad-based radical reform program to ensure the financial system's accountability to shared social objectives. The transition to an SDR-based system would have several advantages over the present state of affairs. It would alleviate the pressure on the United States (as reserve-currency nation) to maintain the dollar's value through high interest rates (Epstein 1985:648). And lower interest rates in one nation (coupled with controls on capital movements—see "Jetsetting Capital" below) are a precondition for a globally orchestrated lowering of rates. Furthermore, an SDR-based system would provide the basis for easing the liquidity crises faced by LDCs.[9] It is generally agreed that world economic recovery and an easing of LDCs' debt burdens requires an increase in international liquidity (Williamson 1984:72–73). Presumably, the Global Bank could make decisions regarding liquidity creation based on the needs of all nations (Epstein 1985).

Targeting Exchange Rates

An important caveat is in order here, however. Today's high interest rates are induced not only by the status of the U.S. dollar as the reserve currency; a second culprit is the freewheeling foreign-exchange market.

Since floating exchange rates were adopted in 1973, foreign-exchange markets have become the world's biggest casino (see Figure 3.1). Massive swings in exchange rates derive from currency traders' speculations regarding changes in values of national currencies. On an average business day, currency traders buy and sell some $600 billion worth of currencies (*Business Week*, 10 September 1990, 62).

Wild fluctuations in exchange rates have important distributional consequences. By impairing the competitiveness (and hence sales) of a nation's goods in the world economy, currency appreciations may lead to production slowdowns and increases in unemployment. At the same time, such "strengthening" of a nation's currency increases its ability to import goods cheaply. Thus, currency appreciations may redistribute income from exporters (and workers in export-oriented industries) to importers. Conversely, currency depreciations improve competitiveness and may lead to an increase in employment in export-oriented industries.[10]

Proponents of free currency markets argue that each nation's currency will find its "natural" level through the operation of supply and demand. But the sight of nervous central bankers intervening daily in foreign-exchange markets contradicts this view. These bankers fear that a precipitous decline in the value of a currency will trigger a flight from interest-bearing assets denominated in that currency. This is because the foreign owners of these assets find the real value of their holdings reduced when the relevant currency is depreciated. Hence central bankers worldwide must maintain high interest rates in the battle to support currency values as a hedge against capital flight. The dampening of world interest rates, then, is predicated on some mechanism for coordinated exchange-rate stabilization.

One such mechanism cited by many progressive and mainstream analysts is the establishment of democratically selected target exchange-rate zones (see, e.g., Bergstrand 1984; Greider 1988; Roosa 1984; Wachtel 1986). Target zones would involve the determination of an international consensus regarding an appropriate and globally feasible range around which currency values could fluctuate. Governments would then be expected to maintain their exchange-rate values within a proscribed zone, through a combination of macroeconomic stabilization policies and coordinated intervention in the foreign-exchange market (Bergstrand 1984:6–7).[11]

Jetsetting Capital

In the midst of the Great Depression and again in the post–World War II period, British economist John Maynard Keynes presented a compelling case for the necessity of control over inward and outward capital movements (see Crotty 1983; Keynes 1933:52). Keynes's vision was guided by neither autarky nor isolationism, but rather by an overriding aim to insulate domestic economic experiments from internationally initiated disruptions. From his vantage point, the success of domestic economic and political experiments was uniquely dependent upon the adoption of controls over the international movement of money (Crotty 1983:60–61).

Controlling Capital in the Twentieth Century

Broadly speaking, capital controls are measures aimed at influencing the timing, character, and volume of international capital movements. International capital movements fall into two classes: portfolio investment (PI) refers to the ownership of bank accounts, securities, and bonds of corporations or governments located in a country other than the one in which the investor resides; direct foreign investment (DFI) refers to the ownership of real estate or a controlling interest in a company located in a country other than the one in which the investor resides. In all cases (except when referring to the loss of manufacturing jobs as plants are relocated overseas) I refer to controls on PI.[12]

Over the last thirty years, capital controls have been implemented by Northern and Southern nations in an effort to maintain the autonomy of domestic economic policy. The United States' Interest Equalization Tax of 1964 and the Voluntary Foreign Credit Restraint Act of 1965 sought to restrict the magnitude of capital outflows.[13] Before June 1988, nations of the European Economic Community (EEC) experimented extensively with a broad range of controls aimed at influencing both inflows and outflows. And until the heavy hand of IMF conditionality all but suffocated their autonomy, LDCs explored various approaches to delinking domestic and international asset markets in order to pursue policies directed toward national objectives.

Laissez-faire Comes Home to Roost

The untimely demise of capital-control policies is but one casualty of the laissez-faire revolution of the 1980s. Restrictions on capital movements, the free-marketeers assert, violate the sacrosanct freedoms of private citizens and enterprises to chase returns across the globe. In their view, respect for private-property rights precludes government interference in the breakneck trading of financial exotica by self-proclaimed "soldiers of fortune" with "no alliances" except, of course, a commitment to their personal or institutional objectives (Wachtel 1988:788).

The ramifications of capital's freedom have not been lost on average citizens of Northern and Southern nations. For example, North American manufacturing workers who lost their jobs when their companies moved production abroad and LDC poor whose real purchasing power declined with successive currency depreciations are no strangers to the consequences of capital flight.[14] For Argentina, Mexico, and Venezuela, the amount of capital flight has been estimated to be nearly equal to their total national indebtedness (Rodriguez 1987:130). The magnitude of capital flight has forced officials of international banks and multilateral lending agencies to confront the consequences of free capital markets. Scores of domestic policymakers—including Jimmy Carter in 1978–79, Jamaica's Michael Manley in the mid-to-late 1970s, and France's François Mitterrand in the early 1980s—learned firsthand that wealth holders exercise veto power over national economic policy so long as capital mobility remains unrestricted (Pastor 1987:30).

Voting with Their Feet

The tyranny of integrated financial markets ultimately thwarts the ability of national governments to pursue expansionary monetary policy. Wealth holders can cast their votes against low-interest-rate policy by moving their capital abroad. This flight frustrates the expansionary project by suppressing the value of the domestic currency at the cost of reduced purchasing power.

It is self-evident that the ability of wealth holders to veto a societal agenda flies in the face of the most fundamental democratic principles. A genuinely democratic international financial system would not exempt some groups from national obligations while extending to them national protections. Democratic control over capital transfers is a minimum quid pro quo for public protection of capital from domestic and foreign threats (see Greider 1988).

Reining in Capital

Taking a leaf from Keynes, progressive economists have prescribed a broad spectrum of capital controls that, if implemented, would go some distance toward ensuring that monetary policy serves social objectives (see, e.g., Crotty 1989; Dornbusch 1986; Epstein 1985; Greider 1988; Pastor 1987). A radical program would entail outright restrictions on speculative capital transfers. More moderate programs might include measures designed to regulate the timing of capital transfers (Crotty 1989:98) or increase the transactions cost of speculative transactions. Similarly, a uniform tax could be imposed on intercurrency transactions. In this vein, economist James Tobin (1978) proposes to reduce speculative transfers through the imposition of an internationally uniform tax—administered by national governments over their geographic jurisdictions—on all conversions of one currency into another.[15]

Clearly, the successful and evenhanded implementation of capital controls depends on the political will of national governments. Measures such as the Bank Secrecy Act of 1970—which requires that all U.S. financial institutions file ownership information on all foreign and domestic cash transactions over $10,000 (Felix 1985)—could be extended to other nations. Such measures would ensure the integrity of capital-control programs and could conceivably be enforced by the Global Bank.

A New Bretton Woods?

It is neither dearth of enthusiasm nor vision on the part of progressives that stands to impede the implementation of global policy coordination. Until recently, proposals to radically reform the international financial order seemed doomed by the lack of political will parading behind patriotic appeals to national sovereignty. Today, however, there is some evidence of changing sentiments. In particular, recent instances of monetary collaboration (around the dollar crisis) by the West's Group of Seven suggests a growing realization that the gravity of the global economic crisis may necessitate some degree of formal policy coordination. And, of course, there is precedent for cooperation in the agreements that govern the operation of international financial institutions (e.g., minimum bank reserve requirements) (Epstein 1989:117). Indeed, as these examples suggest, there is nothing inherently progressive about policy coordination per se. *Progressive* financial coordination requires a *dramatic shift in political agendas*. In the absence of this political shift, there is no reason to doubt that coordination will continue to be based on the imperatives of capital.

More heartening, perhaps, is the emergence of a global vision in the form of trade and currency unions in Latin America, Africa, and the Caribbean. The 1992 plan for Western European economic unification also offers some hope. And despite prevailing conventional wisdom, some types of capital controls continue to be used by a wide range of nations. At the end of 1988, 127 of the 152 member states of the IMF maintained some type of capital control. South Korea, Brazil, and Japan are among the most notable examples where capital-control programs (and other restrictions on the financial sector) have played a role in promoting economic development.

The outcome of these internationalist gestures is uncertain. Nevertheless, it appears that the moment is propitious for progressives to introduce into current debate radical measures to recast the international financial system. Important opportunities have been created by nationals of LDCs who are actively questioning the legitimacy of their nations' debt and the intervention of the IMF into domestic affairs. Similarly, activists in DCs, particularly in the United States, have challenged the practices and regulatory structure of lending institutions based in rural and urban centers. On a modest scale, they have also successfully operated their own financial institutions (examples include the banks operated by the carpenters' trade union and the South Shore Bank in Chicago). Many have also drawn attention to the similarities between the U.S. farm crisis of the 1970s and the LDC debt crisis of the 1980s and 1990s, and have linked unemployment in DCs to austerity programs in LDCs. Due to the energy and openings created by these and other forms of activism, radical programs to recast the international financial system can be envisioned.

Thus, grass-roots activism and the global economic malaise have created opportunities that remain to be fully exploited. It is in this spirit that radical reform programs involving democratic control over financial regulation and institutions, monetary-policy coordination, and international cooperation are presented here.

ACKNOWLEDGMENTS

Thanks to Jerry Epstein and George DeMartino for critical feedback on earlier drafts of this chapter. Thanks also to Kevin Crocker for graphics work and to Emily Kawano, Jessica Nembhard, and Brenda Wyss for helpful comments.

NOTES

1. Much of what follows appears in a different form in Grabel 1989a and 1989b.

2. The discussion of Bretton Woods draws on Aliber (1987), Block (1977), Epstein (1985), Moffit (1983), and Wachtel (1986); for detailed histories of the international monetary order, see these sources.

3. This was referred to as the "Triffin Paradox," after the Yale economist Robert Triffin, who first identified it.

4. For a discussion of trends in U.S. interest rates, see Moffit 1983.

5. Even the recent initiatives of today's Fed chairperson, Alan Greenspan, to reverse the recent recession by loosening monetary policy have proven to be too little, too late. The Fed's ability to reduce rates significantly in this instance has been limited by the hesitancy of the German and other central banks to lower their own interest rates (see the section "Jetsetting Capital").

6. Policy coordination may be said to occur "whenever countries modify their economic policies in what is intended to be a mutually beneficial manner, taking account of international economic linkages" (Group of Thirty 1980:4–5).

7. The voting rights of IMF member governments depend upon their financial contributions: about half of the votes are controlled by eight nations, and the United States' share of the total vote is about one-fifth (Wachtel 1987:11–12).

8. This idea is similar to J. M. Keynes's 1942 plan for an international clearing union (see Crotty 1983).

9. International liquidity may be thought of as a measure of a nation's ability to finance an external payments deficit. Thus, "liquid" (i.e., readily convertible to a means of payment) central bank holdings of foreign currency and SDRs contribute to international liquidity (Williamson 1984:59).

10. But a sad paradox confronts the LDCs. The vast majority of wage-goods are imported in such countries. Hence, by reducing wage earners' purchasing power, depreciations are impoverishing.

11. Agreed-upon ranges for all currencies would be set (Greider 1988). Enforcement could take place in a number of contexts: the Global Bank could supervise DCs and LDCs; governments could collaborate (Roosa 1984); or discipline could be internally imposed such that errant governments (i.e., governments whose currencies strayed out of their proscribed zone) would be required to provide immediate monetary compensation to those holders of its currency that had been economically disadvantaged by its lack of discipline (Greider 1988). In any of its forms, the transition to a target exchange-rate zone would greatly stabilize currency values and consequently would alleviate the real effects of foreign-exchange gyrations (Wachtel 1986). Moreover, globally coordinated exchange rates would provide the wherewithal for a global reduction in interest rates.

12. The issue of controls on DFI, though critical, is beyond the scope of this chapter.

13. The failure of political will, coupled with developments in international money markets, largely served to undermine these policies. In response to pressure from the financial community, numerous loopholes and special exemptions were granted.

14. Depreciation, or a fall in the value of a nation's currency relative to other nations' currencies, increases the cost of imported goods to domestic residents (and decreases the cost of its exports to other nations). Depreciations are seen as impoverishing because they reduce consumers' purchasing power.

15. In order to thwart the possibility of cloaking speculative transfers under the guise of real trade, the tax would apply to all intercurrency transfers. The tax liability would be proportional to the size of the transaction, and the proceeds would be payable to the Global Bank.

BIBLIOGRAPHY

Aliber, Robert. 1987. *The International Money Game*. New York: Basic Books.
Bergsten, C. Fred. 1984. Discussion. In *International Monetary System: Forty Years after Bretton Woods*, Federal Reserve Bank of Boston, Conference Series, no. 28, 267–71. Boston: Federal Reserve Bank of Boston.
Bergstrand, Jeffrey H. 1984. Summary. In *International Monetary System: Forty Years after Bretton Woods*, Federal Reserve Bank of Boston, Conference Series, no. 28, 1–16. Boston: Federal Reserve Bank of Boston.
Block, Fred. 1977. *The Origins of International Economic Disorder*. Berkeley and Los Angeles: University of California Press.
Buira, Ariel. 1984. Discussion. In *International Monetary System: Forty Years after Bretton Woods*, Federal Reserve Bank of Boston, Conference Series, no. 28, 4–51. Boston: Federal Reserve Bank of Boston.
Crotty, James R. 1983. Keynes and Capital Flight. *Journal of Economic Literature* 21(1):59–65.
———. 1989. The Limits of Keynesian Macroeconomic Policy in the Age of the Global Marketplace. In *Instability and Change in the World Economy*, ed. Arthur MacEwan and William K. Tabb, 82–100. New York: Monthly Review Press.
Dornbusch, Rudiger. 1986. Special Exchange Rates for Capital Account Transactions. *World Bank Economic Review* 1(1): 3–33.
Epstein, Gerald. 1985. The Triple Debt Crisis. *World Policy Journal*, 625–57.
———. 1989. Financial Instability and the Structure of the International Monetary System. In *Instability and Change in the World Economy*, ed. Arthur MacEwan and William Tabb, 101–20. New York: Monthly Review Press.
Felix, David. 1985. How to Resolve Latin America's Debt Crisis. *Challenge* 28(5): 44–51.
Grabel, Ilene. 1989a. Money and People: Redesigning the Financial Sector. Working paper prepared for the Financial Democracy Campaign and the Southern Finance Project. Mimeo.

————. 1989b. Taking Control: An Agenda for a Democratic Financial System. *Dollars and Sense* 151:15–18.

Greider, William. 1987. *Secrets of the Temple*. New York: Simon & Schuster.

————. 1988. The Money Question. *World Policy Journal*, 567–613.

Group of Thirty. 1980. *Toward a Less Unstable International Monetary System*. London: Group of Thirty.

Kenen, Peter B. 1983. Use of the SDR to Supplement or Substitute for Other Means of Finance. In *International Money and Credit: The Policy Roles*, ed. George Furstenberg, 32–61. Washington, D.C.: IMF.

Keynes, John Maynard. 1933. National Self-sufficiency. *Yale Review* 22(4): 755–69.

Makhijani, Arjun and Robert S. Browne. 1985–86. Restructuring the International Monetary System. *World Policy Journal*, 59–80.

Moffitt, Michael. 1983. *The World's Money*. New York: Simon & Schuster.

Pastor, Manuel, Jr. 1987. Capital Flight and the Latin American Debt Crisis. Occidental College, Los Angeles. Mimeo.

Pollin, Robert. 1989. Debt-dependent Growth and Financial Innovation: Instability in the U.S. and Latin America. In *Instability and Change in the World Economy*, ed. Arthur MacEwan and William Tabb, 121–46. New York: Monthly Review Press.

Rodriguez, Miguel. 1987. Consequences of Capital Flight for Latin American Debtor Countries. In *Capital Flight and Third World Debt*, ed. Donald Lessard and John Williamson, 129–44. Washington, D.C.: Institute for International Economics.

Roosa, Robert. 1984. Exchange Rate Arrangements in the Eighties. In *International Monetary System: Forty Years after Bretton Woods*, Federal Reserve Bank of Boston, Conference Series, no. 28, 104–18. Boston: Federal Reserve Bank of Boston.

Tavlas, George S. 1990. International Currencies: The Rise of the Deutsche Mark. *Finance and Development* 27(3): 35–38.

Tavlas, George S., and Yuzuru Ozeki. 1991. The Internationalization of the Yen. *Finance and Development* 28(2): 2–5.

Tobin, James. 1978. A Proposal for International Monetary Reform. *Eastern Economic Journal* 4(3–4): 153–59.

Wachtel, Howard. 1986. *The Money Mandarins*. New York: Pantheon.

————. 1987. *The Politics of International Money*. Transnational Issues, no. 2. Amsterdam: Transnational Institute.

————. 1988. The Global Funny Money Game. *The Nation*, 2 January, 784–90.

Williamson, John. 1984. International Liquidity: Are the Supply and Composition Appropriate. In *International Monetary System: Forty Years after Bretton Woods*, Federal Reserve Bank of Boston, Conference Series no. 28, 59–77. Boston: Federal Reserve Bank of Boston.

4 BOB SUTCLIFFE

Immigration and the World Economy

The Political Importance of Migration

The majority of the inhabitants of most of the developed countries can trace their ancestry back to inhabitants of the same or nearby areas in the epoch before modern economic development took place. A few developed countries, however, are now inhabited by people whose ancestors migrated from elsewhere during the epoch of modern capitalist development.

Thinking about development, however, is dominated—albeit often unconsciously—by the first (European) and not the second (American) model. Insofar as people imagine the future elimination of world poverty, it is usually through the progressive development of all countries of the world and not, at least partly, through the large-scale migration of poor people to richer countries.

Yet it is clear that the queue of people in Third World countries who either are consciously trying to emigrate to rich countries or would try if not obstructed by legal obstacles runs into many millions. And the issues that emerge from this demand for migration are ones of extreme political importance in many countries. In Western Europe the question of how much immigration to allow from the Third World countries is one of the dominant issues of contemporary politics. And so are the social issues that arise from the presence in those countries of people with origins in the Third World. In the United States the question of immigration has always been in the center of the political debate. Even in Japan, where the size of the immigrant population is much smaller, the question is still a live issue.

This chapter outlines the role that migration from poor to rich countries might play in the elimination of world poverty in the foreseeable future. The question is not a simple one, because there are no clear analytical guidelines. Few, if any, schools of thought in the social sciences, economics in particular, have any general perspective on the question. Most share the assumption that people are supposed to stay in their "own" countries. I want to put forward a very different perspective: that immigration will and

84

should play a major part in the reduction of world poverty; that socialists in rich countries should advocate the elimination of all restrictions on immigration in their countries; in short, that the rallying cry for "open borders" is both important and progressive.

International Movements of Population

Human populations have always shown a strong tendency to shift their habitat, sometimes over short, sometimes long distances. The growth of industrial capitalism has led to two major forms of movement: migration from the country to the town due to industrialization and to the destruction of rural rights and ways of life; and migration between cities in search of work, due to the prevalence of "free" labor. The development of capitalism led to a vast increase in such intranational migrations. Few people in modern capitalist societies have failed to experience at least one major change of domicile during their lives.

International migration has often had the same economic and social roots as internal migration, but it is still a qualitatively different phenomenon. Unlike intranational migration (except in a few instances), international movements require people to overcome an additional set of constraints—the legal barriers to migration. It is almost a defining characteristic of the modern nation-state that it erects frontiers and a set of regulations to determine who may cross them and for what purpose. The immense bureaucratic apparatus surrounding modern international travel (frontiers, frontier guards or immigration officers, passports, visas, work permits, vaccination certificates) is almost entirely an achievement of the twentieth century. No country in the modern world has open borders; all of them try to control immigration of outsiders to their territory.

In spite of this, during the epoch of the modern nation-state, major moves of population over national borders have occurred. And migration has played an important role in the modern economic and social history of many countries. During the nineteenth century millions of Europeans migrated to the Americas in search of some way out of their economic plight at home. During the decade of 1905–14 the United States each year admitted one immigrant for every eighty-three members of the existing population (during the 1980s the annual ratio was one for every four hundred residents) (Chiswick 1988:101). And in the fifteen years before the First World War, Italy (now a center of attraction for immigrants from Africa) lost in emigration between 1.5 and 2 per 100 of its population (see Figure 4.1). These ratios are among the highest recorded anywhere, but none of the presently developed countries was unaffected by the migrations. There was in the nineteenth century very little voluntary migration from the countries that now constitute the Third World to the developed countries. Most

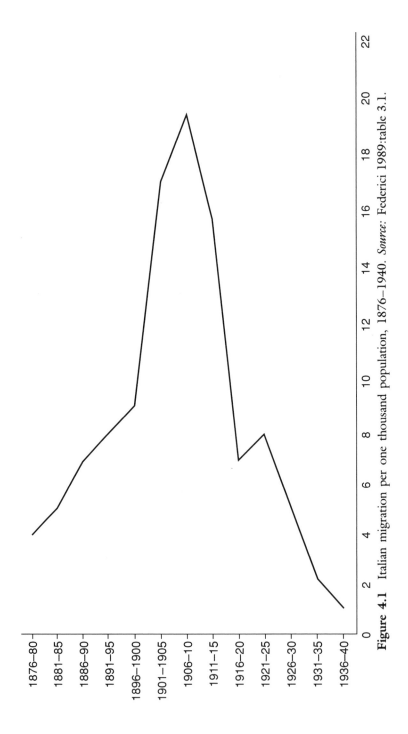

Figure 4.1 Italian migration per one thousand population, 1876–1940. *Source:* Federici 1989:table 3.1.

TABLE 4.1
Migrations of the Post–World War II Boom

Source Countries	Destination Countries	Years
West Indies, North Africa, Turkey, South Asia	Western Europe	1950–1973
South Asia, East Asia, Egypt	Middle Eastern oil-producing countries	1973–1986
Caribbean, Central and South America, East Asia, South Asia	United States	1964–

Source: Federici (1989:52), table 3.1.

of the migration in that direction was forced, due to the slave trade at the start of the century and to various indentured-labor schemes in the latter part. A certain number of Europeans migrated to the Third World, however, either to Latin America, where they came to constitute part of virtually all social classes, and to Africa and Asia, where they became more of a privileged settler elite.

Between the two world wars international migration was severely curtailed because of a more restrictive policy imposed by the United States in the 1920s and later because of restrictions applied by other countries during the Great Depression. The restrictions on migration were partly responsible for the deaths of millions of would-be migrants from Nazi-controlled areas of Europe.

The enormous boom of the world capitalist economy after World War II led to a renewed upsurge of international migration, this time increasingly from poor to rich countries. Since the beginning of the postwar boom there have been three major migrations (summarized in Table 4.1).

Western Europe

The migrations to Western Europe during the 1950s, 1960s, and early 1970s were in part determined by the colonial relationship. Relatively liberal migration laws applying to colonies and former colonies allowed many West Indians and South Asians to migrate to the United Kingdom, and many North Africans to migrate to France. The governments of both European countries began by encouraging such immigration to ease labor shortage problems but ended up by controlling it through overtly racist immigration controls. In West Germany, which was left without colonies, the migration came largely from Spain, Portugal, Italy, Yugoslavia, and especially Turkey. Workers arrived as part of a state-organized plan to provide guest-workers (*Gastarbeiter*).

In all of Western Europe there has always been much confusion and conflict over what should be the rights of the Third World immigrants. Were they really just "guests," expected to return to the country of origin when they had outstayed their welcome, or were they theoretically supposed to be integrated into the society? Opinion in Europe still ranges between demands for full civil rights and demands for forcible repatriation.

The migration was severely curtailed with the renewal of mass unemployment in the Western European economies after the crisis of 1973. Pressure to reduce Third World immigration grew further at the end of the 1980s with the upsurge of westward migration by residents of the collapsing Stalinist states of the East, especially into West Germany. Figure 4.2 shows the size of the non-native population in the countries of Western Europe. This varies from over 6 percent in France to less than 1 percent in Spain, Portugal, Ireland, and Greece. The average for the European Community (EC) is 2.5 percent. Immigrants compose a larger percentage of the labor force than of the population.

In 1993 the EC plans to abolish its internal frontiers and institute the free internal movement of labor. The plan to increase the freedom of movement of Western European workers, however, has been linked to restricting the freedom of entry of workers from the Third World. The countries of the EC that already have a fairly rigorous control of immigration (such as Britain, France, and Germany) are reluctant to lower their frontiers until there is a guarantee that the other countries (especially Italy and Spain) are prepared to toughen their restrictions against Third World immigration. These latter countries, therefore, are under immense pressure to tighten their borders against North Africa and to expel immigrants who have entered illegally. In 1991 the Italian government included for the first time a minister for immigration, whose task is to "close the door," and Spain initiated visas for North Africans. These countries have their own reasons for restricting immigration, but they also wish to avoid the opprobrium of being the ones to impose burdensome restrictions on Third World people. As a result, they would prefer the EC as a whole to impose the restrictions.

In Germany the feeling against Third World immigrants has hardened following reunification and the entry of many thousands of Eastern Europeans. And in France the demands of the extreme right National Front for the forcible repatriation of Third World immigrants has shifted the whole of the political spectrum on the issue. The establishment parties still mouth antiracist platitudes but also talk, in the words of President Mitterand, of the approach of a "threshold of tolerance."

In short, immigration is a major political issue, and in light of present trends, Third World immigrants in Western Europe can expect less demand

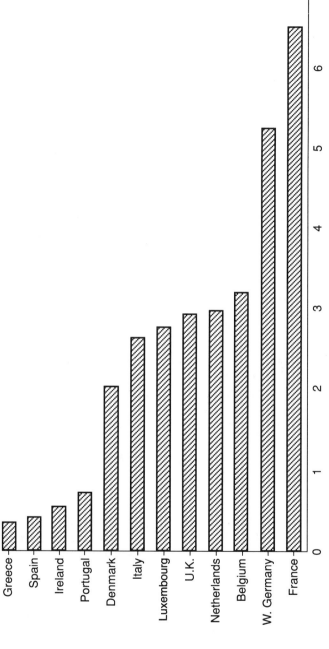

Figure 4.2 Non-EC immigrants as a percentage of EC population, ca. 1989. *Source:* Buchan and Wiles 1990.

for their services, more controls on their movement, and even more demands for their expulsion.

The Middle East Oil Producers

Just as the demand for immigrant labor in Europe began to wane, so in a number of oil-producing countries it began to rise. The rise in oil prices during the 1970s allowed an enormous increase in consumption and investment in a few oil-producing countries, especially around the Persian Gulf, and this resulted in an acute shortage of labor.

Figure 4.3 shows how important immigrant labor had become by the start of the 1980s in the oil-producing countries of the Middle East. These workers were recruited in neighbouring Arab states and later from points east—especially from India, Pakistan, Bangladesh, and even farther east (see Figure 4.4). The rights of these workers are in most cases even fewer than those of immigrants in Europe. The prevailing bias is that their role in the society should not outlast their having a job. When their work ends, they are supposed to return to the place from which they came. These workers constitute such a remarkably high proportion of the labor force of the oil-producing countries that there is a clear reason why the undemocratic governments of those countries—in which immigrants are the majority but have absolutely no political rights—will wish to guard against any autonomous political or trade-union movements developing among the workers.

Since the mid-1980s the decline in the price of oil has led to a major economic shock in the producing countries and reduced the demand for immigrant labor (although recent data are not available for this to show up on Figure 4.4). Here, too, the prospect in the short term is a reduction in the amount of work available and the maintenance of rigid controls against immigrants organizing to improve their lot. The war of 1991 further cut back the demand for immigrants partly as a result of the political spite of Kuwait and Saudi Arabia against Jordan (and the Palestinians) and Yemen, which are major sources of migrant workers and which had not opposed Iraq in the war.

The United States

A proportion of Third World immigration into the United States is of the same kind as that into the Middle East: workers are recruited for very low pay for short periods, mostly in seasonal agricultural activities, after which they are obliged to return home. The great majority of the immigration to the United States, however, is very different; it is of people who mean to come for a long time, perhaps for the rest of their lives. And once they are in the United States—even many of those who originally entered illegally—they obtain the right to stay and other civil rights. There is no doubt that many aspects of the lives and treatment of immigrants from

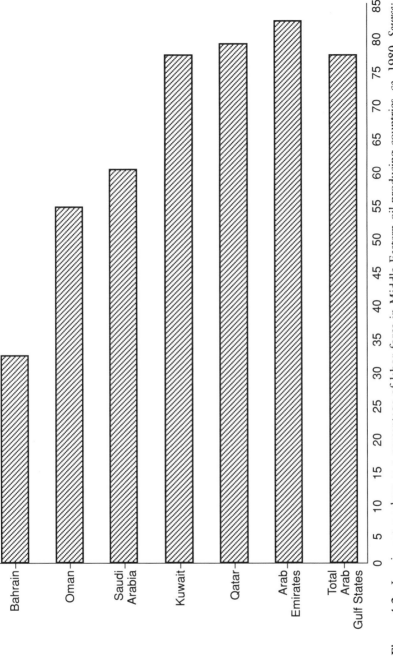

Figure 4.3 Immigrant workers as a percentage of labor force in Middle Eastern oil-producing countries, ca. 1980. *Source:* Owen 1985:table 3.

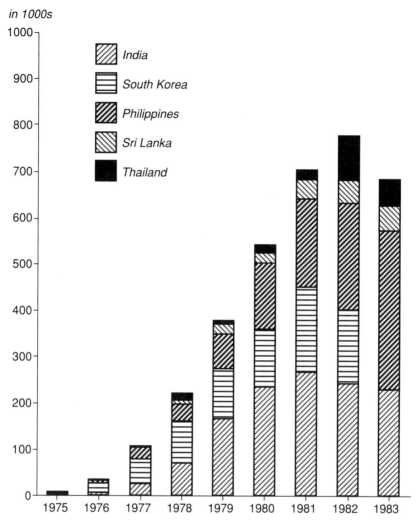

Figure 4.4 Migrant workers from Asia in the Middle East, 1975–1983. *Source:* Huguet 1989:table 6.1.

Third World countries in the United States are deplorable. Nonetheless, their situation is much better than that of their counterparts in Western Europe or the Middle East. Since the political weight of immigrants in the history and politics of the United States has been great, it is hard to imagine now that, despite racism and prejudice, this will not continue to be true.

Immigration to the United States (although still much lower relative to the size of the population and even in absolute numbers than in the first decade of this century) has grown enormously since the change in the immigration law in 1964. This abolished the old quotas based on the existing structure of the population and instituted equal quota limits for all countries. And immigration has to some extent also grown because of illegal immigration, which is only partly and erratically policed. The total number of immigrants has risen, and an increasing number of them come from the Third World—especially, in the latest period, from Asian countries.

This surge of immigration has been closely associated with important changes in the U.S. economy. Immigrant workers furnish the labor force in three areas of the economy. First, they fill various professional posts, such as doctors and engineers, in which the number of qualified U.S. personnel is insufficient to meet the demand. Second, they occupy a disproportionate number of the rapidly expanding low-paid service jobs that have grown alongside the high-paid financial and other services in the major cities (Sassen 1988:ch. 3). The sharp growth of inequality in income distribution in the United States is in part a reflection of this development. And third, immigrants have been a major constituent of the great expansion of low-paid manufacturing jobs in the Southwest in areas such as clothing and electronics. This phenomenon of reindustrialization of part of the United States on the model of the newly industrializing countries (NICs) of the Third World could not have happened without immigrant labor, often coming from the NICs themselves. In addition, a significant number of immigrants have set up their own businesses.

As a democracy with pretensions to the defense of civil rights, the United States finds itself in something of a dilemma regarding immigration. Too rigid enforcement of the laws involves extremely repressive actions that, when publicized, can cause an international loss of political face and can even prejudice domestic votes because immigrants from the Third World form an increasing share of the electorate. The United States likes to present a liberal international image, though this is partly hypocritical. It publicly opposed British forcible repatriation of Vietnamese "boat people" from Hong Kong in 1990, and yet it forcibly repatriates around one million illegal immigrants a year. It has condemned the Soviet Union for restricting the emigration of Jews, and yet in 1990 it increased its restrictions on the immigration of Jews from the USSR. It has the largest number of people infected with the HIV virus, and yet it has imposed harsh restrictions on the immigration of infected people. These contradictions are some of the things that keep immigration regulations a leading issue in United States politics.

Migration in the Contemporary World Economy

Some of the forces that foster migration are strengthening. These are the poverty, lack of employment, and failure of development in the Third World countries; the rapid growth and employment opportunities in some developed areas; the disparity between the Third World and developed countries; the knowledge of the opportunities and of the disparities; and the existence of sizable immigrant communities in the developed countries.

Even so, labor remains a very immobile factor of production. Capital is able to move much more freely around the world economic system than labor. The controls on capital movements are mostly against its emigration from a country, not its immigration; with labor it tends to be the opposite.

In general, a number of highly skilled professions enjoy a good deal of freedom of movement of labor (e.g., airline pilots and doctors), but with only a few exceptions, unskilled workers are confined of necessity to the country where they were born. And those who leave often have to endure exceptional dangers in their efforts to get somewhere else.

The economic significance of labor migration, however, is considerable partly because of its role in filling gaps in labor supply but also because it leads to large flows of money (remittances) sent by emigrants to their families. These outward and inward flows are summarized in Figure 4.5. For some countries, migrant labor provides a large proportion of the labor force (e.g., the oil-producing countries of the Gulf: see Figure 4.3); for some countries, work abroad provides a large proportion of the jobs available to nationals (e.g., Jordan and Yemen); for some countries, the remittances provided by migrants constitute a large proportion of the income of the migrants' own families; in some cases remittances are large in relation to export earnings (in 1988 more than 50 percent in five countries: see Figure 4.6); in some cases they are high even in relation to the national income of the country itself (more than 10 percent for four countries in 1988: see Figure 4.7).

The money transfers resulting from migrant labor are already significantly redistributing the income of the world. The home remittances of migrant workers are in many cases more significant than official aid flows. Several countries receive more money in the form of labor migrants' transfers of funds than they do in official aid (see Figure 4.8). And in some "host" countries, the migrants from the Third World transfer more money to their country of origin than the host country provides in the form of official aid (see Figure 4.9). And private remittances are often put to better use than official aid.

In some countries the presence of a family member in a developed country can make all the difference between a family's poverty and its economic survival. In the long run, of course, remittances by long-term migrants tend to decline, especially if some of their family emigrate to join them. But a rising rate of migration will continue to swell the important international flow of remittances.

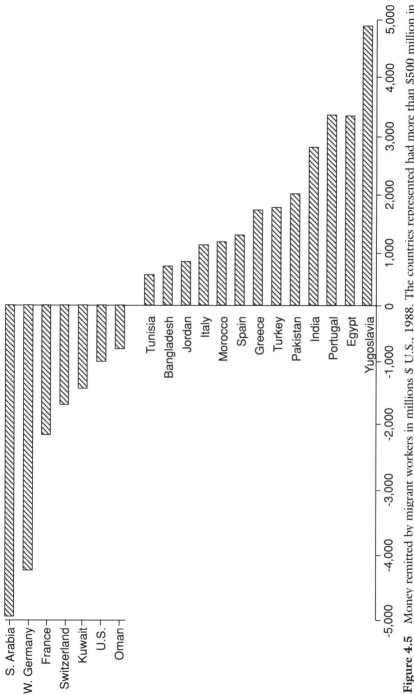

Figure 4.5 Money remitted by migrant workers in millions $ U.S., 1988. The countries represented had more than $500 million in net loss or gain. *Source:* World Bank 1990:table 18.

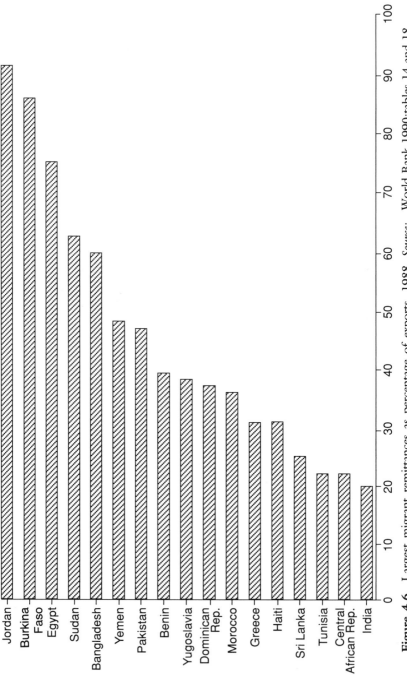

Figure 4.6 Largest migrant remittances as percentage of exports, 1988. *Source:* World Bank 1990:tables 14 and 18.

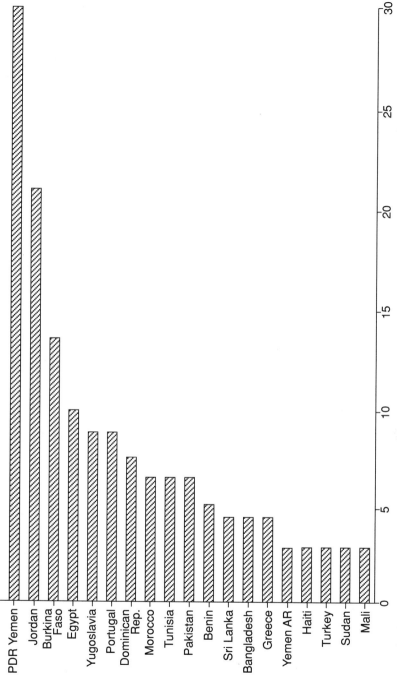

Figure 4.7 Largest migrant remittances as percentage of GDP, 1988. *Source:* World Bank 1990:tables 3 and 18.

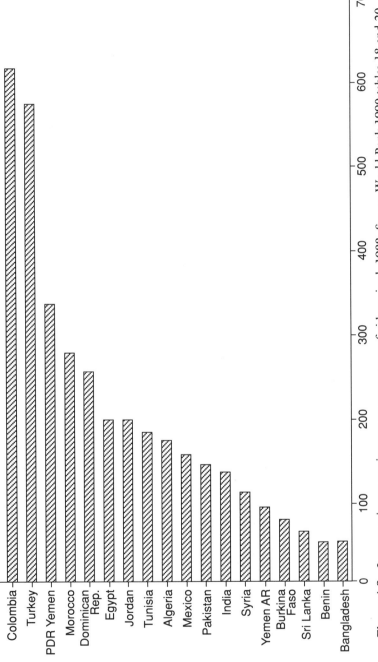

Figure 4.8 Largest migrant remittances as percentage of aid received, 1988. *Source*: World Bank 1990:tables 18 and 20.

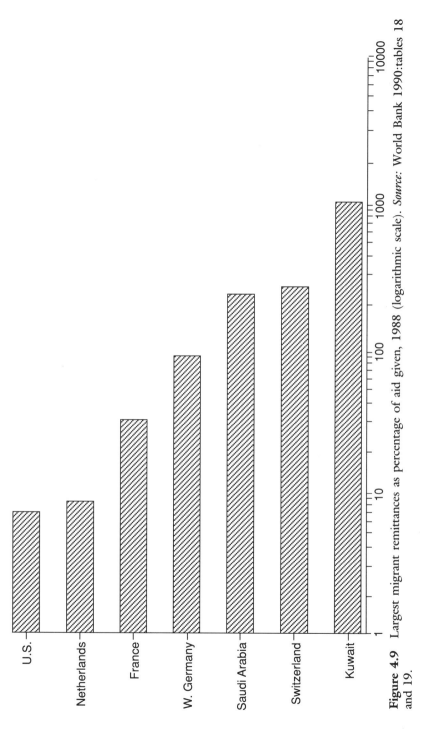

Figure 4.9 Largest migrant remittances as percentage of aid given, 1988 (logarithmic scale). *Source:* World Bank 1990:tables 18 and 19.

Immigration and Political Economy

The information in the previous two sections shows beyond doubt that immigration is an important factor in the world economy. And yet for the most part we will search for it in vain in the economics textbooks, even in those about international economics or economic development. Labor has always been regarded in economic theory as a factor of production that is movable within countries but, in general, not between one country and another.

A famous theorem of neoclassical economics postulates that with the free movement of goods, but not of factors of production, the prices of factors of production will be equalized. It is more common nowadays also to advocate the free movement of capital. The IMF, the World Bank, and their proponents, for instance, increasingly insist that underdeveloped countries open their borders without restriction to foreign capital. But they never advocate that the developed countries should open their borders without restriction to labor immigrants from the Third World.

If we expect economists to be consistent, this is surprising, perhaps particularly so in the case of the more dogmatic adherents of free market neoclassical economics. If the free movement of goods and capital is regarded as such a good thing, then why not the free movement of labor? Adam Smith, after all, argued strongly against the measures that still restricted the free movement of labor within countries in the nineteenth century, although he did not refer directly to international migration. Yet it seems to be true, as one writer on immigration recently asserted, that "no neo-classical economists have argued for the free movement of international labor" (Weiner 1990:150). This could be put down to a belief that international labor migration is culturally undesirable either for the migrant or for the receiving country. In the former case, the view is paternalistic; in the latter case, it must be regarded as nationalist, xenophobic, or racist.

By way of partial exception, a recent major study by an economist of the laissez-faire school concludes that immigration to the United States at present levels is generally beneficial to the existing residents, that it could be expanded without problems, but that an overall limit on the numbers of immigrants should be imposed and individual rights to immigrate should become a marketed commodity (Simon 1989:329–35). The same study shows that, contrary to popular opinion, existing immigration to the United States almost certainly expands, rather than reduces, the number of jobs for existing residents and that immigrants (especially illegal ones) contribute considerably more to public revenues than they receive in public spending. This is mainly because immigrants tend to be younger than the existing population, and so they finance part of the social security of the existing residents (Simon 1989:chs. 5 and 6). It should be noted that this kind of positive argument, based exclusively on the value of immigrants to the existing U.S. population, cannot be extended to the arrival of the dependents of immigrant workers, especially elderly ones.

Most development economists, radical or conservative, never touch the question. The reason is the deep-seated attitude that all people have their countries and in general ought to stay where they are. Development and the elimination of poverty are nearly universally conceived as things that should take place in all countries. No one ever argues that the way out of underdevelopment is for large numbers to move to the developed countries. The view that everyone should stay at home is a fundamental element of nationalism, religious separatism, and all other nonuniversalist cultural ideas, which are in general the dominant ones.

In fact, however, cultures are not always best preserved by people staying where they are; they are all too easily eroded by cultural imperialism. And cultures sometimes preserve themselves very effectively in exile. Similarly, there is no reason to believe that the quickest, surest way to the meeting of economic needs is for people to stay put in their "homelands," appealing as that idea may be for other reasons.

Certainly, nationalism has often been a force that has fostered economic development. Yet European economic development did not take place without vast emigrations. They did not for the most part harm the development of Europe, and they advanced the development of the countries of settlement and improved the material life of most of the migrants, compared with what it would have been if they had not migrated. There is no reason to think that the same could not be true in the Third World today. For the migrants, migration may be a way of enjoying a better job, earning money for themselves and their families, improving their environment, escaping from various forms of social and personal oppression, or gaining a more fulfilling, interesting, and adventurous life. But we should not overglorify the joys of migration, certainly not as it often takes place in practice; it is sometimes an almost obligatory escape from oppression and poverty, although it is seldom the very poorest members of a community who are able to migrate away from their problems.

Nonetheless, it is possible for migration to offer to the individual migrant an expansion of working opportunities, of income, of access to many resources and facilities lacking in his or her place of origin. And in the right conditions this can take place without others being harmed. Since capital is free to move and labor is not, the freedom to migrate, if exercised in the right way, will strengthen workers in general against capital and be of particular benefit to workers in poor countries who are now confined by immigration restrictions to ghetto labor markets. For these reasons, Samir Amin is surely right when he says that "the progressive unification of the commodities and capital markets alone, without being accompanied by gigantic migration of populations, has absolutely no chance of equalizing the economic conditions in which different peoples live" (1990:112).

Three major objections to this positive view of migration should be examined. The first is based on the fact that those who find it easier to migrate are those with the highest qualifications and skills. The resulting "brain drain" from the Third World is often argued to be detrimental to its prospects of economic development and so to the welfare of others who are left behind. The United States in recent years has received four-fifths of its skilled immigrants from the Third World (see Figure 4.10).

The brain drain seems to accentuate inequalities in the development of nations and to involve wasted development expenditure. Arguments against it appear to be arguments against migration, albeit of a certain kind. It seems wrong, for instance, that a doctor educated at public expense in the Third World, where health needs are so acute, should be treating rich Americans or Europeans. The Third World country loses the skills of its citizen, and these are seldom replaced by skills from elsewhere. Yet to see migration as the problem here is to continue to view the question of development as a national and not a universal one. A more universalist approach would see this problem not as being caused by international migration but by something more basic: the fundamentally unjust distribution of income in the world that allows the rich in America or Europe, or indeed the Third World, to have their medical needs more than adequately met, while the poor, in developed countries as well as the Third World, suffer enormous

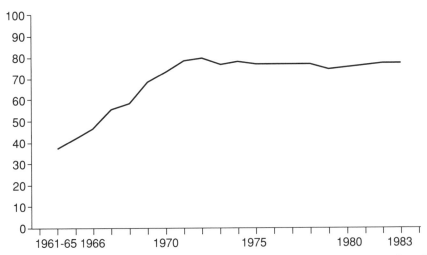

Figure 4.10 Skilled immigrants from developing countries as percentage of total skilled immigrants to United States, 1961–1983. *Source:* d'Oliveira e Sousa 1989:table 12.1.

health problems. A Third World doctor treating only the rich is no worse, by this way of looking at things, than an American or European doctor doing the same.

The brain-drain argument is often used to suggest that countries from which there are many skilled migrants will find their development inhibited. But this is not always true in practice: much of the current emigration is not from countries that are stagnating for lack of skilled labor. Some of the Asian migration to the United States is from countries that continue to experience tremendous economic success (for instance, South Korea) and that from the point of view of their own economies have a superabundance of skilled workers. And even in economically much less successful countries, there is often no work for skilled workers, which suggests, among other things, that it is not the brain drain by itself that is responsible for the loss of skills, but the many other causes of underdevelopment that prevent available skills from being used.

A second argument used against migration, from the standpoint of development, is that migrants frequently suffer the worst economic conditions and enjoy the fewest rights in the countries to which they migrate and that therefore massive migration is something that should not be encouraged, because it creates a class of underprivileged citizens. But this often paternalistic argument ignores the fact that most of the recent migrants choose to migrate because they believe that migration will improve their material life. And most migrants try to establish themselves in their new country rather than return home. It is certainly true that many migrants suffer terrible discrimination and oppression and that many of them are defrauded. But again, this is not an argument against migration but against discrimination, oppression, and fraud. This argument against migration may be decisive for an individual faced with a choice in the real world; but as a general intellectual argument against migration it misses the real point. In any case, discrimination may be less likely if immigrant communities are larger and can thus acquire more political and social weight.

Within developed countries themselves, progressive-minded people frequently argue against the practice of immigration control, especially when these controls are applied in an evidently racist manner. Yet very few advocate absolutely free immigration. In fact, there has always been a sizable number of people within the Left and the labor movement who argue for strict immigration controls as a necessary measure to protect labor from the competition of superexploited immigrant workers. This is the third common argument against more migration.

Certainly, one would expect that the swelling of the labor force from immigration would have some bad effect on the wages and conditions of workers through competition in the labor market. Many economists conclude that immigration, if it is of unskilled workers, will bring economic benefits to both capital and more highly paid workers in the host country but will tend to reduce the wages of the unskilled workers already there.

The implication of this argument is that immigration may improve the distribution of income in the world by benefiting the immigrant, but it may also worsen the distribution in the receiving country because the existing poor there will lose and the existing rich gain. Or, in other words, there will be a redistribution of income from the poor of the receiving country to the immigrants and to the rich of the receiving country. This seems to pose a very uncomfortable trade-off, so it is important to look carefully at the validity of the argument.

There is one reason this argument, if valid at all, is less true today than in the past. In recent years there has been a vast increase in the mobility of certain kinds of capital. This means that immigration is not necessary for foreign workers to be placed in competition with domestic workers in the same labor market; they are already in competition because some capitalists regard the whole world as their field of operations. If they cannot get the labor they need in the developed countries, they will look elsewhere. In this case (especially true in "footloose," as opposed to "rooted," industries) it is not migration but the mobility of capital that creates the depressing effect on unskilled wages.

The evident fact that Third World migrants in developed countries often work in very low paid jobs may give an exaggerated idea of the extent to which they depress the wages of existing workers. Some of these jobs would not exist in the absence of the low-paid migrants, either because the activity would not be profitable or because it would be mechanized.

Even if unskilled immigrants ready to work for relatively low pay may exert a depressing effect on wages in some sectors, this effect at present is diminished or eliminated because existing immigration as a whole has a stronger tendency to raise wages by raising demand.

Moreover, discrimination and racism, which bring about the division of workers, have a depressing effect on the bargaining power of labor. If immigrant workers are subjected to racist and xenophobic discrimination within the host society, they will as a consequence have to live at a lower economic level and will have more of a depressive effect on the labor market in general. Sometimes the very sections of the labor movement that have supported immigration controls (in the interests of labor) have at the same time participated in racist and xenophobic practices against immigrants. Their argument can therefore be partially self-fulfilling.

In addition, illegal immigrants can be much more economically discriminated against than legal immigrants, since they are under a constant threat that increases employers' control and reduces workers' bargaining power. Any depressive effect of immigration on the labor market, therefore, is accentuated by the fact that some migrants are illegal. What is that an argument for? For some it will be seen as an argument for enforcing immigration laws more rigorously. But that simply means more repressive deportations, more profiteering by those who organize illegal immigration, and even worse conditions for those who make it and become illegal migrants. From this point of view, protection implies a reduction of the civil rights of people from the Third World. So a better way to diminish the bad effects of illegality of immigrants would be to abolish the laws that make them illegal, in other words, to allow free immigration.

If both racism and illegality allow immigration to depress the competitive wage rate more than would otherwise be the case, it is possible in theory to compensate for some of the depressive effect of mass immigration by simultaneously reducing discrimination and removing restrictive immigration laws.

But there remains the possibility that these compensatory effects will not be sufficient to eliminate completely the tendency of immigration to lower unskilled wages. And this tendency may be a good deal stronger if the removal of all immigration control leads to a massive increase in immigration. This still does not constitute a valid argument against immigration as such. It should rather be seen as a reason for combining freer immigration with measures to improve the economic position of all the poor and lower-paid in the receiving countries. Such measures could include raising the minimum wage, strengthening the trade unions, fiscal redistribution, employment creation measures, improved welfare provisions, improvements in state-financed medical care, and so on. A general program of radical economic reforms could allow immigrants from the Third World to improve their material lot without the price being paid by the most economically vulnerable section of the population of the receiving country.

Freedom of Movement?

The demand of people from the Third World to migrate to developed countries is immense and growing. And, on present trends, it will grow even faster. It is so strong that many people are prepared to take incredible risks in order to cross borders illegally. But will these potential migrants be allowed to migrate?

Already the airports and frontier posts of the developed countries are the site of many abusive and racist controls. Stronger control of immigration from the Third World into developed countries, advocated by many, implies the development of a more repressive state apparatus. The effects of this would be felt not only by immigrants from the Third World but also by citizens of the advanced countries, especially by members of ethnic minorities. This itself is a strong argument for the abolition of controls.

The freedom to move is important and, within countries that have any pretensions to democracy, would now be hard to restrict. I have argued here for the extension of such freedom internationally through the abolition of immigration controls. Many people fear that such a move could have bad results in which both migrants and residents suffer and only the undeserving rich benefit. But a careful examination of the arguments against free immigration suggests that in general they are not valid.

Moreover, there are good reasons to think that freedom of movement between countries, in combination with other measures, could lead to a fairer distribution of world income. These other measures would include policies and mobilizations against racism and xenophobia, the lifting of restrictions on trade unions and the spread of trade unionism among immigrant workers, the expansion of welfare rights for inhabitants of developed countries, stronger minimum wage laws, a vast expansion of the transfer of development-oriented resources to the Third World, and measures to stop exploitation of freer immigration. My argument against immigration control, therefore, is for greater personal freedom for citizens of the Third World, giving them more choice about how to improve their material welfare. But it is in no way a laissez-faire argument. It is part of a program that would include many other radical social measures designed to expand freedom and improve the distribution of income.

That is not to say that freedom of immigration should only be advocated when all those other measures are being implemented. It is an important thing to fight for in its own right. Although the prospects of free immigration at present look small, any opening of borders can only have the effect of bringing home to more and more people the message that we live in one world and that the economic lives of people within it are intolerably unequal.

Immigration will not be the unique solution to that inequality, although it can play a significant part. The alternative, restricting migration, is certainly a way in which the inhabitants of the developed countries are relieved of the need to regard world inequality as their concern.

BIBLIOGRAPHY

Amin, Samir. 1990. *Eurocentrism*. New York: Monthly Review Press.
Buchan, David, and John Wiles. 1990. The Intolerance Threshold Nears. *Financial Times*, 12 March, 22.
Chiswick, Barry R. 1988. Illegal Immigration and Immigration Control. *Journal of Economic Perspectives* 2(3): 101–15.
d'Oliveira e Sousa, J. 1989. The Brain Drain Issue in International Negotiations. In *The Impact of International Migration on Developing Countries*, ed. Reginald Appleyard, 197–212. Paris: OECD Development Center.
Federici, Nova. 1989. The Causes of International Migration. In *The Impact of Inter-*

national Migration on Developing Countries, ed. Reginald Appleyard, 47–62. Paris: OECD Development Center.

Huguet, J. W. 1989. International Migration from the ESCAP Region. In *The Impact of International Migration on Developing Countries*, ed. Reginald Appleyard, 93–108. Paris: OECD Development Center.

Owen. E.R.J. 1985. *Migrant Workers in the Gulf.* London: Minority Rights Group.

Sassen, Saskia. 1988. *The Mobility of Labour and Capital.* Cambridge: Cambridge University Press.

Simon, Julian L. 1989. *The Economic Consequences of Immigration.* Oxford: Basil Blackwell.

Weiner, Myron. 1990. Immigration: Perspectives from the Receiving Countries. *Third World Quarterly*, January, 140–66.

World Bank. 1990. *World Development Report.* New York: Oxford University Press.

5 TOM RIDDELL

U.S. Militarism and the Global Economy

Military activities—weapons, armed services, arms transfers, the proliferation of increasingly lethal technologies, and wars—are one of the dominating and often disturbing public priorities of the world. Vast amounts of global resources are allocated by governments and other actors to the pursuit of national defense and military power, be it global or regional.

> At the beginning of the 1990s, global military expenditures exceeded $1 trillion. More than 5% of world economic output is devoted to national military budgets; regular armed forces include in excess of 25 million people; and annual arms exports total about $50 billion. (Sivard 1989)

> From the late 1970s to the early 1990s, the five permanent members of the United Nations Security Council sent over $160 billion worth of military equipment to Middle Eastern countries, including $53 billion to the number one importer, Iraq. (Associated Press 1991)

> The United States–led 1991 Persian Gulf War against Iraq, following its invasion of Kuwait in August 1990, cost upwards of $60 billion for the military operations and an additional $20 billion for increased economic assistance to the "frontline" states of Egypt, Jordan and Turkey. (Defense Budget Project 1991a; Bowsher 1991)

Why is so much money devoted to military spending, and what relationship does this have to the world economy? This chapter will not attempt to provide a global answer to these monumental questions. But certainly, in the last decade of the twentieth century, the United States is the dominant military power in the world; and it is worthwhile to focus on U.S. military spending and to analyze its purposes. Perhaps this exercise can shed some light on the broader questions. (See also the note on world military spending and arms transfers at the end of the chapter.)

U.S. Military Spending in the 1980s and 1990s

Tables 5.1 and 5.2 summarize recent trends and projections of U.S. military spending. The budget category identified here is the "national defense" function in the federal government's budget; it includes the entire budget of the Department of Defense, the nuclear weapons portion of the Depart-

TABLE 5.1
U.S. Military Spending, FY 1980–1996

Fiscal Year	Outlays, Contemporary $ (Billions)	Outlays, 1992 $ (Billions)	Budget Authority, Contemporary $ (Billions)	Outlays as % of GNP	Outlays as % of Federal Spending
1980	134	236	144	5.0	22.7
1985	253	320	295	6.4	26.7
1990	299	325	303	5.5	23.9
1991[a]	299	308	286	5.3	21.2
1992[a]	295	295	291	4.9	20.3
1993[a]	292	281	291	4.5	20.1
1994[a]	287	265	292	4.2	20.1
1995[a]	289	257	295	3.9	19.6
1996[a]	293	252	298	3.8	19.0

Source: Cain 1991.   [a]Office of Management and Budget(OMB) estimates.

TABLE 5.2
U.S. Military Spending, Rates of Real Growth

Fiscal Years	Budget Authority	Outlays
CUMULATIVE GROWTH		
1980–85	54.9	35.7
1980–92	19.7	25.0
1980–96[a]	5.7	6.9
1991–96[a]	−12.6	−18.1
AVERAGE ANNUAL GROWTH		
1980–85	9.2	6.3
1986–90	−2.7	0.3
1991–96[a]	−3.9	−4.1

Source: Cain 1991.   [a] OMB estimates.

ment of Energy's budget, the Selective Service System budget, and some miscellaneous budgets.

The early 1980s witnessed the largest peacetime expansion of military spending in U.S. history. This military buildup actually began in the late 1970s under the Carter administration in response to the Soviet invasion of Afghanistan and the taking of U.S. hostages in the wake of the overthrow of the shah of Iran. It was accelerated by the Reagan administration, which was intent on restoring the image and the reality of the United States as the world's number-one superpower. The Reagan buildup, heavily concentrated on weapons procurement, significantly increased spending for both conventional and nuclear forces. From FY 1980 to FY 1985, *budget authority* (what Congress authorizes for current and future spending) increased by 54.9 percent in real terms (over and above inflation) and *budget outlays* (what actually gets spent in each fiscal year) increased by 35.7 percent (see Table 5.2). Military outlays grew from 5.0 percent to 6.4 percent of GNP and from 22.7 percent to 26.7 percent of total federal spending.

By the mid-1980s, however, Congress and the U.S. public had become less tolerant of the rapid expansion of the military budget. It became clear that Reagan had exaggerated the Soviet threat during the 1980 presidential campaign; the public grew tired of the nuclear-weapon-brandishing rhetoric of Reagan, Vice President George Bush, and Secretary of State Alexander Haig; the budget deficit had exploded from increased military spending and the 1981 tax cuts; and there was profound impatience with a prolonged series of procurement scandals stemming from the weapons buildup. Beginning in FY 1986, the military budget started to decrease in real terms. From FY 1986 to FY 1990, budget authority decreased by an average annual rate of 2.7 percent, and outlays (which lagged behind the decrease in budget authority) increased a mere 0.3 percent per year.

By the early 1990s, two conditions created a new environment for even further reductions in military budgets. First, in mid-1990 it was clear that the deficit was out of control again. The 1990–91 recession and the bailouts of the financial industry by the federal government broke the back of the Gramm-Rudman-Hollings Act, which established targets for deficit reduction. The deficit was to be just over $100 billion for FY 1990 and to be entirely eliminated by FY 1993. Instead, the actual deficit for FY 1990 was $220 billion, and the expectations were that the FY 1991 deficit would be well in excess of $300 billion! After months of negotiations, the Bush administration and Congress reached a "budget summit" agreement in October 1990. The subsequent Budget Enforcement Act set ceilings for the military budget and for discretionary international and domestic spending for FY 1991 through FY 1996. The result of these limits is that the federal deficit is projected to decrease gradually from over $300 billion in FY 1991 to about $50 billion in FY 1996 (U.S. Congress 1991). The relevance of the budget deficit agreement is that there are absolute spending limits on the military budget over the near future.

The second factor that contributed to reducing military spending was the apparent end to the cold war. With ongoing fundamental economic, political, and military change in the Soviet Union under Mikhail Gorbachev's leadership and the accompanying wave of liberalization throughout Eastern Europe, the cold war fog of U.S.–Soviet tension and NATO–Warsaw Pact opposition seemed to evaporate. The Berlin Wall came down and Germany was reunified, Gorbachev unilaterally removed troops and military supplies from Warsaw Pact countries, the wealthy capitalist nations discussed economic assistance with the Soviet Union, and political reform swept through Eastern Europe. In reaction, public opinion in the United States began to focus on the opportunities for a post–cold war "peace dividend"—reducing the military budget and reallocating spending to urgent domestic priorities. In fact, the "peace dividend" is contained in the ceilings on military spending agreed on at the October 1990 budget summit. These ceilings, along with similar limits on discretionary international and domestic spending, are scheduled to contribute to deficit reduction into the mid-1990s.

The January 1991 budget submission from the Department of Defense was the first to reflect these new realities. It presented budget requests for fiscal years 1992 and 1993 and budget projections for FY 1994–96. These figures call for average annual real decreases of about 4 percent in both budget authority and outlays. Cumulatively, this amounts to a 20 percent reduction of real military spending by the mid-1990s. There will be a corresponding 20 percent reduction in active duty personnel, from 2,069,000 to 1,653,000. Military outlays will fall from 5.3 percent to 3.8 percent of GNP and from 21.2 percent to 19.0 percent of total federal spending (Cain 1991). This amounts to a significant cutback in U.S. military spending for the 1990s. It should be noted, however, that both budget authority and outlays by FY 1996 will remain higher in real terms than in FY 1980 (see Table 5.2).

In addition, despite the cutbacks in personnel, some weapons contracting, and spending, U.S. military forces will retain global nuclear and conventional capabilities. Walter S. Mossberg, a *Wall Street Journal* reporter, after examining the cutback proposal and soliciting evaluations from experts and policymakers, concluded, "Even the slimmed-down U.S. military currently planned for 1995 would remain an awesomely huge force, able to deploy just as many planes, ships, tanks and troops as the U.S. sent to the Gulf—with units left to spare. . . . Most senior Pentagon officials also say that even at reduced levels, the U.S. would have a lopsidedly large force to field against any foreseeable Third World threat" (Mossberg 1991).

In its plans for the mid-1990s, the Pentagon identifies five contingencies that its forces need to be prepared for: a war in Europe, a war in Korea, other major regional conflicts (e.g., the Middle East), a minor regional conflict, and ongoing counterinsurgency-narcotics activities. A task force of the independent Defense Budget Project in Washington, D.C., has concluded:

> According to DoD's analysis of U.S. military forces planned for fiscal year 1995, U.S. forces will possess impressive capabilities even in these highly demanding scenarios. The United States will be capable of deploying the forces necessary in all of these scenarios, except in the early stages of a short-warning war in Southwest Asia or if two regional contingencies occur simultaneously or in rapid succession. . . . Even after the planned reductions, U.S. military forces will be adequate to meet U.S. security needs and even to repeat the Desert Storm deployment if necessary. (Defense Budget Project 1991b)

Despite the projected cutbacks, the United States will remain a military superpower, with massive nuclear forces and global intervention capabilities.

Will It Happen?

Whether the gradual real decreases in U.S. military spending will proceed as planned into the mid-1990s depends on a number of factors. Very clearly, it will depend on how U.S. policymakers analyze the aftermath of the Persian Gulf War. Has Saddam Hussein been contained? Has his capacity to produce modern weapons of mass destruction been curtailed? Is it possible to organize a meaningful peace conference (or conferences) to resolve the myriad problems of Israeli–Arab and Israeli–Palestinian relations? Will permanent U.S. naval and ground forces remain in the Persian Gulf area?

Some analysts are certain to argue for expansions of U.S. military capabilities. The tactical weaknesses of the U.S. conduct of the war centered on insufficient knowledge of enemy capabilities and plans; this could require accelerated development of battlefield intelligence mechanisms. Given five months to get ready for war, airlift and sealift capabilities were sufficient; but with less warning, U.S. military forces would like quicker and more expansive mobility resources and more extensive prepositioning of supplies. The smart bombs, the stealth planes, and the advanced electronics all performed well in the context of the war plans. But should not U.S. forces be equipped with more of these proven resources? In other words, there will be pressures from the military and from its private corporate suppliers to reverse the decline in military spending. The debate about the needs for this equipment will also not be limited to the geographic territory of the Middle East.

The entire "budget enforcement" agreement, in fact, contains the possible seeds of a reversal of declining military budgets. In other words, the projected decreases depend on the continuation of the whole October 1990 deficit reduction package. The past efforts of the Gramm-Rudman-Hollings legislation hardly inspire confidence. The signal characteristic of the original (1985) and revised (1987) versions of this plan to balance the federal budget was that it would always happen in the future. And, when it became impossible to reach agreement on cutting spending or raising taxes, the whole budget-making process got delayed, and all of the targets got pushed further into the future. Perhaps this latest agreement has the virtue of removing budget setting from public attention and will, therefore, make it less political. On the other hand, there are still a lot of pressures on the federal deficit. Military planners will argue for their own increased needs, while those concerned about both long-run and short-run domestic priorities are also arguing for more resources, and the financial crisis in the banking industry shows no signs of relenting on its demands for federal insurance funds. These conflicting concerns express themselves in the political debate over the federal budget; they will continue to threaten the fragile budget agreement to reduce the deficit. As such, the scheduled military budget reductions in the near future are not a certainty.

Of course, the limitations on military spending could always come unraveled in the context of unanticipated crises, developments in the former Soviet Union or in other parts of the world. All of the funding for Operations Desert Shield and Desert Storm was placed outside the military budget ceilings in the October 1990 budget agreement. About $3 billion fell in FY 1990, and the rest of the more than $60 billion fell in the FY 1991 budget. The net cost of the war, however, was minimal, since the United States received pledges of contributions from Germany, Japan, South Korea, the United Arab Emirates, Kuwait, and Saudi Arabia totaling $54.6 billion (Defense Budget Project 1991a; Riddell 1991). If there are further crises in the Middle East, or elsewhere, there is no guarantee that the costs of military operations will not be added to future military budgets or that other countries will share the bill. On the other hand, with the breakup of the Soviet Union in 1991 and the election of Bill Clinton as president in 1992, there were also factors that held out promise for even further reductions in U.S. military spending in the mid-1990s.

The Goals and Objectives of U.S. Military Spending

What are the goals and objectives of the $300-billion-a-year U.S. military budget? What have they been, and what will they be in this period of transition to lower levels of spending?

The Post–World War II Era

The United States has had a consistent commitment to high levels of military spending and worldwide forces throughout the post–World War II period. The most common explanation for this has been the U.S. reaction to the Soviet threat and the cold war. Yet there has also been a purposeful U.S. political economic strategy that has required a global military presence.

The United States emerged from World War II as the world's dominant political, economic, and military power. Basically, the world capitalist system was restructured with the United States as the hegemonic power. U.S. policymakers took advantage of this position to structure a global political economy that encouraged international economic activity, was based on "free market" private-property arrangements, and provided extra benefits to corporate interests in the United States and elsewhere. Capitalism has always been an international system. Production for profit requires the expansion of markets, and capitalists are always looking for new market opportunities, cheaper labor, and cheaper raw materials. The whole world offers the most expansive environment for capitalist activity.

The Great Depression of the 1930s offered the bitter lesson to Western policymakers of what can happen when international trade almost totally disappears. The depth and persistence of the depression were significantly a result of the collapse of trade following the 1929 stock market crash and a round of protective and retaliatory tariffs. The policy prescription during and after the war was to create an international economic and financial system that encouraged and maintained a free trade regime, within the context of free markets and capitalist institutions. To this end, the General Agreement on Trade and Tariffs was created to facilitate tariff reductions and to stimulate international trade. The International Monetary Fund was established to develop rules and mechanisms for the exchange of currencies and the settlement of balance-of-payments results in a manner that accommodated free trading patterns. The orthodox economic logic to this was the theory of comparative advantage, which argues that all parties benefit from this expansion of trading opportunities. An open international economy would encourage economic growth for all, thus contributing to the process of economic development for even the poorer, newly independent countries of Africa, Asia, and Latin America.

This global political economy also required arrangements for keeping the peace. In other words, it needed a leader. The United States was in the position to assume this leadership role. It is often suggested that the United States took this role with reluctance, but there is much evidence to suggest that it was also purposeful. Although the theory of comparative advantage concludes that everyone gains from trade, it also acknowledges that more-powerful countries are likely to gain more. U.S. leadership in the creation and the maintenance of the global economic system ensured access to markets, raw materials, cheap labor, and investment opportunities. These advantages were particularly important for U.S.-based multinational corporations. The bottom line of what used to be called the "free world" system, and what others have referred to as Pax Americana, has always been the preponderance of U.S. military power—both nuclear and conventional. The Soviet threat was one of communism challenging capitalism, and the response was to strive for nuclear superiority to contain Soviet power and expansionism. Movements and wars for national liberation were also interpreted as threats to the global, "free world" system and required military mobilizations and wars in response. Consequently, after World War II, the United States for the first time in its history developed a worldwide military establishment. Prior to World War II, the United States devoted about 1 percent of its GNP to the military; since then military expenditures have averaged about 6 percent to 7 percent of GNP (Riddell 1982, 1988).

The Transition to a "Slim Trim" Pax Americana

In the 1990s, with the decline of the cold war, the collapse of the Soviet Union, and in the aftermath of the Persian Gulf War, the United States finds itself in a new international environment. How will it define its goals and objectives in this new context?

Most of the budget and force reductions will be concentrated in Western Europe, as a result of the emerging post–cold war relationship between the United States and the Commonwealth of Independent States. Already there have been agreements to reduce intermediate-range nuclear forces and conventional forces in Europe, as well as a start on the actual reduction of strategic nuclear forces on both sides. Without the cold war, what will the mission of U.S. military forces be?

Even before the Persian Gulf War, U.S. policymakers and military officials were beginning to develop answers to that question. A 1988 report from a group formed by the Reagan administration (the Commission on Integrated Long-Term Strategy) looked around the world and saw new threats everywhere beyond Europe and argued that the United States must practice "discriminate deterrence" and have forces to respond: "We must diversify and strengthen our ability to bring discriminating, non-nuclear force to bear where needed in time to deter aggression" (Ikle and Wohlstetter 1988). Echoing that redefined goal of U.S. foreign and military policy, a 1989 series of articles on "world leadership in the 1990s and beyond" in the *Wall Street Journal* also clarified the linkage of global military power to economic issues:

> Clashes of economic interests—cutting across national frontiers, disrupting social orders and profoundly affecting general populations—can be every bit as divisive and dangerous as political disputes, and also have the ability to lead to military conflicts.
>
> So, as the world becomes more multipolar—with economic leverage and even political-military power being more widely dispersed among nations—it

isn't necessarily becoming a safer, gentler globe. And as nations become more interdependent, they aren't necessarily becoming more cooperative.

In short, there is every reason to believe that the world of the 1990s will be less predictable and in many ways more unstable than the world of the last several decades. The need, then, is all the greater for a global leader to protect peace and prosperity. (House 1989)

In May 1990, the *New York Times* published its own series of articles on the post–cold war U.S. military and how it was redefining its missions to focus on Third World conflicts and the necessity for rapid deployment of forces globally. This emphasis on "low-intensity conflict" would require Army, Navy, Marine Corps, and Air Force capabilities. Air Force Secretary Donald Rice declared that his motto for the Air Force was "global power, global reach" and explained that "sharp, short duration operations where we punch hard and terminate quickly will characterize our use of power. The American people are rightly intolerant of conflicts that last longer than warranted and cause unnecessary suffering and loss" (Gordon 1990). Given this emerging redefinition of U.S. objectives, the military began preparing the appropriate plans for contingencies. In October 1990, the *Wall Street Journal* reported that during the summer of 1990 General Colin Powell, chair of the Joint Chiefs of Staff, had ordered Pentagon analysts to revise Middle East war plans "to defend Saudi Arabia's giant oil fields against threats from its neighbors," rather than to respond to a Soviet attack on Iran. General Norman Schwartzkopf oversaw the development of computerized war games between U.S. and Iraqi forces within this scenario. Consequently, in August, Powell was able to present President Bush with a plan for a massive deployment of U.S. forces to the Gulf (Pasztor and Seib 1990).

In essence, the global power projection capabilities of U.S. forces in defense of U.S. objectives in the world (as defined by policymakers) have not changed. What has happened is that there has been and will continue to be a scaling down of total forces, mostly in Europe and in strategic nuclear forces and some weapons systems. And there is a refocusing on "new" missions, which, in fact, is a reinforcing of military planning that has been in place throughout the post–World War II period. It simply has a new name. George Bush calls it the "new world order," implying that the United States will be able to follow the model of the Persian Gulf War, where the international community lent political, moral, and military force in opposition to Saddam Hussein's invasion of Kuwait. But it was always clear that the entire operation was under U.S. leadership and that the forces allied against Iraq were motivated just as much, if not more so, to preserve stability in the region and U.S. and Western access to Middle East oil as they were to respond to "aggression."

Military analyst Michael Klare (1990) identifies the new approach of U.S. policy as the "geo-strategic" option. Economist James Cypher (1990) calls it "global militarism." In a world of economic, political, and military challenges, the United States will continue to take the superpower route to protecting the operation of the global system—free commerce, open sea lanes, access to resources (particularly oil), international investment, and so forth. In a world no longer bipolar, the United States can pursue a renewed and reinforced hegemony over its allies (because it still "pulls the trigger") and the Third World. The global military forces that are required will now be prepared primarily for "low intensity conflicts" and "mid-intensity conflicts" as opposed to war with the Soviet Union (Klare 1991). It is a scaled-down, "slim trim" Pax Americana. "Despite the president's fervent dreams for a new world order, a policy designed to demonstrate our superpower status while advancing America's geopolitical and economic interests is unlikely to result in international cooperation. Rather, it will produce a new Pax Americana in which U.S. soldiers are the principal instrument of regional stability" (Klare 1991).

Consequences and Alternatives

The consequence of a continued commitment to global hegemony despite the expectation of reduced U.S. military budgets into the mid-1990s is twofold. On the one hand, it reinforces worldwide militarism—the threat of force, the brandishing of force, and the resort to the use of force. On the other, it carries enormous opportunity costs—the fundamental cost of military spending is that those resources are not available for other purposes.

For the United States, continued large military budgets, though smaller than in the recent past, and a strategy of global dominance forgo the opportunity to take a "geo-economic" approach to developing the U.S. economy and its ability to compete in international markets at the end of the twentieth century (Klare 1990). This would require investing resources in education, health, scientific research and development, and infrastructure. At the moment, the commitment to these priorities is woefully inadequate, and the resources are not available. While the Bush administration preferred to focus attention on its "victory" over Saddam Hussein in the Persian Gulf War and on the "end of the Vietnam syndrome," the challenge for the Clinton administration will be freeing up resources for domestic economic development (perhaps at the expense of the military budget).

Global military- and social-spending analyst Ruth Leger Sivard (1989) points out:

> The priorities of the world are even further askew. Six times as much public research money goes for research on weapons as for research on health protection. Every minute 15 children die for want of essential food and inexpensive vaccines, and every minute the world's military machine takes another $1,900,000 from the public treasury. The chances of dying from social neglect

(from malnutrition and preventable disease) are 33 times greater than the chances of dying in a war. . . . The gap in per capita income between the developed and developing countries is now over twice as large as it was 30 years ago; the gap in public health expenditures per capita is four times as large. . . . Since 1960 developing countries have increased their military expenditures twice as fast as living standards, measured by per capita income.

Militarization in the Third World limits the pursuit of economic and social development. And militarization in the developed world limits the ability to provide resources to assist in creating global, sustainable development.

Much progress toward reordering world priorities in the post–cold war period could be made if the United States, instead of trying to reestablish military superiority and planning for intervention, would unilaterally scale back its forces. The opportunity exists. The Center for Defense Information in Washington, D.C., composed of retired military officers, has recently compiled a list of arguments for a radical change in U.S. military objectives: U.S. forces in foreign countries do not help to defend the United States, other countries can provide for their own defense, the world does not need a U.S. global police force, military forces do not assure economic access and political influence, U.S. forces are not necessary to deter Japanese and German rearmament, and reducing U.S. forces could save billions of dollars (1991b). According to this logic, the primary purpose of U.S. military forces should be to defend U.S. territory. Foreign forces are costly and do not assure U.S. influence or advantage even with friendly countries. Diplomacy should become a more effective tool of foreign relations. And allocating resources to education, science, and other domestic priorities is more likely to improve U.S. competitiveness in the world's economy. The center has constructed an alternative military budget for FY 1995 that calls for reducing spending by a third—$200 billion instead of $295 billion (Center for Defense Information 1991a).

However, such a significant further cutback in military spending requires an effective political argument in favor of alternative priorities and against those prevailing now. The logic would have to focus on the excessive resources devoted to military forces. It would have to articulate an alternative vision of global relations, less reliant on arms transfers and force, more dependent on international diplomacy, and less influenced by U.S. self-interest. Moreover, it would have to mount an argument for taking seriously the myriad neglected domestic priorities of the United States and the world. Obviously, this is a radical agenda—one that challenges the status quo, the corporations, the military, the power brokers—but it is also one that offers a clearly alternative and hopeful vision of the world's future.

Data Appendix

WORLD MILITARY SPENDING AND ARMS TRANSFERS

By the late 1980s and early 1990s, the countries of the world were spending around $930 billion to $1 trillion annually on their military budgets. The following data represent military spending for selected countries in 1989 (in billions of U.S. dollars, at 1988 value):

North America		China	11.0
Canada	9.8		
United States	289.1	Far East	
		Japan	29.5
European Community	152.1	South Korea	8.1
Soviet Union	270.0	North Korea	1.8
Warsaw Treaty Organization	19.5	Taiwan	6.3
Middle East		Australia	5.9
Egypt	4.0		
Iran	5.7	Africa	
Iraq	10.7	Libya	2.0
Israel	3.8	South Africa	3.5
Saudi Arabia	14.5		
		South America	
South Asia		Argentina	3.0
India	9.6	Brazil	3.9
Pakistan	2.8		

Source: Saadet Deger, World Military Expenditure, in *SIPRI Yearbook 1991: World Armaments and Disarmament* (Stockholm International Peace Research Institute) (Oxford: Oxford University Press, 1991), 145, 156–57, 169–73.

This spending has been fueled by the example of the rivalry among the world's leading military superpowers and an international system that relies heavily on the threat and the use of force to pursue national and regional objectives. Arsenals include conventional weapons and sophisticated instruments of mass destruction.

Global military spending has also spawned a growing trade in arms. The following data represents the leading suppliers and the leading recipients of arms deliveries to the Third World from 1983 to 1990 (in billions of current U.S. dollars):

LEADING SUPPLIERS		LEADING RECIPIENTS[a]	
Soviet Union	131.4	Saudi Arabia	48.1
United States	45.5	Iraq	39.6
France	25.0	India	21.3
United Kingdom	15.6	Iran	14.5

China	13.2	Afghanistan	14.3
Germany	6.6	Syria	13.8
Italy	4.8	Cuba	12.6
Czechoslovakia	4.1	Vietnam	12.4
North Korea	3.1	Egypt	9.7
Spain	3.0	Libya	9.7
Poland	2.9		

Source: Richard F. Grimmett, Conventional Arms Transfers to the Third World, 1983–1990. Washington, D.C.: Congressional Research Service, Library of Congress, 2 August 1991.
ᵃThese figures would be even larger with the inclusion of military assistance from the leading suppliers. Military sales and assistance is often used to gain regional advantages and can contribute, in turn, to regional hostilities. Certainly, the arms trade to the Middle East has contributed to instability and conflict there. Following the Persian Gulf War, there have been many calls for an arms embargo to the region.

WORLD PRIORITIES

Since 1974, Ruth Leger Sivard, previously the chief of the economics division of the U.S. Arms Control and Disarmament Agency, has been publishing an annual account of world military and social expenditures. She tracks annual military, health, and education spending for every country in the world, as well as information about weapons arsenals, the arms trade, wars, and the environment. Her data dramatically show the tilt in world priorities toward military activities. The following table shows her report's rankings of the top twelve military spenders in indicators of social development in 1987:

Country	Economic/ Social Standing	GNP Per Capita	Education	Health	Environment
United States	9	8	8	16	135
Soviet Union	19	26	15	30	136
W. Germany	10	12	15	11	129
United Kingdom	16	21	21	9	131
Japan	7	5	14	12	127
Iran	72	60	72	76	95
Italy	25	19	40	23	114
Saudi Arabia	52	33	69	57	137
China	91	117	73	72	122
India	110	114	102	96	115
Iraq	72	59	74	76	108

For the United States, Sivard compares ranking of measurements of military power and social development:

Military Power Category	*Rank*
military expenditures	1
military technology	1
military bases worldwide	1
military training of foreign forces	1
military aid to foreign countries	1
naval fleet	1
combat aircraft	1
nuclear reactors	1
nuclear warheads and bombs	1
nuclear tests	1
arms exports	2
armed forces	3

Social Development Category	*Rank*
percentage of the population with safe water	1
percentage of school-age children in school	1
female literacy rate	4
male literacy rate	4
per capita public education expenditure	8
GNP per capita	8
maternal mortality rate	13
per capita public health expenditure	14
life expectancy	15
infant mortality rate	18
population per physician	18
total fertility rate	20
percentage of population with sanitation access	20
under 5 mortality rate	22
percent infants with low birth weight	36

Source: Ruth Leger Sivard, *World Military and Social Expenditures 1991* (Washington, D.C.: World Priorities, 1991), 27, 46.

The world's leading superpower sets the example for the world's priorities. To meet the social, economic, health, education, and environmental goals of the world and its member nations will require the reallocation of vast resources.

BIBLIOGRAPHY

Associated Press. 1991. Allies Push "Secure Zone" South. 6 May.

Bowsher, Charles H. 1991. The Administration's Proposal for Financing Operations Desert Shield and Desert Storm. Statement by the comptroller general of the United States, before the Committee on the Budget, United States House of Representatives, 27 February.

Cain, Stephen Alexis. 1991. Analysis of the FY 1992–93 Defense Budget Request. Defense Budget Project, Washington, D.C., 7 February.

Center for Defense Information. 1991a. A New Military Budget for a New World. *Defense Monitor* 20(2).

———. 1991b. The U.S. as the World's Policeman? Ten Reasons to Find a Different Role. *Defense Monitor* 20(1).

Cypher, James. 1990. Military Spending after the Cold War. Paper presented to the Association for Evolutionary Economics at the Allied Social Sciences Association meetings, New York, 28–30 December.

Defense Budget Project. 1991a. Desert Shield/Storm Costs and FY 1991 Funding Requirements. Defense Budget Project, Washington, D.C., July.

———. 1991b. Responding to Changing Threats: A Report of the Defense Budget Project's Task Force on the FY 1992–97 Defense Plan. Defense Budget Project, Washington, D.C., June.

Gordon, Michael R. 1990. Army and Air Force Fix Sights on the Changing Face of War. *New York Times*, 21 May.

House, Karen Elliott. 1989. As Power Is Dispersed among Nations, Need for Leadership Grows. *Wall Street Journal*, 22 February.

Iklé, Fred, and Albert Wohlstetter. 1988. *Discriminate Deterrence*. A report of the Commission on Integrated Long-Term Strategy. Washington, D.C.: U.S. Government Printing Office.

Klare, Michael T. 1990. Policing the Gulf—and the World. *The Nation*, 15 October, 415–20.

———. 1991. Behind Desert Storm: The New Military Paradigm. *Technology Review* 94 (May/June): 28–36.

Mossberg, Walter S. 1991. Even the Scaled-Down Military Machine Planned for '95 Would Leave the U.S. a Still-Potent Force. *Wall Street Journal*, 14 March.

Pasztor, Andy, and Gerald F. Seib. 1990. Force in Gulf Reflects Colin Powell's Vision; It's Big and It's Mobile. *Wall Street Journal*, 15 October.

Riddell, Tom. 1982. Militarism: The Other Side of Supply. *Economic Forum* 23 (1): 49–70.

———. 1988. U.S. Military Power, the Terms of Trade, and the Profit Rate. *American Economic Review* 79(2): 60–65.

———. 1991. The Gulf War and the U.S. Economy. *Z Magazine*, March, 63–66.

Sivard, Ruth Leger. 1989. *World Military and Social Expenditures*. 13th ed. Washington, D.C.: World Priorities.

U.S. Congress. Congressional Budget Office. 1991. *An Analysis of the President's Budgetary Proposals for Fiscal Year 1992*. Washington, D.C.: U.S. Government Printing Office, March.

6 KIARAN HONDERICH

Cocaine Capitalism

The only law that the narco-terrorists do not break is the law of supply and demand.
—Virgilio Barco, president of Colombia

Defining the Problem

Half of all Americans say they have had a relative or close friend who has
had a problem with illegal drugs (U.S. Senate 1989:8).

Cocaine-related hospital emergencies in the United States rose nearly 600
percent between 1983 and 1987 (U.S. Senate 1989:8).

An estimated 70 percent of all violent crime in the United States is drug-
related (U.S. Senate 1989:8).

The prison population in the United States rose from 329,821 in 1980 to
627,402 in 1988; the United States is now ranked first in the world in
the proportion of its population kept behind bars (Trebach 1989:40).

In Bolivia, illegal exports of coca paste and cocaine are estimated to earn
between $400,000 and $600,000 per annum, as much as the value of
all legal exports combined (NACLA 1991:14).

By now, we are all accustomed to these kinds of statistics, often
thrown together in combination with lurid imagery of addiction and violence to demonstrate that the United States and Latin America face a problem, identified in general terms as drugs. This chapter presents an economic
analysis of the trade in cocaine between Latin America and the United
States in the 1980s and of the so-called drug war waged against it by the
Reagan and Bush administrations.

An economic analysis is sorely needed to understand the structure of
incentives within the trade itself and, equally important, within the drug
war. Until it is clear who is gaining what, and why, in the current situation,
we have no hope of prescribing viable alternatives. Such an analysis needs to
make connections between the cocaine trade and other economic and politi-

123

cal events of the 1980s, ranging from the Latin American debt through bank deregulation, to the covert activities of the CIA. Tracing the passage of cocaine through the Latin American and U.S. economies is much like X-raying the passage of barium through the intestinal workings of global capitalism in the 1980s.

Which Problem Is Which? Illegality, Enforcement, Addiction

Three quite distinct phenomena underlie the drug problem: the existence of addictive drugs (or perhaps people's propensity to become addicted to certain drugs); the illegality of some addictive drugs; and the strategies used in the war on addictive drugs during the 1980s. Such a separation is important because many of the problems attributed to cocaine have actually arisen because of its illegality or because of the drug war. This is as true of the effects of cocaine on the inner cities of the United States as it is of its effects on the Colombian political system.

To start with the drugs themselves, there is no question that cocaine, especially in the form of crack cocaine, can be physically and mentally harmful to its users, and quite addictive.[1] However, we would expect many fewer overdoses and toxic deaths from cocaine and heroin if they were made legal and sold, like cigarettes or aspirin, in doses with clearly stated levels of potency and purity, and with legal recourse available to enforce those levels. If somebody bought a macaroni and cheese dinner that turned out to be laced with strychnine, they—or their next of kin—could sue Kraft for a lot of money. That option was not open to the families of the seventeen people known to have died from a batch of doctored heroin sold in New York over a period of several hours in the "Tango and Cash" incident in 1990 (*New York Times*, 2 August 1991).

Third parties, too, are affected by addiction in a number of ways: families and friends of addicts suffer emotional anguish, and complete strangers may be robbed or mugged or may become victims of random violence. The illegality of drugs plays a major role in all of these effects. Much of the pain for those close to an addict is caused by the fear that the addict will overdose, will end up in prison, will resort to robbery or prostitution, will contract AIDS, or will be murdered. All of these possibilities are enhanced or even caused by the illegality of the drug: overdosing, for reasons explained above, and imprisonment, for obvious reasons. The possibility of resorting to robbery or to prostitution, with its attendant danger of AIDS infection, may be less obviously a result of illegality, but like the violence surrounding drugs, it arises partly because the price of drugs is increased by their illegality.

Illegality, and the law enforcement mechanisms that accompany it, drives up the price of drugs partly by driving sellers to compensate themselves for the risk of confiscation or imprisonment. This legal constraint also effectively rations the drugs: not everyone who wants to buy cocaine or marijuana can get hold of them; and just as Nintendo games become more expensive if there is a craze for them and not enough to go round, so the effect of rationing drugs is to drive up the price and thus the profits to sellers.[2] This has the benefit of reducing demand, but it also has several bad effects. In the United States it increases the incentive to enter the drug trade and causes turf battles between groups who want access to the profits; it also increases crime by users, since their habit becomes more expensive. In Latin America it means small groups of individuals are receiving huge amounts of money, which they can use to buy political influence and, if necessary, sophisticated weapons in case their governments should try to enforce the antidrug laws.

The profits available have also created severe contradictions within successive U.S. administrations. Although some agencies seem genuinely dedicated to eradicating the supply of drugs, other groups have found the flow of funds available from drugs irresistible, particularly when they want to engage in activities for which they cannot gain legal funding.

Finally, while the drug trade has provided a sometimes irresistible source of financial power, the war on drugs has provided other forms of currency. Those using this currency might be racist law enforcement officials who have found a new excuse to arrest, harass, or physically brutalize black and Hispanic men; interventionists who can justify military aid to or even invasions of Latin America by conflating popular insurgency with "narcoterrorism"; or politicians seeking easy political capital.

One question remains: Why do people become addicted to drugs? Or to break the query down further, Why do some people become addicted and not others? And why do the numbers of people addicted change over time? A complete analysis of addiction is obviously impossible in this chapter, but it is worth considering the relevance of economic factors. Certainly, rich people as well as poor people both use and become addicted to drugs, but it seems likely that use is more apt to become abuse if the user is poor and unemployed and has little power over her or his surroundings. Data on this issue is extremely limited (for reasons to be discussed below), but the argument is certainly supported by the observed fact that cocaine and crack abuse rose in the 1980s at the same time that income inequality in the United States increased and the poorest section of the population grew steadily poorer.

The development of crack, a smokable form of cocaine, was also a factor in the increase in drug abuse. Crack was developed as the mass-market version of cocaine; it is available in relatively cheap doses, each providing a short and intense high followed quickly by the desire to repeat the experience. Crack was also developed as a response to illegality; the need to smuggle and to sell and consume in secrecy encouraged the development of a concentrated substance (compare crack vials to the sacks of coca leaves transported in the Andes) that does not require much equipment or expertise in its consumption. In essence, crack is a fast-food version of freebase cocaine, the earlier "home-cooked" smokable form of the drug.

What the Problem Is Not: The Role of Race

The United States is under siege, invaded from outside its borders . . . [by] devilish combinations of chemicals that are destroying our youth, sapping our vitality and eroding our sense of moral and ethical values . . . [and by] foreign governments who seek to poison the youth of America and destroy the future of the nation. (John F. Collins, former mayor of Boston, *Boston Globe*, 16 April 1988)

The American people must understand much better than they ever have in the past how [our] safety and that of our children is threatened by Latin drug conspiracies [which are] dramatically more successful at subversion in the United States than any that are centered in Moscow. (General Paul C. Gorman, former head of U.S. Southern Command in Panama, in U.S. Senate 1989:1)

The reading of the problem I reject is the fable of foreign governments and "Latin drug conspiracies" combining to undermine the defenses of an innocent and woefully unprotected United States. Obviously it is both comforting and convenient to blame villainous outside forces for the ills of U.S. society, but this story is seriously wrong in its analysis and its consequences.

The analysis is wrong in putting the Latin American cart(el) before the U.S. horse. As in so many other respects—economic, political, and cultural—development in the Latin and Central American countries involved has been shaped less by their own long-term interests than by the demands of the U.S. market and by U.S. foreign policy. The economies and cultures of countries from Bolivia to Mexico have been irrevocably altered by the huge sums of money available for cultivating, processing, and smuggling cocaine for the U.S. market, by the drug war, and by the interplay between drug traffic and the foreign-policy goals of various branches of the U.S. government. Central and South Americans have certainly not been helpless in this process—the entrepreneurs of the Colombian cartels have in many ways been model capitalists—but if Latin American cocaine had not been available, U.S. consumers would quite probably have turned to heroin or to designer drugs like ice or ecstasy with Made in the USA labels on them. In Jesse Jackson's words, "People are not being force-fed drugs. They are volunteering for this slow suicide. . . . This time the enemy is us" (1989).

For many, part of the attraction of the "outside contaminants" reading is undoubtedly its racist subtext; connections are made between "Latin drug conspiracies" outside the country and the "aliens" within: the blacks, Hispanics, Chinese, and other ethnic groups who have been blamed in each wave of drug hysteria, from the Chinese opium smokers who were said to be luring innocent whites into their dens in the last quarter of the nineteenth century to the supposed carriers of the marijuana virus of the 1930s—"50% of the violent crimes committed in districts occupied by Mexicans, Turks, Filipinos, Greeks, Spaniards, Latin-Americans and Negroes may be traced to the abuse of marijuana."[3]

Is this racism based on any facts? Evidence on the distribution of cocaine and crack abuse among economic and racial groups is unreliable, given that many studies fail to include groups like the homeless or those without telephones; however, there are several studies that indicate that it is relatively even. For instance, the National Institute on Drug Abuse's household survey reported in 1988 that blacks accounted for only 12 percent of the nation's drug purchases—exactly their proportion of the U.S. population—and 80 percent of all illegal drug transactions involved at least one white (Duster 1990).

Reliable data on who sells drugs are even harder to get. If we use arrest data as an approximation, we must consider that police operations, according to many, may target some groups of sellers more than others. The drug trade is thoroughly integrated into the U.S. economy, with Americans of all colors and classes involved at every level, from importation through wholesaling to laundering of the eventual profits. There does seem to be some racial pattern in the level at which people are involved, however; as Jefferson Morley (1989) describes it, the "new entrepreneurs" selling at street level are more likely to be black, partly because the U.S. economy offers them so little else in the way of employment or income opportunities. There are, however, many more white members of what he calls the "professional middle class" of criminals: "members of a wealthy, highly skilled, professional class, many of whom do not have previous criminal records, some of whom are highly respected members of their community. They are attorneys, accountants, bankers and money brokers." In other words, enormous numbers of Americans are prepared to engage in drug importing or selling or the laundering of profits and will slot into the process at whichever point their education and social background dictate.

But what is not evenly spread is the overall impact of crack and the drug war. Some urban communities have become "no-go" areas, brutalized by poverty, addiction, and violence. This is largely because economic conditions were already so bad there in the early 1980s that selling drugs represented a unique opportunity for young men to gain income and status. These areas have now become focal points for selling, with suburbanites coming in to buy and then returning to their protected communities. As argued above, it may also be true that drug users are more likely to be entirely taken over by their habit if the economy offers them few prospects of growth or development.

What It Also Is: Legalized Death

There is one thing to be learned from the "outside contaminants" reading. What it partly springs from is frustration and anger directed at people who knowingly produce and sell a substance responsible for misery and death and who, when they live in other countries, are very difficult for us to punish or stop. But this is the nature of international capitalism, and we would do well to remember that frustration when we hear the complaints of developing countries whose economies and cultures are suffering from the behavior of U.S.-based corporations.

A particularly close parallel can be drawn with trade in substances that have been defined as legal and therefore not part of the drug problem, such as tobacco. The Federal Center for Disease Control reported that 434,175 Americans died from smoking in 1988, while heroin, cocaine, and marijuana were estimated to account for 3,600 deaths a year.[4] This death toll is currently being exported by U.S. and European tobacco companies to Africa and Asia, using advertising linking cigarettes with "Western sophistication" to sell high-tar, highly addictive cigarettes at low prices while telling African governments that smoking is not harmful and that health warnings are counterproductive (*London Sunday Times*, 13 May 1990). Tobacco companies argue that tobacco differs from cocaine because it only harms those who choose to smoke it, and not innocent bystanders.[5] The problems with this argument are such that it hardly deserves to be called an argument: innocent bystanders harmed by others' smoking include, first, passive smokers (estimated to account for an additional 37,000 deaths a year in the United States); second, the children whose food intake will be reduced because their parents need the money for cigarettes; third, those who will be deprived of medical care as African and Asian hospitals are filled with cancer and emphysema patients; and fourth, those people materially and personally affected by the deaths of friends and relatives.

The Drug Trade

The 1988 report of the Senate Subcommittee on Terrorism, Narcotics and International Operations, chaired by John Kerry of Massachusetts, estimates that 60 percent of all illegal drugs produced in the world are consumed in the United States, that twenty million Americans regularly smoke marijuana, nearly six million regularly use cocaine, and half a million are addicted to heroin. Calculations of the amount of money involved in the drug trade vary enormously, and there are obvious problems with getting reliable information, but the estimate of the 20 June 1988 edition of *Fortune* magazine—that the global drug trade may run up to $500 billion a year, about the same value as total U.S. exports of merchandise and services for that year—is by this time a relatively modest one.

One important fact about the global profits from drugs is that the majority of the money is remaining within the rich countries who buy most of the drugs. The *Economist* estimated in 1988, for example, that of retail cocaine sales in Europe and the United States of around $22 billion in 1987, only around $2 to $5 billion, or 10 to 20 percent, went to Latin America, with the rest going to middlemen. Of the Latin American money, they estimate that around half went to Colombia, with the remaining half being shared evenly between Bolivia and Peru.

The structure of the cocaine industry in Latin America is as follows: hundreds of thousands of peasant producers based primarily in Peru and Bolivia grow coca plants, usually on a relatively small scale, and either sell the leaves as they are or more often convert them into coca paste to sell to processors. Processing the paste into cocaine base and then cocaine hydrochloride is principally done in labs in Colombia, a more industrialized country than Peru and Bolivia and, so, better equipped for this technical process.[6] While coca is cultivated on a small scale by very large numbers of peasants—Rensselaer Lee estimated in 1988 that around 20 percent of the Peruvian and Bolivian populations were directly employed in the drug trade in one way or another (1988)—the processing and export stages are handled by highly coordinated Colombian cartels, run by some of the richest men in the world.

Fortune magazine estimated in 1988 that the price structure of one kilogram of cocaine starts at around $500 received by peasants for 500 kilograms of coca leaves (enough to yield one kilogram of cocaine), increases to $4,000 per kilogram of cocaine hydrochloride, $18,000 per kilogram wholesale in the United States, and finally a U.S. street price of $135,000 for the amount of crack cocaine produced from one kilogram of cocaine. Even though it is clear from this that the peasant producers are getting a tiny share of the eventual price, in the 1980s coca was an enormously profitable crop compared to the alternatives. It is also hardy, pest free, and very easy to grow, which made it by far the best income alternative available to many Peruvians and Bolivians.

There were a number of reasons for the boom in cocaine production in the early 1980s. One was the increase in demand in the United States, and a second that the Andean countries, like many other Third World nations, urgently needed foreign exchange to pay off enormous external debts. In the early 1980s they were faced with rising interest rates (caused in large part by the ballooning U.S. government deficit) and falling legal export revenues, caused by a lethal combination of falling demand, increased protection from the industrialized countries, and falling prices for any legal exports they did manage to sell.

Lee notes that during the period 1980–86 the Bolivian economy experienced negative GNP growth of 2.3 percent a year and an increase in the official unemployment rate from 5.7 percent to 20 percent. From 1984 to 1986 the prices of their principal export alternatives—oil, tin, and natural gas—fell, to the extent that legal export earnings fell by 25 percent in Bolivia and 20 percent in Peru. It is no surprise then that many farmers and entrepreneurs in Latin America embraced the cocaine trade; indeed, given that parts of rural Bolivia and Peru contain examples of the worst poverty in Latin America, it is frightening to imagine what might have happened there if that life (death) line had not been available.

The fact that cocaine was, and remains, such an attractive income source does not mean that its effects on Latin America have all been salutary. In some ways the economic effects are like those of many other commodity booms, with the profits tending to go to luxury consumption, real estate investment and speculation, and capital flight, rather than productive investment to help long-run development in the Andean nations. These effects are exaggerated in this case, since the illegality of cocaine discourages legitimate investment of the proceeds, and also means governments do not receive as large a share of the profits through taxation as they would with a legal commodity.[7]

As noted above, the illegality of drugs has also had severe political effects in a number of countries. In Colombia it created a small group of rich and powerful druglords who corrupted and attacked the legal and political system, especially when the U.S. drug war put pressure on the Colombian government to be entirely uncompromising over issues like extradition.

During the 1980s this pushed Colombia into a state of siege, with assassinations of justices and politicans becoming commonplace; but there were other political effects there too. Before the rise of the cocaine trade, Colombia, far from being a peaceful democracy, had been engaged in political, economic, and often violent struggle at least since the 1950s, when the civil war known as La Violencia took as many as 350,000 lives. During the 1970s Colombia's poor and excluded formed massive movements to wrest power from a deeply entrenched elite; when the latter proved unwilling to reform peacefully, many of those involved in the movements turned to guerrilla warfare. The response of the elite was to launch a dirty war against not only guerrillas but union organizers, peasants, opposition politicians, and anyone else considered to be a threat to "stability"—a dirty war that has killed eight thousand peasants, workers, and politicians since 1986

(NACLA 1990). The injection of drug profits has, if anything, slowed the process of reform by creating a nouveau riche class, wealthy druglords who played a central role in the 1980s in setting up and funding right-wing death squads. In this respect, the druglords have been acting in cooperation with the Colombian military and occasionally with the government.

In Peru, on the other hand, the drug trade has tended to strengthen the principal insurgent group, the Maoist Sendero Luminoso, or Shining Path. This is not because they have actually been running drugs, but because they have acted as intermediaries between peasant producers and the middlemen who purchase the coca leaves or paste, bargaining to increase the share of eventual profits received by the peasants. This has strengthened them both financially—they tax these transactions—and politically, by increasing their popular support among the peasants whose livelihood they protect. Whether this seems like a beneficial political effect or another bad one depends on whether one sees the Sendero Luminoso as a progressive force or as a potential rerun of the Khmer Rouge (NACLA 1989).

Latin American governments meanwhile have been put in a difficult situation. Aware of the dependence of their economies on drug profits and on the foreign exchange generated, they are nevertheless shaken by political forces catalyzed by the emergence of a drug-enriched class or by the growth of insurgencies, and are pressured by the U.S. government to be uncompromising in a fight that could trigger right-wing terrorism or, in the Peruvian case, push peasants into sympathy with the Sendero Luminoso.

Aside from the countries involved in growing and processing cocaine, many countries in Central America and the Caribbean have been used as stopping points in smuggling routes up to the United States and for money laundering, with varying degrees of government involvement. These have included Mexico, Cuba, the Bahamas—in 1988, 50 to 60 percent of all the cocaine and marijuana entering the United States transited through Bahamian territory[8]—and Panama. In Panama the dictatorships of Torrijos and then Noriega were deeply implicated in the drug trade at many levels; in the words of the publisher of the Panamanian opposition newspaper, Panama became the only country where the "formal military institutions were entirely controlled by the multinational narco-mafia" (*Frontline* 1990). During the 1970s and 1980s, Noriega is believed to have created "a political system in which Panamanian government became controlled by personal loyalties to Noriega, cemented by graft and corruption, and substantially funded with narcotics money" (U.S. Senate 1989:83). It is alleged that he made Panama into a major money-laundering center, allowed members of the Medellin cartel to build cocaine-processing laboratories in his country, and sold them protection and asylum. He is also said to have used his supporters to smuggle narcotics directly (U.S. Senate 1989:79–97).

The War on Drugs

If we take the aim of the war on drugs as being to reduce the supply and increase the price of cocaine, thereby reducing its consumption, the war waged through the 1980s was clearly a failure. The Kerry report documents that the street price for a kilogram of cocaine in the United States plummeted from $60,000 in 1980 to approximately $9,000 in 1988 (U.S. Senate 1989:9). More recently, the *New York Times* of 25 November 1990 reported of the Bush phase of the war that administration officials "could not be sure if imports of cocaine . . . had been cut by even 5% in the last year." While cocaine trafficking through the Caribbean into Florida had been reduced, traffickers had simply redirected it through Central America and Mexico; meanwhile, cultivation of heroin poppies was said to be rising in Guatemala, Mexico, and Colombia.[9]

The main problem with the drug war is that it has been largely aimed at the wrong places: at interdiction and buy-and-bust operations. Given the kind of profits involved, and given people's ingenuity in cirvumventing legal controls, interdiction is always going to spur creative new forms of smuggling. Another reason it is a misguided strategy is that smuggling costs are only a small share of the total distribution costs of cocaine—the landed cost of cocaine is less than one-tenth of the retail price—so that even increasing smuggling costs dramatically through interdiction has a very small effect on the street price of cocaine. A RAND study concludes that "unless interdiction can very substantially increase the costs of smuggling, effective interdiction will have modest effects on total cocaine consumption" (Reuter, Crawford, and Cave 1988:xi).

Direct military intervention in the producing countries would be no better; coca cultivation is already spreading to other Latin American countries, and finding every field of coca and every processing laboratory in Latin America would not be feasible. Even if it were possible to stamp cocaine out, it is reasonable to assume that a fair proportion of users would move on to heroin—there is already some evidence of this happening—or to "designer drugs." Nonetheless, there is a strong likelihood that the U.S. government will move further in this direction, a likelihood increased by the January 1992 announcement that the Bush administration was preparing to send $10 million in military aid to Peru, with the intention of sending $25 million more once the military demonstrates better antidrug and human rights efforts. The Peruvian military has a poor human rights record, and two months before this announcement, American officials accused members of the army of taking payoffs from drug traffickers and blocking the Peruvian police's antidrug efforts.[10]

We should recognize the interest the Pentagon has in expanding the drug war to fill the gap left by the end of the cold war: its antinarcotics spending increased to a projected $1.2 billion for 1992, from $440 million in 1989.

In contrast, one area the war on drugs has focused little energy on is money laundering, both in the United States and abroad. The Kerry report argued that money laundering is so crucial to the operation of the Colombian drug cartels that restricting it "is the most important action the United States government can take in challenging seriously the operations of the large traffickers" (U.S. Senate 1989:120). Money laundering involves taking illegally earned cash and putting a legal gloss on it through the banking system; a check—particularly one drawn on a fictitious corporation—will not arouse the kind of suspicion a sack of used notes would. In the United States, the Bank Secrecy Act of 1974 requires that all cash transactions in excess of $10,000 (including deposits into banks) must be reported to the Internal Revenue Service; this is intended to crimp money laundering. However, such regulations do not exist in many other countries, and even inside the United States it has been very poorly enforced.

The recent revelations about the BCCI have included allegations that it engaged in money laundering; however, contrary to the impression given by some accounts, it is by no means unusual in this. The increased internationalization of banking in the 1970s and 1980s and international competition to deregulate have both made it easier for banks to engage in money laundering and cut down on the regulatory apparatus that would detect them.

Jefferson Morley (1989) gives an account of the rise and fall of one investigation in Florida, Operation Greenback. This operation was launched in 1979, in the wake of media publicity about the tripling of cash surpluses in Florida banks between 1970 and 1976, from $576 million to $1.5 billion (a large gap between deposits of cash and payouts is taken to be a good indication of money laundering); but within a year of George Bush's appointment as leader of the drug war in March 1982, he downgraded the operation from an interagency task force to a single unit inside the U.S. attorney's office in Miami.

It is hard not to find a racist pattern in the emphases of the drug war: attacks have been concentrated on Latin American growers and suppliers and on U.S. street-level sellers, rather than on banks or—to a lesser extent—buyers, with the result that in the United States a quarter of black men in their twenties are now imprisoned, on probation, or on parole. Between 1985 and 1988, drug prosecutions of white juveniles dropped 15 percent while jumping 88 percent for minority youth; although 80 percent of drug users are white, the majority arrested are black (Beers 1991).

Meanwhile, a 1989 survey showed nearly 67,000 people on drug treatment waiting lists, and the House Select Committee on Narcotics and Control concluded that only one-fifth of the people who need treatment get it. Understandably, this situation has led many people to the conclusion that the drug war can only be understood as a racist conspiracy. A *New York Times*/WCBS-TV News poll conducted in New York City in June 1990 found that 60 percent of black people interviewed thought the statement that the government "deliberately makes sure that drugs are easily available in poor Black neighborhoods in order to harm Black people" was true, or possibly true.

But another explanation for the debacle is what I call the saprophytic one. A saprophyte is a type of fungus that grows on dead or decaying matter, and both the drug trade and the war on drugs have spawned swampfuls of them. The fungi include politicians who have used the drug war for self-aggrandizement and as a distraction from the underlying issues of poverty and inequality.[11] They also include those who have used the drug trade itself, and the prime example of this behavior in the United States is the CIA.[12] There are now a large number of cases where the CIA is widely believed to have been, at a minimum, complicit in drug-running activities undertaken by groups they had decided to support as assets in the cold war. Examples range from supporting Chinese Nationalist troops in Burma in the 1950s, as they transformed that country's Shan states into the world's largest opium producer, to supporting the drug running of Hmong tribesmen in Laos from 1960 to 1975, to supporting Afghan guerrillas during a major expansion of their heroin exports (McCoy 1991). In Latin America, former DEA agent Michael Levine (1990) alleges that the CIA supported the so-called cocaine coup of General Garcia Meza in Bolivia in 1980—"the first time in our history that drug dealers took over a government" (Szykowny 1990).

The common thread running through these events is that in the pursuit of the cold war anything was tolerated. Overlooking or on many occasions actively aiding the drug-running activities of allies is a way to give them covert aid when none, or not enough, is forthcoming through legal channels. The Nicaraguan Contras are a more recent example of this; the Kerry report found strong links between the Contras and drug runners, and found that "in each case, one or another agency of the U.S. government had information regarding the involvement either while it was occurring, or immediately thereafter" (U.S. Senate 1989:36). In cases where cold war policies have come into conflict with the aims of the drug war, cold warriors have usually won.

Perhaps the most surreal failure of U.S. drug policy is the case of Panama. U.S. relations with Noriega can be framed by two events: in 1971 two undercover CIA contract agents are said to have watched as Noriega demanded his cut of a four-hundred-pound marijuana deal, and in 1989 U.S. soldiers in the midst of an invasion that took perhaps thousands of civilian lives apparently found fifty pounds of cocaine in his refrigerator.[13] The first event and all succeeding evidence of Noriega's drug dealings were suppressed—DEA files on drugs in Panama were denied to legislators who requested them during the Panama Canal Treaty debates, and then disappeared entirely (*Frontline* 1990). In the second case, the cocaine of course turned out to be tamale flour. Noriega is currently accused of having spent fifteen years manipulating the DEA and the CIA—which at one point were paying him $100,000 a year as an informant. The DEA regarded him as a friend of the United States as late as 1986, expressing their "deep appreciation for the vigorous anti–drug trafficking policy" that he had adopted,[14] and the CIA given his support for the Contras, was apparently willing to overlook any drug dealing.

Another view of the situation is that the CIA was using him in its Contra war, and when their program of covert support for the Contras ended, he became expendable (Scott and Marshall 1991). As the *New York Times* said in 1990, Noriega's alleged drug dealing was "relatively small scale by Latin American standards . . . American officials strongly suspect high-ranking military officers in Honduras, Guatemala and El Salvador of similar, and in some cases even greater involvement in drug dealing—yet have not taken harsh action against them" (*New York Times*, 1990).

Despite its ineffectiveness in reducing supply, the Bush administration claimed to be winning the drug war, in large part because of surveys released in December 1990 and January 1991 showing an apparently dramatic decline in cocaine use. There was much skepticism about survey results during the last election campaign, and particularly about generalizing from them to the whole population; the survey by the National Institute on Drug Abuse, which showed a 45 percent decrease in casual cocaine use, omitted groups like prison inmates and the homeless, among whom addiction is most prevalent (*New York Times*, 20 December 1990); and the survey by the University of Michigan's Institute for Social Research, which showed a significant decline in cocaine use among high school students, failed to include high school dropouts, who are thought to be among the heaviest users (*New York Times*, 25 January 1990). At most, then, it seems likely that cocaine use is falling among the middle class; as Mark Kleiman of Harvard University put it, "drug use appears to be dropping down the social scale."

If drug use among some sectors of society has been falling dramatically despite the failure of the drug war to reduce supply and increase price, it seems clear that it has been falling for other reasons. High school students in 1991 are much more aware of the dangers of cocaine abuse than they were in 1981, both because of education programs in their communities and because the effects are all too visible around them. This really confirms the argument that the most effective way to reduce drug abuse is through education and treatment and, if it is really decreasing primarily among the middle class, through regenerating the economies of the inner cities—not through law enforcement.

Alternatives

If so many of the problems around drugs actually arise from their illegality and the war on drugs, is the solution simply to legalize some or all narcotics? Is the drug trade just one more example of the axiom that no one should tamper with any markets, for any reason? The situation is really not that simple; what is needed is not an end to regulation, but implementation of different forms of regulation.

Legalization might be able to erase some of the behavior that has grown up around drugs, but many of the problems that have been described above would be perpetuated in other ways, while others would worsen: drug addiction would increase, and the cocaine-dependent economies in Latin America would suffer an enormous loss of income. One argument made for legalization is that drug use is and should be a matter of individual responsibility—the government has no business "legislating morality" and should pull out and leave people to make their own decisions. Although this is a forceful argument, it neglects the fact that some individuals and communities would be affected much more than others by such "freedom," not because some people have no will power or have bad morals, but because their economic circumstances are so bad that a fast and reliable high is an irresistible option. And those economic circumstances have largely not been of their own making.

What is needed is an attack on the causes of drug addiction, which should include the following components:

Drug treatment should be available free and on demand. The problem we are supposed to be declaring war on should not be confused with its victims. This does not mean, however, that all treatment is equally good, or that it is a panacea: recovering addicts who leave programs, only to return to their original circumstances, are highly unlikely to remain "clean."

Inner-city regeneration should be a top priority and should include aid in starting small businesses to tap some of the entrepreneurial skills displayed by drug dealers. (This aid should include job training and credit for those shut out by banks because of their race or lack of connections.)

The Latin American nations profiting from cocaine need to be given real alternatives. This means writing off much of their debt, ensuring stable markets and fair prices for other exports, and allowing them autonomy in their choice of economic systems.

On an individual basis, we need to be extremely wary of the rhetoric of the drug war. Each time a proposal is put forward we need to be clear-eyed about whose interests it will serve, what their motives are, and how the policy might end up being perverted. If cocaine and heroin were legalized and taxed by the government, for example, they could become an enormous source of revenues, which, like the revenues from cigarette taxation, would at least produce conflicts of interest within government, since it would stand to gain financially from increased use. In addition to political pressure for national reforms, community-level action has to be taken—redirecting law enforcement efforts, building or strengthening treatment programs, and fighting poverty and homelessness.

Finally, we should think about what the drug trade has revealed about some American institutions. Two examples that have been addressed in this chapter are the CIA and the banking system; in both cases the drug trade has illuminated underlying problems that would continue to exist even if cocaine disappeared overnight. The CIA has consistently given a priority to the cold war, justifying support of allies who were involved in repression and human rights abuses of their own populations as well as aiding drug traffickers to sell to the United States. Now that the cold war is over, it is time to clarify their proper objectives and set limits on covert activity. The banking system must be reformed to serve needs other than those of the banks, speculators, and criminals. Some form of democratic accountability is needed; ideally this should be on a global level, or we run the risk that capital will just flow out of the U.S. economy.

Polls taken by the *New York Times* and CBS show that the proportion of the population that believes drugs are the largest problem facing the country has fallen from 65 percent in September 1989 to around 5 percent in January 1992 (*New York Times*, 1992). This drop in concern did not occur because the drug war has been won—the suffering caused by drugs and the drug war remain enormous—but because other issues such as the Gulf War and the state of the U.S. economy increased in importance. One benefit of this is that the level of inflammatory rhetoric is likely to drop off; we must seize such an opportunity to fight a very different form of war on drugs.

NOTES

1. There is no evidence that the coca leaves from which cocaine is derived, and which inhabitants of the Andes have been chewing for thousands of years, are particularly harmful. On the contrary, they are reported to contain nutritional value and to help the chewer overcome the effects of fatigue and altitude sickness.

2. Enforcement policies were unsuccessful on their own terms, since the price of cocaine fell dramatically in the United States during the 1980s. Even so, it remained higher than it would have been if cocaine had been legalized.

3. Harry Anslinger, the drug czar of the 1930s, quoted in Ronald Hamowy (1987:27). The change in marijuana's image over the last fifty years ("those addicted to marihuana . . . become bestial demoniacs, filled with the mad lust to kill"—news story in 1936, in Hamowy 1987:20) should make us a little cautious of the hyperbole surrounding this decade's "devilish combination."

4. "Death Toll from Smoking Is Worsening," *New York Times*, 1 February 1991; and Boaz 1988. David Boaz does not clarify whether this figure includes drug-related homicides.

5. Many tobacco companies also argue that smoking has "not been established to be the cause of disease," but I will not waste time on this claim here.

6. This situation is changing in the 1990s; as the Colombian government has managed to weaken or destroy the Medellin cartel, processing has been moving to Bolivia.

7. Individual members of governments have certainly been enriched through corruption or direct participation in the drug trade. This has not been generally helpful for national development, though.

8. This situation is also changing; increased interdiction efforts in the Caribbean have had the effect of shifting smuggling to a route through Panama and Mexico (U.S. Senate 1989:14).

9. By some accounts, drug consumption is declining. However, I argue that the drug war cannot plausibly take much credit for this.

10. "In Shift, U.S. Army Will Aid Peru's Army Against Drugs and Rebels," *New York Times*, 25 January 1992. This is not a new development; U.S. marines have been secretly training Peruvian marine units for more than two years, and Drug Enforcement Agency officials have also been based there. However, the fifteen trainers included in the new package, and the military aid sent with them, will be used not only for antidrug training but for training in antiterrorist warfare against the "narcoterrorists" of the Sendero Luminoso.

11. Edward Jay Epstein argues in his book *Agency of Fear* (1990) that Richard Nixon's motive in launching the first drug war, in 1972, was to wrest political control of his government from the hands of the different law enforcement agencies (examples are the FBI, Customs, the Internal Revenue Service, and the CIA) who held power. Narcotics were blown into a "national crisis" to make reorganization possible.

12. Many foreign governments have also been accused of using both the drug trade and the war on drugs in a cynical fashion; those accused have included countries hostile to the United States, such as Syria and Cuba, as well as countries aligned with them, like Panama and Thailand.

13. Estimates of the number killed during the invasion, including U.S. and Panamanian civilians as well as the military, run from the United States' figure of 500 up to the figure coming out of the University of Panama, 12,000 (Zimbalist 1990).

14. Letter from DEA administrator Jack Lawn, quoted in the Kerry report (U.S. Senate 1989:92).

BIBLIOGRAPHY

Beers, David. 1991. Just Say Whoa! *Mother Jones*, July/August, 36–56.
Boaz, David. 1988. Let's Quit the Drug War. *New York Times.* 17 March.
Duster, Troy. 1990. Criminal Justice and Criminal Injustice. Testimony delivered to the U.S. House of Representatives Subcommittee on Legislation and National Security, 2 July.
Epstein, Edward Jay. 1990. *Agency of Fear.* London: Verso.
Frontline. 1990. The Noriega Connection. PBS documentary, 31 January.
Hamowy, Ronald. 1987. Introduction: Illicit Drugs and Government Control. *Dealing with Drugs.* San Francisco: Pacific Research Institute.
Jackson, Rev. Jesse. 1989. Drug Use Is a Sin. *New Perspectives Quarterly* 6(Summer): 8–11.
Kerry report. *See* U.S. Senate 1989.
Kwitny, Jonathan. 1987. *The Crimes of Patriots.* New York: Simon & Schuster.
Lee, Rensselaer Lee, III. 1988. Why the U.S. Cannot Stop South American Cocaine. *Orbis* 32(Fall): 499–519.
Levine, Michael. 1990. *Deep Cover: The Inside Story of How DEA Infighting, Incompetence, and Subterfuge Lost Us the Biggest Battle of the Drug War.* New York: Delacorte Press.
McCoy, Alfred W. 1991. *The Politics of Heroin: CIA Complicity in the Global Drug Trade.* New York: Lawrence Hill.
Morley, Jefferson. 1989. Contradictions of Cocaine Capitalism. *The Nation,* 2 October.
NACLA. 1989. Coca: The Real Green Revolution. *Report on the Americas* 22(6): 12–38.
———. 1990. Colombia Cracks Up. *Report on the Americas* 23(6): 13–38.
———. 1991. *Report on the Americas* 24(1): 14–15.
Reuter, Peter, Gordon Crawford, and Jonathan Cave. 1988. *Sealing the Borders: The Effects of Increased Military Participation in Drug Interdiction.* Santa Monica: RAND Corporation.
Scott, Peter Dale, and Jonathan Marshall. 1991. *Cocaine Politics: Drugs, Armies, and the CIA in Central America.* Berkeley and Los Angeles: University of California Press.
Szykowny, Rick. 1990. A Funny, Dirty Little War. *The Humanist* 50 (September/October): 15–42.
Trebach, Arnold. 1989. Accepting the Presence of Drugs. *New Perspectives Quarterly* 6 (Summer): 40–44.
U.S. Senate. Subcommittee on Terrorism, Narcotics, and International Operations of the Committee on Foreign Relations. 1989. *Drugs, Law Enforcement, and Foreign Policy.* Washington, D.C.: U.S. Government Printing Office. (Referred to in text as Kerry report.)
Zimbalist, Andrew. 1990. Why Did the U.S. Invade Panama? *Radical America* 23(2/3): 7–13.

7 DIANE FLAHERTY

Can Markets Work in Eastern Europe?

The democratic movements of Eastern Europe came to power recently with broad popular mandates for sweeping change. But change has deteriorated into chaos, and the new governments find themselves fighting off political opposition and presiding over accelerating economic decline. There are now two choices: quicken the pace of reform and suppress dissent or retreat to more gradual dismantling of the old systems.

In deciding which choice to make, perceptions about what went wrong with earlier, more modest reforms play an important role. Previous moves toward markets are often seen to have failed because they did not go far enough in clearing out economic and political barriers to change. In this view, only a quick and radical reform, a "big bang," can put these countries on the right path.

The economic reforms of the 1960s and 1970s did indeed leave many undesirable institutions in place. Conventional wisdom blames resistance to change on greedy bureaucrats and lazy workers inherited from central planning. The obvious cures then are privatization and bankruptcy, which force everyone to compete for a job.

In this headlong rush to the market, two basic questions are swept aside. First, what *can* the market do for countries like these? Even in theory, can we expect Eastern Europe to become a region of South Koreas and Singapores? Second, in the real world of inherited nonmarket institutions and attitudes, how can markets be created?

To answer these questions and judge what the future of reform in Eastern Europe might be, we can look at the experience of the country that already has tried radical market reform. Twenty-five years ago, Yugoslavia opened its economy to the discipline of the market as Poland and Hungary are doing now. The results were disastrous, and unfortunately there are strong indications that the same problems are already arising in the rest of Eastern Europe. There are alternatives, however, based in broader worker and popular participation, that offer some hope of improving efficiency

140

while at the same time avoiding the inequality associated with introducing markets.

How Eastern European Countries Have Done Economically

Central planning overall did well in achieving high rates of growth of national income until the end of the 1970s. Between 1965 and 1975, for example, Eastern European countries as a whole grew faster than the United States and West Germany (U.S. Congress 1985:118). Even while growing fast, however, these countries had many problems. Economic benefits were not distributed equally or according to work. Workers in industries favored by the central plan earned higher wages and enhanced nonwage privileges such as access to better food supplies at subsidized prices. Social benefits such as health care and education were seen to go disproportionately to the party elite. Social costs such as pollution were too often ignored in the drive to increase industrial output. Relative neglect of industries producing consumer goods held back improvement in the standard of living. In some countries, the majority of farmers and rural workers lived in near poverty, their incomes held down to guarantee low food prices in the cities. Urban workers had little say in how their factories were run, and worker apathy was becoming a drain on productivity.

To a large extent, these problems arose from the strategy for economic growth pursued by Eastern European governments. Wary of participating in the world economy as agricultural countries, they pushed to industrialize and become independent as rapidly as possible. Industrialization in turn required a high level of investment at the expense of consumption and low prices of food at the expense of farmers to subsidize workers. Although this growth strategy overall achieved a more well-rounded and self-sufficient economic structure, it rested on a strictly hierarchical, top-down system in which firms were told what and how much to produce at what prices and for whom.

By the early 1960s, frustration with the one-party system and the pervasive power of the government compounded dissatisfaction with the strategy for industrialization. Absence of a significant popular voice in decisions meant scant hope of changing economic priorities in favor of consumers, farmers, or the environment. At the same time, the growth strategy itself ran into trouble. After achieving a large part of its economic promise, industrialization began to lose steam, and political dissent sharpened.

The 1980s: Economic Slowdown

The current move toward markets in Eastern Europe comes at the end of a decade in which conditions of work and life began to fall far short of both expectations of the people and promises of governments. Figures 7.1–7.4 show growth of the economy overall (growth of gross social product [GSP]), of industry and agriculture, and of real wages and employment during the 1980s. From the figures, we can see that growth on average for all the countries was only 2 to 3 percent a year. Agricultural output in several countries fell. This is a very weak performance compared to the 1960s and early 1970s, when the economies grew 8 to 10 percent a year.

As a result of slow growth, fewer and fewer jobs were created. In Hungary, the number of jobs actually fell throughout the 1980s. Real wages and incomes also grew by very little in most years, and in some cases declined. Again, the stagnation in the 1980s was more alarming because it came after many years of wage growth of nearly 6 to 8 percent.

A second concern was that, because the economies were becoming less efficient, future growth was going to be even worse. Figures 7.5–7.8 give the standard indicators of efficiency, including productivity growth of labor and capital (productivity is measured by the output produced by a unit of an input, such as an hour of labor) during the 1980s. From the figures, we can see that labor productivity in most countries did not do too badly, but capital productivity fell in all the countries. This means that expensive investment in building factories and new machines was not doing its job of helping the economy grow faster. People sacrificed for the future by accepting lower wages to pay for the investment, but they were getting less and less in return.

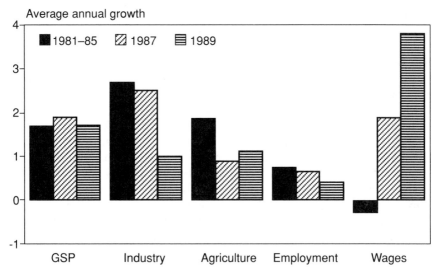

Figure 7.1 Overall economic performance (expressed as percentages) for Czechoslovakia, 1981–1989. *Source:* United Nations 1990.

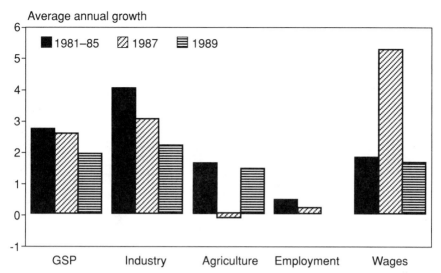

Figure 7.2 Overall economic performance (expressed as percentages) for German Democratic Republic, 1981–1989. Employment data for 1989 are not available. *Source:* United Nations 1990.

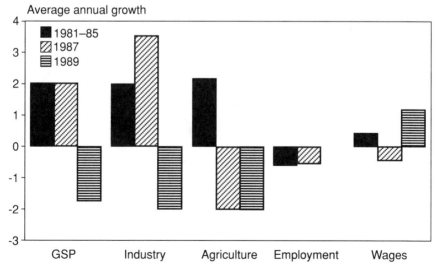

Figure 7.3 Overall economic performance (expressed as percentages) for Hungary, 1981–1989. Employment data for 1989 are not available. *Source:* United Nations 1990.

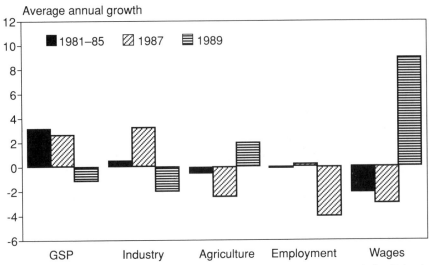

Figure 7.4 Overall economic performance (expressed as percentages) for Poland, 1981–1989. *Source:* United Nations 1990.

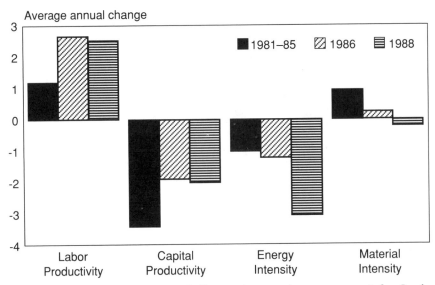

Figure 7.5 Economic efficiency indicators (expressed as percentages) for Czechoslovakia, 1981–1988. *Source:* United Nations 1990.

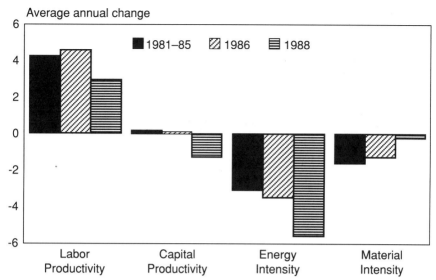

Figure 7.6   Economic efficiency indicators (expressed as percentages) for German Democratic Republic, 1981–1988. *Source:* United Nations 1990.

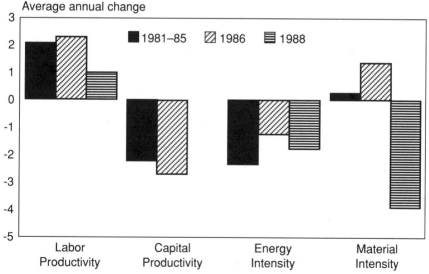

Figure 7.7   Economic efficiency indicators (expressed as percentages) for Hungary, 1981–1988. Capital productivity data are not available for 1988. *Source:* United Nations 1990.

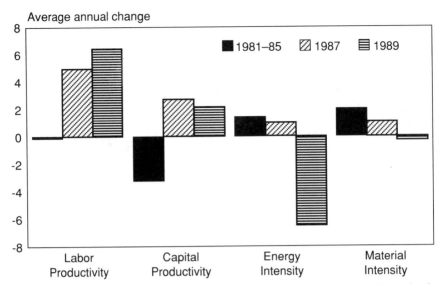

Figure 7.8 Economic efficiency indicators (expressed as percentages) for Poland, 1981–1989. *Source:* United Nations 1990.

Another indicator of efficiency is how much energy is used to produce the nation's output, called the energy intensity. Figures 7.5–7.8 show changes in intensity of energy use in the 1980s. What we would like to see is a gradual decline, telling us that the economy is becoming more effective in using energy. A rapid decline, however, often means that the country is simply collapsing. According to Figures 7.5–7.8 only in Poland is there a poor picture of energy intensity, first increasing and then falling dramatically in 1989. This is a pattern of deteriorating efficiency throughout the 1980s followed by severe economic contraction.

Figures 7.5–7.8 also give the material intensity of production, which measures the total resources used up to produce national output. In most countries material intensity either increased or fell by only a little during the decade. This means that efficiency either improved very slowly or deteriorated. The numbers for material intensity paint a slightly worse picture than for energy intensity and, along with the capital productivity numbers, show that the economies were beginning to run out of steam in the 1980s.

Trouble was brewing in foreign debt, too. At the beginning of the 1970s, debt was very low, but by the mid-1970s, depressed world economic conditions made it harder to export. At the same time, most countries were experiencing shortages of some important goods, like modern machinery and consumer goods. Once restrictions on trade were lifted, imports made up for lack of goods produced at home. In the worst case, Poland, net debt in 1989 was more than 36 times larger than in 1970. As imports rose and exports fell, it became increasingly difficult to pay back the foreign debt used to finance imports.

Another way to understand the economic conditions in Eastern European countries is to compare them to relatively poor Western countries, like Greece, Portugal, Spain, and Turkey, whose average annual growth in the first half of the 1980s was about 1.8 percent a year. From 1986 to 1989, though, their growth rose to just under 4 percent. So, although Eastern Europe did about the same or a little better in the early part of the decade, it did somewhat worse by the end. When people in these countries looked to the West, they saw that their standard of living was falling further and further behind. On the other hand, inflation was much worse in Western Europe, averaging between 20 and 30 percent a year for the whole decade. When corrected for this high inflation, wages in the Western countries virtually stagnated from 1980 to 1989 (United Nations 1990).

Overall, then, we cannot say that the economic performance of Eastern Europe was a disaster compared to the poorer countries of Western Europe. But at this point, we need to remember that economic statistics do not tell the whole story behind the passion for reform. Equally important are people's perceptions of economic performance and their concerns about concentration of political power. The ideology of socialism has created expectations of basic rights like job and income security. When even these rights were compromised as a result of economic slowdown, the gap between the theory and experience of socialism became too wide to ignore.

For example, it was a public scandal when inflation in Hungary reached 5 percent in the early 1980s. The country had never experienced such inflation before. People believed that economic stability and relative equality of income were rights in a socialist country. They simply would not accept either the inflation itself or its effect of widening income inequality. A level of inflation that in other parts of the world is accepted with resignation in Eastern Europe helped foment revolutionary movements.

The 1990s: Economic Collapse

Economic reform, however, has not been the cure for all these economic ills. Introduction of markets, together with privatization, was supposed to improve efficiency, output, exports, inflation and eventually the standard of living. In fact, the Eastern European economies have performed much worse after reform. Each country's degree of economic deterioration following reform depends on how radical the change has been.

In Poland, where reform has been most radical, the collapse is most complete. Whereas the economy grew by little more than 4 percent overall in 1988, it contracted by 12 percent in 1990. Industrial output, which increased by more than 5 percent in 1988, fell by 23 percent in 1990, and consumer prices soared by 585 percent. Consumers were hurt further because food output fell by almost 26 percent and consumer goods production by 37 percent during the year. Farmers, who were supposed to be helped most by reform, saw the prices they had to pay for goods rise by 50 percent more than the prices they received for their products (EIU 1991c).

These figures for the whole year obscure what happened in the months immediately after reform. Prices rose by 78 percent in January 1990 and 23 percent in February (Lipton and Sachs 1990), while unemployment grew from 50,000 people in January to 266,000 in March. Because of the inflation coupled with unemployment and falling wages, real earnings of workers had fallen 37 percent by the end of June. Production dropped dramatically. Sales of industrial output fell by some 13 percent in January and February, and by the end of June, the total decline for the year so far was 25 percent (EIU 1990).

There was some improvement in the second half of 1990, and further improvement was hoped for in 1991 in output and prices, with an estimated low but positive growth of output of 2.4 percent and a decline in inflation to "only" 60 percent. These expectations seem optimistic, however, if we look at the bankruptcy rate in early 1991: in February, two-thirds of all Polish firms were considered to be facing bankruptcy (EIU 1991c).

Foreign trade shows a pattern different from that of output, prices, and employment, by performing better at the beginning than at the end of the year. Unemployment and falling wages squeezed demand for imports so that in the first three months of 1990, imports fell by 14 percent. At the same time, exports rose by 36 percent. Still, the foreign debt remained so big that paying only the interest took 40 percent of export earnings at the middle of the year (EIU 1990). By the end of the year, exports had fallen by 35 percent from their peak in the early summer, and imports had fallen only by 16 percent (IMF 1991). This added to the foreign debt, which was estimated to be $4.6 billion in 1991, much greater than the $1.8 billion in 1989. The problem these numbers highlight is that any recovery in the Polish economy will push up imports and reduce exports as Poles buy more of both imports and goods that could be exported. The Polish economy is then stuck in a dilemma. Recession is good for foreign trade but bad for Polish output; on the other hand, economic recovery is bad for foreign trade and can increase the foreign debt burden.

Other countries in the region are having similar problems. Hungary and Czechoslovakia saw national output fall by 3.5 percent and 4.5 percent respectively in 1990. Their foreign debt, on the other hand, is expected to rise, but much more slowly than Poland's. In fact, these countries, which have opened themselves to market forces very gradually and cautiously, are not yet experiencing anything like the dramatic collapse of the Polish economy.

Still, time since reform has been short, and it is not fair to judge the ultimate effect of markets by what has happened so far. Many advocates of reform argue that soon the positive side of market forces will take hold and Eastern Europe will begin to grow faster than before. On their side is the deceleration of Polish decline in the second half of 1990, which slowed economic collapse to a somewhat more gentle decay. On the other side, the rate of inflation in Czechoslovakia in early 1991 was over 50 percent a month, and the most pessimistic estimate of inflation for the entire year was only 50 percent (EIU 1991a).

How Economic Reform Is Supposed to Work

Free market theories in fashion now in Eastern Europe are based on the idea that when each individual is allowed to pursue his or her own self-interest, everyone benefits. Maximizing profit is the same as maximizing the welfare of society as a whole.

This vision of the free market depends upon the economy being competitive. Competition means that only those who produce goods at the price and quality consumers want will survive. For this to happen, there must be no companies powerful enough to "corner the market," to control what is produced and set any price they want.

Free market theory calls on markets to discipline inefficient producers, and discipline takes the form of bankruptcy for companies and unemployment for workers. So, in the short run, if the economic reforms are working, there should be a rapid rise in unemployment. But, in theory, as the economy as a whole becomes more efficient, job opportunities will be created in successful businesses. Eventually, the rate of job creation will be high enough to provide employment for all those who used to work in the inefficient firms.

The key policy for change is opening up the economy to the world market by removing subsidies for exports and restrictions on imports and allowing the value of each country's currency to be set by international demand for the currency, which depends on how attractive the country's products are to customers abroad. Governments are also out of the business of deciding how much each firm can keep of its export earnings and how much it can borrow abroad. These are now to be decisions made by independent, profit-maximizing private companies. Foreign investment is encouraged by generous tax laws, and each firm is free to negotiate terms with the investors (with some broad limits on degree of foreign ownership).

These policies are designed to force the economy to change what and how it produces. It should give up on those products it cannot produce competitively and switch to products it can. In practice, this means concentrating on consumer goods and raw materials and giving up on trying to export machinery or other industrial goods. While the change is taking place, unemployment will rise as workers are laid off from industrial jobs, but the theory argues that workers will be rehired in the new, expanding export sectors.

During this time, foreign debt will probably also increase, not decrease. This happens because the drive to compete on the world market pushes companies to import the most up-to-date and efficient technology. Firms will have to borrow money, mostly from abroad, to pay for these imports, and so debt goes up. But debt, like unemployment, is expected to be temporary. Once the companies use the new technology to reduce costs, they will be able to export more and repay the debt. The foreign trade situation will also worsen, because consumers will now be free to import any goods they want (and can afford). But again, when the market has forced companies at home to switch to efficient consumer goods production, the problem will be solved automatically.

All of this optimism depends upon workers and owners of firms being disciplined by the market. For workers, unemployment is only a part of this discipline. Wages, too, must fall, because Eastern European firms are going to compete in the world market on the basis of low-wage labor.

Wages are reduced in two ways. First, companies simply pay less: the actual money wage falls. Second, inflation eats away at the purchasing power of wages; when this happens, the real wage, rather than the money wage, falls. As a central policy of reform in Eastern European countries today, prices of most goods are free to seek their market levels. Because prices were artificially low before reform, this has meant high inflation immediately after reform. Necessities have been particularly hard hit. As a result, real wages have taken a big fall in the past year in all these countries.

The theory of free markets expects inflation, too, to be temporary. As soon as producers see that they must compete to survive, supplies of goods to the market will increase and prices will fall. Even if money wages go down, prices will go down still more. In the end, the real wage will rise and people will be better off.

Not only that, but even during the transition period people will be better off, despite lower real wages. An idea now popular among Western economists is that the higher prices mean shorter lines. Your quality of life is supposed to be improved by not having to wait in line even if your real wage is less. Another version of this thinking is that consumers are better off having goods available even if they cannot afford most of them, because what they *can* afford is there (Lipton and Sachs 1990).

Restructuring the financial sector is called for as well. A Western-style fractional reserve system will be established in which banks are free to lend at market interest rates instead of simply disbursing predetermined grants from the central plan. Even a stock market is called for as a way to generate and allocate financial capital. The argument is that investment decisions in the past have been made according to political power of various industries, not their economic potential. If, instead, the banks lending the money must now show a profit, they will not lend to the big dinosaur companies but to the emerging dynamic companies.

The market model concludes that the sacrifices called for are not that big. Drastic cuts in both real and money wages are largely offset by improved quality of life. In any case, the sacrifices will not last that long, because efficiency is rising and growth will be higher. After a brief transition period, everyone will be better off.

What Yugoslavia Means for Economic Reform

This same optimism was felt in Yugoslavia in the mid-1960s, when the economy was radically "marketized," but two things went wrong. First, the effects of reform were much worse than expected. Second, the disastrous impact of reform made the whole notion of market discipline politically dangerous. Reform not only failed to deliver the goods, it disillusioned people about the whole process of fighting the system.

What Went Wrong with Reform

There have been two periods of reform in Yugoslavia, the first lasting from the mid-1960s to the mid-1970s and the second including almost the entire decade of the 1980s. In general, reforms included the same changes now being suggested in the rest of Eastern Europe, with the exception of privatization. The economy was opened to the world market, firms were supposed to be left to sink or swim in the currents of capitalist prices, social services were financed by local communities and not the central government, and bankruptcy and unemployment were accepted.

The most obvious result of reform was inflation. In the first six months after the early reforms, inflation rose to 85 percent. In the middle of the 1980s, the annual inflation rate rose to 100 percent, and preliminary results for 1990 show 2000 percent (Federal Statistics Office of Yugoslavia 1990).

The source of the most rapid inflation in Yugoslavia has been investment booms. This has been very upsetting to market theorists because excess investment was a major weakness of central planning that reform was supposed to eliminate. How did this happen? What were the motives and what were the opportunities behind inflation?

Motive came primarily from the pressure on firms to modernize and compete. To the extent that reform thrust firms into newly competitive markets to sink or swim, they were forced to modernize. Modernization in turn depended upon borrowing, hence on pressuring the sources of funds, the banks. Communities, too, put pressure on banks because they did not simply accept growing unemployment but insisted that banks save local companies.

Opportunity came first from the transformation of the financial system. The entire banking system was reformed, with regional and local banks given more resources and power to make loans. In theory, because banks were now profit maximizers who also had to compete, they would not give in to pressure to make risky loans. In this way, only companies and individuals with the right collateral or with sound investment plans would get access to money.

In practice, however, the new banking system was loosely controlled at best. It never developed into the theoretically ideal system with strong central policing of lending policies. The best description is that it operated like the U.S. savings-and-loan industry, with little regulation but a lot of collusion between borrowers and lenders. Banks simply gave people and businesses the loans they requested, regardless of creditworthiness. As a result, banks created the classic inflationary situation in which too much money is chasing too few goods.

The poorer regions of the country have suffered worst from the new system. Unemployment rose quickly after the 1960s reform, reaching 20 percent by the early 1970s. Prior to the civil war, the situation became bleaker still, with some estimates saying 40 percent of youth in the poor areas were out of work. For comparison, unemployment in the richest region, Slovenia, had been less than 1 percent in the last few years. Income differences between poor and rich regions also grew rapidly. While the average total income for a family in a poor area was about 70 percent of that of a family in a rich area in 1965, in 1970 the rate was less than 60 percent and it was down to 50 percent by 1987 (Federal Statistics Office of Yugoslavia 1989).

Because reform hit so hard in poor regions, people there had the strongest incentive to find and use whatever loopholes there were in the banking system to get more loans. And they did this very well. The biggest employer in one of the poorest regions of the country, a food-processing company called Agrokomerc, financed its operations by a combination of shady deals with banks and IOUs to its suppliers. When the scheme began to fall apart, the government had the choice of letting the firm go bankrupt, laying off a large part of the work force of a desperately poor province, or bailing it out.

The government reluctantly paid for the bailout. It really had no choice, because the economic cost of "letting the market decide" was so high that it was politically impossible. Almost always, when the government tries to hang tough with the banks, antigovernment riots or ethnic fighting over a shrinking economic pie break out.

This pattern, in which reform causes a serious economic problem and the government intervenes to curb the worst effects, became normal operating procedure. For example, when controls on imports and exports were relaxed, the foreign-trade deficit exploded. Firms began to import most of the machinery they needed to modernize and become competitive. Consumers began to import luxury goods not available at home and also to buy goods that used to be set aside for export. Imports went up and exports went down.

The government then stepped in to try to contain the damage by fixing some prices and setting some quotas, setting off a vicious cycle. Whenever the government loosened controls, people rushed to import, fearing the opportunity would be temporary. The foreign-trade deficit would shoot up, and the government would crack down even harder next time.

Still, we cannot conclude that reform had no successes. It did achieve a great increase in one export, labor. The massive unemployment in the poor regions sent workers to Western Europe, from which they sent German marks back home. The money they sent back, called remittances from abroad, is counted like exports in measuring the foreign-trade deficit. For many years, it was enough to offset the boom in imports and loss of exports following reform. Not until recession in Western Europe forced Yugoslav workers to return home did the real cost of reform become apparent.

Why Reform Went Wrong

In dealing with simultaneous inflation, unemployment, and foreign debt, the government faced a chronic dilemma. One approach is to ignore the consequences of reform, arguing, as has become fashionable now, that the patient is so sick the cure itself might be dangerous. The only alternative is to violate the coherence of the reform package by counteracting its worst effects. This is the course that Yugoslavia chose, and this is why the so-called soft budget constraint (government bailout) returned, and even grew softer, in periods of economic reform. The budget constraint was allowed to soften whenever the costs of reform became economically unsustainable or politically unmanageable.

Neither approach worked. Where reform continued, its effects were not short-lived, as promised. Unemployment persisted in the poor regions in spite of the belief that low-wage labor would attract investment. Yugoslavia did not find secure markets for its exports even when it did what the theory said and switched to less ambitious products. On the other hand, where the principles of reform were violated, uncertainty about policy itself became a source of instability.

The underlying problem has two parts. First, the market model applied to Yugoslavia and proposed for other countries is largely inappropriate. Second, even if marketization theoretically could succeed, the nature of existing institutions made it difficult for markets to work.

Yugoslavia was a small, relatively resource-poor country. When it followed the free market prescription to trade with capitalist rather than social-ist countries, it was severely handicapped by its size and resource base. Nonetheless, it was able to compete at first, if not in the advanced capitalist countries themselves, at least in Third World markets. For example, Yugoslavia exported ships to India and tractors to many developing coun-tries. At the beginning, it was able to get dollars or other "hard" currencies for these exports and pay off some of its foreign debt. Then the world recession of the early 1970s devastated the economies of the countries that were buying Yugoslavia's industrial exports. The only way to continue sell-ing was to offer generous credit terms. Eventually, however, the credits were not repaid in full and Yugoslavia's deficit soared.

Where Yugoslavia did try to export to the United States and other advanced countries, it ran into trouble immediately. Because Yugoslavia from early on had a Western orientation, it had built up good marketing talent and connections with Western distributors. From its marketing cre-ativity, it came up with a new product: fruit juice in foil containers that can be punctured with an attached straw. For a while, this product was on the shelves of even small-town groceries in the United States. The problem was that the product was so successful that it was soon imitated by Dole and Del Monte, which had the resources to undercut Yugoslavia's prices.

This is the competitive process at work. In the market model, for Yugoslavia to have an efficient economy, it had to go through this shake-out. Its job was to go back to the drawing board and find other products that even for a short time could compete in the West. But this process is very expensive and disruptive, requiring large expenditures in research and development and producing high social costs from displacement of workers. Perhaps a rich country can absorb these costs, but poor countries often cannot.

In the 1980s, Yugoslavia switched its overall export strategy. With the notable and disastrous exception of the Yugo car, foreign-trade policy gen-erally accepted the impossibility of exporting industrial goods. The country resigned itself to going back to exporting what poor countries usually do, raw materials and agricultural products. Unfortunately, when it tried, it found that the logical markets for these goods, Western European coun-tries, were almost completely closed.

Through the European Economic Community, or the Common Mar-ket, these countries had gotten together to protect their farmers from com-petition. At the same time that free markets were being prescribed for Yugoslavia, free markets did not exist in the developed countries. Some products, like beef, were banned entirely, while others, like fruits, faced high tariffs that effectively made them uncompetitive in Western Europe.

The experience of foreign trade has taught some sad lessons. Even with low-wage labor, and even in traditional exports, Yugoslavia could not compete. Worse, its failures were to a large extent beyond its control. It did not lack marketing or creative skills or stick with an out-of-date strategy. The problems were deeper. First, the cards are stacked against countries like Yugoslavia in a world market in which free markets do not exist. Second, even if markets did exist, the costs of adjusting to rapid changes in competition and demand are much harder for small, poor countries to bear.

The second problem for free market reform is barriers to the creation of markets. A capital market was not created partly because banks continued to act under political pressure rather than according to profit maximization. Moreover, after reform, capital mobility declined substantially due to the effects of reform on regional relations. Firms in richer regions chose to keep their capital at home, even in cases where more profitable opportunities existed in the less developed regions.

Nor was a conventional labor market created in Yugoslavia. One reason for its absence is the socialist ideology of full employment; it is very difficult to lay off workers, and this difficulty translates into higher unemployment among young people just entering the work force. Another reason is that Yugoslavia was legally a self-managed economy: according to its constitution, workers' councils ran their companies. This means that workers had a say in whether they were laid off or not, with obvious consequences for job security.

There are many other examples to illustrate the same point. The punch line is that it is wildly optimistic to expect markets to exist or to be created quickly in the countries of Eastern Europe.

Lessons for the Future

The experience of Yugoslavia does not mean that any introduction of markets is bad. The countries of Eastern Europe need to improve their efficiency, and some form of marketization is useful for that purpose. However, achieving stability even with limited marketization is a delicate process that requires a powerful and engaged central government.

Yet a government introducing reform will be a government under siege. The more radical the reform, the more pressing the need for coherent macroeconomic management of the transition. But at the same time, the more radical the reform, the greater the economic misery and the stronger the political opposition to change.

This is the central dilemma of reform that Yugoslavia's experience highlights for us. Those economists who argue that the misery will not be deep understate the negative aspects of the market. Those who argue that the adjustment will be quick underestimate political resistance to deteriorating living and working conditions.

But is it possible that the other countries of Eastern Europe are somehow immune from Yugoslavia's troubles? After all, Yugoslavia was especially plagued by some barriers to reform, like ethnic rivalries and power of workers. More important, Yugoslavia never tried the cornerstone of other reforms, privatization. Economic advisers to many Eastern European countries argue that without privatization markets cannot be expected to work. Reformers also argue that the debt positions of the other Eastern European countries will be better than Yugoslavia's, for two reasons. First, generous international help will flow into Eastern Europe to support the newly democratic governments. Second, the creation of stock markets in these countries is said to be a potent source for capital. Clearly, the more capital can be raised domestically, the less has to be borrowed from abroad.

Can, then, privatization, foreign loans, and a domestic stock market avoid the troubles Yugoslavia had with reform? For privatization, there are a few important bits of evidence that we can gather from what already has happened in Poland, the country that has pursued privatization most vigorously.

The first step in privatization is to set a value on the assets to be sold to private companies and individuals. The question then is, How can a value be determined without an already existing market? One answer the Poles have tried is auctions, in effect creating a market by collecting bids. Unfortunately, the auctions have not worked, mainly because potential large buyers, mostly foreigners, have been too concerned about economic and political instability to jump in.

One group has been willing to buy up assets: those who used to manage the firms when they were under the control of central planners. Because of this, even the very small sales achieved so far have not borne out expectations of bringing in new, competitive blood. On the contrary, buy-outs have made the economy more concentrated and therefore less competitive (EIU 1991c).

Perhaps more telling, despite the lack of foreign interest in Polish assets, a political backlash against reform now attacks the very concept of foreign ownership. In the recent elections, the challenger to Lech Walesa found his constituency by criticizing the Solidarity government for being willing to give away the national wealth to foreign exploiters. The net result has been that even with a high and rising unemployment rate and low wages, Poland cannot make itself attractive enough to sell its assets at bargain-basement prices. Among the foreign business community, if not among academic economists, the economic and political fragility of reform is an open secret.

Privatization is such an elusive goal because reform is so disruptive. Is it nonetheless possible that the disruption will be less severe than in the Yugoslav case? If so, maybe foreign investors will soon come into Poland. After all, it is true that Poland, and in fact all other Eastern European countries, have nothing like the ethnic hatreds that have torn Yugoslavia apart.

Unfortunately, Poland (and most of the other countries) does have something similar to deal with in conflict between workers and farmers. Every time in the past the government has tried to make prices approach market levels, there have been riots. When food prices go up, urban workers suspect peasants of getting rich at urban expense and take to the streets. When prices of industrial goods go up, peasants revolt because they think workers are profiting by charging farmers sky-high prices for industrial goods. Poland's way of reducing the tension between workers and farmers has been to import enough goods to keep the prices down. This is an important source of the tremendous foreign debt the country is now saddled with as it attempts its most radical change. By the end of 1989, Poland's foreign debt service was four and a half times larger than its export earnings (United Nations 1990). Other countries are somewhat better off, particularly Czechoslovakia, which has implemented little economic reform in spite of dramatic political changes. Still, no country of the region today can afford to smooth the reform process using imports without substantial foreign help.

Are foreign loans perhaps a way out? New credit would allow Poland and the other countries to avoid large price shocks in the short run. In the longer run, foreign capital would allow importation of technologies that would reduce the costs and prices of Polish goods and help exports.

Some Eastern European countries have received support from the West in their transition to capitalism. In a July 1989 economic summit, the United States, Japan, and major Western European nations agreed on special help for Poland and Hungary. In early 1990, the program was extended to Bulgaria, Czechoslovakia, East Germany, and Romania. The goals of the support are to provide emergency food aid and to foster markets by a variety of training and investment plans. Many other agencies and countries have participated as well. A partial sum of international commitments to Hungary and Poland for 1990 and beyond, including only the largest donors, comes to about $6.5 billion for Hungary and $10 billion for Poland (United Nations 1990).

International financial organizations also have pitched in. The International Monetary Fund allowed Poland to draw on $723 million of standby credit in 1989, and the World Bank projected a total of around $4 billion for 1989–92. With such support, it may be possible for Poland to defer repayment of some of its loans to commercial banks to the tune of $1 billion a year (United Nations 1990).

A rough estimate for total aid to Poland is something like $18 to $20 billion over the next few years, and to Hungary, $8 to $10 billion. These numbers are large, amounting to almost half of each country's debt, and are cause for optimism that the debt burden will not be crushing.

Still, there are reasons for concern. Although debt relief and direct aid are large, a number of other factors have hurt the debt positions of these countries. The terms for loans have become more than twice as stiff in the past two years, so that when the countries have to turn to banks to finance the rest of their debt, the payments double. The source of debt has also become less favorable. Eastern European countries borrow more now from nonbank sources of credit, mainly governments of other countries. These loans are more costly because they often require that the borrowing country pay a higher price for imports from the lender country (United Nations 1990).

A final caution is that the cost of importing basic necessities, like food and oil, can rise suddenly. Not only is the world price of oil volatile, but the Eastern European countries now have to purchase a larger share of their oil at the world price, since they no longer get most of their oil (or food) at subsidized prices from the former Soviet Union. The World Bank has estimated that the cost in lost subsidies over the next three years may be $50 billion for the region.

Another proposed source of funds is a stock market. In the free market theory, a stock market would induce people to invest rather than spend and thus would provide additional sources of capital. The underlying assumption is that stock markets in developed capitalist countries perform two critical functions: they allocate savings to the most profitable investment opportunities and encourage the efficient use of existing assets. Evidence does not support these assumptions, however. Most corporations depend upon retained earnings rather than stock issues to raise capital, and prices of stocks are not related systematically to the performance of companies. In short, the stock market neither induces people to save more nor imposes competitive discipline on companies (Singh 1989). If well-developed stock markets in advanced capitalist countries cannot perform the assumed functions, is it reasonable to expect infant stock markets in noncapitalist countries to do better?

So we are back to foreign debt as the more likely source of capital. The ultimate test of whether debt is manageable or not is the use to which the borrowed money is put. In the past, Eastern European countries have borrowed to smooth over political problems caused by economic decline; the money they have borrowed they have used to import scarce goods. The theory of market reform says that now, because of privatization and competition, new opportunities exist for efficient use of the debt.

The obvious flaw in this theory is that there is still a strong incentive for the government to use the debt to maintain political stability. Again, the dilemma of reform is that it creates such economic pain that political pressure explodes. The reformers argue that political democracy provides the safety valve for people's economic frustration. In this view, elections can buy time for governments by damping public reaction against the impact of reform. However, the example of Poland shows that even with a workers' party in power, the political honeymoon is very short. In Czechoslovakia, too, major strikes have already broken out, the most serious over gasoline price increases (EIU 1991a).

Is Capitalism the Way Forward?

The lesson from the Yugoslav experience of twenty-five years and the Polish experience of almost two years is that it will be extremely difficult to turn Eastern Europe into a region of market economies. Because markets are so disruptive, their operation must be limited if governments are to stay in power.

It may seem, then, that existing market economies have little to teach Eastern Europe. In fact, we can look both to the experience of Yugoslavia and to some poor capitalist economies to see the likely future of Eastern Europe. What Poland, Hungary, and Yugoslavia have in common with countries like Mexico, Chile, and Bolivia is a set of policy prescriptions that were tried already in Latin America during the 1970s and 1980s. The same economists who advised the Chilean government of General Augusto Pinochet are behind current Polish government policy.

Briefly, the performance of poor capitalist countries since their reforms has been terrible. Although the free market economists brag about Chile and Bolivia, we do not have to look very deeply to see that their policies have done virtually nothing to improve the standard of living. In Bolivia, the alleged success of marketization rests upon its almost overnight cure of runaway inflation by massive contraction of state-sector employment. Yet, five years after the "big bang" treatment of inflation, unemployment refuses to fall, and economic growth has been negligible.

In Chile, held up as the shining example of the virtues of unrestrained markets, there have been a few years of high growth. Unfortunately, they were followed by years of rapid decline, so that from 1973 to 1989, the overall yearly growth rate was less than 1 percent. And this pitifully low growth came at the expense of democracy and basic human rights. Even if we would accept loss of democracy in order to achieve a decent economic standard of living, Chile shows that repression is no guarantee of economic progress. All repression can do is distribute the pain of market adjustment to groups with no political power.

The two fundamental lessons of market reform in poor countries are forcefully expressed by Rudiger Dornbusch, an MIT economist who is by no means a radical. On the relation between economic reform and political stability, he has noted that "what markets consider a sufficient policy action may simply be beyond the political scope of democratic governments" (Dornbusch 1989:17). Democracy may not be able to enforce the inequality resulting from reform, which does not bode well for the political hopes of the new democratic parties of Eastern Europe.

But the second lesson is perhaps even more disturbing. In discussing why Bolivia was able to cure runaway inflation but not to return to economic growth, Dornbusch argues that market reforms fail more often than not because "the income distribution issues produce a serious inflation and recession problem, or because . . . the trimming back of credit growth and devaluation produce a deep recession and no investment boom, not in the first year and not for many years" (Dornbusch 1989:14).

In other words, the prognosis is for a long period of stagnation and class conflict. The market model simply does not consider that those who lose from reform will react (at least in a democracy) or that pushing the economy into recession to make it more competitive drives away potential investors by rendering future growth and profits highly uncertain.

Can Anything Be Done?

Eastern Europe has only negative lessons to learn from experiences with the policies advocated by the free-marketeers. There are some places to look for positive examples, however. The Hungarian reform of the 1960s and 1970s was successful in many respects. Unlike the current reforms, it was designed to be introduced gradually, after people were educated about its goals and effects. It was also less ambitious, in that efficiency was to be a long-run and not an overnight goal. The reasoning behind the reform was that people would accept change if they were convinced that the government knew what the costs would be and was ready to contain them temporarily while people adjusted to the "discipline of the market." Hungary both improved efficiency and avoided massive unemployment or wage declines.

Other Eastern European countries would do well to follow the outline, if not the details, of the Hungarian approach. The gradualist approach encouraged a basic transformation of agriculture, in which farmers went into business with the factories processing their produce in what were called combinations. From these arrangements, farmers got higher and more stable prices and also more choice over what to produce, without letting the market completely set prices. In this way, agricultural price increases were contained, and workers' real incomes did not suffer.

Industry has been more resistant to change in Hungary. Here the better model to follow might be something like Japan. But Japanese success depends in part upon large-scale government intervention, the exact opposite of free markets. In Japan, the government works with and limits business to make sure that investment goes into the newest technologies. The government also protects Japanese producers from world market forces, allowing them to get used to new technology gradually. Also, for a small but significant proportion of Japanese workers (around 15 percent today), no labor market exists. Job security is virtually guaranteed, so workers tend not to fight against new technology.

In Japan, competition is not free; it is managed to achieve specific goals. The market is not allowed to decide by itself what is produced and how. After thirty years of this policy, Japan clearly does not have to rely on agricultural and raw materials exports, whose markets and prices are notoriously unstable. Another top priority has been to support and control research and development, putting investment only into the best new processes and products. The market is not allowed to decide by itself what is produced and how. It works more like a check on decisions taken elsewhere.

Like Hungary, Japan has many features that we perhaps would not want in our ideal society. For example, both are highly regimented and hierarchical societies. The point, however, is that both countries have pursued independent development strategies that have had major successes. It is these countries, and others like them, that we should study to find ideas for Eastern Europe, because they have avoided the misery of radical market transformation while still using markets to improve efficiency.

Finally, the Eastern European countries can learn from experiences with worker participation. Repression or unemployment are not the only ways to get workers to work harder. Many experiments have found that workers who have more power are more committed, enthusiastic, and productive. Rather than ask people to sacrifice still more to raise investment in new factories and machines, all participation asks them to do is take control of their workplaces. When they do, the savings in supervisory personnel alone can often be substantial.

In these times of popular clamor for democracy, worker participation is the one strategy for change that builds upon democratic rather than hierarchical values. Because participation fits in with demands for empowerment sweeping across Eastern Europe, it is much more likely to succeed than artificial transplants of market institutions. Although it cannot solve all the problems, like foreign debt or out-of-date factories, giving workers more control over their factories may be the most promising first step toward improving productivity and democracy in Eastern Europe.

BIBLIOGRAPHY

Dornbusch, Rudiger. 1989. Short-term Macroeconomic Policies for Stabilization and Growth. Department of Economics, MIT, Cambridge, Mass. Photocopy.
Economist Intelligence Unit (EIU). 1990. *Country Report: Poland*, no. 3. London: The Economist.
———. 1991a. *Country Report: Czechoslovakia*, no. 2. London: The Economist.

————. 1991b. *Country Report: Hungary*, no. 1. London: The Economist.

————. 1991c. *Country Report: Poland*, no. 1. London: The Economist.

Federal Statistics Office of Yugoslavia. 1989, 1990. *Statistical Yearbook of Yugoslavia*. Belgrade: Savezni Zavod za Statistiku.

International Monetary Fund (IMF). 1991. *International Financial Statistics*. Washington, D.C.: IMF.

Lipton, David, and Jeffrey Sachs. 1990. Creating a Market Economy in Eastern Europe: The Case of Poland. Department of Economics, Harvard University, Cambridge, Mass. Photocopy.

Singh, Ajit. 1989. The Institution of a Stockmarket in a Socialist Economy: Notes on the Chinese Economic Reform. Faculty of Economics, Cambridge University. Mimeo.

United Nations Economic Commission for Europe. 1990. *Economic Survey of Europe*. Geneva: United Nations.

U.S. Congress Joint Economic Committee. 1985. *East European Economics: Slow Growth in the 1980's*. Vol. 1. Washington, D.C.: U.S. Government Printing Office.

8

JAMES CROTTY

The Rise and Fall of the Keynesian Revolution in the Age of the Global Marketplace

The United States emerged from World War II as the unchallenged leader of world capitalism, in virtually complete control of its own economic destiny and with the power to establish a new economic order, both domestically and internationally. By the early 1950s, the new economic order was solidly in place. Domestically, we had a Keynesian welfare–warfare state in which fiscal and monetary tools were to be used to guide our capitalist economy toward stable economic growth with full employment. Internationally, we had U.S. hegemony, a degree of military, political, and economic dominance in world affairs that would assure relative stability, the free movement of capital across national boundaries, and, eventually, an increasingly free movement of merchandise. Domestic growth would provide the economic foundation for international dominance. International dominance would assure the stability and access to markets and resources needed for domestic growth. By 1966, with the U.S. economy in the midst of a decade-long expansion, Keynesian economists celebrated the total victory of the Keynesian regime over the instability and inequality of the laissez-faire capitalism of the prewar era.

Yet just twenty years later, in 1987, Fed Chairman Paul Volcker, noting "how vulnerable our own financial markets and our own economy have become to what other people think," warned Americans that "we are obviously in danger of losing control of our own [economic] destiny" (*Wall Street Journal*, 19 May 1987). And in 1988, Felix Rohatyn declared that Volcker's worst fears were now facts:

> More than two hundred years after the Declaration of Independence, the U.S. has lost its position as an independent power. . . . We now conform to the classic model of a failing economic power: with increasingly high levels of foreign debt, a constantly depreciating currency, and a continuing negative trade balance, whether the dollar is rising or falling. . . . We are becoming as constrained, in some ways, as other large external debtors such as Brazil and Mexico. (1988:8)

163

Less than one generation ago, the United States was prosperous and powerful, the banker to the Western world. Today the United States is economically unstable and in hock to its allies, unable even to formulate macropolicy without the consent of its creditors.

In the body of this essay I attempt to explain why the Keynesian regulatory system was powerful enough to help promote prosperity in the early postwar period yet was too weak to prevent the instability and decline of the past fifteen years. I also investigate the role played by the emerging globalization of the world economy in the rise and fall of the Keynesian state and the loss of U.S. economic independence. I conclude by asking: Where do we go from here? Can Keynesian macropolicy recreate prosperity in the coming decades? And if not, what is to be done?

A Theory of Keynesian Macropolicy

Of course, we cannot address these questions without reference to a theory of modern capitalism and a theory of Keynesian regulation that can elaborate the conditions under which macropolicy can effectively promote its advertised goals of high employment, a high rate of growth, and a "fair" distribution of income.[1]

Keynesian economists provided one such theory. They acknowledged that capitalism has one major structural flaw, but only one. It has no internal mechanism to keep total national spending or what economists call aggregate demand at the full-employment level. When, as in the 1930s, spending or aggregate demand falls precipitously, and corporation managers face depressed sales and factories operating at half capacity, they have no economic incentive to employ the jobless or invest in additional capacity. But, Keynesians argued, this weakness can be corrected by nonradical government fiscal and monetary policy that can raise and lower national spending without interfering with the efficiency of capitalist markets. Keynesian regulation is not socialism; it was never designed to *directly* control investment, production, and jobs. Rather, by controlling the level of national spending, it was intended to enable private business to perform in the public interest.

On the other hand, radical critics of mainstream Keynesianism have always argued that the Keynesian theory of macropolicy itself had a major structural flaw—its erroneous assumption that once macropolicy was wisely set, profit signals would *automatically* motivate those private enterprises that are in direct control of employment, production, and investment to make decisions supportive of balanced full-employment growth. The relation between policy and economic performance, the radical argument went, is mediated by the complex conditions and varied institutions that determine profitability. In the absence of more direct public control over economic outcomes, profit signals can frustrate as easily as facilitate macropolicy effectiveness.

The radical critics were right. The story of the rise and fall of the Keynesian regime is the story of the creation and destruction of an integrated set of domestic and international institutions (described in the next section) that supported high profits and strong growth in the early postwar U.S. economy. In this section I develop the theoretical background needed to understand this story by discussing the conditions required for macropolicy effectiveness. As a simple matter of logic, two such conditions are needed.

First, policymakers must be able to control the level of national spending. To do so, they must be free to manipulate taxes, government spending, and interest rates in pursuit of domestic objectives.[2] They cannot do so, however, when international problems dominate domestic objectives. For example, concern over a large trade deficit may rule out fiscal stimulation, or difficulties with an unstable exchange rate may restrict the government's ability to manipulate interest rates.

Furthermore, changes in policy must be capable of generating significant alterations in the level of aggregate demand. Yet various complications may interfere with the connection between policy change and demand response. For example, the Fed cannot lower the interest rate to stimulate spending if its attempts to do so create heightened inflationary expectations that push interest rates upward. Also, the Fed cannot adequately control U.S. interest rates and credit availability when financial markets are thoroughly international and money can flow into and out of the country to counter the Fed's moves.

Second, policy-induced changes in aggregate demand must induce the desired changes in domestic objectives. For macropolicy to be effective, changes in aggregate demand must cause changes in domestic production, employment, income, and capacity utilization instead of changes in prices and in the demand for imported goods. The experience of the 1970s and early 1980s made it clear that national spending can grow at a rapid rate while domestic production and employment are stagnant or even declining, if increased spending is primarily reflected in rising prices rather than increased production. Events of the mid-1980s showed that a substantial proportion of increased aggregate demand can "leak" into the foreign sector in the form of increased demand for imported goods; in 1986, for example, net import growth lowered gross national product (GNP) by about 3.6 percent.

Beyond these short-run factors, however, there is a long-run issue that is more basic, more suggestive of the extent to which Keynesian macropolicy is fundamentally flawed. Even if the problems of inflation and import leakage are overcome, to attain the key domestic objective of raising the rate of growth of potential output and labor productivity, an expansion of aggregate demand must raise the pace of corporate investment spending or, to use economists' terms, raise the rate of capital accumulation. Unfortunately, there are times when macropolicy is unable to ensure that investment will respond positively to an increase in aggregate demand.

Vigorous and sustained capital accumulation takes place when the typical corporation confidently believes that the average profit rate it expects to receive over the expected life of its new plant and equipment significantly exceeds the return it could expect to get on financial assets, and when it feels that its current financial position will permit it to shoulder the risks inevitably associated with capital investment.

We know what the determinants of the rate of profit on capital already in place are. The profit rate on capital in any period will be high if sales are strong and capacity utilization high, if competitive pressures are not intense so that output price is attractive, if wages are modest in comparison with worker productivity (so that labor's share of corporate revenue is modest), and if raw material costs are low. If these conditions hold and the interest rate is low, corporations will be pleased with the return on domestic investment (provided only that the return on foreign capital is not significantly higher).

Now, it is clear that macropolicy may be helpless to create this set of conditions if they are not present in the economy to begin with. Under the best of circumstances macropolicy can stimulate or retard aggregate demand and affect the rate of interest—that's all. It has no direct power to control capital–labor conflict (which affects the profit share of sales revenue), rearrange price–cost relations, or change the degree of competition.

But the problem is yet more complex because corporations will undertake major new capital-spending projects only if they are convinced that the rate of profit on this capital will remain high on average for some ten or twenty years. In other words, in order for macropolicy to be able to stimulate an investment boom, it must be able to create an environment seen by the typical corporation as not just temporarily profitable but stably and predictably profitable over long periods of time. The insights of both Keynes and Marx can help us understand why the re-creation of such an environment has been beyond the power of the Keynesian regulatory apparatus for the past two decades.

In Keynes's theory, volatile expectations of future profits and inherently speculative financial markets are the Achilles' heel of modern capitalism. In the unplanned and unpredictable world of unregulated, or laissez-faire, capitalism, he argued, there is no way that corporations can ever *know* the future state of the economy. Therefore, expectations of future profits are prone to shift back and forth between periods of optimism (when things have gone well for a while) and pessimism (when optimistic expectations are disappointed by the onset of economic difficulties) because there is no solid knowledge of the future to hold them in place. Investment spending will shift up and down with these volatile profit expectations.

The particular institutional foundation of the early postwar economy did provide some stability and predictability to the economic environment, and this helped stabilize investment spending during these decades. However, once that foundation began to unravel, profit expectations became unrooted and destabilized, corporations lost confidence in their ability to forecast future profits, and a preference developed for the safety of short-term financial assets rather than the risk of plant and equipment investment. These developments blunted the incentive to invest.

Keynes also believed that unregulated financial markets are unstable. Stock prices, bond prices, and long-term interest rates, which influence business investment, are determined in markets that are, in essence, casinos in which buyers gamble that prices will rise and sellers gamble that they will fall. In Keynes's view, such markets are inherently speculative; each player tries to predict how long the other players will stay in or get out of the market. Since rising prices reward and embolden buyers and punish sellers, and vice versa, both upswings and downswings tend to be self-reinforcing. The instability of financial markets (so evident in the 1980s) makes investment spending even riskier and more unstable than it would otherwise be.

He made an analogous argument in his work on international finance. He believed that unregulated international financial flows would generate instability in domestic interest rates and in the balance of trade and balance of payments and, therefore, in domestic production, employment, and investment. For the last twenty years of his life, Keynes was a strong supporter of strict government controls on the movement of goods and, especially, money across national borders. In the absence of such controls, he believed, effective national economic planning in pursuit of full employment and a more equitable income distribution would not be possible (a point to which I return below).[3]

Marxian theory has traditionally stressed the contradictory relation between capital accumulation and profitability as the most important impediment to balanced growth in capitalist economies. In Marxian theory, investment is stimulated by a high profit rate. However, an investment boom can create economic conditions—such as a low unemployment rate that weakens capital's control over labor and erodes the profit margin, or excess productive capacity—that eventually lower the profit rate. A low profit rate in turn will cause a decline of investment and a subsequent economic downturn. Consequently, in Marxian theory there is no counterpart to the early postwar Keynesian tale of the potential for endless prosperity and no foundation for the modern Keynesian theory of macropolicy.

Several interesting Marxian explanations of the crisis of the past two decades contain two creative variations on the traditional Marxian theory of the dynamics of profit-rate determination. The first recognizes that unregulated free markets alone can never maintain the high average rate of profit required for long-term prosperity. Rather, the argument goes, long-term prosperity requires an internally coherent and stable set of institutions and policies powerful enough to shore up the profit rate and hold back the onset of crisis over long periods of time.[4] The second variation is that capitalist competition is ultimately structurally and institutionally corrosive. The disruptive power of competition may be stifled for a time by forms of domestic monopoly or by international schemes of market segmentation, but it eventually breaks down all barriers and erodes the institutional status quo.

The most persuasive of Marxian analyses of the outbreak of instability in the past twenty years combines these two innovations in a dialectical way. The prosperity of the early postwar period, it is argued, was made possible by the creation of an effective institutional structure to sustain profitability during and after World War II. But the process of two decades of economic growth and the corrosive forces of competition spawned by that growth caused changes that weakened that structure, ultimately rendering it incapable of sustaining a high profit rate. With the collapse of this institutional foundation for stability and profitability, the instability and stagnation of the current period emerged.

The important point to note is that the constellation of institutions and forces that permitted Keynesian macropolicy to be effective in the first twenty years or so of the postwar period could not reproduce themselves forever. Yet once they eroded, Keynesian regulation would be unable to function effectively. Keynes's theory of financial instability and Marx's theory of profit determination turned out to be right, and Keynesian macrotheory wrong.

Internationalization and the Decline of the Keynesian Regime

Stable long-term growth was possible in the 1950s and 1960s because the international and domestic institutional structures of the period kept the average profit rate high and the rate of accumulation strong. The following institutional factors contributed to this prosperity.

First, this was a period of relative stability and predictability in international economic relations because the institutions that mediated these relations were stable and effective. The United States used its virtual monopoly of international military, economic, and political power to construct and control these structures of dominance. Under U.S. hegemony, exchange rates were stabilized, national markets were kept open to trade and investment, and the raw materials of the Third World remained cheap and abundant. This environment helped sustain a strong trend rate of growth in international trade and investment and provided low-cost imported raw materials to the industrialized world.

Second, there was relative labor peace. The industrial conflict of the 1930s and 1940s induced capital to enter into an implicit and limited "accord" with labor. Organized labor ended its struggle for greater control of the labor process and for control of corporate investment policy in return for official recognition and acceptance by the country's economic and political elite. Workers in the core of the economy achieved a reasonably high rate of real wage growth in the 1950s and 1960s through struggle within the confines of the accord. For its part, capital achieved stability and predictability in its relation with workers and a high trend rate of productivity growth through technical progress and labor-saving investment. Thus, high profit margins could be maintained in a noninflationary environment in spite of rising real wages. And capital was free to reduce union power by investing in the antiunion South and overseas where, of course, there was no accord with labor.

Third, under the stimulus of rising real wages and family incomes made possible by the accord, demand for domestically produced goods and services grew at a strong average rate. Domestic demand was sustained by the growth of the auto industry, the construction of the highway system, the growth of housing and consumer durables in the process of suburbanization, and by government spending on defense and social programs. But export markets were also important, especially in the early postwar years.

Fourth, competition was stabilized and restricted in the core of the economy through the collusion of small numbers of powerful firms and, until the late 1960s, the absence of serious foreign competition. This not only supported high profit margins, it gave corporations the confidence in future profitability that is essential for capital accumulation.

Fifth, not only did the corporate and household sectors enter the period free of significant indebtedness, they owned significant quantities of government bonds or had large savings accounts accumulated during the war. Investment and consumption decisions thus were not constrained by financial burdens. Moreover, the abundance of accumulated corporate and household savings contributed to the low interest rates of the era.

Sixth, U.S. financial markets were insulated from foreign financial markets throughout most of this period. Very little money flowed from one country to another. As a result, through the late 1960s the Fed had reasonably firm control over U.S. interest rates and the rate of growth of domestic money and credit and could use this control to pursue domestic objectives relatively unconstrained by international problems.

In sum, in the first two decades of the postwar period, international as well as domestic institutions supported both stability and high profits in the U.S. economy. Positive trade balances, cheap and stable sources of imported raw materials, and the stability and predictability of the fixed exchange rates of the Bretton Woods system all strongly contributed to the maintenance of U.S. markets and U.S. profit margins. High average profit rates in turn fostered solid growth and a strong rate of investment. At those times when the government wanted to stimulate the economy, it found that corporations would indeed respond to increased national spending by raising production, employment, and investment because it was profitable for them to do so.

Thus, Keynesian regulation was successful in stimulating investment in the 1950s and 1960s in spite of its fundamental structural flaws because the determinants of the profit rate were held in a favorable position and because there were few domestic or international constraints on the use of policy to pursue domestic objectives. However, by 1973 at the latest, it had become clear that the long phase of stable postwar prosperity had come to an end, because the institutions that made it possible crumbled one by one. The effectiveness of macropolicy crumbled with them. Most noteworthy from our perspective is the extent to which the collapse of these institutions and practices and the economic dynamics of the fifteen years that followed was effected by, and in turn affected, the pace and character of the internationalization of production and finance.

First, twenty years of growth and change caused a redistribution of economic and political power among the leading capitalist nations. As U.S. control of international economic events eroded, international rivalry in trade, foreign investment, and access to raw materials broke out. With the decline of U.S. hegemony, the foundation of international institutional stability crumbled. One key reflection of this change was the collapse of the Bretton Woods system in the early 1970s. From that point on, exchange rates fluctuated wildly, adding a new source of uncertainty and instability to the economy. After 1970 the pace of the globalization of financial markets accelerated; the Fed's control of domestic interest rates and the supply of credit weakened continuously.

Second, contradictions embedded in the limited capital–labor accord eventually led to its collapse. Capital had undermined the basis for the accord from the beginning by accumulating capital in nonunion areas. Then in the late 1960s industrial conflict broke out as low unemployment rates helped spark an upsurge in labor militance that contributed to a significant decline in the average profit rate. Of course, capital responded with a multidimensional attack on labor that included support for a high unemployment macropolicy, union-busting tactics, and labor-saving investment. One important weapon in capital's arsenal was its ability to discipline U.S. labor by threatening to substitute foreign for domestic investment and to use foreign rather than domestic components. When key industries like autos and electronics "ran away" on a large scale in the 1970s, the entire U.S. labor movement was weakened. By the early 1980s the volume of U.S. foreign investment seeking cheap labor was substantial.

Thus, the labor militance of the late 1960s and early 1970s eventually accelerated the speed with which U.S. corporations internationalized their operations, a process that in turn helped destroy the power of the U.S. labor movement. Even so, the defeat of U.S. labor was a mixed blessing for U.S. capital. The late 1970s and 1980s have seen a low trend rate of productivity growth and stagnation in real wages and median family incomes. In turn, stagnant working-class income contributed to the rise in household indebtedness of this period, as families struggled to maintain their living standards by borrowing, and it constrained domestic demand, making U.S. industry ever more dependent on foreign markets.

Third, the OPEC oil price increase of 1973–74 inaugurated a period of volatility in petroleum prices and, to a lesser degree, in the price of other raw materials. The end of U.S. hegemony meant the end of guaranteed supplies of cheap imported raw materials.

Fourth, in the 1970s and 1980s both the domestic and the international economies became debt-laden and crisis-prone. Following each of the two OPEC oil price hikes in the 1970s, the Eurodollar market was flooded with dollars deposited by OPEC countries just as stagnant economic conditions overtook Europe and North America. With a huge supply of interest-earning deposits and a weak demand for loans in the First World, multinational banks poured money into the Third World. By 1982, Third World debt was $500 billion; by 1989, it was $1.4 trillion. Financial fragility not only crippled the Third World's ability to buy exports from the developed countries and from its own member nations, it made the solvency of the Third World dependent upon the continued existence of a large U.S. trade deficit (because exports to the U.S. are the major source of dollar earnings paid to banks) and upon low real interest rates on their variable-rate loans.

Domestic financial fragility evolved alongside its international counterpart. The relative indebtedness of nonfinancial corporations increased dramatically from the mid-1960s through 1970 as competitive pressure kept investment spending high while the profit rate declined. It held steady at this higher level until the 1980s, then leapt up again in the Reagan years as corporate America engaged in an orgy of financial speculation with borrowed funds. For example, from 1983 through 1990 the value of mergers and acquisitions of U.S. corporations totaled $1.3 trillion, almost all of it financed by debt. Household indebtedness began its ascent after 1975, as families strove to maintain living standards in the face of stagnant or declining real incomes. The ratio of nongovernment debt to GNP grew by about 40 percent in the 1980s. Meanwhile, banks and other financial institutions relied on increasingly speculative, short-term sources of funds and used them to support ever riskier classes of loans. And of course federal government debt exploded under Reagan and Bush, while the United States emerged as the biggest debtor nation in the world.

Fifth, beginning in the late 1960s the intensity of foreign competition confronting U.S. corporations began a dramatic rise. European, Japanese, and Southeast Asian corporations as well as foreign subsidiaries of U.S. corporations successfully penetrated U.S. markets. The rise in the intensity of competition naturally reduced the domestic rate of profit. Since this was also an era of wildly fluctuating exchange rates, which caused instability in the prices of imported products, the rate of profit became more unstable even as it declined.

This set of institutional and structural changes drastically eroded the necessary conditions for macropolicy effectiveness. After 1970 the use of policy to pursue domestic objectives would often be constrained by problems in the international sector, while the links between policy moves and domestic production and employment became ever more tenuous and uncertain. More important, the trend rate of net capital investment was retarded by two aspects of these developments that Keynesian regulation was powerless to control. First, these structural changes lowered the rate of profit. Second, they dramatically increased the degree of uncertainty associated with expectations of future profit rates and simultaneously increased corporate debt burdens; thus, the capacity of corporations to tolerate risk declined just as capital accumulation became riskier.

Macropolicy under Reagan–Bush: The Collapse of Keynesian Regulation

Entering 1983, with the unemployment rate close to 11 percent, we could look back at fifteen years of instability and stop–go macropolicy and a decade of low growth, high inflation, high unemployment, and the lowest average rate of net capital accumulation in the postwar period. The Reagan expansion that began that year represents the latest phase in the long process of decline in the potential of macropolicy to achieve its traditional domestic objectives. To be sure, Reaganomics did help achieve an average rate of growth of real GNP of almost 4 percent per year from 1983 through 1988 in a context of moderate inflation. But the means used to generate these results left the U.S. and world economies more unbalanced and financially precarious than at any time since the 1930s, and they left macropolicy passive and powerless. The Reagan years demonstrated that in the present era it takes ever more extreme policies to achieve modest short-term gains, policies that only make our long-term situation more intractable. And the Bush years proved that extraordinary fiscal and monetary policy stimulation is now required to avoid economic stagnation.[5]

Reagan's fiscal policy can be summarized concisely. He raised military spending and cut or restrained social programs (other than Social Security and Medicare), raising federal spending as a share of GNP while skewing its priorities to adhere to his reactionary ideology. Meanwhile, he slashed the tax obligations of the rich and of the corporations they own. These policies led to an explosion of the federal budget deficit that began in the second half of 1982 and continues to this day, more than tripling federal debt held by private investors. This orgy of regressive debt-financed fiscal stimulation was the driving force behind the Reagan expansion, but the rising incomes of the expansion also fed the U.S. demand for imports. Simultaneously, the stratospheric real or inflation-adjusted interest rates caused by Volcker's tight money policy were attracting financial capital inflows that raised the exchange value of the dollar by some 60 percent between 1980 and 1985. Since a high exchange rate for the dollar lowers the price of imported goods, this dollar appreciation made it ever easier for foreign companies to penetrate U.S. markets.

As a result, the U.S. trade deficit, which had averaged about $30 billion a year from 1980 through 1982, accelerated rapidly to about $160 billion in 1987. These net imports were, in effect, bought on credit from foreigners. The inflow of foreign "loans" that financed these cumulative U.S. trade deficits quickly destroyed the U.S. position as the world's largest creditor nation, a position that had taken many decades to construct. The U.S. net international investment position was that of a creditor to whom was owed about $364 billion in 1982; by the end of 1989 the United States owed the rest of the world about $440 billion. In other words, the debt-fueled fiscal policy that helped create the expansion of 1983 through 1988, in combination with the Fed's high-interest-rate monetary policy, also made U.S. economic health dependent on foreign credit. The $143 billion in foreign funds that entered the United States in 1986, for example, was far greater than total net business investment in plant and equipment that year.

Between 1985 and 1990 the value of the dollar declined by about 40 percent. This decline first helped stabilize the trade deficit, then contributed to its slow decline. Even so, U.S. debt to the rest of the world will continue to grow in the face of a long string of foreseeable trade deficits in excess of $100 billion.[6] As a result, foreign creditors are able to exercise an increasing degree of influence over U.S. government economic policy. When they disapprove of U.S. policy, they will withdraw their funds from U.S. markets. This will cause a decline (and could cause a collapse) in U.S. financial markets and in the value of the U.S. dollar. The resulting rise in interest rates and decline in stock, bond, and even real estate prices will pressure U.S. officials to adopt policies more to foreign investors' liking. Keep in mind that foreign lenders dislike high growth and low unemployment because the inflation that often accompanies them erodes the value of their assets, and like all creditors, they dislike the low interest rates needed to sustain high growth.

Of course, the enormous trade deficits and the growth of U.S. dependence on foreign capital are not the only dangerous side effects of Reaganomics. Debt-dependence, financial fragility, poverty, inequality, and the deterioration of our natural environment and our economic infrastructure all increased in the 1980s. Nevertheless, this brief discussion of policy and performance under Reagan–Bush should provide an adequate background from which to undertake an assessment of the prospective state of macropolicy in the next decade.

Keynesian Regulation in the 1990s: Prospects and Problems

Prospects for the effective use of government economic policy in pursuit of traditional domestic economic objectives in the coming decade are so dim as to be almost invisible. The Keynesian regulatory mechanism is feeble, constrained by numerous developments, many of which have their origin in the globalization of the economy. The U.S. economy is now deeply imbedded in global markets that are literally out of control.

The necessary conditions for the effectiveness of macropolicy discussed at the beginning of this chapter will provide the framework for my evaluation of the contradictions confronting policymakers in the current era. The first condition was that policymakers must be free to pursue domestic objectives. Today and for the foreseeable future, policy seems constrained from moving aggressively either to stimulate or to restrain economic growth by international problems or the threat of domestic and international financial crisis.

The limitation on expansive monetary policy lies primarily in U.S. dependence on foreign capital and the generally speculative nature of international financial flows. Should monetary policy be used to lower U.S. interest rates (thereby making foreign financial investment in the United States less attractive), it is feared that a flight from the U.S. dollar will take place, causing a sharp decline or even a potential collapse in the exchange rate and in U.S. financial markets generally. For example, foreign lending to the United States slowed dramatically in 1990 in response to a simultaneous fall in U.S. and rise in foreign short-term interest rates. The potential of a dollar collapse is perhaps greater than is commonly realized. In 1987 *private* foreign capital flows to the United States virtually dried up. According to the *New York Times* (1 January 1988), "official [i.e., foreign government] intervention to directly support the dollar [in 1987] amounted to between $100B and $140B or almost all of America's current account deficit." Imagine the U.S. interest rate level that would have been required to attract an additional $140 billion in private foreign lending in 1987 if this foreign-government lending had not taken place.

Expansionary fiscal policy is similarly constrained. The long string of record-breaking peacetime budget deficits racked up by the Reagan–Bush administrations created a consensus view in financial markets that deficit reduction should be our number-one fiscal priority, the onset of recession in late 1990 and its deepening in 1991 notwithstanding. As a result, there has been no effective political support for a policy of deliberately and substantially raising the deficit—currently estimated to be as high as $400 billion in fiscal 1992—in order to fight recession. And even if there were, expansionary policy could, by destroying financial investor "confidence," trigger a rise in long-term interest rates that would counteract to some extent the expansionary effect of the fiscal policy.[7] The use of fiscal stimulation to raise the growth rate (or even simply to prevent a recession) is now out of the question.

But policies designed to slow growth face a major constraint as well: the precarious condition of domestic and international financial markets. Can our overleveraged corporations, our overindebted households, and our speculatively financed banks withstand a long and deep recession without triggering a wave of bankruptcies and a financial crisis? How much more financial carnage would have accompanied the current recession if the Fed had not been able to lower short-term interest rates in 1991? Can the debt-laden countries of the world avoid bankruptcy if real interest rates rise dramatically or if U.S. demand for their exports collapses during a recession? At some point in the near future we may find out. The key point is that fear of these adverse developments may constrain the severity of restrictive policy in the coming years.[8]

The second condition for policy effectiveness is that changes in policy must be capable of causing significant change in the level of aggregate demand. Several links between policy and aggregate demand have been seriously weakened since 1970. First, as noted, the degree of control exercised by the Fed over domestic interest rates and money and credit growth has declined substantially. Second, expansionary fiscal policy tends to raise the inflation rate, which causes an outflow of foreign funds that raises interest rates, thus countering to some extent the intended thrust of the policy. Third, supply-side tax cuts ostensibly designed to raise the percentage of national income devoted to saving and investment have been spectacularly ineffective. The personal tax cuts of the early 1980s were followed by the lowest personal savings rates in postwar history (a fact that did not deter President Bush from proposing even deeper cuts in the capital gains tax). And the huge corporate tax cut in 1981 failed to stimulate investment spending. With a low profit rate, a stagnant national and international economy, excess capacity, and general uncertainty, corporations quite rationally chose to combine their tax cuts with corporate borrowing to finance massive speculation through mergers, acquisitions, stock buy-backs, and general casino action.

The final condition for policy effectiveness is that policy-induced changes in aggregate demand must have the desired effect on domestic economic objectives. Inflation has not been a severe problem since 1982, though it could become one in the foreseeable future. The main short-term problem in the mid-1980s has been import leakage, a problem that will continue to burden policy for many years.

However, it is the long-term problem—the precariousness of the link between increased aggregate demand and increased capital investment—that constitutes the most deeply rooted, intractable impediment to effective Keynesian regulation in the current period. In spite of all the Reagan-era tax breaks, the net rate growth of the capital stock was lower on average in the expansion of the 1980s than it had been in the late 1970s, which in turn was lower than in the late 1960s and early 1970s. Indeed, at its peak year in 1985, real net investment was no higher than it had been in 1979.

Keynesian macropolicy seems powerless to rekindle capital accumulation because it cannot remove all the institutional and structural, domestic and international impediments to sustained investment growth that developed in the 1970s and 1980s. Keynesian regulatory mechanisms cannot change the institutional determinants of the expected profit rate, and they cannot restore stability and predictability to profit expectations. Nor can they recreate financial robustness by removing the debt burdens that restrict demand and threaten crisis in so many sectors of our economy and in so many nations of the world. They cannot even produce a low inflation-adjusted long-term interest rate.

Thus, I conclude that the Keynesian regulatory mechanism is bankrupt. No doubt policy can still be used to dampen short-term bursts of inflation or to generate short-term growth spurts. But the aggressive use of policy for an extended period in pursuit of either expansion or contraction seems out of the question. And the use of policy to recreate another era of stable prosperity by rekindling a long-term investment boom is virtually impossible. The necessary conditions for the effective use of policy in pursuit of domestic objectives have been destroyed, not least of all by the internationalization of production and finance. We seem once again to be at the mercy of the anarchic forces of capitalist markets over which we have little control, just as we were in the 1930s before the creation of the Keynesian state.

What Is to Be Done?

The new global economy is structurally biased against the interests of working people. The pressure on national governments to attract financial capital has raised real interest rates while concern with the balance of trade has led to generally restrictive policies that lower imports and hold down export prices by lowering economic growth and raising unemployment. With high average rates of unemployment around the Western world, labor is perpetually in retreat and capital perpetually dominant. Moreover, internation competition to attract multinational capital investment and financial flows from world markets has pressured national governments into deregulating their economies; international capital flows to those countries that least constrain it. In other words, we live in an era in which markets are global but regulatory mechanisms are national, class-biased, inherently inadequate, and crumbling under the onslaught of international and inter-nation competition.

So the question naturally arises, What is to be done? The analysis used here suggests the need for a democratically constituted regulatory system with more direct public control over the broad contours of the domestic economy than was granted to the Keynesian state. Democratic principles demand that any new regulatory mechanism be popularly constituted and controlled. It is obviously beyond the scope of this chapter to discuss blueprints for a new and more powerful system of economic regulation. Nevertheless, one thing seems clear. Unless the ultimate power to determine such key economic outcomes as the rate of unemployment, the distribution of income and wealth, the level and quality of social services, and the size and composition of investment is taken from the owners of private capital and the dictatorship of the profit rate and placed in the public domain, our economic future will be bleak indeed.

The logic of this essay also suggests the need for more autonomy from the instability and irrationality of the international marketplace. Keynes was right when he argued in the 1930s and 1940s that government controls over the movement of goods and, especially, money across the nation's borders are an essential precondition for effective national economic planning. The internationalization of finance and production has made the need for such autonomy even more pressing today. In the absence of capital controls, any attempt to pursue genuine full employment or other progressive objectives will bring forth the wrath of the international capitalist class in the form of capital flight, a run on the currency, an assault on domestic financial markets, and rising interest rates. These developments will make it impossible to achieve progressive goals.

Of course, the imposition of capital controls does not mean the elimination of international financial flows; it means, rather, their regulation. Under capital controls, the government has the authority to set the conditions under which money can lawfully enter and leave the country. For example, the government might permit unregulated income flows (such as interest payments, dividends, or profits), controlling only the investment and repatriation of the original capital itself. And it might allow capital to be repatriated some months after the government has been notified of the owner's intention to withdraw the funds, a time period that could be altered in length depending on conditions in financial markets.

Opponents of capital controls have questioned their practicality and their efficiency. One argument is that capital controls would raise the cost to the United States of foreign borrowing because they reduce the liquidity of foreign-held assets. They probably would. But they could also help dramatically reduce our reliance on foreign capital because they would remove a powerful impediment to full employment and domestic financial market regulation. Under controls, we could generate a much higher level of domestic saving and could channel these funds away from financial market and real estate speculation toward productive public and private investment. Another objection is that in today's complex telecommunications-based international financial casino, effective capital controls would be technically impossible to construct. The counterargument is that the technical capability of monitoring telecommunications and processing vast quantities of data has itself undergone a revolution; the ability of the U.S. intelligence apparatus to perform such tasks is a case in point.

The most important and convincing evidence in support of the effectiveness of capital controls is historical rather than theoretical. The most successful competitors in world trade in recent decades have made significant use of capital controls to achieve both domestic and international economic objectives. Countries such as Japan, South Korea, and Taiwan come immediately to mind. Until recently, Japan used strict capital controls to keep its large pool of national savings inside the country, providing Japanese corporations with a plentiful supply of low-cost capital to finance all their investment needs. Without controls, this money would have fled to the United States and Europe in search of higher interest rates. Japan's capital controls also prevented foreign investors from gaining control of important sectors of the economy and ensured that Japan was not burdened and constrained by foreign debt. South Korea used capital controls to make sure that the large quantity of foreign grants and loans they received was used for domestic capital formation rather than for imported luxury goods or foreign financial speculation. Neither the Japanese nor the South Korean "miracles" would have been possible without the use of capital controls as an integral component of a government-conceived and government-directed plan for economic development.

Finally, it should be noted that progressive activists have argued that support for capital and trade controls reflects an insular nationalist perspective, one that rejects solidarity with the economic and political struggles of working people around the globe. The fact that a regime of capital and trade controls might be supported by a national chauvinist political movement does not imply that a progressive internationalist economic and political agenda can do without them. Why should a reduction in the degree of control exercised by the international capitalist class over the economic destiny of the United States be harmful to the interests of working people in other countries? On the contrary, the imposition of capital and trade controls would make it possible for a new system of economic regulation to generate sustained full employment, which in turn could help maintain a stable demand for imports and remove the material foundation for protectionist sentiment among U.S. workers.

The bottom line is this: Capital mobility gives the wealthy classes around the globe veto power over the economic policies and priorities of every nation. No progressive, democratically controlled system of economic regulation can function effectively if it does not break that veto power through the imposition of capital controls.

ACKNOWLEDGMENT

This is a revised version of an essay first published in *Instability and Change in the World Economy*, edited by Arthur MacEwan and William K. Tabb. Copyright© 1989 by Arthur MacEwan and William K. Tabb. Reprinted by permission of Monthly Review Foundation.

NOTES

1. For the purpose of this paper, I abstract from the class-biased nature of actual policy formation and focus on the potential of the system to achieve its stated policy goals. Of course, I recognize that in practice, policymakers are generally uninterested in pursuing such a labor-empowering objective as sustained full employment and that they rarely muster much enthusiasm for progressive income or wealth redistribution.

2. I consider standard international policy objectives such as trade balance and a stable exchange rate to be constraints on the ability to attain domestic goals rather than as goals in and of themselves.

3. For a discussion of Keynes's less publicized, more radical views on macrotheory and macropolicy, see Crotty 1983.

4. David Gordon helped popularize the idea that an articulated set of economic and political institutions and practices are required to sustain the rate of profit and the rate of capital accumulation. He coined the term *social structure of accumulation* to represent his particular version of this concept.

5. Economic performance under President Bush was dreadful. The average annual rate of growth of real GNP during his administration was about 0.7 percent—the worst record since Herbert Hoover. Without the improvement that occurred in our trade balance during his term (an improvement that recently came to a halt), there might have been no growth at all. The economy sank into recession in 1990, then moved on to the weakest economic recovery of the postwar era, growing at about half the normal rate. Astoundingly, over the six quarters of recovery through late 1992, the number of private-sector jobs actually declined. From 1989

through 1991 the rate of unemployment rose from 5.2 percent to 7.5 percent while real median family income fell by about 5.0 percent. Two million more people were added to the poverty rolls in 1991 alone.

6. The trade deficit declined substantially in 1990 and 1991, falling to $75 billion in the latter year. However, the main cause of this accelerated decline in the deficit was the economic slowdown and recession of the period, rather than some quantum leap in American productivity. Stagnant incomes and production levels always lead to a falloff in the value of imports. If and when the economy experiences a new expansion, the trend deficit should return to amounts in excess of $100 billion, which is the consensus forecast for the 1993 trade deficit.

7. Economist Alan Blinder stressed this problem in his *Newsweek* column. "Tax cuts might not even work in the current environment. Suppose a relatively small tax reduction—and the huge budget deficit precludes more than that—induces a relatively large adverse reaction in the bond market. Then, rising interest rates might cancel out any stimulus from the tax cut, leaving the deficit larger and the economy no better off" (19 December 1991).

8. The idea that macropolicy is relatively powerless in the current era has become part of the common wisdom. The *New York Times* observed that "as recently as the early 1970's most economists thought they knew how to take the sting out of recessions. What was needed to offset swings in private demand, they argued, was some combination of tax cuts and government spending, plus an increase in funds available for bank loans. . . . [However,] there is no longer anything approaching a consensus on the virtue of intervention in a crisis of current dimensions" (11 December 1991).

The *Wall Street Journal* made a similar observation. "Ever since World War II, the federal government has employed fiscal and monetary policy to battle recessions. But [17 months into] the current slump—so far at least—it has been reluctant to resort to fiscal stimulus. . . . Meanwhile, the Federal Reserve, though much more active, has been singularly ineffective. With lenders shaky and overextended consumers and businesses hesitant to borrow, the Fed has little to show for two years of easing" (9 December 1991).

BIBLIOGRAPHY

Crotty, James. 1983. Keynes and Capital Flight. *Journal of Economic Literature* 21(1): 59–65.
Gordon, David. 1980. Stages of Accumulation and Long Economic Cycles. In *Processes of the World System*, ed. Terence Hopkins and Immanuel Wallerstein, 9–45. Beverly Hills: Sage Publications.
Rohatyn, Felix. 1988. Restoring American Independence. *New York Review of Books*, 18 February, 8–10.

II

CHANGES IN THE
INDUSTRIALIZED WORLD:
NATIONS AND MULTINATIONALS

9
JULIET B. SCHOR

Global Equity and Environmental Crisis: An Argument for Reducing Working Hours in the North

Modern methods of production have given us the possibility of ease and security for all; we have chosen, instead, to have overwork for some and starvation for the others. Hitherto we have continued to be as energetic as we were before there were machines; in this we have been foolish, but there is no reason to go on being foolish forever.
—*Bertrand Russell, "In Praise of Idleness," 1935*

Poverty, Growth, and Global Inequality

For economists, a salient feature of global relations is the wide disparity in standards of living and standards of well-being between the North and the South. The North is rich; the South poor. Estimates of per capita income for 1987 show that the average income in the OECD stood at $14,670, with the U.S. figure even higher at $18,530. By contrast, in the World Bank's low-income countries (comprising 60 percent of the world's population), the average person earned only $290. Middle-income countries were much closer to the bottom end of the scale, with an average figure of $1,810 (World Bank 1989:table 1).

Other measures tell a similar story. The infant mortality rate (for children under five), thought by UNICEF to be the best summary statistic of overall social development, also reveals tremendous global inequality. The United States had an infant mortality rate of 13 (per 1,000 live births) in 1987, while 63 nations, with a total population of 2 billion, were at over 100 (UNICEF 1989:table 1). Similar inequalities are found in literacy rates, life expectancy, access to safe water, and the like.

Figures on resource use also highlight global inequity. The rich countries consume a disproportionate share of the world's resources. The developed countries (accounting for 26 percent of the world's population) consume 85 percent of the world's paper, 79 percent of its steel, 86 percent of other metals, and 80 percent of commercial energy (WCED 1987).

One obvious method of redress is to redistribute resources and in-

183

come on a world scale. There are a variety of mechanisms through which a North–South resource transfer could be effected: direct foreign aid, the SDR link, recycling of trade surpluses, policy-induced increases in commodity prices, reduction of OECD tariff barriers against the South, or the regulation of transnational corporations.

A thoroughgoing redistribution could solve both the problem of global inequity and that of absolute deprivation, and shows clearly that the "development problem" is not due to overpopulation. A total leveling of world GNP would provide a per capita income figure of $3,644 (in 1988 dollars).[1] Although this amount is clearly inadequate to keep the population of the OECD out of nationally based definitions of poverty, it would be a princely sum in South and East Asia and sub-Saharan Africa, where 65 percent of the world's population lives. It is also far higher than that enjoyed even in the upper-middle-income countries, which include much of South America. Even a modest redistribution of 10 percent of the per capita income of the OECD (which would leave average income at $13,203), would be sufficient to increase income in the low-income countries by $388, which more than doubles current levels. A 20 percent redistribution would raise income in the poorest countries by $776. This would put those countries over $1,000, while leaving the OECD in absolute affluence.

Redistribution carries moral appeal to many, but it has proven difficult to implement. After decades of "development dialogue" between North and South, foreign aid remains a trivial portion of national income. In the 1980s, official aid programs were eclipsed in the wake of the debt crisis. To pay interest and principal on their loans, Southern debtors were forced to provide net transfers to the North. According to World Bank estimates, between 1982 and 1988, net transfers from developing countries were $85 billion (1988:29–30). This is redistribution with a vengeance.

The political difficulty with a North-to-South redistribution is not hard to identify. The rich countries, and particularly the rich within them, benefit from the current structure of inequality. As was painfully apparent in the debate over a New International Economic Order, the wealthy are unwilling to give up much without a fight.

This may be why the Brandt report stressed the self-interest of the North in aiding the South. The commission report argued:

> The North–South debate is often described as if the rich were being asked to make sacrifices in response to the demands of the poor. We reject this view. . . . Above all, the achievement of economic growth in one country depends increasingly on the performance of others. The South cannot grow adequately without the North. The North cannot prosper or improve its situation unless there is greater progress in the South. (Brandt Commission 1980:33)

The macroeconomic developments of the 1980s cast doubt on this assumption of strong commonality of economic interests, at least in any narrow sense. The impact of economic adversity has surely been softened in the North by the decline in the price of oil and other commodities, as well as by the net resource transfers from the South. The Brandt Commission's position brings to mind a disturbing question: if the rich and powerful would be so much better off by helping the poor, why are they so resistant?

The political impediments to a large-scale North–South redistribution are formidable. Given the magnitude of redistribution schemes in both the present and at least the foreseeable future, redistribution will be at best a necessary, rather than sufficient, solution to the economic problems of the South. The stinginess of the North is too great. Thus, it seems clear that redistribution must be coupled with some other strategy.

The strategy that development economics has identified has been, of course, the strategy of growth. During the forty or so years that "development" has existed as a subfield of economics, its dominant premise has been the need to maximize growth in developing countries. What Amartya Sen (1983) has called the "major strategic themes" of development—industrialization, rapid capital accumulation, mobilization of underemployed manpower, and an economically active state—are all essentially strategies for growth. Even the critics of standard development approaches—underdevelopment theorists, basic-needs advocates, Marxists, or those criticizing growth without development—underscore the need for at least some type of growth in some types of output.

The record of the 1960s and 1970s shows considerable success in achieving rapid growth in the South, although the gap between North and South has widened. From 1960 to 1973, average annual growth rates in the LDCs were 6.3 percent. From 1973 to 1979, the rate fell to 5.2 percent. Population growth reduced the extent to which increases in output were able to raise living standards, because per capita growth rates were considerably less, approximately 2.6 percent over the period. Since then, a substantial number of poor countries have experienced absolute declines in per capita GNP. On average, per capita income growth in LDCs during the 1980s was only 1.8 percent.

For the most part, the economic failures of the 1980s have been met with the conviction that higher growth is needed, either from the North, which would act as a locomotive, or originating in the South itself. In recent years, however, growth itself has come under considerable scrutiny as environmental awareness has become widespread. The scope of environmental degradation now occurring on a world scale has called into question the feasibility of growth.

The Environmental Constraint on Growth

Today's environmental crisis is multifaceted, encompassing a wide variety of ecological problems. Among the major aspects of environmental degradation are toxic wastes, air and water pollution, global warming, the depletion of the ozone layer, deforestation, desertification, soil erosion, and the loss of plant and animal species.[2]

The diversity of environmental problems implies a diversity of causal factors. Some problems are primarily local, others global. Some are primarily the result of patterns of production and consumption in the rich countries. Others result from the pressures of population and development in the poor nations. In some cases, we can point to a single chemical or process that is producing destructive effects. In other cases, the apparently seamless web of an entire life-style is implicated.

A key point is the link between environmental degradation and aggregate output growth. Although choice of technology and product and numerous other factors are key determinants of the extent of environmental degradation, it is difficult to deny the role of growth itself. More production of steel and autos creates more air pollution and global warming, more newspapers and houses lead to the felling of more trees, more food generally implies more pesticides, and increased output in the petrochemical industry is accompanied by a rise in toxic substances. Green political movements, especially those in Western Europe, have argued in favor of zero growth, on the grounds that the environmental effects of growth outweigh the needs of affluent societies for more production.

The conclusion that growth is environmentally destructive implies that there is some (in principle) identifiable relation between growth and environmental change. Therefore, we can also identify a maximum feasible rate of growth of world output, relative to any degree of environmental degradation, stasis, or reconstruction. For example, if we begin with a goal of no change in the environmental status of the earth (no further degradation, no reconstruction), then, given the existing set of technologies and patterns of production and consumption, we can in theory specify a feasible rate of growth of output. (There is no guarantee this rate would even be a positive number, but for the purposes of the present argument, speculation about its actual value can be deferred.) The relation between output growth and environmental change is called the growth–environment frontier.

If we assume that there is the capacity for environmentally beneficial change in technology and in patterns of production and consumption (an outward shift of the growth–environment frontier), then higher rates of growth of output will be compatible with the goal of no environmental change. Over the short run, however, except under extremely favorable, and most likely unrealistic, assumptions about technological change and the transformation of production and consumption, it is hard to imagine that the environmentally feasible rate of world output growth could be higher than the rates we have actually experienced during the last few decades.

Clearly, a reduction in growth alone cannot solve the environmental crisis, and as noted above, the environmentally feasible rate of growth may be too low to be politically acceptable, given current production and consumption patterns. Realistically, a reduction in the world's growth rate will have to occur in concert with other measures, such as alterations in energy use, regulation of toxic and other polluting substances, and reforestation. My emphasis here on growth is not intended to minimize the urgency of those tasks. However, in the absence of dramatic technological break-throughs, for the medium term at least, it is difficult to conceive of a solution to the environmental crisis that does not include a decrease in growth.

But reducing growth is a formidable task. Growth has been the cornerstone of the economic and political structures of most of the nations of both the capitalist and socialist worlds. Reversing that trend would be difficult to engineer even under the most auspicious conditions, and conditions now are not auspicious. Rather, we are facing environmental crisis at a time when a large fraction of the world's population is malnourished, without adequate health care, housing, or productive employment. In short, growth is becoming constrained at a time when "basic needs" are far from being met on a widespread scale around the world. We are on the horns of a profound dilemma.

For those who care about meeting those needs *and* beginning to undo the damage we have been doing to our planet, a globally uniform reduction of growth is not acceptable. Instead, an unequal allocation of feasible growth rates, like those between North and South, appears to be a plausible solution to the dilemma. If our goal were progress toward the equalization of income and wealth on a global scale, we might advocate that all growth occur in the South. Given the existing disparities in output, this would mean a very large percentage increase in the South. For example, a 1 percent world rate of growth is currently equivalent to an increase of $171 billion in GNP, which translates into a 5.6 percent rise in the LDCs. If the world growth target were set at 2 percent, LDCs would be able to grow 11 percent and still remain within the target. This is far higher than these countries have actually been able to grow, even under the relatively favorable conditions of the 1970s.[3]

Just as the reduction of world growth is not a sufficient but may be a necessary condition for environmental regeneration, aggregate income growth in the South is necessary but not sufficient for increasing welfare. As numerous critics of development policy have argued, changes in income distribution, the devolution of political and economic power to the people at the bottom, the provision of resources to satisfy basic needs, and other measures are imperative. However, it is unlikely that poor countries can solve their problems without increases in aggregate levels of output.

The Case for Reduced Working Hours in the North

Thus far, my argument has been that a reallocation of growth on a global basis is a policy measure that would address both environmental and equity concerns simultaneously. Can a case be made for implementing this scenario?

Perhaps so, but bear in mind that what was politically astute in the Brandt Commission's approach was the assumption that the North would not act altruistically. Policies that provided benefits for both North and South were seen to have a higher likelihood of success. Whether the proposals of the commission were in fact mutually beneficial is of course another story, and a plausible case can be made that they were not. But whatever the answer to that question, it does seem clear that the debate over the commission's proposals should teach us a lesson about Northern intransigence.

How does a policy to reallocate growth to the South fare on the grounds of regional self-interest? Is it likely to be politically popular in the North? Are the economics of low or zero growth feasible?

Assume that the North adopts a zero output growth target, allowing all growth to occur in the South. For the sake of simplicity, assume also that there is no population growth in the North. With no growth in output permitted, all productivity growth must be channeled into shorter hours. If the North maintains a rate of annual productivity growth of 3 percent, and if we assume a base work year of 1,800 hours, which is roughly the current average for manufacturing workers in the North (Bureau of Labor Statistics 1989), then within ten years annual hours would stand at 1,340. In just over twenty years, total labor time worked per person would be halved. The North could have either a four-day work week with six months of vacation each year or alternating-year work schedules with paid sabbaticals in between. Money income (adjusted for inflation) would be constant.

Economic Feasibility

Is this an economically feasible scenario? It is impossible to give a comprehensive answer to this question within the confines of this chapter.

In the South, the dominant effect will occur as a result of the stimulus to Southern growth that Northern demand now provides. Since the interwar years, the South has relied heavily on exports to the North to bolster its growth rate. It is difficult to know precisely what the impact of prolonged zero Northern growth will be, as it is far beyond the range of current experience. However, we do have current estimates of elasticities of Southern to Northern growth. For example, the World Bank's estimate of this elasticity within the "central" range of Northern growth (3.7 percent GDP growth) in 1986–87 is that a decline of one percentage point of Northern GDP growth will result in approximately a one percentage point decline in the South. The decline will be largest in those countries that are probably most able to afford it, namely manufacturing exporters. Primary commodity exports are only half as responsive as manufactures. At lower rates of Northern growth the elasticity is less.

For those who advocate a "locomotive" strategy of Southern growth, these effects will be sufficient to reject the no-Northern-growth scenario (e.g., Lewis 1980). However, a significant body of opinion has argued that dependence on Northern demand is a damaging structural relationship that the South ought to overcome. Self-reliance, selective delinking, and the growth of South–South trade have commanded widespread attention as the only feasible long-term strategies to overcome Southern dependence and achieve true development (Diaz-Alejandro 1978; Streeten 1981: ch. 10; Taylor 1982, 1991).

If the critics of the locomotive relationship are too optimistic and if the South cannot expand production sufficiently in the face of zero Northern growth, then compensatory mechanisms may be necessary. Reductions in tariffs, quotas, and nontariff barriers would expedite Southern growth. The North currently erects higher protective barriers to Southern goods than it does within its own territory. Given the beneficial effects that massive reductions in working time can be expected to have on unemployment, protectionist pressures in the North may eventually be eased.

It may also be worth noting that for some countries, namely, primary-commodity exporters, even current scenarios predict a long-term decline in demand from the North, given ongoing shifts toward services and away from traditional manufacturing processes. Alternative strategies for growth are probably already inevitable.

Political Context

As is often the case with social transformations, economic feasibility is less of a problem than political viability. In the case of hours reductions, the perspective of neoclassical theory would counsel that such a policy would reduce social welfare and be unpopular as a result.

In mainstream economic theory, the determination of labor hours depends on workers' choices: they look at the wage rate being offered by the employer, and they are free to decide how much they want to work and how much leisure they want; if the employer wants them to work more than they want, they simply find an employer who will provide the right mix of work and leisure time.[4] By this argument, workers in the North are already working just the amount that they want. Therefore, if this is true, Northern workers would oppose any reduction in their work hours.

I believe this view to be seriously flawed. In order to argue that point, I begin with a weak claim, which is that this neoclassical, or mainstream, position is not sustainable in the face of evidence on labor markets and consumption patterns. In fact, hours reductions might be preferred by Northern workers.

Working Hours and Economic Theory

Institutionalist and Marxist economists have long argued that businesses and governments set hours and that worker choice is strictly limited. Neoclassical economists countered weakly that workers can choose the number of jobs they work or the number of years they are in the labor force, but clearly these options provide only limited flexibility. In recent years, these issues have been explored in the labor economics literature. There is now an accumulating body of evidence, for the United States at least, that suggests that constraints on hours are widespread.

The lack of free choice in hours is strongly supported by survey data in the United States. For example, in the Panel Study on Income Dynamics, 85 percent of working male heads of households reported that they faced some kind of hours constraint (minimum, maximum, or both) (Kahn and Lang 1987). Of those surveyed, 15 percent could work more but not fewer hours, 27 percent could work fewer but not more, and 43 percent could work neither more nor less. For a substantial fraction of workers, these constraints are binding.

I have argued elsewhere that capitalist firms have strong incentives to maintain long hours for their workers (Schor 1987). The argument is in the spirit of Marx (1976), and notes that long hours facilitate the firm's control over workers. Long hours also increase the size of the unemployment pool, which improves the terms on which firms can hire labor. Firms also prefer long hours in part because they can save on fringe benefits and utilize factories and equipment more intensively.[5]

If employers are generally in the position of exercising power over employees, then the firm's preference for long hours will result in a systematic bias in that direction. Indeed, the history of the trade-union struggle for shorter hours suggests the plausibility of this view. That history also reveals that hours have been reduced under two general circumstances. The first is during recessions or depressions, when hours reductions are a form of involuntary underemployment. The second is when trade unions are powerful enough to pressure employers or the state into reducing hours.

The growth of capitalist production was associated with an increase in hours, and the mid-nineteenth century represented a peak in levels of working hours in industrialized nations (Schor 1987). Since the mid-nineteenth century, hours have fallen substantially. In the United States, weekly hours were roughly halved between 1850 and 1950. Similar reductions obtained in many Western European countries. For the most part, the industrialized countries of the North followed a common path of dramatic reductions in working time.

Trends in Working Hours in the OECD

Since the Second World War, however, trends in hours in the North have diverged. Hours in Western Europe have continued to fall substantially, while those in the United States have remained relatively constant. Any discussion of the postwar period, however, should also consider Japan, where hours are far longer than in other countries at comparable stages of development. Table 9.1 presents total hours worked per employee in manufacturing in twelve countries of the North between 1950 and 1988. The divergence of trends is evident. In Western Europe, hours have been reduced on average slightly over 20 percent since 1950, while in the United States there has been almost no reduction (1.8 percent only).

The divergence in hours trends suggests that the North is not homogeneous on the issue of hours reductions. The political and economic contexts of Western Europe, the United States, and Japan differ considerably.

TABLE 9.1
Hours Worked per Employee in Manufacturing: International Comparisons

	1950	1960	1970[a]	1979	1988	% Decrease 1950–88
Belgium	n.a.	2,022	1,870	1,638	1,565[b]	n.a.
Canada	2,048	1,949	1,918	1,859	1,887	7.9
Denmark	2,232	2,080	1,829	1,639	1,618	27.5
France	1,955	1,955	1,872	1,712	1,618	17.2
Germany	2,293	2,068	1,889	1,717	1,619	29.4
Italy	1,851	1,918	1,905[c]	1,738[c]	1,849[c]	0.1
Japan	2,298	2,509	2,269	2,159	2,180	5.1
Netherlands	2,088	2,116	1,893[d]	1,669[d]	1,579[d]	24.4
Norway	2,047	1,972	1,794	1,572	1,558	23.9
Sweden	2,131	2,003	1,744	1,513	1,499	29.7
U.K.	2,138	2,118	1,939[e]	1,886	1,856	13.2
U.S.	1,978	1,940	1,913	1,907	1,942	1.8

Source: Bureau of Labor Statistics 1989.
[a]Series undergoes some revisions from 1970 for most countries.   [b]1987.   [c]Based on full-time job equivalents.   [d]Based on worker-years.   [e]1971.

The case that hours reductions would be welfare enhancing is most straightforward for Western Europe. This is because reductions in work time have remained a major demand of the trade-union movement throughout the post–World War II period. This has been true both during the years of rapid growth and since the onset of stagnation after 1979. In fact, since 1979, popular pressure for fewer hours has increased considerably. In earlier years, the case for lower hours was cast primarily in terms of the enhanced quality of life made possible by more leisure. Since 1979, the movement has stressed the potential of shorter hours to reduce unemployment. However, the growth of postindustrial and "green" thinking has also had a strong influence on the debate over work time. Green tendencies have stressed freedom from alienating and environmentally destructive labor and the need for more time to engage in community-enhancing and socially productive activity. The German struggles over shorter hours are perhaps the most well known, but similar conflicts have been occurring throughout Western Europe.

The growth in labor pressure during the 1980s for reduced hours has not been particularly successful, with gains in leisure time below the achievements of earlier decades. The relative failure of the movement can be attributed in part to heightened economic adversity and competitive pressures, as well as the growth of business hegemony and conservative economic ideology. It may also be that emphasis on the ability of hours reduction to cure unemployment weakened the case, on account of considerable evidence that unemployment would not respond substantially. Anne van Lancken (1986) observed that a stalemate on hours reductions had taken hold by the mid-1980s, which could only be broken by common, EEC-wide agreements, owing to strong competitive intra-European pressures.

Trade-union support for hours reductions remains strong, but it has been argued that this demand has "lost its mobilizing power and popularity with the workforce" on account of its failure to create jobs, continuing employment insecurity, and the heightened intensity of work and lower wages that often accompanied hours reductions in the 1980s (van Lancken 1986:14). However, the literature is optimistic about the prospects for hours reductions if common, Europe-wide agreements can be made (van Lancken 1986). Particularly in the context of European unification, common agreements can achieve hours reductions without intra-European competitive effects and can thereby overcome the negative pressures on wages and the pace of work. It is quite possible that popular agitation for more free time will increase substantially during the 1990s.

In the United States, the case for hours reductions hinges on its peculiar trend in market hours, that is, hours worked in the paid labor force outside the home. Despite a doubling of productivity since 1950, it appears that per capita working hours in the United States have not fallen. Unfortunately, the data on total hours worked from the National Income and Product Accounts was discontinued in 1979. However, between 1950 and 1979, that measure shows a rise in annual hours per person (Schor 1987: table 1). A separate estimate, based on survey data from the Current Population Survey, has been done for the years 1969–87, and it also shows an increase, from 1,249 to 1,350 hours per year (Leete-Guy and Schor 1993: table 1).

Part of what is going on is that a higher proportion of the population is engaged in paid work as a result of increased women's labor-force participation. But in the last twenty years, hours per labor-force participant have risen as well (Leete-Guy and Schor 1992:table 5). One reason is that it is becoming more common for one worker to hold more than one job. A second is that paid time off has only increased by about 8.6 days. American workers have only about half as much vacation, holiday, and paid leave time as their Western European counterparts (Leete-Guy and Schor 1993:table 14). The larger picture is perhaps best seen in the manufacturing-hours data in Table 9.1. Hours per employee have just not fallen in forty years.

Perhaps the most obvious explanation for the rise in hours is that, unlike in Western Europe, unions in the States after World War II did not wage a serious battle to reduce work time. This failure represented a departure from a long tradition of resistance to long hours. The reasons are various: the expulsion of the Communist unions from the AFL and CIO, labor's acceptance of "the American dream," the early institution of premium pay for overtime work, and the relative weakness of labor and strength of business in both the economic and political arenas.[6]

There are growing signs that long hours are beginning to take a toll on U.S. families and, in particular, on the women in them who are responsible for the bulk of domestic labor. Arlie Hochschild's recent book, *The Second Shift*, provides a sobering picture of the time squeeze facing employed parents. Media accounts of overwork appear regularly, and according to the Harris poll (Harris 1988), Americans report 16.6 median hours of weekly leisure, down from 26.2 hours in 1973.

The overwork that American workers may be experiencing does not translate easily into effective political support for hours reductions. The erosion of union power relative to that of management, the preponderant influence of business on state policy, and the hegemony of laissez-faire doctrines militate against legislated reductions in hours. However, growing environmental and feminist awareness suggest that support for hours reductions may come from historically unexpected quarters. The United States is unlikely to take the lead in a Northern initiative to lower work time, but it may well be willing to follow greener allies in Europe.

Japan presents a third model of postwar work time. As is well known, Japanese workers toil far longer than others in the North. Annual hours of work in 1984 were estimated at over 2,100 (Yamada 1985). The five-day week is not yet common, applying to only about 25 percent of the work force. Annual paid leave is short, and only 60 percent of granted paid leave time is even taken by employees. (Public holidays, set at sixteen or seventeen per year in large firms, do exceed Western standards, however.)

The trends in working hours in post–World War II Japan are unlike those elsewhere. The immediate postwar restructuring led to increasing hours, from an average of 2,338 in 1955 to 2,432 in 1960. After 1960, however, hours fell steadily, as prosperity-induced labor shortages and companies' recruitment efforts led to reduced hours. By 1975, hours had fallen by 15 percent to 2,064. However, after 1975, hours began to rise again. This trend has not yet abated, despite the fact that the Japanese economy has performed so well in recent years.

According to Yamada, "working time has become a central labour policy issue" (1985:715). Unions have now taken it up as one of their main demands. The Ministry of Labor has also set reduced working hours as a major priority. The state is hoping to use decreases in work time as part of its response to international pressure to reduce the trade surplus. Firms have taken a predictable position, arguing that hours reduction must be in line with productivity advances. However, productivity growth in Japan is sufficiently rapid that this should not be a major obstacle.

Thus, political support appears to be quite favorable for a policy of declining work hours. What is more problematic in Japan is an acceptance of zero or slow growth. Japanese businesses and the state are heavily committed to a fast-growth, high-investment, export-oriented economy and notoriously inattentive to environmental concerns. It is likely that tremendous international pressure will be necessary to induce Japanese policymakers to conform to a zero-growth scenario.

Ultimately, I believe the case on the welfare impact of reducing work hours is most convincingly made by what workers themselves say about the issue. There is an interesting coincidence of survey results that argues well for the zero-growth–hours-reduction proposal. Apparently, workers in all three regions have expressed their support for trading off future income in favor of leisure. In a very detailed 1980 U.S. study, 84 percent of all workers indicated that their preference was to give up at least 40 percent of future income for increased leisure; 49 percent wanted to trade *all* future pay raises for more free time (Best 1980). A 1978 EEC survey also found that "in a straightforward choice between shorter hours and better pay in the European Community, more respondents to a survey favored the former—both overall and in six countries out of the nine" (Clarke 1983:140). And in Japan, a mid-1980s survey of younger workers revealed that they are not different from their counterparts in the West on this issue, "probably" preferring a reduction of working time to a wage increase (Yamada 1985:704–5).[7]

These surveys reveal a very different picture from those concerned with current hours and income, which typically ask, Would you be willing to give up an hour of pay for an hour of free time? In those surveys a majority of workers in many countries consistently answer no. I have argued elsewhere (Schor 1987, 1992) that their negative answers are due to a strong aversion to reducing any given level of consumption and should not necessarily be seen as expressing satisfaction with current working hours. If consumption is habit-forming, as Scitovsky (1976) and others have argued (convincingly, I think), then queries about current hours become rather meaningless. More relevant are those on future income cited above, which speak to the zero-growth scenario.

Of course, the fact that workers say they would like more leisure in the future in no way implies that they will get it. Indeed, I argued above that business is particularly averse to shorter hours. However, a touch of optimism on this score may not be out of place. Technological developments, worker preferences, and increasing environmental pressure may render business's opposition less vigorous than in the past. Declining labor supply in the North may force corporations to be more responsive to workers' needs for time. An energetic social movement consisting of greens, labor, and advocates for the South will be necessary to make this scenario a reality. I expect the leadership for such a movement would come from Europe, with the United States and Japan strictly followers.

From the perspective of the early 1990s—fraught as they have been with unemployment, declines in real wages for many, and heightened international competition—the prospect of a four-hour workday may strike some as hopelessly utopian. But as environmental oblivion appears more and more possible with every passing year, one cannot but wonder if those who think we can continue with the status quo are not the utopians. If those of us in the North can free ourselves from the need to consume more and more each year, as well as from the competitive economic institutions that pit us against each other, liberation from work is plausible. However, it will require no less than a profound cultural transformation. In the words of Andre Gorz, "For 200 years our societies have been dominated by the productivist ethic which has sanctified work as mortification and sacrifice, as a renunciation of life and pleasure, of the freedom to be oneself." The time has come to "destroy it and replace it with an ethic which privileges the values of voluntary cooperation, self-determination, creativity and the quality of our relations with each other and with nature" (1985:107).

ACKNOWLEDGMENTS

This chapter was prepared for the Symposium on Global Issues of the World Development Institute, Boston University. I would like to thank Prasannan Parthasarathi, Danny Schydlowsky, Paul Streeten, and the members of the symposium. Research assistance was provided by Deepak Bhargava. This is an abridged version of an article that originally appeared in *World Development* 19 (1) (1991): 73–84; *World Development* is published by Pergamon Press Ltd., Oxford, U.K.

NOTES

1. Calculated as total world GDP ($17.125 trillion) divided by total population (4.699 billion). Data from World Bank 1989.
2. See Brown et al. 1989 and previous years, WCED 1987, and United Nations Environment Programme 1987 and other years.
3. Growth rates were calculated on the basis of GDP figures from World Bank 1989.
4. I will assume a one-period model here, abstracting from decisions about future versus present consumption, which would unnecessarily complicate the discussion.
5. Labor historians have long recognized this point. There are two excellent, recent studies by Benjamin Hunnicutt (1988) and David Roediger and Philip Foner (1989), both of which provide extensive documentation of capitalists' resistance to shorter hours.
6. Both Hunnicutt (1988) and Roediger and Foner (1989) discuss labor's inactivity. See also my *Overworked American*.
7. I have not yet found comparable survey data for all Japanese workers.

BIBLIOGRAPHY

Best, F. 1980. *Exchanging Earnings for Leisure: Findings of an Exploratory National Survey on Work Time Preferences*. R&D Monograph 79, Employment and Training Administration, U.S. Department of Labor.
Brandt Commission. 1980. *North South: A Programme for Survival*. London: Pan Books.
Brown, Lester, et al. 1989. *State of the World Atlas*. New York: W.W. Norton.
Bureau of Labor Statistics. 1989. Underlying Data for Indexes of Output Per Hour, Hourly Compensation, and Unit Labor Costs in Manufacturing, Twelve Industrial Countries, 1950–1988. Office of Productivity and Technology, June.
Clarke, Oliver. 1983. The Work Ethic: An International Perspective. In *The Work Ethic—A Critical Analysis*, ed. Jack Barbash et al., 121–50. Madison, Wis.: Industrial Relations Research Association.
Diaz-Alejandro, Carlos. 1978. Delinking North and South: Unshackled or Unhinged? In *Rich and Poor Nations in the World Economy*, ed. A. Fishlow et al. New York: McGraw-Hill.

Gorz, Andre. 1985. *Paths to Paradise: On the Liberation from Work.* Boston: South End Press.

Harris, Louis. 1988. *Americans and the Arts.* Project report of Louis Harris and Associates, Inc. New York: Louis Harris and Associates.

Hochschild, Arlie. 1989. *The Second Shift: Working Parents and the Revolution at Home.* New York: Viking Penguin.

Hunnicutt, Benjamin Kline. 1988. *Work without End: Abandoning Shorter Hours for the Right to Work.* Philadelphia: Temple University Press.

Kahn, Shulamit, and Kevin Lang. 1987. Constraints on the Choice of Work Hours: Agency vs. Specific-Capital. Working paper no. 2238, National Bureau of Economic Research, Cambridge, Mass.

Leete-Guy, Laura, and Juliet B. Schor. 1990. Is There a Time Squeeze? Estimates of Market and Non-Market Hours in the United States, 1969–1987. Harvard University, Cambridge, Mass. Mimeo.

———. 1993. Assessing the Time Squeeze Hypothesis: Estimates of Market and Non-Market Hours in the U.S., 1969–1989. *Industrial Relations,* forthcoming.

Lewis, W. Arthur. 1980. The Slowing Down of the Engine of Growth. *American Economic Review* 70(5): 555–64.

Marx, Karl. 1976. *Capital.* Trans. David Fernbach. Vol. 1. New York: Vintage.

Roediger, David, and Philip Foner. 1989. *Our Own Time: A History of American Labor and the Working Day.* London: Verso.

Russell, Bertrand. 1935. *In Praise of Idleness and Other Essays.* New York: W.W. Norton.

Schor, Juliet B. 1987. Toil and Trouble: Leisure in a Capitalist Economy. Harvard University, Cambridge, Mass. Mimeo.

———. 1992. *The Overworked American: The Unexpected Decline of Leisure.* New York: Basic Books.

Schor, Juliet B., and Samuel Bowles. 1987. Employment Rents and the Incidence of Strikes. *Review of Economics and Statistics* 49(4): 584–92.

Scitovsky, T. 1976. *The Joyless Economy: An Inquiry into Human Satisfaction and Consumer Dissatisfaction.* Oxford: Oxford University Press.

Sen, A. K. 1983. Development: Which Way Now? *Economic Journal* 93:745–62.

Shapiro, Carl, and Joseph Stiglitz. 1984. Equilibrium Unemployment as a Worker Discipline Device. *American Economic Review* 74(3): 433–44.

Streeten, Paul. 1981. *Development Perspectives.* New York: St. Martin's Press.

Taylor, Lance. 1982. Back to Basics: Theory for the Rhetoric in North–South Negotiations. *World Development* 10(4): 327–35.

———. 1991. Economic Openness—Problems to the Century's End. In *The Limits of Liberalization,* ed. Tariq Banuri, WIDER Studies in Development Economics. Oxford: Oxford University Press.

UNICEF. 1989. *The State of the World's Children.* Oxford: Oxford University Press.

United Nations Environment Programme. 1987. *The State of the World Environment.* Nairobi: UNEP.

van Lancken, Anne. 1986. A Long Way to Shorter Hours. Brussels. Mimeo.

World Bank. 1988. *World Development Report.* New York: Oxford University Press.

World Bank. 1989. *World Development Report.* New York: Oxford University Press.

World Commission on Environment and Development (WCED). 1987. *Our Common Future*. Oxford: Oxford University Press.

Yamada, Narumi. 1985. Working Time in Japan: Recent Trends and Issues. *International Labour Review* 124(6): 699–718.

10 GERALD EPSTEIN

The United States as a Debtor Country

The United States, once the world's largest creditor nation, is now the world's largest debtor, owing more money to foreigners than it is owed by them. This turnabout has come swiftly. As recently as 1985 the United States was in the black; four years later U.S. foreign debt stood at more than $650 billion—roughly 12 percent of its gross national product (GNP). And in the next few years, most economists agree, U.S. foreign indebtedness could reach $1 trillion.

Although no one disputes America's increased dependence on foreign capital, what all of this borrowing means for the United States and the world is less obvious, as the range of "expert" opinion on the subject suggests. To investment banker Felix Rohatyn (1989), it represents a loss of U.S. "economic independence." America's international debt, he contends, has made us more vulnerable to the vagaries of foreign capital and less able to influence world events. Harvard economist Benjamin Friedman (1988) warns of a "day of reckoning" when we, our children, or our grandchildren will have to pay for our sins of profligacy. And according to William Cline of the Institute for International Economics, we will pay either by fire (a financial panic as foreigners lose confidence and abruptly withdraw their funds) or by ice (a long, slow, painful decline in our standard of living as we hand over more and more of our earnings to foreigners in debt payments). For these analysts, it is time to face the music and tighten our belts, to cut government spending, raise taxes, and end our national "consumption binge."

Keynesian economist Robert Eisner (1990) disagrees. The United States is not really that much in debt, he argues. And besides, a little debt is a useful thing, providing demand for goods and services that keeps the economy—ours and the rest of the world's—growing and prospering. In fact, say the supply-siders, we should celebrate. Foreigners want to invest here because our brand of supply-side capitalism, which is now being embraced by converts from behind the former Iron Curtain, has been so profitable. Foreign investments, Arthur Laffer contends, will make our economy even more productive, profitable, and cheery.

Each of these views has its supporters, but despite their popularity, they provide at best only a partial explanation of America's international debt position. What is missing from all of these views is an understanding of the role the globalization of U.S. corporations has played in the creation of the country's foreign-debt problem. Paradoxically, the United States is today the world's largest debtor in part because it is also the world's largest overseas investor and home to many of the world's largest multinational corporations. In an age of globalized production, these corporations have progressively abandoned their commitment to the United States, with negative consequences not only for America's balance of payments but also for the U.S. standard of living.

In many ways America's international-debt problem is thus a symptom of a larger and more serious problem—the mobility of capital. By failing to come to grips with this problem, all of the currently popular responses to our foreign-debt problem—which range from cutting the budget deficit to curbing foreign investment in the United States—can only make matters worse.

U.S. Foreign Debt: An Overview

Each year billions of dollars enter and leave the United States in search of a profitable return. These flows of investment cumulate in stocks of U.S. assets held abroad and foreign assets held in the United States. When the stock of assets held by Americans abroad is larger than the stock of assets held by foreigners here, the United States is said to be in a net creditor position. Conversely, when the stock of assets held by foreigners in the United States is greater than that held by Americans abroad, the United States is in a net debtor position, as it has been since 1985 (see Figure 10.1).[1]

Foreign investment here and U.S. investment abroad can take several forms. Most foreign investment involves buying financial assets, either stocks or bonds. The main distinction between different types of financial investments is whether or not they confer "control" over the company in question. Those that do are called direct investments; those that do not are called portfolio investments. Since it is extremely difficult to determine whether a particular investment confers actual control, an arbitrary figure is chosen for statistical purposes. Thus, if an investor buys 10 percent or more of the stock of a company, it is regarded as a direct investment; ownership of bonds or less than 10 percent of a company's stock constitutes a portfolio investment. Currently, foreign investment in the United States consists largely of portfolio investments—government securities held by foreign

Billions
$U.S.

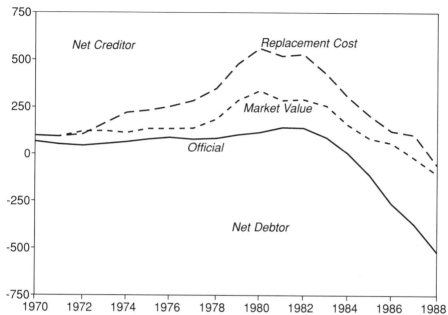

Figure 10.1 U.S. international position, 1970–1988. *Source:* Eisner and Pieper 1990.

governments and portfolio investments held by private interests. Together these made up 79 percent of all foreign investment in 1988; foreign direct investment, on the other hand, made up 18 percent.

Even though direct investment constitutes a small portion of total foreign investment, there is little doubt that the share of foreign direct investment in the United States relative to the size of the economy has increased. From 1977 to 1988, foreign direct investment in the United States grew threefold, from controlling less than 2.5 percent of the economy's capital stock to around 7.5 percent. The proportion of manufacturing assets controlled by foreign companies is even greater, having risen from 5 percent in 1977 to 12.5 percent in 1987. As a result, by 1987, foreign-owned companies provided about 5.4 percent of all manufacturing jobs in the United States.

Who are the leading foreign investors? When many Americans think of foreign investment in the United States, they think of Japan. A look at the data, however, suggests that concern about Japanese investment is exaggerated (see Figure 10.2). True, since 1980 the Japanese share of total foreign direct investment has grown threefold and at a rate faster than that of

Billions
$U.S.

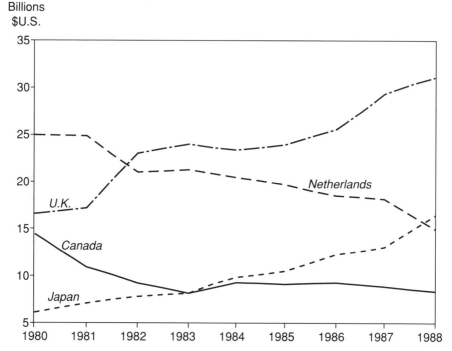

Figure 10.2 Foreign direct investment in U.S. by country of origin, 1980–1988.
Source: Graham and Krugman 1992.

the other major investor countries. But it is important to realize that the Japanese, relative newcomers, started with a small share, about 7 percent. And while their share of foreign investment has grown quickly, so too has that of Great Britain, making up in part for the declining share of Dutch and Canadian investment. Indeed, Britain's share of foreign direct investment is almost twice that of Japan's (30 percent versus 16 percent in 1988), yet since the Beatles arrived, one has not heard much about a British invasion.

There are three competing images that economists employ to explain America's foreign-debt situation. In the first, the United States is a rising corporation, revitalized by Ronald Reagan's supply-side magic. In this view, the rising corporation is so profitable and so competitive that other corporations naturally want to get a piece of the action. They invest in the corporation to get a share of its spectacular profits. Far from being a sign of decline, therefore, foreign investment in the United States is a sign of success. By implication, America's net debtor status is nothing to worry about.

Appealing though this image is, it fails to provide a satisfactory explanation. If the United States were truly a rising corporation, one would expect most foreign investment to be direct investment—the better to profit from the extraordinary strength of U.S. business. But most foreign investment in the United States is portfolio investment; indeed, a good 20 percent has been in government securities.

Moreover, what foreign direct investment there has been has not been used to build new plants here, as one would also expect if the United States were truly a rising corporation. Instead, most of this investment has been used to acquire already existing plants. In 1989, for example, foreign companies spent $64 billion to acquire U.S. companies but only $9 billion to establish new ones (*Survey of Current Business*, May 1990, 23).[2]

The second image used to explain America's indebtedness is that of the United States as one big family working to earn a living and spending money to consume. There are two kinds of families according to this view: the good thrifty family that never spends more than it earns and saves the rest for the future, and the bad spendthrift family that spends more than it earns and has to go into debt to support its profligate habits. It is not hard to see what kind of family the United States has been. Living well beyond its means, it has had to borrow substantially from foreigners.

By this logic there are two main culprits. The first is the American consumer, who, we are told, has been on a consumption binge. The second is the U.S. government, which has also overspent and undertaxed. To make up the difference between its spending and its earnings, the United States has had to borrow.

Although these arguments have some basis in fact—more so than the first explanation—as they are commonly presented, they are still highly misleading. First, take the idea that "we" have been consuming too much. On the face of it, this appears to be true.[3] In the 1970s, average consumption accounted for 89.6 percent of disposable income. In the early 1980s that figure rose to 91.8 percent; and in the latter half of the decade, to 93.1 percent. But averages deceive. A closer look at the figures makes clear that one group in particular was largely responsible for the increase in consumption—the wealthy. The wealthiest 20 percent of the population increased their consumption 11.2 percent annually from 1981 to 1987, accounting for approximately 80 percent of the overall increase in U.S. consumption during that period, while the poorest 20 percent of the population increased their consumption by only 1.6 percent in the first half of the 1980s, and the next 20 percent decreased their consumption by 3.5 percent. Hence, it was not Americans as a whole who were on a consumption binge, but rather the richest Americans.

It comes as no surprise that the wealthy increased their consumption as much as they did, given the dramatic increase in income they experienced. Before taxes, the real income of the wealthiest 10 percent of the nation's families rose, on average, 21 percent from 1979 to 1987, while that of the poorest 10 percent fell by 12 percent. It is estimated that the fraction of Americans who are "rich" nearly doubled from 1979 to 1987; meanwhile, the fraction of families living below the poverty line increased by 15 percent (Krugman 1990:4–6).

Wealthy Americans were able to go on a spending spree in part because of changes in government policy. Thanks to Reagan's tax cuts, the average tax rate for the wealthiest 1 percent of Americans fell by 6 percent between 1977 and 1988, and for the wealthiest 5 percent by 2.6 percent. The burden on the poorest 10 percent meanwhile increased by 1.6 percent, and on the poorer 50 percent by an average of 0.6 percent (U.S. Congress 1987:48; Phillips 1990:83). Contrary to supply-side claims, the tax cuts contributed to the government budget deficit, and because the wealthy favored consumption over saving, the tax cuts led to a reduction in private savings as well.

Partisans of the spendthrift-family explanation lay much of the blame for the buildup in U.S. foreign debt not just on private consumption, they blame large increases in public consumption—the government budget deficit—as well. The logic is simple: the more the U.S. government spends in relation to what it earns in taxes, the more it has to borrow. And because of the country's low private-savings rate, more and more of that borrowing is from abroad. The Reagan-era tax cuts contributed greatly to the budget deficit, but they represent only one side of the ledger. On the other side were enormous increases in government spending, in particular the big-ticket item of the 1980s, military spending. The increases alone in military expenditure from 1981 to 1987—close to $600 billion—amount to 90 percent of America's foreign-debt accumulation in those years.

Thus the spendthrift-family explanation contains some elements of truth. A few members of the family—namely, America's wealthy—indeed went on a consumption binge in the 1980s. And government expenditure did increase, particularly in the form of military spending. At the same time, the tax burden on these wealthiest Americans and their corporations went into a free fall. These trends reduced national savings and contributed to increased borrowing from abroad.

Yet this analysis is of little use for policy purposes unless we ask the following question: Why has the government pursued these policies? A major force driving these policies has been the globalization of the American corporation. The ability of U.S. corporations to move abroad has made it more difficult to tax them for their share of the military spending they desire to help support their global operations.

The third image used by economists to illustrate America's debt situation is that of a declining corporation. According to this view, U.S. industry is no longer competitive in world markets. As a consequence, the United

States is running a large trade deficit that can only be financed by borrowing from abroad. When Americans buy more VCRs and cars from abroad than we sell to foreigners, we have to borrow money to pay the difference, just as any household would have to go into debt if it bought more goods than it could afford.

This argument, too, contains some important elements of truth. The United States has fallen behind its competitors in many key sectors and product areas. From 1980 to 1988, for example, the U.S. share of world automobile exports dropped 46 percent, computer exports 36 percent, microelectronic exports 26 percent, and machine-tool exports 17 percent. As a result, the U.S. trade imbalance widened significantly in manufactures, and the high-tech sector registered a deficit for the first time ever.

Yet few analysts acknowledge that here, too, the decline of U.S. exports relative to imports is connected to the globalization of U.S. corporations. For if the United States as a nation has become less competitive, U.S. multinational corporations have not. This is evident from the fact that while the U.S. share of world manufacturing exports fell from 17.1 percent in 1966 to 11.7 percent in 1986—a drop of more than two-thirds—U.S. multinationals essentially maintained their share of the world market, and the foreign affiliates of U.S. multinationals actually increased their share from 8.0 percent to 9.8 percent in the same time period (Kravis and Lipsey 1989).

What these data suggest is that many major U.S. corporations are abandoning the United States as a production site and are moving abroad, where they continue to do quite well. Partly as a result, the U.S. trade position has deteriorated to the point where the United States must borrow to finance its imports.

In short, whatever model we use to explain the roots of the U.S. debt problem—whether it be that we spend more than we produce (the spendthrift family) or that we import more than we export (the declining corporation)—the globalization of U.S. corporations has played a central role. Analyzing the United States as a world debtor without U.S. multinational corporations is like presenting Shakespeare's *Hamlet* without the prince.

U.S. Multinationals and U.S. Foreign Debt

While foreign direct investment in the United States has raised concern in many circles, it is, paradoxically, U.S. direct investment abroad that provides the missing link in a complete explanation of America's growing international-debt problem. To be sure, foreign direct investment in the United States has grown rapidly in the past decade, but U.S. direct investment abroad has been growing at an even faster rate since the mid-1980s (see Figure 10.3). Indeed, for much of the past twenty-five years U.S. invest-

Billions
$U.S.

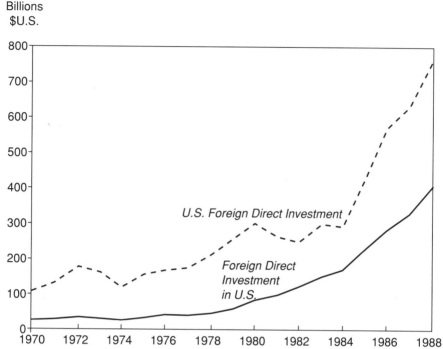

Figure 10.3 Foreign direct investment in U.S. and U.S. foreign direct investment abroad (market values), 1970–1988. *Source:* Eisner and Pieper 1990.

ment abroad has outpaced investment at home, reflecting an apparent decision by many large American corporations to reduce their commitment to the United States as a production site. Moving production abroad may have helped U.S. multinationals maintain their competitive edge, but it has also had far-reaching and detrimental consequences for the country and its balance of payments.

To begin with, the multinationalization of U.S. business has, as suggested earlier, exacerbated the U.S. trade deficit. Increased production and exports on the part of U.S. corporations outside the United States have meant reduced production and exports for companies within the United States. In some cases they have also resulted in increased U.S. imports from foreign-based U.S. multinationals.

Thus, although the United States now runs sizable trade deficits each year with countries such as Japan, Taiwan, and Singapore, it is U.S. multinationals based in these countries that are often the leading contributors to this trend (Reich 1990).[4] IBM-Japan, for instance, employs eighteen thousand Japanese workers and is one of the country's largest exporters of computers. Texas Instruments employs more than five thousand people in Japan to make advanced semiconductors; almost half of these semiconductors are exported, many to the United States. In Taiwan, U.S. multinationals—AT&T, RCA, and Texas Instruments—figure among the largest exporters; U.S. corporate production there is responsible for more than one-third of Taiwan's trade surplus with the United States. And Singapore's largest private employer is a U.S. multinational—General Electric—that accounts for a large share of that country's exports.

These are not isolated examples. In fact, the production and sourcing practices of U.S. multinationals account for a substantial share of the U.S. trade imbalance not only with Taiwan and Singapore but also with Mexico, South Korea, and other newly industrializing countries. According to a recent study, by 1986, U.S. multinational corporations were exporting more goods from their overseas affiliates than they were from the United States (Kravis and Lipsey 1989: 3 n. 12).

Of course, it is conceivable that moving production abroad does not necessarily result in the loss of production and jobs at home, as defenders of U.S. corporate practices argue. It is possible, for example, that foreign-based U.S. firms would import inputs from their U.S. affiliates, thus boosting production and employment at home. However, true though these arguments might have been in the 1960s and 1970s, they have no basis in fact in the 1980s. Recent studies suggest a decline in U.S. exports to countries experiencing increases in U.S. multinational production (Kravis and Lipsey 1988). These same studies also indicate that as U.S. multinational corporations increase employment in their foreign subsidiaries, they draw down the number of workers in their U.S.-based operations. Moreover, U.S. multinationals tend to reduce their investment at home as they increase their investment abroad.[5] This lack of investment, economists of all stripes agree, is one of the principal causes of America's trade and competitiveness problem.

It is relatively easy to see, then, that by weakening America's trade position the multinationalization of U.S. business has contributed to the U.S. accumulation of debt. The United States now exports less than it imports and thus must borrow the difference from abroad, at least in part because U.S. multinationals have moved production overseas. If U.S. corporations had invested more in production at home over the past decade, the U.S. trade deficit today would be smaller. So would America's borrowing needs.

If the multinationalization of U.S. business helps to explain the U.S. debt problem when we think of the United States as a declining corporation, the multinationalization of U.S. business has also exacerbated America's debtor status when we look at the United States as a spendthrift nation. First, the multinationalization of U.S. business has helped to increase the U.S. budget deficit. Although the causal relations among the budget deficit, the trade deficit, and foreign borrowing may have been exaggerated in the past, there can be little doubt at this point that the federal budget is contributing to our international-debt problem. What is not appreciated is that U.S. multinational corporations have contributed to the budget deficit on both the revenue and expenditure sides of the equation.

On the revenue side, for every dollar invested abroad that would have been invested at home, the United States loses employment and tax income. It is estimated that 3.4 million U.S. jobs were lost in the 1977–86 period as a result of U.S. foreign direct investment abroad. This translates today into a tax loss of about $30 billion a year.[6] To this figure, however, one needs to add the quite considerable tax losses that arise as a result of the various tax advantages that U.S. multinationals enjoy.

U.S. tax laws—riddled with loopholes despite recent reform efforts— give U.S. multinational corporations numerous opportunities to reduce their liabilities to the U.S. government. To begin with, U.S. multinational corporations do not always have to pay U.S. taxes on their earnings abroad; the law grants foreign countries the opportunity to tax these firms first. Only if the foreign tax rate is lower than the U.S. rate do U.S. multinationals have to pay U.S. taxes (in which case they pay the difference between the two rates). In other words, firms get a foreign-tax credit for taxes paid to foreign governments—to the tune of $21.5 billion in 1986, the latest year for which data are available (Mose 1989–90). This is a far more generous provision than would be the case if corporations were only allowed to deduct the taxes paid from their gross income, as they do with any other business cost.

Often, however, U.S. firms are able to avoid paying even those taxes. This is because U.S. law allows a U.S. firm to defer tax payments until it repatriates its profits back to the United States. As a result, firms can simply reinvest their overseas profits in foreign countries, thereby avoiding U.S. taxes indefinitely. The countries that host U.S. firms are not necessarily any richer as a result. For U.S. multinationals often seek to further avoid taxes by shifting profits to foreign countries that have low tax rates.

One of the most common ways of shifting profits is through transfer pricing. Transfer prices are what firms charge themselves for inputs bought from their subsidiaries. By manipulating these prices, multinational corporations can spirit their profits to low-tax havens. A firm may have its subsidiary in a low-tax country overcharge for an input, for instance, thus lowering the recorded profits in the high-tax country and raising the recorded profits in the low-tax country.

The opportunities for such tax evasion are clearly not hypothetical. In a recent study of more than 12,000 foreign subsidiaries of 453 U.S. firms, it was found that 8,277, or 69 percent of them, paid no dividends, interest, rent, or royalties to their U.S. parent corporations in 1984 and therefore had to pay no U.S. taxes at all on their foreign earnings. Or, to put it another way, 433 of the 453 parent U.S. corporations had at least one foreign entity that made no payments to its parent and therefore generated no U.S. tax liabilities (Hines and Hubbard 1989).

The ability of U.S. multinationals abroad to protect their profits from taxation has serious repercussions for the U.S. fiscal balance. Consider that in 1984 the United States netted only $6.4 billion in taxes on foreign-source income totaling $64 billion. That represents an effective tax rate of 10 percent. With the changes stemming from the 1986 tax reforms, this figure is likely to fall to about 4 percent. This is a good deal for U.S. multinationals, which are now earning over 25 percent of their income abroad. But for the U.S. government, which is highly dependent on corporate income tax as a source of revenue, the consequences are quite damaging—more so than for other advanced capitalist countries because these rely to a greater extent on progressive income taxes and value-added taxes, which are harder for companies to evade.

How much tax revenue could be generated if the tax laws were changed? In particular, what would be the effect of eliminating deferral and substituting tax deductions for the foreign-tax credit? According to analysts at the Treasury Department, eliminating deferral would have increased taxes by $4.2 billion in 1984, the latest year for which such estimates are available. Although this may not seem like much in dollar terms, it nonetheless represents a 65 percent increase in tax payments on foreign-source income for that year (Goodspeed and Frish 1989: table 1).[7] If, in addition, the United States had substituted deductions for foreign-tax credits, there would have been a further increase of nearly $21 billion in tax revenue.[8] The total increase—roughly $60 billion in 1989 dollars if one also factors in the $30 billion in taxes lost by U.S. direct investment abroad—represents about 40 percent of the $150 billion federal budget deficit for that year, or 55 percent of the $106 billion borrowed from abroad (see Table 10.1).

TABLE 10.1
U.S. Multinational Corporations' Contribution to the U.S. Budget Deficit and Foreign Borrowing in 1989 (Inflation Adjusted, 1989 Dollars)

Lost Revenue	Loss in Billions $	Loss as % of Budget Deficit	Loss as % of Foreign Borrowing
From job loss	30	20	27.5
From tax code loopholes	30	20	27.5
Total	60	40	55.0

Sources: Author's estimates.

Naturally these estimates are very rough and assume, among other things, that firms do not resort to other ways of avoiding taxes. But the fact remains that for many firms these changes would remove a large incentive to produce abroad. And if companies can be induced to shift production back to the United States, the benefits will be considerable: more jobs, more income, and, of course, more tax revenue.

The loss of tax revenue from these forms of tax evasion and reduction is in some ways less serious than the indirect costs associated with the shift of U.S. multinational production abroad. Most striking among these is the change in attitude that the management of U.S. multinational corporations has undergone. Since World War II, as U.S. firms have shifted more and more of their operations overseas, their sense of identity has ceased to be closely associated with their country of origin. This is reflected in remarks by Charles Exley, the head of National Cash Register, who said that National Cash Register was not a U.S. corporation but was a world corporation that happened to be headquartered in the United States.

There are serious, indeed deadly, consequences that follow from this change in attitude. As U.S. multinational corporations feel less tied to the United States, they are less willing to pay to maintain the quality of domestic productive factors that in the past would have been necessary to the success of their operations—an educated work force and a sound infrastructure. They are less willing to support U.S. public investment because they no longer see themselves as directly benefiting from it. As a result, U.S. productivity falters and brings down the U.S. standard of living and competitiveness along with it. As a result, Americans are less willing and able to pay taxes, which also exacerbates the U.S. budget deficit, and U.S. firms are less competitive with foreign firms, which harms the U.S. trade deficit. Once again, any way you look at it, this refusal by multinational corporations to engage in sufficient private investment and support sufficient public investment, helps generate the U.S. international-debt problem.

An economist might argue that the market will correct this problem. By this reasoning, U.S. or Japanese multinational corporations may not wish to pay taxes back home, but they can be expected to support taxes in countries where they do produce—not for reasons of altruism but because of their need for skilled technicians, modern communication systems, efficient transportation facilities, and the like. In reality, however, it does not work this way. A corporation can always threaten to move to another country if taxes get too high—an option that each corporation knows is available to all other corporations. In classic free-rider fashion, each corporation benefits from the effect that other firms' propensity for flight has on the host government. Collectively, corporations are thus able to cow governments into maintaining low rates of taxation. In the end, all nations and even the corporations themselves suffer as a result, since revenue is simply not available for needed investments in physical and human infrastructure. The invisible hand of perfect capital mobility, far from solving the problem, only aggravates it.

At the same time that U.S. multinationals have become less dependent on domestic infrastructure, they have become more concerned with maintaining a hospitable international environment for trade and investment and with preserving their competitive position in key markets abroad. They have thus tended to be supportive of increased U.S. military spending, which they see not only as contributing to a secure environment for their investments but also as strengthening their bargaining position with countries dependent on the United States for military security—countries such as South Korea, Saudi Arabia, and the European Community. The days when U.S. multinationals could expect the U.S. military to intervene to protect their investments in banana republics may be over, but as was vividly illustrated by the Gulf War, a strong U.S. military posture abroad has tended to accord indirect benefits to U.S. multinationals. It is no accident that Western Europe has tended to treat U.S. investment more favorably than that from Japan, or that Japan grants U.S. multinationals greater access than it does European firms.

As a result of this change in orientation, one would expect U.S. corporations to support a strong U.S. military and diplomatic posture abroad while showing less willingness to pay taxes to finance domestic education and infrastructure programs. This is precisely what one has seen for the past two decades and particularly during the Reagan years, when U.S. multinationals lobbied hard not only for lower taxes but also for increased military spending. As Thomas Ferguson and Joel Rogers document in their book, *Right Turn* (1986), the U.S. multinational corporate community contributed heavily to candidates and political organizations favoring increased military spending in the 1978–82 period—the incipient years of America's largest peacetime military buildup ever. Although the ideological Right took this military expansion further than many in the business community thought prudent, corporate America's support was clearly critical to the formation of a national consensus that sanctioned the buildup in the first place.

The lobbying efforts paid off. Corporate taxes, as a share of federal, state, and local revenue, have declined sharply from a high of 45 percent in 1945 to roughly 10 percent in 1988. Meanwhile, there has been a dramatic increase in military expenditures relative to total expenditures, and especially relative to expenditures on domestic infrastructure. U.S. military stock grew by 700 percent from 1973 to 1987, while the ratio of public capital to employed worker actually fell in the same period (Munnell 1990).

In these ways, then—through diminished tax contributions and support for increased military spending—U.S. corporate activity abroad bears substantial responsibility for the budget deficit. And to the extent that the

U.S. budget deficit is linked to U.S. net foreign borrowing, as is widely believed, the operations of U.S. multinationals have contributed directly to the accumulation of U.S. foreign debt.

Moreover, the change in public spending priorities that U.S. multinationals have helped to bring about threatens to exacerbate the consequences of that borrowing. The lack of U.S. multinationals' support for spending on public infrastructure, in general, and their unwillingness to pay taxes, in particular, have resulted in declining rates of public capital investment. Yet as recent studies demonstrate, adequate public infrastructure is critical to the productivity of private investments. Lower public capital investment means lower productivity growth. And that, in turn, means that future foreign-debt-servicing burdens will be more onerous than they would be otherwise.

It should be clear from the preceding discussion that the real problem is not the nationality of corporations but the lack of correspondence between the interests of multinational corporations and the communities in which they operate. Capital and production, able to move freely around the globe, have turned the multinational corporation—regardless of national origin—into a "foreign" entity in relation to the community in which it operates.[9] In this age of international capital mobility, it seems that Adam Smith's invisible hand—which has always been imperfect in translating self-interest into common good—has developed severe arthritis.

America's Foreign Debt: The Real Dangers

Just as it is important to establish clearly the sources of America's foreign debt, so is it important to appreciate the true dangers of that debt. The conventional wisdom argues that the United States has been borrowing excessively and that as a result the country has become vulnerable to the whims of its foreign creditors. But the real problem is not so much the level of foreign debt, high though it may be. Rather, the real problem is that the United States has essentially been squandering the large sums it has been borrowing, while its public policies have failed to respond to the effect that the globalization of U.S. corporations has had on investment and income patterns in the United States. The net result is that the United States has been investing insufficiently in its productive capacity—a trend that, if unchecked, will lead to accelerating economic decline, an increasing burden on middle- and working-class Americans, and a loss of economic control.

By historical standards, the United States is by no means an excessive borrower. At the moment, America's net foreign debt stands at 10 percent of its gross national product (GNP). This is comparable to the level of debt the country sustained for nearly fifty years beginning in the early nineteenth century (see Figure 10.4). Of course, if current trends continue, the U.S.

% GNP

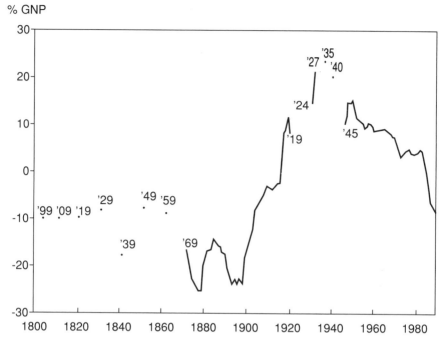

Figure 10.4 U.S. net investment position as a percentage of GNP, 1799–1987. *Source:* Epstein 1989.

debt will approach 30 percent of GNP by 2000; this would certainly represent an unprecedented degree of indebtedness.

More serious than the current level of debt, however, is the fact that the United States has not been investing what it has been borrowing. On average during the 1980s, the United States borrowed about 2.6 percent of its net national product (NNP) from abroad and invested less than 5 percent (see Figure 10.5). Compared with other large debtors, this is a disturbing pattern indeed. By contrast, in the nineteenth century the United States borrowed about 1 percent of its NNP and invested 14 percent. Moreover, it invested this capital in railways, canals, factories, and other productive resources, as opposed to the wasteful ends to which borrowed funds are put today. Productive capacity expanded as a consequence, and the United States had no trouble servicing its foreign debt in the decades that followed.

The experience of the past decade could not be more different. The money the United States borrowed from abroad was not used for productive investment—for automating our factories or for upgrading the skills of our work force. Rather, it went into foreign investment, exotic military systems, and luxury consumer imports, some of which is connected to the multinationalization of U.S. firms and none of which added to the nation's

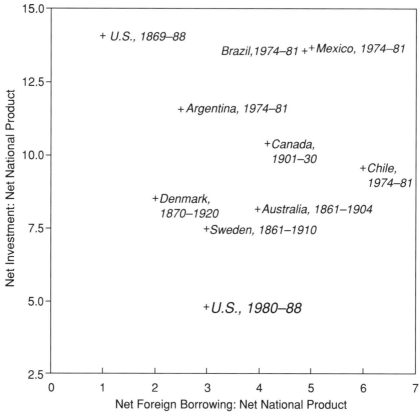

Figure 10.5 Net investment and net foreign borrowing relative to net national product. *Sources:* Kuznets 1955:19–107.

economic strength. Thus, the United States accumulated major financial liabilities without adding real assets to the nation's productive capacity that would enable it to service and pay off these liabilities in the future.

The United States, in short, has been operating like a huge and irresponsible savings and loan. By borrowing as much as we have, without investing in our productive capacity, we have condemned ourselves and our children to a lower standard of living in the future and our nation to a slow economic decline.

A false sense of danger leads, naturally enough, to mistaken prescriptions. Currently there are three popular, though wrongheaded, policy responses to the U.S. international-debt position. The first is to cut the U.S. budget deficit by cutting spending and raising taxes. But cutting government spending—which, if past practice is any guide, would reduce public investments in education, roads, research and development, health, and day care, programs that add to our social infrastructure and promote productivity growth—would only further reduce the competitiveness of the United States and lead to further increases in foreign borrowing. The second, under the guise of enhancing U.S. competitiveness, is to use U.S. diplomatic and political clout to open other countries to U.S. foreign investment. The North American Free Trade Agreement currently being negotiated is a prime example. But by facilitating foreign investment by U.S. MNCs, this policy would only make the hollowing out of the U.S. worse. The third popular policy is to place curbs on foreign investment in the United States. But the problem is not foreign investment per se; it is the destructive effects of unregulated international investment—both domestic and foreign—that are undermining our economy. Focusing attention on investment only by foreigners only diverts attention from the real issues. To be sure, there is clear value to some of these efforts. Regulating foreign investment to minimize the destructive effects of speculative mergers and acquisitions on the U.S. industrial base; ensuring that foreign multinational corporations operating in the United States pay their fair share of taxes; insisting that foreign multinational corporations abide by environmental, labor, and anti-discrimination standards; and reducing the power of the foreign corporate lobby through campaign finance reform—all are steps in the right direction. But if these efforts are directed only at Japanese and other foreign corporations—to the exclusion of U.S. multinational corporations—they will not succeed in redressing the real problems associated with America's foreign debt.

Restoring Control, Reversing Decline

The United States clearly lacks a fair and economically coherent strategy for managing its international debt problem. The Bush administration's approach—cutting the budget deficit and opening other countries to U.S. investment—amounts to nothing more than a program of squeezing America's poor and middle class to free up savings and investment capital for U.S. corporations to invest abroad. And calls by Congress to curb foreign investment, although they may appeal to certain xenophobic impulses, are no more promising.

The obvious alternative to these simplistic solutions is a long-term strategy of strengthening the productive capacity of the U.S. economy so that we can begin to earn at least as much as we spend and thus be able to reduce our debt relative to the size of our economy. Many of the elements of such a strategy have gained currency over the years—for instance, major increases in public and social investment, expanded research and development, improved education and worker retraining, progressive taxes on the wealthy and speculative activities, dramatic cuts in military spending, and international debt relief to revive U.S. export markets in the developing world. As important as these various measures are, however, they will not add up to a coherent strategy unless we come to grips with the basic problem of capital mobility and the globalization of U.S. corporations. How to maintain adequate levels of public and private investment and at the same time ensure rising wages and environmental standards in an age of global corporations and international capital mobility is the dominant question of the 1990s.

There are, of course, no easy answers to this question. But it is an issue that can no longer be ignored or wished away. And it is a matter of concern not just for the United States. Eastern Europe, which faces a capital shortage yet lacks the political infrastructure to regulate investment, is especially vulnerable to the vicissitudes of foreign investment. So is Latin America, many of whose countries are now under pressure from the United States to further relax restrictions on capital flows.

In today's interdependent world economy, where the mobility of capital threatens to ratchet down living standards for the great majority, what is needed is a global regulatory framework for multinational corporations—a set of common standards for labor rights, tax and wage rates, and environmental standards, as well as the means, both national and international, to enforce them. Such a regulatory framework, it is clear, will not emerge, at least not initially, from the lengthy and often empty exercises that have characterized treatment of this issue to date, including the effort begun in the 1970s under the auspices of the United Nations to establish a code of conduct for multinational corporations. Little will be accomplished until nations and communities take it upon themselves to exert more control over multinational corporations.

But what control can communities possibly exercise over today's global corporations? In isolation, of course, small communities are virtually powerless; yet large communities or collectives of smaller ones operating in unison have considerable power at their disposal. The establishment of an integrated European economy in 1992, for example, creates the opportunity for these nations to exercise significant control over multinational corporations. The United States, too, is large enough to wield such control. And if it were to pursue negotiations with its neighbors, leading to common policies governing the regulation of multinational investments, instead of its current efforts to form a free trade zone with Canada and Mexico, the interests of the United States would yet be better served.

In each of these cases, the source of control lies with access to the resources that the multinational corporations want. In the case of the United States, the major "resource" is the U.S. market. In markets characterized by competition among large corporations, profits are intimately tied up with market share. Large corporations gain huge economic rents by having access to markets. These are rents that a government can threaten to reduce if corporations are not willing to invest in a nation's well-being. The United States, for instance, could alter the terms of access to its market that corporations (domestic and foreign) now enjoy. In this way, corporations could be induced to help realize, rather than undermine, national and community goals (Dorman 1989; Honderich 1989).

The purpose of such regulation would not be to shift more investment from one country to another, for this would only fuel investment wars among nations. Rather, the idea is to reduce the power the multinational corporation now has to pit one country against another. In this way a more level playing field would emerge, and multinational corporations would find it more difficult to ratchet down tax rates, public investment, wages, and environmental standards.

One way to accomplish these goals would be through the use of social tariffs (Dorman 1989). If the United States were to adopt a social-tariff system, for instance, companies that reap a cost advantage by producing under labor, environmental, or other conditions that are below certain international standards would have to pay a compensating tax, or tariff, to bring their costs and prices up to the levels faced by companies not violating these standards. The imposition of social tariffs would help level the playing field among firms, since those corporations that do not meet international standards would no longer have cost advantages over those that do. The revenue collected from social tariffs could then be channeled back into public investment or international development assistance to ensure that everyone gained in the process.

Of course, social tariffs by themselves will not solve all the problems associated with the U.S. international debt. As suggested earlier, to protect against further economic decline and to restore fairness to its economic system, the United States must also be willing to increase its investment in public infrastructure and to finance that increase by taxing the wealthy. But here, too, social tariffs can help. Whereas current budget-cutting measures reduce public investment and raise taxes for the lower 60 percent of the population, social tariffs would generate revenue for public investment and would fall on the owners of multinational corporations. Moreover, by removing the cost advantages of relocating production, social tariffs would help tie multinational corporations to the communities in which they operate, making them more likely to support public investment in those communities.

In short, social tariffs would be a much more effective way of increasing public and private investment, reducing the budget deficit, and maintaining U.S. competitiveness than the budget cutting we have witnessed in Washington. The tax revenue generated by social tariffs could be augmented by changes in the U.S. tax code that govern U.S. corporations abroad.

Ultimately the problem is one of political will. It is certainly within the power of Congress and the president to establish conditions in which multinational corporations can operate profitably while better serving community interests. Yet as long as our elected representatives remain beholden to the "special interests" of the wealthy or fail to see, for lack of political courage, the problems posed by the hypermobility of U.S. capital, the bold action that is required to revitalize the country will not be forthcoming. The sources of America's decline are no mystery. What we need to do is muster the resolve to reverse it.

ACKNOWLEDGMENTS

This chapter is a shortened and revised version of the author's "Mortgaging America," which originally appeared in *World Policy Journal* (Winter 1990–91). The author would like to thank Trish Kelly for excellent research assistance and Richard Caplan, Julie Graham, Jessica Nembhard, Arthur MacEwan, and Sherle Schwenninger for extremely helpful comments.

NOTES

1. These stocks, and therefore the country's position as net debtor or net creditor, are difficult to measure accurately because their value depends on the rate at which old holdings appreciate or depreciate, the effects of changes in exchange rates, bankruptcies and defaults, and the like. These valuation problems can create rather large discrepancies among estimates. Robert Eisner and Paul Pieper, among many others, have argued that because U.S. foreign direct investment abroad is undervalued in official statistics, the U.S. net debt position is much less than it seems. Official Commerce Department data have recently incorporated some of Eisner and Peiper's suggested revisions. Figure 10.1 presents their two alternative estimates, with foreign direct investment measured at what it would cost to replace and at what it would fetch at current market prices, along with the official figures. A main point of this chapter, however, is that the U.S. people as a whole benefit little from U.S. foreign direct investment abroad, and therefore its true value is much less than its accounting value. Eisner and Pieper's point thus loses much of its force, since U.S. foreign direct investment abroad, as an asset to offset the debt side of the balance sheet, is actually of much less value than it appears.

2. These figures are based on preliminary data.

3. For the data in this and the next paragraph, see Blecker 1990.

4. See Reich 1990 for most of the data in the following few paragraphs.

5. In a study of the foreign and domestic investment behavior of a small sample of U.S. multinational corporations, Guy V. G. Stevens and Robert E. Lipsey (1988) found that investment abroad and domestic investment tended to be negatively correlated. If this small sample is representative of the behavior of U.S. multi-

national corporations generally, it implies that expansion abroad by U.S. multinationals tends to reduce investment at home.

6. The job-loss estimates are from Norman J. Glickman and Douglas P. Woodward (1989). My estimate of the tax loss is a crude one because it assumes that the net job loss remained 3.4 million. Since some of those 3.4 million no doubt found other jobs, my estimate may exaggerate the tax loss. On the other hand, since others subsequently lost jobs and, moreover, since the jobs lost tended to pay higher-than-average wages, my estimate perhaps understates the tax loss. Also, I only take into account the effects of job loss on federal revenue, not state and local revenue, which further minimizes the estimate of tax loss.

7. These numbers assume the 46 percent corporate rate in effect prior to 1986. The 1986 tax reforms lowered the rate to 34 percent, which would have reduced collections in 1984 to only $2.6 billion on $64 billion of foreign income. The elimination of deferral would have increased collections to $4.5 billion, an increase of almost 75 percent.

8. These estimates are based on extrapolating G. C. Hufbauer's figures to the current period. They should be seen as very rough estimates (Hufbauer 1975).

9. I am not arguing that U.S. corporations in an earlier time were more altruistic and for that reason might have been more willing to invest in education, infrastructure, and the like. The point is that in previous periods the interests of U.S. corporations were more organically connected to those of the communities in which they operated. Of course, in other respects U.S. corporate interests have been in conflict with community interests, as the numerous violations of environmental and labor laws on the part of U.S. businesses attest.

BIBLIOGRAPHY

Blecker, Robert A. 1990. *Are We on a Consumpton Binge? The Evidence Reconsidered.* Washington, D.C.: Economic Policy Institute.
Cline, William R. 1989. *United States External Adjustment and the World Economy.* Washington, D.C.: Institute for International Economics.
Dorman, Peter. 1989. Worker Rights and International Trade Policy. Smith College, Northampton, Mass. Mimeo.
Eisner, Robert. 1990. Debunking the Conventional Wisdom. *Challenge* 33(3): 4–11.
Eisner, Robert, and Paul J. Pieper. 1990. The World's Greatest Debtor Nation? *North America Review of Economics and Finance* 1(1): 9–32.
Epstein, Gerald. 1989. The United States as a World Debtor. University of Massachusetts, Amherst. Mimeo.
Ferguson, Thomas, and Joel Rogers. 1986. *Right Turn.* New York: Hill & Wang.
Friedman, Benjamin M. 1988. *Day of Reckoning: The Consequences of American Economic Policy under Reagan and After.* New York: Random House.
Glickman, Norman J., and Douglas P. Woodward. 1989. *The New Competitors: How Foreign Investors Are Changing the U.S. Economy.* New York: Basic Books.
Goodspeed, Timothy, and Daniel Frish, 1989. U.S. Tax Policy and the Overseas Activities of U.S. Multinational Corporations: A Quantitative Assessment. U.S. Treasury Department, Office of Tax Analysis, Washington, D.C. Mimeo.

Graham, Edward M., and Paul R. Krugman. 1992. *Foreign Direct Investment in the United States.* 2d ed. Washington, D.C.: Institute for International Economics.

Hines, James R., Jr., and R. Glenn Hubbard. 1989. Coming Home to America: Dividend Repatriations by U.S. Multinationals. Working paper no. 2931, National Bureau of Economic Research, April.

Honderich, Kiaran. 1989. Rent Seekers' Revenge: The Use of Rents to Control International Trade. Williams College, Williamstown, Mass. Mimeo.

Hufbauer, G. C. 1975. A Guide to Law and Policy. In *U.S. Taxation of American Business Abroad,* ed. G. C. Hufbauer. Washington, D.C.: American Enterprise Institute.

Kravis, Irving B., and Robert Lipsey. 1988. The Effect of Multinational Firms' Foreign Operations on their Domestic Employment. Working paper no. 2760, National Bureau of Economic Research, Cambridge, Mass.

———. 1989. Technological Characteristics of Industries and the Competitiveness of the U.S. and Its Multinational Firms. Working paper no. 2933, National Bureau of Economic Research, Cambridge, Mass.

Krugman, Paul. 1990. The Income Distribution Disparity. *Challenge* 33(4): 4–6.

Kuznets, Simon. 1955. International Differences in Capital Formation and Financing. In *Capital Formation and Economic Growth: A Conference,* ed. Moses Abramovitz, 19–107. Princeton: Princeton University Press.

Mose, Vergie. 1989–90. Corporate Foreign Tax Credit by Industry, 1984. In *Statistics of Income Bulletin,* 57–81. Washington, D.C.: U.S. Department of Treasury, Winter.

Munnell, Alicia H. 1990. Why Has Productivity Growth Declined? Productivity and Public Investment. *New England Economic Review* (Federal Reserve Bank of Boston), January/February, 3–22.

Phillips, Kevin. 1990. *The Politics of Rich and Poor: Wealth and the American Electorate in the Reagan Aftermath.* New York: Random House.

Reich, Robert. 1990. Who Is Us? *Harvard Business Review* 90 (January/February): 53–64.

Rohatyn, Felix. 1989. America's Economic Dependence. *Foreign Affairs* 68(1): 53–65.

Stevens, Guy V.G., and Robert E. Lipsey. 1988. Interactions between Domestic and Foreign Investment. Working paper no. 2714, National Bureau of Economic Research, Cambridge, Mass.

U.S. Congress. Congressional Budget Office. 1987. *The Changing Distribution of Federal Taxes: 1975–1990.* Washington, D.C.: U.S. Government Printing Office.

11

JULIE GRAHAM

Multinational Corporations and the Internationalization of Production: An Industry Perspective

For several decades now, leftists have understood the activities of multinational corporations (MNCs) as part of a process called the "internationalization of productive capital" or the "globalization of production." This refers to the extension of (industrial) production to previously nonindustrialized parts of the world and, more commonly perhaps, to individual firms engaging in production in more than one nation. On the home front, the internationalization of production and the multinational corporations that carry it out are viewed as major causes of plant closings and industrial decay, as operations that were formerly performed in the United States are moved overseas. Workers experience job loss and communities lose their industrial base as employers seek more profitable opportunities in other parts of the world.

This is a compelling story, and I think it is true. But I want to be very careful here, because I think it is true in a limited way. It conveys what has happened, and is happening, in certain industries (or segments of industries), and it describes the experience of certain regions and workers. But there is a danger in seeing the internationalization of production as the major process going on in the U.S. (or world) economy or as the principal cause of job loss and industrial decline. When internationalization looms large, other factors are obscured. And these factors can be just as responsible for worker dislocation and community decline as the internationalization of production.[1]

In this chapter, I first set out a particular conception of the internationalization of production that I call the "capital flight" story. This story presents internationalization as the work of MNCs and tells us why and where they are going. Though it may seem like a caricature of the internationalization process, it is actually an amalgam of stories that are prevalent on the Left.

I then present alternative perspectives put forward by leftists who argue that the internationalization of production (1) is not as extensive or

221

consequential as the capital flight story would lead us to believe or (2) is a major feature of the world economy but does not generally involve capital flight. I show that disagreements over the extent of international production are sustained and supported by quantitative indicators that point in contradictory directions.

In order to sort out these conflicting perspectives, I examine the internationalization of production in various industries. I show that production is scarcely internationalized at all in some major U.S. industries, such as steel and insurance, but highly internationalized in others. In those, however, international production takes a variety of forms and has a variety of effects, only a few of which are captured by the story of capital flight.

Finally, I take a brief look at what all this means for politics on the Left. If we are concerned with job loss, worker dislocation, and community decline, it is important to recognize that the internationalization of production is only one contributor to these processes, one that plays a major role only in certain industries and communities. It is also important to recognize that internationalization takes a variety of forms, not limited to capital flight (or even direct foreign investment) by U.S.-based MNCs. Since organizing and action often emerge within the context of particular industries and communities, the specific circumstances of each industry are important catalysts of opposition and change. It is my goal to put international production in its industrial context(s), in order to contribute to strategies for dealing with plant closings, job loss and industrial decline.

International Production: A Story of Capital Flight

Many people see the internationalization of production as part of a process of capital flight. From this perspective, internationalized producers are "fleeing" countries where workers are unionized and relatively well paid and seeking out workers in poorer countries where labor is cheap and subject to the discipline of a repressive state. In addition to labor militancy and costs, other factors may contribute to the flight of capital—including high taxes, environmental restrictions, and the existence of a welfare state. These things, common in wealthier nations, may be avoided in poorer countries that are trying to encourage foreign investment.

The principal actor in this story is the multinational corporation, a large-scale business organization with plants in two or more countries. MNCs provide an institutional framework for rapid capital mobility. Scanning the globe for profitable investment opportunities, they can shift vast resources around the world within the bounds of a single firm. As "stateless corporations," MNCs can play nations and communities against each other, holding them hostage to demands for subsidies and threats to close plants and remove jobs.

The compelling image of the "global factory" is perhaps the most familiar representation of the production activities of the MNC. In this model, MNCs locate the various phases of a multiphase production process in different countries and regions, seeking the cheapest combination of labor with appropriate skills to perform the requisite tasks. Higher-level management, research and development, and technology-intensive production are typically located in wealthier countries, while labor intensive fabrication and assembly operations take place in poorer countries around the globe.[2]

Usually portrayed as a footloose corporation with no allegiance to any particular nation or labor force, the MNC continually redesigns the global factory, remaking the geography of production as the map of profitability changes. Not surprisingly, the effects on regional development of international production are largely detrimental. In their home countries MNCs and their global production strategies are responsible for closed plants, lost jobs, and depressed communities. Abroad they create "sterile" branch plants that do not contribute to the development of the host country's economy. Instead they funnel profits to the headquarters of the MNC, draining the host country of the wealth that its labor force produced and contributing to impoverishment rather than growth and development.

The MNC is often seen as a natural and inevitable outgrowth of a capitalist economy, and the internationalization of production as part of an irreversible process of capitalist expansion. According to this view, capital flight is not just the corporate strategy of particular firms at a particular moment but an unavoidable outcome of a system in which corporate profitability is the driving force. Unimpeded by the nation state and undeterred by the opposition of workers and communities, multinational corporations continually seek new profit opportunities, abandoning some communities and temporarily alighting in others as they pursue their relentless quest.

Casting Doubt on the "Capital Flight" Story

Researchers have questioned the capital flight story from a number of angles. Some point to the fact that much international investment is not oriented toward lower labor and other costs. Most productive investment by U.S. firms is market oriented and is therefore, not surprisingly, targeted at Europe. Between 1960 and 1988, for example, 75 percent of U.S. direct foreign investment (DFI) went to relatively wealthy industrial countries, with Canada being the prime target and the United Kingdom the second (Koechlin 1989: 29). Presumably this investment was not oriented primarily toward cheap labor,[3] nor was it likely to be successful in avoiding taxes, environmental restrictions, labor unions, or the welfare state.

Even investment in poorer countries may not be motivated by cost considerations but more by concern over access to final markets.[4] Thus, for the 25 percent of U.S. foreign investment that does go to poorer countries, much of it is not fleeing conditions here but is attempting to access markets that are closed by tariff and nontariff barriers to foreign imports (Gordon 1988:50). In addition, some studies have shown that investment is not particularly responsive to differential rates of profit or to changes in profitability around the globe (Webber and Foot 1988; Koechlin 1989). DFI seems to be attracted by growth markets, political stability, and high-quality labor more than by short-run shifts in profits and costs.

Persuaded by this kind of information about the orientation of investment, most researchers would acknowledge that capital flight is only a small part of the internationalization story. What they disagree about, however, is the *degree* to which production is internationalized. And here the numbers seem to point in contradictory directions, justifying widely divergent interpretations of the international scene. People who see production as internationalized will use one kind of data, while those who see it differently will use a different kind of information to make their point. Researchers arguing, for example, that production is highly internationalized often use data on profits. As Figure 11.1 indicates, government data series on corporate profits show that in 1989 almost 30 percent of U.S. after-tax profits originated overseas and that foreign profits as a percentage of total profits have risen steadily since 1966.

Internationalization advocates also point to statistics on MNCs. The top two hundred industrial MNCs, for example, accounted for 28.6 percent of world GDP in 1980, and U.S.-based MNCs accounted for 14.3 percent of world GDP (Gordon 1988:41).[5] According to the Department of Commerce, MNC-associated imports (including intrafirm imports) accounted for 46.3 percent of total U.S. imports in 1983 (Gordon 1988:49). This seems quite a powerful indicator of internationalization, until we remember that in 1982, imports were only about 10 percent of GNP.[6]

On the other hand, those who wish to argue that production is not particularly internationalized, or that its internationalization has been considerably overstated, tend to use data on investment. From 1960 to 1988, for example, 95.5 percent of total U.S. investment was invested in the United States (Koechlin 1989). For the eight nations that are the major sources of direct foreign investment, the ratio of DFI to total investment is less than 4 percent.[7]

Employment statistics are also invoked to show that the internationalization of production is a relatively minimal phenomenon when considered in relation to the economy as a whole. As Table 11.1 shows, for the United States, overseas employment in 1988 accounted for only 5.3 percent of total (domestic and foreign) employment, and this percentage has fallen since 1977.[8]

Where does all this leave us? We seem to have a very significant per-

% Total
Profits

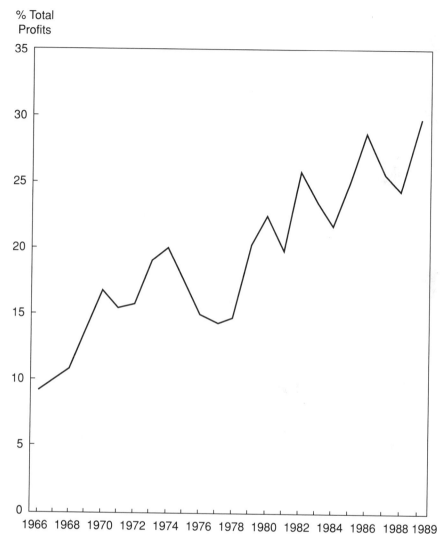

Figure 11.1 After-tax foreign profits as a percentage of total U.S. corporate profits, 1966–1989. *Sources:* U.S. Department of Commerce, *The National Income and Product Accounts of the U.S., 1929–1982*, table 6.21B; idem, *Survey of Current Business*, tables 6.21B (July) and 6.23B.

centage of U.S. corporate profits coming from overseas, yet a relatively insignificant percentage of U.S. investment and employment is associated with the overseas operations of MNCs.[9] It is no wonder that people often give up on numbers and turn to other ways of understanding the phenomenon of internationalization. Some, for example, try to analyze the way it fits

TABLE 11.1
Overseas Employment of U.S. MNCs,[a] 1966–1988

	Employment (in millions)					
Year	Overseas Nonbank	U.S. Civilian	U.S. Bank	U.S. Civilian Nonbank[b]	Total Nonbank[c]	Overseas as % of Total[d]
1966	3.9	72.9	0.8	72.1	76.0	5.1
1977	7.2	92.0	1.4	90.6	97.8	7.4
1982	6.6	99.5	1.7	97.8	104.4	6.3
1983	6.4	100.8	1.7	99.1	105.5	6.1
1984	6.4	105.0	1.7	103.3	109.7	5.8
1985	6.4	107.2	1.7	105.5	111.9	5.7
1986	6.3	109.6	1.7	107.9	114.2	5.5
1987	6.3	112.4	1.7	110.7	117.0	5.4
1988	6.4	115.0	1.7	113.3	119.7	5.3

Sources: "Employment of Nonbank Foreign Affiliates, *Survey of Current Business*, various years; *U.S. Direct Investment Abroad: 1982 Benchmark Survey Data*, 1985, table II.F3; *Economic Report of the President*, 1990, table C-33; "Nonagricultural Industries—Number of Employees," *Statistical Abstract of the United States*, various years. [a]Nonbank foreign affiliates of nonbank U.S. parents. [b]U.S. Civilian minus U.S. Bank. [c]Overseas Nonbank plus U.S. Civilian Nonbank. [d]Overseas Nonbank divided by Total Nonbank.

into a larger picture—a particular historical setting or model of capitalist development—and to convey its significance in qualitative rather than quantitative terms. They question the capital flight story from a different perspective, based on their understanding of how capitalism has developed and changed over time.

International Production and Capitalist Development

Many analysts question the image of the internationalization of production as an inevitable or irreversible process, representing an inherent tendency of capitalist production to expand. They argue that capital flight was a response of certain types of corporations to competitive pressures during the recessions of the 1970s and early 1980s. While some firms invested in overseas locations in order to cut labor and other costs, other firms reduced costs through technological and organizational change at home.

Some people have argued that internationalization is an aspect of Fordist production, in which large, vertically integrated firms produce standardized goods for a mass market. These firms can cut costs by farming out routine and labor-intensive production activities (e.g., assembly) to workers in poor countries who will work long hours for low wages in the "global factory." Fordist mass production, however, is in crisis, and so is the global factory. The Japanese system of production—sometimes called post-Fordist—is in ascendancy. This system is characterized by spatial concentration and integration rather than spatial dispersion. Assembly plants and their suppliers are located within a day's drive of each other to facilitate responsiveness to orders and prompt delivery, cutting down on costly inventory storage and control. Workers are not relegated to a single function but are involved in a continual learning process; such workers are not readily replaceable by cheaper workers overseas. Cost reductions are achieved by continually reevaluating and upgrading each activity in which the firm is involved, not by relocating the production process to an area of cheaper labor.[10]

Other versions of post-Fordist production are based on the model of an "industrial district" rather than on the Japanese model, but they also imply spatial reconcentration rather than further internationalization of production. In many industries, for a variety of reasons, mass production of standardized goods is giving way to small-batch or craft production of specialty goods. This shift in production orientation has been made possible through the application of reprogrammable computerized production equipment, which allows small producers to mechanize their production processes without increasing their scale. Small-scale producers, however, do not function very well in isolation. They do better in clusters, or industrial districts, in which they can share certain resources, like a local pool of labor that has particular skills, or state-subsidized apprenticeship programs and technical schools, or even certain equipment that would be too expensive for any one of them to buy. Spatial proximity facilitates collaboration on design-intensive specialty production and allows for face-to-face contact in a variety of reciprocal subcontracting arrangements. The industrial-district model, then, is vertically disintegrated and spatially concentrated—a network of small interdependent firms operating as suppliers and customers for each other, with their interactions and joint survival facilitated by their proximity.

Instead of being a harbinger of the future, the global factory strategy was the last gasp of Fordism in many industries (Lipietz 1987). As those industries become dominated by post-Fordist approaches to production, many firms will pull back from their international production strategies and attempt to institute more tightly coordinated and spatially concentrated operations. Post-Fordist industrial models like the Japanese just-in-time system and the industrial district militate against the global factory approach to international production. Not only do post-Fordist firms avoid long supply lines, they depend on highly skilled and flexible workers who may be diffi-

cult to find in poorer countries. Spatial clustering rather than spatial dispersion is the post-Fordist footprint, reshaping the industrial landscape and
reconfiguring the map of industry on a world scale.

This does not mean, of course, that industries will no longer be internationalized but that internationalization will assume a post-Fordist guise.
"New forms of international investment and of global networking—international consortia, international subcontracting, licensing and coproduction
agreements, joint ventures, and production-sharing"—are all characteristic
of post-Fordist internationalization (Aponte 1991:70). U.S. MNCs will
need to maintain their presence in other countries (primarily in Europe and
Japan) in order to keep abreast of their competitors in major markets and
respond more quickly to new product and process developments. According
to theorists of post-Fordism, this will often mean sharing research and marketing costs and maintaining access to foreign consumers, capital, and production facilities, instead of directly investing in productive assets overseas.

The Third Road: An Industry Perspective

Both the quantitative indicators of internationalization and the historical
narrative of Fordism and post-Fordism attempt to convince us that production *in the aggregate* is (or is not) internationalized and also to give us some
information about the general form that internationalization takes. But
there is a third approach—which I call an industry perspective—that is less
concerned with making generalizations about the economy as a whole and
more concerned with what is happening in particular industries. From an
industry perspective, production *is* highly internationalized (but only in certain industries) and productive capital *is* fleeing the industrialized world
(but only in certain subsectors of internationalized sectors). This perspective
may help to resolve the debates about the extent and form of internationalization, and it may also suggest some options for political intervention that
were obscured by the aggregate view.

If the economy is made up of different industries, it is clear that general statements about production and where it goes are on pretty shaky
ground. Not many generalizations can cover petroleum refining, eating and
drinking places, apparel, and communications, whether they be generalizations about firm size, technology, labor requirements, or international production. Given their other differences, it makes sense that different industries will differ in their degree and form of internationalization, and that the
impacts of internationalization on the labor force and communities will differ across industries as well.

Not surprisingly, examining the internationalization of production
from an industry perspective yields a patchwork picture of the whole. Many
industries are not particularly internationalized in production. The solid
wood products industry, for example, which produces timber, lumber, and

panels, is a major U.S. industry in which production is not internationalized at all, though trade is highly internationalized. In other industries, like steel, U.S. producers are not internationalized, but producers from other nations are. In still other industries, like automobiles, production is highly internationalized, and this internationalization takes a variety of forms. In the discussion that follows, I examine the nature and extent of internationalization in several industries: steel, automobiles, semiconductors, clothing, and insurance. Since it is not international production per se that concerns us, but the potentially devastating impacts on the workers and communities from which it withdraws (or withholds) jobs, I consider for each industry the ways in which international production contributes to job loss, worker dislocation, and community decline.

Steel

In the 1970s many steel plants in the United States closed, and workers experienced massive job loss, sending traditional steel communities into a prolonged depression. This occurred not because U.S. steel producers were producing overseas but because, among other things, they had not been investing in steel. By failing to appropriately upgrade their existing mills and construct new ones, U.S. steel companies left the market wide open to imports produced by firms in other countries with state-of-the-art technology. Now foreign companies are buying plants in the United States or participating in joint ventures with U.S. steel producers in order to produce the high-grade sheet steel they need for the products they make in the United States (D'Costa 1993).

In Japan and in many newly industrializing countries, most prominently South Korea and Brazil, governments gave priority to the steel industry and protected it from foreign intervention. These countries developed modern steel industries that could serve domestic demand and supply the world (primarily the U.S.) market as well. Fortunately for them, though to the great detriment of U.S. workers and communities in steel-producing regions, both the U.S. government and the U.S. steel industry left the U.S market open to foreign producers of steel.

The history of the steel industry tells more about national and industry priorities for development than it does about international production strategies (Tiffany 1984). If the U.S. government had fostered the development of new technology and tidewater production sites, the United States might still be self-sufficient in steel, and traditional steel communities might still be functioning, though certainly on a smaller scale.

Automobiles

U.S. steel producers ceded a large share of their market to foreign producers, but they never got particularly involved in foreign production themselves. In the automobile industry, on the other hand, U.S automakers lost market share to imports and at the same time established a huge network of plants overseas. Both of these processes undermined automobile workers and their communities in the United States. The automobile industry is the home of the world car, a standardized product produced in a spatially decentralized network of parts suppliers and assembly plants and coordinated by the corporate headquarters of a major auto firm. The existence of such a network allows firms to satisfy a global market while minimizing overall transport costs and to obtain parts from a variety of sources, insuring that each part of the automobile can be procured for the lowest possible price.

The world car has been touted as the supreme achievement of Fordism, realizing economies of global scale. But the world-car model is not the only spatial strategy in place in the auto industry. Many people argue that it has been supplanted by the territorial production complex (Hill 1989). This post-Fordist approach, pioneered by Japanese auto producers, is characterized by regional concentration rather than global dispersion. Japanese auto assemblers' emphasis on just-in-time parts delivery, which has allowed them to reduce drastically the costs of managing, handling, and storing inventories, requires a degree of spatial proximity impossible in the world-car system. Suppliers and subcontractors of Japanese auto firms tend to ring them in concentric circles; distance from the center is based on the nature and frequency of contact, and none is more than a day's drive away (Sheard 1983). Spatial proximity facilitates design collaboration between suppliers and customers, while a continual flow of small orders allows for maximum sensitivity to the market and the early detection of defects, thereby minimizing the waste associated with large batches of defective parts.

The Japanese tendency toward spatial concentration does not keep them from engaging in international production. Because of their concern about possible U.S. restrictions on imports and the rise in the value of the yen, among other things, Japanese auto manufacturers have begun to construct assembly plants in the United States and to replicate the territorial supplier networks that they have built in Japan. These Japanese "transplants" are located primarily on the southeastern rim of the old auto complex so that they can source parts from midwestern suppliers who have traditionally served the Big Three in the Great Lakes region (Mair, Florida, and Kenney 1988). At the same time, they can avoid the union labor that is associated with the north central states and seek out nonunion labor in the rural areas of the south central states.[11]

U.S. automakers are beginning to imitate the Japanese, shutting down some of their distant plants on the West Coast and in the South and reconcentrating their production in or near the old auto-producing region. The Saturn plant built by General Motors in Tennessee is probably the most well-known example of Japanese-style production by a U.S. firm. At this massive integrated production complex, GM is lowering labor costs per unit output through automation, continual upgrading, and zero-defect quality standards.

According to Richard Hill (1989), the current spatial division of labor in the auto industry combines the world-car strategy with the territorial production complex. More expensive, sophisticated, and specialized cars and parts are produced in regional production complexes in the wealthier countries. But automakers in these countries are also situated in an extended spatial network that includes certain newly industrialized countries (NICs) from which they source lower-priced, standardized cars and parts. Major producers in the United States, Japan, and Europe currently have joint ventures with producers in the NICs for a variety of reasons; Japanese automakers, for example, have been involved in producing and exporting from South Korea in order to circumvent import restrictions from the United States. In 1989, 12 percent of all imports to the U.S. market were captive "imports," produced overseas to be sold here with U.S. nameplates (Howes 1993).

The effects of Japanese auto investment in the United States have been assumed by some observers to be an unmixed blessing, since foreign corporations building or buying plants in the United States create or at least maintain jobs. Candace Howes (1991, 1993) points out, however, that the Japanese transplants are creating jobs in the United States at the expense of jobs at the Big Three. The cars produced by the "transplants" are sold in the U.S. market, enlarging the Japanese market share. Thus they continue to displace U.S. cars—and workers—just as Japanese imports have.

Cars produced by Japanese transplants have an advantage over those produced by the Big Three not only because the Japanese plants are more efficient but because of differences in labor costs. The labor force hired by the Japanese is largely nonunion and considerably younger. This means that the cost of health insurance benefits per worker is considerably lower. Because there is no retired work force, pension costs per worker are also much lower. In addition, many of their parts come from transplant suppliers that pay their workers much less than their U.S. counterparts do. Finally, subsidies provided by the states and localities where the plants are located amount to as much as $100,000 per job created. All these things taken together lower Japanese costs per car by as much as $900 below the costs of the Big Three (Howes 1993).

From the perspective of labor in the United States, it is often assumed that imports and foreign investment by U.S. firms are the major causes of job loss in the auto industry. It is less often realized that inward foreign investment can be very important in undermining the power of unions and the economic base of automobile-centered communities. Japanese transplants in greenfield sites are remaking the geography of automobile production,[12] displacing a skilled, relatively well-paid, and diverse work force and replacing them with a predominantly young, white, male, and nonunion labor force (as transplant-produced automobiles displace those produced by the Big Three and as the Big Three emulate the Japanese in their location decisions). Trade and inward direct foreign investment are more important constituents of this labor-replacement process than is an overseas investment strategy by U.S firms, though that strategy still accounts for the export of jobs.

Between 1982 and 1993, according to Howes, the Japanese auto assembly and parts plants will have eliminated "158,000 more U.S. jobs than they will have created." As many as "350,000 unionized workers will have been displaced and 200,000 non-union jobs will have been created, devastating the unions in the auto industry" (1991:16–17). These nonunion jobs will entail comparable wages in assembly plants (though, as we have seen, lower benefit costs) and much lower wages in parts plants, resulting in a huge redistribution of potential wealth from U.S. workers to Japanese capitalists (see also Helper 1991a). Most of all, however, the new jobs are being created in greenfield sites, producing massive dislocation for existing workers and devastating older communities based on the automobile.

Semiconductors

The semiconductor industry has become a well-known instance of the global factory, though its labor force is relatively small—about 300,000 worldwide (Sayer 1986). The most famous product of this industry is the integrated circuit, which is produced in a multiphase process—including design, maskmaking, fabrication, assembly, and testing—that is often spatially dispersed. More specifically, the first three phases tend to be performed in the United States or other developed countries, while assembly, or the application of microscopic circuitry to silicon chips, is often performed in Asia by young women at low wages. The chips are then reimported to the "home" country, where they are used in the production of electronic products like computers and computerized equipment.

Despite its currency, the image of the global factory is not an entirely accurate picture of the international semiconductor industry. In the first place, the model applies largely to U.S. producers. Japanese and European semiconductor firms are much less likely than U.S. firms to assemble semiconductors offshore (Scott and Angel 1988). Second, for most of the history of the U.S. semiconductor industry, offshore assembly has been the strategy of only one type of firm, the large market producer that produces semiconductors for sale. Small market producers and captive producers, firms (like IBM) that produce semiconductors for their own use, have tended to follow a domestic production strategy. Smaller producers restricted themselves to this country in part because they could not afford to establish plants overseas. In addition, they were often operating in niche markets that were more sheltered from the extremes of competition than the market for standardized chips. Captive producers were also sheltered from that highly competitive market and they had the resources to automate the assembly process rather than lower labor costs by moving offshore.

More recently, however, there seems to be a trend toward offshore assembly among small start-up firms and larger captives as well. This reflects the growth of an indigenous semiconductor industry in Southeast Asia to which U.S.-based firms without plants in the region are subcontracting their assembly work. Even those firms like IBM that have automated the assembly phase can now find skilled technical workers who can operate and maintain a relatively automated system much more cheaply than it can be done in this country. According to David Angel (1990), 70 percent of U.S. assembly is now done offshore.

The semiconductor industry is particularly interesting not because of its connection to the global factory but because it is taking root and growing in Southeast Asia. Both upstream suppliers and downstream users have sprung up in a regional complex of indigenous firms, including technical training facilities, centered in Thailand (Scott 1987). This development counters the image of the sterile branch plant in poor countries, which repatriates profits and contributes to underdevelopment rather than industrial growth. The development of the locally owned semiconductor industry in Southeast Asia has been extremely dynamic and relies increasingly on highly skilled workers. Allen Scott (1987) found local producers engaged in all phases of the production process from design to testing, although assembly subcontracting was the major activity at the time. With new firms emerging at an increasing rate across the spectrum of production, it seems that U.S firms operating overseas have once again spawned their competitors of the future.

As a high-tech industry that has spawned industrial districts in the post-Fordist mold (most notably in Silicon Valley but now also in Southeast Asia), the semiconductor industry is often identified as the lead sector in a new wave of industrialization. Unlike the experience of other industries, then, international production in the context of the semiconductor industry is frequently associated with economic development (see Angel 1990; Scott and Angel 1988), both in this country and in certain countries of the Third World. This runs counter to the image of international production as (necessarily) associated with underdevelopment and industrial decline. The experience of the semiconductor industry suggests that, by itself, internationalization is not the problem. The problems with international production have to do with its social, political, and industrial contexts, which will be different in different regions and sectors and will change over time.

Clothing

The clothing industry is another industry in which international production is often organized on the model of the global factory, although international subcontracting to foreign firms is more common than the branch plant strategy. Clothing firms tend to be much smaller and more localized than firms in the automobile and semiconductor industries (see Elson 1989, though) and are often bound together in an international subcontracting network by a major retailing chain in an industrialized country.

The market for clothing, however, has been changing, as have certain other consumer goods markets, with a movement away from standardized goods and toward more specialized or custom goods. A wide variety of styles now coexist where in the past you might have found only a few. Major retailers have promoted this trend, and adjusted to it, by attempting to create a boutique or bazaar shopping environment in place of the old department store with its men's, women's, and children's clothing sections.

As styles proliferate and the pace of change in fashion accelerates, the clothing industry increasingly requires flexibility in production. Computerized retailers like Benetton are extremely sensitive to changes in the market; with each purchase, inventory information can be updated, and retailers can place a continual stream of orders to keep their shelves stocked. No longer do they have to purchase huge lots of garments for an entire season. The ability to be sensitive to signals from shoppers and to adjust orders on a frequently updated basis militates against an overseas production or subcontracting strategy with its great distances and lengthy turnaround times. Increasingly, then, clothing producers and retailers have turned to subcontractors at home (Waldinger 1986). As in the high-fashion segment of the industry or the prototype phase of mass production, retailers, designers, and producers maintain close proximity to facilitate collaboration and the increased number of transactions.

In the major cities of the wealthy nations, an international labor force made up largely of immigrant women works for low wages in the clothing industry.[13] While factories may continue to close, this does not necessarily mean that the work has been shipped overseas. Rather, it is increasingly performed as outwork in homes and sweatshops where compensation and working conditions are unregulated by unions or the government and where patriarchal oppression often compounds capitalist exploitation.[14]

Insurance

In the insurance industry neither production nor trade is particularly internationalized. U.S. insurers have focused on the domestic market, in part because it is the largest in the world but also because other nations have tended to exclude foreign insurers from their jurisdiction. This reflects the fact that insurance companies are major financial organizations that can potentially control a huge proportion of a nation's financial resources. U.S. insurers have so far found foreign markets relatively impenetrable, given the complexity of regulations and the intent to prohibit the dominance of foreign firms.[15]

Insurance production and sales may not be internationalized, but insurance company investment increasingly is. The volume of international loans and portfolio investment by U.S. insurers is on the rise. This form of capital export is potentially just as costly in terms of jobs lost or forgone than other, more familiar forms of overseas movement like the globalization of production by multinational firms.

Insurers have not moved overseas, but they have recently been the source of considerable job loss and worker dislocation. In the 1970s and 1980s, many of the back offices (where workers do not meet the public face-to-face) have been moved from the inner cities to suburban and even rural locations. Insurers cite the differential costs of real estate as a prime reason for these moves; the other reason they give is the labor force (Wissoker and Graham 1993). They are laying off an urban work force made up largely of women of color who are the sole support of their families, in order to hire suburban white women—often with college degrees—who perceive themselves as "second earners" and need to work near home. This labor force satisfies insurers' needs for workers who do not expect much compensation or other satisfaction from their jobs but can handle customer relations and high volumes of computer and paper work (all requiring considerable accuracy and familiarity with a confusing array of policies and regulations). In addition, back-office moves are often associated with labor-saving technological change, producing net job loss as well as worker dislocation.

What Does It All Mean?

From an industry perspective it is clear that the internationalization of production has been a prime cause of plant closings and job loss in some sectors but not in others. In insurance and steel, for example, massive layoffs and worker dislocation have had little if anything to do with international production by U.S. firms.

Even in internationalized industries, job loss may not be predominantly, or even largely, related to direct foreign investment by U.S. firms. In the clothing and auto industries, imports have made huge inroads into U.S.-based production, devastating communities in the older industrial regions. In the auto industry, inward direct foreign investment has (or will) cost many thousands of jobs. Plant closings in the clothing industry are an ongoing trauma for workers in older establishments, but the jobs they are losing are frequently being informalized rather than internationalized.

In all these industries, interregional or intersectoral capital mobility may have the same effects as international mobility and may be used as a threat with the same plausibility and force. In addition, factors besides capital mobility—like bankruptcy schemes to avoid pension liabilities, or monetary policy and exchange rates, or the growth and successful development of other manufacturing nations—may contribute as much or more to layoffs and industrial decline.[16] Clearly not all job loss is traceable to internationalized production, nor does all internationalization necessarily lead to job loss and industrial decline.

Industry studies provide a counterpoint to the story of the global factory and capital flight, recasting to some extent the role of MNCs. Multinational corporations are not necessarily transmitters of underdevelopment and industrial decline (witness the semiconductor industry), nor are they necessarily beyond the control of the nation-state (witness the insurance and steel industries, in which national governments have played an interventionist role in shaping the geography of major corporations).

They are not prevalent in every industry, their strategies are not uniform across industries or over time, and they are not as successful in remaking the globe as their image suggests. Recognizing this allows us to take back some of the power that we have given over to MNCs, which are often constructed in narratives of internationalization as controlling rather than controllable organizations.

The tendency to see MNCs as all-powerful and as a natural outgrowth of capitalism has obscured the ways in which they are constituted and constrained within the regulatory context of the nation-state (Gordon 1988; McIntyre 1991). More specifically, the vision of the MNC as the primary agent of internationalization has obscured the role of the U.S. government in fostering and permitting the internationalization of production. Unlike the governments of many European countries and Japan, the United States has given tax breaks (including import tariff exclusions) to companies producing abroad and importing goods to the United States. The United States is currently entering into a free trade agreement with Canada and Mexico that increases the likelihood that U.S. manufacturing companies will expand production in locations outside the United States (see Larudee, in this volume, Chapter 2). Perhaps most important, the U.S. government has failed until recently to create an institutional framework for industrial policy initiatives or a national forum for industrial policy debate.

Visions and Politics

The restless image of the MNC, scanning the globe for profitable investment opportunities, is an important element in the ideology of competitiveness, which implies that U.S. workers and communities must reduce their demands for decent working and living conditions in order to compete with the rest of the world. According to this version of the competitiveness story, workers and communities are at the mercy of multinational corporations, which discipline them through the threat or actuality of capital flight.

To undermine the ideology of competitiveness, it is important to show the limits of MNCs and of international capital mobility. MNCs are a problem for some workers—a minority of workers—and not for others. Most U.S. workers are not employed in jobs that are easily exported. Instead, they are employed in government, construction, locally based services, agriculture, or in other sectors where production is geographically constrained. Even for the slightly more than 18 percent of U.S. workers employed in manufacturing, many of their jobs are not particularly mobile.

But the international immobility of most employers (including the government) should not reassure us. There are many things corporations can do to jobs besides export them. A major problem for most workers is that corporations do not see themselves as existing primarily—or even incidentally—to provide good and steady employment. If we want the economy to provide jobs, it seems that we will have to direct it toward that purpose. We will have to make decisions that put jobs, rather than other things, first. Creating businesses (and other organizations) that are concerned to provide employment and a stable industrial base will not guarantee everyone a job, but at least it will ensure that jobs and communities are not sacrificed in the pursuit of some other goal.

ACKNOWLEDGMENTS

I am grateful to Jerry Epstein, Katherine Gibson, Carol Heim, Emily Kawano, Tim Koechlin, Mehrene Larudee, and Jessica Nembhard for their helpful comments on earlier drafts of this chapter. In addition, I would like to thank Sam Bowles, Jerry Epstein, and Tim Koechlin for consultations on data series and interpretation.

NOTES

1. Both Richard McIntyre (1991) and Rhys Jenkins (1984) make this point, citing the role of automation, government policy, and exchange-rate shifts, among other factors, in the loss of manufacturing jobs.

2. According to Rachael Kamel (1990:4), multinational corporations "are not a new invention. . . . What is new is the global factory, in which a single manufacturing process is broken down into many steps that are divided among workers in different nations (or different areas of a single country). Management control, as well as research and development and product design, stays in the hand of the parent firm in the United States (or another advanced industrial country). Meanwhile, fabrication of components or final assembly is carried out in Third

World countries like Korea, the Philippines, or Mexico—or in a low-wage area of the United States."

3. As McIntyre (1991:188) points out, however, the choice of a relatively wealthy country as an investment destination does not mean that labor costs (and wages in particular) are completely inconsequential. Much of the manufacturing investment that flowed to Europe, for example, ended up in the poorer European countries, suggesting that labor cost considerations were often involved in the location decision.

4. Well over half the output of U.S. MNCs in the Third World is sold locally (Timothy Koechlin, 1991, personal communication).

5. Of course, this does not mean that they generate most of that income outside their home countries. In fact, for the United States, only 25 percent of MNC income is earned abroad (see Epstein, in this volume, Chapter 10). In other words, U.S. MNCs are big, but they are not necessarily very multinational.

6. *Statistical Abstract of the United States*, 1984, tables 734 and 1451. This means that about 5 percent of final transactions were accounted for by MNC-associated imports.

7. The data supporting this assertion were provided by Timothy Koechlin from an updated and revised version of table 2.2 in Koechlin 1989. This table also shows that, for manufacturing, the ratio of DFI to total investment is slightly higher than for the economy as a whole.

8. Employment statistics tend to overstate the extent of MNC activities abroad. A foreign enterprise is a U.S. affiliate if more than 10 percent of its voting shares are owned by a U.S. firm (although most U.S. affiliates are majority owned). All employees of such an affiliate are included in the published data on U.S. MNC employment; i.e., employment figures are not "prorated" to account for the fact that a foreign affiliate is less than completely owned by a U.S. parent (Timothy Koechlin, 1991, personal communication).

One could argue, and people have, that the figures for total civilian employment in Table 11.1 include all kinds of workers—like government workers, or self-employed workers—who are not subject to internationalization. Therefore, the argument goes, they should be taken out of the total, so that it includes only those workers whose jobs are potentially internationalized. I am interested, however, in indicators of the overall extent of globalization, and it seems to me that figures on jobs that cannot be internationalized are just as relevant to this discussion as figures on jobs that have not been internationalized. The fact that these workers are necessarily domestically based is a constraint on globalization and should be acknowledged.

9. If we want to get even more confused, we can look at data on capital stocks, which shows that approximately 14 percent of corporate tangible (plant and equipment) assets were located overseas in 1989. Unlike both the information on profits and the information on investment and employment, data on domestic assets (Board of Governors of the Federal Reserve System 1991) and on stocks of U.S. DFI abroad (Eisner and Pieper 1990:table 4, updated and revised in personal correspondence with Samuel Bowles, June 1991) suggest that production is moderately internationalized.

10. As a counter to this relatively sanguine portrayal of post-Fordism, see Emily Kawano's discussion, in Chapter 12, of the Japanese system of production.

11. This is not necessarily because they want to pay these workers lower wages but because many Japanese firms feel they cannot institute the Japanese system of labor relations in the context of U.S. industrial unionism.

12. Susan Helper (1991b) finds that the transformation of supplier relations in the U.S. auto industry, which involves both Japanese firms and their U.S. emulators, is more pronounced in the newer auto-producing regions. This finding supports Candace Howes's (1993) contention that Japanese investment is replacing rather than transforming the traditional auto regions and their work forces.

13. Roger Waldinger (1986:89–91) shows that New York, which had a steadily declining share of the national market for the thirty years preceding 1975, held on to a constant market share in the period from 1975 to 1985. He attributes this to changes in some segments of the market that gave smaller, more flexible New York manufacturers an advantage over larger, spatially dispersed firms. The ethnic composition of both the firms and the labor force changed dramatically as the apparel market became more volatile and responsive. Over the period from 1970 to 1980, the number of Chinese-owned garment firms in New York went from 102 to 480 and the proportion of foreign-born workers went from 42 to 56 percent (Waldinger 1986:117).

14. In a fascinating study of this process in London, Swasti Mitter (1986) investigated the strange and very rapid growth of productivity in the clothing industry. Whereas government economists attributed rising productivity to technology and work practices, Mitter showed that it had to do with more and more production being taken on in sweatshops and outwork networks, where workers are not counted as part of the labor force (thus, the apparent rise in output per worker, as output remained constant and employment contracted in the official statistics).

15. It is this situation that the current GATT talks are intended, in part, to remedy.

16. A broad range of factors contributes to job loss and community decline. These may be quite distant from the production strategies of individual firms, or even from the conditions of production and marketing in particular industries. Exchange-rate fluctuations, for example, may have major negative impacts that overshadow their wage and productivity advantages to producers in certain nations (McIntyre 1991). Financial manipulations may result in the disposal of productive assets and the subsequent closing of profitable plants (see, for example, Robert Fagan [1990], who examines closings caused by an Australian firm caught up in the highly volatile global financial system of the 1980s). Changes in demand induced by fashion or by product substitution (as in the case of reduced consumption of steel per automobile), automation and productivity increases, conservation and recycling, and a world of other conditions may negatively affect jobs and the communities those jobs have traditionally sustained.

BIBLIOGRAPHY

Angel, David P. 1990. New Firm Formation in the Semiconductor Industry: Elements of a Flexible Manufacturing System. *Regional Studies* 24(3): 211–21.
Aponte-García, Maribel. 1991. The International Division of Labor in the United States Military Industry in the Caribbean Region. Ph.D. diss., University of Massachusetts, Amherst.

Board of Governors of the Federal Reserve System. 1991. *Balance Sheets for the U.S. Economy, 1945–1990.* Washington D.C.: Federal Reserve.

D'Costa, Anthony. 1993. The Internationalization of Steel Production. In *Trading Industries, Trading Regions,* ed. Helzi Noponen, Julie Graham, and Ann Markusen. New York: Guilford Press.

Eisner, Robert, and Paul Pieper. 1990. The World's Greatest Debtor Nation? *North American Review of Economics and Finance* 1(1): 9–32.

Fagan, Robert H. 1990. The Restructuring of Elders IXL Ltd.: Finance and the Global Shift. *Australian Geographer* 21(1): 90–92.

Gordon, David M. 1988. The Global Economy: New Edifice or Crumbling Foundations? *New Left Review* 168:24–6.

Helper, Susan. 1991a. Comparative Performance of U.S. and Japanese "Transplant" Suppliers: Results of Survey Research in the U.S. Automobile Industry. Department of Economics, Case Western Reserve University, Cleveland, Ohio. Unpublished paper.

———. The Restructuring of Supplier Relations in the U.S. Auto Industry: Do Regions Matter? Paper presented at the annual meeting of the Social Science History Association, New Orleans.

Hill, Richard Child. 1989. Divisions of Labor in Global Manufacturing: The Case of the Automobile Industry. In *Instability and Change in the World Economy,* ed. Arthur MacEwan and William K. Tabb, 166–86. New York: Monthly Review Press.

Howes, Candace. 1991. Transplants No Cure. *Dollars and Sense,* July/August, 16–20.

———. 1993. Unconstructing Comparative Advantage: The Political Construction of World Auto Geography. In *Trading Industries, Trading Regions,* ed. Helzi Noponen, Julie Graham, and Ann Markusen. New York: Guilford Press.

Jenkins, Rhys. 1984. Divisions over the International Division of Labour. *Capital and Class* 22:28–58.

Kamel, Rachael. 1990. *The Global Factory: Analysis and Action for a New Economic Era.* Philadelphia: American Friends Service Committee.

Koechlin, Timothy H. 1989. The Globalization of Investment: Three Critical Essays. Ph.D. diss., University of Massachusetts, Amherst.

Lipietz, Alain. 1987. *Mirages and Miracles: The Crises of Global Fordism.* London: Verso.

Mair, Andrew, Richard Florida, and Martin Kenney. 1988. The New Geography of Auto Production: Japanese Transplants in North America. *Economic Geography* 64(4): 352–73.

McIntyre, Richard. 1991. The Political Economy and Class Analytics of International Capital Flows: U.S. Industrial Capitalism in the 1970s and 80s. *Capital and Class* 43:179–201.

Mitter, Swasti. 1986. Industrial Restructuring and Manufacturing Homework: Immigrant Women in the U.K. Clothing Industry. *Capital and Class* 27:36–76.

Sayer, Andrew. 1986. Industrial Location on a World Scale: The Case of the Semiconductor Industry. In *Production, Work, Territory,* ed. Allen Scott and Michael Storper, 107–23. Boston: Allen & Unwin.

Scott, Allen. 1987. The Semiconductor Industry in South East Asia: Organization,

Location, and the International Division of Labour. *Regional Studies* 21(2): 143–59.

Scott, Allen, and David Angel. 1988. The Global Assembly Operations of U.S. Semiconductor Firms: A Geographical Analysis. *Environment and Planning A* 20(8): 1047–67.

Sheard, Paul. 1983. Auto-Production Systems in Japan: Organizational and Locational Features. *Australian Geographical Studies* 21(1): 59–81.

Tiffany, Paul. 1984. The Roots of Decline: Business–Government Relations in the American Steel Industry, 1945–1960. *Journal of Economic History* 46(2): 407–19.

Waldinger, Roger. 1986. *Through the Eye of the Needle: Immigrants and Enterprise in New York's Garment Trades*. New York: New York University Press.

Webber, Michael, and Simon Foot. 1988. Profitability and Accumulation. *Economic Geography* 64(4): 335–51.

Wissoker, Peter, and Julie Graham. 1993. Restructuring and Internationalizing: Domestic Shifts in the Insurance Industry. In *Trading Industries, Trading Regions*, ed. Helzi Noponen, Julie Graham, and Ann Markusen. New York: Guilford Press.

12 EMILY KAWANO

The Japanese Model of Production: Cooperation or Coercion?

Over the last ten years there has been an explosion of interest in Japanese management and production strategies. This interest has been fueled by the success of the Japanese economy and by concern over the competitiveness of American industry.

The Japanese success story is well known. Emerging from postwar devastation, the Japanese economy grew at a rate that far outpaced that of other industrialized countries (see Table 12.1). Japanese rates of productivity growth have also led the world since the early 1960s (see Table 12.2). At the same time, unemployment has remained remarkably low and stable relative to other industrialized nations (see Table 12.3). Since World War II, Japan's unemployment has remained below 3 percent, despite the oil shocks in the 1970s and Japan's complete dependence on imported oil.

Japan's success has sparked fear as well as interest. Many Americans are afraid that the United States is being threatened by a "Japanese takeover" of American businesses and real estate. Republican representative Helen Bentley of Maryland declared that "the U.S. is rapidly becoming a colony of Japan," and historian Arthur Schlesinger speculated that Japan is seeking revenge on the economic battlefield: "Japan is considerably less repentant than Germany about its aggressions and atrocities of half a century ago and very likely more driven by the desire for vindication and even perhaps for revenge" (Smith 1990).

The racist undercurrent of these fears becomes clear when we consider that in 1988 the total value of Japanese investments in the United States was about half that of Britain's, and only in 1988 did they surpass Dutch investments (see Table 12.4). The level of Japanese investment in manufacturing in the United States has been lower than that of the United Kingdom, the Netherlands, and West Germany. Yet there has never been any alarm about the "British takeover" or the "Dutch invasion" of America, and Germany's economic motivations are not impugned as are those of Japan.

Ironically, while Japan bashing has become increasingly popular, Ameri-

TABLE 12.1
Growth Rates in Real Gross National Product (Annual Percentage Changes)

Country	1961–65	1966–70	1971–75	1976–83	1984–89
U.S.	4.6	3.0	2.2	2.5	4.0
Japan	12.4	11.0	4.3	4.4	4.6
Canada	5.3	4.6	5.2	2.7	4.4
France	5.9	5.4	4.0	2.5	2.4
W. Germany	4.7	4.2	2.1	2.4	2.8
Italy	4.8	6.6	2.4	3.3	3.1
U.K.	3.2	2.5	2.1	1.7	3.4

Source: Council of Economic Advisers 1990.

TABLE 12.2
Labor Productivity (Average Annual Percentage Changes)

Country	1960–73	1973–79	1979–88
U.S.	2.2	0.0	0.8
Japan	8.6	3.0	3.2
Canada	2.8	1.5	1.4
France	5.4	3.0	2.6
W. Germany	4.5	3.1	1.7
Italy	6.3	3.0	1.6
U.K.	3.6	1.6	2.1

Source: Council of Economic Advisers 1990.

TABLE 12.3
Unemployment (Percentages)

Country	1988	1989	1990	1991[a]
U.S.	5.5	5.3	5.5	6.4
Japan	2.5	2.3	2.1	2.3
Canada	7.8	7.5	8.1	9.4
France	10.0	9.4	8.9	9.0
W. Germany	6.2	5.6	5.0	5.0
Italy	12.1	12.1	11.1	11.3
U.K.	8.2	6.2	5.8	6.2

Source: Council of Economic Advisers 1990.   [a]Data for 1991 is projected.

TABLE 12.4
Foreign Direct Investment Position of the United States (in Millions of Dollars)

Country	1984	1985	1986	1987	1988
Japan	16,044	19,313	26,824	35,151	53,354
U.K.	38,387	43,555	55,935	79,669	101,909
Netherlands	33,728	37,056	40,717	49,115	48,991

Source: Statistical Abstract of the United States, 1990. *Note:* Foreign direct investment is defined as ownership of 10 percent or more of U.S. real estate and businesses.

TABLE 12.5
Trade Balances (in Seasonally Adjusted Billions of Dollars)

Country	1988	1989	1990	1991ᵃ
U.S.	− 127.0	− 114.9	− 116.0	− 115.0
Japan	95.0	76.9	58.0	60.0
Canada	9.1	6.8	10.0	15.0
France	− 8.5	− 10.1	− 13.0	− 20.0
W. Germany	79.6	77.0	81.0	66.0
Italy	− 1.2	− 2.0	− 1.0	− 2.0
U.K.	− 37.5	− 39.0	− 35.0	− 33.0

Source: Council of Economic Advisers 1990. ᵃData for 1991 is projected.

can managers, faced with shrinking market shares in key industries and a trade deficit in 1990 of $116 billion (see Table 12.5), have been looking to Japan for salvation. A widely publicized report by the MIT Commission on Industrial Productivity concluded that American industry must revamp the basics of production and industrial relations along the lines of the Japanese model in order to restore economic competitiveness.[1]

In fact, the Japanese model of production has already made considerable inroads in the United States through the efforts of domestic firms, Japanese-owned plants in the United States (transplants), and Japanese–American partnerships. Managers are taking crash courses in Japanese management, the Big Three automakers have all established joint production partnerships with Japanese automakers, and the number of Japanese transplants in the United States within the auto industry alone is projected to reach 250 by the early 1990s (Mair, Florida, and Kenney 1988). And not only the United States is so enamored with the Japanese model. Britain, Australia, New Zealand, and many newly industrializing countries, particularly in Asia, are following similar paths.

Given the intensity and breadth of interest in the Japanese model of production and its potentially profound implications for labor, it is important to consider the perspectives of both its supporters and its critics. I believe that one must move beyond a black-and-white depiction of the Japanese model in order to develop an analysis that will be useful in fighting for a more just and democratic workplace.

According to the positive, or post-Fordist, view, the Japanese model of production replaces the Fordist/Taylorist system—based on mass production, assembly lines, the breakdown of complex jobs into simple repetitive tasks, and the separation of manual from mental work—with a post-Fordist structure based on flexible production, work teams, integrated tasks, and a reunification of manual and mental work. Proponents of the post-Fordist view argue that the antagonistic relationship between workers and management is replaced by a system of mutual accommodation and cooperation. They argue that the Japanese system emphasizes its most valuable resource—its work force—and invests in various practices that maximize their skills, cooperation, and the rate of employee retention.

According to the negative, or superexploitation, analysis, the Japanese model of production is nothing more than souped-up Fordism insidiously disguised as a more progressive system. Proponents of this view claim that workers are subjected to increased levels of speedup, stress, supervision, and pressure. They contend that the high rate of productivity is mainly due to speedup rather than organizational innovation and the maximization of human resources.

Looking beyond issues on the shop floor, one alarming implication of the Japanese model of production is that it may deepen the stratification of society into two tiers: highly paid, skilled workers in large firms in the primary sector, who benefit at the expense of low-paid, less-skilled workers in smaller, subsidiary firms in the secondary sector and temporary or part-time workers in the primary sector.

I argue that the Japanese model of production does offer an alternative to Fordism/Taylorism, but that the picture is neither as rosy as in the post-Fordist analysis nor as bleak as in the superexploitation view. The Japanese model may facilitate speedup and increase levels of stress and control over workers, but because of its dependence on the skills of workers, it also has the potential of giving workers greater bargaining leverage. Whether the Japanese model of production proves to be a step forward or backward for labor will depend on whether workers can gather their power and grasp the levers of change.

Cooperation: The Post-Fordist View

Much of the literature on Japanese firms focuses either on the organization of production, such as the just-in-time (JIT) system of inventory control, quality control (QC) circles and job rotation, or on aspects of industrial relations, such as lifetime employment and enterprise unions (defined below). The two are linked, however, in that organizational structures require the active cooperation, willing or coerced, of workers to make them effective. Cooperation, in turn, hinges on the industrial relations system that motivates workers.

Organization of Production

Mass production as a system of organization and production has reigned supreme over the past century, and nobody did it better than the Americans. But the world has moved on, and now the logic of mass production, with its long production runs of standardized models, is being challenged by flexible production.

Flexible production involves short production runs of different models and the ability to change over from one model to another in minutes. Japanese automobile plants, for example, are able to make die changes in five minutes, whereas the same changes require eight to twenty-four hours in American plants. Japanese firms operate on a product cycle, from the conception to the end of a product run, of seven and a half years, while American firms have product cycles of thirteen to fifteen years (Dertouzos et al. 1989:19). In a world where consumer tastes are highly diverse and change with blinding speed, flexible production is able to respond rapidly to the market without losing the cost advantages of mass production.

The system of flexible production is embedded in new forms of production organization and technology as well as industrial relations. The post-Fordist view argues that a highly skilled labor force is necessary in order for the system to operate efficiently. Technology such as flexible automation, robotics, and computer-controlled machinery must be operated by workers who can change over the machinery, program the computers and robots, and perform general maintenance and repair. Other systems such as QC and JIT (discussed below) also require a highly trained work force. Flexible production cannot depend on a low-wage, unskilled work force, nor can it operate well with a transient work force, because it calls for firm-specific skills that are acquired through experience.

The principle of learning by doing is to channel and apply information generated on the shop floor toward improvements in the production process. In the traditional Taylorist model, knowledge is extracted from skilled workers and systematized by specialists such as engineers and system designers (Aglietta 1979; Clawson 1980). Thus, mental work (conceptualization and planning) is separated from the manual work (the execution of work). Mental work becomes the responsibility of the management and specialists, while the manual work is left to the worker. Although this separation of mental and manual work makes it easier to supervise and control workers, it fails to capture the knowledge that is continually produced by workers' firsthand experience.

Learning by doing overthrows the traditional Taylorist principle of separating mental from manual work, in that it recognizes that the knowledge and skills of workers cannot be appropriated once and for all, because workers generate a constant stream of knowledge through their experiences on the production line. This information is invaluable in upgrading, fine-tuning, and adapting production in the face of the day-to-day unexpected problems and opportunities for change. Learning by doing systematically taps into the knowledge and experience that is continually being generated (Koike 1988; Best 1990).

A component of learning by doing is the QC (quality control) circle. Instead of depending on a team of quality inspectors, everyone is expected to bear the responsibility for quality control. Teams of workers meet on a regular basis to discuss strategies to cut cost, waste, improve quality, decrease accidents, and so forth.

Workers accumulate different skills through job rotation among the various stations within and outside a workshop. Not only does this result in multiple skills, it also enables workers to gain an overall understanding of the production process. The post-Fordist analysis argues that this understanding is invaluable to the generation of new information that can be captured through learning by doing and QC circles.

The JIT (just-in-time) system of inventory control drastically reduces the resources that would otherwise be tied up in the storage, coordination, and management of inventories. Instead of stockpiling large inventories of parts, production is set up such that parts arrive as they are needed, or "just-in-time." This system requires close coordination between the supplier and the manufacturer, as well as between stations on the production line (Sugimora 1977; Aoki 1987; Best 1990). Because the just-in-time system depends on a high degree of coordination and proper timing, it is vulnerable to any disruptions along the line. In order to maintain the delicate system, workers must be able to handle a wide variety of tasks that in a traditional organizational structure would be the responsibility of specialists.

By practically eliminating inventory buffers, the JIT system has the added effect of making problems and bottlenecks identifiable and thereby correctable. A central goal of this form of production in general is to make problems immediately visible instead of waiting till the end of a production run to pinpoint and correct defects.

To a great extent, the success of the organizational structures discussed above depends on the firm's ability to motivate or coerce workers to cooperate. The JIT system, because of its great dependence on coordination and timing, is inherently vulnerable to worker sabotage, no matter how mild. Learning by doing and QC circles depend, at least to some extent, on workers being willing to share their knowledge with management. But why should workers accede to this arrangement?

William Ouchi's popular *Theory Z* (1981) claims that workers, given respect and challenging jobs, are willing to work hard and to contribute to improvements in production. From this perspective the very organizational forms described above are sufficient to explain the cooperative dynamic between workers and management. Organizational structures, however, do not work by themselves. A more compelling explanation within the post-Fordist analysis combines the "dignity of work" argument with the incentive system embodied in the Japanese system of industrial relations.

Industrial Relations

The system of Japanese industrial relations is said to promote cooperation between labor and management. The salient features of this system are often called the "three pillars" or "three treasures" of Japanese industrial relations. These three pillars are:

1. The seniority wage system sets wages on the basis of the worker's length of service to the firm rather than according to his or her job (Koike 1987, 1988). This tends to create an internal labor market where jobs all along the hierarchy are filled from within the firm. Although this practice exists in the United States as well, it is not as extensive as in Japan. These practices encourage long-term commitments from workers who would lose some proportion of their seniority wage if they were to seek alternative employment.

   A drawback of the seniority wage system as it is practiced in Japan, however, is that older workers face semimandatory retirement at the age of fifty-five, particularly in large firms. This is because these older workers are the most expensive to the firm, since wages rise with age. Small firms do not pressure older workers to take early retirement to the same degree, possibly because the seniority wage does not rise as steeply with age as in large firms.

2. Ideally, workers are guaranteed lifetime employment, whereby the employer has a commitment to retain workers even in the face of an economic downturn. In a long-run downturn, workers may be laid off, but this is seen as a last resort (Koike 1987, 1988; Ableggen and Stalk 1985).

   Although it is true that only about a third of the work force in large firms enjoys the maximal degree of security due to lifetime employment, Japanese workers on the whole are more insulated against unemployment resulting from production decreases than American workers. Haruo Shimada compared the response of Japanese and American firms to reductions in production due to the oil shocks from

1973 through 1975. He found that the reduction in employment (for a given decline in output) was two to four times greater in the United States than in Japan (Shimada 1985:69). American firms also responded by cutting back on work hours to a far greater extent than in Japan.

3. Enterprise unions are organized at the plant instead of the industrywide level. Proponents argue that these enterprise unions are better able to navigate between the interests of workers and management, since they operate at the local level (Koike 1987, 1988; Shirai 1983; Gordon 1985).

The Japanese system of industrial relations is credited with securing the cooperation of workers by ensuring a rising wage corresponding to tenure and by providing job security. Enterprise unions facilitate the bargaining process between labor and management by bringing decisions down to the local plant level rather than negotiating on an industrywide basis.

According to what is known as the "culturalist approach," the three pillars of Japanese industrial relations are unique to Japan and are rooted in cultural traditions of groupism and harmony (Ableggen and Stalk 1985; Benedict 1946). It has become apparent, however, that lifetime employment and seniority wage practices are not unique to Japan but are prevalent features of industrial relations in Europe and the United States as well. However, Kazuo Koike (1987, 1988) argues that in Western firms these practices are features of white-collar employment, whereas in Japan they are extended to blue-collar workers also. Thus, not only Japanese white-collar workers but also blue-collar workers strongly identify with the interests of their firms and tend to have long-term employment relationships. Koike calls this the white-collarization of blue-collar workers.

Data on length of service in Japanese firms confirms this long-term employment relationship. Although it is a myth that Japanese workers enter a company right out of school and remain there until retirement, the overall length-of-service profile is much higher in Japan than in the United States (see Table 12.6).

This characterization of the Japanese model of production presents a fairly idyllic picture in which high levels of productivity and quality are maintained through organizational innovation and cooperation between labor and management. This is not the only picture, however, as a more critical analysis of the Japanese model reveals.

Coercion: The Superexploitation Analysis

The superexploitation view argues that Japan's high levels of productivity are not due to innovations in organization or to labor–management coop-

TABLE 12.6
Length of Service in Japan and the United States (Percentages of Male Nonagricultural Employees)

Total Years	United States			Japan			
	1966	*1973*	*1978*	*1962*	*1974*	*1977*	*1979*
Up to 1	23.2	22.4	25.2	9.1	8.4	7.2	7.5
1	8.5	10.5	10.4	10.5	6.5	2.7	2.7
2	6.4	7.4	7.1	10.0	6.9	6.4	6.6
3–4	9.7	13.0	11.9	14.9	13.2	12.3	11.1
5–9	15.2	16.8	16.9	21.4	21.5	22.8	21.7
10–14	11.6	9.6	9.6	16.9	16.6	16.9	17.3
15+	22.2	20.5	19.0	17.7	26.8	31.5	33.1

Sources: Koike 1988:66.

eration, but to increased control over workers and speedup, or "management by stress." Exponents of this view assert that the Japanese model is just the same old Fordist/Taylorist model of production insidiously disguised as a cooperative system and more effective than ever at controlling workers (Slaughter and Parker 1988; Dohse, Ulrich, and Malsch 1985; Stevens and Kato 1989; Kamata 1973).

Organization of Production and Speedup

The JIT system is seen as a primary source of speedup. The reduction of inventory buffers due to JIT leads to the intensification of pressure and stress on workers. If something goes wrong at one point along the line, there is no inventory to cushion the adjustment process. Instead, the whole line comes to a halt. Once the problem is taken care of, workers are expected to make up for the lost time by working faster and longer.

This pattern appears to apply to absenteeism as well. If the workshop is shorthanded, extra workers are not brought in. Rather, the smaller work crew is expected to meet the same production quota by working faster and longer. This pressures workers to minimize absenteeism and to cooperate with efforts to streamline production, simply for the sake of self-preservation (Slaughter and Parker 1988).

Use of a system of stoplights on the production line also reinforces speedup. Lights installed above workstations signal that things are running smoothly (green) or that there is a problem (yellow or red). A yellow light lit over a workstation will bring the assistance of a team leader or supervisor; a red light will bring the production line to a halt. Management has touted the use of stoplights as a way in which workers control the pace of the line, rather than the line controlling the pace of the workers. Critics, however, contend that green lights simply signal that there is too much slack in the line. In response, supervisors ratchet up the pace until yellow and red lights come on. The line is then rebalanced and sped up again.

In these ways the superexploitation analysis claims that much of the increase in productivity results from speedup and increased control, rather than from innovations in organization. To the extent that there has been innovation, it has been in order to further speedup.

Mental Work and Information Flows

The superexploitation analysis contends that contrary to post-Fordist claims, the extent of reskilling and the importance of mental work are minimal. They argue, for example, that job rotation does not amount to reskilling, nor does it give workers a greater overall understanding of the production process. Rather, workers are shifted around to different workstations, all of which require only simple, repetitive skills. This amounts to job widening rather than reskilling. Furthermore, the flexible deployment of workers goes against the job divisions that were carefully set up to provide clear lines of promotion and to prevent job loading, the practice of adding more and more tasks to a workstation (Burawoy 1983).

Critics of the Japanese model also contend that information is tapped from the production line through the participation of the supervisors on the line. Supervisors straddle the boundary between management and worker. They occupy the lowest level of management and, at the same time, the highest rank among workers. Since workers and supervisors work side by side, it becomes impossible for workers to guard any knowledge from management, who might use the information for speedup or greater control (Shimada 1985; Slaughter and Parker 1988; Dohse, Ulrich, and Malsch 1985).

In addition, critics of learning by doing and QC circles argue that they are simply management attempts to shunt more responsibility onto the shoulders of workers. Not only do workers have to perform their prescribed tasks, they also have to check for defects, repair basic mechanical failures, and come up with suggestions for improvements. These responsibilities should belong to management, not to workers (Slaughter and Parker 1988).

Industrial Relations

The superexploitation analysis claims that lifetime employment does not deliver the job security that it purports to. First, it applies only to the one-third of the labor force that is employed in the primary sector. Second, firms may respond to a downturn in demand by transferring workers to other workshops or subsidiary firms that have been less affected by the slowdown (Dohse, Ulrich, and Malsch 1985:139). This may result in an interruption of skill accumulation and a consequent reduction in wages (Koike 1987:308).

The superexploitation view criticizes the seniority wage system for severing the link between wages and job classification. Management is thus able to maximize flexibility in deploying workers to different jobs. This carries the danger of job loading and also reduces workers' control over the labor process.

Enterprise unions are said to stake the interests of workers to the firm where they are employed, because they bargain on the basis of the well-being of the employer; industrial unions, on the other hand, can negotiate packages based on the health of the entire industry, regardless of the state of individual firms within the industry. The well-being of workers in enterprise unions is thus entwined with the fortunes of their employer, and unions are thereby greatly constrained in their bargaining power (Dohse, Ulrich, and Malsch 1985).[2]

The superexploitation analysis argues that the nature of enterprise unions and the weak position of labor in general has left Japanese workers vulnerable to a pernicious system of control and exploitation. Thus, whereas the post-Fordist analysis contends that Japanese industrial relations foster an environment of cooperation necessary to maintain the highly efficient organization of production, the superexploitation analysis argues that industrial relations play a pivotal role in supporting a harsh regime of "management by stress."

Beyond the Shop Floor: Marginalized Workers

The Japanese model of production has consequences for workers that reach far beyond the factory walls. One of the most problematic implications of the Japanese model is the increased stratification between core workers and marginalized workers.

As mentioned above, not all workers enjoy the full benefits of lifetime employment, seniority wages, and corporate welfare. These benefits fully apply only to about one-third of Japan's work force who are employed in large firms (with over a thousand workers) that make up the primary sector. Women, older workers, and minorities, in particular, are concentrated in smaller supplier or subsidiary firms in the secondary sector. These workers are marginalized in the sense that, relative to workers in the primary sector, they receive lower wages, poorer benefits, less job security, and fewer promotional opportunities. Although this is not very different from the dual industrial structure that exists in the United States, the wage gap between the primary and secondary sectors, and male and female workers, is greater in Japan.

In 1981 the female–male wage differential in Japan was 54.1 percent; in the United States in 1980 it was 66 percent. Women in Japan are often employed through their early twenties but stop working when they get married and have children. These women reenter the labor market as middle-aged workers and are paid at around the same level as young single women. Although part of the female–male wage differential may be due to this interruption of work experience, at least half of the differential appears to be due to gender discrimination (Patrick and Rohlen 1987:361).

Japanese firms also heavily employ temporary workers who are completely outside of the sphere of collective bargaining agreements and who usually receive no fringe benefits. Approximately 90 percent of the temporary work force is composed of women.

Minorities in Japan are also marginalized in the labor force. The emphasis on conformity in Japanese corporate culture predisposes it to exclusionary behavior toward minorities such as Koreans, Burakumin,[3] and others who do not "fit in."

The employment privileges of the primary sector, privileges that largely apply to full-time, permanent male workers, are to some extent gained at the expense of workers in the secondary sector. Firms in the primary sector benefit from the low cost of inputs from suppliers in the lower-wage secondary sector, as well as from the low wages paid to women and temporary workers even within the primary sector. The glowing descriptions of Japanese industrial relations are tarnished when we take into account the majority of workers who are outside its scope.

Toward a Progressive Strategy

The Japanese model of production is potentially both promising and threatening to labor; the post-Fordist characterization, then, is overly optimistic. Although some workers are seen as a valuable resource, they may also be subjected to oppressive strategies of production—greater management control, increased stress, speedup, job loading, and capricious job rotation.

The introduction of the Japanese model in the United States has been associated with shutting out unions by locating in "greenfield sites"—rural areas where union organizing has been relatively weak (see Graham, in this volume, Chapter 11). Nissan, for example, chose to locate in Smyrna, Tennessee, where "right-to-work" laws constrain union organizing.[4] Honda, on the other hand, decided to locate in Ohio, a state with a strong union tradition, but chose a rural site far from the more unionized urban centers (Mair, Florida, and Kenney 1988). The lack of a union presence leaves workers vulnerable to oppressive strategies of control.

Finally, the poor treatment of marginalized workers and the prospect of a growing stratification between privileged workers in the primary sector and disadvantaged workers in the secondary sector are disturbing. Japanese transplants in the United States have been accused of discriminating against women, African Americans, and Latinos, and of favoring Japanese over white workers for management jobs (*Wall Street Journal*, 5 October 1990 and 12 December 1990). The post-Fordist analysis not only overemphasizes the positive aspects of the system, it also glosses over these conflictual areas.

On the other hand, the superexploitation analysis is overeager to dismiss the claims of the post-Fordist interpretation. I believe that it is mistaken to write off the Japanese system of production as simply Fordism in disguise. Strategies for worker empowerment that are informed by this interpretation will be ill equipped to grasp the opportunities for increased bargaining leverage.

The Japanese model of production does represent a break from the Taylorist, or scientific-management, principle of separating intellectual from manual work. To some extent at least, the systems of flexible production, flexible technology, learning by doing, QC circles, and JIT require workers' intellectual skills and their cooperation. The JIT system, for example, demands the ability to anticipate as well as solve problems. Workers may also be responsible for programming and repairing sophisticated machinery.

There is at least anecdotal evidence that information flows from the shop floor account in part for the competitiveness of some Japanese firms. At Nissan Chemical, for example, suggestions and input from groups of workers resulted in savings of $2.4 million over a three-year period. At Canon, worker suggestions generated an estimated savings of $1.08 million in one year. Suggestions included energy conservation measures, repairs to equipment, and changes in work procedures (Imai 1986:107).

What this all comes down to is that the Japanese model is dependent on the workers' involvement in maintaining and improving production. This acknowledgment of the value of workers' knowledge and cooperation could strengthen the bargaining position of workers. Alain Lipietz (1987), a French economist, argues that the Japanese model of production puts the working class in a strong position to extract a favorable compromise from firms.

A system of industrial relations that provides greater job security, steady wage increases, and promotional opportunities is a start, but not enough. Workers should demand greater control over the production process to ensure that their input will not be turned against them in the form of speedup and greater management control. It is also reasonable to demand that gains in productivity be shared with the workers who are responsible for those gains. Lipietz argues that these benefits should be shared with workers in the form of more leisure, rather than higher wages. This would avoid the problem of ever-increasing levels of productivity leading to ever-increasing quantities of goods and consumption, which puts a terrible strain on the world's resources (see Schor, Chapter 9 in this volume).

Most important, labor must demand that the privileges in the primary sector be extended to workers in the secondary sector. The inclusion of these marginalized workers is crucial to a progressive response. If labor wins privileges at the expense of women, minorities, and older workers it will fall victim to the divide-and-rule strategy of management. Finally, labor must fight the steady dismantling of social programs, not only to protect the victims who "fall through the safety net" but also to protect their own interests. The weakening of social programs, from unemployment benefits to health care, leaves workers increasingly dependent on company welfare programs, deepening their dependence on their employers.

The skeletal strategy outlined above can form the basis for an ongoing struggle for greater worker control and democratization of production. Whether a progressive version of the Japanese model of production can be achieved or not will greatly depend on whether the labor movement can withstand the attempts to undermine its power and presence. This seems to be a common strategy among firms in the United States that are steering toward the Japanese model. The transformation of the basics of production and industrial relations is already underway in the United States, but whether the outcome will be favorable for working people is still to be decided.

NOTES

1. While America's "competitiveness" is cause for concern, we must also be aware that there are costs to the restoration of our competitiveness. For instance, we should be wary of solutions, such as those promoted by Reaganomics, that come at the expense of increased job insecurity, speedup, lower wages, weakened health and safety standards, gutted environmental legislation, longer work weeks, and exploitative child labor. Looking beyond the level of domestic welfare, we must also question a notion of competitiveness in which some nations emerge as winners, while others are losers.

2. A common misconception about the Japanese labor movement is that it has always been complacent and cooperative with management. In the 1950s, however, there were intense labor struggles with prolonged and widespread strikes led by militant unions. During the Allied occupation of Japan, SCAP (the Supreme Commander for the Allied Powers) played the anti-Communist card against the radical element of the labor movement and succeeded in severely crippling the influence of the militant forces (Gordon 1985). The moderate and more cooperative strands within the labor movement were pushed to the fore and became the dominant force in the unions, which remains true to this day.

3. Burakumin are Japanese outcasts employed in occupations that are consid-

ered unclean, such as those of butchers, leather workers, and morticians. The status is inherited and carries restrictions on marriage and employment.

4. Right-to-work laws prohibit union membership as a condition of employment. This undermines the bargaining power of unions because some workers will "free ride," that is, reap the higher wages and benefits won by unions without paying dues and becoming members.

BIBLIOGRAPHY

Ableggen, James, and George Stalk. 1985. *Kaisha*. New York: Basic Books.
Aglietta, Michel. 1979. *A Theory of Capitalist Regulation: The U.S. Experience*. London: New Left Books.
Aoki, Masahiko. 1987. The Japanese Firm in Transition. In *The Political Economy of Japan*, vol. 1, ed., Kozo Yamamura and Yasukichi Yasuba, 263–88. Stanford: Stanford University Press.
Benedict, Ruth. 1946. *The Chrysanthemum and the Sword: Patterns of Japanese Culture*. Boston: Houghton Mifflin.
Best, Michael. 1990. *The New Competition: Institutions of Industrial Restructuring*. Cambridge: Polity.
Burawoy, Michael. 1983. Between the Labor Process and the State: The Changing Face of Factory Regimes under Advanced Capitalism. *American Sociological Review* 48: 587–695.
Clawson, Dan. 1980. *Bureaucracy and the Labor Process: The Transformation of U.S. Industry, 1860–1920*. New York: Monthly Review Press.
Council of Economic Advisers. 1990. *Economic Report of the President*. Washington, D.C.: U.S. Government Printing Office, February.
Dertouzos, Michael, Richard Lester, and Robert Solow, and the MIT Commission on Industrial Productivity, eds. 1989. *Made in America: Regaining the Productive Edge*. Cambridge, Mass.: MIT Press.
Dohse, Knuth, Jurgens Ulrich, and Thomas Malsch. 1985. From "Fordism" to "Toyotaism"? The Social Organization of the Labor Process in the Japanese Automobile Industry. *Politics and Society* 14(2): 115–46.
Gordon, Andrew. 1985. *The Evolution of Labor Relations in Japan: Heavy Industry, 1853–1955*. Cambridge, Mass.: Council on East Asian Studies, Harvard University Press.
Imai, Masaaki. 1986. *Kaizen*. New York: Random House Business Division.
Kamata, Satoshi. 1973. *Japan in the Passing Lane*. New York: Pantheon.
Koike, Kazuo. 1987. Human Resource Development. In *The Political Economy of Japan*, vol. 1, ed. Kozo Yamamura and Yasukichi Yasuba, 289–330. Stanford: Stanford University Press.
———. 1988. *Understanding Industrial Relations in Modern Japan*. New York: St. Martin's Press.
Lipietz, Alain. 1987. *An Alternative Design for the Twenty-First Century*. Working paper no. 8738. CEPREMAP (Centre D'Etudes Prospectives D'Economie Mathematique Appliquees a la Planification) Paris.
Mair, Andrew, Richard Florida, and Martin Kenney. 1988. The New Geography of

Automobile Production: Japanese Transplants in North America. *Economic Geography* 64(4): 352–73.

Ouchi, William. 1981. *Theory Z*. Reading, Mass.: Addison Wesley.

Patrick, Hugh, and Thomas Rohlen. 1987. Small-Scale Family Enterprises. In *The Political Economy of Japan*, vol. 1, ed. Kozo Yamamura and Yasukichi Yasuba, 331–84. Stanford: Stanford University Press.

Shimada, Haruo. 1985. Perceptions and Reality of Japanese Industrial Relations. In *The Management Challenge*, ed. Lester Thurow, 42–68. Cambridge, Mass.: MIT Press.

Shirai, Taishiro, ed. 1983. *Contemporary Industrial Relations in Japan*. Madison: University of Wisconsin Press.

Slaughter, Jane, and Mike Parker. 1988. *Choosing Sides*. Boston: South End Press.

Smith, Lee. 1990. Fear and Loathing of Japan. *Fortune*, 26 February.

Stevens, Rob, and Tetsuro Kato. 1989. Is Japanese Capitalism "Post-Fordist"? Paper presented to the 8th New Zealand Asian Studies Conference, Christchurch, 17–19 August.

Sugimora, Y., K. Kusunoki, F. Cho, and S. Uchikawa. 1977. Toyota Production System—Materialization of Just-in-Time and Respect-for-Human System. *International Journal of Productivity Research* 15(6): 553–64.

13   LYUBA ZARSKY

From Junior Partner To . . . ?
Japan in the World Economy

Japan's meteoric rise to global economic power is one of the most significant developments of the late twentieth century. The first non-Western country to become an economic superpower, Japan remains the only non-Western member of the Group of Seven (G7) of the world's most powerful nations.[1]

Militarily subordinate to the United States since the end of World War II, Japan catapulted in the 1980s from the status of U.S. junior partner to that of economic equal and rival. Japan has become a major exporter of capital, overtaking the global role of U.S. banks, and a source of technological leadership, challenging many U.S. manufacturing companies.

The American and Japanese economies, however, are highly interdependent: the United States is Japan's largest export market for consumer goods; Japan is the largest buyer of U.S. debt. Moreover, American dominance within the U.S.–Japanese alliance remains the pillar of U.S. military strategy in Asia and the backbone of the Pacific security regime.

Since the late 1970s, U.S.–Japanese relations have been strained by persistent Japanese bilateral trade surpluses. In Japan, U.S. attempts to "pry open" the Japanese market have led to charges of American bullying. In 1989, a prominent Japanese businessman and a politician co-authored an anti-American tirade with the telling title "*The Japan That Can Say No.*"[2]

In the United States, trade-induced economic dislocation, coupled with Japanese technological dominance in many industries and the high visibility of Japanese investment, has fueled an anti-Japanese backlash. Cultural ignorance often lends "Japan bashing" a tinge of racism. With the collapse of the cold war and continued social and economic deterioration in the United States, Japan has become in the minds of many Americans the primary threat to national security. Voicing a widespread sense of siege, a 1991 CIA-funded study warned that Japan "relentlessly" seeks world economic domination and called Japan an "adversary" (Dougherty 1991:167).

258

How did Japan rise to economic power? Is it to blame for U.S. economic woes? What changes must the United States—and Japan—make to live together peacefully as equals? What is Japan's future political and economic role in the world economy?

This chapter sketches some answers to these questions and suggests that American economic policies, rather than Japan, are largely to blame for the U.S. economic decline. It argues that new approaches to economic and foreign policy are required—on both sides of the Pacific—to manage U.S.–Japanese interdependence. For the United States, the task is to develop effective industry and technology policies while striving in its foreign policy to help Japan assume a peaceful role as a global economic superpower. For Japan, the task is to define and embrace a positive contribution to global leadership. Although Japan will choose its own direction, American initiatives could be crucial in determining how the rise of Japan will affect the future of both the U.S. and world economies.

Rise to Power

In the 1960s and 1970s, Japan experienced a period of extraordinarily rapid economic growth. From 1960 to 1969, Japan's GNP grew at an average of 12.1 percent per year, far above the 4.7 percent combined average of the United States, West Germany, France, and Great Britain. Growth remained brisk in the 1970s before settling down to a level more or less commensurate with other Western countries in the 1980s. Nonetheless, over the twenty-five years between 1960 and 1985, Japan grew nearly twice as fast as the United States (see Table 13.1). By 1980, Japan's economy was the third largest in the world, behind only the United States and the Soviet Union. With the collapse of the Soviet Union, Japan has become the world's second largest economy.

TABLE 13.1
Average Annual GNP Growth Rates: A Comparison

Country	1960–69	1970–73	1974–85	1985–88
Japan	12.1	7.5	3.8	4.2
U.S.	4.1	3.2	2.2	3.6
W. Germany	5.7	4.2	1.8	2.6
France (GDP)	5.8	5.6	2.1	2.6
U.K. (GDP)	3.1	3.7	1.3	3.9

Sources: International Monetary Fund, *International Financial Statistics Yearbook*, 1986; *Statistical Abstract of the United States*, 1990.

The immediate source of dynamic growth was Japan's ability to close its technological gap with the West rapidly. World War II had destroyed both a significant portion of Japan's old capital stock and the barriers to trade with the West. Between 1956 and 1973, Japan's capital stock expanded on average by 16 percent per year, much of it imported. The result was a highly productive industrial base made up of cutting-edge technologies. By contrast, the U.S. technological base retained a significant portion of older, obsolete production techniques. Between 1966 and 1985, labor productivity in Japan grew more than two and a half times faster than in the United States (Lincoln 1988:43; Balassa and Noland 1988:6).

Japan's ability to absorb rapidly and diffuse foreign technology was the result of several factors, including its special relationship with the United States, a favorable international climate, and the particular character of its domestic economic institutions, especially those which govern the interaction of government and industry.

The U.S.–Japanese Alliance

Toward the close of World War II, the United States ended the Pacific War with the nuclear bombing of Hiroshima and Nagasaki and established an occupation government in Tokyo. Japan accepted a "peace constitution" drafted by the United States that "forever renounce[d] war as a sovereign right of the nation and the threat or use of force as means of settling international disputes." A bilateral U.S.–Japanese security alliance entrusted responsibility for Japan's external defense to the United States, while Japan provided ports and bases for stationing American military forces. These forces are central to U.S. military strategy not only in Japan but throughout the Asia–Pacific region (Hayes, Bello, and Zarsky 1986). In the past two decades, Japan has also contributed its own expanding "Self-Defense Forces" to the alliance.

The alliance allowed, indeed forced, Japan to focus its energies exclusively on economic development. Economic growth has been the basis of political legitimacy of the Liberal Democratic Party, which has ruled without interruption since 1955. An ideological commitment to growth has had two economic benefits. First, it has generated a high level of political and social cohesion around national economic goals, allowing intellectual and political energies to be directed toward economic development. Second, it has kept military spending at a relatively low level, freeing up national savings for productive investment.[3]

By contrast, the United States, as a global superpower, has shouldered extensive military commitments, especially in Europe and the Asia–Pacific region. For nearly the entire postwar period, U.S. foreign policy has been dominated by military and political, rather than economic and commercial, concerns (Mead 1991). Besides absorbing financial, productive, intellectual, and political resources, the U.S. military posture has generated deep social conflict, evidenced especially during the Vietnam War and by continuing resistance to the military draft. Internal conflict undermines social cohesion and national purpose.

The Japanese economy also got an early boost from U.S. Marshall Plan funds and from regional U.S. military intervention, especially the Korean War, which provided a boom market for struggling Japanese firms. To service the needs of the war effort, the United States provided technological know-how to Japanese firms for mass production of textiles, metal products, fuels, munitions, and vehicles. Indeed, an American-supervised vehicle-production complex known as "little Detroit" helped to lay the foundation for the future development of Japan's automotive industry (Spencer 1967: 62).

Open Global Economy

At the global level, Japan has benefited from the openness of international trade. The General Agreement on Tariffs and Trade (GATT), signed in 1948, organized world trade around the principle of multilateral "free trade." Access to European and North American markets meant that Japan could import needed production technology and export finished goods.

Japan was already a significant economic power on the eve of World War II. Despite the existence of exclusive European-dominated economic blocs, Japan's share of world trade totaled 4.1 percent by 1938, about equal to that of France. With a significant portion of plant and equipment destroyed in the war, Japan's trade share fell to less than 1 percent in 1948. However, the skill, know-how, and cultural attitudes needed for rapid industrial growth remained in place. With American financial and technological assistance, plus access to rapidly growing American and global markets, Japan resumed its high-growth trajectory. By 1970, its share of world trade had jumped to 6 percent (see Table 13.2).

TABLE 13.2
Shares of World Trade: G7 Countries in Percentages

Country	1938	1948	1970	1980	1990
Japan	4.1	0.8	6.0	6.6	7.7
U.S.	10.0	10.0	6.6	11.6	13.3
Canada	3.0	3.0	4.9	3.2	3.6
Britain	14.0	12.0	6.5	5.5	5.6
France	4.0	5.0	5.8	6.1	6.6
Germany	9.0	2.0	10.0	9.3	10.6
Italy	2.0	2.0	4.4	4.3	4.9

Sources: For 1938 and 1948, see Rostow 1978:table II-8. For 1970 and 1980, see Council of Economic Advisers, *Economic Report of the President*, 1985, table B-105.

Trade promotion became an important part of Japan's economic strategy in the 1970s and 1980s, when domestic growth slowed. Net export (i.e., exports minus imports) expansion accounted for about 8 percent of GNP growth between 1973 and 1979, rising to 38 percent between 1980 and 1985 (Lincoln 1988:39).[4] However, Japan's trade emphasis is not out of step with other industrial countries. By 1990, Japan's share of world trade had risen only to 7.7 percent (see Table 13.2).

Industrial and Technological Policy

Although favorable external conditions were helpful, Japan's rise to the global technological frontier was propelled primarily by internal forces. Most important was the framework of its domestic economic institutions, especially those which govern relations between government and markets.

Unlike the United States, the Japanese government has played a significant role in setting the pace and direction of private economic development. The Ministries of Finance (MOF) and International Trade and Industry (MITI) help to promote industries with a high potential for economic growth and technological change and to generate a high level of savings, which provide funds for investment.

Dubbed the "capitalist developmental state" (Johnson 1982), Japan has managed its economy not as a centrally planned, command economy such as existed until recently in China and the Soviet Union; or a regulated, social democratic, market economy such as exists in central and northern Europe; or a "free market" variant of the U.S. economy. Rather, it comprises a particular public–private-sector cooperative approach, which uses government financial and industrial policies in a market economy to promote high-learning, high-technology industries. Emulating the Japanese model, South Korea and Taiwan have likewise achieved rapid growth rates.

Japan's interventionist industrial policy "affected where and how much investment occurred, what kinds of skills and technological learning took place, and by its influence on the production profile of the economy . . . ultimately affected the pace and direction of technological innovation and diffusion" (Dosi, Tyson, and Zysman 1989:33).

Central to Japan's strategic industrial policy is government support for technology-oriented research and development. Firms that join designated nonprofit research consortia, usually based at universities, can qualify for government subsidies in the form of grants, low-interest loans, tax benefits, and use of public research facilities. In the 1950s and 1960s, these research consortia helped to diffuse cutting-edge, foreign technologies rapidly throughout Japanese industry. In the 1970s and 1980s, they became hotbeds for new technologies in targeted industries such as telecommunications and computers.

One important feature of the consortia is that they promote collaboration, both in basic and applied research, among rival firms. "Cooperative R&D has been ubiquitous in Japan's leap from a position of technological backwardness to one of world leadership in just a few decades," concluded a recent MIT study (Levy and Samuels 1988:4). The study found a "startling acceleration" in the 1980s in the number of new institutions that generate knowledge in Japan, all of which involve competitive firms (Levy and Samuels 1988:10).

Differences between countries in rates of technological learning are an important source of competitive advantage in trade (Grossman and Helpman 1991). While the Japanese government has nurtured commercially promising industries, the United States has targeted, to the extent that it can be said to have targeted at all, militarily relevant industries. The Pentagon's research-and-development programs, as well as its procurement policies, are the primary, though implicit, form of U.S. industrial policy. Industries with military applications, such as aviation, computers, and lasers, have received substantial government investment.[5] And although there have been commercial spin-offs, the result has been to skew U.S. technological innovation toward military uses rather than commercial advantage.

Japan's rise to economic power was thus primarily the result of technological advantages arising from being "the new kid on the block"—advantages that the United States enjoyed vis-à-vis Great Britain earlier in this century—from its exclusive policy focus on economic development and from its unique approach to industry and technology policy. This approach included the protection of targeted infant industries from international competition until they were able to compete. As long as the United States retained technological, financial, and trade dominance, it tolerated Japanese deviations from American concepts of "free markets" and "free trade." The emergence of persistent U.S. trade deficits with Japan in the late 1970s, however, created tensions in the alliance. When U.S. trade deficits with the world mushroomed in the 1980s, American policymakers became increasingly unwilling to tolerate national differences in economic management.

Managing—and Mismanaging—Interdependence

The economies of Japan and the United States are highly interdependent. In 1988, the United States absorbed 34 percent of total Japanese exports. Although the Japanese market is less important to the United States, accounting for only about 12 percent of exports in 1988 (see Table 13.3), inflows of Japanese capital have financed the large U.S. external debts of the 1980s. The United States also depends on Japan for important high-technology imports, including computer components crucial to the U.S. military.[6]

Policymakers, legislators, and the general public in both countries have not managed interdependence very well. The United States has defined

TABLE 13.3
U.S.–Japanese Interdependence

	1970	1975	1980	1985	1988
Trade					
Japanese exports to U.S. (% total Japanese exports)	31.2	20.2	24.5	37.6	34.1
U.S. exports to Japan (% total U.S. exports)	10.8	8.9	9.4	10.6	11.8
U.S. trade deficit with Japan (U.S. $ billions)[a]	1.4	1.7	8.7[b]	29.8	52.6
Investment					
Japanese DFI in U.S. (% of total Japanese DFI)[c]	19.6	21.8	24.7	30.4	NA
Japanese DFI in U.S. (% of total DFI in U.S.)[c]	1.7	2.1	5.7	10.4	16.2

Sources: Statistical Abstract of the United States; International Monetary Fund, *Direction of Trade Statistics*; Healey 1991; Nakamura 1982.   [a]Balance on bilateral merchandise trade. [b]1979.   [c]Accumulated stock of direct foreign investment.

and pursued two primary foreign policy objectives in Japan: first, the reduction of Japan's trade surplus via Japan's movement to more "free market" policies under the rubric of "fair trade"; and second, an increase in Japan's military contribution to defense. These objectives are problematic from the viewpoint both of U.S. economic welfare and world peace.

On the Japanese side, the management of interdependence has often focused on resisting or slowly giving in to American bullying tactics, rather than developing forward-looking, independent policies. Although the Japanese economy is much more deregulated and open than it was a decade ago, Japan has still to develop a global political and economic perspective commensurate with its economic power.

Trade Deficits and Industrial Policy
In the late 1970s, Japan's newfound economic strength translated into growing trade surpluses with the United States, Western Europe, and other countries. For deficit countries, a trade imbalance is problematic because it means that foreign producers are gaining larger shares of domestic markets,

displacing local producers and the jobs they generate. The problem is especially acute if the loss of domestic market share occurs in the manufacturing sector. Japan is a heavy importer of oil and other raw materials, and its exports are heavily concentrated in manufacturing. Moreover, a persistent trade deficit means an accumulation of foreign debt to pay for the excess of imports over exports. A deficit with one country need not be of concern as long as there is an offsetting surplus elsewhere. For the United States, the problem is that its trade is in deficit to the world as a whole. Japan simply has the single largest share of it.

The primary U.S. response to the bilateral trade deficit was to accuse Japan repeatedly of protectionist "foul play" and to pressure it to open up. U.S. trade representative Carla Hills once claimed she would use a crowbar if necessary to pry open the Japanese market. U.S. trade negotiators consistently used the threat of a protectionist Congress to try to win concessions from their Japanese counterparts (Prestowitz 1988).

The United States has identified both tariff and, increasingly, nontariff import barriers in Japan. In general, nontariff barriers encompass a variety of means to discourage imports, including government subsidies and tax breaks to domestic producers; quotas, embargoes, and other constraints on volume; and regulatory and administrative hurdles. Policies that favor domestic over foreign producers are contrary to the spirit, if not the practice, of the General Agreement on Tariffs and Trade, which provides for a global framework based on "free trade."

American charges of unfair obstacles to U.S. imports in Japan often focus on "cultural barriers" such as difficult-to-penetrate retailing networks, political favoritism, "groupism," and the close relations between governmental agencies, banks, and corporations. One study identified as an unfair trade barrier the fact that most businesspeople in Japan speak only Japanese. In essence, the U.S. strategy has been to pressure the Japanese to be more like Americans (Romberg and Yamamoto 1991).

Is Japanese protectionism responsible for its trade surpluses, especially with the United States? Although not all economists agree, studies point toward the conclusion that current levels of protection for manufactured products in Japan are in line or below those in other OECD countries. This includes both tariffs, which were cut by half in 1981, and nontariff trade barriers. Japan's import penetration ratio (the ratio of imports to GDP) in manufacturing has until recently been relatively low, but studies suggest that closed domestic markets are not to blame. Rather, Japanese firms seem to have garnered a cost, quality, or other advantage in selling to the domestic market (Barbone 1988).

Although Japan's manufacturing sector is relatively open to imports, other sectors, especially agriculture, are highly protected. In 1984, the nominal rate of agricultural protection in Japan was three times higher than in the European Community and thirty-five times higher than in the United States (Hayami 1990). Indeed, Japanese agriculture is probably the most protected in the world, the legacy of the cultural importance of rice production and the political weight of farmers. American attempts to increase Japanese imports of U.S. goods have focused largely on food items such as oranges and rice.

Other U.S. complaints center on the financial sector and barriers to direct foreign investment, especially for big infrastructure projects such as construction and telecommunications. Since the early 1980s, Japan's highly regulated financial sector has undergone a process of deregulation. Nonetheless, barriers to foreign participation remain. Moreover, government infrastructure procurement policies do tend to favor Japanese companies.

Thus, reduction of Japan's trade barriers would primarily benefit U.S. agricultural exports and promote U.S. direct foreign investment in Japan. While this would ease bilateral tensions and improve the U.S. debt position, it would do little to create jobs for U.S. workers or boost the long-term prospects for the manufacturing sector.

In general, Japanese trade barriers offer only a partial explanation for Japan's enduring trade surpluses. More important are the cost and quality advantages gained by high levels of innovation in Japanese manufacturing companies. Innovation puts Japanese firms on a dynamic path of technological development. According to one study, American manufacturing firms have become increasingly uncompetitive because they are locked in an obsolete, nondynamic production paradigm based on mass production and administrative hierarchies. Rather than technological improvements, gains in market share are often sought through marginal changes in product, process, and style. Japanese and American manufacturing companies are on distinctly different technological trajectories (Cohen and Zysman 1989).

"Unfair trade is often only a minor reason for a U.S. industry's decline," concluded an Office of Technology Assessment study, "secondary to the ability of foreign firms (often aided by industrial policies) to lower production costs, acquire new technologies, and make genuinely superior products at a good price" (Office of Technology Assessment 1991:14).

American economic policies are also to blame for the persistent trade deficit and the general U.S. economic decline. Ideologically committed to neoliberal, "hands-off" economic policies, successive U.S. administrations in the 1980s were hamstrung in fashioning industrial policies to adjust to the new competition from Japan. Adjustment entails helping uncompetitive "sunset" firms or industries move to other production activities; nurturing high-growth industries, especially those with high technological potential; and cushioning the blows of income loss to displaced workers in uncompetitive firms by maintaining income while providing retraining for the new "sunrise" industries. Adjustment, in short, is another term for proactive industrial policy. Instead, U.S. policy has aimed primarily at protecting existing manufacturing industries and promoting exports of raw agricultural products.

Precisely how to nurture new industries should be a matter of public debate, since much is at stake in terms of income distribution among regions, as well as between big and small businesses, and employers and workers. Approaches could include targeted research-and-development programs, including joint ventures with Japanese research agencies; government lending programs for innovative small businesses excluded from private credit markets; and tax credits or other incentives for high-potential infant industries. The point is to move toward a coherent national industrial policy, without adopting a beggar-thy-neighbor, neomercantilist posture antagonistic to Japan and other countries. Without effective industrial and technological policies, strains between the United States and Japan could intensify to the breaking point. With them, relations could be improved while gaining the benefits of economic interdependence.

Although an American approach to industrial policy must be homegrown, studying the Japanese model could provide guidance. "What Americans and others may learn from Japan," concludes a study by the Berkeley Roundtable on the International Economy, "is how to design a set of economic institutions, based on capitalist rules, that are more conducive to rapid growth, high productivity, and rapid technological change than the institutions characteristic of contemporary American capitalism" (Dosi, Tyson, and Zysman 1989:33).

Exchange-Rate Blues

Even though it first appeared in the late 1970s, the U.S. trade deficit with Japan increased considerably between 1980 and 1986. In 1980, the deficit amounted to around $9 billion. By 1986, it had jumped to over $54 billion.

This increase was caused in large part by an overvalued dollar created by U.S. fiscal and monetary policies. In the early 1980s, the United States pursued expansionary fiscal but tight monetary policies. Increased government spending, largely to finance the largest military build-up in U.S. peacetime history, combined with high interest rates to drive up the value of the dollar, making imports cheaper and exports more expensive. As a result of the superdollar, the U.S. trade deficit exploded from about $25 billion in 1980 to nearly $125 billion by 1985. Japan accounted for about a quarter of the total deficit.

Besides driving up the value of the dollar, U.S. domestic economic policies generated a huge external debt. Tax cuts reduced government revenues just as expenditure increased. Tight monetary policies reduced credit for investment, generating an economic contraction that further reduced government revenues. In 1986 alone, the federal government was in hock to the tune of $221 billion. To finance both the trade and the government deficits, the United States borrowed heavily in international financial markets, especially from Japan. From its position as the world's largest net creditor in the late 1970s, the United States became the world's largest net debtor by the mid-1980s.

Worries about the ballooning Japanese surplus and U.S. trade and fiscal deficits led to a meeting of the G7 nations at New York's Plaza Hotel in 1985. The governments agreed to try together to push down the value of the dollar and drive up the value of the yen. Over the following years, central bank currency-market intervention via the Plaza Accord halved the yen–dollar exchange rate.

The strategy has had some success. Japan's balance-of-payments surplus with the world economy peaked in 1987 and declined thereafter by $10 to $15 billion. For two reasons, however, the bilateral deficit with the United States has persisted. First, American consumers continued to purchase Japanese goods, in part because Japanese companies slashed profit margins rather than raise prices, and in part because, when prices did go up, the corresponding drop in purchases was smaller. In other words, American preference for Japanese goods meant that the total value of imports changed little.

Second, Japanese imports of U.S. manufactured goods did not increase substantially. Rather than U.S. manufactured goods, the high-yen, high-growth Japanese economy sucked in imports primarily from neighboring East Asian countries such as Korea, Taiwan, the Philippines, and Malaysia. Although the U.S.–Japanese trade deficit stopped growing in the late 1980s, it did not decrease.

One explanation for the failure of exchange-rate changes to restore trade balance is that the dollar is still overvalued. With most of world trade denominated in dollars, there are global pressures driving up its value. Moreover, the United States is a "safe haven" for deposit of the world's finances. Deposits into U.S. banks create demand for dollars, pushing up the dollar's value. Finally, global floating exchange rates create opportunities for currency speculation. The dollar's role as international money militates against its role in promoting U.S. exports.

Failing to consider substantial changes to its own policies, the United States has adopted an increasingly strident posture. Japan was included on a list of "unfair traders" and threatened with retaliation under congressional legislation known as Super 301. The U.S.–initiated bilateral Structural Impediments Initiative aimed to change underlying economic patterns in Japan, such as high savings and low consumption. For its part, Japan points the finger at low U.S. savings rates, high rates of government spending, lack of American work discipline, and the deterioration of productive capacities as the causes of the trade deficit. By the late 1980s, Japan came to be characterized by Americans as lean, mean, and menacing, while Japan saw the United States as lazy, profligate, and bullying.[7]

Japan as Global Superpower?

Japan's rise to economic power has generated debates in Tokyo, Washington, and beyond concerning Japan's international responsibilities. Shielded under the U.S. security umbrella, the Japanese government has focused on domestic economic growth. In international affairs, it has followed U.S. foreign policy and shunned global entanglements. Although there is widespread recognition that Japan needs to emerge from its cocoon and embrace "internationalism," there is no consensus as to what direction it should take.

The U.S. position has been that Japan's economic power should be accompanied by a concomitant military commitment within the rubric of the U.S.–Japanese alliance. The United States has pressed Japan to "share the burden" of its own defense, as well as that of regional security in the Asia–Pacific region and beyond.

To some extent, the Japanese have obliged. The Japanese Self-Defense Forces have accepted responsibility for policing sea lanes a thousand miles out from Japanese shores. Japanese forces are functionally and operationally integrated with U.S. forces in Asia and participate in regional U.S. military exercises. Japan's military spending has increased substantially in absolute terms—it was the sixth largest in the world in 1987—though it has remained around 1 percent of GNP.

There is substantial popular resistance in Japan, however, to expanding the size or role of the military. The Japanese people suffered greatly in World War II, generating a deep aversion to war and fear of domestic right-wing military elements. Strong public opinion in defense of the peace constitution prevented Japan from sending troops to the Gulf War in 1991, despite strong U.S. pressure. Japanese citizen groups ran a full page ad in the *New York Times* that claimed that 55 percent of Japanese opposed the war (AMPO 1991).

There is also regional resistance to an expanded Japanese military role. Asian countries, including China and the Philippines, remember the brutality of Japan's expansionary drive in the 1930s. They are willing to accept Japanese economic and even political leadership, but they would not accept an independent military role. Alienating them could jeopardize Japan's significant trade and investment interests in the region.

Blocked from independent military expansion, the primary currency of Japan's global role is money. With its large accumulated trade surpluses, Japan became in the 1980s the world's leading net exporter of capital. Net outflows (i.e., outflows minus inflows) of long-term capital mushroomed from $3 billion in 1977 to nearly $137 billion in 1987. Over the ten-year period, total long-term net capital outflows amounted to over $450 billion (Healey 1991:36).

The lion's share of Japan's capital outflows—nearly three-quarters between 1977 and 1987—took the form of portfolio investment, that is, purchase of financial assets. In effect, Japan became the banker to the world. More precisely, as the largest consumer of the spiraling U.S. government debt, Japan became the banker to the United States. Portfolio investment in the United States accounted for 48 percent of total Japanese portfolio investment between 1980 and 1986 (Balassa and Noland 1988:124).

The United States also receives the largest portion of Japanese direct foreign investment (DFI), that is, investment in productive enterprises. By 1985, the United States accounted for 30 percent of Japan's global stock of DFI. Japan's share of direct foreign investment in the United States rose from less than 2 percent in 1970 to over 16 percent in 1988 (see Table 13.3).

Besides the United States, Japanese monies have flowed heavily to Western Europe and Asia, especially Southeast Asia. In Europe, direct investments aim mainly to position Japanese companies in lucrative domestic markets. In Asia, Japanese companies seek supplies of raw materials as well as cheap-labor production sites for manufacturing industries no longer competitive in Japan. Southeast Asian countries export heavily to the Japanese market, creating a nexus of investment and trade integration.

The debate about the meaning of "internationalism" often centers on the extent to which Japan is or should be a regional, versus a global, power. The regionalists hold that Japan's primary economic and security interests lie in Asia. Therefore, foreign-policy objectives should focus there. Japan can further its regional goals, they argue, through bilateral diplomacy as well as by becoming a leading force in emerging regional organizations such as the Asia Pacific Economic Cooperation group. Japan is already the heavyweight in the regional Asian Development Bank. There are even voices, including domestic right-wing military elements, calling for Japan to become the leading military power in the region.

The globalists contend that since Japan's well-being depends on a well-functioning global economic system, it must actively participate in the broader international arena. Given Japan's money power, the most appropriate arenas in which to raise its profile would be in institutions that manage world finance. This includes the International Monetary Fund, where Japan recently became the second-largest vote-holder, and the World Bank. Japan has also taken a prominent role in helping to resolve the Third World debt crisis.

Beyond managing the world's money, however, there is a growing sense that Japan should contribute to maintaining global order and promoting economic development. There are several ways to do so. The United States has proposed the path of increased military spending in the context of a continuing security alliance with the United States. Such an alternative, however, risks rekindling domestic Japanese militarism, with both domestic and regional repercussions. Neighboring Asian countries accept a growing military role for Japan as long as it remains firmly lodged within the U.S. alliance. Over the long term, however, there is no guarantee that it would do so. An independent and highly armed Japan would greatly undermine the region's sense of security.

The Japan Socialist Party and progressive citizen groups argue for another alternative. They propose an independent Japan committed to the promotion of international peace. Japan would use its peace constitution and economic weight as a basis for a strong peace-and-development diplomacy in the context of the United Nations (AMPO 1991). Besides seeking peaceful resolution to conflict, Japan would also become a champion of international economic and environmental cooperation. In the Pacific, a multilateral common security system would replace the U.S.–Japanese alliance as the linchpin of regional peace and stability.

To date, the Japanese government has taken a third path. It has used its money power to appease both U.S. pressures for "burden sharing" and domestic pressures against militarization. Legislatively blocked from sending troops, Japan contributed $13 billion toward the U.S. war effort in the Gulf. It has also greatly increased its official aid flows to developing countries. In 1989, Japan overtook the United States to become the world's largest source of aid, earning it the appellation "aid superpower." In the minds of Japanese policymakers, aid substitutes for a larger Japanese military contribution.

Historically, most nations that have become as economically powerful as Japan have become important military powers as well. Japan could potentially avoid such a fate either by remaining wedded to financial diplomacy or by embracing peace and development diplomacy. Either alternative reduces the likelihood that Japan will become a military superpower. Ironically, U.S. "burden-sharing" policy increases it.

The emergence of a new economic power brings both opportunities and dangers to the rest of the world. To date, the American response to the rise of Japan has been shackled by an ideological commitment to "free market" policies and by a misguided attempt to slough off onto Japan the costs of its own, self-defined global military role.

The embrace of sound U.S. industrial policies would go a long way not only toward easing bilateral tensions but also toward setting a solid domestic economic foundation for the future. Promoting an Asia–Pacific common security system and encouraging Japan to accept a nonmilitary global role would enhance prospects for regional and world peace. Without a shift in these directions, Japan will continue to be blamed for U.S. economic woes, bilateral relations will deteriorate, and Japan's peaceful assumption of global coleadership will be far from assured.

NOTES

1. The G7 countries are the United States, Germany, France, the United Kingdom, Italy, Canada, and Japan.

2. The authors are Akio Morita, chairman of Sony, and Shintaro Isihihara, a member of the Japanese Diet. An unofficial translation of the booklet, produced by an agency of the U.S. Department of Defense, caused such an uproar in the United States that the authors refused to allow an official English translation.

3. On the other hand, the growth focus has also kept a lid on social spending. Compared to most other developed countries, Japan provides few social services.

4. The contribution of net exports to GNP growth is calculated by weighting the growth of exports and imports by their shares in GNP. Net exports are exports minus imports. The percentage share of net export growth to GNP growth is calculated by dividing the former by the latter.

5. The two primary government agencies providing support for industry development are the Department of Defense and the National Aeronautics and Space Administration.

6. Concern about dependence on foreigners for strategically important components led to the creation of the SemaTech project, involving the federal government and computer chip manufacturers in an effort to regain a U.S. competitive edge.

7. The racially tinged paranoia that has seeped into U.S. political and intellectual circles is evident in the CIA-funded report quoted earlier, which was leaked to the press in June 1991. The preface to the report entitled *Japan: 2000* states, "The Japanese as a people are driven by pride, nationalism, and down-right irrationality. . . . Mainstream Japanese . . . are creatures of an ageless, amoral, manipulative and controlling culture" (Awanohara 1991). Cultural stereotypes also abound in Japan. In February 1992, Japanese Prime Minister Kiichi Miyazawa caused a diplomatic storm when he described American workers as lazy and illiterate.

BIBLIOGRAPHY

AMPO. 1991. The Gulf War, Japan, and the "New World Order." *Japan-Asia Quarterly Review* 23(1): 2–39.

Awanohara, Susumu. 1991. Paradigm Paranoia. *Far Eastern Economic Review* 152(26): 15.

Balassa, Bela, and Marcus Noland. 1988. *Japan in the World Economy*. Washington, D.C.: Institute for International Economics.

Barbone, Luca. 1988. Import Barriers: An Analysis of Time-Series Cross-Section Data. *OECD Economic Studies* 11(Autumn): 155–66.

Cohen, Stephen S., and John Zysman. 1989. Diverging Trajectories: Manufacturing

Innovation and American Industrial Competitiveness. In *Politics and Productivity: The Real Story of Why Japan Works*, ed. Chalmers Johnson, Laura D'Andrea Tyson, and John Zysman, 39–55. New York: Harper Business.

Dosi, Giovanni, Laura D'Andrea Tyson, and John Zysman. 1989. Trade, Technologies, and Development: A Framework for Discussing Japan. In *Politics and Productivity: The Real Story of Why Japan Works*, ed. Chalmers Johnson, Laura D'Andrea Tyson, and John Zysman, 3–38. New York: Harper Business.

Dougherty, Andrew. 1991. Japan 2000. Rochester Institute of Technology, Rochester, N.Y. Draft.

Grossman, Gene, and Elhanan Helpman. 1991. *Innovation and Growth in the Global Economy*. Cambridge, Mass.: MIT Press.

Hayami, Yujiro. 1990. Japan. In *Agricultural Protectionism in the Industrialized World*, ed. F. H. Sanderson. Washington D.C.: Resources for the Future.

Hayes, Peter, Walden Bello, and Lyuba Zarsky. 1986. *American Lake: Nuclear Peril in the Pacific*. New York: Viking Penguin.

Healey, Derek. 1991. *Japanese Capital Exports and Asian Economic Development*. Paris: OECD, June.

Johnson, Chalmers. 1982. *MITI and the Japanese Miracle: The Growth of Industrial Policy, 1925–1975*. Stanford: Stanford University Press.

Levy, Jonah D., and Richard J. Samuels. 1988. Institutions and Innovation: Research Collaboration as Technology Strategy in Japan. The MIT Japan Program, Center for International Studies, Massachusetts Institute of Technology, MITJSTP 89-02.

Lincoln, Edward J. 1988. *Japan: Facing Economic Maturity*. Washington, D.C.: Brookings Institution.

Mead, Walter Russell. 1991. Saul among the Prophets: The Bush Administration and the New World Order. *World Policy Journal* 8(3): 375–420.

Nakamura, Takafusa. 1982. *The Postwar Japanese Economy: Its Development and Structure*. Tokyo: University of Tokyo Press.

Office of Technology Assessment. 1991. *Competing Economies: America, Europe, and the Pacific Rim*. Washington, D.C.: U.S. Congress, Office of Technology Assessment.

Prestowitz, Clyde. 1988. *Trading Places: How We Allowed Japan to Take the Lead*. New York: Basic Books.

Romberg, Alan, and Tadashi Yamamoto. 1991. *Same Bed, Different Dreams*. New York: Council on Foreign Relations.

Rostow, W. W. 1978. *The World Economy: History and Prospect*. Austin: University of Texas Press.

Spencer, Daniel L. 1967. Military Transfer of Technology: International Techno-Economic Transfers Via Military By-products and Initiative Based on Cases from Japan and Other Pacific Countries. Howard University, report to U.S. Department of Defense, Washington, D.C., March.

14 JULIET B. SCHOR
The Great Trade Debates

International trade is proving to be a vexing issue for the U.S. Left. In contrast to the certainty with which leftists approach most political questions, this one brings forth confusion and intellectual insecurity. There is an almost total absence of anything that could be called a left, or radical, position. We have some tired platitudes—"Neither free trade nor protectionism is the answer"—but beyond them lurks an intellectual void.

The inevitable consequence is that the Left has splintered. Some have joined the ranks of the liberals and neoliberals, or the "neomercantilists," as I call them. Neomercantilists are concerned with what they perceive as a dramatic, long-term decline of American competitiveness. Their central analytical category is the nation in its relation to other nations. Like the mercantilists of the seventeenth century, they believe that economic well-being is achieved by the accumulation of assets. For the original mercantilists the aim was the accumulation of gold. In the modern rendition, the objective is paper assets. That is, they advocate policies that will allow the country to run trade *surpluses*, thereby permitting Americans to accumulate reserves of foreign currencies, that is, claims on foreigners' wealth.

The crux of the new mercantilism is a partnership between the state and the corporations that is directed toward improving the country's position in the international marketplace. Specific proposals include industrial policies, reorientation of the educational system, increased civilian research and development, and pressure on allies to buy more American products. Left-wing neomercantilists can be found almost everywhere, in organizations such as the Democratic Socialists of America and in think tanks such as the World Policy Institute and the Economic Policy Institute.

Other leftists have adopted the protectionist stance of the AFL-CIO. Although individual affiliate unions do differ, the basic thrust of organized labor has been that unfair foreign competition is robbing U.S. workers of jobs and that the government should intervene to protect employment. The Japanese and Western Europeans have erected barriers to U.S. goods

274

(hence, the call for a "leveling of the playing field"), while the poor countries are fingered for low wages. (A trade unionist once explained this position to me with the quip that "the AFL–CIO doesn't think we should buy goods from any countries that commit the sin of being poor.")

The key analytic focus of organized labor's approach is the fusion of class and nation. The class interest in high-wage employment is promoted through a national response, which implies a coalition of union, state, and corporation. Albeit with misgivings, many on the Left have tacitly acquiesced to this position, believing that to oppose it is political suicide.

There is much to be said about neomercantilism and protectionism. Later I consider these perspectives in more detail. In the meantime, it may help to point out that nearly all these approaches start with the category of nation. But nation may no longer be the fundamental category. If we have moved from an "international" to a global economy, our analytic and political categories must take account of that change.

The first step toward understanding the transformation of the international economy is a step back in time, into the history of U.S. involvement in the international economy. This history will frame the issues in their proper perspective and allow us to ask some very basic questions about class, nation, and world. Exactly how did the international economy work in the postwar period? Is the United States really in decline? What do we mean by a national economy in a world of multinational firms? How can we sort out the effects of intracapitalist competition and worldwide stagnation?

To answer these questions we need to begin fifty years ago, when the outlines of today's world economy were taking shape. We can then use this background to analyze the contemporary situation and current debates on international trade, concluding with views on what a radical alternative could be.

What the New Deal Really Dealt: Free Trade

The standard histories of the postwar international economic system begin in Bretton Woods, New Hampshire, at the 1944 conference that established the International Monetary Fund, the World Bank, and a fixed exchange-rate system based on the U.S. dollar. The focus on these institutions is excessive and reveals a technocratic bias in the interpretation of history. In fact, the story should begin much earlier, with the Smoot–Hawley tariff of 1930.

Whatever its actual effects—many contend that it caused the Great Depression, although the academic scholarship suggests otherwise—Smoot–Hawley is important as the last major protectionist act in the United States. Until this time, the nation had been staunchly protectionist. For decades, both political parties, capital, and labor had stood for high tariffs. American industry had prospered behind a wall of protection. Woodrow Wilson failed with the League of Nations because he could not scale this wall.

The 1930s witnessed the demise of protectionism. At the time, only a fraction of manufacturing corporations had significant overseas operations or trade, but they were large and important companies. They sought international expansion as the solution to the stagnant markets they were facing domestically. The financial sector was already internationalized, as each major banking house had ties with European banks. This coalition of manufacturing and financial institutions came to constitute a formidable political bloc in favor of "free trade" and "corporate internationalism."

In the voluminous literature on the New Deal, this story goes unmentioned. Thanks to the pioneering work of Tom Ferguson, we can now identify the real deal of the New Deal: internationally oriented corporations and banks shifted into the Democratic party, agreeing to support social reforms, in return for which there was a dramatic turnabout on the trade issue. Henceforward, the Democratic party became the party of internationalism and free trade. Eventually, the Republicans were forced to go along, but not until much later.

In retrospect, the shift away from protectionism is not surprising. Free trade has always been the religion of the strong, preached self-righteously to the weak—for a simple reason: in a free market the big players win. The weak seek "protection" from the ravages of the strong. Britain invented the gospel of free trade when it dominated the world. As American capital grew strong enough to challenge Britain's dominance, it too converted.

Colonizing the Colonizers

Throughout the depression, and then during the war years, the free traders were hard at work. Ensconced at the State Department, they argued for their worldview in idealistic terms, citing principles of open access, nondiscrimination, and the economic benefits of free trade. They faced considerable opposition. At home, they had to contend with nationally oriented capitalists, labor, and a plethora of other interests that had developed over the long years of protection. Abroad, they sought to dismantle the protectionist barriers that had developed in the interwar period and to end the special (often exclusive) access that the European colonial powers enjoyed within their extensive system of "imperial preference." The Americans wanted access to the British Empire, but they would have to force their way in.

As it happened, wartime distress provided the means to realize these aims. Lend-lease aid was given, contingent on Britain's promise to end imperial preference. Throughout the war, the Americans conducted themselves with an eye to these objectives. After the war, Marshall Plan aid carried a requirement for recipient countries to sign free trade pledges.

But America was out for more than markets. There was also the issue of access to raw materials. Most important was wresting control of oil from Britain in the area known as the "Middle East" (but which, in a less Eurocentric world, would be called West Asia). As it turned out, political and diplomatic maneuvering during and after the war succeeded in nudging out the British; the U.S. share of the oil rose from a small fraction to nearly 60 percent.

America's attempts to subdue the European powers can also account for its contradictory stance on decolonization. During the war and its immediate aftermath, the United States trumpeted noble ideals of anti-imperialism and self-determination, illustrated by its support for the United Nations. But these ideals turned out to be little more than props once the Europeans had been decisively relegated to subordinates. By the mid-1950s the United States had assumed global responsibility for maintaining the crumbling empires, as the war in Indochina was to reveal.

In retrospect, subordinating the capitalist classes of the imperial powers was a relatively simple affair. In the Continental countries and Japan, their association with the fascist regimes left them weak. They had no choice but to rely on American largess after the war. The British too went quietly, preferring junior-partner status to all-out war with the Americans. It was labor that posed a greater threat.

In the aftermath of World War II, the working classes of Europe were not particularly sympathetic to American designs. Communist parties had gained widespread support and credibility by their leading role in the anti-fascist resistance. In Britain, a spirit of egalitarianism permeated the air. Social democracy and even more radical currents of grass roots democracy were gaining ground.

These possibilities provoked a strong American response. In the Continental countries, Nazis and their collaborators were recruited to infiltrate and destroy the workers' movements. Trade unionists from the AFL were dispatched to Europe, where they helped engineer splits in the French and Italian labor movements. The cold war propaganda machine was turned on. And most important, Marshall Plan aid was enlisted in the fight against Europe's workers. In the end, the combination of muscle and money proved too powerful; American-style, pro-American unions triumphed, and more-radical options were foreclosed.

So the American corporations and government got what they wanted. A corporate internationalist, free trade regime prevailed. (The fact that there were tariff walls around Europe, as well as much of the non-European cap-

italist world, did not matter; what was important was that American companies were now inside those walls.) The United States stepped to the head
of the line for resources in the poor countries.

And finally, the safety and security of American overseas investment—
a central concern of multinational companies—came to be guaranteed by
the American state. Beginning in the early 1950s, just as business started
expanding its overseas operations, the government started a massive military
buildup. Eventually, the United States would assume a worldwide military
presence (totaling over 350 bases today), which actively protected capital
throughout the postwar period.

Surpluses and Deficits:
The Fifties, Sixties, and Seventies

As a consequence of these developments, American power came to be the
dominant feature of the world economy. The United States had an overwhelming advantage in productivity, size of capital stock, and military
strength. The postwar struggles gave Americans the upper hand politically
as well. The result was an international order created to enhance American
interests. This is the context in which the institutions created at the Bretton
Woods Conference must be understood.

The Bretton Woods Conference yielded two innovations. The first
was the creation of the International Monetary Fund (IMF) and the International Bank for Reconstruction and Development (the World Bank). Interestingly, the IMF and the World Bank played virtually no role in the
reconstruction of Europe and Japan. They were immediately pushed out of
the picture, in large part by conservative forces in the United States who
saw them as too European and too Keynesian. This helps explain why these
institutions, originally designed to aid the West, eventually came to be the
main multilateral disciplinarians of the poor countries, a group that was
virtually ignored in the postwar exercises of international restructuring.

The second innovation was a system of international monetary transactions built around the U.S. dollar. The price of gold was set at $35 per
ounce, thereby creating a gold–dollar standard. All other currencies were
pegged to the dollar. This pegged, or "fixed," exchange-rate system was in
effect until the early 1970s, at which point the United States put the world
on a pure dollar standard and allowed currency values to "float" in a foreign-exchange market.

The gold–dollar, and later the pure dollar, standard was a gold mine
for the United States—figuratively and almost literally. By turning the dollar into a substitute for gold, it was as if the country had just been given a
nearly unlimited supply of gold that it could "mine" at what it cost to print
dollar bills (i.e., virtually nothing). The bottom line of the dollar-based sys-

tem was that the United States could run persistent trade deficits because the dollar was both the national and international currency. That is why the United States is the only country in the world that could have gotten away with what it did from 1982 to 1986—running up a cumulative balance-of-payments deficit of more than $500 billion. The gold–dollar standard also turned out to be a boon to U.S. banks, which got a competitive advantage from worldwide use of the dollar. They used that advantage to multinationalize themselves even more fully.

In addition to the benefits it provided for this country, the fixed exchange-rate system helped create a truly global economy by facilitating the flow of U.S. capital abroad. This globalization is key to understanding today's trade problems. Here is how it happened.

After the war, U.S. goods were in great demand. Had the dollar been allowed to rise in response to this demand, U.S. products would have become prohibitively expensive. By keeping the dollar undervalued, the system allowed the United States to run a consistent excess of exports over imports—a surplus on the (merchandise) trade account. The United States also had a surplus on what is called the *current account*, which is just the trade account plus income from services, tourism, some government purchases and sales, remittances, and overseas investment income. Throughout the 1950s and 1960s, the United States had a surplus on current account.

The surpluses of the 1950s and 1960s are just the reverse of America's deficits in the 1980s, which were brought on in part by an overvalued dollar. Japan and West Germany have been replicating the earlier U.S. experience—undervalued currency, current account surplus.

The flip side of the current account is the *capital account* (see Table 14.1). The capital account measures the changing ownership of assets (or capital), rather than goods. It is the mirror image of the current account, because flows of goods and services must be balanced by changes in the ownership of assets (or capital). For example, if the United States is running a current account deficit (buying more that it is selling), foreigners

TABLE 14.1
Trade Accounting

Decade	Trade Account	Current Account	Capital Movements	Value of the Dollar
1950s	surplus	surplus	outflow	fixed
1960s	surplus	surplus	outflow	fixed
1970s	deficit	near balance	no change	falling
1980s	deficit	deficit	inflow	rising

must necessarily be accumulating U.S. assets. This is today's situation; Japanese and Germans are accumulating U.S. assets.

The American current account surplus of the 1950s and 1960s allowed U.S. corporations to accumulate foreign currencies and use them to set up shop abroad. America's predominant competitive position plus the fixed exchange rate system were what gave U.S. corporations the incentive and the means to branch out around the world.

The developments of the fifties, sixties, and seventies yielded a globalized economy along the lines envisioned by multinational capitalists. This globalization is the product of capital's switch to free trade and corporate internationalism during the Great Depression. The growth in American power as a result of the war led to the consolidation of corporate internationalism in the late 1940s and early 1950s. Through the workings of the international economy in the ensuing three decades, the promise of this corporate internationalism has been fulfilled.

Neomercantilism and the "Yellow Peril"

By 1980 a group of patriots was sounding the alarm. America is in decline, in danger of being taken over by a race of people who know how to make a better car. Apparently we have been flipping too many hamburgers. We should be making more medical instruments and jet engines. We must become more competitive.

These alarmists are the neomercantilists. Their central claim is that U.S. industry has become uncompetitive. They use words like "world class" and "first rate." Productivity growth has slowed, management has lost the ability to think long-term, research-and-development efforts have been diverted to economically useless military applications, and our educational system has deteriorated. (Japanese children are in school more hours and they study math and science.) We invented the VCR and then did not even produce it.

Neomercantilists cover the political spectrum from Right to Left (Kevin Phillips to Lester Thurow). They reside in universities (especially business schools) and think tanks. Some corporations have them. Labor unions have some, and among the great mass of ordinary citizens, many neomercantilists can be found.

I myself have never been convinced by neomercantilist claims. As I read the numbers, they do not bear out the neomercantilist case.

Is America Declining?

The recent trade deficits have lent urgency and credibility to the view that American industry is in decline. The surge in imports in the 1980s necessarily has reduced the market share of many U.S. producers.

But this evidence is not particularly relevant. About 80 percent of the trade deficit is attributable to an appreciation of the dollar and global depression. These are *macroeconomic* imbalances. The neomercantilists point to a *microeconomic* problem.

Still, the neomercantilists might still be right that there is a long-term loss of U.S. competitiveness. We need to look to the decades before the 1980s, as they often do, to assess their claim.

By many measures, the relative position of the United States in the world economy has declined since the 1950s. U.S. exports as a share of all world exports fell from 20 percent in the early 1950s to about 12 percent now. The American share of world output has fallen, and the gap between our living standard and that of other rich countries has virtually been eliminated. There is also clear evidence of long-term relative decline in auto, steel, footwear, textiles and apparel, and other individual industries.

What should we conclude from these statistics? The first point to remember is that the U.S. share *had* to fall. America began the postwar period with a productive capacity that far outstripped any other country's. Recovery around the world ensured a declining position.

We should adopt a proper perspective on this decline, remembering a now (in)famous observation made by George Kennan at the end of the Second World War, that while the United States had about 50 percent of the world's wealth, it had only 6.3 percent of its population. The only reasonable thing to think about the decline of the American share is to be glad that it happened.

Second, the pattern of decline does not support the neomercantilists' fears: virtually all of the fall in the U.S. share came before 1973. Since then, there has been almost no change. This suggests that catch-up by other nations, rather than U.S. incompetence, is to blame.

Finally, the decline of specific industries does not imply general decline. It is only to be expected that the United States will move away from labor-intensive production, especially now that modern technologies can be replicated around the globe, in both high- and low-wage countries.

Yellow Peril

Many neomercantilists will contend that the aggregate figures hide a dangerous trend: the challenge from East Asia. The U.S. share has been maintained since 1973 by gains relative to Western Europe (its traditional rival) and the so-called LDCs (less-developed countries), but the real problems are with Japan and the Gang of Four (South Korea, Singapore, Taiwan, and Hong Kong). These countries have become formidable producers of manufactured goods, on the basis of greater exploitation of labor (wages, hours, and intensity of work), more-efficient management, and strategic planning. (Interestingly, their highly egalitarian distribution of wealth and income is rarely mentioned.)

I have always found these discussions to be deeply infused with racism and national chauvinism. East Asians are geniuses because their inventories are "just-in-time." Ours are always-too-late. They are automatons in the factory. We are lazy and shiftless. They plan ahead. We demand instant gratification. Need I point out the obvious similarities to the explanations of Afro-American poverty in this country?

The racism comes in another, subtler form. These countries are viewed as homogeneous entities. What about their internal dynamics? For instance, do Japanese or Korean corporations and government have too much power and workers too little? That would explain why labor is more exploited. And it would lead us to a different conclusion about our own trade policy. Instead of worrying about the yellow peril, the neomercantilists might investigate why conservative (right-wing) forces have so much power in these countries. They might even be led to examine the role the United States has played historically in helping to create and maintain these authoritarian capitalist regimes.

Companies versus Nations

Of course, throughout the discussion lurks the sticky question of defining the United States of America. Earlier in this chapter I discussed the multinationalization of U.S. corporations. The trade surpluses of the 1950s, 1960s, and 1970s led to a large outflow of capital. American corporations set up shop abroad. They now have overseas assets approaching one trillion dollars.

This globalization has profound implications. For example, roughly two-thirds of all U.S. foreign trade now involves multinational corporations.

In 1985, American multinationals shipped $70 billion worth of products from their foreign affiliates into the United States, an amount equivalent to 60 percent of the total trade deficit. These are U.S. companies selling to U.S. consumers. But they are producing in other countries—in many cases because labor is more exploited there than here at home.

It is true that the extent of globalization has slipped slightly since its peak in the late 1970s. But this is the predictable result of a large trade deficit (which must be accompanied by capital inflow to the United States). A second factor is the depressed state of both Western Europe and Latin America, two major areas of overseas investment. As the trade deficit falls and growth in these areas resumes, there is every reason to think that there will be a continuation of the trend toward multinationalization.

The existence of the multinational corporation casts a different light on the decline of America. While the country's share of export markets has declined, the multinationals' share has not. Overall, multinationals have held a steady 18 percent of world manufacturing exports since the 1950s. The record inside and outside the United States has differed significantly, however. Their domestic operations have been losing market share, while foreign affiliates have gained. It is likely that the cause for this divergence is less reinvestment and modernization in U.S. facilities. If the neomercantilists are really concerned about competitiveness and lagging productivity, one solution would be to prohibit overseas investment.

Protectionism: Labor's Trade Woes

For the most part, labor has not jumped on the neomercantilist bandwagon. Unions are dubious of corporate pleas for competitiveness, which are often thinly disguised hustles for wage concessions. (There is of course a degree of yellow perilism in labor, but it takes a different form.)

By and large the part of the labor movement that is active around trade issues has defined the problem as one of unfair competition: from low-wage countries and from countries who inhibit access to their markets. The thrust of the union response is to inhibit access to the U.S. market— that is, protectionism.

Like most economists, I'm against protectionism. But for different reasons. Protectionism subverts class solidarity and creates an alliance among domestic labor, capital, and government. Protectionism is insidious because it defines foreign workers as the enemy.

It should come as no surprise that the unions have adopted protectionism. Their political allegiances since the Second World War gave them little choice. They painted themselves into an uncomfortable corner by entering a political alliance with capital and state in defense of empire. Labor joined in the creation of the American-dominated world economy. It accepted the bipartisan foreign-policy consensus—a fancy term for the fact that Democrats and Republicans alike supported imperialism. This political alliance is still reflected in labor's participation in organizations such as the Trilateral Commission and the National Endowment for Democracy.

Having adopted the political goals of empire, labor was virtually forced to accept the economic suppositions. Commitment to free trade, at least rhetorically, was de rigueur. Although labor had never been enthusiastic about "free markets" and "free trade," there was little harm done. The United States faced no competitive challenge.

The unions did well in the international economy. Cheap raw materials, strong demand for exports, and profitable overseas operations contributed to a rising standard of living. But this prosperity was not long-lasting.

By the 1970s, the landscape was changing. Unions began to complain about job loss due to overseas investment. Imports were displacing U.S. production. The offsetting effects of exports were not relevant, because unions were organized on an industry basis.

By the 1980s, the unions were being decimated by wage concessions, plant closures, imports, and *maquiladoras* on the Mexican border. Free trade had come back to haunt them. Protectionism is about the only strategy the unions can seize on if they do not want to alienate their friends in high places. It is not anticorporate and not antigovernment. It is not too threatening because it is practically impossible to build a viable political coalition in favor of it. It allows the intelligentsia to mock the workers for advocating such a backward position.

All in all, it is hard to avoid the conclusion that labor has not yet come to terms with its imperial role. This failure underlies its current position and prevents it from advocating a genuinely proworker stance. For example, along with import restrictions, labor has been advocating sanctions against countries that do not respect labor rights, such as South Korea. This is more than a bit hypocritical. The Department of International Affairs of the AFL-CIO has been undermining trade unions in poor countries for forty years.

Instead of trying to keep out products made in countries where the average income is three hundred dollars per year, American unions should take an internationalist position. They should do things that will raise wages overseas, not lower them. Examples include support for a provision to force multinationals to pay the U.S. minimum wage abroad, restrictions on overseas investment, organizing the *maquiladoras*, and opposition to U.S. military aid for antiunion governments. The labor movement needs to begin acting on a *class* basis.

Class-based Internationalism

If neither the neomercantilists nor those in the labor movement have come up with a reasonable position on the international economy, who has? Certainly the laissez-fairers in the Reagan and Bush administrations did not. If we do not like the free market domestically, there is no reason to think it is any better internationally. Nor is isolationism (the extreme form of protectionism) the answer. It is economically inefficient, culturally unappealing, and sounds too much like a step backward.

We are left with internationalism. We need to counter capital's form of internationalism with one of our own. We need to supplant nation as the dominant category in the great trade debates and insert class in its place. Here are five principles that could form the basis of a "left" position on trade.

Imperialism in Decline

The neomercantilists are worried about the decline of American industry. We should worry about the decline of American imperialism. What can we do to help?

I argued above that industry is not in the dire shape some have claimed. Nevertheless, it is true that American hegemony (i.e., dominance) has eroded. The United States is still the richest, most productive, and most powerful country in the world. But the gap has narrowed substantially. It will continue to narrow. (This is the political chord being struck by the neomercantilists.)

The appropriate response is not to try to put America back on top. Even if the alternative appears to be the ascendance of Japan to top-dog position. The appropriate response is to advocate democratic and egalitarian international relations. Reject hegemony altogether. Urge international cooperation and disarmament.

As an aside, we may speculate that the ascendance of a new hegemonic power may not be inevitable. The classical Marxian theories of imperialism have been based on the existence of strong national capitalisms fighting for markets and raw materials. Certainly the last twenty years must be understood as a period of intensified intracapitalist competition. And yet, the rise of global corporations suggests that nation-states may be increasingly irrelevant. The bourgeoisie may be integrating itself internationally. It is still too early to know.

Prosperity versus Competitiveness

Neomercantilists claim that their ultimate goal is not competitiveness but a high standard of living for Americans. Apart from the obviously exclusionary nature of this objective (why not a high standard of living for other nations as well?), it is not clear that we should trust their formulation. Increased international competition is not likely to benefit most people, because it intensifies downward pressure on costs (i.e., wages).

If we want to raise our standard of living, productivity is the key (as many neomercantilists acknowledge). But we need to worry about our own rate of productivity growth, not the Japanese rate. If the Japanese have a higher productivity growth (and thereby become more competitive), it just means that we can buy their goods more cheaply.

If we want prosperity, we should pursue it directly, through more rational and humane social and economic relations, rather than by entering an international rat race.

Reflation versus Mercantilism

One example of rationality would be to reflate the world economy, after nearly a decade of depression. This could be done by "recycling" the Japanese trade surplus to the poor countries, which would use it to buy U.S. goods and help reduce our trade deficit. Or the International Monetary Fund could just put some money into the accounts of its poorer member countries. Reflation is an easy thing to do, made difficult only by the opposition of wealth holders fearful of inflation and companies wary of the effects of sustained growth on labor and other costs. It is a far better solution to our trade problems than the neomercantilist desire to run trade surpluses.

Controlling the Multinationals

Gaining a measure of control over our multinational corporations is an essential part of any left strategy. Domestically, multinationalization erodes unions' influence over management, paving the way for strikebreaking, wage concessions, and plant closures.

Multinationalization also contributes to militarization: America's 350 military bases around the world are not merely there to promote the interests of the U.S. state. They are also there to protect American-owned capital, as they have done repeatedly throughout modern history. If we are truly interested in peaceful and democratic international relations, we will need to address this defense of property.

We should simultaneously attempt to control multinationals' current activities and inhibit further globalization. Extending U.S. labor, consumer, and environmental regulations to overseas operations would be a beginning.

Labor Internationalism

We must also try to organize these giant corporations on a global scale. But to do this, U.S. unions will have to adopt a fundamentally new approach to foreign unions. They will have to tolerate political differences. The AFL-CIO's practice of shunning—that is, banning contacts with unions whose politics it does not like—will have to end.

But labor internationalism means more than this. It also means creating an identification and common project with workers around the world to replace the existing identification with capital. It means labor must think about the effects of the policies it proposes not just on American workers but on workers elsewhere. It must advocate policies that aid both, such as reflation or control of multinationals, rather than policies that divide (protectionism).

Forty years ago capital went international. It is time now for labor to do the same.

ACKNOWLEDGMENT

The Great Trade Debates are reprinted from *Zeta Magazine* 1 (January and March 1987) with permission.

III

THE THIRD WORLD IN THE
GLOBAL ECONOMY:
FAILED MODELS AND NEW APPROACHES

15 MANUEL PASTOR, JR.

Managing the Latin American Debt Crisis: The International Monetary Fund and Beyond

Throughout the 1980s, the International Monetary Fund (IMF) played a major role in managing the international and intranational conflicts caused by the nearly half-trillion dollars of Latin American debt. Fund missions shuttled from country to country, recommending austerity programs that opened the door to debt rescheduling. Under IMF direction, a much-feared international financial calamity was avoided. At the same time, Latin American growth rates and living standards fell dramatically.

By the middle of decade, the IMF's approach to the Latin American crisis was increasingly viewed as misplaced. Wayward debtors, such as Argentina and Brazil, adopted stabilization programs not in keeping with the IMF's free market thinking; in 1985, Peru unilaterally limited debt service to a fixed percentage of its export earnings. The United States responded with the so-called Baker Plan, a program designed to partially restore flows of commercial credit. When this plan yielded little success at resurrecting loan flows or resuscitating the regional economy, the United States shifted gears and, in late 1989, suggested a new approach based on rewarding more conservative regimes with partial debt relief. This framework, labeled the Brady Plan after the U.S. Treasury secretary who introduced it, recognized the need to reduce debt levels and rekindle growth; unfortunately, it proposed to do this with the same sort of orthodox conditions the IMF imposed on debtors in the earlier phase of debt management. Whether the same approach with new rhetoric can produce a regional economic recovery remains in serious doubt.

The Debt Crisis: Competing Views

Table 15.1 presents select balance-of-payments data from 1977 to 1990, the last years of Latin America's rapid debt accumulation and the ensuing period of crisis. As is clear from the table, both Latin American current account deficits and net external borrowing grew steadily from 1977 until

289

TABLE 15.1

Trade Balance, Current Account, and Basic Transfer for Latin America and the Caribbean, 1977–1990 (in Billions of Current U.S. Dollars)

	1977	1978	1979	1980	1981	1982	1983	1984	1985	1986	1987	1988	1989	1990
Exports (fob)	50.6	54.4	71.9	94.4	100.6	91.1	91.9	101.4	96.5	81.1	91.5	105.5	116.2	128.3
Imports (fob)	51.1	58.3	73.5	96.4	103.5	83.7	62.5	63.7	63.4	64.6	72.6	82.5	87.2	99.4
Trade balance	-0.5	-4.0	-1.6	-2.0	-2.9	7.4	29.3	37.8	33.1	16.4	18.9	23.0	28.9	28.9
Net services	-11.1	-15.8	-20.6	-29.0	-40.6	-48.9	-40.3	-41.1	-38.2	-37.2	-32.9	-39.0	-41.8	-42.5
Interest payments	-8.1	-12.3	-16.4	-26.4	-38.4	-45.2	-40.1	-43.8	-41.1	-36.5	-33.7	-36.6	-40.1	-39.6
Current account	-11.6	-19.0	-21.1	-29.8	-42.0	-40.3	-9.1	-1.0	-2.2	-16.9	-8.5	-10.0	-6.9	-6.9
Net external borrowing	19.4	28.0	30.5	38.6	56.1	40.0	16.8	12.8	5.3	9.3	9.0	4.9	11.6	25.7
Basic transfer	11.3	15.7	14.1	12.2	17.7	-5.2	-23.3	-31.0	-35.8	-27.2	-24.7	-31.7	-28.5	-13.9

Sources: 1983–90 figures from IMF 1991a; 1982 figures from IMF 1990; 1981 figures from IMF 1989; 1980 figures from IMF 1987; 1978 figures from IMF 1986; 1977 figures from IMF 1985. Note: As defined in the text, the "basic transfer" is net external borrowing minus interest payments (Stewart 1985). Since the interest-payments measure here includes dividends and other investment income not related to foreign direct investment, the measure of basic transfer reported above is biased downward (more negative) throughout the whole period.

1982.[1] The merchandise-trade balance was roughly in balance in this time period; the largest regional deficits in this category occurred in 1974 and 1975 (− $7.3 billion and − $9.4 billion respectively [IMF 1980:99]). Indeed, between 1974–75 and 1979–80, the trade deficit as a percentage of the current account deficit fell from more than 50 percent to less than 10 percent (IMF 1980:99; IMF 1987:157, 170). On the other hand, interest payments were rising dramatically, partly because of debt financing of previous trade deficits. This, in turn, led to increasing debt and an even higher structural level of interest payments.[2]

Both Fund economists and U.S. Treasury officials have blamed Latin America's pre-1982 increase in deficits and debt on domestic policy, particularly fiscal expansion and exchange-rate overvaluation (Weisner 1985; Enders and Mattione 1984). More-liberal economists have focused on the impact of external factors such as the decline in industrial country growth and unfavorable terms of trade (see Cline 1983, 1984; Diaz-Alejandro 1984; Dell and Lawrence 1980; Taylor 1986). In this view, Latin American policies may have needed correction, but the regional scope and simultaneous nature of the crisis clearly suggest that the causes were more international in nature.

Radical explanations of the crisis have coupled the standard focus on Latin borrowing with an equal focus on the practices of international bankers. In this view, capitalist economies are characterized by cyclical and endogenous shifts in finance. In an initial period of "overlending," banks aggressively seek new clients in order to protect market share; when either exogenous shocks or endogenous instability trigger payments difficulties, banks collectively retreat from the market in a sort of "panic."[3] This certainly squares with the experience in Latin America. In the 1970s, there was a dramatic increase in Latin America's access to international capital markets and therefore a relaxation of the usual constraints on domestic policy. In the 1980s there was an equally dramatic abandonment of the region by private lenders. This severely limited economic growth and created intense adjustment and inflation difficulties.

Radical analyses also differ from mainstream accounts in stressing *both* external and internal factors. My own regression analysis of the determinants of the current account in nineteen Latin American countries in the period of rapid debt accumulation (1973–82) suggests that (1) external variables such as U.S. growth, real interest rates, the terms of trade, and capital availability played a role; and (2) that when the effects of these external variables are accounted for, exchange-rate management had a significant impact, but fiscal policy did not (Pastor 1989).[4] Disentangling the relative contribution of external and internal factors is certainly important for both analysis and policy. However, the importance of both sets of factors suggests that Washington's nearly exclusive attention to Latin American economic restructuring is not sufficient to resolve the problem.

Radical analyses also attempt to go beyond the *proximate* causes of Latin America's debt problems and link together the various external and internal factors in a general theory of capitalist crisis. On the external side, left analyses usually place Latin America's debt accumulation within the context of a crisis of capitalism in the core of world economy, particularly in the United States (Frank 1984). This crisis in core countries produced a decline in growth in the United States and other advanced capitalist countries, and this had negative effects on Latin America's terms of trade and export performance throughout the 1970s. The resulting external deficits, which might have required severe trade adjustments in an earlier period, found available financing from Western banks that had a relatively abundant supply of capital but faced lagging loan demand from core customers. The response by profit-hungry bankers was a turn toward Southern borrowers.[5]

As for the internal factors causing debt accumulation, Jeff Frieden has argued that "overborrowing" resulted from the exhaustion of import substitution in the late 1960s. Seeking to maintain accumulation in the 1970s while simultaneously avoiding direct foreign investment, local capitalist classes and governments turned to a strategy of debt-dependent development (Frieden 1985:26–27; MacEwan 1986a). I have suggested that in the Southern Cone the so-called policy mistakes of overvaluation and fiscal "excess" were deeply imbedded in the monetarist/authoritarian models of accumulation adopted there (Pastor 1987b:158). Overvalued exchange rates, for example, reflected an attempt to maintain cheap consumer imports and easy private access to foreign funds in order to shore up the thin social bases for authoritarian regimes among middle and upper classes. Similarly, the refusal of these regimes to reduce domestic absorption during the 1979–82 period can be linked to the need to maintain authoritarian regimes' fragile claim to legitimacy—the economic success they had been partially able to achieve.[6] Naturally enough, the analysis of the "internal" reasons for deficits and debt differs substantially among countries and is the object of intense research and debate.[7] What is most crucial is the need to go beyond a "policy errors" approach and understand the "underlying structural and institutional forces" (Dietz 1986:1044) that produced rapid debt accumulation by Latin American governments and firms.[8]

It was the shift toward restrictive monetary policy in the United States that turned Latin America's structural difficulties into conjunctural crisis (Cypher 1986:10; Pastor 1986). The U.S. policy was, in part, a response to various symptoms of the U.S. crisis: high inflation and a falling dollar. The monetary restriction did reduce inflation and increase the value of the dollar by raising U.S. interest rates, but at the cost of a dramatic recession in the United States. The resulting world slowdown led to declining export volume and falling prices for Latin America's products; in 1982, the worst year of world recession, export revenues for the region fell by 10 percent. At the same time, high interest rates swelled interest payments on the region's previous debt (most of which had been contracted with variable interest rates) and "pulled" flight capital north.[9] With outpayments rising and revenues falling, international reserves dwindled; between 1979 and 1982, Latin America's official reserves and reserves as a proportion of imports fell by over 30 and 50 percent, respectively. Meanwhile, the real-interest-rate burden from Latin America's perspective—the nominal rate minus the change in its export prices—rose dramatically, reaching nearly 20 percent in the years 1981–83.

By late 1982, when oil-rich Mexico announced its inability to make debt payments, the problem had become painfully clear. Banks responded by raising "spreads" (the interest charge above a standard loan rate, such as the U.S. prime or the London Interbank Offer Rate [LIBOR]) and reducing the availability of new credit to the entire region; given the previous debt financing of interest payments noted above, this reduction in new capital simply aggravated payments problems. Countries sought to adjust for falling exports and reduced credit by restricting imports; between 1981 and 1983, regional imports fell by around 40 percent (see Table 15.1). Since 65 to 80 percent of Latin American imports were intermediates used in production (see IADB 1984:43), growth slowed; indeed, one estimate suggests that Latin American output loss between 1980 and 1983 was approximately $361 billion (in 1987 dollars)—almost enough to pay off the entire regional debt.[10] The growth slowdown and concurrent payments problems lowered capitalist confidence, reducing foreign investment inflows and pushing out flight capital. The balance of payments was pressed from every side. Led by Mexico, Latin America began turning to the official purveyor of bridge financing and advice, the IMF.

The Power of the IMF

In one sense, the turn to the Fund was quite normal; in the postwar world of international finance, the IMF has enjoyed the designated role of "lender of last resort," a job that involves the provision of short-term finance and harsh adjustment programs to countries in balance-of-payments difficulties. However, the shift toward the Fund in the 1980s was quite a departure from the previous decade. Between 1979 and 1981, even as many observers worried about underlying debt problems in Latin America, less than a third of the countries in the region were operating under Fund arrangements, and IMF officials were complaining that Fund resources were being "underutilized." In addition, program countries' observance of performance clauses had deteriorated substantially, signaling a relative reduction in the Fund's power to enforce its arrangements.[11]

The diminution in IMF influence in Latin America partly reflected the rising Third World challenge to Fund policies. Sustained politically by leaders such as Julius Nyerere in Tanzania and Michael Manley in Jamaica and nurtured intellectually by dependency and structuralist economists, critics argued that IMF programs were recessionary and punished deficit countries for trade problems that were either endemic to the development process or the result of external and uncontrollable factors (Payer 1974; Abdalla 1980; Krugman and Taylor 1978; Dell 1982).

The IMF responded to the political and ideological challenge in a variety of ways. On the one hand, it expanded resources by developing new credit facilities and loosening the conditions attached to their use. At the same time, Fund economists issued the results of cross-country studies, showing that Fund programs had no consistently negative impact on the rate of growth (Reichmann and Stillson 1978; Donovan 1982).[12]

Despite the attempt to both placate the growth critics and prove them wrong, Third World countries continued to avoid the IMF. For Latin America, the reason lay largely in its new independent access to international finance. Commercial lenders were interested in the region partly because of the fall in real interest rates in the industrialized countries. In the United States, for example, historically high inflation meant that the real interest rate that might be earned from U.S. loans—the so-called prime rate minus the change in a U.S. price index—was quite low (though usually positive) throughout the 1970s (see Table 15.2). Lending to Latin America with an extra charge, or "spread," was sufficient to return the real rate to that which had been earned from U.S. customers in the 1960s. On the other hand, the general rise in the prices of Latin America's commodities meant that the real interest rate from the borrowers' view—the nominal interest rate minus the inflation in export prices—was mostly negative (see Table 15.2). It was a situation that could make even prudent governments eager to borrow; given the confluence of this financial situation with the exhaustion of old accumulation models in Latin America and the need and desire to maintain development, rapid debt accumulation became common.

Through the 1970s, this increased access to external credit essentially relaxed the previous constraints on current account deficits; as a result, the regional deficit more than tripled between 1973 and 1980 (IMF 1980:99). Such growing deficits traditionally would have frightened away private lenders and forced the borrowers to adopt a regime of IMF conditionality. But with profit rates weakening in the industrial world, international banks discovering the growing loan market in the Third World, and Latin American countries eager to take advantage of their new access to credit, the previous reluctance to lend to deficit countries was put to one side. Given the availability of independent financing, fewer countries adopted Fund programs, because fewer countries *had to*.

Thus, the percentage of Latin American countries operating under

TABLE 15.2

Interest Rates from the Perspectives of Latin Borrowers and U.S. Lenders

Year	Nominal	Real Latin	Real U.S.
1961	4.5	− 4.0	3.4
1962	4.5	7.5	3.4
1963	4.5	6.3	3.3
1964	4.5	− 6.2	3.2
1965	4.5	− 8.1	2.9
1966	5.6	9.5	2.7
1967	5.6	4.0	2.9
1968	6.3	6.8	2.2
1969	8.0	7.9	2.7
1970	7.9	− 0.6	2.2
1971	5.7	− 2.1	1.6
1972	5.2	− 3.2	2.0
1973	8.0	− 23.5	2.0
1974	10.8	− 40.5	0.3
1975	7.9	2.7	− 0.9
1976	6.8	− 2.2	1.3
1977	6.8	− 10.6	0.5
1978	9.1	15.6	1.7
1979	12.7	− 6.9	2.0
1980	15.3	− 7.3	2.6
1981	18.9	18.2	9.1
1982	14.9	22.1	8.9
1983	10.8	15.7	7.6
1984	12.0	15.1	7.8
1985	9.9	16.4	6.4
1986	8.4	21.6	6.5
1987	8.2	8.7	4.5
1988	9.3	—	5.4
1989	10.9	—	6.2
1990	10.0	—	4.8
PERIOD AVERAGES			
1961–66	4.7	.8	3.2
1967–72	6.5	2.1	2.3
1973–80	9.7	− 9.1	1.2
1981–85	13.3	17.5	8.0
1986–90	9.4	—	5.5

Source: IMF 1991b. *Note:* As defined in the text, the nominal rate is the U.S. prime rate. The real interest rate from the point of view of Latin borrowers is calculated as the U.S. prime rate minus the rate of change of the Western Hemisphere export price index (calculated logarithmically); the real interest rate from the point of view of U.S. lenders is the U.S. prime minus the U.S. inflation rate (derived from the Consumer Price Index).

IMF programs fell by half between 1966–70 and 1979–81.[13] In the late 1970s, even countries in serious balance-of-payments difficulties, like Jamaica and Peru, tried to bypass the Fund altogether and obtain payments financing directly from private creditors.[14] Although these efforts were ultimately unsuccessful, the fact that countries even attempted to reject the Fund's financing and advice in favor of private credit and stabilization programs of their own design indicated a general weakening of the Fund's institutional power.

The decline in Fund influence was dramatically reversed with the emergence of the debt crisis in 1982. Cut off from new private credit due to the ongoing banker "panic," Latin America found that the "lender of last resort" was now the negotiator of first resort. With countries seeking both short-term relief and the IMF's aid in renegotiation of long-term loans, the 1970s' resistance to IMF-sponsored stabilization programs was rapidly overcome. By 1983, three-quarters of the Latin American countries were operating under some sort of IMF arrangement; moreover, *all* of the programs in this period were so-called upper-credit-tranche arrangements involving a high degree of conditionality. As the decade proceeded, most of the remaining one-quarter of Latin America also fell under IMF control and the few countries that escaped direct IMF intervention were often under indirect IMF supervision.[15]

This control over the region was reinforced by a subtle but significant transformation of the IMF's relationship with private bankers. Throughout the 1960s and 1970s, banks had often withheld new credit until a country agreed to an IMF-sponsored stabilization program; the banks took this as a "seal of approval" and *followed* the IMF, pouring new loans onto a fire presumably already dampened by Fund advice. In the early years of the debt crisis, however, bankers were generally seeking to reduce their own exposure. This posed a classic collective-action problem; while it was profitable for each *individual* bank to insist on prompt repayment and refuse new credit, the pursuit of such self-interest by creditors en masse would leave debtors with no resources to refinance and every incentive to default (Lipson 1981).

The banks therefore needed the Fund to organize a "creditors' cartel" that would both dictate macroeconomic policy to debtors *and* force individual banks to continue the "involuntary lending" that was necessary for the system as a whole. Beginning with the Mexican case, IMF officials approached international creditors directly and indicated that Fund credit to problem debtors would be withheld unless there was a fresh inflow of capital from the bankers as well (Cline 1984:30). This gave the Fund an effective monopoly over credit lines to Latin America.

In a capital-scarce world, then, the IMF became a sort of global capitalist planner, enforcing the collective self-interest of the banks and using its new leverage to determine the macroeconomic policy of almost all of Latin America.[16] Even as the Fund took on these global tasks, it carefully maintained a case-by-case approach that blamed the crisis on various domestic "mistakes" and maintained separate negotiations between itself and individual countries; this helped to ensure that the creditors' unity of interest would not be mirrored by the organization of a debtors' cartel. With its power expanded, the Fund imposed austerity with little concern for political constraints. What were the policies the Fund promoted, and what were the effects?

Latin America under the IMF

Despite its implicit view that the Latin American crisis had emerged as the result of separate and unrelated poor policies in individual countries, the IMF recommended virtually the same package to all of Latin America: devaluation, reduction of fiscal deficits (with the presumption that monetary contraction would follow), and decreases in real wages (usually by freezing nominal public sector wages—and therefore indirectly private-sector wages—in the context of ongoing inflation). In addition, the Fund argued for the relaxation of controls on trade and capital flows in the international sphere, as well as the elimination of subsidies and other government interferences. Indeed, the only price the IMF wished host governments to regulate was the price of labor.

Although this policy package of devaluation, fiscal restriction, and wage repression might be problematic under any circumstances, it was particularly inappropriate in the context of a global economic slowdown. Devaluation, for example, was unlikely to improve export growth given the slow economies of the North. Moreover, the simultaneous devaluation by a large number of countries eroded away the benefits expected when such a policy is pursued by an individual country.[17] The deliberate attempt to reduce fiscal deficits in the midst of global slowdown exacerbated the Latin slowdown. In contrast, many countries could have sharply reduced their deficits and avoided the growth costs had they engaged in an action the Fund sought desperately to forestall: the refusal to give up scarce tax revenues to repay old loans.

As for wage repression, this faced the same problem as devaluation: it yielded little export advantage when Northern markets were stagnant and every other debtor was pursuing the same policy. On the domestic side, wage cuts hardly seemed necessary to relieve excess demand, since domestic consumption was already curtailed due to collapsing export demand, attempts to restrain government spending, and an output decline resulting from the curtailment of intermediate imports. Finally, slack demand and excess capacity meant that lowering wages to improve cost conditions would not necessarily attract new local or foreign investment.

And consistent with its penchant for removing controls on the economy, particularly those on trade and capital flows, the IMF insisted that devaluation and inflation reduction would be sufficient to attract capital "back home" and warned that any attempt to impose capital controls would only shake capitalist confidence and result in more flight. Such reliance on the "magic of the marketplace" was misplaced in the midst of a generalized economic and social crisis and does not readily follow from the low levels of flight evidenced by those developing countries with capital controls (Taylor 1986:57; Pastor 1990). Moreover, econometric work on the flight problem suggests that while such controls do not prevent capital flight in the face of extremely poor policy, they do "muffle" the effects of policy changes or external shocks on outward capital flows: in short, they slow flight down (Pastor 1990).

What were the results in Latin America in this era of IMF control? Turning back to Table 15.1, we can note that the region was able to turn a trade deficit of $2.9 billion in 1981 into a decade-ending trade surplus of $28.9 billion. This was not primarily due to export success—exports did not recover their 1981 value for seven years—but rather to a sharp and sustained reduction of imports. The painfully achieved trade surplus was the real counterpart to what has been termed the "basic financial transfer" due to the debt: net inflows of capital minus interest payments (Stewart 1985). The "basic transfer" sank from an average inflow of $14.2 billion from 1977 to 1981 to an average outflow of $28.9 billion from 1983 to 1989, representing a distributional shift of annual flows toward the North amounting to nearly 6 percent of Latin American GDP.

The macroeconomic costs of this redistribution were severe. Whereas Latin America's annual growth rate averaged 5.8 percent between 1968 and 1980, the 1981–90 period saw growth average a mere 1.1 percent. Gross capital formation—investment in future development—fell from 23.3 percent of GDP to 18.4 percent over the same period. The decade's slowdown was accompanied by an increase in regional inflation from 60.7 percent in 1981 to nearly 800 percent in 1990 (see Table 15.3). Despite the ongoing austerity, Latin America made only modest headway in improving the ratio of debt to GDP (see Table 15.4).

The international redistribution of resources in this period was accompanied by regressive redistribution on the domestic level. This should come as no surprise given the performance of Fund-type policies before the debt crisis hit; in Pastor 1987a I found that the most consistent and statistically significant effect of an IMF program in Latin America between 1965 and 1981 was a reduction in labor share of income. In the period between 1982 and 1986—when the IMF was providing macroeconomic advice to most of

TABLE 15.3
Latin America under the IMF: Behavior of Certain Key Economic Variables

	Average 1969–80	1981	1982	1983	1984	1985	1986	1987	1988	1989	1990
Growth rate of real GDP (RGDP)	5.8	-0.2	-1.1	-2.8	3.7	3.3	4.7	2.4	0.2	1.4	-0.9
Growth rate of per capita RGDP	3.3	-2.2	-3.4	-5.0	1.4	1.1	1.6	1.2	-1.9	-0.6	-2.8
Inflation rate (weighted avg.)	34.3	60.7	67.1	108.7	133.5	145.1	87.4	131.3	286.2	533.4	769.8

	Average 1978–80	1981	1982	1983	1984	1985	1986	1987	1988	1989	1990
Fiscal surplus as % of GDP (weighted avg.)	-1.1	-5.6	-5.8	-5.7	-4.2	-3.8	-5.0	-6.6	-5.3	-4.9	0.1
Fiscal surplus as % of GDP (median)	-2.6	-5.3	-5.4	-4.9	-4.7	-3.2	-3.4	-2.5	-3.3	-2.9	-1.8
Gross capital formation as % of GDP	23.5	23.3	21.2	17.4	17.1	18.4	18.1	19.8	20.3	20.0	18.4

Sources: The Western Hemisphere series in IMF 1985, 1986, 1987, 1988, 1989, 1990, 1991a. The 1978–80 average figures used 1978 figures from IMF 1986.

TABLE 15.4
Latin America under the IMF: Behavior of Certain Debt-Related Variables

	Average 1978–80	1981	1982	1983	1984	1985	1986	1987	1988	1989	1990
External debt in billions $ U.S.	191.7	288.8	331.2	344.5	359.3	367.8	382.4	421.2	411.2	411.7	432.7
Growth rate of real debt[a]	12.7	13.1	7.5	0.1	0.4	– 0.5	1.4	6.5	– 5.7	– 3.9	1.0
External debt as % of GDP	32.8	39.8	43.0	46.8	46.4	45.2	43.9	44.3	39.6	37.9	37.1
Debt service as % of exports[b]	37.0	43.9	53.6	43.2	40.8	42.3	46.1	40.0	44.3	31.5	28.5
% of debt service devoted to interest payments	44.9	55.8	60.8	72.2	70.6	69.7	65.7	52.5	54.6	59.4	53.0

Sources: Western Hemisphere series from IMF 1985, 1986, 1987, 1988, 1989, 1990, 1991a. The 1978–1980 average used 1978 figures from IMF 1986:188, 242, 249, 250. The 1978 growth of nominal debt used 1977 figures from IMF 1985:262. [a]The real debt is figured as the nominal debt divided by the U.S. GNP deflator. This is similar to a measure used in Cline 1983:14–15. [b]Debt service includes both amortization and interest payments.

Latin America—various measures of wage share deteriorated for the vast majority of Latin American countries for which data exists (see Pastor and Dymski 1990).[18]

The domestic macroeconomic and distributional problems were made worse by a capital flight mostly unchecked by IMF-style "liberalization" policies. By 1987, the capital that Mexican and Argentine citizens had stashed abroad amounted to around 75 percent of their countries' total external debt (see Table 15.5). The continuing outflow of domestic wealth exacerbated the investment and growth difficulties.[19] It also contributed to a perverse dynamic in which the poor tightened their belts to make interest payments to international bankers, while the bankers returned a significant portion of those payments to domestic Latin elites.[20]

The Fund argued that the deteriorating economic performance and extraordinary domestic redistribution were due to factors beyond its control.[21] It is true that almost no policy would have worked well in the context of slowed growth in the advanced capitalist nations, high real interest rates, falling terms of trade, and a nearly total credit embargo by private banks. But the IMF surely shares some blame both for stressing a set of domestic adjustments that fit poorly into the global conditions and for failing to use its power to lobby for changes in the negative policies of core countries. Instead, it concentrated on domestic adjustment in Latin America, a trend that reflected the IMF's project of "disorganizing" debtors by dealing with them on a case-by-case basis. Yet requiring individual country adjustment in the context of global slowdown was a bit like telling the depression-era

TABLE 15.5
Capital Flight from Four Latin American Countries, 1973–1987
(Millions $ U.S.)

Country	Capital Flight (CF)	Change in External Debt (CED)	CF as % of CED	Stock of Foreign Assets Relative to External Debt
Argentina	29.4	48.0	61.3	76.9
Brazil	15.6	96.6	16.1	18.3
Mexico	60.9	95.4	63.9	73.3
Venezuela	38.8	29.4	132.1	131.5

Sources: Data for the calculation of both debt and capital flight come from the World Bank's *World Debt Tables* and the International Monetary Fund's *International Financial Statistics,* various years. *Note:* The estimates of capital flight are derived following the procedure described in Morgan Guarantee Trust 1986 and Pastor 1990.

unemployed to retrain—it simply did not address the real causes of the problem.

Although it is difficult to distinguish the "IMF effect" from the generalized crisis,[22] Latin America's poor performance while under IMF direction irrevocably associated the Fund with austerity, stagnation, and regressive redistribution; it is no wonder that the signing of a Fund agreement often brought an "IMF riot."[23] In fact, the Latin American impression of the IMF attitude ruling in the mid-1980s may be neatly summarized by a Mexican cartoon of the era. In it, a working-class Mexican is hanging from a scaffold while a well-dressed man with a briefcase is reaching into the dying worker's pocket to take the last of his money. The briefcase is stamped "IMF." If debt management was to move further, clearly a new approach was in order.

Beyond the IMF

By 1985, the IMF's ability to manage the Latin American crisis seemed increasingly in doubt. Argentina and (in early 1986) Brazil launched heterodox stabilization programs that explicitly rejected free market orthodoxy and instead used wage–price controls to quell inflation. Peruvian President Alan García attacked the Fund in his inaugural address, then promptly limited debt payments as a percentage of exports and allowed the country to fall into arrears on IMF payments. In 1987, Brazil suspended interest payments on its debt and refused to deal openly with the Fund. The Fund seemed increasingly exhausted as a vehicle for resolving the crisis.

The United States responded by proposing the so-called Baker Plan.[24] In contrast to the IMF image of austerity without end, the Baker Plan presented an image of growth: the multilateral institutions would provide new loans, private creditors would be pressured by Washington to do the same, and debtor countries would adopt "new growth-oriented" policies. Unfortunately, the Baker Plan promised only $29 billion in public and private funds over three years to the fifteen largest debtors, a sum that amounted to less than a quarter of just the interest payments on these countries' previously acquired debt.[25] The "growth-oriented" policies turned out to be pretty much what the Fund had already recommended but had labeled "austerity": liberalization, devaluation, monetary restriction, and deficit cutting. Indeed, the very targeting of the Baker funds to the fifteen largest debtors—rather than to the fifteen poorest countries—indicated that the United States continued to be primarily interested in protecting the financial stability of the banks. The previous IMF-based strategy had been dressed in new "growth-oriented" clothes, but few in Latin America were fooled.

By 1989, with the crisis persisting and a new administration in Washington, a new approach was unveiled. Called the Brady Plan, after the treasury secretary who announced it, it represented a new U.S. recognition that what stood in the way of Latin American economic recovery was the debt itself. The previous Baker Plan's promised new loans from commercial creditors had not materialized and were, in fact, not likely until macroeconomic stability was achieved. Stability, in turn, was difficult as long as the high levels of existing indebtedness made domestic capitalists reluctant to make long-term investments.[26] To restore growth, lessen social conflict, and eventually resurrect Latin creditworthiness would require some degree of debt reduction.

The Brady Plan signaled a significant shift in U.S. policy in two ways. First, it modestly shifted the prism of policy away from the financial side and toward the economic and political needs of Latin America. This shift indicated both that U.S. banks had finally managed to reduce their excessive exposure to LDC debt,[27] a phenomenon that made the financial fixation less pressing, and that the growth and social crises in Latin America showed few signs of abating; it also reflected the U.S. concern that the previous approach, relying on new official loans while commercial creditors cut back, "could lead to a situation in which the debt problem would be transferred largely to the international institutions, weakening their position."[28] Second, the Brady Plan explicitly recognized the need for long-lasting debt relief and proposed a specific mechanism by which private creditors would reduce debt obligations by exchanging them for bonds partially backed by the United States and international financial institutions. In return, debtor countries would continue with orthodox adjustment packages and try to lure flight capital back home. Although the projected debt reductions were small, the new principle of debt reduction—in stark contrast to the IMF's previous attempt to maximize debt service at the cost of domestic stability and social justice—was most welcome.

In July 1989 Mexico became the first Brady Plan country. President Carlos Salinas de Gotari came on television (symbolically enough, right after the Miss Mexico contest) and optimistically announced that "life will be easier" because a debt agreement had been reached in principle with the banks. Several weeks afterward, the president hosted a debt-relief celebration at the National Palace, with Mexican businessmen and political leaders using up some of the projected foreign-exchange savings in the form of imported whiskey. Although it took until early the next year to complete the detailed arrangements with the banks, the Mexican government was obviously pleased. The question was whether their people and others in Latin America should have been just as happy.

The simple answer is no. Mexico did achieve a sizable reduction in its debt-service obligations. Offering private creditors the choice between exchanging loans for bonds discounted by 35 percent, reducing interest rates, or extending fresh credit, Mexico was able to reduce its annual net outflow on debt by over $1.5 billion (Cohen 1991:48). This reduction in the service burden, however, was not accompanied by a significant reduction in the actual debt, since Mexico was required to take on new IMF and World Bank debt to collateralize the discounted bonds (Lissakers 1991:243). At the same time, the trade liberalization Mexico adopted as part of its new free market thinking took the trade account from near balance in 1987 to a deficit of over $7 billion in 1991, a slide that more than consumed the modest Brady Plan savings.[29] Growth did recover, but real wages remained stagnant, and the external side was nearly as fragile as in the early 1980s. Meanwhile, Mexico's most significant achievement—the reduction of inflation from nearly 160 percent in 1987 to less than 20 percent in 1991—was accomplished through the sort of wage–price controls that orthodox theory usually rejects.[30]

In fact, the problem with the Brady Plan was that it coupled small steps in the right direction—debt reduction and relief—with large strides toward making IMF-style orthodox management a permanent feature of the Latin American economic landscape. The timidity of even Mexico's proposed option for a 35 percent reduction in the debt's face value, unusually large because of the geopolitical importance that country has for Washington, can be noted by looking at the actual discounts prevailing in the secondary market for LDC debt. This is a market in which banks resell loans to other banks as well as to those interested in exchanging debt for investment in those countries where such programs are in place; as a result, the price of a resold loan provides some idea of the bank's real valuation of the prospects of payback. By these standards, Mexico's debt, selling at fifty-six cents on the dollar in June 1991, had an implicit discount of 44 percent; Argentine and Brazilian debts at that time enjoyed discounts of around 70 to 75 percent (see Table 15.6).[31] Clearly, the Brady Plan's originally projected goal of 20 percent discounts for most debtors does not reflect market realities and is unlikely to ease the burden of debt service sufficiently.

As for the movement toward solidifying orthodox management, it should be acknowledged that there are some positive elements of the new "Washington Consensus" on appropriate policy (Williamson 1990). The elimination of excessive government deficits and the adoption of competitive exchange rates are necessary for Latin America to regain ground on both the domestic and external sides. But the excessive focus on liberalization should be a cause for concern. After all, those Latin American economies that liberalized most during the 1970s—the so-called Southern Cone experiments in Argentina, Chile, and Uruguay—did not escape the global crisis and, in fact, were among the most financially unstable when the shocks of the early 1980s arrived (Felix 1986).

More important, the East Asian export economies, often celebrated as the alternative to Latin American models, did not become successes through

TABLE 15.6
Latin American Debt in Secondary Markets, June 1991

Country	Value of Bank Loans in Cents/Dollar	Country	Value of Bank Loans in Cents/Dollar
Argentina	23.1	Honduras	22.0
Bolivia	11.0	Mexico	55.9
Brazil	31.8	Nicaragua	4.0
Chile	88.0	Panama	15.0
Columbia	75.0	Peru	7.8
Costa Rica	40.5	Uruguay	62.0
Ecuador	24.0	Venezuela	60.0

Source: LDC Debt Report, 17 June 1991, 2, offers price reported (selling price is lower than the figures above).

the adoption of unfettered markets. As Andrew Berg and Jeffrey Sachs note, "several of the most outward-oriented economies [in Asia] have highly *dirigiste* governments, with highly regulated trade" (1988:278). Alice Amsden, pointing to Korea's nationalized banking system, government-set export targets for private producers, and strict controls on capital flight, suggests that one crucial ingredient in the East Asian story was exactly the ability of the state to "*discipline big business*, and thereby to dispense subsidies to big business according to a more effective set of allocative principles" (1990:16). This seems a far cry from the retreat of the state and a free hand for private capital usually espoused by orthodox logic.

Equally important is the failure of the "Washington Consensus" to treat effectively the regressive income distribution plaguing Latin America. The theory of "trickle-down" growth is, of course, firmly entrenched in mainstream economics as well as in recent U.S. policy: poor countries are expected to suffer worsening distribution as part of the overall development process (Ahlusalia 1976; Lecaillon et al. 1984). Recent research, however, has suggested that unequal distribution is inefficient as well as unfair. Jeffrey Sachs (1987), for example, argues that highly unequal distribution can produce social pressures on the government and induce it to engage in destabilizing macroeconomic policies. Econometric research suggests a positive association between income inequality and debt problems (Berg and Sachs 1988); Gary Dymski and I (1990) demonstrate that for a set of eight Latin American debtors, those countries with worsening distribution (holding constant other factors) were able to obtain more loans from private banks but were also more prone to wind up in debt difficulties.[32] Shifting the distributional burden onto workers through orthodox policy may please local capital, but it does not seem to guarantee better economic performance.

A new approach to the debt crisis must begin by removing the financial prism through which the debt crisis has been viewed. It is only through such a prism that the last decade—in which Latin America continued servicing the debt at the cost of deteriorating economies and worsening social tensions—can be labeled a success. If the focus of policy were changed, policy itself could be altered. Debt relief could be targeted to those countries most in need and not those posing simply the largest threat to international bankers. And conditions to relief could center on policies designed to alleviate unemployment, restore growth, and raise the living standards of the poorest citizens.

A new and more progressive approach is technically feasible and could even include some policies associated with the current strategy. Previous Latin American import-substitution efforts, for example, can rightly be criticized for their effects on both distribution and growth (Pollin and Alarcon 1988); overvaluation is to be avoided, since such an exchange-rate policy cheapens imports and does not necessarily enhance domestic development; and the state need not be as large and sprawling as it has been in Latin America to guarantee the sort of effective interventions that will remedy distributional inequities and keep investment at home.

There are, however, strong political limits to a shift in the debt-management strategy. The constraints are not simply those posed by the United States and the International Monetary Fund; although the previous orthodox strategies have certainly been designed with international financiers in mind, they have also "in fact serve[d] the interests of the ruling groups" within Latin America itself (MacEwan 1986b:8) by redistributing income and reducing the state's power over domestic capital. As a result, it will not be enough to challenge Washington; if Latin America is truly to move beyond the wreckage left by large debts and a decade of IMF-style management, its popular sectors will have to struggle for the political power necessary to transform economic policy. The question for the United States is whether we will be allies or obstacles in the attempt to create and implement a socially just model of development for our Southern neighbors.

ACKNOWLEDGMENT

This essay is an updated version of Manuel Pastor, Jr., "Third World Debt and the IMF," *Latin American Perspectives* 16(1) (Winter 1989), reprinted by permission of Sage Publications. Copyright © Sage Publications, Inc.

NOTES

1. The data reported in Tables 15.1 through 15.4 are from the Western Hemisphere series from various issues of the IMF's *World Economic Outlook*. Al-

though this series includes data from a number of small Caribbean nations, I refer to the various series as representing Latin America. When I refer, however, to the number of countries under Fund arrangements, I am confining myself to a nineteen-country set that excludes the various Caribbean nations; this is the country set categorized as Latin America in the IMF's *International Financial Statistics* and has constituted the country set for a number of empirical investigations (Pastor 1987a, 1989).

2. Dooley et al. (1986) also stresses the role of the nontrade components of the current account in Latin American debt accumulation. See also Dietz 1986:1036.

3. For a radical perspective on the instability of capitalist finance, see MacEwan 1990. For a more mainstream but equally pessimistic view of endogenous financial cycles, see Kindleberger 1978.

4. For a similar exercise by Fund economists, with slightly different results, see Khan and Knight 1983.

5. Why did presumably rational bankers lend to a region that had, almost to a country, defaulted on international bonds and loans in the crisis of the 1930s? Howard Wachtel (1986:127) suggests that these risky practices were rooted in the "deregulation" of the international monetary system brought about by the breakdown of the Bretton Woods system. Others locate the process earlier, suggesting that it was the "dollar overhang" of the 1960s—when the United States, with the dollar as the key currency, could run persistent payments deficits and so expand worldwide liquidity—that allowed the creation of the unregulated Eurodollar market so key to future loans to Latin America (MacEwan 1986a, 1990; Block 1977). In both views, OPEC surpluses and petrodollar recycling exacerbated the lending phenomenon but they did not cause it. For one thing, the two major waves of liquidity expansion occurred prior to the oil price increases of 1973 and 1979; for another, the OPEC surpluses "are best explained as a symptom of the decline and breakup of U.S. hegemony" (MacEwan 1986a:189).

6. For another treatment of the structural reasons for debt accumulation, as well as a progressive policy alternative, see Cavanaugh et al. 1985.

7. See Frieden 1991 for a comparative study of five countries' experiences.

8. For detailed reviews of the Southern Cone (Argentina, Chile, and Uruguay) experiments, see Foxley 1983 and Ramos 1986.

9. Over 60 percent of the total Latin American public or publicly guaranteed external debt and almost all of the nonguaranteed debt bear variable rates (Stewart 1985:193, 200).

10. This calculation is explained in Pastor 1986:194, 250. Briefly, I estimated 1980–83 GDP figures for a scenario where the 1967–76 growth rates had obtained (all data from IMF 1985). I then subtracted the actual output from the counterfactual to obtain the lost output. There were several estimates drawing upon different data bases and using different exchange-rate conversions; I present the most conservative estimate here. The figure there was for 1984 dollars: I recalculated to 1987 dollars using the inflation of the U.S. GNP deflator as reported in the IMF 1987:125.

11. Direct evidence on country observation of various performance clauses (especially fiscal) is detailed in Beveridge and Kelly (1980). This decline in country "obedience" is in striking contrast to the levels of such "obedience" in the 1960s; for the latter, see Reichmann and Stillson 1978 and the interpretation of their results in Pastor 1987b:72.

12. These results on growth were later confirmed by researchers outside the IMF (Killick 1984; Pastor 1987a).

13. By Latin America here, I mean the nineteen countries identified under the Latin American rubric in the IMF's *International Financial Statistics*. The definition of operating under an IMF program is given in Pastor 1987a and 1987b and follows Donovan 1982.

14. For more on the Peruvian case, see Stallings 1979.

15. Colombia, for example, sought IMF blessings for its stabilization efforts, even though it had no formal program, in part to reassure its foreign creditors.

16. Speaking of the Fund's role in the early 1980s, Ron Phillips (1983:62) has likewise referred to the IMF as "functioning in the global capitalist interest—a kind of global collective capitalist."

17. While devaluation might be expected to slow capital flight (by raising the price of foreign assets), it is also likely that rapid devaluation shakes capitalist confidence and so spurs capital flight.

18. For an IMF defense of the distributional consequences of Fund programs and policies, see Johnson and Salop 1980 and Sisson 1986.

19. In Pastor 1990:4–5, I calculate that potential interest earnings on the stock of capital flight in 1987 amounted to nearly 75 percent of the import bill in Argentina and nearly 60 percent of the import bill in Mexico; an increase in repatriation by 25 percent of those earnings could raise the growth rate by 2.6 percent in Argentina and 1.9 percent in Mexico. For one progressive suggestion about how to make use of those earnings to further Latin American growth, see Felix 1985.

20. Another source of distributional friction has been the treatment of private external debt. Early in the debt crisis, Western banks and local elites pressured Latin American governments to "consolidate debt"—that is, to absorb what had been privately contracted external loans. The banks, of course, wanted assurances of repayment and held the rescheduling of publicly contracted loans "hostage" to a government agreement to take over these private-sector liabilities. Elites had equally strong incentives: given their inability to service debt, bankruptcy was threatening. Although this *socialization* of the private debt differed slightly by country, the essential logic involved the conversion of private sector dollar loans into local currency obligations payable to the state, often utilizing special exchange rates that reduced the real obligations and thus constituted a subsidy to private borrowers. The government, in turn, took on the burdensome foreign-currency obligation and reduced government services to the poor in order to finance both debt service and the resulting private subsidies; apparently, laissez-faire can be abandoned when international creditors and local rulers stand to lose in the market they nominally celebrate. The aforementioned assumption of private liabilities occurred in Argentina, Mexico, Chile, Ecuador, and elsewhere. For discussion of this phenomenon, see Diaz-Alejandro 1984:379, Rodríguez 1987:138, and Felix 1986:107.

21. For example, the terms of trade for the Western Hemisphere fell 30 percent between 1980 and 1988, stabilizing at this new lower level in 1989 and 1990 (data from IMF 1988, 1989, 1990, 1991b).

22. For example, distinguishing the "IMF effect" from the generalized external influences would require that we separate countries with programs from countries without—a difficult task in the 1980s, since almost all Latin American countries were directly or indirectly under Fund supervision.

23. In the Dominican Republic in 1984, for example, the announcement of an IMF program brought riots that left 60 people dead, 200 wounded, and 4,300 arrested. Upon subsequently rescinding the IMF pact, Dominican economic planning minister L. Orlando Haza explained, "It is not that we are unwilling to put our own house in order. It is that we want to keep our house and not let it go up in flames." This quote is from "Verbatim: Rebuffing the IMF," *New York Times*, 3 June 1984.

24. Karin Lissakers (1991:229) suggests that the Baker Plan was a direct and hastily conceived response to the Peruvian debt limits as well as the general erosion of support for IMF-style debt management.

25. This figure is calculated by taking the interest payments series for the fifteen heavily indebted countries in the years 1986–88 as reported in IMF 1991b:131. A review of the Baker Plan is in George 1988:189–94.

26. For more on the relation between the debt "overhang" and investment and growth, see Sachs 1989 and Pastor 1992.

27. Benjamin Cohen (1991:49) reports that U.S. bank provisions against developing-country loans rose from 5 percent in 1986 to an average 50 percent by June 1990. Lissakers (1991:237) notes that the Latin American exposure of the nine largest U.S. banks as a percentage of their capital fell from 177 percent in 1982 to 84 percent by the end of 1988.

28. The statement is from a March 1989 address by U.S. Treasury Secretary Nicholas Brady, as quoted in Lissakers 1991:234.

29. The trade deficit for 1991 is an estimate based on the figures for the first two quarters of 1991 as reported in the March 1992 issue of the IMF's *International Financial Statistics*.

30. Macroeconomic results for other Brady Plan countries—Venezuela, Costa Rica, and the Philippines—have been even worse in the wake of debt-relief arrangements (Cohen 1991:48–49). See also Lissakers 1991:243–44.

31. The figure for the Mexican debt in Table 15.6 is for the par value debt. Even the post-Brady discounted Mexican debt was selling well below face value in the time period covered in the table.

32. The actual technique used in arriving at this conclusion entailed regression analysis of the determinants of loan volume to the eight countries over the period 1973–82, followed by logistic analysis of whether those factors that prompted lending were equally effective at predicting arrears and other payments problems. See Dymski and Pastor 1990.

BIBLIOGRAPHY

Abdalla, Ismail-Sabri. 1980. The Inadequacy and Loss of Legitimacy of the International Monetary Fund. *Development Dialogue* 2: 25–53.
Ahlusalia, Montek S. 1976. Income Distribution and Development: Some Stylized Facts. *American Economic Review* 66(2): 128–35.
Amsden, Alice H. 1990. Third World Industrialization: "Global Fordism" or a New Model? *New Left Review* 182 (July/August): 5–31.
Berg, Andrew, and Jeffrey Sachs. 1988. The Debt Crisis: Structural Explanations of Country Performance. *Journal of Development Economics* 29(3): 271–306.
Beveridge, W. A., and Margaret R. Kelly. 1980. Fiscal Content of Financial Pro-

grams Supported by Stand-by Arrangements in the Upper Credit Tranches, 1969–78. IMF *Staff Papers* 27 (June): 205–44.

Block, Fred L. 1977. *The Origins of International Economic Disorder: A Study of United States International Monetary Policy from World War II to the Present.* Berkeley and Los Angeles: University of California Press.

Cavanagh, John, Fantu Cheru, Carole Collins, Cameron Duncan, and Dominic Ntube. 1985. *From Debt to Development: Alternatives to the International Debt Crisis.* Washington, D.C.: Institute for Policy Studies.

Cline, William R. 1983. *International Debt and the Stability of the World Economy.* Washington, D.C.: Institute for International Economics.

———. 1984. *International Debt: Systemic Risk and Policy Response.* Washington, D.C.: Institute for International Economics.

Cohen, Benjamin J. 1991. What Ever Happened to the LDC Debt Crisis? *Challenge* 34(3): 47–51.

Cypher, James M. 1986. The Crisis of the Third World and the Theory of Dependency: What Is the Relationship Now? Paper presented at the annual meeting of the Allied Social Science Association, New Orleans, December.

Dell, Sidney. 1982. Stabilization: The Political Economy of Overkill. *World Development* 10(8): 597–612.

Dell, Sidney, and Roger Lawrence. 1980. *The Balance of Payments Adjustment Process in Developing Countries.* New York: Pergamon Press.

Diaz-Alejandro, Carlos. 1984. Latin American Debt: I Don't Think We Are in Kansas Anymore. *Brookings Papers on Economic Activity* 2:335–403 (including comments and discussion).

Dietz, James L. 1986. Debt and Development: The Future of Latin America. *Journal of Economic Issues* 20 (December): 1029–51.

Donovan, Donal J. 1982. Macroeconomic Performance and Adjustment under Fund-Supported Programs: The Experience of the Seventies. IMF *Staff Papers* 29 (June): 171–203.

Dooley, Michael, William Helkie, Ralph Tryon, and John Underwood. 1986. An Analysis of External Debt Positions of Eight Developing Countries through 1990. *Journal of Development Economics* 21:283–318.

Dymski, Gary A., and Manuel Pastor, Jr. 1990. Bank Lending, Misleading Signals, and the Latin American Debt Crisis. *International Trade Journal* 6(2): 151–91.

Enders, Thomas O., and Richard P. Mattione. 1984. *Latin America: The Crisis of Debt and Growth.* Washington, D.C.: Brookings Institute.

Felix, David. 1985. How to Resolve Latin America's Debt Crisis. *Challenge* 28(5): 44–51.

———. 1986. On Financial Blowups and Authoritarian Regimes in Latin America. In *Latin American Political Economy: Financial Crisis and Political Change*, ed. Jonathan Hartlyn and Samuel A. Morley, 85–125. Boulder, Colo.: Westview Press.

Foxley, Alejandro. 1983. *Latin American Experiments in Neoconservative Economics.* Berkeley and Los Angeles: University of California Press.

Frank, Andre Gunder. 1984. Can the Debt Bomb Be Defused? *World Policy Journal* 1 (Summer): 723–43.

Frieden, Jeff. 1985. On Borrowed Time. *NACLA Report on the Americas* 18 (March/April): 25–33.

———. 1991. *Debt, Development, and Democracy: Modern Political Economy and Latin America, 1965–1985*. Princeton: Princeton University Press.

George, Susan. 1988. *A Fate Worse than Debt: The World Financial Crisis and the Poor*. New York: Grove Press.

IADB (Inter-American Development Bank). 1984. *External Debt and Economic Development in Latin America: Background and Prospects*. Washington, D.C.: IADB.

IMF (International Monetary Fund). 1980. *World Economic Outlook, 1980*. Washington, D.C.: IMF.

———. 1985. *World Economic Outlook, 1985*. Washington, D.C.: IMF.

———. 1986. *World Economic Outlook, 1986*. Washington, D.C.: IMF.

———. 1987. *World Economic Outlook, 1987*. Washington, D.C.: IMF.

———. 1988. *World Economic Outlook, 1988*. Washington, D.C.: IMF.

———. 1989. *World Economic Outlook, 1989*. Washington, D.C.: IMF.

———. 1990. *World Economic Outlook, 1990*. Washington, D.C.: IMF.

———. 1991a. *International Financial Statistics*. Washington, D.C.: IMF.

———. 1991b. *World Economic Outlook, 1991*. Washington, D.C.: IMF.

Johnson, Omotunde, and Joanne Salop. 1980. Distributional Aspects of Stabilization Programs in Developing Countries. IMF *Staff Papers* 27 (March): 1–23.

Khan, Mohsin S., and Malcolm D. Knight. 1983. Determinants of Current Account Balances of Non–Oil Developing Countries in the 1970's: An Empirical Analysis. IMF *Staff Papers* 30(4): 819–42.

Killick, Tony. 1984. The Impact of Fund Stabilisation Programmes. In *The Quest for Economic Stabilization*, ed. Tony Killick, 227–59. New York: St. Martin's Press.

Kindleberger, Charles. 1978. *Manias, Panics, and Crashes*. New York: Basic Books.

Krugman, Paul, and Lance Taylor. 1978. Contractionary Effects of Devaluation. *Journal of International Economics* 8:445–56.

Lecaillon, Jacques, Felix Paukert, Christian Morrisson, and Dimitri Germidis. 1984. *Income Distribution and Economic Development: An Analytical Survey*. Geneva: International Labour Office.

Lipson, Charles. 1981. The International Organization of Third World Debt. *International Organization* 35 (Autumn): 603–31.

Lissakers, Karin. 1991. *Banks, Borrowers, and the Establishment: A Revisionist Account of the International Debt Crisis*. New York: Basic Books.

MacEwan, Arthur. 1986a. International Debt and Banking: Rising Instability within the General Crisis. *Science and Society* 50 (Summer): 177–209.

———. 1986b. Latin America: Why Not Default? *Monthly Review* 38 (September): 1–13.

———. 1990. *Debt and Disorder: International Economic Instability and U.S. Imperial Decline*. New York: Monthly Review Press.

Morgan Guarantee Trust. 1986. LDC Capital Flight. *World Financial Markets* (March): 13–15.

Pastor, Manuel, Jr. 1986. Long Shadow of Global Debt. In *Economic Report of the People*, Center for Popular Economics, 185–207. Boston: South End Press.

————. 1987a. The Effects of IMF Programs in the Third World: Debate and Evidence from Latin America. *World Development* 15(2): 244–62.

————. 1987b. *The International Monetary Fund and Latin America: Economic Stabilization and Class Conflict.* Boulder, Colo.: Westview Press.

————. 1989. Current Account Deficits and Debt Accumulation in Latin America: Debate and Evidence. *Journal of Development Economics* 31(1): 77–97.

————. 1990. Capital Flight from Latin America. *World Development* 18(1): 1–18.

————. 1992. Private Investment and Debt Overhang in Latin America. In *The Political Economy of Investment, Saving and Finance: A Global Perspective*, ed. Gerald Epstein and Herbert Gintis. Oxford: Oxford University Press.

Pastor, Manuel, Jr., and Gary Dymski. 1990. Debt Crisis and Class Conflict in Latin America. *Review of Radical Political Economics* 22(1): 155–78.

Payer, Cheryl. 1974. *The Debt Trap: The IMF and the Third World.* New York: Monthly Review Press.

Phillips, Ron. 1983. The Role of the International Monetary Fund in the Post–Bretton Woods Era. *Review of Radical Political Economics* 15(2): 59–81.

Pollin, Robert, and Alarcon, Diana. 1988. Debt Crisis, Accumulation Crisis, and Economic Restructuring in Latin America. *International Review of Applied Economics* 2(2): 127–54.

Ramos, Joseph. 1986. *Neoconservative Economics in the Southern Cone of Latin America, 1973–1983.* Baltimore: John Hopkins University Press.

Reichmann, Thomas M., and Richard T. Stillson. 1978. Experience with Programs of Balance of Payments Adjustment: Stand-by Arrangements in the Higher Tranches, 1963–72. IMF *Staff Papers* 25(June): 292–310.

Rodríguez, Miguel A. 1987. Consequences of Capital Flight for Latin American Debtor Countries. In *Capital Flight and Third World Debt*, ed. Donald R. Lessard and John Williamson, 129–44. Washington, D.C.: Institute for International Economics.

Sachs, Jeffrey D. 1987. Trade and Exchange Rate Policies in Growth-Oriented Adjustment Programs. In *Growth-Oriented Adjustment Programs*, ed. Vittorio Corbo, Morris Goldstein, and Mohsin Khan, 80–102. Washington, D.C.: World Bank.

————. 1989. The Debt Overhang of Developing Countries. In *Debt, Stabilization, and Development: Essays in Memory of Carlos Diaz-Alejandro*, ed. Guillermo Calvo, Ronald Findlay, Pentti Kouri, and Jorge Braga de Macedo, 291–325. Oxford: Basil Blackwell.

Sisson, Charles A. 1986. Fund-Supported Programs and Income Distribution in LDC's. *Finance and Development* 23(March): 30–32.

Stallings, Barbara. 1979. Peru and the U.S. Banks: Privatization of Financial Relations. In *Capitalism and the State in U.S.–Latin American Relations*, ed. Richard R. Fagen, 217–53. Stanford: Stanford University Press.

Stewart, Frances. 1985. The International Debt Situation and North–South Relations. *World Development* 13(2): 191–204.

Taylor, Lance. 1986. Economic Openness—Problems to the Century's End. Paper prepared for the Macroeconomic Policies Project, World Institute for Development Economic Research, Helsinki.

Wachtel, Howard. 1986. *The Money Mandarins: The Making of a New Supranational Economic Order*. New York: Pantheon.

Weisner, Eduardo. 1985. Latin American Debt: Lessons and Pending Issues. *American Economic Review* 75(2): 191–95.

Williamson, John. 1990. What Washington Means by Policy Reform. In *Latin American Development: How Much Has Happened?* ed. John Williamson, 5–20. Washington, D.C.: Institute for International Economics.

16

JESSICA NEMBHARD

Foreign Aid and Dependent Development

Countries use external finance (foreign loans, direct foreign investment, foreign aid) for a variety of reasons—particularly if their domestic resources are not enough to finance economic expansion, social programs, necessary imports, defense, or debt servicing. In none of its forms, however, does external financing come without cost. In the 1970s, low-interest foreign loans seemed ideal, but by the 1980s, interest rates skyrocketed and debt servicing became unbearable for most borrowers. The debt crisis brought stabilization conditions and austerity measures directed by the International Monetary Fund (IMF). Direct foreign investment also has its downside, most notably that decision and profit making escape local control. Multinational investors use a country's cheap labor and resources and give little in return.

Foreign aid is supposed to be beneficial and neutral, but the analysis in this chapter will show that although foreign aid often seems helpful and innocuous, even generous, in more cases than not, it has destabilizing and impoverishing effects. Its presence and impact take control of the economy out of the hands of national governments and localities and put it into the hands of foreign countries, aid bureaucracies, and national elites. A country indulging in foreign aid relations often finds itself entrapped in preconceived economic models and prescriptions, following policies and supporting projects antithetical to its goals, and undermining its own economic strategies.

Aid distribution has less to do with need and philanthropy than it does with military strategy, political policy, and capitalist expansion. Teresa Hayter found foreign aid to be "merely the smooth face of imperialism"; it has "never been an unconditional transfer of financial resources" (1971:7, 15).

It is the purpose of this chapter to explore the ways in which the giving and receiving of aid promote dependent capitalist development and further exacerbate the differences between rich and poor—to show that the

314

rules of access to economic aid favor the private sector, capitalist development, and external control.

Aid: What Is It, Who Gives It, and Who Gets It?

For the purposes of this chapter, the term *foreign aid* refers to transfers of resources (often financial) from governments, through official and international institutions, to other governments, on concessional terms. Analysis focuses on nonmilitary economic aid for development purposes. Also considered in this chapter is government-to-government or multilateral institution-to-government lending, where the concessional, or grant, element may be ambiguous.[1]

There are several different types of aid that are given by governments and multilateral organizations: project aid, program aid, in-kind food or commodity aid, and technical assistance. The bulk of aid is given in the form of project aid, although in the last two decades aid is increasingly being disbursed in the form of program aid.

Project aid is assistance given for a specific economic activity, a particular plan, and may be used only for the project specified—to buy certain materials or to pay certain salaries and setup costs. Project aid generally entails the transfer of a specific capital asset or of directed technical assistance.

Program aid is a broader category, providing transfers to a country for general economic assistance, for "budget support or balance of payments support" (Payer 1974). Program aid provides a cash sum "available for the benefit of the entire recipient economy or a sector of it, and is normally accompanied by policy discussions" (Cassen 1987).

According to Cheryl Payer, the shift from project aid to program aid has been gradual, starting in the 1960s and escalating in the 1980s. This shift in the form of support was initiated by the United States.

> The problem with "project" aid, from the U.S. point of view, was that it gave the donor too little leverage over the economic policies of the recipient country. This disadvantage was especially pronounced if the project itself was dearer to the heart of the aid-giver than to that of the recipient. The aided country would accept the project, and then spend the rest of its budget on items that might not be "rational" in the eyes of the donor. The switch to "programme" aid, which was not tied to the importation of equipment for a specific project (though still tied to procurement in the donor country), could give the donor leverage over the entire economic programme of the recipient. . . . disbursements could be tied to specified performance criteria. (1974:30)

Aid is given bilaterally, from one government to another, and multilaterally, from an international organization to a country. Although bilateral aid is still more prevalent, multilateral aid has been increasing steadily. In

1987, 64 percent of development assistance was disbursed from bilateral sources, 22 percent from multilateral sources, and 14 percent from non-governmental sources (World Bank 1990:128, figure 8.2).

The Donors

Governments of industrialized countries in North America, Western Europe, Japan, (what used to be) the USSR, Eastern Europe, and OPEC countries all give aid either directly or through international agencies. In 1988, U.S.$51 billion in bilateral aid was disbursed in official development assistance[2]—$48 billion from Western countries (members of the Organization for Economic Cooperation and Development, or OECD) and $2 billion from members of the Organization of Petroleum Exporting Countries (OPEC) (World Bank 1990: table 19).

To understand the significance of the amount of aid disbursed by industrialized countries, I provide a few comparisons. The $22 billion a year (estimated in 1984) spent in the United States on cigarettes was more than the combined dollar value of aid given by the three largest Western donors (the United States, Japan, and France) in 1986. The total *annual* value of world aid at the end of the 1980s was roughly equivalent to the combined amount that the United States and the former Soviet Union (before the USSR's economic downturn) spent on military expenditures in *one month* (at $1.5 billion a *day*) (Hancock 1989:43).

The United States has traditionally dominated bilateral aid giving in terms of value of aid and amount. However, when aid is calculated as a percentage of a country's gross national product (GNP), the United States is one of the smallest aid givers (see Table 16.1). In 1988, Saudi Arabia, Norway, the Netherlands, Sweden, and Denmark were the top givers as a proportion of their own GNP (see Table 16.1).[3] In 1990, Japan became the largest donor of foreign aid, in terms of value of disbursements (Islam 1991).

The bulk of U.S. bilateral aid is channeled through the U.S. Agency for International Development (AID), which has been the largest and most influential bilateral aid institution. In the 1980s, the United States reduced its role in providing development aid, allocating more aid as security assistance than as actual development assistance. Robert Wood points out that now "well over half of economic aid . . . [from the United States, excluding food aid,] is channeled through the Economic Support Fund . . . , which is formally subordinated to the pursuit of U.S. military and strategic objectives" (1986:11). In fact, in 1986, only about 8 percent of U.S. aid could be classified as "development assistance devoted to low-income countries" (World Bank 1990:127–28). In multilateral aid, the United States is a major financier of the World Bank, which gives it the most voting power.

Multilateral aid is provided by international organizations and institu-

TABLE 16.1
Official Development Assistance (as a Percentage of Donor's GNP)

Country	1965	1975	1985	1988
Australia	0.53	0.65	0.48	0.46
Belgium	0.60	0.59	0.55	0.40
Canada	0.19	0.54	0.49	0.50
Denmark	0.13	0.58	0.80	0.89
France	0.76	0.62	0.78	0.72
Germany, F.R.	0.40	0.40	0.47	0.39
Japan	0.27	0.23	0.29	0.32
Kuwait	—	4.82[a]	3.25	0.41
Libya	—	0.66[a]	0.58	0.52
Netherlands	0.36	0.75	0.91	0.98
Norway	0.16	0.66	1.01	1.10
Saudi Arabia	—	5.95[a]	2.86	2.70
Sweden	0.19	0.82	0.86	0.89
U.K.	0.47	0.39	0.33	0.32
U.A.E.	—	8.95[a]	0.29	—
U.S.	0.58	0.27	0.24	0.21

Sources: World Bank, *World Development Report 1989* (New York: Oxford University Press, 1989), table 19; and for 1988, World Bank 1990:table 19.   [a]Figure is for 1976.

tions—mostly multilateral development banks and several agencies of the United Nations. The World Bank is the largest multilateral aid donor. In 1988, net disbursements of concessional assistance from multilateral donors was approximately $8.8 billion: about $3.8 billion from the World Bank's International Development Association; about $1.2 billion from other multilateral development banks; and another $3.8 billion in total from the United Nations Children's Fund (UNICEF), the United Nations Development Program, and the UN's World Food Program (World Bank 1990:129).

The question often arises whether aid giving from Scandinavia, China, the former USSR, and Eastern Europe is different from that of the United States and Western Europe. Although there has traditionally been little analysis of and data on aid from state socialist and social democratic governments,[4] researchers in the field find little practical difference between donors, particularly in the case of ensuing dependence on aid and lack of local participation and control. Idrian Resnick (1981), for example, found that of the many donors in Tanzania (including Swedish and Eastern bloc donors), only the Chinese (People's Republic) were unobtrusive and truly philanthropic in their aid giving. They were the only ones who asked the Tanzanians what they needed (instead of telling them what they were going to give), gave without asking anything in return, and actually got their hands dirty helping. Furthermore, Gunnar Myrdal (1984:161) has lamented that by the 1980s, Sweden had gradually abandoned its long-standing principle of giving aid with no strings attached. It remains to be seen how the character of Japanese aid develops, now that Japan is the largest bilateral donor.[5]

The Recipients

After World War II, Western and Eastern Europe received aid from the United States as part of the reconstruction programs under the Marshall Plan. As those regions recovered, aid giving was increasingly transferred to the Third World. Underdeveloped ("developing," "less-developed") countries receive aid, as do relatively powerless countries. But mostly, countries favored by the donor for military, ideological, and other strategic reasons receive aid, regardless of whether they are middle-income, newly industrializing, or the poorest of states.

Contrary to popular belief, the poorest countries do not receive the bulk of foreign aid, particularly when measured in dollars per person. In 1988, approximately 41 percent of official development assistance was disbursed to middle- and high-income countries (World Bank 1990:127). The top receivers of official development assistance in 1988 were India, China, Indonesia, Bangladesh, and Egypt (see Table 16.2). The same countries have qualified each year, throughout the decade of the 1980s, as the highest receivers of aid in dollar terms (although their exact ranks fluctuate).[6] India and China, although the top dollar recipients and among the poorest of nations, receive some of the least aid per capita: $2.60 and $1.80 per person respectively.

Throughout the decade, Israel (classified as a high-income economy by the World Bank) received the most aid per person (by a large margin) of any recipient—$279 in 1988—followed by Botswana with $128 per person and Jordan with $109 (see Table 16.2). In addition, Israel has continuously been one of the top receivers of nominal aid. Per capita aid to Central American and Caribbean countries increased dramatically from 1977 to 1984. Tom Barry and Deb Preusch (1988:3) found that economic aid to Central American countries increased sevenfold in the 1980s, mostly from increased U.S. aid.

What Are the Motives for Aid Giving?

In its modern form, aid giving began with the Marshall Plan and was essentially a U.S. phenomenon. The United States used aid to help its World War II allies, to bolster the international capitalist system, to secure markets for its exports and open up other communities to its investments, and to guarantee military and political allegiances.

TABLE 16.2
Top Fifteen Recipients of Official Development Assistance
(from All Sources, in 1988)

Country	Net Disbursement (millions $ U.S.)		Per Capita Disbursement ($ U.S.)
India	2,098	Israel	279.30
China	1,990	Botswana	127.70
Indonesia	1,632	Jordan	108.80
Bangladesh	1,592	Papua New Guinea	101.90
Egypt	1,537	Gabon	98.30
Pakistan	1,408	Mauritania	96.60
Israel	1,241	El Salvador	83.40
Tanzania	978	Senegal	81.20
Ethiopia	970	Jamaica	80.30
Sudan	918	Somalia	73.40
Mozambique	886	Costa Rica	69.90
Philippines	854	Central African Rep.	68.40
Kenya	808	Honduras	66.40
Sri Lanka	599	Lesotho	64.40
Zaire	580	Zambia	63.30

Source: World Bank, *World Development Report 1990* (New York: Oxford University Press, 1990): table 20 (for countries with populations over 1 million).

Aid is supposed to help narrow the gap between the industrialized North and the underdeveloped South. Almost everyone, however—from U.S. presidents and congresspeople to aid-agency bureaucrats around the world to international economists—agrees that foreign aid, even economic and development aid, is essentially a foreign-policy tool for a donor.[7] Governments and official agencies give aid to reward less powerful countries for their political and economic cooperation, to promote military alliances, and to suppress redistributive and revolutionary movements.[8] President John F. Kennedy candidly remarked in 1961 that "foreign aid is a method by which the United States maintains its position of influence and control around the world and sustains a good many countries which would definitely collapse or pass into the communist bloc" (Hancock 1989:71).[9]

Aid is also an economic tool to promote an international "free" market system and provide markets for the goods and services peddled by the businessmen, corporations, and financial institutions affiliated with the donor. Although aid was used heavily as a weapon in the cold war and has often been justified on those grounds, it actually has a more pervasive and permanent function in international relations. Foreign aid is an integral part of the

international financial and commercial economic system and has played a
major role in the worldwide internationalization of capital and interdependence of economies (Wood 1986:5). It helps open societies to industrialized countries' products, promote private investment, and legitimize
world capitalist development—keeping countries that were former colonies
dependent on Western technology, products, and expertise and perpetuat-
ing Southern countries' provision of labor and other raw materials to maintain the industrialized North's way of life.

Although the rhetoric about aid began, in the 1970s, to reflect a concern for helping countries alleviate poverty, the new rhetoric was little more
than that. Even the World Bank and the OECD's Development Assistance
Committee admit that development aid has been disappointingly ineffective
at reducing "extreme poverty," often because a preponderance of the aid,
particularly bilateral aid, has "simply not been concerned with economic
development or poverty reduction" (World Bank 1990:127).

When we think about aid, we do not generally think of it in terms of
the donors' military and political strategy or the donors' economic needs.
We tend to think of aid solely as a gift from a rich country to a poor
country—to help the poor country. We ignore donors' hidden agendas and
the ways in which donors benefit. Yet for aid recipients these are the overwhelming realities that color and stain the giving of aid.

The Impact of Foreign Aid on Recipient Societies

Aid has most certainly been effective at solidifying alliances for donor countries, opening up markets for corporations affiliated with the donors, and
creating economic dependence between donors and recipients. But has aid
effectively helped recipients? The consensus from the literature on development aid is that recipients have not benefited as much as the donors. The
most liberal and radical, as well as the most conservative, critics share a
common assessment that foreign-aid giving has not significantly helped to
reduce poverty in recipient societies and rarely fosters self-reliance or un-
equivocally enhances economic growth.

The problems with receiving aid fall into several almost universal categories: (1) aid promotes and exacerbates inequalities, (2) it fosters dependent and ecologically unsound development, (3) most aid is "tied" in some
form or another, (4) aid creates debt, and (5) there is little local participation in securing and allocating incoming aid and in designing and implementing aid projects.

Inegalitarian Development

Foreign aid exacerbates domestic and global inequalities.[10] Stephen
Hellinger, Douglas Hellinger, and Fred O'Regan (1988:164), among many

others, note that "there has been no period during the forty-year history of U.S. economic assistance when the vast majority of that aid has bypassed the privileged members of . . . [recipient] societies." The assumption behind aid giving has always been that development should be achieved by promoting and supporting private enterprise, using foreign technology and products, and letting the market rule. Once businesses and international trade are thriving, growth rates are supposed to increase, and some portion of the new wealth is expected to trickle down to appease the poor.

Because of its bias toward large projects and the promotion of certain segments of the private sector, foreign aid disproportionately benefits local elites and multinational entities (corporations and financial institutions), the private sector, and the donor countries more than the local poor or even the recipient government itself. Aid has tended to exacerbate initial inequalities and bolster the powerful and the wealthy in recipient countries. Graham Hancock (1989:192) finds that in many countries where aid is plentiful, the poor "suffer the most abject miseries," often "not in spite of aid but because of it."

Aid giving often results in making the poor poorer, especially if the receiving society is characterized by severe inequalities in income and power. It privileges domestic elites by leaving poorer sectors out of projects altogether, by allowing local elites to control projects and use the resources for their own personal benefit, or by doing projects that have no relevance to alleviating poverty or redistributing income. For example, the tubewell irrigation project in Bangladesh was designed on paper to help irrigate land for small farmers. In practice all the wells, however, have been located on lands belonging to the top 1 percent of rural families, who often charge their neighbors a fee for use of the well (Hartmann and Boyce 1983:256–67).

Electrification projects have similar consequences, aiding local elites and transnational corporations. For example, the Akosombo Dam built with aid money in Ghana has provided the U.S.-owned VALCO aluminum plant with hydroelectric power at rates substantially below production cost for more than twenty years. This is a plant that does not even use Ghana's domestic bauxite; it imports bauxite from Jamaica and refines it in Louisiana. In addition, the electric lines pass over many poor villages on their way to electrifying the capital's prosperous suburbs. To enable the rich to have electric light and air conditioning, 1 percent of Ghana's population, the majority of whom were rural poor, were displaced in order to build the dam, and hundreds of thousands of the neighboring poor have been disabled by river blindness disease and water-borne parasites from the reservoir created by the dam (see Hancock 1989:140).[11]

Also, projects to build new roads in rural areas tend to benefit the more prosperous farmers who already produce enough surplus. The new roads allow them to sell their excess crops at urban markets or for export. They are then able to use their increased earnings to buy up the land of their worse-off neighbors—poor farmers who then have no livelihood (Lappé, Schurman, and Danaher 1987:64).

In addition, aid giving helps local elites engage in capital flight. The private sector relies on aid monies to finance new investments, thus freeing up their own money—derived from their increased profit-making abilities and increased status—or even sometimes using the aid money itself, to invest and save outside the recipient country. When asked where the U.S. aid was going, for instance, a U.S. Embassy official in Honduras answered that "most of it ends up in private bank accounts in Miami" (Lappé, Schurman, and Danaher 1987:129).

Frances Lappé, Joseph Collins, and David Kinley (1980:11) conclude that aid fails to help the poor, because it is based on a fundamental fallacy: that aid can reach the powerless even though channeled through the powerful.

Dependent Development

Although development and growth are considered to be the goals of foreign-aid giving, those are rarely achieved. None of the studies reviewed for this chapter provide any overwhelming evidence that aid makes a significant or necessary contribution to a nation's economic development (e.g., see Riddell 1987). Moreover, Volker Bornschier, Christopher Chase-Dunn, and Richard Rubinson (1978) find that the cumulative, long-term effect of stocks of direct foreign investment and aid is a decrease in the relative rate of economic growth in recipient economies. Aided countries have not experienced much economic growth and have come to rely on foreign imports; highly technical, inappropriate, and capital-intensive production; high consumption; and export promotion. The development models used and the projects promoted are dictated by aid agency bureaucrats (usually located in Washington, D.C., or London or Paris) using theories and models that have little correspondence to the reality of Third World economies.

In addition to taking resources out of the recipient country and benefiting donors and national elites, aid giving and the provisions under which aid must be accepted, used, and distributed create distortions—market and social distortions—within the country. Projects alter conditions in the local markets and are controlled by certain elements of the already powerful private sector, further tipping the scales against the have-nots. Agricultural projects and food aid, for example, tend to alter market conditions such that local products end up selling at lower prices, rendering local small farmers unable to make a living. In Haiti, Frances Lappé, Rachel Schurman, and Kevin Danaher (1987:89) found that small farmers do not even bother to bring their produce to market the week food aid arrives.

Aid resources tend to be allocated and concentrated into big projects that are not self-sustaining.[12] For example, projects and programs are made larger than necessary, requiring large expenditures on goods and services, or are made to depend on imports, bypassing local goods and services and creating excessive foreign exchange needs. Often public services and public enterprises are curtailed or privatized, which results in cutting off needed services.[13]

Most aid donors tend to believe that countries will only develop if economic activity focuses on export promotion and if government enterprises are privatized. Such a focus, however, often makes a country more dependent on the international economy, on foreign trade, and on the beneficence of local private and transnational corporations—and thus less oriented toward local needs, local control, and self-sufficiency.

One of the most common export projects promoted by aid agencies is the exportation of nontraditional or specialty crops such as winter vegetables, herbs, and ornamental plants. Farmers are encouraged (and sometimes coerced) to concentrate on producing one crop for export, such as broccoli, brussels sprouts, or cashews, and to give up their subsistence farming—corn, rice, beans, yams, and the like (which guaranteed them some level of subsistence).

In Honduras, for example, small farmers were coerced into planting cashews instead of their usual corn crop. They had been promised $40 per hundred pounds but were subsequently paid only $7.50. In Guatemala, U.S. AID funded a somewhat successful project whereby local small farmers produced broccoli, cauliflower, and other winter vegetables for a wholly owned U.S. subsidiary. Farmers were to be provided with credit, advice, and an assured price. However, under the contract, farmers were required to sell all of their harvest to the company, but the company was not obliged to buy all that they produced. When the farmers began to double the projected volume of vegetables, the system went into disarray. For periods of time the company suspended purchases of some kinds of the vegetables, prices plummeted, and quality standards increased (see Lappé, Schurman, and Danaher 1987:73–77). The farmers were left with an oversupply of vegetables that they were not allowed to sell elsewhere, and an unstable and insecure market for specialty crops. They, of course, now had to buy most of the food staples they had previously grown themselves.

In addition, such projects run into problems in relation to the international economy. The farmers have no real guarantees that their exports will be successful. Often after a project has been implemented, trade arrangements change, and U.S. and Western European markets close to such exports.

At issue here is not just a change from relatively secure, traditional crops to more precarious ones; there is also the change from self-sufficiency to dependence on food imports. Zaire, for instance, was a food exporter immediately after independence in 1960. More recently, after twenty years of association with aid giving, it spends more than $300 million a year on food imports (Lappé, Collins, and Kinley 1980:31). South Korea has had a similar experience (see Lappé, Schurman, and Danaher 1987:94–95).

Aid projects also have adverse ecological consequences, both locally and globally. The desertification and destruction of the Brazilian rain forests from aid-sponsored cattle-raising projects is a well-known example (see Hancock 1989). Hydroelectric power projects also devastate needed forests and expose neighboring villages to new diseases and hazards.

In addition, aid in the 1980s was aimed less and less at fostering long-term development strategies, while it was made more and more contingent upon implementing stabilization and austerity programs to curtail government spending and lower inflation levels. Country experiences show that not only has the International Monetary Fund promoted stabilization and austerity packages for Third World countries (as part of its function as the international agency to address countries' short-term balance-of-payments problems), but also multilateral aid agencies and bilateral aid agencies have adopted their own stabilization policies, and require recipient countries to settle with the IMF as a precondition for receiving foreign aid.

Tied Aid

Even as an aid to development, foreign assistance is always conditional (Hayter 1971; Wood 1986:26) and never neutral (Hartmann and Boyce 1983). Aid is usually given with strict provisions about how it is to be used—what project, how financed, what products and equipment to buy and from whom, what staff at what salaries, and what government structure, agencies, and advisors are to be used.

Foreign aid is "tied" by almost every donor, often because the money or capital given is required to be used for procuring goods and services from the donor country. For example, 70 per cent of U.S. foreign aid expenditures return to the United States in the form of purchases of U.S. goods and services.[14] Even the money the United States gives to the multilateral banks for their aid projects returns to U.S. coffers. A recent report on the self-interested nature of U.S. economic bilateral and multilateral aid found that the money spent by the multilaterals on U.S. goods and services "greatly exceeds our contributions to them."[15]

Even program aid, which does not specify projects, does specify economic and political policies that should be pursued, as well as personnel and salaries, and continues to stipulate where goods and services are to be bought. Most "negotiations" between aid agencies and recipient governments are to secure agreement from the receiving country on the provisions in the plan as set out by the aid agency and to promote "policy dialogues."

To qualify for U.S. bilateral aid, for example, a country must sign a Memorandum of Understanding, which sets out the ways in which U.S. AID wants the assistance used.

Policy dialogues are meetings with recipient government ministers at which AID officials provide "inputs to policy formation, planning and the design and implementation of management and administrative systems."[16] Recipient governments are also expected to hold similar dialogues with other U.S.-sponsored organizations, including private-sector groups. U.S. AID staff and any other officials attending such a dialogue expect to be given access to complete financial information about the internal affairs of the government, including the budget and records of the nation's central bank (Barry and Preusch 1988:26). Barry and Preusch conclude that

> the conditions imposed by the economic aid agreements restrict each government's range of political and economic options, and in a very real way undermine the sovereignty and democratic process of each country. A.I.D. tells the government what bills to introduce into the legislature and often withholds the release of promised economic assistance until the bills are passed. (27)

The World Bank has similar relations with recipient governments, attempting to influence all the activities in the sectors in which it sponsors projects (Payer 1982; Payer quoted in Torrie 1983:83). The World Bank expects laws and taxation policies to change to suit the "needs" of the projects and to make the sector conducive to more projects of the same sort. Moreover, Lappé, Collins, and Kinley (1980:49) find that in some countries, the World Bank lends funds for and places foreign advisors into key government ministries. Similarly, James Mittelman (1980:154) notes that international agencies have "penetrated key state apparatuses in Tanzania." In Nicaragua, a World Bank confidential report (written in 1980, after the new Reagan administration changed some of the key World Bank bureaucrats) admitted that the World Bank had taken on the role of negotiating with the Nicaraguan government for projects that promote the domestic private sector. In the report, the author insisted that new "clear and consistent rules of the game for the private sector," acceptable to the World Bank, were a precondition for further lending (Conroy 1985: 52).

Lack of Local Participation

There is little if any local participation in the structure of aid giving. Aid agencies have their own staffs who design and implement programs. Foreign staff often determine project sites according to their own convenience and comfort rather than according to a country's needs. They may insist on foreign evaluators and foreign products. The assumption is that the aid staff have the knowledge and the experience to make the decisions, that they know better than the recipient government officials or any other indigenous personnel. Recipients' own professionals and experts are almost always considered inferior and are not consulted. Sometimes even the recipient government's own needs are not taken into account.

Hancock (1989) provides many examples where local personnel who were more qualified than the aid officials were underutilized or not utilized at all. He strongly supports the criticism that aid organizations are "inherently ethnocentric, paternalistic and non-professional" (22).

Few aid programs are channeled through community and grass-roots organizations, and little aid actually reaches the poor: "I am still skeptical as to how far official aid is capable of reaching the poor after it has gone through the double filter of the governments of the aid-giving and the aid-receiving countries, each naturally pursuing its own political and economic goals."[17] Few aid programs or projects attempt to promote empowerment and self-reliance (in fact, empowerment and self-reliance are antithetical to the major motivations for aid giving). For Harry Magdoff, the entire structure of aid and imperialism prevents recipient societies from controlling and utilizing their own resources and defining their own capacities.[18]

Finally, aid projects also tend to suffer from implementation problems: implementation requirements and constraints are not fully considered; information needs are not fully anticipated. There is a generalized lack of experienced management, inappropriate technology is used, and project sizes are often disproportionate (too big or too small). Both coordination and sustainability are wanting. There are few mechanisms for learning by doing or for sharing of information, particularly at the local level.

Aid and Debt

Aid giving creates debt problems. In the first place, much aid, although on concessional terms, still is not in grant form and must be repaid with interest. Since the 1960s (coinciding with a change in the countries receiving aid, from the Marshall Plan to Third World aid), aid has increasingly been given as loans that must be repaid. The terms are still concessional—below the market rate—but most are no longer outright grants. In fact, more than half of all official aid is now "given" as loans (Wood 1986:234).

In 1970, the World Bank was already collecting more in payments on debt service than it was giving out in new loans (Wood 1986:77). In 1983, almost half of the long term public debt of Third World countries was official debt, even though by market standards much of this official debt from capital and commodity aid was given under concessional terms (Wood 1986:234). By 1988, both the IMF and the World Bank were receiving billions of dollars more in repayments than they disbursed.[19]

Second, aid projects often require local financing and create needs for expensive and capital-intensive imports that end up being financed by foreign debt. "Counterpart funds"—the money that the recipient government puts in itself or raises elsewhere—are often required as part of an aid deal. Counterpart funds may constitute anywhere from 20 percent to 60 percent of the total cost of a project, tying up a country's scarce financial resources (Lappé, Collins, and Kinley 1980:90) and often requiring other outside funding.

Third, aid receiving allows local elites to engage in capital flight; through corruption and other measures that give them control over much of the incoming money, they are able to send out their plunder to foreign bank accounts. Donors end up receiving more than they gave, and the recipient governments and their poor repay more than they ever received (Wood 1986:14).

Is There Any Good Aid?

It is difficult to find examples of unequivocal successes from the receipt of official foreign aid. All analysts, however, seem to agree on the ingredients that might produce favorable outcomes from aid giving. Aid giving needs to be designed and structured more from the bottom up—as a response to programs and projects initiated by democratic governments and grass-roots local organizations. It needs to be given without conditions and tying, and as grants, not loans. It should be given directly to local groups, bypassing local elites, corrupt governments, and local aid bureaucracies. Aid giving should not be a big business or bureaucracy, and its institutions should be peopled more by representatives of the recipients than by representatives of the donors. Aid must contribute to alleviating poverty and inequalities and must not be used to reward military and political allies or promote international private enterprise and unequal "free" trade.

Lappé, Schurman, and Danaher (1987:112) note one example of a successful project in which food aid was "reconceived as a tool of empowerment." Food aid was distributed by the international agency Caritas to a women's group in Lima, Peru. The aid helped to launch cooperative kitchens that save fuel, time, and costs. These successful cooperative kitchens have been moving significantly toward self-sufficiency—that is, no longer needing any aid.

Strategies

If most aid does not reach the poor in recipient countries and does not contribute to alleviating poverty and inequalities or to fostering economic growth, then is it worth it? The answer to that question obviously depends upon who asks. Aid seems to satisfy donors' motives. But it falls short of recipients' expectations and international concerns for economic equality, egalitarian development, and the reduction of poverty.

The aid-giving system should allow recipients to decide for themselves whether to continue receiving aid and under what circumstances and conditions. Recipients need the information, the power, and the opportunities to fashion aid giving to suit the needs of their economies and particularly the needs of their poor. Concerned citizens affiliated with donors should work to help make the conditions right, in their own countries and internationally, for aid actually to serve the recipients and not the donors.

Alternatives to continuing the foreign-aid process as currently constituted fall into two rather contradictory strategies: (1) radical strategies that call for the dismantling of the present structure of aid giving or the total elimination of aid, and (2) short-term, temporary strategies that do not actually solve the fundamental problems of aid giving and receiving but lessen the undesirable consequences. Dismantling the current structure of aid giving would entail putting control into the hands of the recipients. It would require international or coordinated actions—taking the international economy out of corporate and dominant industrialized nations' hands, promoting regional coordination and delinking. Cosmetic strategies include making aid less blatantly destructive, targeting aid to the reduction of poverty and inequality, diversifying the composition of aid and the number of donors to a country, and increasing local democratic control over aid.

To Receive Aid or Not to Receive Aid:
What Could Recipients Do?

External finance tends to keep countries in economic dependence rather than help them gain independence. Payer (1974:210–11) suggests that "nations have failed to develop not because they had too little international money, but because they had too much." It may not be only the network of inevitable ties and coercions that accompanies aid but also the physical act of accepting foreign resources that is the problem, creating reliance on and preferences for foreign enterprise, technology, and goods.

If foreign aid exacerbates domestic as well as North–South inequalities and perpetuates unequal dependencies, then a country may be better off not receiving aid. From the point of view of the recipient, aid is only useful and worthwhile if the receiver actually receives more than it has to give up. Therefore a recipient should only agree to the disbursement if there is a strong probability that the aid will be used productively and constructively, if it would actually reduce poverty or at least not further immiserize the population, and if it is under the control of democratic and grass-roots elements of the society. There may be only a very narrow set of circumstances under which a country would be better off with external finances.

Doing without foreign aid from the North means that former recipients must reorganize and reorient their economies. They must become self-sufficient and self-reliant, or at least regionally so. Delinking and selective delinking (disassociation from the prevailing international economy) strategies have been proposed by varying sources.[20] Such strategies emphasize reducing dependencies on industrial countries' models of development, products, and consumption values. They might entail withdrawing from trade and foreign debt arrangements with industrialized countries.

Regional cooperation, South–South cooperation, is an option to be considered in conjunction with delinking or partial delinking. This strategy might include the promotion and establishment of regional and Third World planning and trade associations; the pooling of resources, technology, and finances; and joint investment projects.

What Can Citizens of Donor Countries Do?

The most important thing that citizens of donor countries should do is to find ways to support the efforts of recipients. Let the recipients do the initiating and donors do the responding and supporting. Support may entail creating solidarity organizations with citizens from recipient countries, passing legislation in donor countries to provide aid without ties and in the form of outright grants, and facilitating the repudiation of recipients' foreign debt.[21] Citizens of donor countries should be informed, should know what their aid dollars are doing and the consequences of their aid giving.

Citizens of donor countries should help to create national and international conditions such that recipients can embark upon egalitarian development, can get aid in the form and under the terms that they want and need, and can withdraw from the aid cycle if they want—without economic and political repercussions. Citizens in donor countries can help recipients to alter the structure of the multilateral organizations, which would entail changing voting rights and eliminating behind-the-scenes power plays. They should support the New International Economic Order (NIEO) proposed by the Non-Aligned Movement to restructure the world's trading and financial arrangements and reorganize the structures of world production.[22]

Citizens in donor countries can help to reshape the structures—relations and conditions—of aid giving and receiving.

Aid should be more directly and clearly related to alleviating poverty, empowering the poor and other low-status members of recipient societies, and creating self-reliance.

The recipients of aid should be chosen according to their ability to generate and support local processes of participatory democracy. Donors should provide aid only to governments that have shown a commitment to equitable development and a capacity to promote such development and bypass the elites.

The top-down approach should be replaced by a bottom-up approach—the poor and local grass-roots organizations should define their own needs. Disbursal and implementation of projects should be decentralized through local groups, site-specific community organizations, and church and women's groups.[23]

ACKNOWLEDGMENTS

The author thanks James Boyce, Cheryl Payer, Gerald Epstein, and Julie Graham for helpful comments and editorial advice. This chapter is a version, written specifically for this volume, of a research project entitled "The Impact of Foreign Aid on Recipient Economies: Some Questions to Ask." The research and writing were completed while the author was the recipient of a National Science Foundation Graduate Fellowship (1988–91).

NOTES

1. The term *foreign aid* generally includes military and financial grants, commodity and food giveaways (or at least sales of foodstuffs below the market value), technical assistance, short-term financial transfers for specific programs and projects, or long-term "soft" development loans. More specifically, much of the literature focuses on aid as the transfer of resources on concessional terms, that is, under terms of grants or "soft" long-term loans with low, fixed interest rates, usually for the purpose of development.

Official development assistance (ODA) is aid undertaken by official agencies with the objective of promoting the economic development and welfare of recipient countries, and consists of a grant element of 25 percent or more (criteria of the Development Assistance Committee [DAC] of the Organization for Economic Cooperation and Development [OECD], the guardian of official aid information [Cassen and Associates 1986:2]).

2. This does not include aid from the former Soviet Union and countries in Eastern Europe or China. One figure given for Soviet aid is $3.8 billion in 1986 (Hancock 1989:43). U.S. aid that same year was $9.6 billion, $10.1 billion in 1988 (World Bank 1990:table 19).

3. Note here, however, that the total amount of aid disbursed from those countries individually or collectively is small, particularly compared to worldwide totals. International aid giving has been dominated continuously by the United States (and perhaps, in what was the socialist world, by the former USSR). The characteristics of aid giving described in this chapter continue to be significantly influenced by U.S. agencies, although Western European aid and Canadian aid have increased in importance, and Japanese nominal aid is now highest. This new era of aid giving, however, is distinguished not so much by the change in the largest donor as by the narrowness of the gap between the amounts given by the top two donors and the absence of the USSR as a patron to fledgling alternative economies.

4. For a discussion on aid and trade between the former "Eastern bloc" and Third World socialist countries, see Deere and Malinowitz, Chapter 22 in this volume, "Third World Socialism and the Demise of COMECON."

5. This chapter summarizes the effects of aid giving from the 1950s to the

1980s, particularly U.S. aid, which dominated during that time. An assumption is that Japanese aid, until the late 1980s, was relatively inconsequential and not very different from the prevailing character of foreign-aid giving presented here. Future analyses of aid giving will need in-depth, longitudinal studies of the development of Japanese aid—its form, character, and consequences, and the motives for its distribution (Islam [1991] begins this tradition). I suspect, however, that the problems described here will continue to be of concern regardless of the change in the top donor.

6. In 1987, the top-ten receivers were (in descending order) India, Egypt, Bangladesh, China, Israel, Indonesia, Sudan, Tanzania, Pakistan, and the Philippines (World Bank 1989:table 20). And in 1980, Egypt, Israel, India, Indonesia, Bangladesh, Turkey, Portugal, Pakistan, the Philippines, and Syria were the top receivers (Lappé, Collins, and Kinley 1980:18). Many of these same countries are also the top recipients of military assistance (Lappé, Collins, and Kinley 1980:24).

7. Alfred Maizels and Machiko Nissanke (1984) used an econometric study to analyze motivations for aid and found, as many other studies have indicated, that for bilateral aid, "allocations are made largely (for some donors) or solely (for others) in support of donors' perceived foreign economic, political and security interests."

8. Robert McNamara, when he was head of the World Bank, said that military aid can help stabilize countries, but is not enough: "Our economic assistance is designed to offer a reasonable alternative to [revolutionary] violence" (Mittelman 1980:157).

9. President Nixon was even more blunt in 1968: "Let us remember that the main purpose of aid is not to help other nations but to help ourselves" (Hancock 1989:71).

10. In a review of empirical studies on the effects of economic dependence on growth and inequality, Bornschier, Chase-Dunn, and Rubinson (1978) conclude that foreign investment and aid increase economic inequality within countries.

11. For other electrification examples, see Hancock 1989, Hartmann and Boyce 1983:273, and Lappé, Schurman, and Danaher 1987.

12. For example, Frances Lappé, Joseph Collins, and David Kinley (1980: 38) found that in the late 1970s, the construction cost per mile of a road project in Pakistan was $62,500 and that each advisor cost $7,500 per month.

13. See Lappé, Schurman, and Danaher 1987 on the inefficiencies in the Jamaican health-care system that resulted from the "rationalization" efforts (read "privatization") promoted by aid agencies.

14. From a U.S. AID report cited in Lappé, Schurman, and Danaher 1987: 70; the same figure also appears in Barry and Preusch 1988:44, from the House Committee on Foreign Affairs publication on foreign-assistance legislation, fiscal years 1986 and 1987. In addition, for every $1 billion given in foreign aid, 25,000 jobs are created in the United States (Barry and Preusch 1988:44).

15. Vicki Hicks, Who Does Foreign Aid Really Help? *Farm Journal*, May 1985, cited in Barry and Preusch 1988:44.

16. Testimony of Frank C. Conahan, director of the National Security and International Affairs Division, at hearings before the Senate Subcommittee on For-

eign Operations of the Committee on Appropriations, 14 March 1984, in Barry and Preusch 1988:26.

17. Hla Myint, comment to Gunnar Myrdal (1984:172).

18. Harry Magdoff, Capital, Technology, and Development, in *Imperialism: From the Colonial Age to the Present* (New York: Monthly Review Press, 1978), 223. Quoted by Payer (1982:359).

19. Graham Hancock (1989:188) shows that the IMF received net payments totaling almost $8 billion during 1986–88, and the International Bank for Reconstruction and Development (the World Bank) received net payments of $1.9 billion in 1988.

20. The most comprehensive proposal seen by the author is the delinking process set out by Jacobo Schatan (1987), based on Dieter Senghaas's "imperative of dissociation" (The Case for Autarchy, *Development* 22, no. 1 [1980]: 3–10). Schatan's proposal includes the promotion of new social values to create different consumption patterns (disavow false notions of progress and stop imitating the North), the promotion of new production relations (create communal societies and produce more efficiently with communal labor and organization), and regional import substitutions and self-sufficiency (113–20). See also summaries of delinking theories by Samir Amin and Carlos Diaz-Alejandro, in Stallings 1986:55–56.

21. If interest rates had remained low, or if initial disbursements had been grants, then most of the debt outstanding today would have already been repaid. The economies of many countries would be much better off if a good portion of their foreign-exchange earnings did not have to be spent on continued debt payments.

22. For discussion of the provisions of the NIEO, see Manley (1987), chs. 10, 11, 12, and the conclusion.

23. Many of the suggestions in this section were inspired by Hellinger, Hellinger, and O'Regan 1988 (see esp. ch. 8, "Constructing a New Aid System").

REFERENCES AND BIBLIOGRAPHY

Barry, Tom, and Deb Preusch. 1988. *The Soft War: The Uses and Abuses of U.S. Economic Aid in Central America*. New York: Grove Press.

Bhagwati, J. N., and E. Grinols. 1975. Foreign Capital, Destabilization, and Feasibility of Transition to Socialism. *Journal of Development Economics* 2(2): 85–98.

Bornschier, Volker, Christopher Chase-Dunn, and Richard Rubinson. 1978. Cross-national Evidence of the Effects of Foreign Investment and Aid on Economic Growth and Inequality: A Survey of Findings and a Reanalysis. *American Journal of Sociology* 84 (November): 651–83.

Broad, Robin. 1988. *Unequal Alliance: The World Bank, The IMF, and the Philippines*. Berkeley and Los Angeles: University of California Press.

Cassen, Robert, and Associates. 1987. *Does Aid Work?* Oxford: Clarendon Press.

Chenery, Hollis B. 1964. Objectives and Criteria for Foreign Assistance. In *The United States and the Developing Economies*, ed. Gustav Ranis, 80–91. New York: W.W. Norton.

Conroy, Michael E. 1985. External Dependence, External Assistance, and Economic

Aggression against Nicaragua. *Latin American Perspectives* 12(2): 39–68.

The Debt Crisis Network. 1986. *From Debt to Development: Alternatives to the International Debt Crisis.* Washington, D.C.: Institute for Policy Studies.

George, Susan. 1988. *A Fate Worse than Debt: The World Financial Crisis and the Poor.* New York: Grove Press.

Griffin, Keith. 1970. Foreign Capital, Domestic Savings, and Economic Development. *Oxford Bulletin of Economics and Statistics* 32 (May): 99–112.

Griffin, Keith, and J. L. Enos. 1970. Foreign Assistance: Objectives and Consequences. *Economic Development and Cultural Change* 18:313–27.

Hancock, Graham. 1989. *Lords of Poverty: The Power, Prestige, and Corruption of the International Aid Business.* New York: Atlantic Monthly Press.

Hartmann, Betsy, and James K. Boyce. 1983. *A Quiet Violence: View from a Bangladesh Village.* London: Zed Press for Food First.

Hayter, Teresa. 1971. *Aid as Imperialism.* Harmondsworth, Middlesex: Penguin.

Hayter, Teresa, and Cathy Watson. 1985. *Aid: Rhetoric and Reality.* London: Pluto Press.

Hellinger, Stephen, Douglas Hellinger, and Fred M. O'Regan. 1988. *Aid for Just Development: Report on the Future of Foreign Assistance.* Boulder, Colo.: Lynne Reinner.

Horowitz, David. 1967. Narrowing the Gap through International Aid. In *Fiscal and Monetary Problems in Developing States,* ed. David Krivine, 46–57. New York: Praeger.

Islam, Shafiqul. 1991. *Yen for Development: Japanese Foreign Aid and the Politics of Burden-Sharing.* Washington, D.C.: Council on Foreign Relations.

Lappé, Frances Moore, Joseph Collins, and David Kinley. 1980. *Aid as Obstacle: Twenty Questions about Our Foreign Aid and the Hungry.* San Francisco: Institute for Food and Development Policy for Food First.

Lappé, Frances Moore, Rachel Schurman, and Kevin Danaher. 1987. *Betraying the National Interest.* New York: Grove Press for Food First.

Loxley, John. 1986. *Debt and Disorder: External Financing for Development.* Boulder, Colo.: Westview Press.

Maizels, Alfred, and Machiko K. Nissanke. 1984. Motivations for Aid to Developing Countries. *World Development* 12(9):879–900.

Manley, Michael. 1987. *Up the Down Escalator: Development and the International Economy (a Jamaican Case Study).* Washington, D.C.: Howard University Press.

Mittelman, James H. 1980. International Monetary Institutions and Policies of Socialism and Self-reliance: Are They Compatible? The Tanzanian Experience. *Social Research* 47 (Spring): 141–65.

Myrdal, Gunnar. 1984. International Inequality and Foreign Aid in Retrospect. In *Pioneers in Development,* ed. Gerald M. Meier and Dudley Seers, 151–72. Washington, D.C.: Oxford University Press for the World Bank.

Papanek, Gustav F. 1972. The Effect of Aid and Other Resource Transfers on Savings and Growth in Less Developed Countries. *Economic Journal* 82(327): 934–50.

Pastor, Manuel, Jr. 1987. *The IMF and Latin America: Economic Stabilization and Class Conflict.* Boulder, Colo.: Westview Press.

Payer, Cheryl. 1974. *The Debt Trap: The International Monetary Fund and the Third World*. New York: Monthly Review Press.

———. 1982. *The World Bank: A Critical Analysis*. New York: Monthly Review Press.

Resnick, Idrian N. 1981. *The Long Transition: Building Socialism in Tanzania*. New York: Monthly Review Press.

Riddell, R. C. 1987. *Foreign Aid Reconsidered*. London: James Currey.

Schatan, Jacobo. 1987. *World Debt: Who Is to Pay?* London: Zed Books.

Stallings, Barbara. 1986. External Finance and the Transition to Socialism in Small, Peripheral Societies. In *Transition and Development: Problems of Third World Socialism*, ed. Richard Fagen, Carmen Diana Deere, and Jose Luis Coraggio, 54–78. New York: Monthly Review Press.

Tendler, Judith. 1975. *Inside Foreign Aid*. Baltimore: Johns Hopkins University Press.

Torrie, Jill, ed. 1983. *Banking on Poverty: The Global Impact of the IMF and World Bank*. Toronto: Between the Lines.

Weissman, Steve, and members of Pacific Studies Center and North American Congress on Latin America. 1975. *The Trojan Horse: A Radical Look at Foreign Aid*. Rev. ed. Palo Alto, Calif.: Ramparts Press.

Wood, Robert E. 1986. *From Marshall Plan to Debt Crisis: Foreign Aid and Development Choices in the World Economy*. Berkeley and Los Angeles: University of California Press.

World Bank. 1990. *World Development Report 1990: Poverty*. New York: Oxford University Press for the World Bank.

17 ANTHONY GUGLIELMI
The Crisis of Plenty: Africa

But the people cried in unison: . . . You seize men's wealth, then, you dress in robes of friendship and instruct them to join in the pursuit of the villain who has robbed them.

And there and then the people crucified the Devil on the Cross, and they went away singing songs of victory.

—*Ngugi Wa Thiong'o,* Devil on the Cross

The decade of the 1960s seemed to assure a bright future for Africa. With the advent of political freedom, many Africans anticipated a golden age of wealth and social improvement, not for just the few but for the entire continent. The long centuries under European domination were coming to an end and many expected that the advent of political freedom would enable Africans to claim full partnership and recognition among the nations of the world. With time and determination Africa would harness its natural resources, create a fully functioning industrial economy, and establish itself on an equal footing with the other regions of the globe.

The perspective of the 1990s yields a much grimmer vision of Africa's future. For no one can look at Africa today and not recognize that this land is in the throes of a full scale economic and political crisis. With a birth rate that hovers around 3 percent (highest for a continental area), a growth rate in per capita agricultural production that is negative in many parts of the continent, and a debt service that was equivalent to 123 percent of the value of export earnings on primary commodities (the principal element in Africa's exports), Africa is starving and getting poorer each year (Amin 1989:7).

Because the subject of sub-Saharan African underdevelopment is such a broad and complex topic for this limited format, it will suit my purpose more to focus on a single country that illustrates some of the general characteristics of an Africa caught up in the dilemma of mounting debt and declin-

335

ing revenues. To this end, I have selected Zambia, a country that depends almost exclusively on copper production for its revenue and has in the last decade seen its debt balloon to unimagined proportions.

But before engaging the reader in this investigation, I think it appropriate to lay some groundwork in the history of sub-Saharan African underdevelopment and to provide a synoptic view of the geopolitical significance of natural-resource extraction in this region and its effect on world capitalist development.

Roots of the Crisis

Is this Africa, with its growing population and hungry children, a result of misdirected policies, incompetence, and the misfortunes of nature, or is it the result of complex structural factors? Some, including the World Bank, blame most of Africa's problems on the domestic policies of the nation-states.[1] But African scholars like Samir Amin (1990:7–23) and Basil Davidson (1980:32–45), drawing on their deep knowledge of the continent and its problems, take issue with the views that attribute Africa's problems primarily to the policies of the African countries themselves. They point to the long history and continuing reality of Western political interventions in African affairs and to the policies of "modernization" so heavily touted by the West as the solution to Africa's economic backwardness.[2] In the afterglow of the freedom movements of the 1960s, Africans wholeheartedly embraced Western programs for economic development. But as Amin notes, "the history of the past three decades for Africa can be described as the history of the failure of the so-called 'modernization' strategies" (Amin 1990:36).

Looking back several centuries, Davidson traces the disintegration of African societies and their economies to the European forces opening up the slave trade, which destroyed some of the more prominent and advanced economic centers on the continent. For example, the East African Swahili trading centers were sacked by the Portuguese in the sixteenth century. In addition to politically and militarily weakening Africa, undermining its ability to resist the future colonial takeover, the slave trade depopulated and deskilled the continent. Up until "the 17th century Africa was not inferior to the rest of the world. Indeed it was because Africa's mining technology was superior to that of southern Europe that skilled African miners were taken into slavery . . . to operate the gold and silver mines of South America" (Onimodo 1988:14). From 1451 to the enactment of the 1833 English Abolition Act, experts estimate that between 50 and 160 million people were removed from Africa. African population growth did not recover from this blow until the early 1900s; from 1750 to 1900 the African population growth rate was zero, hovering around 124 million (Onimodo 1988:14–15).

In the violent colonial "adventure" that followed the slave trade, Europeans not only bore away the wealth of Africa, they also installed their political and economic institutions, laws, and educational system, imposing their cultures on a defenseless population. Private property, a fierce economic competition based on an individualistic ethic—all the ideological accoutrements of Western capitalism did not mesh well with these fundamentally communal societies.

Constrained by the colonial institutional apparatus, Africans, in some cases, willingly cooperated in reproducing and reinforcing the Westernization of their nations—so much so, in fact, that in the postcolonial period, Africans struggled with the problem of how to restore pride in being African. In the period from 1960 to 1975, movements for Pan-Africanism and negritude captured the imaginations of many who wanted to define what it means to be African as distinct from a "white" European, and what it means to have an African culture (consciousness) as distinct from a European culture. But the movement for political and cultural independence was also accompanied by wars of liberation, wars that sprouted up throughout the continent and continued for decades (in the Congo, Guinea Bissau, Angola, and Zimbabwe).

Having gained a modicum of independence and political autonomy, many new African leaders found that the struggle for economic independence and development would prove harder than the military struggle, for the centers of economic power, world finance, and consumer markets lie in the West. Without access to finance, Africa could not build the industrial base it so needed and desired, and without sufficient demand for its exports, Africa could not earn the foreign exchange to pay its debts and maintain a proper standard of credit, so necessary to a country's ability to borrow funds on world financial markets. The cultural agenda, then, gave way to the more pressing and complex task of nation building, and the greater part of that task fell to the construction of a viable domestic economy. In accordance with mainstream thinking on development, African leaders agreed to recognize the economic principles of "modernization." The analysis developed in the West and applied to less-developed countries characterized their economies as having a backward agricultural sector and an infant modern industrial sector. To modernize an economy, then, it was necessary to develop the more advanced industrial (urban) centers. What this meant in practice was a massive influx of foreign borrowing to boost industrial growth in these countries at the expense of the rural areas.[3]

Three decades after the advent of "modernization," the failures are evident. In the 1960s, exports grew by 7.2 percent, but in the recessionary years of the 1970s, exports grew by only 2 percent, as African economies suffered from the economic downturn in the industrialized North. As world oil prices rose, so did African indebtedness. By 1985, African debt service took 30 percent of its foreign earnings. This was exacerbated by a $25 billion trade deficit. The terrible 1980s resolved the boom or bust cycles of the 1970s into a morass of economic stagnation: the growth rate in industrial production was less than 1 percent, and in agriculture it was negative.[4]

Natural Resource Abundance and Poverty

Studying Africa is like looking at a modern sculpture: everything depends on the position you take in viewing the subject. On the one hand, Africa is gifted with an abundance of natural wealth; on the other hand, it is a region overflowing with social inequities, unmanageable debt, and an alarming growth in environmental hazards. This is the poorest region in the world, yet it encompasses within its borders the most varied and abundant deposits of resource wealth in the world. As one interested entrepreneur has stated:

> To the crowded Europe, Africa holds the promise of a frontier land still susceptible of great expansion . . . its riches in strategic minerals are impressive. In industrial diamonds, columbium, cobalt, chromium, and beryllium, Africa either heads the list of world producers or stands close to the top. It is a significant producer of tin, manganese, copper, antimony; and its reserves of iron ore and bauxite are just beginning to be tapped. The uranium of the Congo and South Africa has contributed to the unfolding of the atomic age. . . . To this mineral wealth, Africa adds through its agriculture a variety of foodstuffs and industrial materials such as cocoa, coffee, tea, vegetable oil, cotton, and pyrethrum. *The United States has a direct interest in many of these products, but it is probably of less importance to assure its own access to Africa's resources and markets than to make sure that its European allies are not cut off.* (Onimodo 1988:3; emphasis added)

All the developing countries, and especially those in Africa, are a rich source of natural resources. For many raw materials—for example, strategic minerals, coffee, cocoa, tropical timber, and oil—they are the world's primary sources. Without a ready and stable supply of raw materials at affordable prices, the industrialized nations of the North would not be able to produce the automobiles, ships, high-performance jets, and other high-tech commodities that have become an integral part of the modern capitalist world. The output price of manufactured goods might well rise to prohibitive heights if supplies of minerals are interrrupted or the price of these minerals rises significantly. On the other hand, some manufacturing firms might not be able to adjust production to rising prices, and therefore they would have to close their operations.

The foreign dependence of the industrialized nations will only increase as their domestic supplies of these minerals decline. To illustrate the generality of world mineral distribution, of which Africa is a more prominent and specific case, Table 17.1 underscores the sensitivity of the Northern industrialized countries to the realities of mineral distribution.

It is important to note that the percentages of reserves are the current geological estimates of the minerals in the ground that are economically recoverable at current technological capabilities. Based on these estimates, which always change as mining firms undertake further exploration, it is evident that the lion's share of strategic minerals lies in the developing countries. Current geological estimates confirm that if new reserves are discovered, they will be found in either inaccessible regions like Siberia, which would lead to higher mineral prices as a result of increased mining costs, or in the less-developed countries where the ore deposits are of a richer quality and less costly to mine.

Table 17.2 dramatizes the specific case of the developed nations' resource dependence on African mineral imports and helps again to underscore the importance of an unimpaired flow of mineral stock from the South to the North. This table, though somewhat dated, illustrates the degree to which the industrialized countries depend on the resource flows from the African continent. In terms of the world demand for these minerals, in 1973 Africa produced the following world share of fuel and nonfuel minerals: 84 percent of cobalt, 80 percent of gold and diamonds, 46 percent of vanadium, 37 percent of platinum, 33 percent of chromium ore, 32 percent of manganese, 29 percent of phosphate, 24 percent of antimony, 21 percent of uranium, and 10 percent of all crude oil (Lanning 1979:110–11). With such mineral wealth, the industrial potential of the region should

TABLE 17.1
World Mineral Reserves (Percentages)

	Industrialized Countries	Former and Present Centrally Planned Economies	Developing Countries[a]
Bauxite	31.1	3.6	64.3
Copper	28.9	8.9	62.2
Chromium	0.7	1.0	98.3
Manganese	8.0	38.3	53.6
Nickel	25.7	15.3	59.0
Tin	5.4	29.9	64.7
Tungsten	20.9	10.1	69.0
Cobalt	8.1	22.1	69.8
Platinum	1.4	15.1	83.4

Source: Mikesell 1979.   [a]South Africa is included under this category because these resources are part of the continental resource base of Africa.

TABLE 17.2
Consumption Based on Mineral Imports (Percentage of Imports from Africa, 1970)

Minerals	U.K.	France	W. Germany	Japan	U.S.[a]
Chromium	56.4	—	52	62	19
Manganese	30	46.5	68	27	55
Cobalt	—	14.3	—	84	17.9
Copper	31	21	26	—	—
Platinum	39	—	—	—	15.6
Bauxite	65	—	60	—	—

Source: Lanning, 1979:112–13.   [a]More recent figures for 1983 show that 74.5 percent of U.S. chromium imports come from Africa (55.7 percent from South Africa). From 1979 to 1983, 60 percent of all U.S. imports of cobalt came from Zambia and Zaire. Also, in 1983 Guinea (West Africa) supplied 45 percent of U.S. imports of bauxite. Japan imports virtually 100 percent of the platinum group minerals from South Africa (U.S. Bureau of Mines 1985:139, 178, 19, 607).

be assured, but there are serious obstacles to the African nations' capacity to utilize these resources for industrialization; one is the shortage of money capital, and a second is the inability of African markets to generate sufficient demand to make large-scale industrialism profitable.

Resource extraction, however profitable in the short term, can, under certain conditions, pose a long-term threat to a nation's future economic development. Unrestrained and mismanaged resource extraction can deplete mineral reserves too fast, and without alternative export commodities to substitute for declining mineral exports, the country may well find itself in a position where it has to borrow increasingly from foreign capital to provide for the nation's basic social needs. Because government revenue is the only source of long-term funds for the country's social infrastructure (hospitals, schools, roads, etc.), African mining nations become vulnerable to severe budget deficits when either the price of minerals or world demand falls precipitously, as it often does. Without a diverse mix of export products (economic diversification) to sell on the world market, African countries cannot spread the risk of revenue loss due to market uncertainties in the demand for and the price of any one export commodity.

Often, to overcome revenue declines in mineral exports, a country will increase its extraction rate. This, of course, creates additional problems with respect to the environment. The mineral extracted is only a small portion of the mined material; the greater portion is mine waste, which is a significant source of water and air pollution. Some of this waste is acidic, fouling local streams and waterways and killing the organic matter present; mine tailings, or mine waste, are also a prominent source of dust particles in the atmosphere, which cause lung maladies and related health problems.

And to increase the profit from mining, African nations have added additional smelting and refining capacity to their mining extraction infrastructure (this additional capacity also requires extensive foreign borrowing). While this may increase the profit on the refined mineral product, it also adds particulate matter and sulfur dioxide (in the case of copper) pollution to the atmosphere. Although there is little in the way of a concrete study on the environmental effects of mining in Africa, the U.S. experience in this area leaves no doubt as to the possible damages being inflicted on the African ecosystems.

A Case Study in Disaster: Zambia

The reader should be advised that any conclusions based on a country-specific study should not be used to generalize about other African nations or other developing countries. Comparisons with other countries will naturally arise with respect to certain details, but one should avoid attempts to oversimplify the problems or solutions of a region as vast and complex as Africa. With that principle in mind, I now turn to the double disaster in Zambia: falling copper prices and rising debt.

Zambia is located in central southern Africa and possesses some of the richest copper reserves in the world. With the nationalization of the copper mines in 1971 (Zambia gained a 51 percent controlling interest in the distribution of mine revenues but still left the marketing and management control to the foreign multinationals, such as Britain's Anglo-American Corporation and the U.S.-owned American Metal Climax Company), the 7.6 million Zambians stood to make some significant economic gains from the ownership of these mines.[5] Following the 1972 fall in world copper prices, however, potential gains were significantly eroded (Seidman 1975:362). What had once seemed to be a panacea for Zambia's chronic poverty turned into a nightmare.

Copper in the Zambian economy has brought diminishing returns for the populace at large but an increasing concentration of power and wealth into the hands of the Zambian elites, as well as an increasing dependence on the infrastructure of international capitalism. In the past, it had been rather easy to identify the colonial powers as the chief exploiters of African labor, but with the emergence of the African national state, an African elite, capitalist class has used the cloak of nationalism to transform themselves into "champions of the people" while accruing wealth from the control of export revenues.[6] The seeds of collaboration between African national leaders and multinational lending agencies and corporations were planted during the nationalist movement of the 60s; it has proved profitable for both domestic and foreign capital (Markovitz 1987:12–19).

Many economists characterize Zambia as a classic example of a re-source rich, mineral-exporting country that is unable to escape the cycle of boom or bust (the business cycle) within the highly competitive world commodity market. Because its copper production represents only a small share of the total market, Zambia must adjust its economic and social objectives to meet the fluctuating demand of the industrial countries.

What this means in hard economic terms becomes more apparent if we recognize that copper exports make up 90 percent of the total exports of the country (Seidman 1975:359). Copper exports are the single most important source of valuable foreign exchange, which provides the currency to buy medical supplies, textbooks, new and replacement technology, and other needed imports. The continued development and growth in just meeting basic human needs, therefore, depends almost exclusively on the stability of the world price of copper. Although the distribution of mine revenues is not shared equally among all income classes, a fall in mine revenue means a cut in services to those least able to afford them. A fall in the world price of copper similiar to that of 1972 could and did lead to serious shortfalls in needed foreign exchange, which further reduced the ability of the Zambian government to provide necessary human services to the populace (Seidman 1975:362). As copper prices fall, national income is reduced, and the quality of life declines.

To understand why and how the price of copper can have such a devastating impact on the Zambian economy, we must take a closer look at the institutional nature of the Zambian nation and its relation to international capitalism. For lack of space, I will focus on only three major aspects of the nation-state problem in Zambia: the state as a source of funding for social programs, state debt, and the unequal distribution of power and income.

State Apparatus

The state in developing nations has had to take on the role of the primary investor in social infrastructure. Schools, roads, hospitals, and housing had to be built as the new nations emerged in the 1960s. In Zambia, as in other countries, only the national government possessed the necessary capital and desire to invest in what foreign capital judged as nonprofitable investments.

The single most important income-generating source for the government, now and in the beginning of its existence, is and was the copper mines. But the mines were owned by foreign multinational firms, and the government could obtain only limited revenues from the taxation of mine output. Mine output as well as marketing and wages were controlled by the co-owners of the mines, Rio Tinto Zinc and Anglo-American, at least until

1975, when the Zambian government took complete control of mine operations and marketing (Nwoke 1987:147).

This was done to gain more control over mine output, which gave the government, in conjunction with other copper producing nations (CIPEC, or Intergovernmental Council of Copper Exporting Countries),[7] the ability to raise copper prices and, therefore, to increase government mine revenues; but there was a downside to this process. The government chose to increase its source of foreign exchange, but it also created more indebtedness for itself. To buy out the multinationals, it had to borrow from foreign banks. As the main controlling interest in the mines, it also had to bear the lion's share of any investment costs incurred by them. To offset the increased cost of replacing depreciated mining equipment and also to augment mine output with new investment, Zambia hoped to increase its share of mine revenues by increasing its share of mine ownership. But such was not to be, as mineral prices fell and Zambia found itself saddled by a debt that ballooned with each passing year throughout the decade of the 1980s.

As the nation continued to borrow on its assets, principally the copper mines, it became more dependent on the foreign-exchange flows generated by copper mine revenues to sustain its financial position vis-à-vis the international banking system. Simply stated, if government revenues, used to finance both social programs and debt obligations, fell because copper prices dipped below their previous levels, then the government was compelled to renegotiate its loans with a promise to commit a greater share of its future income to repay the country's debt.

During the 1980s, therefore, government revenues fluctuated with the cyclical rise and fall of world copper prices, and the Zambian government found itself by 1985 in default on its foreign loan obligations. In 1985 the Zambian government was headed for total collapse. Its foreign debt had grown to $4 billion, second in Africa only to the Sudan. Unable to pay its debt service, the government went hat in hand to the International Monetary Fund (IMF) and the World Bank for foreign credits to stabilize its financial standing.

As part of its agreement to extend credit, the IMF demanded that Zambia submit to a planned restructuring of its economy. Through structural adjustment programs, or SAPs, the debtor nation agreed to change government policies that were responsible for altering free market forces. Price supports and subsidies that reduce the market prices of foodstuffs and transportation would have to be removed; prices, then, would be determined only by supply and demand: in practical terms this meant that while the price of food would be allowed to rise, wage income would fall or remain constant. The lower-income or poor households would, therefore, be unable to afford the most basic of human necessities. Exchange rates would also have to be adjusted downward. Thus, the value of the Zambian kwacha would fall with respect to the dollar. In 1985–86 the kwacha fell from 2.23 to 15.25 kwacha to the dollar. Zambians paid higher prices for imports, including oil, and earned less for their exports, especially copper.

While the IMF refers to its programs of restructuring as the hope of the future, developing countries refer to them as economic austerity. The purpose of the SAPs is twofold: first, to reduce the government deficit by curtailing social spending; and second, to reduce the balance-of-payments deficit by reducing imports and increasing exports. What was the result in this case? First, government debt rose from $3.8 billion in 1984 to $5.1 billion in 1987. With the severe cuts in government spending, total debt continued to rise. One reason for this was that the price of copper continued to fall, which reduced government revenue. And since the debt had to be paid back in dollars, the government found itself unable to meet its debt service.

At what cost, then, was government spending curtailed? Health and education, for which the state is the primary funding source, were the first programs to be cut. "At some rural health centers, essential drugs like chloroquine and penicillin are in short supply. And in 1986, immunization programmes had to be curtailed" (Cheru 1989:136–37). Health-care professionals as well as doctors left the country as real wages fell in these professions. Education services were curtailed in the rural areas where the political fallout would be felt the least. Primary education, which affects the poor the most, was targeted for cuts, whereas higher and middle-level education, which affects the middle- and upper-income classes, was left untouched. The subsidies on maize were removed, and this, coupled with the decline in the value of the kwacha and the fall in real income, has led to problems of nutritional deficiency among the poorer strata of Zambian society.

These last points illustrate one important fact of life in many developing countries: in times of economic stress, it is the poor, rural peasants and underemployed workers (especially African women, who both work and bear the greater burden of child rearing) who suffer the most from these austerity programs. Their political power is not yet sufficient to enforce a more just and equitable sharing of the burden among the population at large. As with many other African countries, Zambia suffers from a maldistribution of income and unequal political relations. Policies that favor and protect the privileged classes, as in the above example, worsen the economic conditions for the masses and only intensify the internal decay of national life brought on by the IMF and World Bank structural adjustment programs.

Faced with a mounting debt and a lack of economic diversification within its economy, Zambia is trapped in a downward spiral of impoverishment, debt, and chronic food shortages. Buffeted by the fluctuating world price of copper and hampered by growing income inequalities between the city and the rural areas, Zambia faces a bleak future indeed.

What Can Be Done?

Although the richness of Africa's natural resources attracted European capitalists to the continent, Africans have not yet been able to appropriate those riches for their mutual benefit. How then will Africans escape the downward spiral of poverty in the future?

This question has stimulated a considerable debate from within and outside Africa, but to date, no single developmental strategy has won the day. However, a short list of strategies has emerged, and these do seem to offer some hope of escape from the grinding and increasing pauperization of the continent. There are four principal development themes that I believe have gained credibility and prominence among Africans in the last decade: self-sufficiency, regional economic planning and delinking, sustainable development, and popular participation in economic planning.

The concept of self-sufficiency and activism in economic development gained the center stage in sub-Saharan Africa in 1980 with the signing of the Lagos Plan of Action in Nigeria. Fifty African state representatives came together to espouse the idea "that Africa's development could not be merely a passive result of the world system or evolution of the European Economic Community. . . . a new self-reliant development strategy arose from this crucial idea" (Amin 1990:57).

The central tenets of the Lagos Plan of Action focused on the need for regional economic cooperation, avoidance of short-term sectarian interests, a firm rejection of stabilization policies, and the need for long-term planning for growth rather than the short-sighted thinking that seeks to shore up the state by relying on resource-export earnings. But the Lagos resolution failed to challenge Africa's role as a primary supplier of resources to the industrialized North (Amin 1990:57). The real weakness of the Lagos Plan of Action was that it did not initiate either concrete plans or actions to implement its design: it was empty rhetoric (Onimodo 1988:200).

If African nations are to realize their plans to develop an independent and viable modern society, they will have to create an institutional climate that can match their plans to reality. It is to achieve these objectives that the regional economic cooperative organizations were founded, many initiated before or at the same time as the signing of the Lagos Plan.

The Economic Community of West African States (ECOWAS), formed in 1967, is the largest regional economic group in Africa and includes many of the Francophone states as well as the former English colonies Nigeria and Ghana. The diverse colonial heritage of the sixteen member states is just one of the major problems to be overcome in creating a well-functioning regional unit. These countries speak different colonial languages and have inherited incompatible institutional structures; their trade and finance are also tied to the economies of their former colonial masters. Suspicion of each other's motives is common, since smaller nations are afraid that they will be overrun by the more powerful states such as Nigeria (Nigeria has the largest army and is the wealthiest state among the sixteen members). For these reasons, among others, ECOWAS has had limited success in setting up joint projects, though more success in intraregional trading and in creating common military defenses (Okolo 1990).

The South African Development Coordination Conference, or SADCC, includes the frontline states that surround South Africa: Angola, Zimbabwe, Mozambique, Botswana, Zambia, Lesotho, Swaziland, and Malawi. In 1980 these states came together to form a regional economic union whose primary objective was to delink their economies from South Africa. Their dependence is demonstrated by the following conditions:

Six of the nine states have South Africa as their main trading partner.
In four of the nine states, South African firms control the retail trade.
Four of the nine states use South African ports for shipping.
Six of the nine states have migrant workers in South Africa.
South Africa runs a trade surplus of $1.7 billion with eight out of the nine
    countries.

Doing business with South Africa has inhibited these countries from developing their own industrial infrastructures. One example is the frustration of efforts to realize the excellent port capabilities at Beira in Mozambique, which have in the last decade been attacked and rendered unfit by the Renamo rebels supported by South Africa. Shipping out of Beira instead of South Africa would mean increased and needed revenues for war-torn Mozambique and reduced transportation costs to other SADCC members.

This is only one example of how regional cooperation and delinking would aid economic development in southern Africa. The SADCC plan specified that each country would develop those resources in which it has a definite advantage. Once developed, the project country would share the results with the other participants according to a planned arrangement. But South African military destabilization of these SADCC states has taken its toll, and further economic reorganization along these lines appears to be in a state of limbo (Hanlon 1984:1–12).[8]

The objectives and methods of the regional economic groups reflected the consensus reached in the Lagos Plan: to advance industrial and agricultural development in Africa as soon as possible. The environmental question, while given a place in the overall agenda, still remained a stepchild of the industrial objective. But other voices sounded a counterpoint to this position, and none was more prominent or persuasive than the chorus that issued from the Brundtland report published in 1987. Often associated with Gro Brundtland, chairwoman of the World Commission on Environment and Development, the report's proper title is *Our Common Future*.

Although the title is simply stated, the report is comprehensive and radical. It challenges the basic economic wisdom of the last two hundred years, that industrial growth should everywhere and at all times be the highest objective of modern society: "Failure to manage the environment and to sustain development threatens to overwhelm all countries. Environment and development are not separate challenges; they are inexorably linked. Development cannot subsist upon a deteriorating environmental base" (World Commission 1987:37).

The Brundtland report espouses the concept of sustainable development, as opposed to the uninhibited industrial growth of advanced capitalism. Sustainable development recognizes the vulnerability of environmental systems and the need to preserve the resource base for future generations. What is even more critical to the developing world, where poverty is pervasive, is the emphasis placed on meeting "human needs by increasing productive potential and by ensuring equitable opportunities for all" (World Commission 1987:44).[9]

The concerns of the Brundtland report have been echoed in the Arusha Conference report (1990), entitled the *African Charter for Popular Participation in Development*: "Furthermore, Africa's grave environmental and ecological problems cannot be solved in the absence of a process of sustainable development which commands the full support and participation of the people."

Sustainable development rejects unrestrained mining of the nation's minerals or the clear-cutting of forests to provide urban elites with the foreign exchange to buy luxury imports. Sustainable development demands popular participation because it cannot succeed without the broad-base support of the rural and urban poor. Many nongovernmental organizations in Africa that are working on developing sustainable agricultural programs need the support of government policies that are not directed at the urban centers only.

In Zambia, as in many African countries, democratic participation remains, perhaps, the most important revolution yet to come. It is inconceivable that African elites will voluntarily give up some of the privileges of their position. It is further inconceivable that having been trained in Western economic thinking and often supported by Western military alliances, these same elites will embrace and act on the concepts outlined in *Our Common Future*.

Although the political reform movements taking place in Africa today are a prerequisite to the redirection of public policy away from the urban centers—with their poverty and hopeless millions waiting to gain access to the all too few jobs—and toward a more comprehensive and equitable program of agricultural self-sufficiency and industrial development, they will not suffice to address the immediate demand to renegotiate the African debt with foreign lenders.

The most hopeful sign in this regard was the formation in 1989 of the African Alternative Framework to Stuctural Adjustment Programs (AAF-SAP). Signed and approved by most of the African heads of state and given the stamp of approval by the General Assembly of the United Nations, AAF-SAP outlines a plan of attack whereby African governments draw up "broad and flexible" programs in conjunction with the World Bank and IMF to restructure the African economies under a set of conditions that will neither undermine the nations' economic growth nor engender a widening of environmental problems and food shortages. The response from the World Bank and the IMF has been favorable, opening up channels for continued negotiation, but much remains to be done, not the least of which is the resolution of social and political unrest that disturbs the continent today.

ACKNOWLEDGMENTS

The author wishes to thank Julie Graham and Jessica Nembhard for helpful comments on previous drafts.

NOTES

1. The World Bank has included in its list of structural sins by African states the following: trade and exchange-rate policies designed to protect infant industries, overextended public sectors, policies that distort agricultural prices, and policies that favor urban growth at the expense of rural areas. Although there is some truth here, it is still only a partial analysis, and they leave out the factors of external intervention by the Western states, as well as the bias of the World Bank itself.

2. Witness the recent case of U.S. support for the UNITA rebels in Angola. Jonas Savimbi, head of UNITA, was a paid agent of the Portuguese in the war to oust the colonial power and is also on the payroll of the CIA. History records U.S. involvement in the assassination of Patrice Lumumba, prime minister for the Congo, in 1960 and with the fascist South African government. And this is only the U.S. level of intervention. France, Britain, and Portugal also have a long history of political intrigue and military adventurism in Africa.

3. An increasing reliance on foreign capital and high wage growth in urban centers was a prerequisite to this mix of industrial growth and modernization. As a result of these policies people migrated in large numbers to the cities only to find that unemployment and urban poverty awaited their arrival. There were too many people chasing too few jobs. This urban poverty is now a hallmark throughout the

developing world, and plans to cope with this problem have yet to produce any concrete results.

4. The growth rate in food production per capita in sub-Saharan Africa was 0.2 percent in the 1960s but fell to -0.9 percent between 1970 and 1982.

5. In the 1970s, even as the world market price of copper fell, government revenue from the mines was approximately equal to a quarter of the Zambian gross domestic product (GDP).

6. "The consumption of consumer imports is almost entirely shaped by the demands for luxury items of the top 10% of the population that accumulates over half, and perhaps as much as three-fourths, of Zambia's national income in the form of high salaries, profits, interest and rent. The remaining 90% . . . earn little more than bare subsistence wages" (Seidman 1975:363).

7. CIPEC was formed in 1967 and included Zambia, Zaire, Chile, and Peru. CIPEC, as an organization of copper producers, was formed to counter the influence and control of transnational mining companies. In time, members sought to use their combined market power to increase copper prices. In 1973 the countries of the European Economic Community (EEC) and the United States imported 45 percent of their copper from CIPEC countries, and Japan imported 60 percent. CIPEC failed to duplicate in the copper market the control OPEC had been able to exert over oil prices, for two reasons: the collapse of a unified political will among CIPEC countries, largely due to the fall of Allende in Chile in 1973 and to the CIA-backed government of Mobutu in Zaire; and the 1974 collapse in demand for world copper as a result of high oil prices and a recession in the United States (Nwoke 1987:112–39).

8. Mozambique has fought a civil war with RENAMO rebels trained and funded by South Africa that has left 100,000 dead and over one million homeless. Malnutrition stalks the survivors, since rebels have carried out a slash-and-burn policy throughout the country. Angola has just come out of a ten-year civil war with the UNITA rebels sponsored by South Africa and the CIA. The countryside is in ruins, thousands have been crippled by land mines, and the country is desperate for peace.

9. The question has been asked by critics of the Brundtland report, What is meant by "productive growth"? This is a hard question to answer because many ecologists and sustainable-development specialists believe that we do not need to reform the industrial process but rather need to reassess the value system that helped to create the process in the first place. In short, we need a revolution in thought similar to the one that occurred five-hundred years ago in science. This seems to go further than *Our Common Future* intended.

BIBLIOGRAPHY

Amin, Samir. 1990. *Maldevelopment*. London: Zed Press.
Arusha Conference. 1990. *African Charter for Popular Participation in Development and Transformation*. Arusha, Tanzania: United Republic of Tanzania.
British–North American Committee. 1976. *Mineral Development in the Eighties: Prospects and Problems*. Washington, D.C.: National Planning Association.

Brundtland report. *See* World Commission on Environment and Development.

Cheru, Fantu. 1989. *The Silent Revolution*. London: Zed Press.

Davidson, Basil. 1978. *Let Freedom Come: Africa in Modern History*. Boston: Little, Brown.

———. 1980. *Cross Roads in Africa*. Nottingham: Russell Press.

Hanlon, Joseph. 1984. *SADCC: Progress, Projects, and Prospects*. London: The Economist.

Lanning, Greg. 1979. *Africa Undermined: Mining Companies and the Underdevelopment of Africa*. London: Penquin.

Markovitz, Irving Leonard, ed. 1987. *Studies in Power and Class in Africa*. New York: Oxford University Press.

Mikesell, Raymond. 1979. *New Patterns of World Development*. Washington D.C.: National Planning Association.

Nwoke, Chibuzo. 1987. *Third World Minerals and Global Pricing*. London: Zed Press.

Okolo, Julius Emeka. 1990. The Development and Structure of ECOWAS. In *West African Regional Cooperation and Development*, ed. Julius Emeka Okolo, 19–52. Boulder, Colo.: Westview Press.

Onimodo, Bade. 1988. *A Political Economy of the African Crisis*. London: Zed Press.

Seidman, Ann, ed. 1975. *Natural Resources and National Welfare*. New York: Praeger.

Thiong'o, Ngugi Wa. 1982. *Devil on the Cross*. London: Heinemann.

U.S. Bureau of Mines. 1985. *Mineral Facts and Problems*. Washington D.C.: U.S. Department of the Interior.

World Commission on Environment and Development. 1987. *Our Common Future*. New York: Oxford University Press. (Referred to in the text as the Brundtland report.)

18 HÉCTOR SÁEZ

The International Economy and the Environment in Latin America

This chapter explores the ways in which government economic policies, multinational corporations, and international development institutions shape the environment in Latin America. Most conclusions can readily be extended to other countries in the Third World.

In particular, I argue that the benefits and costs of the exploitation of natural resources are distributed unequally among classes, countries, and generations: poor countries (and people) and future generations bear the greatest costs of environmental degradation, while those who today wield wealth and power reap the greater benefits.

Latin American countries are highly dependent on foreign trade to satisfy their consumption needs. Their exports are mostly primary products: raw materials from agriculture and mining. In many cases, a few primary products account for more than 50 percent of total export earnings. Primary industries depend on the availability and quality of natural resources. Shortsighted management of these resources has adverse consequences for the current satisfaction of basic needs and for future economic growth.

Agriculture

Latin American countries inherited from the colonial era two conditions that are closely linked to past and present environmental destruction: (1) land concentration in the hands of the few, and (2) production to satisfy demand in remote places. The production of sugar, coffee, cocoa, bananas, cotton, soybeans, and beef for export markets has been given priority by governments and by landed classes, often at the expense of staple food production. Deforestation, soil degradation, and the loss of biotic resources have greatly accelerated in the last fifty years, but they are not new; the stage for the present environmental crisis was set during the last five centuries.

International economic forces have played an important role in these

351

processes (Sáez 1992). In the late nineteenth century, U.S. companies invested in coffee, banana, and sugar production in Central and South America and the Caribbean. This led to the development of capitalist relations of production and to the use of modern agricultural technology. In the last decades, foreign capital has moved away from agricultural production to the food-marketing and -processing industries. However, this does not reduce its effect on agricultural development in Latin America. Roger Burbach and Patricia Flynn point out that "food processing companies based in the United States, for example, have a far-reaching impact on agricultural production through their financing, technical assistance, and purchase contracts with local growers" (1980:103). Production for international markets decreases the amount of the agricultural output geared toward meeting basic needs in Latin America and explains in part why so many Latin Americans are malnourished.

In recent decades, the U.S. government, international development agencies such as the World Bank and the Inter-American Development Bank (IADB), multinational corporations, and national governments have invested large sums in the "modernization" of Latin American agriculture. Production for export has boomed since the 1950s. The use of imported machinery, fertilizers, and pesticides has increased in large commercial holdings of land.

Despite attempts to redistribute land, this development strategy has exacerbated the inequality in land distribution. The provision of infrastructure and agricultural credit is geared toward large holdings. Meanwhile, peasants pushed out of the best agricultural land exploit natural resources in fragile ecosystems or migrate to city slums. Small farmers, facing increasing competitive pressures, engage in intensive and environmentally aggressive cropping patterns (see Redclift 1989).

Latin American commercial agriculture has become dependent upon chemical pesticides, which kill natural defenses against pests. At the same time, pests become more resistant to pesticides owing to natural selection. Stronger pesticides are then applied more often. The resurgence of malaria in many areas of Central and South America has been associated with increased use of pesticides (Chapin and Wasserstrom 1983). Pesticide use affects both workers in the Third World and consumers in the First World (see Weir and Shapiro 1981). However, pesticides are increasingly being used that reduce poisoning risks for consumers, though not for workers who handle and apply them (Wright 1986).

Large-scale beef production is a factor in the destruction of Latin American rain forests. More than one-third of the deforestation of the Brazilian rain forest between 1966 and 1975 was associated with cattle ranching (Skinner 1985). Around 66 percent of all arable land in Central America was dedicated to beef production in 1983 (Nations and Komer

1983). Nearly 90 percent of Central American beef exports go to the United States, where beef consumption rose from 85 pounds per person per year in 1960 to 134 in 1980. Swift-Armour, United Brands, and King Ranch are among the multinational firms engaged in cattle ranching in Latin America.

Logging

The worst enemy of South American rain forests, however, may prove to be the nascent logging industry. As tropical forest resources are depleted elsewhere in the world, foreign logging companies are beginning to gain access to the rain forests of Latin America. Around 2.4 percent of Third World exports of log and processed wood came from Latin America in 1980, but it is estimated that 63 percent will come from Latin America in the year 2000 (Scott 1989).

Japan, the world's largest importer of tropical timber, received its first timber shipment from Brazil in November of 1988. Analysts estimated that in 1989, Japan would import forty thousand cubic meters of raw logs from Brazil each month. Japanese importers needed to overcome an obstacle, however, a nominal ban on the exports of Brazilian logs. According to David Swinbanks and Alun Anderson (1989:103), Japan circumvented this obstacle "by taking timber from areas cleared for a hydroelectric project financed with overseas aid." Swinbanks and Anderson suggest that in the future, Japanese "aid" will pour into Brazil. Specifically, the Japanese may finance a road linking the western Amazon with the Pacific coast in Peru, which could serve as an outlet for timber exports. This road was earlier financed by the World Bank and the IADB, but in 1985 congressional and public pressure in the United States stopped the disbursement of funds for the project because of its destruction of the environment and of the habitat of indigenous people of the area.

In the extraction of tropical hardwoods, loggers typically take a small fraction of the trees, but careless practices destroy much of the remainder. Timber companies are interested in profits from logs, not the environmental importance of the rain forest. The same is true for commercial farmers, cattle ranchers, and mining companies.

As long as the rights over the rain forest are not in the hands of local communities and indigenous people, whoever extracts forest resources will lack the incentive to do so in a sustainable way. Robert Repetto (1990) points out that the limited periods of time covered by government concession agreements with logging companies encourage the depletion of the resource as fast as possible, with little regard for future generations. At the same time, commercial logging often prevents local dwellers from managing the forest and capturing the revenues from the sale of its products, part of which could be reinvested in resource renewal and community development.

The undervaluation of the rain forests also contributes to their mismanagement and depletion. The economic value of the rain forest is not merely that of the few commercial hardwood species. A study conducted by three North American scientists in the village of Mishana, Peru, concluded that other forest resources, including edible fruits and latex, could yield in Peruvian markets up to $6,820 per hectare; the same area would yield $490 in timber. They also note the "immeasurable" nonmarket value of the rain forest, since deforestation leads to species extinction, loss of soil fertility, changes in the microclimate, droughts, flooding, and possibly to changes in the climate of the earth (Peters, Gentry, and Mendelsohn 1989).

Mineral Extraction

Minerals were the greatest attraction to European colonizers in their "encounter" with Latin America. Today Peru and Bolivia are respectively the world's largest producers of silver and antimony, and Chile and Brazil are the second largest producers of copper and iron, respectively. Minerals constitute 38 percent of Peru's exports and 46 percent of Chile's.

International interests continue to play an important role in Latin America's mineral industries. Foreign corporations provide much of the financing and technology for mineral extraction and capture much of the ensuing profits. As a result, the benefits accrue primarily to foreign firms and their domestic partners. Mineral extraction imposes two social costs, however, that are borne by the people of the developing countries. First, mining and mineral processing generate large quantities of solid and liquid waste, destroy vegetation and landscapes, and produce airborne dust and waterborne sediments. For example, studies have found dangerous levels of mercury contamination, a result of gold mining, in the state of Rondonia in Brazil (Martinelli et al. 1989).

Second, mineral resources are nonrenewable. To maintain the income-generating base of a country for future generations, part of the receipts from the sale of nonrenewable resources must be invested in other income-generating activities in that country. If the profits accrue to foreigners, however, or to domestic capitalists who invest abroad or consume rather than invest locally, the future income-generating ability of the country is diminished.

These costs are illustrated in the exploitation of the world's largest iron deposit, discovered in eastern Amazonia (Brazil) by Meridional Co., a subsidiary of U.S. Steel. The iron ore project is now being developed with an initial budget of $3.6 billion, including $500 million from Japan, $600 million from the European Coal and Steel Community, and $300 million from the World Bank. The project is yielding 10 million tons of low-priced iron per year for Japanese firms and 13.6 million tons of iron for European firms. Brazil now supplies 50 percent of the iron consumed by the European Economic Community, with "enormous gains to the European steel industry" (Treece 1988). This project is causing widespread pollution and the destruction of hundreds of thousands of hectares of rain forest, devastating the habitat of thousands of indigenous people. As usual in these development schemes, the victims have had no participation in decision-making regarding this project and have reaped no benefits from it.

Importing Industrial Pollution

In this century, Latin America has experienced a profound transformation and development of its industrial base, partly as a consequence of national industrial policies. Most industrial centers in Latin America face acute pollution problems as a consequence of these industrial development policies. However, industrialization and pollution also have an international dimension. Multinational direct foreign investment in Latin America spans a large spectrum of industries besides agriculture and mining, including minerals, pharmaceuticals, chemicals, electronics, and apparel. Often, even firms that comply with environmental standards in their countries of origin take advantage of the leniency or lack of environmental legislation or enforcement in their host countries, even when comparable legislation is in place.

Technological transfers from industrialized countries to developing countries often bring with them the environmental problems of air and water pollution and toxic waste management. Developing countries often do not have the pollution-abatement technology that industrialized countries have. More important, the governments of developing countries often lack the power or the willingness to enact and enforce environmental regulations. Their priority objective is to attract foreign investment, and they compete with each other for it.

Environmental regulations in the North and the lack thereof in the South may induce some MNCs to relocate. U.S. firms, for example, have shifted the production of trioxide to Peru, the chemical intermediate furfural to the Dominican Republic, and pesticides to Mexico, Brazil, and Colombia (Leonard 1984).

In 1987, the U.S. and Mexican governments signed an agreement whereby toxic wastes produced by U.S. firms under the *maquiladora* assembly operations were to be returned to the United States. Research conducted by Jane Juffer, an associate director of Pacifica News Service, concluded that even though most of the U.S. assembly plants operating in Mexico produce some kind of toxic waste, there is little evidence that any of it has been returned to the United States: "The companies have poured chemical wastes down drains, dumped them in irrigation ditches, left them in the desert, burned them in city dumps and turned them over to Mexican recycling firms not qualified to handle toxic waste" (1988:24).

People who live near the industrial parks and work in the plants are directly affected. Many of these neighborhoods have no electricity or municipal water. Water is delivered by truck and often stored in fifty-five gallon drums that are obtained from the plants and formerly contained toxic substances.

Ironically, the United States is being affected as well. Juffer (1988:3) reports that the New River, which empties near Palm Springs, California, carries "at least a hundred types of toxic chemicals" that are presumed to be dumped by companies operating in areas near the river.

International Finance, Debt, and the Environment

Economic development strategies in Latin America have been financed in part by international development agencies and commercial banks. The lending portfolios of commercial banks are not available for public scrutiny. Nevertheless, we can get a sense of the impact of international financing on projects that affect the environment by looking at the lending activities of multilateral development banks (MDBs). Their funding often guarantees additional financing from commercial sources for the same projects.

A large number of the development projects funded by the MDBs directly affect the environment. More than half of the World Bank's projects are in agriculture, rural development, energy, and transportation (Rich 1985). Dams constructed for irrigation and electricity have covered thousands of square kilometers of rain forest with water. Peasants and indigenous peoples displaced by these projects are left with no land and little means of subsistence. The loss of species is incalculable. In many cases, the lack of watershed management results in quick sedimentation of dams, thus reducing their useful life.

The World Bank is the most important of the MDBs. After much pressure from nongovernmental organizations, the World Bank created in 1987 a new environmental department and environmental assessment unit for in-the-field analysis. Yet observers monitoring the extent and the effectiveness of the World Bank's environmental program report disillusionment. Bruce Rich (1990) argues that the program is the "emperor's new clothes," and identifies many reasons that it does not live up to expectations. Most salient are the lack of priority accorded to environmental concerns by the bank, the lack of public accountability in donor and borrower countries, and the borrowing governments' resistance to environmental prerequisites.

Today, the countries of Latin America pay much more in debt service than they receive in new lending. The solution to the debt crisis, as conceived by the World Bank and the IMF, are the familiar stabilization or structural adjustment policies. To reschedule the debt and to obtain more financing, governments must adopt free market, export-oriented, foreign-investment-inducing, and social-spending-reducing policies. Aimed at "liberating" resources for debt repayment, these policies have caused increases in unemployment and decreases in the standard of living in most Latin American countries.

While unemployment increases and real wages fall, poor people escalate the pressure on resources by intensifying subsistence agriculture in marginal lands, expanding the agricultural frontier to the rain forest, and relying more on fuelwood. At the same time, governments, in their need to generate foreign exchange to pay the debt, intensify the exploitation of resources and eliminate their environmental protection programs. For example, the rate of growth of mining production in Latin America more than doubled from 1983 to 1987, and oceanic fishing along the coasts of South America has grown at a yearly average of 16 percent (Brzovic Parilo 1989:13, 17). Between 1974 and 1986, the area under food crop production dropped 26 percent in Ecuador, while the production of four cash crop items increased 171 percent. Shrimp exports grew to $360 million a year, but one hundred thousand hectares of mangrove forests disappeared as a result (World Resources Institute 1990). Susan George reports that

> Brazil does have the equivalent of an environmental protection agency, but its budget has been cut to the point that it can barely pay its employees. . . . Costa Rica is asking for private donations to maintain its national parks. . . . Mexico recently eliminated fifteen governmental under-secretaries, four of them environment-linked. (1988:167)

Democracy, the Economy, and the Environment

Natural resources in Latin America have been decimated as a consequence of the region's socioeconomic structure, domestic economic policies, and its international economic relations. The wealthy and powerful have benefited from the degradation of the environment. Meanwhile, poor people in Latin America are displaced from fertile agricultural land, poisoned by pollution, and left unemployed by adjustment policies. Future generations lose too, as natural resources are squandered for short-term profit.

To protect the environment, a very different development strategy is needed:

Increase the amount of resources under the ownership and control of communities of peasants and indigenous peoples. Land redistribution can alleviate pressures on marginal lands and fragile ecosystems and can improve nutritional standards while giving rural inhabitants incentives to sustainably manage land resources. Rights over minerals should be shared with communities affected by mining. Profits captured by communities should be targeted to local development. Companies found in violation of health, safety, and environmental standards should face stiff penalties, such as the deprivation of mining rights.

Strengthen peasants' productivity and willingness to produce food for domestic consumption. International development banks and agencies must shift their focus from large-scale, export-oriented projects to the development of appropriate small-scale agro-forestry technology and projects aimed at satisfying the needs of the urban population.

Require that international development agencies and banks accede to civic participation in project planning and independent monitoring of their development projects. This is especially needed in ongoing large-scale projects. Monitors should include members of organizations in affected communities, national and international nongovernmental organizations, and other interested parties that are traditionally excluded from decision making regarding development policies. Information in their possession should be freely available to the public.

Seek to make international economic relations more equitable and democratic. Industrialized countries should accept partial responsibility for the debt. Environmental protection regulations should take precedence over free trade. Institutions that oversee, manage, and finance international economic activity should be accountable to the public in partaking countries.

BIBLIOGRAPHY

Berkes, Fikret, and David Feeney. 1990. Paradigms Lost: Changing Views on the Use of Common Property Resources. *Alternatives* 17(2): 48–55.

Brzovic Parilo, Francisco J. 1989. Crisis económica y medio ambiente en America Latina y el Caribe. Paper presented at Seminario Sudamericano Sobre Nuestro Futuro Común, Santiago, Chile.

Burbach, Roger, and Patricia Flynn. 1980. *Agribusiness in the Americas.* New York: Monthly Review Press; NACLA.

Chapin, Georgeanne, and Robert Wasserstrom. 1983. Pesticide Use and Malaria Resurgence in Central America. *The Ecologist* 13(4): 115–26.

Juffer, Jane. 1988. Dump at the Border: U.S. Firms Make a Mexican Wasteland. *The Progressive* 52(10): 24–29.

Leonard, H. Jeffrey. 1984. *Are Environmental Regulations Driving U.S. Industry Overseas?* Washington D.C.: Conservation Foundation.

Martinelli, Luis Antonio, J. R. Ferreira, B. R. Forsberg, and R. L. Victoria. 1989. Gold Rush Produces Mercury Contamination in Amazon. *Cultural Survival Quarterly* 13(1): 32–34.

Nations, James D., and Daniel I. Komer. 1983. Rainforests and the Hamburger Society. *Environment* 25(3): 12–20.

Peters, C. M., A. H. Gentry, and R. O. Mendelsohn. 1989. Valuation of an Amazonian Rainforest. *Nature* 339 (29 June): 655–56.

Redclift, Michael. 1989. The Environmental Consequences of Latin America's Agricultural Development: Some Thoughts on the Brundtland Commission Report. *World Development* 17(3): 365–77.

Repetto, Robert. 1990. Deforestation in the Tropics. *Scientific American* 262(4): 36–42.

Rich, Bruce. 1985. The Multilateral Development Banks, Environmental Policy, and the United States. *Ecology Law Quarterly* 12(4): 681–745.

———. 1990. The Emperor's New Clothes: The World Bank and Environmental Reform. *World Policy Journal* (Spring): 305–29.

Sáez, Héctor. 1992. Agriculture and Land Degradation in Latin America. University of Massachusetts, Amherst. Photocopy.

Scott, Margaret. 1989. The Disappearing Forests. *Far Eastern Economic Review* 12 (January): 34–38.

Skinner, Joseph K. 1985. Big Mac and the Tropical Forests. *Monthly Review* 37(7): 25–32.

Swinbanks, David, and Alun Anderson. 1989. Japan and Brazil Team Up. *Nature* 338 (9 March): 103.

Treece, David. 1988. Brutality and Brazil: The Human Costs of Cheap Steel. *Multinational Monitor* 9(2): 24–26.

Weir, David, and Mark Shapiro. 1981. *The Circle of Poison*. San Francisco: Institute for Food and Development Policy.

World Resources Institute. 1990. *World Resources 1990–91*. New York: Oxford University Press.

Wright, Angus. 1986. Rethinking the Circle of Poison: The Politics of Pesticide Poisoning among Mexican Farm Workers. *Latin American Perspectives* 13(4): 26–59.

19

MARIBEL APONTE-GARCÍA

The Internationalization of the U.S. Military Industry: A Caribbean Case Study

Traditionally, radical economic analyses of U.S. militarism at the international level have focused on the functions that militarism serves for capital accumulation: securing sea lanes of communication, contributing to U.S. capitalist hegemony, and limiting the spread of socialism in the international arena. These functions are taken to promote capital accumulation by increasing profits and by reproducing the conditions necessary to preserve the capital accumulation process (Riddell 1986; O'Connor 1978; Baran and Sweezy 1968; Smith and Smith 1983).

Radicals associate Third World militarization with military intervention, war, and military assistance funding and training. In their view, the role militarism plays at the international level necessarily leads to an expanding U.S. military budget. They claim that the defense of the empire obliges the U.S. government not only to create and finance a series of military blocs, an extensive network of military bases, and a gigantic national military apparatus (O'Connor 1978; Baran and Sweezy 1968), but also to enter into military alliances that institutionalize military assistance programs (Baran and Sweezy 1968). They also claim that since most of the research-and-development activity necessary to attain technological superiority is financed by military and space programs, the government has to expand the military budget to improve technology. Finally, since the United States depends on capitalist industry to produce military equipment and supplies, military industrialists have developed an influential lobby that promotes the continued expansion of U.S. military spending.

There is more to economic militarization than the facts stated above. From an economic viewpoint, Third World countries can be militarized in two ways: through military assistance funds or through the internationalization of military production. The first form of militarization is generally recognized by radicals. In fact, a political practice organized to protest against U.S. military assistance to Third World countries is built around this analysis. But leftist economists have largely ignored the way Third World econ-

360

omies are militarized through U.S. military production at the international level. The Left's political project of dismantling the warfare state, or the military–industrial complex, centers on military production within the United States. It excludes military production at the international level.

This blind spot in radical analyses of Third World militarization has persisted despite the fact that Third World economies have been drawn into the military–industrial complex of the United States. The nature and extent of Third World military production and the ways in which it affects economic development in the Third World should not be further ignored. This is particularly important now, when U.S. military expenditure is being cut back, and economic conversion to civilian production is an issue for Third World countries and their workers, just as it is for workers and communities in the United States.

How is U.S. military production organized at the international level? What are Third World countries producing for the U.S. military industry? What does this process imply for the people who live in these countries? These are the questions this chapter seeks to address by analyzing the Caribbean as a case study of U.S. military production at the international level.

The U.S. Military Industry and Its Internationalization

U.S. military production is organized at the international level through the U.S. military industry. The U.S. military industry is the sum of all the private firms and government suppliers that produce equipment or parts or provide services for the Department of Defense (DOD). It comprises a complex amalgam of industries ranging from electronics and apparel to engineering and housekeeping services. In that sense, the U.S. military industry is an industry of industries.

The U.S. military industry is also constituted of many different types of firms. There are large multinational corporations operating throughout the world, smaller U.S. or foreign firms, and U.S. or foreign government suppliers. The complex mosaic of all the different participants forms what is called the structure of the U.S. military industry. This industrial structure is constituted of prime contractors, subcontractors, parts suppliers, and government suppliers.

Prime contractors are those firms directly selected by the DOD through contract bidding competition. The top one hundred defense contractors are usually large multinational corporations that outcompete other firms in bidding contests. Prime contractors then subcontract to smaller firms (subcontractors and parts suppliers) on a year-by-year basis to have either goods assembled from parts or components supplied by them or to acquire raw materials and assembled components. A parts supplier can be a subsidiary of a prime contractor's parent company, or it can be an independent firm to which the prime contractor simply contracts out the production work. But a parts supplier, different from the subcontractor, can also act as a direct DOD contractor. In addition, both contractors and subcontractors can be U.S. or foreign firms and can be located within the United States or in other countries. Government suppliers include government armories, arsenals, and dockyards where ammunition and military equipment are produced, in-house laboratories, the arsenal system of military departments, and the naval shipyards where military-related research is carried out. Government suppliers are almost entirely from the United States, although foreign governments participate through arms collaboration agreements or sale of products exempted from the Buy American Act.

The production and structure of the U.S. military industry became increasingly internationalized after the 1960s. Until then, procurement of U.S. military equipment was mostly carried out by U.S. firms within the United States. After this time, however, the production of goods for the U.S. military industry began to shift abroad. Four main forces contributed to the growing trend toward foreign production of U.S. military goods, as discussed below.

One was that top contractors were multinational corporations that already carried out some phases of production outside the United States. Consequently, although contracts were awarded to U.S. corporations, military components were sometimes actually manufactured or assembled in foreign countries and reexported back to the United States.

A second was that the shrinkage of the U.S. military industry's network of parts suppliers spurred growth in offshore procurement. The network of parts suppliers within the United States had shrunk because the way the DOD did business with them—imposing government regulations that ignored allowances for real costs, interrupting and delaying procurement, and refusing to provide funds, plants, space and equipment—imposed low rates of return on their investment, compared to that of the top DOD contractors (Gansler 1980). The shrinkage of the supplier base created industrial bottlenecks and supply problems in areas affecting almost all major weapons systems (Gansler 1982). Consequently, although the U.S. military industry was tied to mass production—since it needed to produce identical pieces of equipment, interchangeable parts, and standardized goods in large volumes—the supplier network for parts and components necessary to carry out military production within mass production shrunk. The DOD, in search of an alternative network of suppliers, turned to offshore producers that manufactured components and supplies in high volumes and at low costs (Gansler 1980).

A third was that U.S. market shares in arms sales had deteriorated. In the 1970s, the United States lost ground to the Soviet Union, France, West

Germany, Israel, and Brazil (Klare 1984). As Europe and the Soviet Union consolidated their arms industries, fierce competition led to marketing strategies based on offsets (Tuomi and Vayrynen 1982). Offsets are industrial and commercial compensation practices required as a condition of sale for military-related exports. Direct offsets allowed foreign countries to produce certain components or subsystems when they purchased weapons systems from the United States; indirect offsets allowed them to tie the purchase of U.S. arms to the sale of their own nonmilitary goods (Neuman 1985; Defense Systems Management College 1987).[1] Since prime contractors depended on foreign military sales to maintain volume and profits, and since foreign governments had been successful in linking military purchases to offset agreements, DOD procurement from firms located abroad grew after the 1960s (Gansler 1986).

The fourth was that before the end of the cold war, the United States moved toward establishing collaboration agreements in arms and weapons systems development. Through these agreements, the United States sought—within the context of its fiscal crisis—to share the burden of maintaining a military system dependent on continuous technological innovation of sophisticated weapons, transportation, and communication systems. It also sought to standardize equipment that could strengthen allied compatibility for integrated international military operations and U.S. force deployment worldwide. These agreements—sometimes negotiated as offsets—were mostly structured with Europe and Japan, and oriented toward the production of arms: tanks, helicopters, antitank rockets, aircraft and vessels. Less-developed countries with which the United States has signed coproduction programs include Taiwan, Korea, Israel, Turkey, and Egypt (Klare 1984). In the late 1980s, the United States signed an agreement on military–industrial cooperation with Brazil and was discussing long-term cooperative programs with Mexico (Defense Systems Management College 1987). As corporations and governments entered into these agreements, offshore procurement grew.

In sum, DOD offshore procurement, from both U.S. firms and foreign firms located abroad, increased markedly since 1960. As a result, the DOD became dependent on foreign sources for parts and components. Many industrial sectors have been affected by these trends (U.S. Congress 1987).

It is within the context of the U.S. military industry's dependence on mass production—as discussed above—that the militarization of the Caribbean region must be understood. The structural dependence of the U.S. military industry on mass production led it to expand production in the Caribbean region as the network of DOD suppliers within the United States contracted. The growth in DOD contracts awarded to Caribbean countries was also partly the consequence of multinational corporations, potential contractors or subcontractors for the DOD, operating in the region.

Caribbean Militarization

Throughout the 1979–88 period, the economies of the Caribbean Basin Initiative (CBI) countries and of Puerto Rico and the Virgin Islands were militarized in terms unparalleled during the post–World War II era.[2] The militarization process incorporated the Caribbean economies into the industrial structure of the U.S. military industry. It also integrated some of these countries into the financial and commercial network of U.S.-sponsored military assistance programs.

Militarization took place through two different mechanisms available to the U.S. government to pursue its objectives: military contract awards, and *repayable* or *nonrepayable* military assistance.[3] Through these two mechanisms, the U.S. government channeled approximately $15.8 billion to the Caribbean region over the 1979–88 period. Caribbean Basin Initiative countries, Caribbean Basin Initiative contributors[4] (Colombia, Mexico, and Venezuela), and U.S. territories in the Caribbean (Puerto Rico and the U.S. Virgin Islands) received, respectively, $5.1 billion, $1.6 billion, and $9.1 billion. Department of Defense contracts awarded to Caribbean countries during the 1979–88 period constituted 53 percent of total military expenditures in the region.

The Caribbean Basin Initiative as an
Economic–Military Strategy

The CBI is a constantly evolving package of programs intended to augment trade and capital flows between the United States and the basin. It includes, among others, bilateral and multilateral aid programs and military aid and assistance programs. The trade aspect of the initiative is covered by the economic provisions and stipulations of the Caribbean Basin Economic Recovery Act (CBERA), which granted duty-free treatment to a number of products from Caribbean countries that complied with specific requirements.

In general terms, the CBI is a broad policy formulated in response to the geopolitical and socioeconomic changes taking place within some Caribbean countries—the Sandinista revolution in Nicaragua and the New Jewel's triumph in Grenada, both in 1979, El Salvador's civil war, Central America's political instability, and some of the eastern Caribbean islands' independence—which were creating alternative models of economic development and threatening to break down Cuba's isolation. As part of the U.S. strategy to regain military superiority on a world scale and military hegemony in the Caribbean region during the 1979–88 period, the CBI must be evaluated, at least partly, as a mechanism designed to link the Caribbean economies to the military industry of the United States and to reinforce the existing military assistance and aid programs made available through U.S. government funds.

Initially conceived in the early 1980s, the CBI was finally implemented in 1984 and was to be extended for a period of twelve years. In 1985, Vice-President George Bush announced that countries participating in the CBI would be allowed to compete for government contracts. For the *first time* in U.S. history, the U.S. military industry would incorporate into its structure, as a policy initiative, the Caribbean region beyond its territories (U.S. Virgin Islands and Puerto Rico). This served to promote military production in the region. It also allowed the U.S. military industry to create a Caribbean supplier network within the institutional framework and advantages offered by the CBI.

Coupled with the component of military production in the Caribbean, the CBI also strengthened military assistance programs such as the Foreign Military Sales Program (FMS), the Military Assistance Program (MAP), the International Military Education and Training Program (IMET), and the Economic Support Fund (ESF). As a result, the CBI led to an increase in total military expenditures in the region for the 1979–1988 period, as discussed below.

Military Production and Assistance in the Caribbean

The Department of Defense classifies its data on contracts by category. Each contract falls into one of four categories, or functions: research and development, supply and equipment, construction, or services. At the same time, each one of these categories contains different subcategories, termed industries. The industry category serves to identify whether the contract awarded in research and development is related, for example, to electronics or weapons systems and, similarly, whether the contract awarded for supply and equipment is related to apparel or pharmaceutical products.

The awarding of DOD contracts in the Caribbean during the 1979–88 period followed a pattern of specialization by function and region. Furthermore, within functions, there was also a specialization among industries. In general terms, U.S. military production in the Caribbean was concentrated in industries included within the supply-and-equipment function or within construction. Industries in which U.S. multinational corporations had production and assembly operations in the Caribbean—textiles and apparel; tools; electrical, electronic, and communication equipment—received the bulk of military contracts awarded to the region.[5]

Although these contracts were allocated to industries in the Caribbean where U.S. multinational corporations were already involved, military contracts were awarded mostly to countries that housed U.S. military installations or were, during the 1980s, undergoing military escalation with the support of the United States. In other words, the internationalization of production did not result in the indiscriminate awarding of contracts to Caribbean countries simply on the basis of lower economic costs. Instead, the awarding of military contracts in the Caribbean was used as an implicit DOD industrial policy—conditioned by political and geostrategic factors— to promote U.S. military production where strategic military bases were located or where a social movement opposed to U.S. military presence existed or could form, threatening U.S. security interests. For this reason, it was in the interest of the U.S. government that local businesses, in addition to multinational corporations, also received awards.

During the 1979–88 period, the U.S. military industry awarded over $7.9 billion to the Caribbean region. Most of these contracts were awarded to the U.S. Caribbean territories ($4.8 billion), while the CBI countries attained the second position ($2.5 billion). Furthermore, different functions were concentrated in specific countries. For instance, the U.S. Caribbean territories dominated both in research and development and in supplies and equipment, while CBI countries dominated in both services and construction awards.

During the first four years of the post-CBI period (1984–88), the countries awarded the most dollars in DOD contracts were Puerto Rico and the U.S. Virgin Islands, Venezuela, Panama, the Bahamas, Honduras, El Salvador, Mexico, Antigua and Barbuda, and Barbados, in that order.[6] What Puerto Rico, the U.S. Virgin Islands, Panama, Honduras, Antigua and Barbuda, and the Bahamas shared was housing U.S. military installations.[7] Mexico was also strategically important because it was considered part of the U.S. security zone.

The inclusion of El Salvador and Barbados in this group reflects the military escalation that took place in both countries during the post-CBI period. In the case of El Salvador, as civil war intensified in 1984, and as the U.S. government pushed for "elections" while the Frente Farabundo Martí para la Liberación Nacional (FMLN) controlled 81 of 261 municipalities, the U.S. government pumped in funds to "stabilize" the situation. Consequently, awards destined to El Salvador increased from $1.4 million during the pre-CBI period (1979–83) to $131 million during the post-CBI period (1984–88). Although, unlike El Salvador, Barbados was not undergoing a civil war, its military escalation was related to its pivotal strategic role in the invasion of neighboring Grenada and in the formation of the Regional Security System (Phillips 1988).

Since the U.S. Virgin Islands is a petroleum-refining site, whereas Mexico and Venezuela are petroleum producers, contracts awarded to these countries were concentrated in the petroleum and petroleum derivatives industry.[8] Awards for Trinidad and Tobago, Mexico, the U.S. Virgin Islands, and Jamaica decreased from the pre- to the post-CBI period. It seems that the underlying cause of the decrease was the contraction in the petroleum and mineral industries that characterized the period. Even then, the significant amounts destined for the U.S. Virgin Islands and Mexico still placed them in the group of countries receiving the most dollars in DOD contracts during the early years of the post-CBI period.

In the case of Puerto Rico, all industries experienced post-CBI increases, including fuel, lubricating oils, metals and ores, and the operation of government-owned buildings and facilities. El Salvador experienced 100 percent increases for seven of the nine industries awarded contracts in that country. Panama also obtained large shares of DOD contracts during the first four years of the CBI period in the tools, electrical and electronic equipment, communications equipment, and the furniture and office supply and equipment industries.

Military assistance funds can be subdivided into repayable and nonrepayable kinds. There were increases in repayable military assistance for all countries during the early years of the CBI period. This increase was substantial in El Salvador and Honduras, which together registered $1.1 billion for the period, equivalent to 83 percent of the total awarded the CBI region during that time.

Nonrepayable military assistance also increased substantially for many countries. El Salvador and Honduras obtained the lion's share, followed by Panama, Costa Rica, and Guatemala. Other countries—Belize, Grenada, Haiti, and St. Christopher and Nevis—experienced 100 percent increases during the early years of the post-CBI period.

The increase in repayable and nonrepayable funds can only be understood as a response to the civil war in El Salvador, increasing instability in Guatemala, and the military escalation that some Central American countries—particularly Honduras—experienced as the United States waged its destabilization policy against Nicaragua. In the case of Grenada, the destabilization campaign launched by the United States against Maurice Bishop, and the subsequent U.S. invasion, explains the increase. On 25 October 1983, five thousand U.S. marines and green berets invaded the island with the support of aircraft carriers and nuclear submarines. Scores of civilians died. U.S. troops remained on the island until 1985, and even then, some U.S. soldiers were left behind to train the local police force. Soldiers from the eastern Caribbean, principally from Jamaica, remained on the island until 1986 (Remo Bisso 1988).

In sum, the militarization of the Caribbean, and particularly of the Caribbean Basin Initiative countries, involved an increase in two different types of military expenditures—DOD contracts and repayable and nonrepayable military assistance funds—over the 1979–88 period.

Vieques and the Vieques Economic
Adjustment Program

The island of Vieques, a civilian municipality of Puerto Rico, provides a case study of the militarization process in the Caribbean. The Vieques Economic Adjustment Program (VEAP), an economic development program designed to stimulate U.S. military production, was implemented in the 1980s in the face of growing community opposition to U.S. military bases, political instability in the Caribbean region, and structural problems plaguing the U.S. military industry.

Vieques comprises an area of about 33,000 acres, 69 percent of which is "owned" by the U.S. Navy. It is part of the Roosevelt Roads military base located at Ceiba, Puerto Rico, only a few miles away. Roosevelt Roads is a geopolitical bastion from which the U.S. Navy and the Atlantic fleet of NATO can conduct bombardments and maneuvers throughout the year and can control access to and launch invasions in Central and northern South America as well as Caribbean Basin countries.

Vieques magnifies the contradictions that a small island community affected by U.S. military activities experiences. The U.S. Navy's control over the island impedes Viequenses from carrying out an economic development process based on access to the land and its coastline to develop fishing, tourism, and agriculture. Due to the high levels of unemployment, the population has been forced to migrate; many people live on welfare; and others depend on the scarce jobs available to civilians at the U.S. base. This situation generates contradictory sentiments among the population. There are those who see their welfare as dependent on the presence of the U.S. Navy—for instance, those employed at the base and some local businesspeople. There are others who see their difficulties as linked to the U.S. presence—for instance, local fishermen.

During the 1970s, a group of Viequenses organized the Crusade Pro Vieques Rescue (CPVR), which grouped the Fishermen's Association and other anti-Navy Viequenses under the leadership of Carlos Zenón. Political and civic organizations from the rest of the island of Puerto Rico opposed to the U.S. Navy's presence in Vieques also formed the National Committee Pro Vieques Rescue (NCPVR). Toward the end of the 1970s, the CPVR and the NCPVR constituted an anti-Navy movement. Although it represented a minority group in terms of the local population and had its own internal contradictions, this social movement organized protests during the late 1970s that—within the wider context of political instability in the region and the structural difficulties faced by the U.S. military industry—paved the way for the design and implementation of the Vieques Economic Adjustment Program.

The Vieques Economic Adjustment Program is an economic development program designed by the Pentagon, in coordination with the Department of Defense and the government of Puerto Rico, to foster the economic interests of the U.S. military industry in a way that helped solve the structural problems it faced, diffused social protests, and could be replicated elsewhere later on (U.S. President's Economic Adjustment Committee 1985). In 1983, the governor of Puerto Rico, Carlos Romero Barceló, and the U.S. Navy signed the VEAP, whereby the Navy maintained access to the training and ammunition storage facilities, as well as the right to launch operations and mobilizations from Vieques, in exchange for an economic development program that would increase employment and allow the islanders to use some land—if the Navy agreed—for civilian projects and activities. The Pentagon sold the program as a solution that combined U.S. national security objectives with community development goals.

During 1983–85, $40.2 million was channeled or committed to implement the VEAP. DOD contracts made up the bulk of the funds (51 percent), followed by foreign private funds (21 percent). DOD contracts were funneled through its top ten contractors worldwide, many of which already had subsidiaries in Puerto Rico, and some, like General Electric, in Vieques. The DOD also helped obtain funds from federal programs such as the Small Business Administration and the U.S. Department of Housing and Urban Development.

Puerto Rico's fundamental role in the implementation of the program was to provide most of the capital requirements needed, including the construction of new buildings in which to locate plant operations, and improvements and expansion of Vieques' civilian airport and of the ferry's terminal facilities. Government funds were committed to these projects, although private funds from the island were also used to execute the plan.

Manufacturing operations obtained the bulk of the funds. Seven firms were established, all owned by foreigners or nonlocal residents. In services and tourism, funds reached local businesses in just a few cases. By 1988 most companies had shut down operations.

The VEAP was designed not only to contain a movement that opposed U.S. interventionism and militarism but also to make the Vieques' industries dependent on the military industry of the United States in order to strengthen the role of Puerto Rico as a military bastion. It was also designed to benefit the U.S. military industry by granting DOD contracts to island firms that could produce at lower costs than U.S. mainland contractors.

In 1988, Carlos Zenón and Ismael Guadalupe, spokespersons for the CPVR, denounced the VEAP for attempting to buy out the people of Vieques or lead them to migrate (Andreu-Cuevas 1988). The VEAP's objectives were successful to the extent that its false promises generated expectations among the people that served to undermine the anti-Navy struggle. On an island where unemployment rates sometimes reached 50 percent, anti-Navy activists, for example, went to work in DOD-sponsored projects. As political repression in Puerto Rico escalated against the Left and the independence movement, arrests for political participation in the anti-Navy movement increased. Political activists served prison terms, and one of them, Angel Rodríguez Cristobal, was murdered in Florida while serving a sentence. This marked a setback for the anti-Navy movement at a time when it faced many other problems.

The success or failure of the VEAP cannot be evaluated in terms of whether it helped foster community development, because the program was not created for that purpose. Instead, the VEAP sought to secure U.S. military interests on the island, and that the VEAP did help achieve. Vieques experienced a reduction in DOD contract awards after 1985 due partly to the cyclical nature of military production. Also, however, DOD funds diminished once the political objectives of undermining the anti-Navy movement in Vieques were attained.

Analysis and Conclusions

The contradictions generated by the way the DOD does business with the supplier network for parts and components, the consolidation of the multinational corporations, and the fierce competition within arms industries have all served to spur growth in offshore procurement and to undermine—within the United States—the network of suppliers necessary to carry out military production with mass production.

The incorporation of Caribbean countries into the structure of the U.S. military industry has provided the U.S. military industry with an alternative supplier network. Through the incorporation of Caribbean economies, the U.S. military industry seeks a production network that can be activated on short notice during times of crisis and that is located close to home. The Caribbean network of suppliers allows the United States to expand production easily during times of mobilization—as they did in Puerto Rico during the Gulf War—and to contract it as needed. Notwithstanding the end of the cold war, the United States needs to maintain a regional infrastructure from which to secure civilian and military products in case of mobilization.

As a consequence, production within the U.S. military industry has been restructured within the institutional framework and advantages offered by the CBI. Caribbean production is concentrated in nonarms industries focused on goods that are fundamental to the functioning of the military industry (e.g., uniforms, underwear, pharmaceutical products, canned food, tents) and that must be mass-produced.

Vieques exemplifies the links among the military, economic, and political components in U.S. DOD industrial policies. The militarization of the

Caribbean is essentially the VEAP on a regional scale. The basic ingredient of the VEAP—the awarding of military contracts to secure military interests—was replicated in Puerto Rico, Panama, Honduras, and other countries where the U.S. sought a military stronghold, pursued the construction of military infrastructure, and desired to quench an opposition movement. As in the case of Vieques, military contract awards to the Caribbean region were related to the geopolitical interest of establishing, renegotiating, or preserving strategic interests and military facilities in the region.

What the CBI has brought about has not been security through development, but development through security. A process of militarization has taken place not just through aid and armaments sales but through the incorporation of Caribbean industry into the military industry of the United States. It is, of course, the security of U.S. military interests and the development of U.S. multinational corporations that have benefited the most.

How the U.S. military industry will be restructured at the international level during the post–cold war era and what implications these processes will have for the Caribbean region are yet to be seen. However, at present, some tendencies and their implications for the Caribbean can be outlined.

The cutbacks in military spending will affect both the top contractors and the network of suppliers. Which firms will be most affected is an issue of controversy. Some argue that the U.S. network will fare better than the top DOD contractors; because it tended to manufacture components and parts that were geared toward civilian markets but that also had military uses, a smaller portion of their business depended on military contracts. Others argue that top DOD contractors might fare better because they can confront declining demand by diversifying into civilian products or by entering into corporate mergers (Weidenbaum 1992).

The Caribbean network will be affected by cutbacks but will remain as a structure to be activated if need arises. The Caribbean will be affected through the impact on top DOD contractors carrying out production in the region and through the Caribbean network of suppliers of parts. The impact will also depend on the instability of the post–cold war era.

The post–cold war era might become increasingly unstable. Although the U.S.–Soviet superpower dynamic has receded, Third World countries might experience growing instability as distinctions between developed and less-developed countries become acute in a world economy of blocs. Moreover, Europe might arise as a military power with goals of its own and resign from NATO to form its own military structures (Rodríguez-Beruff and García-Muñiz 1993).

In order to maintain military strength within the context of cutbacks and possible growing instability, the United States has opted for restructuring its military forces around the concept of Special Operation Forces

(SOF). This will allow the United States to retain the capability of deployment and intervention in conflict zones around the world with reduced forces capable of fighting effectively in varied scenarios (Rodríguez-Beruff and García-Muñiz 1993). It will require increased standardization of equipment and communication systems necessary to carry out coordinated maneuvers and operations among allies.

For the Caribbean, this would imply that the military infrastructure of bases and installations could be rearticulated and, moreover, that military assistance funds might decrease and that military production will be cutback and reactivated only in times of crises in order to comply with the changing situations worldwide (Rodríguez-Beruff and García-Muñiz 1993).

In sum, considering the industrial component of militarization at the international level has allowed us to broaden the concept of Third World militarization. This approach has served to illustrate how that militarization is tied to the dynamics of the international economy and the globalization of production and to industrial policies that seek to promote U.S. interests by combining geopolitical, social, and economic elements.

In general terms, the U.S. Left associates the term *Third World militarization* with U.S. military intervention and war. Its political practice, therefore, presents an anti-interventionist, an antiwar, and an anti-military assistance stance. But militarization goes beyond military intervention and war and involves complex relations at the international level among militarism, the economy, and society. Political practice and the peace movement should not ignore these facts. The arguments in this chapter have been presented with the hope that they might serve to inform alternative political practices that articulate the complex relations at the international level among militarism, the economy, and society. For radicals and liberals, the time is ripe to demand conversion plans, as evidenced by the varied proposals of defense conversion legislation in the United States (Weidenbaum 1992). We need a peace movement that calls for demilitarization and military conversion on an international scale.

ACKNOWLEDGMENTS

I am grateful to Julie Graham, Juan B. Aponte, Jorge Rodríguez-Beruff, and Humberto García-Muñiz for their helpful comments.

NOTES

1. "For example, McDonnell Douglas agreed to use its best effort to purchase $100 million of Israeli goods over a ten-year period in connection with the sale of its F-15 aircraft to Israel" (Neuman 1985:187).

2. The term "Caribbean Basin" was first coined back in 1971 by a group of scholars headed by James D. Theberg at Georgetown's Center for International and

Strategic Studies. The Theberg group produced a report entitled "Russia in the Caribbean," in which they asserted that the Caribbean Basin region—including the Central American mainland, the Caribbean islands, and the states bordering Caribbean waters (Colombia, Guyana, Mexico, Panama, Surinam, and Venezuela)—should be seen as a single strategic entity and as part of the U.S. "mare nostrum" (Black 1985:19).

I will use the term *Caribbean Basin* throughout the chapter in reference to the countries that were originally designated as beneficiaries under the Caribbean Basin Initiative (Antigua and Barbuda, the Bahamas, Barbados, Belize, the British Virgin Islands, Costa Rica, Dominica, the Dominican Republic, El Salvador, Grenada, Guatemala, Haiti, Honduras, Jamaica, Montserrat, the Netherlands Antilles, Panama, St. Christopher and Nevis, St. Lucia, St. Vincent and the Grenadines, and Trinidad and Tobago) as well as the countries that were to be, originally, contributor states to the Caribbean Basin Initiative (Mexico, Venezuela, and Colombia).

Puerto Rico and the U.S. Virgin Islands are the remaining territories the United States holds in the Caribbean area. Thus, I have classified these two as Caribbean territories.

3. The repayable-funds category includes U.S. foreign military sales, foreign military construction sales, and commercial exports to Caribbean countries made directly from U.S. private manufacturers but controlled by the U.S. government through its Arms Export Control Act. The nonrepayable-funds category includes all those programs where the U.S. government offers nonrepayable grants of military assistance: Military Assistance Program Merger Funds, used solely to meet obligations of the recipient countries for payment of FMS purchases and not available to finance procurements from U.S. private suppliers; the International Military Education and Training funds, for which the U.S. government receives no dollar reimbursement; and the International Narcotics Control funds. To evaluate nonrepayable funds, I used military assistance funds as a parameter.

For Puerto Rico and the Virgin Islands, I used the operational expenditures of the military apparatus as a parameter of nonrepayable military assistance funds (based on Rodríguez-Beruff's methodology). This included the net operating expenditures of the Department of Defense and of the Veterans Administration, Veterans benefits transfer payments, and federal grants received by some sectors of the government. Repayable funds included the Veterans Housing Guaranteed and Insured Loans.

4. These were the countries that were to be, initially, contributors to the CBI. Afterward, however, they declined to comply with this role for diverse reasons. For instance, one of the areas of disagreement was the exclusion of Cuba and Nicaragua for political reasons.

5. This does not imply that the bulk of the business of these industries in the Caribbean is military contracting.

6. Total CBI figures for the 1979–88 period differ from those mentioned above ($1.6 rather than $2.5 billion) because the Netherlands Antilles has been excluded. The Netherlands Antilles' severe fall in petroleum exports distorted the analysis of CBI figures for DOD contract awards.

7. Approximately half the contracts destined to the Bahamas, for example, were concentrated in the operation of buildings and nonbuildings facilities. This

country is the site of two shore facilities for the U.S. Navy's antisubmarine program, which serves to monitor traffic from the Gulf of Mexico to the Atlantic Ocean through the Straits of Florida. All other countries within this group also house military installations.

8. The severe fall in petroleum exports seems to be linked to the shift in refining activities from Caribbean countries to the United States. As expressed by Carmen Deere and her colleagues (1990:29), "U.S. government efforts to discourage offshore refining in favor of the domestic refining industry (as well as periodic efforts to encourage energy conservation) have led to heavy disinvestment by U.S. multinationals that had built up the petroleum sector in Trinidad-Tobago as well as offshore refining in the Dutch Antilles, the Bahamas, and the U.S. Virgin Islands."

BIBLIOGRAPHY

Andreu-Cuevas, Luis A. 1988. Denuncia comité fracaso industrial en Vieques. *El Vocero*, 12 May, 104.

Baran, Paul, and Paul Sweezy. 1968. *El capital monopolista*. Mexico: Siglo XXI.

Black, George. 1985. Mare Nostrum: U.S. Security Policy in the English-Speaking Caribbean. *North American Congress for Latin America* (NACLA) 19(4): 13–48.

Deere, Carmen D., Edwin Meléndez, Marcia Rivera, Peggy Antrobus, and Lynn Bolles. 1990. *In the Shadows of the Sun: Alternative Development Policies for the Caribbean*. Boulder, Colo.: Westview Press.

Defense Systems Management College. 1987. *Management of Multinational Programs: A Handbook for Managers Entering the World of International Acquisition*. 2d ed. Fort Belvoir, Va.: Defense Systems Management College.

Gansler, Jacques. 1980. *The Defense Industry*. Cambridge, Mass.: MIT Press.

———. 1982. Can the Defense Industry Respond to the Reagan Initiatives? *International Security* 6(4): 102–321.

———. 1986. U.S. Dependence on Foreign Military Parts: Should We Be Concerned? *Issues in Science and Technology* 2(4): 17–18.

Klare, Michael T. 1984. *American Arms Supermarket*. Austin: University of Texas Press.

Neuman, Stephanie. 1985. Coproduction, Barter, and Countertrade: Offsets in the International Arms Market. *Orbis Phil* 29(1): 183–213.

O'Connor, John. 1978. *La crisis fiscal del estado*. Barcelona: Márquez.

Phillips, Dion. 1988. The Creation, Structure, and Training of the Barbados Defense Force. *Caribbean Studies* 21(1–2): 124–57.

Remo Bisso, Roberto. 1988. *Guía del Tercer Mundo*. Argentina: Ediciones Colihue.

Riddell, Tom. 1986. Marxism and Military Spending. *Journal of Post-Keynesian Economics* 8(4): 574–80.

Rodríguez-Beruff, Jorge, and Humberto García-Muñiz. 1993. Cambio estratégico global y nueva política militar de Estados Unidos: Su impacto en América Latina y el Caribe.

Smith, Ron, and Dan Smith. 1983. *The Economics of Militarism*. London: Pluto Press.

Tuomi, H., and R. Vayrynen. 1982. *Transnational Corporations, Armaments, and Development*. New York: St. Martin's Press.

U.S. Congress. House Committee on Banking, Finance, and Urban Affairs. Subcommittee on Economic Stabilization. 1987. *The New Industrial Base Initiative*. Hearings before the Subcommittee on Economic Stabilization. 100th Cong., 1st sess. Washington, D.C.: U.S. Government Printing Office.

U.S. President's Economic Adjustment Committee, Office of the Secretary of Defense. 1985. *Economic Adjustment Program for Vieques, Puerto Rico*. Washington, D.C.: The Pentagon.

Weidenbaum, Murray L. 1992. *Small Wars, Big Defense*. New York: Oxford University Press.

20

ROBIN BROAD
JOHN CAVANAGH

No More NICs

For more than a decade the most common policy advice to developing countries the world over has been a simple formula: copy the export-oriented path of the newly industrializing countries, the celebrated NICs. These economies—Brazil, Hong Kong, Mexico, Singapore, South Korea, and Taiwan—burst onto world manufactures markets in the late 1960s and the 1970s. By 1978 these six economies plus India accounted for fully 70 percent of the developing world's manufactured exports. Their growth rates for gross national product (GNP) and exports were unequaled.

No wonder the call was sounded for others to follow. Dozens have tried. But with the possible exceptions of Malaysia and Thailand, no country has come close. Why not? The answer lies in far-reaching changes in the global economy—from synthetic substitutes for commodity exports to unsustainable levels of external debt—that have created a glut economy offering little room for new entrants.

Despite these shifts, the foremost international development institutions, the World Bank and the International Monetary Fund (IMF), continue to promote the NIC path as the way for heavily indebted developing countries to escape the debt crisis. Yet in 1988, eight years into a period of reduced growth in world markets, the bankruptcy of this approach should be all too apparent. By the end of the 1970s, the World Bank had singled out the four Asian NICs as models to be studied by a second rung of developing countries. Having mastered the production of textiles, clothing, shoes, simple consumer electronics, and other light manufactured wares, the four NICs were moving into more sophisticated products like automobiles and video cassette recorders. Therefore, the Bank argued, as the NICs' level of industrial development advanced, they would abandon the more basic industries to other countries.

But the World Bank did more than offer the intellectual underpinnings for this development theory. In the late 1970s it positioned itself as a central actor in pushing would-be NICs up the ladder to the NIC rung. In

May 1979, World Bank President Robert McNamara, in an address to a United Nations Conference on Trade and Development (UNCTAD) meeting in Manila, called for developing countries to "upgrade their export structure to take advantage of the export markets being vacated by more-advanced developing countries" (1979:15). McNamara added that the Bank would move to the forefront of this new "program of action" (1979:27). To do so, however, the Bank needed to move beyond its more traditional project lending with a new instrument that would maximize its leverage with developing countries. Loans for hydroelectric dams, highways, and urban renewal, among other projects, had made the Bank the key international development player; but they did not confer on the Bank adequate leverage for the proposed global restructuring.

Consequently, the Bank turned to a new set of policy prescriptions dubbed "structural adjustment," the key ingredient of which was structural adjustment loans (SALs). These large loans—targeted toward broad sectors and heavily conditioned on a recipient's economic reforms—sought to hasten the new international division of labor whereby the would-be NICs would mimic the established NICs' light-manufactures export successes. The SALs were "the World Bank's best weapon yet," a close aide to McNamara said in 1981.[1] Designed to enhance efficiency and export orientation, they carried a broad set of policy prescriptions that focused on trade-related economic sectors.

Who are these would-be NICs that the World Bank and the IMF hoped to push up the development ladder? According to various classification systems, including those of the World Bank, this group comprises up to thirty second-tier less-developed countries (LDCs) across Africa, Asia, and Latin America.

These would-be NICs largely received the big loans and amplified attention from the Bank during the later 1970s and early 1980s. Of the nine LDCs rewarded with structural adjustment loans of more than $50 million as of mid-1982, seven were would-be NICs and one was a NIC. Moreover, the IMF's attention largely complemented the Bank's. Of the twenty LDCs that by mid-1982 had received one of the IMF's extended-fund facilities—highly conditioned loans with a ten-year repayment period—of more than $50 million, twelve fell into the would-be NICs grouping and two were NICs.

More insight into the Bank's role in the would-be NICs can be gained by looking at one illuminating case, the Philippines. By the end of Ferdinand Marcos's administration in February 1986, the Philippines had borrowed more than $4.5 billion from the World Bank in more than one hundred project and program loans. The country was, in the words of Gregario Licaros, one of Marcos's central bank governors, the "guinea pig" for structural adjustment. Indeed, one of the Bank's first SALs was a $200 million loan geared specifically toward restructuring the Philippine industrial sector. Its final approval by the Bank in September 1980 capped two years of intense policy-related dialogue between the Bank and Philippine government officials. Aided by its benevolent image as a bestower of funds for long-term development projects, the World Bank was able to take on the short-term stabilization role traditionally played by the IMF.

After a record Philippine balance-of-payments deficit of $570 million in 1979, the Bank put together the 1980 SAL package, which was attached not to a specific project but to a group of policies stipulating an export-oriented course for Philippine industry. Former high-ranking Philippine officials, including both proponents and opponents of the reforms, agree that the negotiations marked a critical juncture in the Philippine development path. Tariffs were slashed. Protective import restrictions were lifted. The exchange rate began a steady and steep devaluation, while export- and investment-promotion policies diverted resources from domestically oriented output. New free-trade tax havens, using generous incentives for transnational corporations (TNCs) to exploit low-cost Filipino labor, were established across the archipelago. Individual light manufacturing industries, such as textiles, cement, food processing, furniture, and footwear, were slated for restructuring according to World Bank specifications.

During this period, similar policies were pushed in other would-be NICs. World Bank SALs to the Ivory Coast, Kenya, Pakistan, Senegal, and Turkey—like the Philippine SAL—all concentrated on improving export incentives and performance. In Thailand, where a central bank official vowed in mid-1979 that the World Bank's policies would "never be listened to or followed by top people here,"[2] the government implemented economic policy changes almost identical to those of the Philippines a few years and a SAL later. In other cases, notably Chile and Indonesia, would-be NICs followed the Bank's blueprint for development without a formal SAL.

NIC Rivalry

In effect the World Bank was helping to create a group of countries that would compete against each other to become NICs. The result was two vicious battles—one to offer cheaper, more docile labor forces and more attractive financial incentives to lure TNC assembly lines away from the other countries, and the other to win scarce export markets.

This competition soon became clear to each would-be NIC. As a deputy governor of the Philippine central bank remarked in a 1980 interview, "We've got to always be careful now, always watching, on the lookout for other [developing] nations' next moves. . . . And then we've got to make sure we meet their offer and better it."[3] Sri Lanka's advertisement in the 16 October 1981 issue of the *Far Eastern Economic Review* said it well: "Sri

Lanka challenges you to match the advantages of its Free Trade Zone, against those being offered elsewhere. . . . Sri Lanka has the lowest labor rates in Asia." Variations on that appeal were issued by one would-be NIC after another, putting TNCs in a choice position from which to bargain the most lucrative investment or subcontracting deals.

The competition encouraged labor repression and exploitation. One Manila-based TNC executive explained in a 1981 interview, "We tell the [Philippine] government: you've got to clamp down [on labor]. . . . Or we threaten to move elsewhere. And we'll do just that. There's Sri Lanka [and] now China too."[4]

Most of the Bank's public documents sought to play down the problems associated with rivalry among the would-be NICs. But the Bank was not unaware of the potential zero-sum game. In a January 1979 working paper assessing the LDCs' manufacturing export potential, two leading Bank economists, Hollis Chenery and Donald Keesing (1979:47), forecast that "the increasing number of successful competitors may make it increasingly difficult for new comers to get established" and that the success of a "few" could leave "too little" opportunity for the rest.

Yet who had set in motion this chain of competition? An October 1979 World Bank report had counseled the Philippines to take advantage of the fact that its wages had "declined significantly relative to those in competing countries," notably Hong Kong and South Korea (1979a:2). Almost simultaneously, as reported in the *Southeast Asia Chronicle* in December 1981, the Bank helped steer Indonesia onto a parallel course, advising that "incentives for firms to locate there rather than in some other Southeast Asian country . . . must be provided" (Kelly and Rocamora 1981:16). Meanwhile, Sri Lanka received a $20 million World Bank loan to establish a new export platform for apparel subcontracting, and the Bank pushed the People's Republic of China (PRC), Thailand, and some of the Caribbean Basin countries into the light-manufactures arena as well.

The competition among would-be NICs was further exacerbated by the exporters of an earlier era, the Asian NICs of Hong Kong, Singapore, South Korea, and Taiwan. World Bank theory to the contrary, these countries were not abandoning textiles, apparel, and electronics assembly as they moved into higher stages of industrialization. Indeed, since the 1960s the Asian NICs had been spreading throughout the entire range of industry—from light to heavy, from unsophisticated to sophisticated—leaving little space for would-be NICs.

The export performance of the Asian NICs between 1979 and 1985 illustrates this point. Their combined exports leaped from $60.5 billion to $113.9 billion, a stunning 88 percent increase during years of slow global economic growth. More sophisticated "strategic" industries like telecommunications, complex electronic equipment, and motor vehicles were encouraged by NIC governments through various tax holidays and subsidized loans. Over this period South Korean motor vehicle exports rose from $300 million to close to $1 billion, and Hong Kong telecommunications and sound equipment rose from less than $1.6 billion to more than $2 billion.

On a regular basis, export surges in these high-value-added industries captured newspaper headlines. Little attention was paid, however, to the continuing rapid NIC export growth in traditional light manufactures. Through a combination of innovation, cost-cutting measures, upgrading capital equipment, and state and private-sector cooperation, these countries held on to and expanded their markets. Textile and clothing exports from the four grew from $14.6 billion to $23.4 billion over the six years, a 60 percent rise. The Asian NICs enjoyed a rising global market share in the textile and clothing industries. The same rapid growth was noticeable in other light manufacturing sectors. For example, Hong Kong's exports of footwear doubled, from $125 million to $250 million. And South Korea's exports of toys grew from $300 million to $670 million.

Another factor also was inhibiting the would-be NICs' economic ascension—new technologies. The more than a decade that separated the NICs' debut from that of the would-be NICs witnessed technological advances in several sectors that changed the very definition of Third World industrialization.

By the late 1970s, technological innovations, led by the microprocessor revolution, made the global fragmentation of production highly profitable and desirable. Whereas the original NICs had received complete industrial processes such as shipbuilding and machinery, the would-be NICs won marginal segments of scattered assembly lines for semiconductors and consumer electronics, textiles, and apparel. In Sri Lanka, for example, workers in export-processing zones used basic sewing machines to stitch together garments from imported fabric. In the Philippines, female workers in 1980 were performing only one of the ten major operations of electronic production, attaching hairlike gold wires to silicon chips.

As a result, these new global assembly lines left gaping disparities between the gross value of the would-be NICs' industrial export earnings and the actual value added to the product in the developing country. Consider again the Philippine case. When proclaiming the nontraditional-export strategy's supposed triumphs, the Philippine government naturally focused on the higher of the two figures, the gross value of exports. Yet when stripped of import components' costs, the "value added" by the domestic side of production was but a fraction of the export earnings.

With the Philippines importing cartons for its banana exports, cans for some food exports, and a wide assortment of machinery and component parts for its limited apparel and electronic assembly lines, value added in most Philippine industries was quite low. Although a public version of a

1979 World Bank document admitted that the aggregate value added for Philippine nontraditional exports was "at best only 40 percent," a confidential report revealed the precise Bank calculation to be 25 percent (World Bank 1979b; 1981). In other words, for every dollar of nontraditional-export earnings, only twenty-five cents stayed in the Philippines; the rest was siphoned off by import payments. Low value added was a fact of life in the Philippines' part in the new international division of labor.

According to one of the best analyses of electronics subcontracting, the long-term outlook for increasing the amount of value added in developing countries in the industry was bleak. As this December 1981 United Nations Industrial Development Organization report, *Restructuring World Industry in a Period of Crisis*, detailed, the percentage of value added attributable to new LDC microprocessor production lines rose until 1973. By 1977, however, value added in the newest LDC factories had already begun to fall. This downward turn came even as the gross value of semiconductors reexported to the United States soared tenfold from 1970 to 1978. Of the seven LDCs studied, the Philippines was the last to start silicon chip assembly. Entering on the downswing of the curve, value added in its factories was the lowest of all.

Since 1977 a growing share of the value was being held in the electronics companies' home countries. The U.N. report emphasized that "as complexity of circuitry increases, more value added is produced in the early wafer-fabrication stage, i.e., in the United States, in Japan, or in some locations in Western Europe. Furthermore, the more complex, computerized final testing . . . again is usually done in OECD [Organization for Economic Cooperation and Development] locations, particularly in the United States and Japan" (UNIDO 1981:249).

If the production side of the would-be-NIC experience offered less than what was advertised, the marketing side was even grimmer. For light manufactured exports to be the engine of growth for the would-be NICs, world trade—that is, global demand for these products—had to grow each year. There was no way to escape this logic in the aggregate.

But in the late 1970s and early 1980s, at precisely the time when would-be NICs were induced to embark on a nontraditional-export path, these necessary conditions were decidedly absent. Over the decade from 1963 to 1973 the volume of world exports rose at a rapid average annual rate of 8.5 percent. Beginning in 1973, however, an economic deceleration slowed the average annual expansion to 4 percent. By 1980, exports were crawling ahead at only 1 percent per year, and in 1981 they showed no growth. Moreover, 1981 had the dubious distinction of being the first year since 1958 to experience an actual decrease in world trade in current dollar terms, a shrinkage of 1 percent.

Behind these global trade statistics lurked the domestic stagnation of the industrialized economies. According to IMF figures, from 1976 to 1979 the real GNP of industrialized countries grew at a tolerable average yearly rate of 4 percent. By 1980, OECD growth was limping ahead at only 1.25 percent; the next year it increased again by only 1.25 percent. These two years presaged a decade of vastly reduced growth. From 1981 to 1985 world output growth slowed to an average of 1.7 percent per year and trade to 2.8 percent. These aggregate statistics become even more dismal if Eastern Europe and the PRC are excluded: output over the first half of the 1980s grew at an average annual rate of only 1.4 percent in developing countries and 2.3 percent in developed countries.

As more countries battled for the same tepid export markets, prices plunged. Between 1981 and 1985, world prices of food commodities fell at an average annual rate of 15 percent; agricultural raw materials dropped at an average annual rate of 7 percent; and minerals fell 6 percent. The year 1986 proved even dimmer, when a 30 percent decline in the developing countries' terms of trade (the ratio of prices of developing-country exports to prices of their imports) translated into a staggering $94 billion transfer of income to the developed world.

Another pitfall facing the LDCs' export-oriented industrialization was the panoply of quantitative restrictions that had spread to cover fully one-half of global trade. Despite official encomiums to "free trade," the OECD countries increasingly were barricading themselves behind what even President Ronald Reagan's Council of Economic Advisers admitted were "neo-mercantile" policies.

These defensive machinations to moderate the recessionary bite at home were baptized the "new protectionism"—a proliferation of American, European Economic Community, and Japanese trade barriers, notably quotas on LDC-manufactured exports. "New" referred to the dazzling array of nontariff barriers not regulated by the General Agreement on Tariffs and Trade. Voluntary export restraints and orderly marketing arrangements flourished. As the World Bank and the IMF encouraged free trade policies in LDCs, the major voting blocs within those institutions retreated from any semblance of free trade at home. The retreat of free trade became inextricably meshed with the recession: as OECD growth slackened, quotas were tightened. The more successful a particular LDC export category was, the more restrictive the quota became.

By the calculations of the World Bank's own economists in 1979, the most dangerous of the new protectionist barriers was centered in the apparel, textile, and footwear sectors. Yet it was precisely these sectors—along with furniture, wood products, electronics, and other light manufactured exports—that the Bank had pinpointed as the engine of growth for the would-be NICs. The restrictive allotments of the Multi-Fiber Agreement made textiles and apparel perhaps the most heavily controlled sectors in international trade. As a result, the LDCs' share of textile and apparel exports began to shrink in the early 1980s.

Did the World Bank adequately address the impact of slow global economic growth and rising protectionism on its policy directives? As early as 1974 the Bank understood certain pitfalls that the 1970s and 1980s might hold for export-oriented industrialization. That year McNamara, in an address to the board of governors, noted: "The adverse effect on the developing countries . . . of a reduction in economic growth in their major markets would be great. There is a strong—almost one-to-one—relationship between changes in the growth of OECD countries and that of oil importing nations" (1974:12). The Philippines was especially vulnerable, the Bank acknowledged in a country program paper two years later, "with international trade the equivalent of almost half of GNP" (1976:6). And in his May 1979 address to the UNCTAD conference in Manila, McNamara noted that the World Bank had perceived the onset of the new protectionism as early as 1976.

Yet in the late 1970s and early 1980s, Bank officials who were planning Third World development strategies continually made assumptions that ignored slow growth and rising protectionism. Their model, grounded in theories of free trade and comparative advantage, posited the absence of such conditions. They opted instead for what was termed "one set of reasonable assumptions" without explaining their legitimacy. The set of "reasonable" assumptions about trade and protectionism that underpinned the Bank's structural adjustment reports and advice to would-be NICs was some permutation of the following: industrial countries were to grow 4 percent annually in the 1980s, "worldwide economic recovery" stood on the horizon, and "no major setbacks" would occur in major markets.

Did Bank economists really believe this? In the Philippine example a wide chasm between these assumptions and the private assessments of Bank officials was revealed time and again during interviews conducted by one of the authors in the early 1980s. One World Bank consultant and member of the Bank's appraisal mission for its first Philippine SAL, John Power, privately admitted his doubts about a successful outcome of Philippine export-oriented industrialization given the gravity of the "world situation."[5] Yet a 1979 book he coauthored as background for the Philippine SAL, *Industrial Promotion Policies in the Philippines*, refused to give credence to any such misgivings. In a similar case of conflicting assessments, a January 1979 study by the Bank economists Chenery and Keesing (1979:43) acknowledged existing "severe import restrictions" imposed by key developed countries and increasingly smaller quotas for up-and-coming LDC manufactures exporters. But in another working paper, published about two years later, the Bank economist Barend de Vries (1980:17) argued that "considerable opportunities" existed for Philippine nontraditional exports.

The potential effects of this unsubstantiated optimism about the Philippines and other would-be NICs were never seriously considered by World Bank officials. The development prescriptions of Bank officials were transformed into a kind of dogma: "The more hostile the external environment, the more urgent" the need for restructuring, an August 1980 *Report and Recommendation* urged (World Bank 1980a:31). In one instance, a World Bank director took the floor at the executive board's final meeting on the Philippine SAL to question the management's scenario of Philippine "dynamic" export-led growth in light of "an adverse environment [including] lower than projected growth rates in industrial countries and increased protectionism." The board chairman's response epitomized the Bank's unquestioning attitude: "If the environment turned out to be more adverse than projected, then the ultimate benefits under the adjustment program would be reduced, but the nature of the adjustment needed would not be changed" (World Bank 1980b:8). But such a response was no more than conjecture. No hard evidence and no computer runs were offered to answer what should have been a basic question: If world trade did not grow, and if key markets became increasingly protected, would export-oriented industrialization be the optimal route to growth?

The Bank's 1981 *World Development Report*, in fact, did present formally a quantitative global model incorporating "slower industrial [country] growth" and "increased protectionism." But the exercise was at best questionable; at worst, it was deceptive. Although lower than either the accompanying best-case scenario or previous *World Development Report* estimates, the low-case scenario for 1980–85 still promised growth rates higher than what transpired. Indeed, over the past nine years the Bank consistently has projected average developing-country export growth rates of more than 5 percent per year; between 1981 and 1986 the actual annual growth rates averaged instead a negative 0.4 percent.

In any event, the low-case projections were largely ignored in the plans and projections for specific countries. When incorporating global growth estimates in aggregate economic work for various LDCs, the Bank used figures closer to high-case yields. This was done without any caveat mentioning that the Bank also had somewhat less optimistic forecasts.

It was becoming increasingly clear that the World Bank had no vision of development in a world economy of curtailed growth. To a large extent, Bank officials had equated growth with development. To them, development did not primarily mean providing adequate food, clean water, clothing, and housing—in short, offering a standard of living consistent with human dignity. Those had become secondary concerns to be met through growth. In the Bank's view, no growth meant no development and therefore could not be considered seriously.

In recent public World Bank documents, slow growth in the world economy is still viewed as a short-term or cyclical aberration that does not undermine the basic soundness of the Bank's structural adjustment advice. Indeed, as late as its 1987 *World Development Report*, the Bank was still stressing that the world economy was continuing to "expand," albeit at a "modest and uneven" rate (iii). That outlook enabled the Bank to continue unabashedly to counsel "the outward-oriented trade policies which have proved so successful for the NICs in recent years" (11).

A New World Economy

World Bank forecasts notwithstanding, global stagnation is likely to prove harder to shake than most would like to believe. Aside from protectionism pressures, a series of corporate developments has stunted demand globally, leaving increasing numbers of people at the margins of market activity. Prominent among these developments are the commercial banks' handling of the Third World debt crisis, corporate substitution for Third World raw materials, and labor-saving technological innovations in the developed world.

The debt crisis arose inevitably from the export-oriented development strategies, which depended on heavy borrowing for infrastructure and in many countries fed corruption and capital flight. In the early 1980s, as oil prices and interest rates rose and primary commodity prices fell, country after country announced its inability to service debts owed to banks in the developed world. In rapid succession the creditor banks sent these countries through IMF austerity programs, which prescribed a kind of shock treatment to bring countries' balance of payments out of deficit. Wage freezes, currency devaluations, and government spending cuts reduced imports into the Third World; indeed, many countries wiped out trade and national budget deficits within a few years. But the lowered wages and imports also dampened global economic growth.

Technological breakthroughs in substitutes for Third World raw materials also hurt growth performance in the developing world. A single anecdote typifies the impact of longer-term corporate development on commodity markets. Until 1981 the largest consumer of the world's sugar was Coca-Cola. That year, in a move rapidly emulated by other soft drink giants, Coca-Cola began to shift its sweetener from sugar to corn syrup. Western consumers might not have viewed the change as significant, but it displaced millions of Third World sugar workers for a product produced within industrial countries.

Advances in plastics, synthetic fibers, food chemistry, and biotechnology are bringing similar far-reaching changes to other raw material and commodity markets. Cumulatively these substitutions have pushed tens of millions of Third World workers into the margins of the marketplace, further curbing global demand.

Likewise, new corporate technologies are transforming developed-country economies. The computer revolution, the major technological breakthrough of the last two decades, is strikingly dissimilar from earlier technological breakthroughs. The advent of electricity and the automobile, for example, generated millions of jobs in related industries and sparked economic booms in the leading countries. The microprocessor revolution has also created millions of jobs. However, applications of microprocessors have spread through almost every manufacturing and service sector in uses that are labor saving. Bank tellers, supermarket checkout clerks, assembly-line workers, and others are all joining the ranks of the unemployed. This phenomenon is reflected in Western Europe, where for seventeen straight years the unemployment rate has risen.

The result of these three changes is that all over the world, industry is turning out more than consumers can buy. The new global glut economy prevails despite the billions of people with enormous needs and wants but with little ability to buy.

As world economic growth has slowed, so have the Third World activities of its central private institutions: TNCs and banks. Much of the growth of the 1960s and 1970s was based on a rapid expansion of production around the world by subsidiaries of such TNCs as Ford, John Deere, and Texas Instruments. Western banks followed to provide financing. Then, after 1973, they became major economic actors in the developing world in their own right as recyclers of billions of petrodollars.

This is no longer the case. Banks and corporations go where there is growth and, hence, profit. Since the early 1980s the Third World basically has stopped growing; many countries have even slipped backward. Consequently, U.S. banks in the 1980s returned home for new short-term rewards—consumer credit, corporate mergers, and the get-rich-quick gimmicks of financial speculation.

Again, the statistics are stark. In 1983 international bank lending to developing countries, excluding offshore bank centers, totaled $35 billion. By 1985 a mere $3 billion in new lending had trickled in.

Yet the changing world economy has created a desperate need to rethink the kinds of adjustments that will produce growth and development. At the very least, the adjustment strategies must be built on realistic assumptions. The NICs were the product of a radically different world economy. That they cannot be replicated in the 1980s is an indication of how much that world economy has changed.

Rather than increase their reliance on a hostile world environment, developing countries should try to reduce this dependence and diversify trading partners and products. This approach implies a careful restructuring of trade and financial linkages to conform with a development logic that is driven by internal economic forces.

If economies can no longer be pulled along primarily by external growth, stronger internal buying power must be generated. The great challenge is to transform crushing social needs into effective demand and then to meet that demand by turning first to domestically produced goods and services, next to the region, and only after that to the wider world market. In most developing countries this development framework implies vast internal adjustment quite different from the World Bank's brand of structural adjustment. Most of the Third World's people cannot afford to purchase many goods and services. Wages are locked into rock-bottom subsistence rates; wealth and income are heavily skewed toward a relatively small, wealthy elite. As a result, spreading income more evenly requires, for a start, extensive land reform, progressive taxation policies, and guarantees of worker rights.

To offer more specifics on internal demand-driven development strategies is risky. Vastly different resource bases and social strata among countries suggest that a country-specific approach is essential. Indeed, the sin of universality in development strategies was perhaps the central weakness of IMF and World Bank adjustment programs. Further, the successful implementation of any development strategy depends on its acceptance by entrenched interests in that country. However desirable comprehensive agrarian reform may be in the Philippines, for example, a powerful landowning group has substantial influence in the government and is likely to block serious reform efforts.

These caveats noted, a few general principles for development in a hostile world economy can be sketched out. Most would-be NICs remain predominantly agricultural societies; hence the starting point of internal demand-led development must be in farming. Two undertakings are central to increasing buying power in the countryside: redistributing wealth and raising productivity.

Agrarian reform remains the major means of redistributing wealth and income and thereby increasing the effective purchasing power of the rural population. The people in Third World rural areas are largely either poor tenants or agricultural workers who earn only subsistence wages. They have meager resources to consume in the marketplace. Only through agrarian reform can this population begin to produce a surplus that can be translated into consumption. In economic terms, small farmers have a higher "marginal propensity" to consume than larger ones, and much of their consumption could be satisfied by locally produced products.

Raising productivity depends in large part on upgrading infrastructure—from irrigation and roads to credit institutions and marketing channels. In this area, as in efforts to upgrade social infrastructure through health, education, and nutrition loans, the World Bank could play a positive role by providing loans and technical assistance. In many respects, this emphasis would return the Bank to its original purpose as a development bank. In all loans, the Bank would do well to work closely with producer and neighborhood associations and cooperatives and other nongovernmental organizations that have proliferated in developing countries of late.

From this starting point, industrialization based on maximizing industrial linkages with agriculture makes great sense. In particular, three strands of industry could be encouraged:

Agricultural inputs. An agricultural sector with rising productivity will need locally produced fertilizer, pesticides, water pumps, and a wide range of tools, from plows to tractors.

Processing farm products. From cocoa and coffee to sugar and cotton, increased domestic processing offers more foodstuffs for local consumption and increases the value added of exports.

Consumer goods. As purchasing power grows in the countryside, so does the market for locally produced textiles, clothing, shoes, bicycles, refrigerators, and other consumer goods. Here, too, World Bank loans could help by improving the technology of small and medium-sized industries.

The cycle of agriculture-linked industrialization does not stop there. As industry grows, the increased buying power of industrial workers provides an expanding market for farm goods from rural areas. Agriculture and industry would grow in tandem. It is worth pointing out that, popular myths notwithstanding, South Korea pursued this basic strategy in its earliest phase of industrialization.

This agriculture-linked industrialization strategy should not be confused with import-substitution policies for industrialization. Those were decidedly different—more capital- and import-intensive, often dependent on protecting inefficiencies, and less sensitive to creating markets for new production. Nor does agriculture-linked industrialization shun exports. Rather, it focuses on exporting products offering higher value added.

In a highly interdependent world, such demand-centered development does not and cannot imply autarky. What cannot be produced locally is produced nationally. What cannot be produced nationally is purchased from regional partners—which suggests the importance of revitalizing regional integration institutions. Only for those products for which regional producers cannot satisfy demand is trade necessary with countries on the other side of the globe. Domestic needs should shape trade patterns rather than vice versa.

Beyond domestic market policies in agriculture and industry, development strategies should seek to curtail the wasteful economic activities that are rampant in some countries. These range from large, unproductive landholdings and capital flight to production and export monopolies and cronyism. Rooting out these practices is a monumental political task, threatening as it does entrenched groups of speculators, moneylenders, landlords, and bloated militaries. Development strategies must also pay closer attention to the pressing need to maintain fragile natural resource bases around the world. The disappearance of rain forests, plant and animal species, clean rivers, and clean air has become the dominant trend in too many countries.

Most observers continue to view the Asian NICs as role models. And they offer glowing imagery in support of their views: Asian NICs have "already taken off," and the rest of the noncommunist Southeast Asian countries are "on the runway revving" up to follow, as former Japanese Foreign Minister Saburo Okita has described it.

The would-be NICs have fallen for such prophecies for nearly a decade. Now is the time to demand not imagery but a realistic assessment of options. The debate on adjustment and development should be reopened; strategies that proclaim that the only option is greater dependence on an increasingly hostile and turbulent world economy need to be challenged. It is time to ask whether any more developing countries can really hope to become the South Korea or the Hong Kong of the early 1990s.

ACKNOWLEDGMENT

1. Excerpted and reprinted with permission from *Foreign Policy* 72 (Fall 1988). Copyright © 1988 by the Carnegie Endowment for International Peace.

NOTES

1. Interview conducted by Robin Broad with World Bank official (anonymity requested), 4 March 1981.
2. Interview conducted by Robin Broad with Bank of Thailand official (anonymity requested), July 1979.
3. Interview conducted by Robin Broad, 2 December 1980.
4. Interview conducted by Robin Broad, 13 February 1981.
5. Interview conducted by Robin Broad with John Power, World Bank consultant and professor of economics, University of Hawaii at Manoa, 29 October 1980.

BIBLIOGRAPHY

Bautista, Romeo, and John H. Power, et al. 1979. *Industrial Promotion Policies in the Philippines.* Manila: Philippine Institute for Development Studies.
Chenery, Hollis B., and Donald B. Keesing. 1979. *The Changing Composition of Developing Country Exports.* World Bank Staff Working Paper 314 (January). Washington, D.C.: World Bank.

de Vries, Barend. 1980. *Transition toward More Rapid and Labor-Intensive Development: The Case of the Philippines.* World Bank Staff Working Paper 424 (October). Washington, D.C.: World Bank.

Kelly, John, and Joel Rocamora. 1981. Indonesia: A Show of Resistance. *Southeast Asia Chronicle* 81 (December): 16–25.

McNamara, Robert. 1974. *Address to the Board of Governors, Washington, D.C., September 30, 1974.* Washington, D.C.: World Bank.

———. 1979. *Address to the United Nations Conference on Trade and Development, Manila, Philippines, May 10, 1979.* Washington, D.C.: World Bank.

UNIDO. 1981. *Restructuring World Industry in a Period of Crisis—The Role of Innovation: An Analysis of Recent Developments in the Semiconductor Industry.* New York: United Nations.

World Bank. 1976. *Philippines: Country Program Paper.* Washington, D.C.: World Bank.

———. 1979a. *Industrial Development Strategy and Policies in the Philippines.* Report 2513-PH, vol. 1. Washington, D.C.: World Bank.

———. 1979b. *Philippines: Domestic and External Resources for Development.* Report 2674-PH. Washington, D.C.: World Bank.

———. 1980a. *Report and Recommendation of the President of the International Bank for Reconstruction and Development on a Proposed Structural Adjustment Loan to the Republic of the Philippines.* Report P-2872-PH. Washington, D.C.: World Bank.

———. 1980b. *Summaries of the Discussions at the Meeting of the Executive Directors of the Bank and IDA, September 16, 1980.* Washington, D.C.: World Bank.

———. 1981. *Philippines: Staff Appraisal Report on the Industrial Finance Project.* Report 3331-PH. Washington, D.C.: World Bank.

21

JOSÉ TÁVARA

Development Strategies in
Latin America: Which Way Now?

It has been fashionable to refer to the 1980s as the "lost decade" for many countries in the Third World. In fact, most of the economic and social indicators show a dismal picture for the decade. In the case of Latin America, real per capita gross domestic product fell by 7 percent between 1980 and 1988, after an almost 40 percent increase between 1970 and 1980 (IADB 1989:1).

The term *lost decade* might be misleading, however, if it is taken to mean that nothing substantial happened in the Latin American region. In fact, one of the most significant features of this period has been the development of new forms of production organization and social institutions as those affected by the crisis have banded together in an effort to survive.[1] Diverse collective initiatives have been organized, such as communal kitchens and primary health-care workshops, along with a wide range of small-scale activities, mostly in commerce and services but also in manufacturing.

Although many of the activities organized in poor urban settlements have been oriented to meeting basic needs, the constitution of producers' associations, industrial parks, and production networks goes well beyond meeting the demands of survival. In fact, the dynamism of these local experiences suggests that new avenues for industrialization have been created amid the crisis, providing far-reaching development lessons. Scholars and policymakers continue to debate the appropriate path to industrial development, but ideas and inspiration are being drawn from initiatives at the community level. These grass-roots experiences herald the emergence of a new politics as well as a new economics of industrial development.

Industrial Strategies in Latin America:
A Brief History

Recent debates over industrial strategy in Latin America have focused on the alleged exhaustion of import-substitution industrialization (ISI) and on

391

the virtues and shortcomings of an alternative model dubbed export-oriented industrialization (EOI). The main advocates of ISI were a group of scholars working at the United Nations' Economic Commission for Latin America (ECLA) since the late 1940s. They argued that the emphasis given to the primary exports sectors (mining and export agriculture) and the absence of an industrial base weakened prospects for autonomous development, accentuating the dependence of peripheral Third World nations on the industrialized world.

The great crisis of 1929 had demonstrated the serious limitations of the primary export model, as Latin America's export earnings—and therefore its import capacity—fell sharply. The dependence of most of the countries of the region on a few export commodities made them more vulnerable to the vagaries of the world market. Continual deterioration in the terms of trade between the center and the periphery, argued the ISI advocates, would condemn Third World nations to permanent stagnation. The only way to reduce their dependence was to develop an industrial base, expand domestic markets, and diversify exports, increasing at the same time the pool of skilled workers and the levels of employment and income per capita.

The Second World War created serious disruptions in world trade, providing further incentives to produce industrial goods domestically. Several policy measures were implemented to promote ISI, such as easy credit and subsidies to new industries, public investment in education and industrial infrastructure, and price controls on industrial inputs. The chief measure, however, was the protection of the domestic market through increased tariffs, import prohibitions, quotas, and the like.

Larger countries such as Argentina, Brazil, and Mexico had already implemented some ISI policies and had achieved a substantial degree of industrial diversification before World War II. ISI gradually became the mainstream strategy in the 1950s and 1960s, and its vigorous promotion led to an acceleration of industrial growth all across the region. Industry's share in GNP for the region as a whole rose from 13 percent in 1928–29 to 23 percent in 1963–64. By the mid-1960s, however, the industrialization process began to show some signs of exhaustion, and during the next decade it became clear that ISI had failed to live up to expectations.

The ISI strategy had not only failed to relieve the foreign-exchange constraint, but ironically it had further accentuated the dependence of Latin American economies, making them more vulnerable to balance-of-payments problems. All the transactions in international trade are denominated in hard currency (mainly dollars). A country with balance-of-payments problems has, by definition, a limited availability of hard currency and is therefore unable to sustain its level of imports.[2]

The new industries created in Latin America had provided the relatively small wealthy classes with domestic sources of supply of consumer durables, including automobiles. Even though production—or assembly— of these goods was done domestically, raw materials, machinery, and spare parts still had to be imported from the industrialized countries. Given the relatively high capital-intensity of these industries as well as their weak linkages with other sectors of the economy, the industrialization process was not only unable to diffuse its benefits to the rest of the economy, but also tended to accentuate marked inequalities in the distribution of income and wealth.[3] Moreover, the increasing dominance of foreign capital in the most dynamic industries as well as in related financial and commercial activities reduced, rather than enhanced, national autonomy.[4]

To be sure, import substitution did achieve some successes, including a sizable reduction in the region's relative dependence on world trade. Total imports diminished from 30 percent of GNP in 1928–29 to 9 percent in 1963–64, and the export share also plunged from 31 percent to 14 percent over the same period. The *volume* of imports from the industrialized nations rose rapidly during the 1970s, however, contributing to a massive accumulation of foreign debt. The oil crisis accelerated the process of indebtedness, particularly for the oil-importing countries of the region. In the 1980s the chickens came home to roost when private banks and international agencies drastically reduced lending and Latin America began to repay its foreign debt. But just as ISI "declared bankruptcy," a new strategy became available to take its place, one that had begun to emerge in academic circles in the late 1960s and that came to be known as export-oriented industrialization (EOI).[5]

The criticisms of ISI put forward by proponents of EOI contained elements of truth that had already been pointed out by some of the early ISI advocates themselves. EOI supporters argued that the protectionist measures and the interventionist policies associated with ISI had contributed to an inefficient industrial structure, unable to compete in international markets. The solution was to restore the market mechanism, dismantling all forms of state intervention and bureaucratic restrictions on entrepreneurial creativity. The discipline of the market would allegedly expand the export capacity of developing countries, particularly in those sectors in which they had comparative advantage. The market would also eradicate the anti-agricultural bias of ISI, improving prices and incomes of agricultural producers. In sum, free markets would eliminate all the price distortions generated by subsidies and other forms of state intervention, promoting a better allocation of resources and improving the distribution of income.

EOI rapidly became dogma in the context of the debt crisis and the conservative offensive of the 1980s. Its main advocates have been multilateral organizations such as the World Bank and the International Monetary Fund, as well as most of the governments of the industrialized countries. The basic policy measures associated with the new strategy include a substantial reduction in the scope of government intervention (elimination of subsidies, privatization of public enterprises, cutbacks in public services, etc.), reduction of real wages and social benefits, liberalization of controls in all markets (imports, labor, land, and finance), incentives to foreign investment, and exchange-rate devaluations.

Most of these policies were designed to increase the competitiveness of Latin American exports and were indeed successful from the point of view of the international lenders: they resulted in substantial increases in exports and made possible a massive transfer of resources in the form of debt repayments.[6] From the point of view of the majority of Latin Americans, however, these policies have been a devastating failure. They have accentuated the vulnerability of the region to fluctuations in world markets and have weakened the prospects for internal integration between the export sectors and the domestic market. They have also led to the continuing impoverishment of larger segments of the population and have aggravated long-standing inequalities in the distribution of income and wealth. Furthermore, these policies have intensified the problems related to rural poverty, migration, and demographic concentration in the cities.

In the case of Peru, for example, the lack of maintenance and investment in sewerage, drainage, and drinking-water facilities, as well as the drastic cutbacks in public services since the mid-1970s, has created the conditions for a cholera epidemic that by mid-May 1991 had already infected 160,000 people and claimed some 1,300 lives. Nurses and physicians in public hospitals, earning miserable salaries and working under primitive medical conditions, have managed to keep the death rate below 1 percent, thanks to the active role played by health-care workshops and grass-roots organizations. They fear, however, that the disease will become even more widespread. Unfortunately, the appalling state of infrastructure and public services is not unique to Peru, and the cholera is reportedly spreading into the Amazon Basin and along the Pacific coast.[7] The World Health Organization estimates that up to 120 million people in Latin America—one-quarter of the region's total population—is at risk from cholera and other diseases.

This situation certainly illustrates the deadly consequences of the greed of international lenders coupled with the corruption and incompetence of the Latin American governments and elites. At the same time, it symbolizes the bankruptcy of the strategies that have been tried in the region and provides some useful development lessons.

A first lesson is that the opposition between "inward-oriented" and "outward-oriented" strategies is false and misleading. ISI did fail to relieve the foreign-exchange constraint, but the unilateral emphasis on export promotion through cutbacks in public services, wage reductions, and devaluations has weakened the domestic market, increased the vulnerability of the labor force, and in the long run is bound to reduce the very export potential that it would allegedly promote.

In the current world economic environment, the achievement of a "genuine"—as opposed to "spurious"—international competitiveness depends upon the development of several capacities, including the capacity to innovate in product and process designs, to develop sophisticated marketing networks, and to upgrade machinery and technology constantly. These capabilities require, in turn, investment in public services, a healthy and educated labor force, new types of relations within and between firms, and new types of institutions. Worker participation in decision-making processes, as well as the quality of education, health, and technological infrastructure, is a crucial ingredient in a truly competitive economy (Fajnzylber 1988).

Latin America has indeed increased exports during the 1980s, but against a background of poverty, inequality, and deterioration in health and public services. The increase in competitiveness claimed by EOI advocates, if it exists at all, has been purchased at too great a cost and does not provide a solid basis for the sustained expansion of exports in the future. In fact, the growth rate of gross domestic investment for the whole region dropped from 7.3 percent for the period 1961–80 to -2.1 percent for the period 1981–88 (IADB 1989:20).

A second lesson is that for an industrial strategy to be successful, the diversification of the export sector must be linked to the expansion of the domestic market. A growing domestic market provides the basic source of demand, particularly during the first stages in the development of new industries and products that can subsequently be targeted to foreign markets. At the same time, it fosters the social and economic integration of wide sectors of the population. The challenge is then to devise policies aimed at selectively expanding both export- and import-substitution capabilities, developing linkages and industrial complexes that diversify and integrate the productive structure, as many researchers have persuasively argued (Fajnzylber 1983; Iguiniz 1986; Torres-Rivas and Deutscher 1986; Ominami 1988).

These lessons, and the general orientations that emerge from them, have so far remained confined to the realm of "alternative policies" advocated by opposition groups. Moreover, the viability of any industrial strategy has been substantially reduced in the context of the debt crisis. Given the traditionally high imported component of investment, the expansion of import substituting *and* export capabilities along the lines proposed by "alternative policy" advocates would strain the balance of payments in a situation of extreme foreign-exchange scarcity.

There seem to be, in addition, other constraints related to what Victor Tokman (1987) calls "the weakness of the protagonists." The problem is the absence of a dynamic entrepreneurial class willing to risk its capital in investment projects that would relax the foreign-exchange constraint and improve the economic prospects of the region. Instead, local capitalists have been prone to send their capital abroad or to assume subordinated positions in alliances with foreign investors.

We are thus left in the uncomfortable position, pretty familiar in academic circles, of allegedly knowing what strategic industrial policies are required to improve the situation of the impoverished population but lacking the environment that would make them viable and the actors and political will to carry them out. As this position does not lead us anywhere, it is necessary to look elsewhere for inspiration and direction.

Territory, Institutions, and Industrial Reorganization

A major lesson of the debates presented above is that a development strategy, to be successful, cannot result from a set of policies crafted by a qualified group of experts. In fact, none of the strategies described above was based upon democratic participation of the majority of the population. Some "small victories" at a local level suggest that the only projects that work are those oriented to support ongoing processes and productive initiatives carried out by the beneficiaries.

The critical question is how—in the absence of unemployment insurance and social benefits—did the "unemployed" population in Latin America manage to survive the 1980s? More specifically, what forms of production organization have been successful in withstanding the crisis? What have been the strategies actually tried "from the bottom up," and how can they inform the design of industrial policies? Whereas the dynamism of collective survival activities has been widely acknowledged and sometimes documented,[8] the question is whether these activities can provide the basis for sustained development.

One of the most significant processes experienced in Latin America during the last two or three decades has been the development of diverse collective initiatives to cope with the most urgent needs (communal kitchens, health-care workshops, etc.), along with a wide range of small-scale activities. It has been estimated, for example, that in 1980 over 40 percent of the urban population in Latin America was working in what came to be known as the "informal sector."[9]

The nature and dynamics of the "informal sector" in the Third World have been hotly debated over the last several years. Widespread frustration with "the weakness of the protagonists" (Tokman 1987) has led many analysts to blame big firms for their lack of entrepreneurial leadership and to advocate massive support for small-scale industries. Several authors celebrate the dynamism of the informal sector (De Soto 1988) and the potential of small-scale manufacturing (Villarán 1987). Yet others have questioned this optimism, suggesting that small firms are unable to sell in international markets, have lower productivity compared to large firms (Lindlein 1988), and are doomed to disappear unless they receive substantial external support (Little, Mazumdar, and Page 1987).

Most studies, however, have focused on individual units, overlooking the role played by the institutional environment and the nature of cooperative interfirm relations. Along the same lines, the debates on industrial development in Latin America have generally stressed factors such as firm size, neglecting the significance of spatial and institutional factors in explaining concrete experiences of local industrialization.

Of course, by itself, neither firm size nor any other single factor can explain industrial development. With respect to size, for example, conventional studies on industrialization have exaggerated the importance of internal economies of scale, and recent changes in technology and organization at a worldwide level have reduced the efficient scale of production in several industries. There are other industries, however, in which relatively large scales of production are still necessary to produce efficiently at low unit costs. Many of these industries—such as chemicals, oil, refineries, cement— produce basic industrial inputs, and some of them generate substantial surpluses and foreign exchange.

It is, therefore, necessary to understand the conditions that determine the development of both large and small firms as well as the relations between them. In other words, the issue is not whether to promote small or large firms, "formal" or "informal" activities, the private or the public sector; rather, it is important to consider two opposite tendencies that have molded the process of industrial development both in the realm of theory and in the realm of practice.

The first tendency—which appears to be predominant, at least until the present—involves the development of "unembedded" business enterprises with no attachments to the territory in which they operate.[10] These firms pursue short-term profits and exploit local resources and labor through a variety of mechanisms that have been extensively documented in the development literature (Kay 1989:114). Typical examples are the multinational subsidiary operating in alliance with "modern" domestic capitalists and local authorities, and subordinated forms of subcontracting and "putting out" systems in which capitalist firms exploit artisan workshops or domestic outworkers (Beneria 1989; Portes 1990).

Alfred Marshall observed seventy years ago that "once an industry has fallen for the greater part into the hands of producers on a very large scale, there is on balance a tendency to a loosening of the ties that bound it to its old home" (1923:288). In the case of Latin America, this tendency can be illustrated by the substantial magnitude of capital that has fled the region through various channels, some of them fraudulent (Diaz-Alejandro 1984).

In fact, the Latin American elites have been sending abroad not only their capital but also their families. It should not be a surprise that they show little concern with the people and the environment in Latin America.

The second tendency, which has coexisted in opposition to the first, involves the development of what has been termed a "socially-oriented private sector," together with its own nonstate institutional sphere (Quijano 1988:112). Contrary to the first tendency, the economic institutions that constitute the engine of this process are wholly "embedded" in local social structures and "attached" to the localities and regions within which they operate. It is obviously difficult to evaluate the extent to which this tendency has developed solid foundations in the heterogeneous and diversified societies of Latin America. There are some signs, however, that

> a democratic form of organization based on solidarity and collective effort, which restores reciprocity as the foundation for solidarity and democracy, is currently one of the most widespread ways of organizing the day-to-day activities and life experiences of a vast portion of the population in Latin America as these people band together in an effort to survive. (Quijano 1988: 112)

Scattered evidence on the spread and dynamism of diverse collective initiatives and community actions supports this seemingly optimistic assessment.[11] A case in point is Villa El Salvador, a district located on the southern edge of the Lima metropolitan area, in Peru. This district was formed in 1971 when some five hundred impoverished families invaded a plot of land and constituted a so-called self-managed urban community. Villa El Salvador represents what is perhaps the most promising and paradigmatic experience of small-scale industrial development at a local level in Peru.[12] This experience is based on broad democratic participation within a dynamic institutional environment constituted by diverse grass-roots organizations such as communal kitchens, church groups, health-care workshops, women's groups, producers' associations, an industrial park, and an active, democratically elected, local government.

The achievements of Villa El Salvador cannot be overemphasized. It now has 250,000 inhabitants, living in relatively neat, self-constructed housing units. Almost two hundred nursery, elementary, and secondary schools have been built, mostly by community volunteers, and the rate of illiteracy has been substantially reduced. The residents of Villa El Salvador have set aside a thousand hectares for agriculture, and are gradually transforming a strip of desert land into a dynamic and environmentally sustainable territory (Annis and Franks 1989).

To be sure, Villa El Salvador is not a paradise. Capitalist private enterprise, understood in the conventional sense—that is, as a profit-maximizing unit that hires wage labor—is the prevailing form of economic activity throughout urban settlements such as Villa El Salvador. The conditions under which large segments of the population survive are so demanding that individualistic attitudes and practices often undermine the links of solidarity and reciprocity that are being patiently constructed. The existence of a sizable number of unemployed workers, for example, provides incentives for the small producers to compete on the basis of low wages, hindering the growth of the domestic market and the development of technical and entrepreneurial skills.

Furthermore, most of the small productive units operating in this context are characterized by low technological sophistication and a limited division of labor. Moreover, the exercise of monopoly power in some intermediate industries that sell inputs to small producers (steel, cement, leather, chemical products, etc.), as well as the subordinated forms of subcontracting referred to above, has obstructed the development of local systems of firms. Under these conditions, access to family labor has tended to reinforce gender inequalities and has further limited the possibilities of accumulation within the family firm.

Nonetheless, it is precisely because of these adverse conditions that complex organizational networks have emerged and developed at a local level as the only viable option for survival. Although the groups that constitute these networks (women's groups, communal kitchens, church groups, producers associations, etc.) have diverse objectives and operate within a context full of conflicts and contradictions, a shared history of struggles against diverse forms of oppression has forged active local communities bound together by strong links of solidarity. As Anibal Quijano acutely observes, the logic of capital interacts with the logic of reciprocity and solidarity and they affect and transform each other.

Perhaps the most suggestive aspect of this interaction is the nature of the institutional environment within which it operates. In fact, the institutions that constitute this environment have tended to build links and develop complex networks that, in some cases, spread across the country. But the main feature of this institutional sphere is that "it does not take the form of an institutional apparatus which sets itself apart from or which places itself above the social practices and the institutions associated with day-to-day life in society." These institutions, therefore, "do not represent a State power, but rather a type of power within society" (Quijano 1988:113).

Policy Implications

The potential of these emerging social institutions and their embedded business enterprises to prevail in the future will certainly depend on the consolidation and expansion of this power within society, but this is a process that requires much more than self-help survival activities. Along with the spread of communal kitchens, self-defense groups and basic health-care workshops, producer groups are uniting to learn how to produce more-sophisticated equipment and how to sell on the world market. Local governments in cooperation with diverse organizations are already promoting small-scale activities in some impoverished districts and localities.

These grass-roots experiences seem to be redefining the very meaning of politics, both in the realm of practice and in the realm of ideas, and may eventually lead to the constitution of a highly entrepreneurial political class. It would not be surprising if they shaped as well the transformation of national political institutions in the years to come. They have themselves become sufficiently institutionalized and seem to provide strategic ingredients for the development of a revolutionary alternative in these times of pessimism, instability, and change.

At the same time, we must admit, paraphrasing Arguedas, that our knowledge is much weaker than our hope. Little is known, for example, about the conditions that determine the constitution and dynamism of territorial systems of firms and how these systems can foster local industrialization and reduce urban poverty. In fact, most of the literature on collective action in the Third World has focused on rural areas where communities are sustained in part by the exploitation of common resources (water, grazing land, fisheries, etc.) (Wade 1988; Ostrom 1990; Uphoff 1989). There is little comparable knowledge of industrial development in urban areas, partly because the "common resources" that can be created and exploited in urban settings, as well as the very processes involved in their creation, are conceptually and empirically difficult to define using conventional analytical tools.

It is certainly urgent to develop a collective research agenda on alternative paths to development in the Third World. In a first stage, it might be appropriate to focus on small victories at the local level, pointing out the specific conditions that explain their success (including personal experiences and human dimensions). A second stage could build upon these case studies, broadening the scope to include comparative assessments of other less successful localities. Finally, research is needed on the sustainability of these local systems, particularly with regard to their performance in a situation of adverse sociopolitical and macroeconomic conditions. This performance can be evaluated, for example, in terms of their capacity to reduce urban and rural poverty, protect the environment, and relieve the foreign-exchange constraint.

With regard to policy alternatives, some implications are clear. In general, the best way to support local experiences of grass-roots development is through decentralization and democratization of existing institutions. Local and regional governments, democratically elected and accountable to their constituencies, must take the lead in the creation of the organizational structure required to support local systems of firms and independent producers. This structure can take the form of a network of quasi-public institutions such as local banks, financial and marketing consortia, service centers, and the like, jointly administered by producers' associations, local governments, and grass-roots organizations. The central purpose of service centers, for example, would be to perform basic functions that many small producers are unable to perform by themselves, such as technical training, research on markets and technology, accounting, marketing, and the provision of other specialized services.

Along the same lines, the major national institutions that formulate and implement fiscal, monetary, and trade policies must be decentralized and democratized to make them truly efficient. The particular institutional design will obviously depend on the peculiarities of each country and region, but the basic idea is the same: to make them more transparent and accountable to the people affected by their decisions.

The limitations of conventional policy tools and existing institutions go hand in hand with the weakness of economic theory to respond to the needs of the people and with the crisis of the nation–state in much of the Third World. A crucial step required to further specify the policy implications of the new strategy ought to be a critical review of the conceptual categories hitherto utilized and a careful evaluation of recent studies on economic organization and collective action.

This task certainly demands the interdisciplinary efforts of historians, geographers, anthropologists, sociologists, and so on. Their efforts will lead to meaningful results, however, only to the extent that they converge with the struggles and initiatives carried out from the bottom up. One of the most stimulating achievements of this convergence might well be to show the existence of common ground on which to build a broad and radical agenda both in the wealthy nations and in the Third World.

ACKNOWLEDGMENTS

The author wishes to thank the editors for their comments on earlier versions of this chapter.

NOTES

1. The term *forms of production organization* refers to the types of relations that exist among the people and institutions involved in the production of goods and services, particularly the relations within the production units, the extent to which workers participate in decision-making processes, the ways in which different firms interact, forms of cooperation and competition, and the roles of and interaction among the local government, producer associations, and other grass-roots organizations, etc.

2. In principle, the availability of hard currency is determined by the country's export earnings (including migrant workers' remittances), although in some

cases a permanent inflow of hard currency in the form of foreign aid, foreign investment, and commercial loans can sustain trade deficits for relatively long periods of
time. In these cases, the country's geopolitical location generally plays an important
role, as the experiences of Cuba, Israel, and Egypt illustrate.

3. Perhaps the most significant economic feature of the Latin American region is the relatively high degree of inequality compared to other regions of the
world. In the case of Brazil, for example, the richest 10 percent of the population get
46.2 percent of the national income, while the poorest 20 percent only receive 4.7
percent. Similar figures for Peru indicate that the richest 10 percent receive 35.8
percent, while the poorest 20 percent only get 4.4 percent of the national income. In
Venezuela these figures are 34.2 percent for the richest 10 percent and 4.7 percent
for the poorest 20 percent, in Guatemala 40.8 percent for the richest 10 percent
versus 5.5 percent for the poorest 20 percent, and in Colombia 37.1 percent for the
richest 10 percent versus only 4.0 percent for the poorest 20 percent. The years for
which these estimates were made are Brazil, 1983; Peru, 1985; Venezuela, 1987;
Guatemala, 1979–81; and Colombia, 1988. The source is the World Bank, *World
Development Report 1990* (Washington, D.C., 1990), 236–37.

4. In the larger countries of the region, import-substitution industrialization
did lead to the development of some capital-goods industries producing a wider
range of machinery and equipment. In the case of Brazil, the state has achieved some
degree of autonomy and bargaining power vis-à-vis foreign capital, but it is still
controlled by powerful domestic elites who have systematically opposed initiatives
and reforms aimed to reduce poverty and inequality. In fact, the World Bank development reports indicate that Brazil, the most industrialized country in Latin America, has at the same time one of the most unequal distributions of income in the
region and in the world.

5. Ian Little, Tibor Scitovsky, and Maurice Scott in 1970 provided one of
the first comprehensive expositions of the new strategy.

6. It has been estimated that the transfers from Latin American countries to
their creditors over the period 1980–87 were equivalent to about two times the
amount involved in the Marshall Plan that contributed to the reconstruction of Europe after the Second World War. See, for example, ADEC-ATC 1989.

7. Health experts fear that native peoples in the Amazon Basin, who have
resisted five hundred years of conquest and "civilization", could now be wiped out
by the cholera epidemic. For statistics on resources and health and sanitation services
in Latin America, see World Resources Institute 1990.

8. See, for example, Hirschman 1984, Uphoff 1989, and the publications of
the Inter-American Foundation, in particular its journal, *Grassroots Development*.

9. See, for example, Portes 1990. The concept of "informal sector" has been
used by different people for different purposes and has generated intense controver-
sies (Bromley 1978; Bromley and Gerry 1979; Tokman 1978). It is commonly used
to refer to a wide range of small-scale activities in industry, commerce, and services.
These ventures are generally unregistered and unprotected and presumably have
many characteristics in common, which justifies their being distinguished from the
"formal sector" constituted by modern capitalist units.

10. The distinction between "embedded" and "unembedded" economic institutions was originally proposed by Karl Polanyi, Conrad Arensberg, and Harry Pear-

son (1957). It is referred to by Clifford Geertz (1963:89) in the context of local development in Indonesia.

11. For the Peruvian case, see Thorp 1989, Franco 1989, and Quijano 1988. Frances Stewart and Gustav Ranis (1990:35) suggest that these experiences are also found in other national contexts in Latin America, although their evidence is not conclusive. Albert Hirschman (1984), on the other hand, introduces the notion of "social energy" to refer to the dynamism of some collective activities—most of them in commerce and services and a few in manufacturing—supported by the Inter-American Foundation, a nonprofit organization specializing in the promotion and financing of grass-roots initiatives.

12. The experience of Villa El Salvador is not unusual in the Peruvian context, but it is certainly the most publicized and perhaps the most dynamic one (Annis and Franks 1989; IPIA 1989).

BIBLIOGRAPHY

ADEC-ATC. 1989. *The Third World Giant Debt*. Lima: Asociación Trabajo y Cultura.

Annis, Sheldon, and Jeffrey Franks. 1989. The Idea, Ideology, and Economics of the Informal Sector: The Case of Peru. *Grassroots Development* 13:9–22.

Beneria, Lourdes. 1989. Gender and the Global Economy. In *Instability and Change in the World Economy*, ed. Arthur MacEwan and William K. Tabb, 241–58. New York: Monthly Review Press.

Bromley, Ray. 1978. The Urban Informal Sector: Why Is It Worth Discussing? *World Development* 6(9/10): 1033–39.

Bromley, Ray and Chris Gerry, eds. 1979. *Casual Work and Poverty in Third World Cities*. Chichester, West Sussex: John Wiley.

De Soto, Hernando. 1988. *El otro sendero*. Lima: Instituto Libertad y Democracia.

Diaz-Alejandro, Carlos. 1984. Latin American Debt: I Don't Think We Are in Kansas Anymore. *Brookings Papers on Economic Activity* 2:335–403.

Fajnzylber, Fernando. 1983. *La industrializacion trunca de America Latina*. Mexico, D.F.: Nueva Imagen.

———. 1988. International Competitiveness: Agreed Goal, Hard Task. *CEPAL Review* 36:7–23.

Franco, Carlos. 1989. *El Peru de los 80s: Un camino posible*. Lima: Centro de Estudios para el Desarrollo y la Participación.

Geertz, Clifford. 1963. *Peddlers and Princes: Social Change and Economic Modernization in Two Indonesian Towns*. Chicago: University of Chicago Press.

Hirschman, Albert. 1984. *Getting Ahead Collectively: Grassroots Experiences in Latin America*. New York: Pergamon Press.

Iguiniz, Javier. 1986. *Sistema economico y estrategia de desarrollo peruano*. Lima: Tarea.

Instituto Peruano de Información Aplicada (IPIA). 1989. *Circuitos productivos: La pequena produccion de villa El Salvador*. Lima: F. Ebert.

Inter-American Development Bank (IADB). 1989. *Economic and Social Progress in Latin America, 1989 Report*. Washington, D.C.: Inter-American Development Bank.

Kay, Cristobal. 1989. *Latin American Theories of Development and Underdevelopment.* New York: Routledge.

Lindlein, Peter. 1988. *Smart Is Beautiful.* Lima: F. Ebert.

Little, Ian, Dipaz Mazumdar, and John Page. 1987. *Small Manufacturing Enterprises: A Comparative Study of India and Other Economies.* New York: Oxford University Press for the World Bank.

Little, Ian, Tibor Scitovsky, and Maurice Scott. 1970. *Industry and Trade in Some Developing Countries.* London: OECD.

Marshall, Alfred. 1923. *Industry and Trade.* 4th. ed. London: Macmillan.

Moser, Caroline. 1978. Informal Sector or Petty Commodity Production: Dualism or Dependence in Urban Development. *World Development* 6(9/10): 1041–64.

Ominami, Carlos. 1988. Doce proposiciones acerca de America Latina en una era de profundo cambio tecnologico. *Pensamiento Iberoamericano* 13:49–65.

Ostrom, Elinor. 1990. *Governing the Commons: The Evolution of Institutions for Collective Action.* New York: Cambridge University Press.

Polanyi, Karl, Conrad Arensberg, and Harry Pearson. 1957. *Trade and Markets in the Early Empires.* Glencoe, Ill.: Free Press.

Portes, Alejandro. 1990. When More Can Be Less: Labor Standards, Development, and the Informal Economy. Distinguished Speaker Series, no. 7. Center for Advanced Study of International Development (CASID), East Lansing, Mich. Mimeo.

Quijano, Anibal. 1988. A Different Concept of the Private Sector, a Different Concept of the Public Sector: Notes for a Latin American Debate. *CEPAL Review* 35:105–20.

Stewart, Frances, and Gustav Ranis. 1990. Macro-Policies for Appropriate Technology: A Synthesis of Findings. In *The Other Policy,* ed. Frances Steward, Hank Thomas, and Ton DeWilde, 3–42. Washington, D.C.: IT Publications in association with Appropriate Technology International.

Thorp, Rosemary. 1989. Surviving Chaos. *New Internationalist* 197:18–19.

Tokman, Victor. 1978. An Exploration into the Nature of Informal-Formal Sector Relations. *World Development* 6(9/10): 1065–75.

———. 1987. The Process of Accumulation and the Weakness of the Protagonists. *CEPAL Review* 26:115–26.

Torres-Rivas, Edelberto, and Eckhard Deutscher, eds. 1986. *Industrializacion en America Latina: Crisis y perspectivas.* San Jose: Facultad Latinoamericana de Ciencias Sóciales y Centro de Estudios Democráticos de América Latina.

Uphoff, Norman. 1989. Drawing on Social Energy in Project Implementation: A Learning Process Experience in Sri Lanka. Cornell University, Center for International Studies, Ithaca, N.Y. Mimeo.

Villáran, Fernando. 1987. *La pequeña empresa: Una alternativa tecnológica para el desarrollo industrial.* Lima: F. Ebert.

Wade, Robert. 1988. *Village Republics: Economic Conditions for Collective Action in South India.* New York: Cambridge University Press.

World Resources Institute. 1990. *World Resources 1990–91.* New York: Oxford University Press.

22
CARMEN DIANA DEERE
STAN MALINOWITZ

Third World Socialism and the Demise of COMECON

During the 1970s there was a virtual explosion in the number of successful revolutions across the Third World, bringing with them the hope that more egalitarian societies could solve the endemic problems of poverty and underdevelopment. Radical, revolutionary regimes came to power during that decade in Africa (Ethiopia, Guinea Bissau, Angola, Mozambique, Somalia, Zimbabwe), Asia (South Vietnam, Laos, Cambodia, Afghanistan), the Middle East (South Yemen, Syria, Libya), and even in the United States' backyard, the Caribbean Basin (Nicaragua and Grenada). They joined the earlier socialist regimes of North Vietnam, North Korea, and Cuba, as well as the progressive experiments of the 1960s and 1970s in Algeria, Tanzania, Chile, and Jamaica, in rejecting dependent capitalism as *the* development path for the Third World.

Most of the revolutionary regimes proclaimed adherence to a vision of socialism as the principal alternative to capitalism. But the content of these visions differed substantially, reflecting in part the unique heritage and circumstances faced by each country. For most, socialism meant a process of transforming the inherited structures of underdevelopment into a new system of production and distribution that would aim at minimum to meet the basic needs of the majority of their populations and end inequality based on class and other forms of privilege.[1] Such a transformation would involve some degree of social rather than private ownership of the productive forces in the economy, as well as some level of planning of economic decision making rather than exclusive reliance on markets for allocation of resources. Not all of the revolutionary regimes considered the state socialist model associated with the Soviet Union and Eastern Europe to be the goal of their transitions. And not all adhered to Marxist–Leninist ideology, by which the revolutionary party maintains a monopoly on state power as the representative of the popular classes.

Besides a commitment to meeting the basic needs of their populations, what many of these revolutionary regimes shared was the search for alternative development paradigms rooted in their own national identity and—particularly among those whose victories had been a product of wars of national liberation or armed insurrections—a commitment to popular participation as a key element of the transition. They also shared anti-imperialist views. Either colonial rule or rule by a U.S.-backed dictator had convinced most of these revolutionary leaderships that the world capitalist system did not work in the interests of their countries and their poor majorities. Rather, capitalist integration had meant the subordination of the domestic economy to the interests of foreign capital and had generated growing poverty, underdevelopment, and blatant internal inequalities between rich and poor.

In addition, many of these revolutionary regimes immediately felt the power and wrath of imperialism firsthand, as the United States, in particular, tried directly or indirectly to undermine their revolutions. Under the Reagan Doctrine, the United States pledged to confront the Soviet Union throughout the Third World through support to counterrevolutionary forces and through outright intervention. Although few of the revolutionary regimes of the 1970s had come to power through direct Soviet support (Afghanistan being the main exception), and although few became economically dependent on the Soviet Union, the United States was determined to ensure the failure of any experiment of a noncapitalist nature.

Even before the demise of state socialism in Eastern Europe and the disintegration of the Soviet Union, the United States had been largely successful in undermining many of these experiments in transition to socialism. By the early 1990s, the United States had invaded Grenada, succeeded through the damage wrought by the Contra war in Nicaragua in having the Sandinistas voted out of power, and forced the Soviets out of Afghanistan through support to counterrevolutionary forces, leading to an impasse in that country.

In addition, in a number of cases (Angola, Mozambique, Ethiopia, South Yemen), the transition was put on hold or aborted due to internal, often ethnic, strife, sometimes abetted by U.S. destabilization measures. In other cases (Syria, Libya, Somalia), the revolutionary regimes ended up being not very socialist and certainly not very democratic. Moreover, the costs of withdrawing from the world capitalist system or of facing the wrath of imperialism also caused several of these regimes to lose their revolutionary fervor early on (Zimbabwe, Guinea Bissau).

Another commonality in these experiments in transition was the difficulty they experienced in transforming the inherited structures of underdevelopment. Far from meeting Marx's precondition—that socialism would evolve out of developed capitalism—many of these countries were among the poorest countries in the world when their revolutions occurred. Most were agro-export economies, heavily dependent on one or two primary products for foreign exchange. Their dependency on the world capitalist market for export revenue and their lack of an industrial infrastructure— which necessitated growing levels of imports to raise living standards (whether to meet basic needs, to modernize peasant agriculture, or to create new industries to meet basic needs and generate employment)—meant that their very survival, let alone transformation, depended on continuing access to world markets and significant aid transfers.

Facing U.S. hostility, many turned to the socialist camp for increased trade and aid. But by the 1970s, the Soviets were unwilling to make major new economic commitments in the Third World, given their own economic stagnation. While a number of countries received Soviet military assistance at some point (Angola, Mozambique, Ethiopia), none received the levels of development assistance that Cuba and Vietnam, revolutions born at the height of the cold war era, received.

Notwithstanding the obstacles, a number of the revolutionary experiments did achieve quite a bit in their initial years. The revolutionary governments in Nicaragua, Grenada, Mozambique, and Angola carried out relatively successful literacy campaigns. Most struggled with limited resources to develop some kind of rudimentary system of national health care, or at least of disease prevention. A few carried out substantial land reforms, breaking the power of the landlord class and giving peasants the possibility to become self-sufficient or modern farmers on cooperative farms (Deere 1986). But as noted above, most carried out these basic transformations in a hostile context, if not on war footing, and the gains in meeting basic needs were subsequently lost.

Of all the countries that have attempted a transition to socialism, the most successful have been those which initiated their transitions in the 1950s, especially Cuba and North Korea (Vietnam's economic development was of course held back by the war). What they have in common, besides their longevity, is that their initial transitions were assisted by substantial Soviet support, partly explained by the intensity of the cold war in that period. Cuba and Vietnam, along with Mongolia, became the only Third World members of COMECON (the Council for Mutual Economic Assistance, also called CMEA), the socialist trading bloc, and received preferential prices for their exports and a guaranteed market, as well as significant amounts of credits to increase their import levels. They also received direct development assistance, often in the form of complete, new factories and considerable technical assistance. For example, Soviet aid to Cuba was estimated as being as high as an annual $2 to $3 billion in the late 1980s, if subsidies on sugar exports, oil imports, military assistance, and technical assistance are totaled.[2] Vietnamese officials estimated that their country re-

TABLE 22.1
Trade with USSR and Eastern Europe as a Percentage of
Total Foreign Trade, 1980

	Imports		Exports	
Country	USSR	Eastern Europe[a]	USSR	Eastern Europe[a]
Afghanistan	52.7	1.0	59.3	2.6
Angola	0.6	4.6	0.8	5.2
Cuba	60.8	12.4	54.3	5.4
Ethiopia	19.3	5.3	9.2	3.5
Mozambique	1.9	11.5	—	—
Nicaragua	0.1	0.1	2.0	0.1
N. Korea	27.0	—	60.8	—
Vietnam	44.4	—	60.8	—

Source: United Nations, *International Trade Statistics Yearbook,* 1986, vol. 1; EIU, *Country Profile: North Korea* (London: The Economist, 1990–91); Kimura 1989. [a]Figures for Eastern Europe include Bulgaria, Czechoslovakia, East Germany, Hungary, Poland, and Romania.

ceived about $16.6 billion in assistance, credits, commodity aid, technical assistance, and written-off loans from Moscow in the last five years of the 1980s (Pike 1991:83).[3]

Table 22.1 shows the percentage of foreign trade that was conducted with the Soviet Union and Eastern Europe in 1980 for a number of Third World countries with revolutionary regimes. Cuba, Vietnam, and to a lesser extent North Korea continued to rely heavily on trade with the COMECON countries, especially the Soviet Union. For countries whose revolutions came later, trade with COMECON members played a much lesser role (Afghanistan again being the exception).

In January 1990 COMECON members agreed to switch to hard-currency trade as of 1991 and stopped the practice of planning five-year trade agreements. One year later, the member countries agreed on plans to dissolve COMECON completely. For Cuba and Vietnam this means the loss of assured markets and the security of the trade agreements, as well as lower prices for their exports and a rising import bill. These as well as other Third World nations have felt a steady reduction in trade credits, aid, and technical assistance from what was the Soviet bloc.

The demise of COMECON motivates the main question of this chapter: Is there a future for Third World socialism without the existence of a socialist bloc? To begin to answer this question, we review the implications of the demise of COMECON for three countries, examining how they have responded to this event and how it may affect their future development possibilities. The case studies include two of the enduring socialist transitions—Cuba and Vietnam—and one of the failures, Mozambique. The three have confronted the current crisis in quite different ways. While Cuba has maintained its commitment to a centrally planned economy, Vietnam has responded by increasing the role of markets in its still largely planned economy. In contrast, Mozambique, which has suffered extreme duress, has largely returned to dependent capitalism. All three are urgently seeking new trading partners and have been forced once again to welcome foreign private investment.

Cuba

The demise of COMECON presented Cuba with a challenge almost as great as the trade embargo imposed on that island in 1960 by the United States, the year after the triumph of the Cuban revolution. Subsequently, after the failed U.S.-sponsored Bay of Pigs invasion by Cuban exiles, the Cuban leadership announced its socialist path and over that decade came to rely increasingly on the socialist bloc for aid and trade. As Cuba became integrated into COMECON trade on the basis of its comparative advantage in sugar production, an initial goal of attaining food self-sufficiency was largely abandoned. Nonetheless, while specializing in sugar exports, the benefits to Cuba from participation in COMECON allowed a significant industrialization effort, one that extended to capital-goods industries in the decade of the 1980s, largely to service the crucial agricultural sector (Zimbalist and Brundenius 1989:87). The demise of COMECON and the disintegration of the Soviet Union have forced the Cuban leadership to again reconsider the nation's development strategy, although not its commitment to socialism.

COMECON countries had accounted for 85 percent of Cuban trade, with the Soviet Union accounting for 71 percent and Eastern Europe 14 percent in the 1986–1988 period (CEE 1988:table XI.18). Cuba relied on the Soviet Union for 90 percent of its petroleum requirements and for most of its food and capital goods imports. Trade with Eastern Europe, though much less important than with the Soviets, had been crucial in certain sectors, with Hungary the major source of buses and the former German Democratic Republic (East Germany) the major source of raw materials for the pharmaceutical industry.

The "Special Period in Peacetime"
By early 1990, Soviet deliveries of wheat and petroleum had become increasingly unreliable, and Eastern European countries refused to renegotiate trade agreements and failed to make contracted deliveries. It has been

estimated that in 1990 Cuban exports to Eastern Europe fell by 50 percent of their 1989 level (EIU 1990a:no.3,21). Over the course of 1990 it also became apparent that the Soviet Union was not going to be able to deliver the 13.3 million tons of petroleum promised for that year. The repercussions for the Cuban economy were daunting, affecting both foreign-exchange earnings and domestic production. Reexport of surplus petroleum and petroleum products had been Cuba's second major source of hard-currency earnings, following sugar. In August 1990, when it was estimated that the oil shortfall would be on the order of 20 percent (it ended up being 25 percent for the year), Cuban officials announced a series of rather severe energy conservation measures. In September, as additional emergency measures—such as extended rationing—were put into effect, it was announced that Cuba was officially in a "special period in peacetime," a period to be characterized by austerity and sacrifice.[4]

The most severe of the conservation measures was a mandated 50 percent cut in energy consumption across all state industries and services. This would come about primarily by reducing the number of work shifts in some industries and by closing down other industries altogether, especially those that were energy-intensive or that relied on scarce imported inputs. To avoid growing unemployment, it was hoped that the "excess" workers released by these industries would work in the agricultural sector, where labor was needed for the renewed drive for food self-sufficiency. Another source of energy conservation would come from reductions in private consumption of gasoline and electricity and in public transportation; bicycles have increasingly filled the streets of Havana. In addition, imports of energy-intensive appliances were cut severely.

The rationing system was extended considerably for both industrial products and foodstuffs. Instead of raising prices to reduce demand for products in short supply, the rationing system controls the quantities available to households in order to ensure their equitable distribution.

New Strategies

Even before the special period went into effect, Cuba had launched a National Food Program, designed to make the country more self-sufficient in food products through major new investments in agriculture and improvements in the food distribution system. Although Cuba had significantly reduced its dependence on food imports over the last two decades,[5] the changing conditions of trade with the Soviet Union and Eastern Europe necessitated deeper measures. The food program was also an outcome of the broader process of "rectification of errors" in the management of the Cuban economy that began in 1986 (Azicri 1990). In that year, Cuba ended its brief experiment with free peasant markets—partly because they were viewed as a corrupting influence and led to growing income and consumption inequalities—and the state began searching for ways to improve the food distribution system while also maintaining the diversity of foodstuffs these markets had provided. The food program aims to lessen Cuba's vulnerability to the ongoing changes in its trade relations by import substitution—producing domestically food products that it previously imported—primarily through massive investments in the land acreage under irrigation and in storage capacity.[6]

In addition to promoting import substitution and pursuing food security, the Cubans are attempting to adjust to the demise of COMECON by diversifying their exports as well as their trading partners. Cuba has pursued diversification of its agricultural exports throughout the last decade and has also invested considerable resources in the biotechnology, medical equipment, and pharmaceutical industries, with an eye toward the hard-currency market. In terms of new trading partners, in recent years trade has been growing most rapidly with China; a five-year trading agreement between the two countries was signed in January 1991, valued at about U.S.$500 million. Cuban officials are also counting on increased trade with Latin America; trade has already increased from an average annual $330 million in the mid-1980s to an estimated $600 million in 1989 (EIU 1990a: no.1, 21).

In the short run, the nations of the former Soviet Union remain Cuba's most important trading partners, but the volume of total trade is declining steadily. The last trade agreement with the former Soviet Union (for 1991) did continue to grant Cuba a preferential (above world market) price for sugar exports, although less than before; nonsugar trade, including petroleum, was at world market prices.

New sources of investment capital are also being sought. Since 1982, Cuba has had a foreign investment law that allows joint ventures with up to 49 percent foreign ownership and profit repatriation in hard currency; it also offers a ten-year tax holiday to investors. Not until 1987, however, did Cuba actively seek out foreign investment. Since then, Spain, Italy, Finland, Mexico, and Venezuela have invested in joint ventures in the tourism sector, reported to total around $800 million in new investment (EIU 1990a:no.4, 20). There are also joint ventures in the electronics, petrochemical, pharmaceutical, textile, and machinery industries. Cuba is currently trying to encourage joint ventures in offshore gas and oil exploration.

In sum, Cuba is attempting to meet the challenge of the post–cold war era by diversifying its trading partners and the composition of its exports, by seeking enhanced food security through import substitution, by relaxing its long-held opposition to foreign investment, and by extending central planning. Somewhat ironically, only by extending central planning—in terms of reduced energy consumption, greater rationing, planned investment in food production, and labor mobilizations—do Cubans believe that they can maintain an equitable distribution of the costs of the general demise of centrally planned economies. They also believe that central planning guarantees a smoother transition to growing trade within the capitalist world economy.

Vietnam

When Vietnam set out on the difficult path of national reconstruction in 1975, the country faced the enormous obstacles left by thirty years of war, first against French colonialism and then against the U.S. intervention. Millions of people had been killed, about five million hectares of forest land had been destroyed or damaged, and the infrastructure and other material resources had been devastated by the heaviest onslaught of explosives in the history of human warfare. Independence and reunification of North and South Vietnam had come at a high cost in every sense of the word.

At the time of formal reunification in 1976, 50 percent of Vietnam's foreign trade was with COMECON countries (Petrasovits 1988:215). North Vietnam's trade with and aid from COMECON as well as China had increased steadily since the Communist party took power in 1954. Vietnamese dependence upon COMECON subsequently increased after reunification, largely because of its growing isolation from other potential sources of aid, particularly after Vietnam's military intervention in Cambodia in 1978, in which they overthrew the Khmer Rouge government led by Pol Pot. China, which backed the Khmer Rouge, now became a bitter adversary. The United States has had a trade embargo in effect since 1975 and has repeatedly blocked Vietnamese attempts to join the IMF or to secure aid from multinational agencies like the World Bank. Other countries, including Japan and some Western European countries, cut back on aid and trade in response to U.S. pressure, especially after the invasion of Cambodia.

Also, in 1978, Vietnam became the third less-developed country to join COMECON and signed a Treaty of Friendship and Cooperation with the Soviet Union. By 1981, 85 percent of its trade was with COMECON (Petrasovits 1988). The Soviet Union was by far the largest trading partner, absorbing well over half of Vietnam's total exports to the COMECON countries, in addition to providing the largest portion of aid.

The largest portion of imports from the COMECON countries consisted of investment goods—machinery, energy, and raw materials—for the development of heavy industry. Basic necessities made up a smaller proportion of imports, although this proportion had grown over the years. Aid from the Soviet Union was instrumental in building up the nation's infrastructure. Vietnam also benefited from a "contract labor" system with COMECON by which more than 200,000 workers yearly were sent abroad on contract, mostly to the Soviet Union and East Germany.

Declining Aid

These economic relations changed drastically in light of the economic crisis and restructuring in the Soviet Union, the sudden changes in Eastern Europe, and the subsequent collapse of COMECON and the USSR. Before, Vietnam benefited from a net inflow of resources, with the other COMECON countries willing to bear the costs until such time as Vietnam had developed economic conditions that would allow it to deal with them as an equal partner. Now, relations with those countries will depend more on the international market than on principles of international solidarity.

Aid from the COMECON countries has been reduced dramatically and in many cases eliminated, and special trade agreements have not been renewed, as in the case of Cuba. Trade is conducted in hard currency at world market prices. Bilateral trade with the Soviet Union was expected to total less than U.S.$1 billion in 1991, down from over U.S.$3 billion in 1990 (Hiebert 1991:25). Trade credits were also reduced, and Vietnam's trade deficit with both the former Soviet Union and Eastern Europe has had to shrink, mainly by Vietnam curtailing its imports. The Soviet Union used to provide Vietnam with 80 percent of its oil requirements at below-market prices. In 1990 they agreed to provide no more than 55 percent and failed to deliver even that much (EIU 1990b:no.4,25). Vietnam is thus forced to find other sources, but with high oil prices on the world market they have no choice but to reduce energy consumption. Industrial production, heavily dependent on oil, is being cut back.

The former Soviet Union has also cut back on supplies of other vital inputs, including fertilizer, steel, and cotton. The shortage of fertilizer and other agricultural inputs has already resulted in declining agricultural output (EIU 1990b:no. 3,20). Cotton is being planted domestically to make up for the loss of Soviet cotton for the textile industry, but most areas lack good prospects for import substitution. Vietnam's response to the growing shortage of supplies is thus to cut back on production, at least in the short run, and to look toward nonsocialist countries for new trading partners, though not with the favorable terms they once enjoyed with their COMECON partners.

The slowdown of production puts strains on the ability to produce enough marketable export products to finance needed imports from new sources. Borrowing to finance Vietnam's growing trade deficit is constrained by the influence of the U.S. blockade on potential sources of loans or aid, including banks, private donors, and other governments, as well as the IMF and World Bank. Vietnam is also encouraging foreign investment, for which oil and gas exploration have drawn the strongest response. The countries accounting for the largest shares of foreign investment have been Great Britain, Canada, the Netherlands, Hong Kong, France, and Australia. Japan, Taiwan, and other East Asian countries are also showing interest in expanding investment as well as trade with Vietnam (EIU 1990b:no.3, 29).

Internal Reforms

The liberalization of foreign investment laws is one of a series of economic reforms begun in 1986. These reforms reduced the scope of central planning and moved Vietnam in the direction of a market-led economy, although one in which a strong centralized administrative apparatus is maintained and the Communist party still keeps its leading role. The hope is that allocation of resources through markets will overcome some of the inefficiencies of central planning and steer the country away from economic crisis. Some dissenting voices in the government believe that the solution is not less planning but better planning, and that too much reliance on the market will jeopardize many of their socialist aims and force the poorest sectors of the population to bear the heaviest costs of adjustment.[7]

The market reforms together with sharp decreases in subsidies and other forms of public spending helped to rein in the high level of inflation caused in part by the increasing prices of imports. But one consequence of these policies was a decline in the standard of living of most of the population and a growing problem of unemployment, aggravated by the return of guest workers from Eastern Europe and the USSR and the demobilization of troops from Cambodia, as well as by layoffs of workers in the scaled-down state sector. They also face increasing social problems, such as declining social services (including health and education), increasing child malnutrition, drug addiction, corruption, and other forms of crime. The reforms called for increased private ownership of enterprises. This was originally aimed at small-scale projects, where central planning is less effective and private control likely to be more efficient. But with the new opportunities and incentives for foreign investment, private ownership increasingly involves large-scale projects owned by foreign corporations. Whatever the economic benefits may be, this process reduces the government's control over the economy without transferring that control to the Vietnamese population.

Vietnam's economic system is in a state of transition whose outcome cannot be predicted with any certainty. Two trends that seem certain to continue are the increasing use of internal market mechanisms and increasing dependence on foreign markets, which, with the demise of COMECON, means increasing dependence on the capitalist world. It remains to be seen how far these trends will go and how they will affect the long-standing revolutionary goals of equality and independence for which the Vietnamese fought so long and hard.

Mozambique

In November of 1990 the People's Republic of Mozambique officially changed its name to the Republic of Mozambique. Earlier, the ruling

FRELIMO party had officially abandoned Marxism–Leninism, renounced its role as the vanguard party of the workers and peasants, and called for multiparty elections. Along with these political changes, Mozambique is pursuing an economic strategy along the lines promoted by the Western capitalist nations. Its Economic Recovery Program, pursued since 1987 with the sponsorship of the IMF and World Bank, calls for private enterprise and market forces as guiding principles for the economy. Although preserving some role for the state to regulate and promote economic growth, it is a long way from the socialist system envisaged by FRELIMO through the long struggle for independence and the early years of national reconstruction following the victory in 1975 over the Portuguese colonizers.

FRELIMO inherited from Portugal a shattered colonial economy that was heavily dependent on neighboring South Africa. In order to maintain its regional dominance, South Africa has engaged in economic, political, and military aggression to destabilize Mozambique. Much of this aggression has been carried out by the South African–backed RENAMO guerrillas. Economic development efforts have consistently been thwarted by RENAMO's terror and destruction and by the need to devote scarce resources to military purposes.

Although there were significant improvements in the quality of life in the early years of the revolutionary government, including impressive advances in education and health, the situation in recent years has grown increasingly desperate. About half of the population of 16 million faces serious food deprivation, and there is danger of even more widespread famine and starvation. An estimated 60 percent of the population are said to be living in conditions of absolute poverty (Ayisi 1991:24). Millions depend on food aid, but outside aid has not been enough. There has been a great deal of difficulty delivering much of the food aid that has arrived, because of RENAMO attacks on roads and other transport facilities, as well as shortages of fuel.

The loss of aid from the COMECON countries led to even greater dependence on the West. The Soviet Union had been important to Mozambique mostly for military aid and for oil imports. Military support has now been cut, and with peace apparently still some distance away, it is not clear who will fill this vacuum. Soviet oil had in the past been provided on credit at favorable terms, accounting for about two-thirds of Mozambique's oil needs. The nations of the former Soviet Union now insist on world market prices and hard-currency payments for their oil, as they are doing elsewhere. Mozambican officials expect their total oil bill approximately to double from having to buy on the open market, although the actual effect will depend on movements in world oil prices. Overall, Soviet aid to Mozambique was reduced from its former level of about $200 million annually to about $90 million in 1990 and has continued to fall (EIU 1990c:38). The emphasis in bilateral relations is moving from aid to trade. This is also true of the Eastern European countries, of which East Germany had been the most important source of assistance.

Assistance to Mozambique from the COMECON countries had always been limited. Mozambique had actually tried to join COMECON in the early 1980s and was turned down. It was clear for most of the decade that the Soviet Union, preoccupied with its own economic problems, would no longer provide Third World revolutionary governments with the massive level of assistance it had once given to Cuba, Vietnam, and Mongolia. Thus, Mozambique had for some years seen little choice but to turn to the West for aid. In fact, the diversion of Western resources from the Third World to Eastern Europe may be a more serious consequence of changes in that region than the loss of Soviet bloc aid.

By the end of 1986, the war had cost Mozambique an estimated $5.5 billion in economic losses. Faced with few options and a deteriorating situation, the government turned to the IMF and World Bank and agreed to implement a structural adjustment program, known as the Economic Recovery Program, which was a condition for receiving loans and development assistance from those agencies. The terms of the program, familiar to many nonsocialist Third World countries, included decreasing state subsidies and other public expenditures, expanding the role of the private sector through privatization of state enterprises and loosening of state controls over the economy, and letting market forces operate more freely to regulate both domestic and international trade and finance.

The austerity measures hit the poorest sectors the hardest, because they lost subsidies on medicines and essential food items as well as other public services. The brief, though modest, appearance of positive growth rates of gross domestic product has more recently been reversed, largely from the war's continuing effects on agricultural output. Nevertheless, the Economic Recovery Program continues, with the reform effort focused on privatization of public enterprises, increasing exports to generate foreign-exchange earnings, and attracting foreign investment.

Much hope for economic recovery is being placed on foreign investment, which the Mozambican government is actively trying to promote. The largest investors have been Great Britain, the United States, the Netherlands, South Africa, Portugal, Spain, and Italy, in that order (EIU 1990c:36). Ironically, South African businesses are now seen as the most promising source of new investments. The Mozambican government is trying to improve relations with South Africa, which, despite being the source of such intense and prolonged destabilization, is now seen as the main hope for economic salvation. South Africa's interest in the region is considered permanent, unlike Western countries, whose resources can suddenly be diverted to other parts of the world.

Internal opposition to the reform program exists. Several members of the Assembly of the Republic (formerly known as the People's Assembly) have argued against the recovery program, which they blame for worsening the plight of the country's already desperately poor people. They claim that all the benefits go to foreign investors, who find it much easier to open bank accounts, obtain land, and start businesses than Mozambicans. Defenders of the program reply that there is no alternative to austerity and appealing to foreign benefactors. They claim that only the war is preventing a more rapid trickling down of the benefits (EIU 1990c:29).

No one doubts that the war is at the root of the country's problems or that the loss of aid from the former COMECON countries aggravated those problems and restricted Mozambique's options. There is also widespread agreement that FRELIMO made many damaging policy errors in the early years of independence. The debate centers on whether it was necessary to abandon rather than reform socialism, on whether such painful austerity measures and the growing inequalities they foster were really the best solution, and on what alternatives there are to throwing the country at the mercy of foreign donors and investors. Opponents of the recovery program feel that the overly centralized system should be replaced by a more democratic socialism encouraging popular participation and grass-roots initiative, rather than top-down decisions by the leadership aiming to reintegrate into the capitalist system. With foreign aid conditional on internal reforms satisfactory to the donor countries and the multinational institutions, many feel that national sovereignty has been unacceptably compromised. On the other hand, the desperate conditions resulting from the devastation of war and the loss of support from the former socialist bloc severely limit Mozambique's options. As one observer put it: "It is very difficult to follow an anti-imperialist policy when you are utterly dependent upon the imperialists to feed your people".[8]

As the profiles of Cuba, Vietnam, and Mozambique illustrate, the demise of COMECON and the undoing of state socialism in the Soviet Union have had tremendous repercussions on Third World revolutionary regimes that had come to depend on their previously assured markets, better terms of trade, and substantial aid. Socialist Third World countries have attempted to meet the new challenge in diverse ways, with Cuba extending central planning, while Vietnam attempts to perfect socialism through greater reliance on market mechanisms and private investment. Mozambique has given up on any transition at all and is currently experiencing the pain, not just of civil war and previous policy mistakes, but of IMF structural adjustment programs designed to create a free market economy.

In this context, the future possibilities for Third World socialism look bleak. But it is important to recall that the Soviet model of state socialism had been rejected by many socialists across the globe long before its collapse in Eastern Europe and its crisis in the Soviet Union. The historical association of socialism with *state* socialism—including rigid central planning, state ownership of all means of production, bureaucratic rule, and lack of democratic practices—for too long distorted the democratic vision of socialism in the Marxist classics and in traditional socialist thought (Bengelsdorf 1986). It also doomed to failure many of the transitions that attempted to copy this model of development under conditions quite different from those in which it had developed in the Soviet Union. Perhaps one beneficial effect of the demise of state socialism for the future of socialism is that the profoundly democratic vision of socialism, grounded in popular participation and democratic practices, might again resurface.[9]

What is also clear is that the end of state socialism does not mean the end of revolution in the Third World. After all, capitalism has also failed to provide very many success stories in the Third World.[10] Moreover, the debt crisis of the 1980s and the structural adjustment policies imposed upon these countries to service their debt—which lowered living standards in most Third World countries to levels prevailing in 1970 or even 1960—continue to demonstrate that the international capitalist system is not a very friendly place.

The fundamental development dilemma for the Third World has yet to be solved, and as long as these countries continue to be plagued by rampant poverty and inequality, revolutionary struggles to create more just systems will continue to erupt. It is important to recall that there are ongoing revolutionary struggles in Guatemala, the Philippines, and South Africa, to name a few. It is also important to keep in mind that revolutionaries do not give up their lives to replicate central planning and bureaucratic rule. What inspires revolutions is the suffering and injustice borne by the poor majority living under Third World capitalism, and the vision of a more prosperous and egalitarian alternative ruled by the "logic of the majority," where, at the very least, basic needs are met.

But the quest for alternative models of development, grounded in the socialist vision of egalitarianism in both the political and economic spheres, and for mixed economies of various shades (with different combinations of planning and markets) is very much contingent upon the role of imperialism. It does not seem likely that with the thawing of the cold war, the world economy will become more hospitable to progressive experiments. On the contrary, it will be harder than ever for a less developed country to defend itself from the economic and military aggression that the United States often unleashes, both overtly and covertly, on Third World countries that attempt to follow a more independent path. The possibilities for progressive change thus depend on changing the policies of the United States and other powerful capitalist nations (including South Africa) and on the development of new and creative strategies for liberatory transformation in the Third World. Such transformations will not come without struggle, and they will require new forms of international cooperation and solidarity.

NOTES

1. See the editors' introduction to Fagen, Deere, and Coraggio 1986 for a more comprehensive discussion of the meaning and goals of socialism in Third World contexts.

2. EIU 1990a:no.2,16. According to Andrew Zimbalist and Claes Brundenius (1989:150), however, these estimates tend to overstate the true level of aid, due to the manner in which the sugar subsidy is calculated, among other measurement problems.

3. North Korea, possessing abundant natural resources and pursuing a self-reliance strategy, has become much less reliant on Soviet aid. See Jon Halliday, "The North Korean Enigma," in White, Murray, and White 1983.

4. The measures were announced in *Granma*, the official daily newspaper of the Cuban Communist party, on 29 August, 26 September, and 1 October, 1990.

5. In 1970, food imports constituted 20 percent of total imports (about the same as in 1958); this ratio was reduced to 9.5 percent in the 1986–88 period (CEE 1988, tables XI.16, XI.18).

6. See Deere 1991 for a more detailed discussion of the National Food Program and its prospects.

7. EIU 1991:12. On intraparty debates over the reform process, see also Pike 1991, and Christine White, "Recent Debates in Vietnamese Development Policy," in White, Murray, and White 1983.

8. Paul Fauvet, "Southern Africa Faces Harsh New Reality," *The Guardian* (New York), 3 April 1991.

9. For a fuller development of this vision and how it influenced the Nicaraguan process, see the essays in Fagen, Deere, and Coraggio 1986.

10. The capitalist success stories are generally held to be South Korea, Taiwan, and Singapore, all countries characterized by authoritarian regimes. Chile has recently been added to this list, as a result of its successful implementation of the neoliberal or structural-adjustment-type policies. After decades of military rule, it finally now has a democratic government, befuddled over what to do with the social tensions generated by the increased inequality that this model of development required.

BIBLIOGRAPHY

Ayisi, Ruth Ansah. 1991. The Problems of Peace. *Africa Report*, March/April, 23–25.

Azicri, Max. 1990. The Cuban Rectification: Safeguarding the Revolution While Building the Future. In *Transformation and Struggle: Cuba Faces the 1990s*, ed. Sandor Halebsky and John Kirk, 3–20. New York: Praeger.

Bengelsdorf, Carollee. 1986. State and Society in the Transition to Socialism: The Theoretical Legacy. In *Transition and Development: Problems of Third World*

Socialism, ed. Richard Fagen, C. D. Deere, and J. L. Coraggio, 192–211. New York: Monthly Review Press.

Comité Estatal de Estadísticas (CEE). 1988. *Anuario estadístico de Cuba*. Havana: CEE.

Deere, Carmen Diana. 1986. Agrarian Reform, Peasant Participation, and the Organization of Production in the Transition to Socialism. In *Transition and Development: Problems of Third World Socialism*, ed. Richard Fagen, C. D. Deere, and J. L. Coraggio. New York: Monthly Review Press.

———. 1991. Cuba's Struggle for Self-Sufficiency. *Monthly Review* 43(3):55–73.

Economist Intelligence Unit (EIU). 1990a. *Country Report: Cuba and Dominican Republic*, nos. 1, 2, 3, and 4. London: The Economist.

———. 1990b. *Country Report: Indochina (Vietnam, Cambodia, Laos)*, nos. 3 and 4. London: The Economist.

———. 1990c. *Country Report: Tanzania, Mozambique*, no. 4. London: The Economist.

———. 1991. *Country Report: Indochina (Vietnam, Cambodia, Laos)*, no. 1. London: The Economist.

Fagen, Richard, Carmen Diana Deere, and Jose Luis Coraggio, eds. 1986. *Transition and Development: Problems of Third World Socialism*. New York: Monthly Review Press.

Hiebert, Murray. 1991. On the Brink. *Far Eastern Economic Review* 152(14):52.

Kimura, Tetsusaburo. 1989. *The Vietnamese Economy, 1975–86: Reforms and International Relations*. Tokyo: Institute of Developing Economies.

Petrasovits, Anna. 1988. Results and Limits in CMEA–Vietnamese Trade Relations, 1975–1985. In *Postwar Vietnam: Dilemmas in Socialist Development*, ed. David Marr and Christine White, 213–24. Ithaca, NY: Cornell Southeast Asia Program.

Pike, Douglas. 1991. Vietnam in 1990: The Last Picture Show. *Asian Survey* 31(1): 79–86.

White, Gordon, Robin Murray, and Christine White, eds. 1983. *Revolutionary Socialist Development in the Third World*. Lexington: University of Kentucky Press.

Zimbalist, Andrew, and Claes Brundenius. 1989. *The Cuban Economy: Measurement and Analysis of Socialist Performance*. Baltimore: Johns Hopkins University Press.

23

BRENDA WYSS
RADHIKA BALAKRISHNAN

Making Connections: Women in the International Economy

This chapter discusses experiences of women in the changing world economy. One of the reasons that the current international economy looks the way it does is that it builds on hierarchical gender relations. Likewise, gender relations can partly be explained by the dictates and dynamics of the world economic system. Gender divisions are continually decomposed, recomposed, or sometimes reinforced by changes in the global economy. By looking at women and the role of gender in economies, we gain critical insight into the workings of the international economy.

Gender is central to how every economy is structured. Feminists commonly distinguish between sex—the biological property of being male or female—and gender—the social attributes of masculinity or femininity. Gender hierarchy in almost all instances places women in an unequal position with respect to men and confers greater status, power, and benefits to men. Although all women share a fundamental subordination to men within gender hierarchies, women's lives and experiences differ according to their race, class, citizenship, age, sexual orientation, marital status, religion, and so forth. In this chapter we highlight both the *common* experiences of women based on gender divisions and the *specific* ways in which different groups of women are integrated into economies. We have focused primarily on women in the Third World and capitalist economies, partly due to our own research interests and partly because we feel it is important to educate ourselves about how our own lives and struggles relate to the lives and struggles of women in the Third World.

Women participate in a variety of productive activities, including work for wages, informal economic activities, housework, and producing new human beings. In the following sections we illustrate how gender relations interact with other economic relations in each of these activities to reinforce, transform, or reduce gender and class domination. Most women in the world participate in more than one of the productive activities discussed, and their experiences in each realm overlap with and influence their

421

experiences in every other realm. Although we have found it easiest to separate various kinds of production for discussion, women cannot separate
these aspects of their lives in reality.

Women's Work

Twenty years ago, development economist Ester Boserup argued that capitalist economic development was eroding women's status. She argued that
Third World women, like women in the United States and elsewhere, progressively lose their traditional roles in agriculture, craft production, and
commerce as capitalist firms come to dominate markets (Boserup
1970:113). Boserup argued that industrial capitalists in Third World countries prefer to employ men rather than women, thereby failing to include
women in new roles in the capitalist sectors of their economies.

Recent studies of women's work in developing countries suggest that
the story is not so simple. In fact, some argue that we are witnessing a
"feminization of the world labor force" (Standing 1989). Unfortunately,
official measures of women's work are biased by the male-dominant gender
relations highlighted in this chapter, so these measures are inadequate.
Women's household production, housework, and informal-sector work often are not counted in official statistics. As a result, "women are frequently
presented as economically inactive members of society even though their
labour . . . is essential for their families' survival" (Anker 1983:709).

For example, the International Labor Organization's definition of labor force activity includes production for one's own consumption;[1] however, applications of the definition often exclude women's work done for
home consumption, while including men's. Furthermore, much of the
growth of women's paid labor has been in what is called the "informal
sector"—for example, women working as market traders or doing industrial
homework. This labor also tends to be uncounted, adding to the invisibility
of women's work in our statistics.

Despite undercounting, global-level statistics indicate growth in the
percentage of women participating in the labor force, as well as growth in
the proportion of labor-force activity provided by women instead of men.
The pace of growth of women's labor-force participation has varied by
country and by region of the world. For developing countries,[2] the percentage of women counted as labor-force participants increased from 37 percent
to 42 percent between 1950 and 1985. But the aggregate growth rate con-
ceals large regional variations. In 1985, women's labor-force participation
rate for Latin America was 25 percent, whereas for East Asia the measure
was 52 percent (Grown and Sebstad 1989:937–38).

Measures of women's participation in wage labor probably are more
accurate than measures of labor-force participation broadly (and ambigu-
ously) defined (Beneria 1989:243). Women make up about one-third of the

TABLE 23.1
Distribution of the Female Labor Force by Sector and Region, 1980 (Percentages)

Sector	Africa and Middle East	Asia	Latin America	Europe	Canada and U.S.
Agriculture	72.5	69.5	14.0	21.0	1.5
Industry	9.0	17.5	17.0	25.8	19.0
Services	18.5	13.0	69.0	53.2	79.5

Sources: Beneria 1989:246, and ILO 1990.

paid labor force worldwide. This share is slowly growing in most places, with the largest increases in Third World countries. In Africa and the former USSR, however, women's paid-labor-force rates appear to have decreased over the past thirty years (Seager and Olson 1986:40).

The distribution of women waged workers across sectors of the economy varies by geographical region and between countries at different stages of capitalist development. In the Third World, female industrial employment increased by 56 percent between 1970 and 1980 (Beneria 1989:244). In the industrialized capitalist countries, however, the growth of women's wage labor has resulted mostly from women's employment in the service sector. For the world as a whole, women continue to be concentrated in agricultural production (see Table 23.1).

Even when women are employed for wages, the jobs women work have less status and lower pay than men's jobs. Women's low wages are partly maintained through occupational segregation: the tendency for women to be excluded from certain activities and professions considered— mostly by the male beneficiaries—to be traditionally male. And in addition to paid activities, women still do most of the unpaid household work, although men are picking up part of the burden in some places. Theories of women's oppression often hold that when women have access to wages or some measure of economic autonomy, they gain bargaining power with the men in their households, which can be translated into a shared burden of housework. Studies from the United States and other industrialized countries suggest, however, that although wages do increase women's power within a marital relationship, most women either do not or cannot use this increased marital power to get men to do housework (England and Farkas 1986:54; see also H. Hartmann 1981b:27 and 1981a:379).

Wage Work: Multinational Corporations and Women Workers

One of the most noted forms of wage work done by women in the world today is factory production on the so-called global assembly line. Many Third World factories producing textiles, pharmaceuticals, and electronic components for export employ a predominantly female work force. This phenomenon has been hailed as a major shift from industrial capitalists' earlier preference to hire male workers in Third World countries and has attracted a lot of attention by activists and researchers. Employing Third World women often is seen as part of a new strategy by multinational capitalists to take advantage of surplus labor pools and low wages in Third World countries. Most explanations of the new strategy focus on the current crises and restructuring in Western capitalism.

The intersection of the history of imperialism and the history of male dominance explains why Third World women are the ideal inexpensive labor force for some employers. Reasons employers give for hiring women are that they can be paid low wages, that they make "docile" or "compliant" workers, or that they have "nimble fingers" better equipped to do certain kinds of production and assembly work. For the women employees, the factory jobs often provide the first opportunity to work for wages and to live independently of their families. In addition, many women workers are the sole or important contributors to their families' survival.

Although the trend toward women's employment by multinationals is difficult to measure, it is pretty clear that it is not nearly so large as people first imagined. An International Labour Organization report in 1985 emphasized that multinational employment is not a numerically large part of employment in Third World countries and that not all multinationals prefer women workers to men. Rather, "multinational employment for women, like total multinational employment, is concentrated in only a few countries, and a few sectors of these countries, in the developing world" (UNCTC/ILO 1985:16).[3] Lourdes Beneria estimates that in 1985 there were probably no more than two million women employed by multinational firms in Third World countries. She argues that those two million workers would make up less than 1 percent of the total female labor force in the Third World and about 3 percent of all worldwide multinational employment for 1985 (Beneria 1989:246–47).

Some working women in the United States and other highly industrialized countries worry that they will lose jobs to their Third World counterparts. Although many of the jobs that moved from the United States to Third World production sites were jobs originally occupied by women (Snow 1983), the loss of jobs for women in the United States has been overstated. In fact, some industries noted for their footloose behavior have actually expanded production here, employing similar cost-cutting strategies (subcontracting, informalization, homework) and a similar low-paid labor force (women and people of color) as in their offshore operations (Snow 1983; Fernandez-Kelly 1989).

Although it is not a numerically large phenomenon, women's work on the global assembly line highlights the important interplay between global economic concerns and gender relations. Women's labor-force participation poses contradictions for capital and male dominance in Third World countries, just as it does in the United States and other highly industrialized countries. In the short run, hiring women in factory production is a profitable strategy for Third World capitalists. But in the long run, this employment threatens the benefits men reap from women working at home as well as the ability of capitalists to continue paying women lower wages than they pay men.

Early discussions of women's employment by multinationals centered around whether this employment was liberating women (a positive change) or subjecting women to a new form of exploitation (a negative change). Speaking on the positive side were those who viewed multinational employment as a step toward "integrating women into the development process." The beneficial results of this integration for women would include increased power and autonomy through earning a wage, working in the public sphere, learning skills, and being free of some of the oppressive aspects of patriarchal families. On the negative side, the jobs were clearly low paid, insecure, low skilled, dead-end, and often hazardous to women's health. Today, most people agree that women's work on the global assembly line has both beneficial and harmful aspects. One of the beneficial outgrowths of the phenomenon is that it has provided an impetus for feminists from all countries to recognize the interconnectedness of their fates and to consider how women's employment in capitalist production changes women's lives and societies.

Women and Informal-Sector Work: Producing Survival

About once every two months, Sophie travels to Haiti, Curaçao, or Panama to buy clothing, shoes, cosmetics, and other assorted consumer goods. She sells them in the little shop she rents in an arcade in Kingston, Jamaica. With her earnings, she supports herself and her six children.

Meanwhile, in her home in Mexico City, Rosa busily sorts metal battery plates into two boxes marked "finished" and "defective." With the U.S. $2.05 Rosa earns per box, she will buy school clothes for her children. Rosa sorts plates only three days each week so that she can keep up with her housekeeping duties.

These two types of informal-sector work—higglering and industrial homework—reflect and incorporate gender roles while at the same time both reinforcing and threatening gender domination. Informal-sector work, rather than the much analyzed global factory production, occupies the energies and time of most women around the world today.

Informal Commercial Importers in Jamaica

Sophie is one of the growing number of informal commercial importers in Jamaica. Jamaican women have a long history of working as small-scale marketers, called *higglers*. But in the past, most women sold agricultural produce or goods manufactured in Jamaica. Informal importers are a new brand of higgler: private individuals who travel abroad to buy goods for resale in Jamaica. The higglers employ a variety of methods to sell their goods. Some wholesale to established stores, others sell on the sidewalks, and many retail goods in arcades recently built by the government.

The growth of informal importers in Jamaica gained momentum in the early 1970s with the migration of traditional businesspersons out of Jamaica. As consumer goods came to be in short supply, import higglers took the place of the traditional suppliers of goods. Higglering has mobilized resources that might otherwise have been idle (particularly earnings unknown to tax authorities), has provided earnings to persons who might otherwise have been unemployed, and has extended the distribution of goods to places not served by the formal establishment (Witter 1989:14).

The vast majority of higglers in Jamaica are women, estimated at around 80 percent in 1985 (Witter 1989:3). A 1985 survey found that most women working as higglers are the sole support for their children. Survey evidence suggests that women go into higglering largely because of the lack of other options. However, higglering has provided an avenue of upward mobility for some women, and a measure of economic independence to those who are successful at it.

Industrial Homeworkers in Mexico City

Like many other women in Mexico City, Rosa does industrial homework. Because homework is often done under illegal conditions, there are no reliable measures of the extent of homeworking in Mexico City. Work is distributed to homeworkers daily, weekly, or by quota. The work is received either directly from a factory or workshop or through a jobber. Homework tasks are simple, repetitive, and monotonous. The work includes garment production, sorting metal pieces for batteries, producing electronic coils, plastic polishing (containers for cosmetics or pharmaceutical), and assembly (toys, cartons, flowers) (Beneria and Roldan 1987).

The pay for homework is based on piecework and is extremely low by Mexican standards. Earnings are unpredictable, since many women do not know whether they will receive work on any given day or week. Like Jamaican higglers, Mexican homeworkers' "choice" of a job is constrained by a lack of alternatives. But, unlike higglers, the majority of Mexican homeworkers have husbands with stable jobs. One reason for the lack of alternatives Mexican women face is their husbands' opposition to women working outside the household (Beneria and Roldan 1987:66).

The Informal Sector

What do importers in Jamaica have in common with Mexican industrial homeworkers? Both kinds of workers could be classified as part of what is often called the informal sector. Depending on the definition employed, informal-sector work is characterized by some subset of the following aspects: very low pay, illegality, irregular and insecure employment, lack of workers' organizations, unskilled tasks, and only indirect links to the capitalist sector. The use of the term varies widely and is often ambiguous. But it suggests economic activity that does not neatly fit traditional categories—work often considered outside the dominant economic system by economists. Here we use the term to denote the hustling, scrounging, juggling kinds of work that people do in order to survive.

Although some economists view the informal sector as an arena of superexploitation of workers, others focus on what they see as positive aspects of the informal sector. They argue that informal work generates survival for countless people who could not manage otherwise, that it is a realm for creative small-scale entrepreneurial activity, that perhaps it holds the key for new kinds of community economic activity in the future.

A 1980 study reported that between 53 percent and 69 percent of all workers in a number of Third World cities were in the informal sector (in Bombay, Jakarta, Belo Horizonte, and Lima). Calculations for several Latin American countries suggest that women make up from 46 to 70 percent of informal-sector workers there (ICRW 1980:68). The history of gender subordination helps explain why so many women are integrated into their economies via participation in informal-sector work. Although the form of women's subordination varies across cultures, all women face limited economic alternatives, so informal activities are often the only options available to them. Women also share the experience of being socialized as the producers and sustainers of life. This means most women are willing to do whatever kinds of work they can find in order to ensure the survival of their families. And even when qualified for a better-paid or higher-status job, some women do informal-sector work because it is more easily combined with child-rearing responsibilities.

The current dynamism of informal-sector work builds on traditional gender roles. For example, some capitalists hire women to do industrial homework at low wages, and since the work is done at home, they avoid government regulation and taxation. At the same time, gender relations are both reinforced and transformed by the informal-sector activities in which women engage. Homework in Mexico City keeps women in their traditional domain while providing them greater economic autonomy and perhaps greater bargaining power with their husbands. And in Jamaica, worldwide and domestic economic trends opened a space for women to make money as import higglers, to learn entrepreneurial skills, to see the world, and to gain greater power to renegotiate their relations with men—both at home and in the larger society.

Domestic Workers

Two of women's economic roles are often overlooked by economists: their roles in housework and biological reproduction. Although maintaining households and producing future generations of people are necessary and valuable aspects of any economic system, theorists often consider these activities outside of the economic realm, calling them "noneconomic" or "not really work." And since these activities make up such a large part of women's lives and contributions to society, devaluing them contributes to women's subordinate status.

Although the responsibility of household work falls primarily on women's shoulders, the relative income and racial position of some women enables them to hire low-paid domestic workers to perform the tasks that are considered their responsibility. The complex interrelation of race, class, gender, and government policy can be seen by examining the case of domestic workers. Here we examine this interrelation in the context of South Africa and Cuba.

South Africa

"In South Africa, poverty, labor controls and a lack of employment alternatives combine to 'trap' about one million black women in domestic service. These women are subject to intense oppression, which is evident in their low wages, long working hours and demeaning treatment by their white female employers" (Cock 1988:205). Employers exert complete control over the lives of the domestic workers, who have no legislative protection regarding minimum wage, job security, unemployment compensation, maternity leave, or paid sick leave.

The South African system of apartheid places the physical mobility of the black African work force under the direct control of the state. Although residence rules very recently have been officially removed, in practice they still exist. According to residence rules, black Africans can only remain in "white" areas when they have fifteen years continuous residence in the same area, ten years of continuous service with the same employer, or have one-year labor contracts (Cock 1988:206). Consequently, black African women's need to support their families often requires them to leave dependent children in the so-called homelands while they go work for white households. In her study of South African domestics, Jacklyn Cock found that domestic servants had an average of 5.5 dependents and that 58 percent were sole breadwinners, in the sense that no one else in their houses was employed in wage labor (1988:207). Black African children must be parceled out to friends and family while their mothers work. And although the mothers spend their days doing housework, they do not have an opportunity physically to maintain their own households.

White women and men, whether they are working-class or elite, benefit from the work of black African domestics. Working-class white women can hire black women at low wages to take care of the household work, which enables the white women to secure employment for themselves in higher-paying formal sectors. Both elite and working-class white men and women enjoy the luxury of having household work done at very low cost and having their children receive constant care. However, while white women retain a position of power over blacks in South Africa, they remain subordinate to white men.

Capitalists in South Africa benefit from the work of domestics by having available to them the labor of white women who no longer are restricted to household work. Because the wages of domestics are so small, capitalists can pay the working-class white women relatively low wages and still be confident that future generations are being raised to be healthy and productive workers.

The system of apartheid organizes different races in a way that benefits white capitalists by maintaining a class structure based primarily on race. The racist system is perpetuated in part by having white children grow up experiencing very asymmetric relations with black Africans and vice versa. These asymmetric relations between white and black Africans are probably the closest in the case of live-in domestic workers. In a system already segregated by race, hierarchical gender divisions place the black African women in the lowest possible position.

Cuba

The history of domestics in Cuba illustrates how a society can consciously change structures of domination. Socialist Cuba inherited the systems of discrimination based on class, race, and sex that are prevalent in capitalist societies. But after the Cuban revolution in 1959, the struggle for women's equality was an integral part of the process of social transformation, socialist revolution, and building a classless society (Larguia and Dumoulin 1986:344). The Federación de Mujeres Cubanos (FMC) was created to facilitate the transition toward an egalitarian society. One of the primary tasks of the FMC was to educate domestic workers and peasant women.

In prerevolutionary Cuba, domestic workers constituted more than a quarter of the women who were classified as economically active. Havana alone had fifty thousand domestic workers. Most domestics were peasants from large families who had migrated to the urban areas looking for work. As in South Africa, domestics were subject to miserable working conditions and low pay. But in Cuba, state policy specifically targeted at changing women's position within a class and gender system helped to alleviate their subordination (Izquierdo 1989:351).

In early 1961 the new government started night schools for domestics in Havana; by December there were sixty schools with an enrollment of twenty thousand students. In these schools the domestics learned skills that would help them get better-paying work and were given instruction in revolutionary ideology. After attending night school the women went to schools of specialization where they studied typing, shorthand, accounting, management of telephone exchanges, or banking skills. During the period of training, the government provided each woman with a stipend to defray the costs of transportation and to help her meet other needs. After leaving school, the newly trained domestics filled positions vacated by the exodus of professionals from Cuba following the revolution.

In a fairly short period of time, domestic workers in Cuba moved into the organized, better-paying sectors of the economy. The successes of the program were great. But even within that revolutionary structure, these domestics were primarily trained for jobs traditionally held by women. The schools set up by the government changed a class system by getting women out of domestic work but at the same time maintained a gender system that conformed with traditional roles.

Population Policy

Childbirth and child rearing are two activities in which women currently play a central role. But even in these activities, relations of gender dominance undermine women's control. Population policies are designed to control or influence women's decisions and practices as producers of new human lives. These policies may be either pronatalist or antinatalist depending on policymakers' perceptions about the needs of their economy. Pronatalist policies provide incentives for women to have many children and are rooted in the desire for a larger labor force and consumer market. Antinatalist policies, on the other hand, try to reduce the population and often are based in the Malthusian ideology according to which a large population is in direct opposition to economic well-being. "Much has been written about the 'population problem' in recent years. 'Overpopulation' is said to be the major reason for poverty of the 'underdeveloped' countries; overpopulation is the 'malaise' and family planning the remedy" (Mamdani 1973:13).

Unfortunately, both pronatalist and antinatalist policies tend to be designed without respect for a woman's right to control her own body and without concern for how the policies will affect women's economic well-being or roles. The targets of population-control policy generally are Third World women. We examine two countries, India and Malaysia, to see the impact of antinatalist and pronatalist policies on women.

TABLE 23.2
Number of Girls Dying for Every 100 Boys Who Die
(Various Years, 1975 to 1985)

Country	Up to 1 Year	1–4 Years
Bangladesh	93	112
Egypt	100	122
Nepal	97	110
Peru	89	102
India	109	300
Pakistan	89	126
S. Korea	86	105
Ecuador	89	105

Source: Seager and Olson 1986.

India

For decades the Indian government has argued the need for population control as a primary mechanism to end poverty. Malthusian ideology flourishes in India, and Indian women are treated as laboratory animals for yet-to-be-tested birth control methods. Dissatisfied with methods of birth control that rely on women's initiative, the Indian government promotes drugs that are long-duration, invasive, and hazardous, such as NET-EN, Norplant, and antifertility vaccines (Saheli 1988).

In India, the rhetoric of population control is couched in terms of decreasing female mortality: government planners argue that the proportion of women in the population is declining because women have too many babies. They suggest that maternal mortality can be diminished via population control measures. But evidence shows that the decrease in the relative female population is primarily due to low levels of survival of girls after birth (see Table 23.2).

Ironically, the very policies promoted as a way to save women's lives seem to be threatening them. Population control policies, coupled with a decreasing social valuation of women's lives, probably contribute to the declining proportion of females in the Indian population. In an economy where the valuation of women is low and where population control is promoted, having a girl child is considered a liability. The economic bases for female infanticide, undernourishment, and sex-selective abortion are very real. The changes in the Indian economy that have decreased the economic value of women are complex. Low wages, high dowry payments, patrilineal inheritance structures, the disappearance of the communal family structure, and increased dependence on a cash economy are but a few strands in the complicated web of reasons women are considered a liability to families.

Although not every state in India shows a decreasing trend, the national ratio of the number of females to every thousand males has gone from 972 in 1901 to 930 in 1981. And as the Indian government continues to target population reduction rather than female survival, the relative number of females in India continues to decline.

Malaysia

While the Indian government strives to decrease births, the Malaysian government strives to increase its population by exhorting women to have five children each. "Dr. Mahathir Mohamed, Malaysia's Prime Minister, announced a policy to achieve a population of 70 million in 115 years as a solution to the country's industrialization and domestic market problems" (Chee 1988:164). The government has asked women whose husbands can afford it to stay home and have babies and for women to marry by age nineteen so they can have five properly spaced children (Chee 1988:166). The government's reasoning behind this new population policy is that heavy industrialization will be necessary in order for Malaysia to become a great society. This will require a bigger labor force and a larger market to sell newly produced goods.

The impact of the Malaysian policy on women is multifold. Having many children in a short span of time can increase maternal mortality, especially among poor women. Of the Malaysian population, 40 percent is considered to live below the poverty line, with inadequate health care and a high level of malnourishment. Policies targeted at increasing the population without structurally changing the government's ability to meet the basic needs of the poor will only increase the poverty level, unemployment level, and further contribute to class divisions in Malaysia (Chee 1988:169). The pronatalist policies of the Malaysian government are likely to have an additional disastrous impact on women, increasing their dependence on men and reinforcing the ideology that women's primary role in society is to be a wife and mother.

Policy

The discussion in this chapter suggests several guidelines for economic policy. First, policies need to be designed with a conscious commitment to promote women's equality and economic well-being. Second, policymakers must address the diversity of women's experiences based on nation, race, and class. Third, policy needs to account for the multiple economic roles of women: as wage workers, unpaid or informal-sector workers, houseworkers, and mothers. Fourth, women themselves are best equipped to design policy to meet women's needs. As we argued in the previous section, strategies dictated by "experts" lack the insight women have into their own lives. Finally, policy strategies and tools must balance short-run and local goals with longer-run and global goals. Short-run, ameliorative approaches are most effective when combined with long-term strategies to establish women's control over the economic decisions that shape their lives. And within the context of an increasingly integrated world economic system, First World and Third World women must coordinate their efforts to create a brighter future.

Examples abound of women organizing for change. Multinational factory workers in the Philippines and Mexico have organized unions, facing violent attacks as a result of their efforts. Informal-sector workers are also organizing. Jamaican higglers have formed two large national associations and have won several concessions from the Jamaican government, although their struggles continue. Organizing is particularly important for women who work as domestics, given the isolation their jobs entail. Domestics have formed organizations in many places, including South Africa. And finally, women are seeking to influence policy affecting their reproductive capacities. Indian women's groups closely monitored trials of the contraceptive NET-EN and petitioned the Indian Supreme Court to halt these drug trials. Indian women have demanded more representation on government decision-making bodies and more direct involvement in research on women's real birth control needs (B. Hartmann 1987:292). Most women's groups focus on the many aspects of women's lives, recognizing the interconnectedness of all their roles. And women are organizing across national borders. Maria Mies (1986:231) describes the joint struggle of Dutch and Thai women against sex tourism in Thailand.

Women's organizing efforts have not been limited to the Third World. Teaching staff and participants in seminars of the Center for Popular Economics have been particularly inspired by the activities of a Springfield, Massachusetts, group called ARISE. The group is an example of women organizing across racial boundaries around economic issues. ARISE formed in 1985 when two African American women and two white women sat down together to discuss the inadequate income and services they were receiving from the Massachusetts Welfare Department. In particular, the women wanted to receive some portion of the child support being paid to the department by their children's fathers. Assertive lobbying got cash flowing through the system to the mothers. In 1986, ARISE became an incorporated nonprofit organization and by 1987 became a local antipoverty agency. ARISE has organized and provided outreach and education to thousands of low-income people. Their most recent campaign to register low-income voters was extremely successful and will have influence far into the future. Low-income people are beginning to be seen as a political force in Springfield and in Massachusetts, in part because of ARISE's efforts.

Women are not powerless to change their roles within society. We have seen that different groups of women are affected differently by the workings of the international economy. But by understanding how the struggles of one group of women are related to the struggles of other groups and then acting collectively, women can make strides to overcome the different forms of domination under which they labor.

NOTES

1. The International Labour Organization recommends that measures of labor force activity include all persons supplying labor for "production of economic goods and services . . . production and processing of primary products, whether for market, for barter or for own consumption" (Anker 1983:713).

2. The World Bank classifies economies according to their gross national product (GNP) per capita. Low-income and middle-income economies are referred to as "developing economies." The 1990 *World Development Report* specifies that low-income economies are those with a GNP per capita of $545 or less in 1988, and middle-income economies are those with a GNP per capita of more than $545 but less than $6000 in 1988. While the World Bank has always specified a particular level of GNP per capita as the dividing line between low-income and middle-income countries, prior to 1989 the bank was ambiguous about the line between middle-income and high-income economies.

3. The employment of women by multinationals is most significant in Brazil, Hong Kong, the Republic of Korea, Malaysia, Mexico, the Philippines, and Singapore. Female employment in multinationals is concentrated in the manufacturing sector, and within that sector in labor-intensive, export-oriented industries such as textiles, garments, and electronics (UNCTC/ILO 1985:93).

BIBLIOGRAPHY

Anker, Richard. 1983. Female Labour Force Participation in Developing Countries: A Critique of Current Definitions and Data Collection Methods. *International Labour Review* 122(6): 709–23.
Anker, Richard, and Catherine Hein. 1985. Why Third World Urban Employers Usually Prefer Men. *International Labour Review* 124(1): 73–90
Beneria, Lourdes. 1989. Gender and the Global Economy. In *Instability and Change in the World Economy*, ed. Arthur MacEwan and William K. Tabb, 241–58. New York: Monthly Review Press.
Beneria, Lourdes, and Martha Roldan. 1987. *The Crossroads of Class and Gender*. Chicago: University of Chicago Press.
Boserup, Ester. 1970. *Women's Role in Economic Development*. New York: St. Martin's Press.
Chee, Heng Leng. 1988. Babies to Order: Recent Population Policies in Malaysia and Singapore. In *Structures of Patriarchy: The State, the Community, and the Household*, ed. Bina Agarwal, 164–74. London: Zed Books.
Cock, Jacklyn. 1988. Trapped Workers: The Case of Domestic Servants in South Africa. In *Patriarchy and Class: African Women in the Home and the Workforce*, ed. Sharon Stichter and Jane Parpart, 205–18. Boulder, Colo.: Westview Press.
England, Paula, and George Farkas. 1986. *Households, Employment, and Gender*. New York: Basic Books.

Fernandez-Kelly, Maria Patricia. 1989. Broadening the Scope: Gender and International Economic Development. *Sociological Forum* 4:11–35.

Grown, Caren A., and Jennifer Sebstad. 1989. Introduction: Toward a Wider Perspective on Women's Employment. *World Development* 17(7): 937–52.

Hartmann, Betsy. 1987. *Reproductive Rights and Wrongs: The Global Politics of Population Control and Contraceptive Choice*. New York: Harper & Row.

Hartmann, Heidi. 1981a. The Family as the Locus of Gender, Class, and Political Struggle: The Example of Housework. *Signs* 6(3): 366–94.

———. 1981b. The Unhappy Marriage of Marxism and Feminism: Towards a More Progressive Union. In *Women and Revolution*, ed. Lydia Sargent, 1–41. Boston: South End Press.

International Centre for Research on Women (ICRW). *Keeping Women Out: A Structural Analysis of Women's Employment in Developing Countries*. Washington, D.C.: Agency for International Development.

International Labour Office (ILO). 1990. *Yearbook of Labour Statistics: Retrospective Edition on Population Censuses, 1945–1989*. Geneva: ILO.

Izquierdo, Elena Gil. 1989. Sharpening the Class Struggle: The Education of Domestic Workers in Cuba. In *Muchachas No More: Household Workers in Latin America and the Caribbean*, ed. Elsa M. Chaney and Mary Garcia Castro, 351–59. Philadelphia: Temple University Press.

Joekes, Susan, with Roxana Moayedi. 1987. *Women and Export Manufacturing: A Review of the Issues and AID Policy*. Washington, D.C.: International Center for Research on Women.

Larguia, Isabel, and John Dumoulin. 1986. Women's Equality and the Cuban Revolution. In *Women and Change in Latin America*, ed. June Nash and Helen Safa, 344–68. South Hadley, Mass.: Bergin and Garvey.

Mamdani, Mahmoud. 1973. *The Myth of Population Control: Family, Caste, and Class in an Indian Village*. New York: Monthly Review Press.

Mies, Maria. 1986. *Patriarchy and Accumulation on a World Scale: Women in the International Division of Labour*. London: Zed Books.

Saheli. 1988. *Saheli*. New Delhi, pamphlet.

Seager, Joni, and Ann Olson. 1986. *Women in the World: An International Atlas*. New York: Simon & Schuster.

Sen, Gita. 1991. Macroeconomic Policies and the Informal Sector: A Gender Sensitive Approach. Paper written for the Conference on Macroeconomic Policies Towards Women in the Informal Sector held by UN/INSTRAW, Rome.

Snow, Robert T. 1983. The New International Division of Labor and the U.S. Workforce: The Case of the Electronics Industry. In *Women, Men, and the International Division of Labor*, ed. June Nash and Maria Patricia Fernandez-Kelly, 39–69. Albany: State University of New York Press.

Standing, Guy. 1989. Global Feminization through Flexible Labor. *World Development* 17(7): 1077–95.

United Nations Centre on Transnational Corporations and the International Labour Organization (UNCTC/ILO). 1985. *Women Workers in Multinational Enterprises in Developing Countries*. Geneva: ILO.

Witter, Michael. 1989. *Higglering/Sidewalk Vending/Informal Commercial Trading in the Jamaican Economy*. Department of Economics Occasional Paper Series, no.4. Mona, Jamaica: University of the West Indies.

GLOSSARY
THE CONTRIBUTORS
INDEX

Glossary

aggregate demand   total spending on goods and services in the economy by households, businesses, government, and foreigners.

antinatalist population policies   policies designed to decrease the birth rate in a society.

balance-of-payments deficit   economic shortfall that occurs when a country earns less income on its exports, and profit and interest on investments abroad, than it pays for imports, and interest and profits on investments from abroad, in a given period of time.

brain drain   the emigration of educated and skilled people, especially from developing countries.

Bretton Woods system   the set of rules, regulations, and institutions (the most important of which are the International Monetary Fund and the World Bank) adopted at an international conference held at Bretton Woods, New Hampshire, in 1944. The United States exercised almost total control of this international financial system until its collapse in the early 1970s. Although the United States remains the most influential country in international financial affairs, it faces increasing competition in this arena, as in so many others, from Japan and Germany.

budget authority   congressional authorization of spending for a particular program, which could last several years, for example, the Trident submarine program.

budget deficit   the shortfall that occurs when a government spends more in a given year than it earns in tax revenue.

budget outlays   the actual amount spent during a fiscal year; for example, the Trident program could have $10 billion authorized over a five-year period during which $2 billion was the average annual outlay.

business cycle   a fluctuation in the level of economic activity (usually measured by gross national product [GNP]) that forms a regular pattern, with an expansion of activity followed by a contraction succeeded by further expansion.

capital   financial and physical assets of a corporation or private wealth-holder: for example, money, stocks, bonds, and equipment. When the term is used for a country, it usually refers only to physical assets, such as land, minerals, and equipment.

capital controls   any government mechanism used to regulate the cross-border flow of money. Common forms of regulations include restricting the conversion of the domestic currency into foreign currencies, limiting the repatriation of investors' foreign-earned interest or profits to their home country, limiting or setting restrictions on foreign ownership of domestic property, and restricting foreigners' bank accounts.

capital intensity   the ratio of capital to labor employed in the process of production. An industry A is said to be more capital intensive than industry B if this ratio is greater in A than in B. For example, the petrochemical industry usually has a higher capital intensity than the garment industry.

capital, or **financial, market**   a market for capital where capital means financial assets. Stocks and bonds are examples of different forms of assets bought and sold in capital markets.

cocaine   a drug that starts its existence as coca leaves (from the coca bush, of which there are a number of different varieties). These leaves are mashed and soaked in kerosene and sodium carbonate to precipitate out **coca paste**, which is about 40 percent pure cocaine. The paste is treated with sulfuric acid and potassium permanganate to produce **cocaine base,** about 90 percent pure cocaine. Then ether and acetone are used on the base to produce **cocaine hydrochloride** (pure cocaine), which is either cut with baby powder, laxative, or other substances and sold in that form, or treated one more time to produce a smokable form, **crack cocaine**.

concessional loan   a subsidized loan, money lent below the market price, that is, at a cost or interest rate lower than the going rate.

conventional forces   non-nuclear weapons, for example, helicopters, machine guns, and the military personnel accompanying them.

Council for Mutual Economic Assistance (COMECON, or **CMEA)**   an intergovernmental organization established in 1949 to promote economic integration and cooperation between socialist countries. Original members were the Soviet Union, Poland, Czechoslovakia, Hungary, Romania, Bulgaria, and East Germany. Mongolia was admitted in 1962, Cuba in 1972, and Vietnam in 1978.

currency appreciation   a "strengthening" of a currency that occurs whenever an increase in demand for that currency raises its "price." When, for example, the dollar appreciates with respect to the peso, the number of dollars it takes to purchase one peso falls. An appreciation of the dollar would be reflected in a shift from ½ to ⅓ in the dollar/peso exchange rate.

currency depreciation   a "weakening" of a currency that occurs whenever a decline in the demand for that currency reduces its "price" in terms of other currencies.

debt-service obligations   the interest and charges due on a debt, including payment of the original amount borrowed.

delinking   economic disassociation; breaking away from the world capitalist system, from dependent development (industrializing based on Western technologies and products and multinational corporations), from dependence on the industrialized countries' products, technology, industrialization, financing, and entrepreneurship; breaking away from patterns of consumption and ecological destruction imported from the North.

dependency   the theory that the poverty of the developing world is due to an economic dependence on the industrialized world. It suggests that even after the colonial period, the industrialized world still controls the economic destiny of the developing nations. Elite power groups in the industrialized countries are in league with the elites of the subregional developing world, and together they manipulate the social, political, and economic institutions to the advantage of the world industrial centers.

direct foreign investment (or **foreign direct investment**)   equity or stock investments in a foreign country sufficiently large to give the investor some control over the corporation. By the U.S. definition, an investor must own at least 10 percent of the stock of the corporation for it to be a "direct" investment.

dollar panic   large-scale sale of dollar-denominated assets.

domestic outworkers   workers who perform specific tasks in their homes under precise contracting arrangements. They are hired on a piece-rate basis by capitalist subcontracting firms or intermediaries, usually to reduce labor costs and to eliminate social benefits. In Mexico this form is normally referred to as *domestic maquila* and is widely used in the garment and textile industries and in the production of electric appliances.

economic austerity   income declines associated with policies, most prominently promoted by the International Monetary Fund (IMF) and World Bank, mandating cutting government spending on social services, reducing real wages, and devaluing the domestic currency, all of which increase the domestic price of consumer goods and thereby lower residents' standards of living.

economic diversification   producing a variety of products within a region. In the case of the developing world this refers to the ability to produce a variety of exports to increase employment opportunities and counter the adverse effect on a country's income from the dependence on one main export good.

emigration   migration away from a country or region.

exchange rate   the price of one nation's currency in terms of some other currency. For example, the U.S. dollar–Mexican peso exchange rate refers to the number of dollars that must be tendered in order to purchase one peso. A dollar–peso exchange rate of ½ means that one U.S. dollar buys two pesos.

Federal Reserve Bank (Fed)   the Fed is the U.S. central bank. The Fed tries to control the money supply (the availability of credit) and be a "lender of last resort" to member banks facing liquidity difficulties.

fiscal policy   the federal government's use of taxes, purchases of goods and services, and transfer payments (such as social security, welfare, or unemployment benefits) to affect the level of income, employment, and inflation in the economy.

flexible production   small-batch production of a wide variety of products, utilizing reprogrammable technology.

Fordism   system of production characterized by use of assembly lines, task fragmentation, Taylorism, and mass production for mass consumption.

foreign direct investment   see direct foreign investment.

foreign-exchange constraint   a constraint that most of the Third World nations face as a result of the limited availability of hard currency, for example, dollars or deutsche marks, to finance imports, debt repayments, and capital outflows in general.

foreign-trade deficit   the excess of a country's imports of goods and services over its exports.

gains from trade   an increase in the total amount of output that can be produced with given resources that results when international trade allows products to be produced where they can be produced most efficiently.

General Agreement on Tariffs and Trade (GATT)   an agreement signed in 1948 by a group of countries that now numbers over one hundred. Trade discussions held in five-year cycles, such as the current Uruguay round, lead to modifications of the original agreement and are usually oriented toward reducing trade barriers.

Generalized System of Preferences (GSP)   a set of exceptions to the general rule that for any GATT country, any tariff reduction granted to one country must be equally granted to all other fellow GATT countries. The purpose of GSP is to give developing countries an extra break, allowing them to export freely to advanced countries by making exceptions to the usual tariffs or quotas.

Gramm–Rudman–Hollings Act   legislation passed originally in 1985 and amended in 1987 that established a process for deciding the federal budget in a timely fashion and a schedule for reducing the budget deficit every year. In 1990, it was superseded by the Budget Agreement Act.

grant   an outright gift of money or equipment; financing that does not have to be repaid, provided from one country or institution to another for a program or project.

greenfield site   a factory location in a previously nonindustrialized region (as opposed to brownfield site).

gross domestic product (GDP)   total amount of goods and services produced in the economy, regardless of whether part of the income accrued to foreign companies or individuals. It does not include income earned by nationals in foreign countries. Communist countries usually define GDP as the value of a country's output *not counting* so called non-productive activities such as legal and professional services. They use this measure of their national output because they believe that nonproductive activities do not contribute to real well-being. Capitalist countries do include such activities in their measure of GDP, so comparing output between capitalist and communist countries is difficult to do accurately.

gross national product (GNP)   the total value, at market prices, of all final goods and services produced in a country in a year. It includes income earned by nationals in foreign countries. It does not include income earned by foreigners in the home country.

Group of Seven (G7)   France, West Germany, Japan, United Kingdom, United States, Canada, and Italy. The G7 meetings are attended by finance ministers, senior officials, and central bank governors.

guest worker   immigrant worker whose right to stay in a country ends when the employment ends.

hard currency   a currency that has a high level of acceptability as payment in international trade. Includes currencies of most industrialized capitalist nations; examples are the U.S. dollar, the British pound, and the German mark. It does not include currencies of most less-developed or socialist nations. Having a hard currency rather than a soft one is desirable because it facilitates international trade; trading partners will accept hard currency in payment for purchases but are wary of getting stuck with soft currencies that can not be changed easily into more reliable currency.

harmonization   establishing a single law or agreement covering several countries.

hegemonic power   the military, economic, and political power wielded by a country to perpetuate its dominance.

immigration   migration into a country or region.

immigration controls   any restrictions on the freedom to move into a country.

import substitution   a strategy to reduce import dependence by establishing industries for domestic production of goods that were traditionally imported. This strategy often involves the use of tariffs, taxes, and subsidies to protect domestic industry.

informal sector   a rather vague term for production units that are perceived as being small and labor-intensive, with relatively low productivity, unorganized and generally lower-paid labor, and operating largely outside the purview of government regulations or assistance.

informalization   the transfer of jobs from the formal sector of the economy (which is recognized and monitored by government agencies) to the informal sector (in which illegal, uncounted, and unrecognized activities take place).

interest rate   the cost of borrowing money or the payment to lenders of money as a percentage per year of the borrowed money. The market interest rate is the going rate for a particular type of loan. Various kinds of loans—for example, loans for buying a home versus loans banks make to one another—are made in different markets and have different interest rates.

internal economies of scale   economies realized when, due to factors of production at an individual firm, the cost per good of production falls as the number of goods produced rises.

International Monetary Fund (IMF)   an international banking institution, initially created as part of the Bretton Woods agreement in 1944, to be a lender of last resort designed to alleviate a country's short-term balance-of-payments problems. It provides short-term loans and usually imposes austerity measures.

jobber   a mediator who links legal and illegal operations in industrial subcontracting (for example, when firms send out production to be done at home in Mexico City). The jobber does not do any production but performs an indirect supervisory role for subcontracted activities. Also, the jobber may perform other functions such as distribution, transportation, or gathering of materials and products.

just-in-time (JIT)   a system of production in which inventories are restocked on a continual basis rather than stockpiled (just-in-case). JIT production is also known as demand–pull production, since things are not produced ahead of time but just-in-time to meet demand. Whatever it is called, the system is seen as minimizing waste by cutting down on costly inventory management and storage and by hastening the detection of defects, among other things.

Keynesian state, or Keynesian regulatory regime   a form of government intervention in the private economy that became dominant in the capitalist world in response to (1) the economic disaster brought on by unregulated free market capitalism in the 1930s and (2) the success of government economic planning in World War II. The core idea behind Keynesian economic theory and Keynesian economic policy is that production, employment, and investment depend on the strength of the national demand for goods and services. If the government can control total national spending, or *aggregate demand*, through the use of macropolicy (i.e., fiscal and monetary policy) and maintain it at a level where both labor and the capital stock are fully employed, then free markets and profit incentives will take care of almost all other potential problems. To solve all the problems of the capitalist economy, the state must complement macropolicy with mechanisms such as antitrust policy and effective regulation of financial markets. Though Keynesian theory and policy take their names and some of their ideas from the writings of John Maynard Keynes, their proponents purposely neglected his more radical prescriptions for regulating the capitalist economy.

liquidity the degree to which one can sell assets for cash on short notice and with no financial loss.

macropolicy the combination of monetary and fiscal policy.

Malthusian ideology a set of ideas inspired by a nineteenth-century clergyman-turned-economist named Thomas Malthus, who maintained that, unless restrained, human population would grow at a geometric rate, while the earth's capacity for food production would increase only arithmetically. In his view, only the poverty and famine brought on by overpopulation, along with war, would keep human numbers down.

maquiladora, or *maquila* foreign-owned plants operating in Mexico, mostly just south of the U.S.–Mexican border, under a special program by which the Mexican government has granted special tax breaks and investment incentives for U.S. investors. The program began in 1965 and was expanded in the 1970s; in 1991 there were over 2,000 plants with about 500,000 workers.

Marxism–Leninism an ideology that emphasizes the role of a vanguard party as the representative of the working class, and the seizure of state power as the means to implementing the transition to socialism.

mass production large-batch production of standardized goods.

migration movement of people from one region of a country to another or from one country to another in order to live or to work on a relatively long-term basis.

modernization the theory that the developing world can be characterized as a dual economy with a backward, basically agricultural sector and a more advanced industrial sector. The backward sector is fundamentally a subsistence economy with excess labor. For a country to develop in the pattern of the industrial North, investment must occur in the more advanced sector, creating employment with increasing wage growth that will draw workers from the less advanced sector. Eventually, with fewer workers, the agricultural sector will have to employ modern techniques to feed the growing urban areas. Through these policies, according to modernization theory, countries will create modern economnic systems. These theories seem to have failed miserably in many African and Latin American countries.

monetary policy the central bank's use of monetary controls (e.g., manipulating the interest rate) in order to affect the level of inflation, unemployment, or the balance of payments.

money wage and real wage   the money wage is the actual amount of money paid for work; the real wage is the money wage corrected for price inflation. If the money wage rises by 20 percent, but the price level rises by 20 percent, the real wage stays the same. Hence, in this case, the purchasing power of wages does not change even with a pay raise.

multicurrency reserve system   a system in which the currencies of several nations serve as reserve currencies.

multinational corporations   corporations that have operations in more than one country.

multinational enterprises   enterprises that own or control production, distribution, services, or other facilities outside the country in which they are based.

net creditor nation   a nation that has invested more abroad than it has borrowed from abroad.

net debtor nation   a nation that has borrowed more from abroad than it has invested abroad.

1981 tax cuts   cuts in individual income tax rates and in corporate taxes that were instituted under Ronald Reagan's first term in office. The tax cuts were intended to invigorate the economy. They were a key part of so-called supply-side economics.

nuclear forces   nuclear weapons and the accompanying forces, for example, long-range bombers, intercontinental ballistic missiles, submarine-launched missiles, and other weapons equipped with nuclear bombs or warheads.

occupational segregation   differences in job assignments based on the ascriptive characteristics of employees. For example, sex-based occupational segregation assigns men and women to different types of jobs on the basis of their gender.

open borders   absence of restrictions on entry to a country.

Organization of Petroleum Exporting Countries (OPEC)   the cartel of large exporters of petroleum.

Pax Americana   the system under which the United States plays a major role in organizing the world's economy and in which the United States takes the main responsibility for enforcing the peace (following, for example, Pax Britannica in the nineteenth century).

petrodollars   money generated by an increase in oil prices and deposited in banks in Europe or the United States.

portfolio investments   investments in government or private assets that do not give the investor effective control, for example, investments in treasury bonds or private bonds.

post-Fordism   system of production characterized by teamwork, task integration, learning by doing, and flexibility.

primary goods   raw materials and foodstuffs. Primary in the sense of not being substantially transformed.

primary sector   large firms (more than a thousand employees) in which jobs are generally characterized by high wages and skills, good promotional opportunities, and job security.

prime rate   the rate of interest banks charge their best corporate customers.

production networks   systems of relatively small, specialized firms with complementary capabilities that jointly produce goods that none of the firms could produce alone.

productivity   the average amount of goods and services produced by each worker. The measure of goods and services is the dollar value of what is produced and does not include the value of things like safety or workers' health. An economy can improve health and safety and become less productive according to conventional measures of productivity.

proletarianization   transformation of property owners, self-employed workers, or other independent producers into people who sell their labor power for a wage.

pronatalist population policies   policies designed to increase the birth rate in a society.

protectionism   advocacy of trade barriers such as tariffs, quotas, or non-tariff measures (like minimum quality standards) to restrict imports of a good and protect domestic production of it from competition.

real weekly earnings   weekly earnings adjusted for inflation, in order to reflect actual purchasing power.

remittances   money sent back by migrants to their country of origin, usually to their families.

reserve currency   the currency accumulated by nations to settle their international accounts with one another.

retaliatory tariffs   tariffs increased by one country in response to another country's increasing its tariffs; this process can lead to a trade war.

secondary sector   smaller firms (less than a thousand employees), often subsidiaries or suppliers of firms in the primary sector, in which jobs are generally characterized by low wages and skills, few promotional opportunities, and job insecurity.

social charter   an agreement or law establishing minimum wages, working conditions, other social safety nets, and environmental and consumer protections throughout several countries.

social tariffs   taxes charged on products that are produced under socially costly conditions—for example, in ways that are environmentally destructive or under conditions that deny workers basic rights.

socialism   no single definition of socialism is universally accepted, but most definitions include some notions of equality, democracy, elimination of class divisions, collective ownership and control of the means of production, and some degree of social planning of the economy.

special drawing right (SDR)   a reserve asset, created by the IMF in 1967, whose value is calculated as a weighted average of sixteen countries' exchange rates.

stabilization policies   policies designed to reduce inflation and balance-of-payments deficits. These policies usually involve austerity: cuts in government spending and reductions in the rate of growth of the money supply.

structural adjustment programs   the policies and programs instituted by the IMF to correct a country's balance-of-payments deficit.

sustainable development   development that meets the needs of the present without compromising the ability of future generations to meet their own needs. It values equitable economic distribution and the importance of environmental balance.

tariff   a tax on imported goods.

Taylorism, or **scientific management**   separation of manual from mental work. Mental work, such as conceptualization, planning, and reorganization, is the domain of management and industrial engineers. Workers carry out the manual work as dictated by management.

terms of trade   the ratio of an index of a country's export prices to an index of its import prices. A decline, or "deterioration," in a country's terms of trade means that the same exports will allow them to purchase fewer imports.

theory of comparative advantage   a theory that shows how two countries can both gain if they produce those goods they can produce most efficiently and then trade those goods for other goods. By concentrating resources in what is produced most efficiently and then trading those goods for other goods, a country can get more output for its resources. The distribution of the gains from trade depends on the relative bargaining power of the two trading countries.

tied aid   aid given under the stipulation that it be used in a specified way, for example, to buy equipment and supplies from firms associated with the donor country.

trade adjustment assistance (TAA; also known as **trade readjustment assistance,** or **TRA)**   temporary benefits and retraining programs for workers displaced from export industries by an unfavorable trade balance; in the United States, this program has never been large.

trade deficit   the shortfall that occurs when in a given period a country buys more goods and services from abroad then it sells abroad.

transfer pricing   prices that one part of a multinational corporation charges another part for goods and services. For example, if a subsidiary of General Motors operating in Mexico sells engines to a General Motors car assembly plant in California, the plant operating in Mexico must set a transfer price for the engines it is selling. If it sets the price too high, the Mexican plant will show a higher profit and the California plant will show a lower profit than otherwise.

transplants   foreign-owned firms operating in countries other than those of the firms' origins.

upstream and downstream activities   activities involved in producing inputs to or using the output of another production process.

Uruguay round   a series of discussions of trade policy, mainly among GATT members, that began in 1986 and were designed to reduce trade barriers wherever possible by mutual agreement.

vertical integration and disintegration   the incorporation or disincorporation of upstream or downstream production activities within a single firm.

voluntary export restraint (VER)   an agreement that one country will limit the amount it exports of a given product to another country. As with Japanese car exports to the United States, VERs are agreed to usually to forestall a harsher or more permanent form of trade barrier like a legislative tariff or quota.

worker dislocation   job loss associated with capital mobility that is offset by job creation elsewhere. Although the individual worker is dislocated, or "displaced," the total number of jobs nationwide stays the same.

World Bank   the major international development agency in the world, created through the Bretton Woods agreement. It is composed of the International Bank for Reconstruction and Development (IBRD), the International Development Association (IDA), and the International Finance Corporation (IFC). Since 1945, they have lent to (in part on concessional terms) and invested in seventy-six countries with commitments of more than $13 billion.

The Contributors

Coeditors

GERALD EPSTEIN received his Ph.D. in economics from Princeton University and now teaches at the University of Massachusetts at Amherst. He has also taught at Williams College and at the New School for Social Research. He is a staff economist with the Center for Popular Economics and a member of the Macroeconomics Project of the United Nations University's World Institute for Development Economic Research (WIDER) based in Helsinki, Finland.

JULIE GRAHAM is associate professor of economic geography at the University of Massachusetts at Amherst and a staff economist with the Center for Popular Economics. Her research interests include the internationalization of production, feminist industrial policy, and the politics of post-Fordism. She is a member of the editorial board of *Rethinking Marxism*.

JESSICA NEMBHARD received her Ph.D. in economics at the University of Massachusetts at Amherst in 1992. She specializes in international finance, macroeconomic policy, and development. Her dissertation is entitled "Capital Controls and Long-Term Economic Growth," and she is the author of *The Nation We Are Making: A Junior History of Belize* (Belize Ministry of Education, 1991). She received a National Science Graduate Fellowship for 1988–91 and an American Economics Association/ Federal Reserve System Minority Fellowship in 1991–92.

Contributors

MARIBEL APONTE-GARCÍA is an assistant professor and researcher of economics at the Graduate School of Business Administration and the Social Science Research Center of the University of Puerto Rico. She holds a Ph.D. in economics from the University of Massachusetts at Am-

450

herst and wrote her doctoral dissertation on the restructuring of the U.S. military industry and the militarization of the Caribbean. At present, she is directing the project "Industrial Restructuring and Alternative Development Models for the Caribbean and Latin America." She is also an advisor on strategic agricultural and industrial development programs to community organizations and farmers' associations in Puerto Rico.

RADHIKA BALAKRISHNAN received her Ph.D. from Rutgers University. She has taught economics and women's studies at Rutgers University, Western New England College, and Wellesley College. Her research interests include gender issues in Third World countries and demographic structures. She has been active in the women's and antiracism movements as well as in antiapartheid and Central American groups.

SAMUEL BOWLES is professor of economics at the University of Massachusetts at Amherst and received his Ph.D. from Harvard University. He has taught economics at Harvard, served as visiting professor at Doshisha University, the University of Siena, and the University of Havana, and has served as economic advisor to the governments of Cuba and Greece. A founder of the alternative economic journal *Dollars and Sense*, Bowles has coauthored *Schooling in Capitalist America* (Basic Books, 1976), *Democracy and Capitalism* (Basic Books, 1986), *After the Wasteland: A Democratic Economics for the Year 2000* (M.E. Sharpe, 1991), and *Understanding Capitalism: Competition, Command, and Change in the U.S. Economy* (HarperCollins, 1992).

ROBIN BROAD is a professor in the School of International Service at the American University in Washington, D.C. She is the author of *Unequal Alliance: The World Bank, the International Monetary Fund, and the Philippines* (University of California Press, 1988). Broad and Cavanagh are coauthors of *Plundering Paradise: The Struggle for the Environment in the Philippines* (University of California Press, 1993).

JOHN CAVANAGH codirects the World Economy Working Group at the Institute for Policy Studies in Washington, D.C. and is, most recently, the coeditor of *Trading Freedom: How Free Trade Affects Our Lives, Work and Environment* (San Francisco: Food First, 1992).

JAMES CROTTY is the former chair of the Department of Economics at the University of Massachusetts at Amherst and is currently professor of economics at that same institution. He holds a Ph.D. from the Graduate School of Industrial Administration at Carnegie Mellon University. He has taught at SUNY–Buffalo and Bucknell University. His teaching and research interests include the effects of the globalization of the U.S. economy, the instability of the financial system, and unemployment. His political activities include work with religious, peace, and social activists.

CARMEN DIANA DEERE is professor of economics at the University of Massachusetts at Amherst and president of the Latin American Studies

Association. She is a specialist in development issues in Latin America and the Caribbean and Third World socialism. Her recent books include *Household and Class Relations: Peasants and Landlords in Northern Peru* (University of California Press, 1990) and *In the Shadows of the Sun: Caribbean Development Alternatives and U.S. Policy* (Westview Press, 1990).

DIANE FLAHERTY is associate professor of economics at the University of Massachusetts at Amherst and holds a Ph.D. in economics from New York University. Her teaching and research interests focus on comparative economic systems, the economies of Eastern European nations, and the organization of labor and technological change. Diane is currently doing research on participatory socialism and economic reform in Eastern Europe.

ILENE GRABEL holds a Ph.D. in economics and is an assistant professor of international economics in the Graduate School of International Studies at the University of Denver. She has worked with the Financial Democracy Campaign on policy research and development and has spoken in forums on the U.S. savings and loan crisis. Her current research focuses on the macroeconomic consequences of financial liberalization.

ANTHONY GUGLIELMI holds master's degrees in resource economics and environmental management and is currently a doctoral student in economics at the University of Massachusetts at Amherst. His present research focuses on industrial districts and the new competition. For the past fifteen years, he has worked on environmental issues, antiracism, and alternative politics.

KIARAN HONDERICH is assistant professor of economics at Williams College, where she teaches international economics, political economy, and women's studies. Her research focuses on power relations in international economics and the international drug trade. She has been an actress in political theater and has been involved in the women's movement and the animal rights movement.

EMILY KAWANO is a doctoral candidate in economics at the University of Massachusetts at Amherst. Her research focuses on labor and work organization in the Japanese production system. She has been active in consumer advocacy groups, community-labor groups, and the environmental movement.

MEHRENE LARUDEE is a doctoral candidate in economics at the University of Massachusetts at Amherst. Her research interests are in the fields of international economics and development. She has been involved in the civil rights, peace, labor, and women's movements and for two years was a teacher in a rural technical school in Nicaragua.

STAN MALINOWITZ is a doctoral candidate in economics at the University of Massachusetts at Amherst. He has worked on community development and popular education projects in Latin America and was a tenant organizer in New York City. His current research interests include Latin American economic development and Third World socialism.

MANUEL PASTOR, JR., is associate professor of economics at Occidental College and holds a Ph.D. in economics from the University of Massachusetts, Amherst. His research has focused on issues of debt, stabilization, and development in Latin America. He has received Fulbright, Kellogg, and Guggenheim fellowships. His publications include *The International Monetary Fund and Latin America: Economic Stabilization and Class Conflict* (Westview Press, 1987) and *Inflation, Stabilization, and Debt: Macroeconomic Experiments in Peru and Bolivia* (Westview Press, 1992). He has also published in such journals as *Latin American Research Review, Journal of Development Economics, Review of Radical Political Economics,* and *World Development.* He has been active most recently in efforts to forge a progressive development alternative for poor communities in Los Angeles.

TOM RIDDELL is associate professor of economics at Smith College and has a Ph.D. in economics from American University. He was one of the original founders of the Center for Popular Economics. His research interests focus on the economics of militarism and public policy. His teaching interests include introductory economics, global economic geography, and public finance. He is coauthor of the popular introductory textbook *Economics: A Tool for Understanding Society* (Addison Wesley, 1991). He has been active in the peace, antiapartheid, and antiracism movements.

HÉCTOR SÁEZ is working on his dissertation at the University of Massachusetts at Amherst. His research focuses on the management of natural resources under different property regimes in Latin American agriculture. Before coming to the University of Massachusetts, Sáez studied economics and geography at the University of Puerto Rico, where he became interested in environmental issues and movements.

JULIET B. SCHOR is senior lecturer in economics and director of studies, Women's Studies, at Harvard University. She holds a Ph.D. from the University of Massachusetts at Amherst and is author of *The Overworked American: The Unexpected Decline of Leisure* (Basic Books, 1992). Juliet was research fellow at the Brookings Institution and is research advisor for the World Institute for Development Economics Research of the United Nations. She coauthored with Daniel Cantor *Tunnel Vision: Labor, the World Economy, and Central America* (South End Press, 1987).

BOB SUTCLIFFE is an economist who specializes in international and development economics. He is the author or coauthor of numerous books and articles including *The Profit System* (Penguin, 1987), *Hard Times* (Pluto Press, 1983), *British Capitalism, Workers, and the Profit Squeeze*

(Penguin, 1972), and *Industry and Underdevelopment* (Addison Wesley, 1971), and coeditor of *Studies in the Theory of Imperialism* (Longman, 1972). He has taught at the University of Massachusetts at Amherst, the Central American University in Managua, and the University of the Basque Country in Bilbao. He now works at Hegoa (South), a Third World documentation and research center in Bilbao.

JOSÉ TÁVARA is assistant professor in the Economics Department at the Catholic University of Peru and researcher at the Centro de Estudios para la Promoción y el Desarrollo (DESCO), both in Lima. He received his Ph.D. from the University of Massachusetts at Amherst with a dissertation entitled "From Survival Activities to Industrial Strategies: Local Systems of Inter-Firm Cooperation in Peru." He has published several articles in Spanish on industrialization and development strategies.

BRENDA WYSS teaches economics at Wheaton College in Norton, Massachusetts. Her research focus is the political economy of women, particularly in the context of Third World economies. She is currently completing her dissertation, which examines Jamaican child support relations in the context of economic crisis and restructuring.

LYUBA ZARSKY is a specialist in environmental economics and in economic and strategic issues in the Asia–Pacific region. She is principal researcher with Nautilus Pacific Research in Berkeley, California. She is the author of *Borders and the Biosphere: Environment, Development, and Global Trade Rules* (Island Press, 1994), co-author of *American Lake: Nuclear Peril in the Pacific* (Viking Penguin, 1986), and editor of CPE's *Economic Report of the People* (South End Press, 1986).

Index

455